Religious Freedom
v.
Equal Protection

FRONTIERS IN POLITICAL COMMUNICATION

Mitchell S. McKinney and Mary E. Stuckey
General Editors

Vol. 47

The Frontiers in Political Communication series
is part of the Peter Lang Media and Communication list.
Every volume is peer reviewed and meets
the highest quality standards for content and production.

PETER LANG
New York • Berlin • Brussels • Lausanne • Oxford

Religious Freedom v. Equal Protection

Clashing American Rights

Edited by
Kevin A. Johnson and Jennifer J. Asenas

PETER LANG
New York • Berlin • Brussels • Lausanne • Oxford

Library of Congress Cataloging-in-Publication Data

Names: Johnson, Kevin A., editor. | Asenas, Jennifer J., editor.
Title: Religious freedom v. equal protection: clashing American rights /
edited by Kevin A. Johnson and Jennifer J. Asenas.
Description: New York: Peter Lang, 2022.
Series: Frontiers in political communication; vol. 47 | ISSN 1525-9730
Includes bibliographical references and index.
Identifiers: LCCN 2021048358 (print) | LCCN 2021048359 (ebook)
ISBN 978-1-4331-6769-0 (hardback) | ISBN 978-1-4331-6773-7 (paperback)
ISBN 978-1-4331-6770-6 (ebook pdf) | ISBN 978-1-4331-6771-3 (epub)
Subjects: LCSH: Freedom of religion—United States. | Equality before the
law—United States. | Discrimination—Law and legislation—United States.
Classification: LCC KF4783 .R4293 2022 (print) | LCC KF4783 (ebook) |
DDC 342.7308/52—dc23/eng/20220128
LC record available at https://lccn.loc.gov/2021048358
LC ebook record available at https://lccn.loc.gov/2021048359
DOI 10.3726/b15461

Bibliographic information published by **Die Deutsche Nationalbibliothek.**
Die Deutsche Nationalbibliothek lists this publication in the "Deutsche
Nationalbibliografie"; detailed bibliographic data are available
on the Internet at http://dnb.d-nb.de/.

Cover: *The Cross of Justitia* by Maia Kaa.
Maia Te Wairemana Kaa is a Māori visual artist/illustrator
based in Ōtautahi, New Zealand.
More artwork is featured on Instagram @maiatewai.

80 Broad Street, 5th floor, New York, NY 10004
www.peterlang.com

Table of Contents

Acknowledgments

This book is the product of the labor of many people. We would like to thank all of those who have contributed to discussions we have had about the clashes between religious freedom and equal protection at academic conferences, panel presentations, informal conversations, and other forms of communication. We especially thank the authors for contributing their essays to this volume and for teaching us about even more of the clashes between these freedoms than we were aware of before beginning this study. We would also like to thank the people at Peter Lang Publishing for their guidance and assistance in the various stages of production and review.

We begin by acknowledging the people whose experiences became the legal facts of the cases and controversies explored in this book. For them, the clash between the First and Fourteenth Amendments has important and sometimes life altering consequences. We thank each of the authors for their contribution to this book and for educating us about situations we previously had no knowledge of, and lines of thought we had not yet considered. We would like to especially thank Dr. Mary Stuckey and the other series editors for their role in providing insightful and generous reviews of the collection. We thank artist Maia Tewai for creating a wonderful piece of artwork for the cover of the book. We are grateful for the people at Peter Lang Publishing who continued to offer their guidance and assistance in the various stages of production and review during the COVID-19 pandemic. We would like to thank the advisory board, the scholars, and the students of the Center for First Amendment Studies at California State University, Long Beach who have also contributed great insights into the project and we appreciate the help. We especially thank Dr. Craig R. Smith for providing feedback on the many ideas that we had for the book. Finally, a special thanks to our family and friends for providing a support network and for listening to our many conversations about equal protection and religious freedom. We hope that the content of this book will become topics of conversation among you and your friends, too.

1. *Religious Freedom v. Equal Protection: Clashing American Rights*

KEVIN A. JOHNSON AND JENNIFER J. ASENAS

American revolutionaries declared the self-evident truths that "all men are created equal," and that unalienable rights are "endowed by their Creator." But are American rights self-evident anymore? Were they ever? Somewhere betwixt and between the Declaration of Independence, the Bill of Rights, Supreme Court interpretations, and government regulations, the "self-evident" nature of rights and their origin in a "creator" has been contested and interpreted by the humans who are the stewards of those endowed rights. These philosophical assertions that declared US independence function differently in practice and it is left to humans to determine to whom and how far rights extend. In this way, creator endowed rights have morphed into "human endowed" rights.

Based on individual perspectives, life experiences, and historical contexts, human interpretation makes the supposed self-evident nature of rights a negotiated matter. For example, "Creator" and "equality" have endured as terms central to American democratic life even as their status has shifted. The self-evident "Creator" has been negotiated in democratic life as a "sincerely" held religious *belief* and is closely aligned with the democratic negotiation of "equality" in American life. Those who *believe* in a "Creator" as self-evident are presumed *equal* to those who do not believe a "Creator" to be self-evident. The result? "Creator" is no longer presumed to be "self-evident." The transformation from the *self-evident* into a *belief* has given rise to clashing American rights of equality and religious freedom. The rights remain deeply engrained in American cultural life, and are deeply contested in our politics.

The words "equality" and "religious freedom" stick to lived experiences in America. The terms themselves may be self-evident as they endure. At the same time, this book demonstrates the way cases that occupy those terms are far removed from the self-evident assumption. A guiding theme that runs throughout this book is that contested notions of "equality" and "religious freedom" are the product of intrinsically rhetorical phenomena. At a basic level, we believe that rhetoric is concerned with the study of persuasion and/as the contestation over meaning in human affairs. It is rooted in the study of phenomena that include: beliefs, pleasures, desires, urgencies, possibilities, potentialities, contingencies, logic and its excesses, changes, becoming, and timing. "Equality" and "religious freedom" are rhetorically contested in terms of their meaning. Different people are persuaded to think about these rights in different ways in different situations. People *believe* different things about these rights, and they take certain *pleasures* in the exercise of these rights. There are competing *desires* about what the rights ought to entail and different senses of *urgency* about when conflicts over these rights ought to be resolved in disputes. There are several *possibilities*, *potentialities*, and *contingencies* built into these rights as they change. The rights continually change in new iterations that are always already in the process of becoming as time unfolds. And yet, there is a certain consistency. So, we proceed in this chapter by examining the emergence, nature, and scope of "equality" and "religious freedom" that have come to be valued, contested, and conflicting terms in American life. We conclude this introductory chapter by sharing a preview of the chapters of this book. Each of the chapters focus on clashes that have emerged over "equality" and "religious freedom."

The Ideal of Equality in the Fabric of American Rights

"Equal Justice Under Law." These are the words etched into the front entrance to the Supreme Court of the United States. They mark the ultimate responsibility of the Court. Although enshrined in the building, equality is nowhere to be found in the original text of the Constitution, nor the Bill of Rights. From the natural rights perspective, equality is "self-evident," and as such, unnecessary to appear in the Constitution because it is found in the "nature of man" preceding the justification for creating the United States in the first place.

Regardless of the absence of equality from the original Constitution and Bill of Rights, the principle is imprinted into the heart of so much of the Supreme Court's jurisprudence. In other words, in its interpretation of the Constitution, the Court has ensured that equality pervades it. For example, the principle is found in the Court's rulings on the First Amendment. In *Rosenberger v. Rectors and Visitors of the University of Virginia*, the Supreme

Court ruled that the government must not engage in viewpoint discrimination: "When the government targets not subject matter but particular views taken by speakers on a subject, the violation of the First Amendment is all the more blatant. Viewpoint discrimination is thus an egregious form of content discrimination. The government must abstain from regulating speech when the specific motivating ideology or the opinion or perspective of the speaker is the rationale for the restriction." Viewpoint discrimination, in other words, is a form of administering legal favor of one viewpoint over another in a manner that runs counter to "equal justice under law." When government targets a viewpoint, it treats that viewpoint unequally compared to viewpoints it does not target.

In fact, equality permeates decisions in nearly every Amendment (except maybe the Third Amendment) in the Bill of Rights. In the Second Amendment case of *McDonald v. City of Chicago*, the Court affirmed Senator James Nye's idea that the Fourteenth Amendment was unnecessary because "blacks, as citizens, 'have *equal right* to protection, and to keep and bear arms for self-defense."[1] In the Fourth Amendment case of *Terry v. Ohio*, the Court affirmed the equal right of every citizen to address questions to other persons and also to ignore an "interrogator and walk away."[2] In the Fifth Amendment case of *Bolling v. Sharpe*, the Court reasoned that equality is inherent in due process, "The '*equal protection of the law*' is a more explicit safeguard of prohibited unfairness than 'due process of law,'. . . But, as this Court has recognized, discrimination may be so unjustifiable as to be violative of due process."[3] In the Sixth Amendment case of *Gideon v. Wainwright*, the Court reasoned, "From the very beginning, our state and national constitutions and laws have laid great emphasis on procedural and substantive safeguards designed to assure fair trials before impartial tribunals in which every defendant stands *equal* before the law."[4] In the Seventh Amendment case of *Parklane Hosiery Company v. Shore*, the Court reasoned an equality rationale undergirding access to jury trials, "The petitioners have advanced no persuasive reason, however, why the meaning of the Seventh Amendment should depend on whether or not mutuality of parties is present. A litigant who has lost because of adverse factual findings in an equity action is *equally* deprived of a jury trial. . . ."[5] In the Eighth Amendment case of *Furman v. Georgia*, Justice Douglas wrote in his concurring opinion, "One cannot read this history without realizing that the desire for *equality* was reflected in the ban against 'cruel and unusual punishments' contained in the Eighth Amendment. In a Nation committed to *equal protection* of the laws there is no permissible 'caste' aspect of law enforcement."[6] In the Ninth Amendment case of *Olff v. East Side Union High School District*, the Court ruled, "The word 'liberty' is not defined in the Constitution. But . . . it includes at least the fundamental rights 'retained by the people' under the Ninth Amendment. . . . One's hair style . . . is certainly fundamental in our constitutional scheme—a scheme designed to keep government off the backs of people. . . . I see no way of allowing a State to set hair styles for patrons of its schools, any more than it could establish a welfare system only for men with crew cuts and women with bobbed hair. Once these lines are drawn, a serious question of *equal protection* of the law is raised."[7] In *Shelby County v. Holder*, the Court upheld a "fundamental principle of *equal sovereignty*"[8] amongst states rights in the Tenth Amendment that prevents "disparate treatment of States"[9] in federal law.

Taken together, the idea of "equality" is pervasive in the Bill of Rights as a matter of Supreme Court interpretations. Of course, the most explicit mention of equality that appears in the Constitution is in the Fourteenth Amendment. Taking effect in 1868, the Equal Protection Clause of the Fourteenth Amendment holds that no state shall "deny to any person within its jurisdiction the *equal protection* of the laws." This clause has been applied to several cases involving state and federal laws. In *Brown v. Board of Education*, the Court ruled on Fourteenth Amendment grounds that, "in the field of public education the doctrine of 'separate but equal' has no place. Separate educational facilities are inherently unequal. . . .We have now announced that such segregation is a denial of the *equal protection* of the laws."[10] In *Reed v. Reed*, the Court invoked the Fourteenth Amendment to apply to sex discrimination, "By providing dissimilar treatment for men and women who are thus similarly situated, the challenged section violates the *Equal Protection Clause*."[11] And, in *Obergefell v. Hodges*, the Court ruled, "the right to marry is a fundamental right inherent in the liberty of the person, and under Due Process and *Equal Protection Clauses* of the Fourteenth Amendment couples of the same-sex may not be deprived of that right and that liberty. The Court now holds that same-sex couples may exercise the fundamental right to marry."[12]

Furthermore, even though the Fourteenth Amendment specifically applies only to the states and makes no mention of the federal government, the Supreme Court has ruled that the Fourteenth Amendment may be applied to understanding the constitutionality of federal laws. Specifically, in the previously mentioned case of *Bolling v. Sharpe*, the Court argued that the Equal Protection Clause of the Fourteenth Amendment may be incorporated into the Fifth Amendment's Due Process Clause. The Court held that even though the Fourteenth Amendment does indeed only apply to the states, the intent of that Amendment may also define the way we think about what Due

Process means in the Fifth Amendment. Put simply, if the federal government violates the standard required of states in the Fourteenth Amendment, then that also may be defined as a federal violation of Due Process.

The applicability of equal protection to the federal government may also have roots in the Constitution's original meaning because of the overarching idea of fiduciary responsibility. Gary Lawson, Guy Seidman, and Robert Natelson argued that, "Federal officials are fiduciaries"[13] based on the original intent. They wrote, "when the Constitution granted power to agents, it did so against the background of fiduciary law."[14] They continued, "the underlying principles—that agents must exercise their authority with care, honesty, and attention to the interests of those who employ them—are as much part of the Constitution as the basic principles of English grammar."[15] While grounding federal equal protection in a fiduciary foundation, they argue, one finds at the very least, "the same kinds of problems, conundrums, and value choices with which the law has wrestled for a century and a half when trying to understand the Fourteenth Amendment."[16]

Whether it be the "self-evident" idea that "all men are created equal" in the Declaration of Independence, or the idea that equal protection is inherent in the fiduciary role of federal officials under their constitutional obligations, or the Supreme Court affirmations of equal protection pervading the Bill of Rights, or the application of the Equal Protection Clause of the Fourteenth Amendment, one thing appears certain—the idea of "equality" is built into the fabric of American rights. As the historical evolution of "equality" suggests, the cultural resonance of the word itself may, indeed, be self-evident (for it hasn't vanished). What is far from self-evident is what that word will come to mean in ongoing cases that dispute either its privileged status in constitutional law when in conflict with other rights, and what it will mean to the lived experiences and realities of American life in the future.

The Ideal of Religious Freedom in the Fabric of American Rights

Just as equality permeates constitutional rights, the same might be said about religious freedom. Thomas Jefferson believed that religious freedom as tied to the "Creator" was "the most inalienable and sacred of all human rights."[17] The colonial and founding generations of America took their "Creator" seriously, and shared an almost exclusively Christian religious faith. As E. Gregory Wallace reminded us, "They believed that religion is unique because it entails duties owed to God. Their principal justifications for religious freedom rested upon the theological premise that God exists and is sovereign over both human government and the individual citizen."[18]

The freedom of religion appears as the first of the five freedoms in the First Amendment in the Bill of Rights. As such, the freedom of religion is often referred to as our "first freedom."[19] And, like the idea of equality, religious freedom permeates the Constitution and the Bill of Rights, both as a matter of the Constitution's text and as a matter of Supreme Court interpretations. In the founding era, "Freedom of religion was universally said to be an unalienable right; the status of other rights commonly found in state bills of rights, such as property or trial by jury, were more disputed and often considered derivative of civil society."[20] James Madison even went so far as to write that the "universal sovereign" precedes any claims of a civil society. In other words, "when the people vested power in the government over civil affairs, they necessarily reserved their unalienable right to the free exercise of religion, in accordance with the dictates of conscience."[21] Regardless of the differences in philosophy between framers like Jefferson and Madison, they agreed to begin the Bill of Rights with religious freedom, declaring that, "Congress shall make no law respecting an establishment of religion, or prohibiting the free exercise thereof."

It may seem a bit peculiar that rationales for religious freedom would appear in Supreme Court cases concerning other rights in the Bill of Rights. Like equality, religious freedom found its way into the Second Amendment case of *Printz v. United States.* Justice Thomas analogized the government restraint on intervening in religious freedom as a rationale for showing similar restraint when it comes to gun rights. He wrote, "The Constitution, in addition to delegating certain enumerated powers to Congress, places whole areas outside the reach of Congress' regulatory authority. The First Amendment, for example, is fittingly celebrated for preventing Congress from 'prohibiting the free exercise' of religion . . . The Second Amendment similarly appears to contain an express limitation on the Government's authority."[22]

The Third and Fourth Amendments are often woven together to form a general right to privacy. The freedom of religion often makes its way into these cases based on the idea that religion is one of those private affairs often exercised in the home, and that troops and police officers may not intrude on that space. For example, in citing both of these freedoms, the Court upheld precedents in *Poe v. Ullman* against police intrusion on teaching religious beliefs in the home, like those of pacificism. The Court ruled, "Mr. Justice Brandeis, writing of a statute which made 'it punishable to teach (pacifism) in any place (to) a single person no matter what the relation of the parties may be,' found such a 'statute invades the privacy and freedom of the home.

Father and mother may not follow the promptings of *religious* belief, of conscience or of conviction, and teach son or daughter the doctrine of pacificism. If they do, any officer may summarily arrest them.' "[23] The Court concluded, "These decisions . . . 'have respected the private realm of family life which the state cannot enter."[24] Religious freedom is, therefore, bound up with the right of privacy in the Third and Fourth Amendments because of the way it is exercised in the home.

Religious freedom is also implicated in the Fifth Amendment. For example, in *U.S. v. Weldon*, the Court reasoned that violating a person's free exercise of religion may inherently violate, in part, a person's Fifth Amendment rights rooted in the Due Process and Self-Incrimination Clauses. The Court noted, "Congress may make no law 'prohibiting the free exercise' of religion, it may not enter the field through investigation and probe the minds of witnesses as to whether they go to church or to the confessional regularly, why they chose this church rather than that one, etc."[25] Even if Congress did make a law enabling the violation of that free exercise, not only would that law be unconstitutional, but the person who would be approached in their religious place of worship may exercise their religious freedom by, for example, confessing to a priest while also exercising their Fifth Amendment right against self-incrimination and *not* confessing to the congressionally authorized investigators.[26]

Religious freedom has been an issue in several constitutional questions in federal and state courts as it relates to the Sixth through Tenth Amendments. For example, in *People v. Gilliam*, the court ruled that the defendant's Sixth Amendment rights were violated when the lower court asked the defendant to choose between exercising his religious freedom to attend religious services on the sabbath, or to attend his voir dire for his case.[27] In the Seventh Amendment case of *United States v. Hillyard*, the court ruled in favor of a member of the Jehovah's Witnesses who objected on religious grounds to fulfilling their jury duty obligation (rooted in the court's obligation to provide a jury under the Seventh Amendment).[28] In the case of *Robbins v. Robertson*, the court ruled that a violation of religious freedom may inherently be an Eighth Amendment violation in certain cases involving religious dietary requirements in the prison context, "by asserting that the only way he could comply with the dictates of his religion was to accept a nutritionally inadequate diet—logically suggests that this same assertion would give rise to an Eighth Amendment claim. That being so, and having reversed the district court's dismissal of the First Amendment claim, we are also obliged to reverse the dismissal of the Eighth Amendment claim."[29] In *City of Wadsworth v. Owens*, the court ruled that a curfew restricting minors from exercising their religious freedom to attend midnight mass was evidence of abridging the Ninth Amendment right "to move freely, without fear of governmental restriction or invasion . . . [T]his right is extended to minors and that before this right may be abridged, the state must show a compelling state interest."[30]

The Tenth Amendment, of course, calls for all powers not delegated to the United States to be delegated to the states. And, while the freedom of religion is protected by the federal government and applies to the states through the doctrine of incorporation, it is notable that every state protects the freedom of religion in their state constitutions. Forty-five of those state constitutions explicitly mention God in their preamble.[31] Aleksandra Sandstrom of the Pew Research Center reported, "God or the divine is mentioned at least once in each of the 50 state constitutions and nearly 200 times overall. . . . In addition to the 116 mentions of God, there are also 14 mentions of a Supreme or Sovereign Being, seven mentions of the 'Creator,' three mentions of 'providence,' four mentions of 'divine,' and 46 instances of the word 'almighty.' "[32]

In addition to the prevalence of religious freedom and practice in court interpretations of the Bill of Rights, the federal government has ensured that such prevalence continues in federal law. Specifically, Congress, with near unanimous support in both the House and Senate, passed the Religious Freedom Restoration Act (RFRA) in order to ensure that the Sherbert Test be used in cases involving federal legislation that affects religious freedom. As such, the Act prevents the government from "substantially burdening a person's exercise of religion even if the burden results from a rule of general applicability." Any government burden placed on a person's exercise of religion must demonstrate that the burden, "(1) furthers a compelling government interest, and (2) is the least restrictive means of furthering that compelling government interest." Thus far, the Court has upheld RFRA in several cases including *Burwell v. Hobby Lobby* and *Tanzin v. Tanvir*, and has even affirmed it as a "kind of super statute, displacing the normal operation of other federal laws" in *Bostock v. Clayton County, GA*.[33] The Supreme Court ruled in *City of Boerne v. Flores* that RFRA does not apply to state governments, prompting a majority of states to implement a RFRA like law either by legislation or state court ruling. Thus, religious freedom continues to be significant and prevalent in the United States.

Taken together, whether it be the "Creator" endowed rights in the Declaration of Independence, or the First Amendment protection of religious freedom, or the many court rulings that highlight the significance of religious rights in defining or influencing the meaning of other rights in the Bill of Rights, or the many legislative acts like RFRA, one theme emerges—religious rights and religious practices appear to be built into the fabric of American life. Thus far, we have noted that both equality and religious freedom appear to be fundamental rights in the United States. There are many Americans who may think of these rights as *inherently* harmonious. Thus, for example, is the belief that "we are all equal in god's eyes." This idea is rooted in the idea that God is the lover of all humanity, equally. Or, for example, the harmonious ideal that we are all equal under the law to practice religion without government interference. These ideals are rooted in the idea of individual choice (i.e., "you have the equal right to your religion if you don't believe in mine."). But, at risk of a bad pun here, "the Devil is in the details."

The Underside of Interpreting Equality and Religious Freedom

As previously noted, one of the guiding assumptions of this book is that "equality" and "religious freedom" are fundamentally complicated by their rhetorical nature. What this means in the world of human affairs is that they become contested, partial, and, as the interpretations are put into practice, consequential. While our training is in the rhetorical tradition, legal scholars may be familiar with the interpretive contests inherent in constitutional interpretation. The most well-known fall into debates concerning originalism versus the living constitution interpretive philosophies. Philip Bobbitt developed a further interpretive breakdown by offering a series of "modalities" that capture the nuance of constitutional interpretation. He argued, "the law is something we do, not something we have as a consequence of what we do."[34] According to Craig R. Smith, Bobbitt "saw constitutional law as a rhetorical practice before the courts and the classroom."[35]

For our purposes, the process of applying terms like "religious freedom" (and related terms "free exercise," etc.) and "equality" (and related terms "equal protection," etc.) in different contexts and cases to particular acts (for example, acts that become subject to litigation) is a rhetorical process. In other words, humans contest what words apply to which acts, whether an act is an act of "religious freedom" and/or a violation of "equality." The classic example in the rhetoric of law is whether we ascribe "self-defense" or "murder" to the shooting of a person. How we define the act comes to correspond to certain types of consequences for the accused. A similar rhetorical process occurs with placing the terms "religious freedom" and/or "equality" to certain actions. How we define the given acts comes to correspond with certain consequences for people.

For example, the exercise of "religious freedom" in practice may have the consequence of denying people "equality." Specifically, there are a number of instances, dating back to the founding era, of *religious freedom exceptionalism*—a term we use to describe the function of rhetorically claiming religious freedom for oneself, while denying that freedom to others. For example, Jacqueline C. Rivers reminds us of how religious freedom was employed unequally in many of the Southern states in particular, "though Southerners claimed religious freedom for themselves, they denied it to others. They subverted the logic of their own documents to uphold a system that enslaved blacks. The Fundamental Constitutions of Carolina were explicitly written, by no lesser man than John Locke, so as to prevent slaves from suing for freedom on the basis of a clause in English Common Law, which prohibited the enslavement of fellow Christians."[36] Religious freedom exceptionalism was not unique to the South. She continued to explain, the founders may have written a "noble statement protecting religious freedom" however, they "*acted* in a way that undermined religious freedom. The very act of formulating the laws of the colonies was a denial of the freedom of enslaved people who shared the faith of the writers."[37]

The negative consequences of the idea of "religious freedom" are perhaps most typified by the way the ideal contributed to the coercion and domination of people who did not confirm to religious norms in America. In her book *Religious Freedom: The Contested History of an American Ideal*, Tisa Wenger documented how, "some of the most frequent and visible articulations of American religious freedom were exclusive, and coercive. The dominant voices in the culture linked racial whiteness, Protestant Christianity, and American national identity not only to freedom in general but often to this freedom in particular."[38] The rhetoric of religious freedom, she continued, "served as an imperial mechanism of classification and control, helping to define not only what counted as religion (or to delineate the good religion versus the bad religion) but also the contours of the racial."[39] Examples from US history include: the expansion of empire in the Philippines, the making of religion on Native American reservations, the making of American whiteness alongside Jewish identity and the tri-faith movement, and the racial limits in the religious freedom of African-American communities.

Similar to "religious freedom," the ideal of "equality" has not been without its own denial of equality. Like *religious freedom exceptionalism*, there is an *equality exceptionalism*--a term we use to describe the function of rhetorically claiming equal protection for oneself while denying it to others. Robert J. Reinstein observed that "the Supreme Court has largely not relied on the Declaration of Independence very much, and when it has, it ruled in *Dred*

Scott that the phrase 'all men are created equal' did not include 'members of the African race.' "[40] Paul Finkelman noted that Abraham Lincoln possessed a tension in his advocacy of equality and the Declaration of Independence in the Lincoln-Douglas Debates, "Lincoln argued that blacks had certain fundamental natural rights, including 'all rights in the Declaration of Independence.' "[41] And in those same debates, Lincoln said, "I am not, nor ever have been in favor of bringing about in any way the social and political equality of the white and black races,-that I am not nor ever have been in favor of making voters or jurors of negroes, nor of qualifying them to hold office, nor to intermarry with white people."[42]

The late Justice Ruth Bader Ginsburg reminded us that the "We" in "We the people" in the Constitution built into the founding document an inequality between those who enjoyed constitutional protection and those who did not, "Think about how things were in 1787. Who were 'We the people'? Certainly not people who were held in human bondage because the original Constitution preserves slavery."[43] She continued, "People who were left out at the beginning—slaves, women, men without property, native Americans—were not part of 'We the people.' "[44] Catharine MacKinnon and Kimberlé Crenshaw explained the constitutional inequality of "equality" thusly, "White supremacy and male dominance, separately and together, were hardwired into a proslavery and tacitly gender-exclusive Constitution from the beginning."[45] They continued, "Enslaved Africans were counted as three-fifths of a person to give political weight to slave owning states; the Electoral College was configured to assure the power of slave states in electing the federal executive officer; no woman or enslaved person was permitted to vote."[46]

The meaning of "equality" is also contested because of individualistic and structural frames of interpretation. Individualistic definitions of "equality" are commonly associated with "discriminatory people" who, because they possess prejudiced attitudes and behaviors, do not believe in equality. The remedy to individualistic equality is typically to sue the discriminatory person for violating the right of the person they discriminated against (and thus denied "equality" to). This is the kind of remedy commonly extended by the courts. For example, in *Oncale v. Sundowner Offshore Services, Inc.* the Court ruled that individual workers discriminated against another individual worker when they subjected the worker to same-sex sexual harassment. In doing so, the person was not treated equally in the workplace. The effect of this individualistic definition of discrimination is the decontextualizing of inequality from any other descriptions beyond the individual. For example, as William Wiecek explained when it comes to race discrimination, "Judges treat racial discrimination as a discrete event, like an intentional tort, even if it is repeated, cumulative, or persistent over time and across space. This approach cuts off the legal wrong of discrimination from the gestalt of its social environment, including the intersection of class, gender, and history."[47]

Defining "equality" strictly in terms of individualism means that structural "inequality" may come to be a defining characteristic of equality's neglect. As Doron Samuel-Siegel, Kenneth Anderson, and Emily Lopynski put it, "Where individual racism is about prejudiced attitudes and behaviors, structural racism is about societal systems."[48] If asked, individually very few in America would be in favor of inequality. This idea, for example, is what Eduardo Bonilla-Silva writes about in *Racism Without Racists: Color-Blind Racism and the Persistence of Racial Inequality in the United States.* He explained, "except for members of white supremacist organizations, few whites in the United States claim to be 'racist.' Most whites assert they 'don't see any color, just people'; that although the ugly face of discrimination is still with us, it is no longer the central factor determining minorities' life chances."[49] He continued, "They publicly denounce blacks for 'playing the race card,' for demanding the maintenance of unnecessary and divisive race-based programs, such as affirmative action, and for crying 'racism' whenever they are criticized by whites. Most whites believe that if blacks and other minorities would just stop thinking about the past, work hard, and complain less (particularly about racial discrimination), then Americans of all hues could 'all get along.' "[50]

For individualist definitions of equality, if people are denied equality, the fault usually lies with the individual for being "unequal." Edward Royce explained the difference well in *Poverty and Power: The Problem of Structural Inequality.* According to Royce, the individualistic perspective on poverty tends toward blaming individuals and their choices for their unequal condition, "They drop out of high school; they reject marriage and sexual monogamy; they have children out of wedlock; they join gangs, do drugs, and commit crimes; and they refuse to stick with a job. . . . [P]oor people are victims of their own bad decisions and lifestyle preferences."[51]

From the structuralist perspective, individuals are victims of inequality for conditions they did not create. Without the working person's consent, politicians and captains of industry make decisions about the structures of society. A structural inequality may result when those in power decide to "downsize the workforce, relocate factories overseas, and impose wage and benefit reductions. They legislate cutbacks in social welfare programs, enact tax cuts for the rich, craft trade agreements that profit multinational corporations at the expense of workers, and pass laws hindering the ability of employees to form labor unions." Those in power also "spend millions of dollars to disseminate the message that the 'free market' is fair and efficient, government programs are wasteful and counterproductive, and poverty is the fault of the poor."[52]

The difference between individualist equality and structural equality may be understood with the example of voting rights arguments. From the individualist equality perspective, every eligible voter has the equal right to vote. This idea finds expression in *Anderson v. Raffensperger*, for example, when the Georgia district court ruled that long lines were not evidence of injury since all those in line voted, and therefore did not violate the equal protection right to vote.[53] From the structural perspective, the long lines are a kind of structural barrier and constitutes a significant violation of equal protection. In the 2004 presidential election, despite lower than expected turnout, Boe Piras explained, "many lines in Ohio were reported to be two to three hours long, some were reported to be seven to nine hours long, and there was one that was as long as twenty-two hours. In that election, an estimated 15,000 voters left polling places in Columbus, Ohio without voting because of long lines."[54] He continued, "it is easy to see how unreasonably long lines at polling places have the real potential to create economic and practical burdens on many employed, voting parents by requiring that voters either miss work or refrain from providing essential childcare in order to vote."[55] From the individualist perspective, all voters are equal because if they all just stand in their lines, they can all vote. From a structural perspective, all voters are not equal because of the structurally unequal demands of time (unequal time in line) and unequal sacrifices based on necessary commitments like work, childcare, etc.

Thus, the individualist notion of equality may define the exercise of the right to vote as "equal" even when different people exercise their right to vote in structurally "unequal" ways by comparing different amounts of time people spend in line. From an individualist perspective, the fact that all participants in line voted is evidence of "equality." From a structural perspective, other structures (i.e., socioeconomic demands) counts of evidence about "inequality." From a structuralist account of "equality," therefore, there are important factors to consider that are not necessarily relevant from the individualist account. Some of these factors include, but are not limited to, the following: (1) the positions of power (e.g., some people have more power over their work schedules than others), (2) The amount of resources available (e.g., some places have more polling places than others), (3) The concern with equity rather than equality (e.g., more resources for areas with problems like parking shortages may be required and less resources for places with plenty of parking) (4) what counts as evidence (e.g., whether a person shows hardship by waiting in line for nine hours, or whether evidence of having voted, despite the wait, is enough to show "unequal" protection).[56]

In sum, both *religious freedom exceptionalism* and *equality exceptionalism* underscore the way both "religious freedom" and "equality" may function to inhibit both freedoms in the way they are practiced. Furthermore, the competing perspectives of individualist "equality" and structural "equality" highlight the rhetorical conflicts over meaning whereby one comes to define "inequality" for the other. While the resolution of structural inequalities is usually recast in the term "equity" to rhetorically shift conversations away from the individualistic frame, the conversations about the nature and scope of "equality" persist. As this book demonstrates, this is particularly the case when the two American rights of "equal protection" and "religious freedom" come into conflict in both legal and cultural contexts.

Preview of Chapters

The range of essays in this volume identify conflicts between "equality" and "religious freedom" relevant to the current historical, political, and cultural moment. They are grouped together in ways that we hope will inform and inspire new lines of sight that may help us collectively understand and come to terms with what our freedoms mean as individuals and as part of a collective. We believe this collection forms a useful way to ground the idealistic concepts of "religious freedom" and "equality" in a manner that bespeaks the practices of those virtues in democratic life.

The first four essays pertain to the role of religious freedom and equality when it comes to the nation's youth. The first two of these focus on the relationships between parents and children. Lindsey A. Sherill examines the conflict between the religious freedom of parents and the equal protection of children to access mandated reporters. Sherill specifically examines the way religious freedom shields cases of child torture, abuse, and neglect when children are denied equal access to the mandated reporters of those crimes. Pamela Morris and Susan Sarapin work through the conflict between equal protection of children and adoption agencies, the religious freedom of adoption agencies, and the issues surrounding government endorsement of religion in supporting religious adoption agencies. They specifically work through the problem whereby 437,000 children are living in foster homes and 125,000 are waiting to be adopted, while at the same time the murky legal situations of sectarian adoption agencies and their religious freedom inhibits their ability to assist an overtaxed child welfare system. One of their fundamental claims is that the lack of legal clarity contributes to the government's failure to meet the needs of children.

The next two essays examine the clash between religious freedom and equality when it comes to educating the nation's youth. Adrienne Hacker-Daniels provides an in-depth analysis of the *Board of Education of Kiryas Joel Village School District v. Grumet* case, involving religious freedom, equal protection for special education, and questions that are homologous to the landmark *Brown v. Board of Education* case. In doing so, she advances the idea that equal protection and religious freedom clashes might be better understand not as a matter of stasis (i.e., the kind of arguments traditionally found in forensic courtroom kinds of rhetoric), but rather as a form of asystatic theory that draws on questions of balance and inconclusiveness. Elizabeth Thorpe examines recent developments in cases that involve the religious rights of prayer in public schools. She suggests that many of the Establishment Clause cases about government endorsement of religion may be less problematic if treated more in terms of Equal Protection Clause jurisprudence. Namely, that the conflict over religious freedom and equal protection appears to be, perhaps ironically, an equal unprotection—people expressing secular viewpoints are more protected than those who express religious viewpoints. These tensions are, of course, more complicated than they appear to be at first glance.

The next set of essays are comprised of three areas of study concerning questions about government endorsements and accommodations of religion. Juliet Dee studies the nature and scope of the Johnson Amendment and its relationship to and with tax codes pertaining to exemptions for religious organizations. Dee highlights the tension between religious leaders who seek to exercise a First Amendment right of electioneering communication for candidates that may be in favor of their interests (i.e., advocating for candidates in favor of upholding religious freedom), and the equal protection of the general public who may in effect be required to subsidize the religious leaders' speech through the tax exemption. Amanda Reid takes up issues pertaining to roadside religious memorials. There are many government regulations pertaining to roadside memorials in terms of religious symbols (i.e., the time, distance between and away from roads, upkeep, and more). Reid suggests that there is a tension in terms of equal protection of the public land use, and the potential for selective nonenforcement of laws that may result in government endorsement of religion concerns. David Dewberry and Pat Arneson review the issue of draft exemption for conscientious objectors. In analyzing the case of *Gibson v. United States*, they argue the difference between equal protection and religious freedom lies in the stark contrast of legal and communication paradigms—potentially irreconcilable differences in the practices of the selective service.

The next set of essays work through equal protection and religious freedom conflicts that have arisen out of the implementation of the Religious Freedom Restoration Act (RFRA). The first two of these essays are on the case of *Burwell v. Hobby Lobby.* Skye de Saint Felix examines the implications of the Court's decision to define corporations' religious freedom based on part of a corporation (i.e., the owners and shareholders, and *not* the employees), and also the impacts that the decision has had for women's equality. de Saint Felix also examines the implications of RFRA and other cases like *Masterpiece Cakeshop v. Colorado* that privilege the freedom of religion over the recognition of gender equality. Joseph Sery examines the rhetorical choices of Justice Alito's majority opinion in *Hobby Lobby.* Drawing on Thomas Goodnight's idea of the "three spheres of argumentation," Sery argues that the primary rhetorical appeal of the personal sphere of argumentation that exists in religious freedom arguments functions to undermine the technical sphere of medical consensus, and in doing so further marginalizes concerns about equal protection in the public sphere of argumentation. Jason Zenor examines the impact of RFRA on Native American sovereignty and religion. Zenor examines the Sioux tribes' loss in their RFRA claim against the Dakota Access Pipeline, specifically to the way Native American rights are rhetorically questioned in terms of their "sincerity" and whether the tests for Native American sincerely held religious beliefs are equally applied to other similar religious freedom claims.

The last set of essays cover a few of the culture clashes that have played out in American life. These essays are less concerned with the way equality and religious freedom have played out in legal conflicts, and more concerned with the implications and lessons to learn from the cultural politics of equal protection and religious freedom. Diana Martínez, Jamila Cupid, and Robert Mejia examine the conflicts between Christian nationalism and the equal protection of migrant people who suffer separation from family members, the enduring of abuse, neglect, assault, and other atrocities. Specifically, they examine elements of visual rhetoric that, from a Christian nationalist framing comes to view immigrants as deficient rather than as human rights abuses, and how that framing impacts the unequal protection of human rights and the perpetuation of citizenship excess. Ann Burnette and Rebekah Fox examine the case of *Masterpiece Cakeshop v. Colorado Civil Rights Commission* in order to account for the complex cultural values that clashed in the case, arguing that the case was never about just a cake but about a fundamental clash between equal protection and religious freedom that permeates

American cultural politics and the right to claim discrimination on the basis of a person's identity and a person's beliefs. Mark Ward Sr. examines the implications of media deregulation and the "equal protection" of proliferating private media spaces. Ward examines the religious freedom claims of Bob Shuler and other televangelists as congruent with privatized equal protection and conflicting with public equal protection. He argues that the rise of the deregulation form of equal protection mirrors the decline of public deliberation and increase in sectarianism. Logan Spence studies the conflict between religious freedom and equal protection in the "war on Christmas." Spence examines the way that the rhetoric of political correctness grew out of a version of equal protection that gave rise to conspiracy theories within American Christian groups who performed a paranoid style by constructing a story about a "war on Christmas."

Conclusion

This collection of essays investigate conflicts between "equality" and "religious freedom" in American life. Whether it be about the welfare and education of our nation's youth, or about government endorsements of religion through tax policies and use of public places, or the religious objections to mandatory military service, or the increasing number of RFRA claims, or the various culture clashes, one thing seems abundantly clear—no book or collection of essays will be able to "resolve" the deep-seated divisions over religious freedom and equal protection. Perhaps the best that we can hope for is to focus on some of the problems (like child torture, for example) that we can all agree on, and work toward productive solutions toward those problems. Perhaps on a more idealistic note, we hope that understanding both "religious freedom" and "equality" as rhetorically contested terms will encourage an expectation of mutuality for working through many of the tensions that are inevitable in democratic life.

At its best, "religious freedom" looks like the United States granting asylum "for a young man from Angola who fled the government after he sought to attend the trial of his religious leader and was attacked and beaten by the police for his religious association."[57] The man wrote, "you have changed the history of my life thank you very much and I hope that as you help me, may you also do, if possible, with more people. Because I was without hope but you gave me hope in my life. You have changed my history, a new history has begun, thanks to all of you for your goodness; you are enlightened beings. May God bless you."[58] Or, religious freedom looks like the role of church life in providing places for assembly of African American communities throughout history. As Allison Calhoun-Brown noted, "Churches have traditionally been viewed as places of stability and strength in the African-American community. From slavery through the long racially segregated history of the United States, when African Americans were prevented from building institutions of their own and precluded from participating in the institutions of mainstream America, churches developed and contained civil society for them."[59] She continued, "In church, one could find politics, arts, music, education, economic development, social services, civic associations, leadership opportunities, and business enterprises. One could also find a rich spiritual tradition of survival and liberation."[60]

At its best, "equality" looks like the achievements of so many "firsts" for identities that have traditionally been underrepresented in honors and occupations. Adeel Hassan reminded us of so many of the recent stories that give us hope for equality.[61] These stories include Chinese railroad workers who were finally recognized for their pivotal role in the construction of the Transcontinental Railroad, Joy Harjo of the Muscogee Creek Nation became the First Native American to hold the post of poet laureate, "Molly of Denali" became the first nationally distributed children's series with a Native American lead, the city Montgomery in Alabama elected its first black mayor, New York City Ballet's "Nutcracker" featured its first black Marie (Charlotte Nebres), Lonnie G. Bunch III became the first African-American to lead the Smithsonian Institution, and Asley James became the first full-time black curator at the Guggenheim. Or, at its best, "equality" looks like breaking up the separate but equal paradigm of segregation in *Plessy v. Ferguson* by establishing what has now come to be a "super-precedent"[62] landmark case of *Brown v. Board of Education*.

At its worst, "religious freedom" looks like children dying because they had no protection against parents who exercised their religious freedom to opt for "faith healing" instead of medical care, "172 children died following faith healing between 1975 and 1995; 140 of them had ailments that, with proper medical care, would have had a ninety percent survival rate. The number of deaths is likely to be even greater than reported."[63] Or, it looks like the hundreds of people who have committed "apocalyptic suicide" by killing themselves after a charismatic figure persuaded them to do so while exercising their religious freedom (often persuaded to believe they are "invincible" because god would protect them from material harm when they, for example, drink poisonous drinks or walk into live gunfire of enemies).[64] Or, it looks like normative religious practices that, implicitly or explicitly, have the effect of shaming people to keep their true selves secret, to live double lives, and experience moments of "cognitive shock, incoherence, and confusion" in a manner that results in self-hatred or diminished self-esteem (and sometimes lashing out at others).[65]

At its worst, "equal protection" looks like de facto segregation in the wake of *Brown v. Board of Education.* Joseph O. Oluwole and Preston C. Green III examine how, for example, the common judicial vehicle of colorblind notions of equal protection result in de facto segregation, which amongst other things, means "that minority students suffer harm in a vicious cycle as they are consigned to lower track placements."[66] Moreover, the adverse reality of this "colorblind equality" means a current reality where, "Latino and African American students attend increasingly segregated schools with 43 percent Latino students and 40 percent of African American students in schools with at least 90 percent minority students."[67] Or, "equal opportunity" looks like a world where the number of billionaires in the world is in the thousands while millions of people struggle to put a daily meal on the table. Or, it looks like tokenism where small numbers of elites select or accompany token minorities with no intention of extending the privileges to other people, making sure the structures remain intact to effectively secure a perpetually marginalized class.

One consistent theme in this book is that these competing terms in American democratic life never exist *solely* at their best or at their worst. Equality and religious freedom encompass some of our greatest hopes and deepest frustrations. The tension must be negotiated through rhetorical processes undertaken with the expectation of mutuality and centered on the lived experiences of the humans they impact. Judgments about the meaning of these terms are consequential. Put simply, interpretation *is* consequential. It is not simply a matter of relegating interpretation to a "*mere* matter of opinion." Interpretation leads to judgment and judgment leads to practice. Together they lead to material consequences. Of course, human affairs is messy. As rhetorical scholars we know this. They must be. We are not the same. We have different lived experiences. And yet, we exist in relation to the language of "equality" and "religious freedom" and must engage the rhetorical economy in a manner that may be (ir)reconcilable with consequence. Such engagement may just be both impossible and necessary, and perhaps that is what makes both "equality" and "religious freedom" endure as rhetorical and (un)satisfying terms.

Notes

1 *McDonald v. City of Chicago*, pp. 28–29.
2 *Terry v. Ohio*, p. 33.

3 *Bolling v. Sharpe*, p. 499.
4 *Gideon v. Wainwright*, p. 344.
5 *Parklane Hosiery Company v. Shore*, p. 335.
6 *Furman v. Georgia*, p. 255.
7 *Olff v. East Side Union High School District*, p. 1044.
8 *Shelby County v. Holder* p. 530.
9 *Shelby County v. Holder* p. 530.
10 *Brown v. Board of Education* p. 483.
11 *Reed v. Reed*, p. 77.
12 *Obergefell v. Hodges* p. 22.
13 Gary Lawson, Guy I. Seidman, and Robert G. Natelson. "The Fiduciary Foundations of Federal Equal Protection," *Boston University School of Law, Public Law Research Paper No. 13–32.* (2013): 25.
14 Gary Lawson, Guy I. Seidman, and Robert G. Natelson. "The Fiduciary Foundations of Federal Equal Protection," *Boston University School of Law, Public Law Research Paper No. 13–32* (2013): 25.
15 Gary Lawson, Guy I. Seidman, and Robert G. Natelson. "The Fiduciary Foundations of Federal Equal Protection," *Boston University School of Law, Public Law Research Paper No. 13–32* (2013): 25.
16 Gary Lawson, Guy I. Seidman, and Robert G. Natelson. "The Fiduciary Foundations of Federal Equal Protection," *Boston University School of Law, Public Law Research Paper No. 13–32* (2013): 41.
17 Thomas Jefferson, "Freedom of Religion at the University of Virginia (October 7, 1822)," in *The Complete Jefferson, Containing His Major Writings,* ed. Saul K. Padover (1969), 957–58.
18 E. Gregory Wallace, "Justifying Religious Freedom: The Western Tradition," *Penn State Law Review*, v. 114 (2009): 489–90.
19 Eric Yordy, "Clamorous Coexistence: The U.S. Commission on Civil Rights and the Internal Battle Between Religion and Nondiscrimination Laws," *William and Mary Policy Review*, v. 8 (2017): 7. Yordy cites several instances of the "first freedom" as resonant in American life.
20 Michael W. McConnell, "The Origins and Historical Understanding of Free Exercise of Religion," *Harvard Law Review*, v. 103 (May, 1990): 1456.
21 Michael W. McConnell, "The Origins and Historical Understanding of Free Exercise of Religion," *Harvard Law Review* 103 (May, 1990): 1512.
22 Justice Thomas, concurring opinion, pp. 937–8.
23 *Poe v. Ullman*, p. 552.
24 *Poe v. Ullman*, p. 552.
25 *U.S. v. Weldon*, p. 117.
26 Confession and information confidentiality issues, of course, are another matter altogether. The point here is that the person may refuse to take part in the investigation if the investigation infringes on their First Amendment right while simultaneously infringing on their Fifth Amendment right against self-incrimination.
27 215 A.D.2d 401, 626 N.Y.S.2d 245, People v. Gilliam, Supreme Court, Appellate Division, Second Department, New York, 94–00351 (May 1, 1995).
28 52 F.Supp. 612, District Court, E.D. Washington, Southern Division. United States v. Hillyard, No. C-3879, November 30, 1943.

29 *Robbins v.* Robertson, United States Court of Appeals, Eleventh Circuit. July 23, 2019, 782 Fed. Appx. 794 2019 WL 3302229 P. 804.
30 *City of Wadsworth v.* Owens, Wadsworth Municipal Court, Ohio. May 28, 1987, 42 Ohio Misc. 2d 1536 N.E. 2d 67, P. 3
31 New Hampshire, Oregon, Vermont, Tennessee, and Virginia do not mention "God" in their preambles. See Christopher Hammons, "State Constitutions, Religious Protection, and Federalism," *University of St. Thomas Journal of Law and Public Policy* 7, no. 2 (Spring, 2013): 231.
32 Aleksandra Sandstrom, "God or the Divine is Referenced in Every State Constitution," *Factank: News in the Numbers.* Pew Research Center. (August 17, 2017). Available at https://www.pewresearch.org/fact-tank/2017/08/17/god-or-the-divine-is-referenced-in-every-state-constitution/
33 While the Court made this determination, it did claim that RFRA was irrelevant to the case insofar as there was no religious liberty claim in the specific case. p. 1754.
34 Philip Bobbitt, *Constitutional Interpretation* (Oxford: Basil Blackwell, 1991), p. 24.
35 Craig R. Smith, "Introduction, Methodology, and Overview," *A First Amendment Profile of the Supreme Court*, ed. Craig R. Smith (Newark, DE: John Cabot U P, 2011), 3.
36 Jacqueline C. Rivers, "The Paradox of the Black Church and Religious Freedom," *University of St. Thomas Law Journal*, 15 (Spring, 2019): 679–80.
37 Jacqueline C. Rivers, "The Paradox of the Black Church and Religious Freedom," *University of St. Thomas Law Journal*, 15 (Spring, 2019): 680.
38 Tisa Wegner, *Religious Freedom: The Contested History of an American Ideal* (Chapel Hill, NC: U of North Carolina P, 2017), 1.
39 Tisa Wegner, *Religious Freedom: The Contested History of an American Ideal* (Chapel Hill, NC: U of North Carolina P, 2017), 3.
40 Robert J. Reinstein, "Completing the Constitution: The Declaration of Independence, Bill of Rights and Fourteenth Amendment," *Temple Law Review*, 66 (Summer, 1993): 362.
41 Qtd. In Paul Finkelman, "Civil Liberties and Civil War: The Great Emancipator as Civil Libertarian" (Book review). *Michigan Law* Review 91 (May, 1993): 1355. Abraham Lincoln, Speech at Quincy (October 13, 1858) *in* 3 WORKS OF LINCOLN, *supra* note 14, at 249.
42 Qtd. In Paul Finkelman, "Civil Liberties and Civil War: The Great Emancipator as Civil Libertarian" (Book review). *Michigan Law* Review 91 (May, 1993): 1355. Abraham Lincoln, Speech at Charleston (September 18, 1858) *in* 3 WORKS OF LINCOLN, *supra* note 14, at 145.
43 Ruth Bader Ginsburg in "5 Inspiring Quotes from Justice Ruth Bader Ginsburg's Lecture in Little Rock, Arkansas," *Clinton Foundation.* (September 9, 2019), available at https://stories.clintonfoundation.org/five-inspiring-quotes-from-justice-ruth-bader-ginsburgs-lecture-in-little-rock-arkansas-5b034176e485
44 Ruth Bader Ginsburg in "5 Inspiring Quotes from Justice Ruth Bader Ginsburg's Lecture in Little Rock, Arkansas," *Clinton Foundation.* (September 9, 2019), available at https://stories.clintonfoundation.org/five-inspiring-quotes-from-justice-ruth-bader-ginsburgs-lecture-in-little-rock-arkansas-5b034176e485
45 Catharine A. MacKinnon and Kimberlé Crenshaw, "Reconstituting the Future: An Equality Amendment," *Yale Law Journal Forum* 129 (December 26, 2019): 344.

46 Catharine A. MacKinnon and Kimberlé Crenshaw, "Reconstituting the Future: An Equality Amendment," *Yale Law Journal Forum* 129 (December 26, 2019): 346.
47 William M. Wiecek, "Structural Racism and the Law in America Today: An Introduction," *Kentucky Law Journal* 100 (2011–2012): 4.
48 Doron Samuel-Siegel, Kenneth S. Anderson, and Emily Lopynski, "Reckoning with Structural Racism: A Restorative Jurisprudence of Equal Protection," *Richmond Public Interest Law Review*, 23 (March, 2020): 139.
49 Eduardo Bonilla-Silva, *Racism without Racists: Color-Blind Racism and the Persistence of Racial Inequality in the United States* (Rowman & Littlefield Publishers, 2006), 1.
50 Eduardo Bonilla-Silva, *Racism without Racists: Color-Blind Racism and the Persistence of Racial Inequality in the United States* (Rowman & Littlefield Publishers, 2006), 1.
51 Edward Royce, *Poverty and Power: The Problem of Structural Inequality* (Rowman & Littlefield, 2018), 17.
52 Edward Royce, *Poverty and Power: The Problem of Structural Inequality* (Rowman & Littlefield, 2018), 17–18.
53 *Anderson v. Reffensperger*, States District Court, N.D. Georgia, Atlanta Division, October 13, 2020.
54 Boe M. Piras, "Long Lines at the Polls Violate Equal Protection and Require Judicial and Legislative Action," *University of St. Thomas Law Journal* 6 (Spring, 2009): 660.
55 Boe M. Piras, "Long Lines at the Polls Violate Equal Protection and Require Judicial and Legislative Action," *University of St. Thomas Law Journal* 6 (Spring, 2009): 668.
56 The analysis of structural factors is super-complicated by a vast array of histories, identities, socio-economies, and the like. This is also because structures themselves are immensely complex, intersectional, and overlapping.
57 Migrant Center for Human Rights, "Success Stories," https://migrantcenter.org/success-stories/ (Accessed December 28, 2020).
58 Anonymous. Many asylum names remain confidential because those who seek to harm the person may continue to seek them out if they know the identity. Migrant Center for Human Rights, "Success Stories," https://migrantcenter.org/success-stories/ (Accessed December 28, 2020).
59 Allison Calhoun-Brown, "Upon This Rock: The Black Church, Nonviolence, and the Civil Rights Movement." *PS: Political Science and Politics* 33, no. 2 (2000): 169–74, p. 169.
60 Allison Calhoun-Brown, "Upon This Rock: The Black Church, Nonviolence, and the Civil Rights Movement." *PS: Political Science and Politics* 33, no. 2 (2000): 169–74, p. 169.
61 Adeel Hassan, "Stories About Equality that Gave Us Hope in 2019," *New York Times (Online)*, (January 1, 2020).
62 The "super precedent" idea has appeared in several Supreme Court confirmation hearings, most notably in those involving Chief Justice Roberts, Justice Alito, and Justice Amy Coney Barrett. The term seems to have been coined in 1976 by Judge (then professor) Posner and Professor Landes. According to Michael Sinclair, a "super precedent" is not necessarily a legal term, though it may be used to refer to a case that is "judicially unshakeable, a precedential monument which may not be gainsaid, akin to having the statute-like force of vertical stare decisis horizontally." See Michael Sinclair, "Precedent, Supre-Precedent," *George Mason Law Review* 14, no. 2 (2007): 365.

63 Rebecca Williams, "Faith Healing Exceptions Versus Parens Patriae: Something's Gotta Give," *First Amendment Law* Review 10 (Spring, 2012): 693.
64 Simon Dein, and Roland Littlewood. "Apocalyptic Suicide: From a Pathological to an Eschatological Interpretation." *International Journal of Social Psychiatry* 51, no. 3 (2005): 198–210.
65 Donald L. Nathanson, "Foreword," p. xiv. The quote is from the foreword, but the rest of the ideas in this sentence may be found in Sally R. Munt, *Queer Attachments: The Cultural Politics of Shame* (New York: Routledge, 2016).
66 Joseph O. Oluwole and Preston C. Green III, "Riding the *Plessy* Train: Reviving *Brown* for a New Civil Rights Era for Micro-Desegregation," *Chicana/o-Latina/o Law Review*, 36 (2019): 65.
67 Joseph O. Oluwole and Preston C. Green III, "Riding the *Plessy* Train: Reviving *Brown* for a New Civil Rights Era for Micro-Desegregation," *Chicana/o-Latina/o Law Review* 36 (2019): 3.

Bibliography

Anderson v. Raffensperger, No. 1: 20-cv-03263 (N.D. Ga. Oct. 13, 2020).

Bobbitt, Philip Chase. "Constitutional Interpretation", 24. Blackwell Publishing, 1991.

Bolling v. Sharpe, 347 U.S. 497 (1954): 499.

Bonilla-Silva, Eduardo. "Racism without Racists: Color-Blind Racism and the Persistence of Racial Inequality in the United States", 1. Rowman & Littlefield Publishers, 2006.

Bostock v. Clayton County, 140 S.Ct. 1731 (2020).

Brown v. Board of Education, 347 U.S. 483 (1954): 483.

Calhoun-Brown, Allison. "Upon this Rock: The Black Church, Nonviolence, and the Civil Rights Movement", 169. *Political Science & Politics* 33, no. 2 (2000): 169–174.

City of Wadsworth v. Owens, 42 Ohio Misc. 2d 1 (1987).

Dein, Simon, and Roland Littlewood. "Apocalyptic Suicide: From a Pathological to an Eschatological Interpretation", *International Journal of Social Psychiatry* 51, no. 3 (2005): 198–210.

Finkelman, Paul. "Civil Liberties and Civil War: The Great Emancipator as Civil Libertarian", *Michigan Law Review* (1993): 1353–1381.

Foundation, Clinton. "Five Inspiring Quotes from Justice Ruth Bader Ginsburg's Lecture in Little Rock, Arkansas", The Clinton Foundation, September 23, 2019. https://stories.clintonfoundation.org/five-inspiring-quotes-from-justice-ruth-bader-ginsburgs-lecture-in-little-rock-arkansas-5b034176e485.

Furman v. Georgia, 408 U.S. 238 (1972): 255.

Gideon v. Wainwright, 372 U.S. 335 (1963): 344.

Hammons, Christopher. "State Constitutions, Religious Protection, and Federalism.", 231. U. St. Thomas JL & Pub. Pol'y 7 (2012): 226.

Hassan, Adeel. "Stories about Equality That Gave Us Hope in 2019." *The New York Times*. January 1, 2020. https://www.nytimes.com/2020/01/01/us/stories-about-equality-that-gave-us-hope-in-2019.html.

Lawson, Gary, Guy I. Seidman, and Robert G. Natelson. "The Fiduciary Foundations of Federal Equal Protection", 25, 41. *Boston University School of Law, Public Law Research Paper* No. 13-32. http://dx.doi.org/10.2139/ssrn.2298762.

MacKinnon, Catharine A., and Kimberlé W. Crenshaw. "Reconstituting the Future: An Equality Amendment.", 344, 346. *Yale LJF* 129 (2019): 343.

McConnell, Michael W. "The Origins and Historical Understanding of Free Exercise of Religion", 1456, 1512. In *Harvard Law Review*, v. 103 (May, 1990).

McDonald v. City of Chicago, 561 U.S. 742 (2010): 28–29.

Michael B.W. "Precedent, Super-Precedent" *George Mason Law Review*. (2007). http://www.georgemasonlawreview.org/wp-content/uploads/2014/03/14-2_Sinclair.pdf

Migrant Center for Human Rights. "Success Stories." *Migrant Center For Human Rights*. January 4, 2021. https://migrantcenter.org/success-stories/.

Munt, Sally R. "Queer Attachments: The Cultural Politics of Shame", *Routledge*, 2017.

Obergefell v. Hodges, 135 S.Ct. 2071 (2015): 22.

Olff v. East Side Union High School District, 305 F.Supp. 557 (1969): 1044.

Oluwole, Joseph O., and Preston C. Green III. "Riding the Plessy Train: Reviving Brown for a New Civil Rights Era for Micro-Desegregation.", 3, 65. *Chicano-Latino L. Rev.* 36 (2019): 1.

Parklane Hosiery Company v. Shore, 439 U.S. 322 (1979): 335.

People v. Gilliam, 670 N.E.2d 606 (1996).

Piras, Boe M. "Long Lines at the Polls Violate Equal Protection and Require Judicial and Legislative Action", 660, 668. *U. St. Thomas LJ* 6 (2008): 658.

Poe v. Ullman, 367 U.S. 497 (1961): 552.

Reed v. Reed, 404 U.S. 71 (1971): 77.

Reinstein, Robert J. "Completing the Constitution: The Declaration of Independence, Bill of Rights and Fourteenth Amendment", 362. *Temple L. Rev.* 66 (1993): 361.

Rivers, Jacqueline C. "The Paradox of the Black Church and Religious Freedom", *U. St. Thomas LJ* 15 (2018): 679–680.

Robbins v. Robertson, No. 16-16021 (11th Cir. July 23, 2019).

Royce, Edward. "Poverty and Power: The Problem of Structural Inequality", 17–18. Rowman & Littlefield, 2018.

Samuel-Siegel, Doron, Kenneth S. Anderson, and Emily Lopynski. "Reckoning with Structural Racism: A Restorative Jurisprudence of Equal Protection", 139. *Rich. Pub. Int. L. Rev.* 23 (2019): 137.

Sandstrom, Aleksandra. "God or the Divine Is Referenced in Every State Constitution." *Pew Research Center* (2017).

Saul, Kussiel Padover. "Thomas Jefferson's Freedom of Religion at the University of Virginia" In *The Complete Jefferson: Containing his Major Writings*, 957–958. New York: Duell, Sloan & Pearce (1943).

Shelby County v. Holder, 133 S.Ct. 2612 (2013): 530.

Smith, Craig. "Introduction, Methodology, and Overview," *A First Amendment Profile of the Supreme Court.* University of Delaware, 2011.

Terry v. Ohio, 392 U.S. 1 (1968): 33.

U.S. v. Welden, 377 U.S. 95 (1964).

United States v. Hillyard, 677 F.2d 1336 (1982).

Wallace, E. Gregory. "Justifying Religious Freedom: The Western Tradition", *Penn St. L. Rev.* 114 (2009): 489–490.

Wenger, Tisa. "Religious Freedom: The Contested History of an American Ideal", *UNC Press Books*, 2017.

Wiecek, William M. "Structural Racism and the Law in America Today: An Introduction", *Ky. LJ* 100 (2011): 1.

Williams, Rebecca. "Faith Healing Exception versus Parens Patriae: Something's Gotta Give", 693. *First Amend. L. Rev.* 10 (2011): 692.

Yordy, Eric. "Clamorous Coexistence: The US Commission on Civil Rights and the Internal Battle between Religion and Nondiscrimination Laws", *William & Mary Policy Review* 8, no. 2 (2017).

Part I. Equality, Religious Freedom, and the Nation's Youth

2. *Child Protection v. Parental Rights: Homeschooling and Abuse in the United States*

LINDSEY A. SHERRILL

While the vast majority of parents who choose to homeschool have the best interests of their children at heart, lax regulations on home education in the United States effectively allow parents to circumvent safeguards meant to protect children from mistreatment and educational neglect.[1] In some cases, this means children receive inadequate instruction; in the worst cases, children suffer abuse and lack access to mandated reporters. Homeschooling regulations (or lack thereof) are the result of powerful lobbying efforts by homeschool advocates, using various legal arguments pitting parental rights and religious practice against the interests of the state while often ignoring children's rights to equal protection. This chapter begins by describing the legal arguments that have resulted in current state laws, the history of homeschooling in the United States, and the motivations of homeschooling parents. It includes an analysis of the rhetoric and positioning of eight homeschool-related organizations, and provides future suggestions for protecting homeschooled children's rights.

Legal Arguments: Protecting Children v. Religious Freedom and Privacy

For much of American history, the idea of equal protection for children went unexamined, with legal precedent resting on the English common law view of children as the property of their parents.[2] One of the United States' first child abuse convictions did not come until the 1870s, and the American Medical Association did not describe medical diagnoses of child abuse until

1962.[3] In 1974, the Child Abuse Prevention and Treatment Act (CAPTA) was passed to offer federal funding for the prosecution and prevention of child abuse.[4]

Several different philosophies make a compelling case for state interest in the protection of children.[5] One such philosophy is vulnerability theory,[6] which considers society to have a universal public and legal responsibility to guard against individuals', particularly children's, vulnerability. Fineman and Shepherd describe a "geography of childhood" built upon family, community, and education. They argue that homeschooling distorts this geography through isolation, lack of exposure to diverse others and ideologies, and creates intentional or inadvertent knowledge gaps; thus, the state has good reasons to regulate or prohibit home education.[7]

Others frame these arguments in terms of three interlocking spheres of children's rights—individual rights, parental rights, and interests of the state.[8] From this perspective, parents have an interest in raising their children, children have an interest in receiving safe, quality education that affords them choice later in life, and the state has an interest in protecting children and producing prepared citizens.[9] This argument rests upon the democratic ideal of checks and balances. Ideally, all of the adults in a child's sphere—family members, teachers, doctors, etc.—should serve as checks against abuse and neglect. This balance may be lost if families isolate, such as in some homeschooling situations. Lupu states it thus:

> Children raised in a regime of separated power are rather less likely to feel at risk and far more likely to feel themselves to be citizens of their larger communities than children raised in a regime of highly concentrated authority. Parents should have substantial power to choose their children's teachers, but there is reason to be troubled, and sufficient constitutional warrant for states to act, when parents choose only themselves.[10]

Others have argued for stronger legislation of children's rights based on the harm principle, or the idea that laws exist to prevent harm to others. Using this principle, scholars have argued that failing to prepare children for the best availability of future options violates their "rights in trust" by limiting potential.[11] However, rights in trust, or presenting children with unlimited future options, may directly clash with parental rights.[12] This clash is particularly difficult when religious convictions compete with state interests; values such as teaching tolerance and broadening minds may undermine parental beliefs. Parents may also argue that some kinds of education, like secular sexual education, are harmful to their children, or that they themselves are harmed by being forced to violate deeply held religious convictions.[13] Others argue that the harm principle comes from a liberal tradition of weighing certain societal goals as superior to others and is thus too subjective to apply to religious freedom arguments.[14]

Fineman and Shepherd state, "The United States is currently the only country not to officially accept the premise that children have rights as individuals, independent of their families."[15] Dwyer concurs:

> There is an attitude at work toward children, one that views them not as persons in their own right but as appendages or property of their parents. . .even highly educated liberals tend to view child-rearing legal issues through an adult-focused lens, perceiving conflicts over regulation of child-rearing as pitting the state against "the family" as a unitary entity represented solely and fully by the expressed wishes of the adults.[16]

U.S. laws have focused on parental rights versus state interests rather than children's rights to equal protection. These cases rest largely on three arguments: first, parental rights are tantamount to unalienable rights; second, religious freedom must be protected at almost any cost; and third, rights to privacy and against government intrusion are sacred. While these rights are valuable in a democratic society, they have often come at the price of vulnerable children's rights. The following sections detail the history and substance of these arguments.

Parental Rights

In the view of many homeschooling advocates, public schools are bastions of authoritarian control while parents are experts on their own children.[17] Nicholas Wolterstorff, a Yale theologian and philosopher often cited by proponents of private and religious education, argued for the preeminence of parental rights: "I am profoundly persuaded that the right of parents to determine the character of their child's education is one of the most fundamental human rights, more fundamental than the right to free speech."[18] This view of parental rights over their children's education has been affirmed by the Supreme Court as well: "[the] primary role of parents in the upbringing of their children is . . . an enduring American tradition"[19] In 1923, *Meyer v. Nebraska*[20] found that parents had a "liberty interest" in the education of their children. *Pierce v. Society of Sisters*[21] allowed parents some say in school attendance rules: "The child is not the mere creature of the state; those who nurture him and direct his destiny have the right, coupled with the high duty, to recognize and prepare him for additional obligations." Parental authority over all aspects of a child's education was further affirmed by 1987's *Care and Protection of Charles & Others*,[22] which broadened parental authority over education previously limited by cases like *Runyon v. McCrary*.[23] *Charles* essentially shifted the burden of proving child educational neglect to the state by arguing that asking homeschooling parents to prove that they were *not* neglecting their children was essentially removing presumption of innocence.[24] In general, rulings on home education legislation have erred on the side of parental rights. These rulings come from the "negative rights" tradition—that is, the belief that laws exist to prevent rights from being taken away rather than affording assistance to maintain rights (such as overseeing that a child's rights not be abused).[25] Yet this upholding of parental absolutism appears inconsistent with state and federal laws giving children the right to education and freedom from abuse and neglect.[26]

Religious Freedom

Many of the strongest parental rights arguments are linked to religious freedom and practice. The homeschooling movement in the United States and the majority of its advocacy has come from religious groups, primarily fundamentalist Christians. Early religious freedom in education cases dealt with the convictions of other groups however, such as *Wisconsin v. Yoder.*[27] Advocates of regulation have argued that *Yoder* has been interpreted too broadly, noting that while *Yoder* can be interpreted to ignore the interests of the child in favor of the parent or religious group, it only applies directly to Amish communities, and if challenged, could be more strictly confined or overturned.[28] Other scholars have argued that religious exceptions to education and neglect statutes are the real violations of First Amendment rights because they allow for unequal treatment (i.e., different levels of regulation) based on religion.[29] One such example is state laws that homeschool students must be taught by a registered teacher—parents may be exempt from this requirement for religious but not secular reasons.[30] Even organizations with religious affiliations, like the Home Education Association of Virginia, have noted religious exemption discrepancies. A section of their website devoted to understanding whether to register as a religious or non-religious homeschooler quotes Virginia statute 22.1–254 (B)(1):

> A school board shall excuse from attendance at school: any pupil who, together with his parents, by reason of bona fide religious training or belief is conscientiously opposed to attendance at school. For purposes of this subdivision, "bona fide religious training or belief" does not include essentially political, sociological or philosophical views or a merely personal moral code.[31]

The website notes that parents and state officials must be especially careful in stating or asking if "beliefs are sincere and present in daily life" as this statement could easily become an unconstitutional religiosity test. This is echoed by other legal arguments which have claimed that asking parents to prove that religion is a reason for their decisions is essentially a religious test, thus violating constitutional law.[32]

Other homeschool advocates argue that *any* regulation, regardless of religious exemptions, is "extremely oppressive."[33] One advocate told *The Christian Post:* "The famous quote, 'the price of liberty is eternal vigilance,' is very apropos here because that's what all of us who believe in educational freedom and parental rights do. We seek to be vigilant so that our God-given right to train up our children is not impeded upon by bureaucrats and legislatures."[34] This argument is often used to connect parental authority to religious freedom—parental objections to regulation are grounded in a disbelief in the legitimate authority of secular powers.[35] The precedent in *Charles* recognized that state regulation of education required parental cooperation, in essence forcing parents to submit to an authority that they did not see as legitimate.[36]

More recent arguments have suggested *Burwell v. Hobby Lobby's* interpretation of the Religious Freedom Restoration Act might be applied to homeschooling and religious accommodation.[37] While *Hobby Lobby* expands the definition of "core aspects" of religion, it is possible that courts will not apply it to educational contexts as it addresses employers rather than parents, and federal rather than state regulations. Others note that long-standing Supreme Court precedent has held that exemptions relating to free exercise can be struck down for purposes of compelling state interests, such as in *Reynolds v. U.S.*'s polygamy prohibitions, suggesting that religious freedom arguments may not be as unassailable as advocates want legislators to believe, and that sensible regulations are allowable.[38] There is also an argument to be made that *children's* religious liberty is being violated if they are given no exposure to other options.[39]

Fourth Amendment Rights

Other arguments against homeschooling regulations have been framed in terms of rights to privacy and against unreasonable search and seizure, pitting child protective services (CPS) against parental rights.[40] This position argues that CPS often overstep constitutional bounds against warrantless searches or use coercion (such as threatening parents with removal of their children) to gain consent to interview children or inspect homes.[41] Advocates of parental privacy rights cite data that up to 71.4% of investigations of child abuse claims are unsubstantiated[42] and that overzealous investigations are themselves abusive.[43] *Calabretta v. Floyd* included children's rights to privacy as well in the ruling: "The government's best interest in the welfare of children embraces not only protecting children from physical abuse, but also protecting children's interest in the privacy and dignity of their homes and in the lawfully exercised authority of their parents."[44]

This fear of state overreach and CPS failure is not entirely baseless. Early homeschoolers were often reported for truancy or neglect by well-meaning relatives or neighbors, leading to many of the early legal fights.[45] There are also extreme cases of CPS overreach, like that of Jessie and Lauren Wallis in the early 1990s.[46] CPS failures are often cited, claiming that attention to non-serious cases strains the system and leads to examples like *State v. Wilkerson*[47] where a *lack* of CPS action allowed a toddler's murder despite repeated reports.[48] In states that do have regulations allowing officials to follow-up on homeschooled children, there appears to be little willingness to do so. For example, it was reported in 2018 that Denver Public Schools, which oversaw 359 registered homeschoolers, had no record of ever initiating a follow-up after a child was withdrawn from school.[49] Also worth mentioning is the disproportionate representation of poor and minority communities in reports that escalate to investigation, an issue that certainly needs addressing in any serious discussion of reform.[50]

Advocates for more regulation argue that there is existing legal structure to support stricter legislation. While due process and privacy have been used to assert parental autonomy, equal protection doctrine allows for relaxation of strict scrutiny standards for protected classes—this reasonably includes children.[51] While *San Antonio v. Rodriguez* affirmed the strict scrutiny standard, it dealt with a limited case and funding allocation, not direct educational neglect by parents.[52] But advocates of deregulation have also seen victories based on strict scrutiny standards. The Home School Legal Defense Association has aggressively lobbied for strict scrutiny, including taking on CPS-involved cases not directly related to homeschooling such as *Jonathan L. v. Superior Court*.[53] Further complicating the issue are rulings like *DeShaney v. Winnebago County Department of Social Services*, which ruled that children cannot file claims against the state for failure of protection, but parents may claim against unlawful intrusion.[54]

Homeschooling in the U.S.

Homeschooling as we know it today began in the mid-20th century, through the efforts of "strange bedfellows"[55] as progressive-left reformers advocated for "unschooling"[56] while fundamentalist Christians used home education to push back against the sexual and cultural revolutions.[57] In the early 1980s two groups led the legal fight for homeschooling—the Home School Legal Defense Association (HSLDA) and the National Home Education Network. These organizations shared a belief in little to no regulation and strong parental authority over education.[58] As parents—largely fundamentalist Christians—began to pushback against school board officials (with whom homeschoolers had previously cooperated), lobbying and legal battles intensified.[59] By 1993, homeschooling was legal in all fifty states.[60]

Homeschooling in the United States has since remained loosely regulated, contrasting with other countries' strict regulation or—like Germany—outright bans.[61] Only two states have provisions to protect homeschooled children from adults in the home with past sex offenses or violent crimes, and no state has specific monitoring for homeschool families with open neglect or abuse cases.[62] Only a few states have any requirements for academic evaluation or registration, and several have "religious practice" exemptions to educational and medical neglect laws.[63] Only six states specifically deny any right to exemptions.[64] Over the past ten years, the legal trend nationally has been toward deregulation, removing and relaxing assessment requirements.[65]

Because of the variations in state laws, true quantification of homeschoolers is difficult.[66] Data from the National Center for Education Statistics estimates that around 1.7 million students were homeschooled in the United States as of 2016,[67] and 10% of students spend at least some time being homeschooled.[68] Demographically, 59% of homeschoolers are white, while 26% are Hispanic, 8% are Black, and 7% are of other races.[69] The growth of the non-white homeschool population has been continuous between 1999 and 2016.[70] While early homeschoolers were traditionally from higher socioeconomic backgrounds, as of 2010, more than half of homeschool families were found to be poor or "near poor."[71] Christian homeschoolers are the majority, but secular families represent about 25% of the homeschooled population.[72] Muslims are the fastest growing subset of homeschoolers, and there are small populations of Adventists, Baha'i, Jehovah's Witness, Quaker, Catholic, Unitarian, and Jewish homeschoolers.[73] There are no secular equivalents to the politicized entities of Christian homeschooling,[74] and no large organization for non-religious or progressive homeschoolers.[75]

Homeschool parents have diverse motivations. In 1991, Van Galen identified homeschool parents as either *ideologues*, whose values clashed with those they saw in public school, or *pedagogues*, who had issues with quality or methods of instruction.[76] Some of the early homeschoolers were influenced by decisions like *Brown v. Board of Education*, which was seen by many as an overreach of parental school choice rights.[77] Since then, more nuanced motivations have been observed: religious conviction, concerns over poor or dangerous school systems, inability to afford private schools, care for students with special needs, bullying, temporary illness, dissatisfaction with academic quality, or work-related reasons (for example, child actors).[78] The most common reason given is concern over the environment of public schools, followed by desire to provide religious or moral instruction. Non-white homeschool families may have additional motivations, such as dissatisfaction with the Eurocentrism inherent in most public school curricula.[79] Parents who chose to homeschool their Black sons particularly expressed a desire to protect them from systemic racial bias and violence.[80] A lack of general trust in institutions may also be leading more communities of color toward home education.[81]

Even religiously conservative homeschoolers are not an ideological monolith. Motivations of the most conservative Christian homeschoolers, those who might be considered the "countercultural right," is predicated on desired isolation from a "sinful" society based on a Biblical exhortation to be separated from "the world."[82] This ideology is often anti-progressive and anti-government, and the academic is interwoven with the religious, emphasizing scriptural knowledge as supreme.[83] A strong distrust of sex education is emphasized by some in this group, which often appears in their materials and in arguments for religious exemptions. "Purity culture" and strict traditional gender roles are often emphasized, especially in groups that identify with Quiverfull ideology (a belief that a woman's role is to bear and raise as many children as possible) and the 1990s Stay at Home Daughters movement, which advocated that girls did not need higher education.[84] This ideology can lead to severe educational neglect of homeschooled girls.[85]

In some extreme cases, homeschooling is used as a means to conceal abuse, truancy, or even kidnapping.[86] While traditional schools offer "checks" in the form of mandatory reporters and other adults, homeschooled students may not have access to help or the knowledge to recognize and report abuse.[87] In a study of cases of child torture, 76% of the victims were homeschooled at some point, with over 46% of those removed from school after an abuse allegation.[88] Homeschooling has also been used by extreme ideologues to prevent race mingling, to go "off-the-grid," and by the anti-vaccine movement to circumvent immunization requirements.[89] These cases—often involving First Amendment religious freedom or Fourth Amendment privacy loopholes—are the basis of argumentation for advocates of stronger homeschool regulation and child protection measures. Most salient to the legal arguments regarding children's rights legislation are the religious arguments these Christian homeschoolers and their proxies, like HSLDA, have levied in court and against legislators. These arguments are based on the idea of "traditional family" and parental authority as Biblical and "God-given," and these assertions undergird much of the religious freedom argumentation.[90]

Analysis: Home Education Organizations' Positioning and Rhetoric

To better understand the stances of the organizations involved in lobbying for and against federal and state abuse and neglect statutes from a homeschooling perspective, an analysis of websites, press releases, and public statements of several organizations was conducted. These organizations include two large, national policy organizations (the Home School Legal Defense Association and the Coalition for Responsible Home Education), two large state organizations (Florida Parent Educators Association and Texas Homeschool Coalition), two research organizations (National Home Education Research Initiative and the Homeschooling's Invisible Children Database), and two lobbying organizations (Family Research Council and ParentalRights.org). The following sections explain the missions of these organizations, their stances on regulation and preventing child neglect and abuse, and finally, their stances on child protection legislation.

Organizational Missions and Stances

HSLDA. The Home School Legal Defense Association was founded in 1983 by attorneys and homeschool fathers, Mike Farris and Mike Smith, and has a current membership of about 80,000 families. The mission of HSLDA is specifically Christian: "To preserve and advance the fundamental, God-given, constitutional right of parents and others legally responsible for their children to direct their education."[91] HSLDA positions itself as a political lobbying and legal defense organization focused on "fundamental freedoms" of parental rights and religion. The news sections of HSLDA's site reveals a pattern of fear-based language around parental rights; that is, the wording of headlines and choices of topics reflect an ideology that government interference is rampant and parents should be constantly warry of losing their own children. As noted above, this fear was not unrealistic in homeschooling's early years. However, despite the full legalization of homeschooling in all fifty states and their own reporting on the drastic decline in false reporting of homeschool neglect cases, the rhetoric of fear and institutional mistrust is evident. A 2008 story describes a Florida homeschool family's interactions with CPS as so traumatizing that their children now require therapy. Others warn of a coming "police state" if mandatory reporter laws are extended to the federal level and describe social workers as constitutionally-ignorant interrogators out to trap good parents through bogus abuse claims. HSLDA also shares overseas examples as warnings of what a country with more regulation might be like, such as a December 2009 post calling a proposed United Kingdom home-school parent background check law "draconian," and blaming the United Nations Committee on the Rights of the Child for the overreach (see more below).

CRHE. Another large homeschool advocacy organization, the Coalition for Responsible Home Education (CRHE), stands in contrast to HSLDA as specifically non-religious and non-partisan, and advocates for stronger regulation of home education. Founded in 2013 by homeschool alumni, CRHE's mission focuses more on children's (rather than parents') rights: "We are committed to providing resources, conducting research, and promoting policy to protect homeschooled children and youth from falling through the cracks if their parents or guardians are unable or unwilling to responsibly educate them. We are. . .committed to ensuring that the interests of the homeschooled child are respected alongside the interests of the homeschooling parent."[92] A main tenant of CRHE is prevention of educational neglect, a form of abuse in which parents are either unable or unwilling to provide adequate academic instruction to their homeschooled children: "We believe parents or guardians should be allowed to choose how to educate their children, but not whether to educate their children."[93]

While CRHE's website places a strong emphasis on reporting and preventing abuse and neglect in home school environments, their approach is measured and careful, particularly in their regard to religious homeschooling. For example, they write, "Religious fundamentalism can in some cases contribute to abuse and neglect. However, abuse and neglect occur in non-religious homeschool settings as well, and many fundamentalist religious parents are able provide their children with a healthy upbringing and sound education."[94] They also include testimonials from parents, including a homeschool mother who frames the need for more regulation in Christian terms, quoting Bible verses and writing "Christian home educators, above all kinds of home educators, should welcome accountability and seek it out," and paraphrasing a quote from Jesus to refer to children in need of protection as "the least of these our brethren."

CRHE is active in political lobbying in various U.S. states and territories. They also propose changes to statutes to further protect homeschooled children, such as a recent proposal to Florida Statute 1002.41 adding background checks on all adults living with home schooled children, oversight for families with verified CPS reports of abuse, interviews with children at the time of annual portfolio review, standardized testing conducted by a teacher unrelated to the children, and the filing of truancy reports for failure to complete yearly evaluations.[95] CRHE also monitors home schooling legislation throughout the United States (such as Florida HB 1059, see more below).

THSC. One of the largest state home education associations is the Texas Homeschool Coalition. Founded in 1986, THSC has served over 100,000 families. THSC defines itself as an explicitly Christian organization focused on "influencing the political process" and parental rights: "We believe raising children is a family's God-given right and calling. . .[Our] values are distinctly Christian, while THSC serves all home schoolers in the state of Texas, regardless of ethnicity, religion or creed."[96]

Like the Home School Legal Defense Association, THSC's website is filled with stories framed to encourage fear of government interference for home school parents. They include members' horror stories of dealing with CPS investigations, and detail THSC's legal efforts in dozens of cases brought against home school families, describing them as "traumatic scenarios." There is a heavy focus on political lobbying, including lists of bills to support or oppose, particularly any regarding regulation or limitation of parental rights.

FPEA. Another large state organization is the Florida Parent-Educators Association. Florida has slightly more restrictive laws than many other states, including requirements for yearly evaluations and allowing home school students to participate in public school activities,[97] and the FPEA website seems to show the organization is satisfied with the current level of regulation. FPEA is a Christian organization, citing "Judeo-Christian principles," but noting, "Acknowledging there is no one 'right' way to educate, the FPEA acts as an ambassador and champion, serving and protecting the rights and choices of all homeschoolers."[98]

A deeper dive into the organization's materials however, shows a more fundamentalist bent, more closely aligned with HSLDA than the home page might suggest. News headlines proclaim "Emergency alert! Parental rights under attack!" There is a description of a proposed immunization bill that leans heavily on conservative arguments against making HPV vaccinations a part of the required vaccine schedule for school aged children. FPEA's arguments include phrases such as "assumes all teenage girls will be sexually active before marriage" and present vaccine side effects as "dangerous and sometimes deadly." Another bill, relating to private and "umbrella" schools is described by FPEA as "a threat to their very existence!"

NHERI. The National Home Education Research Institute (NHERI) publishes the *Home School Researcher Journal* and describes itself as devoted to empirical research. However, multiple sources[99] have pointed toward possible underlying motivations and methodological issues with NHERI's research—NHERI receives at least some funding from the Home School Legal Defense Association,[100] and its links to affiliated organizations include HSLDA and five other explicitly Christian home education associations.

Much of NHERI's published research focuses on rebuffing outside research findings that cast any negative light on homeschooling through often questionable arguments or methodology. For example, a 2017 piece attacks Vicry,[101] mainly on the grounds that qualitative research is not generalizable (which is true, and not a claim Vicry makes). Another post, from 2017, deflects from abuse by homeschool parents by arguing that public school children are susceptible to abuse not only by parents but also by teachers, coaches, and other school personnel. In 2018, NHERI directly attacked the Homeschooling's Invisible Children Database (see below), reporting a lack of statistical difference in abuse rates for high versus low regulation states. This premise is a fallacy in and of itself, since, as noted above, there are no truly "high" regulation states in the United States. Other NHERI research also fails under scrutiny, using small or unrepresentative samples to make sweeping claims, or by using solely religious arguments as legal justifications.[102]

HIC Database. Members of CRHE created their research arm, the Homeschooling's Invisible Children Database, to monitor and track cases of school aged children who were victims of abuse or neglect and were homeschooled at the time of the incident. By contrast to NHERI, HIC is transparent in their methodology and gives detailed descriptions of criteria for inclusion. Their justification for the database is stated as a desire to understand how children may "slip through the cracks" of the system when they are less likely to be seen by mandatory reporters than children enrolled in other education settings. The site is largely straightforward and non-sensationalist, including links to datasets, news articles, and affiliated organizations.[103]

FRC and Parental Rights.org. Two lobbying groups appeared often in the materials of the above organizations, so they were included for analysis. These groups, the Family Research Council and ParentalRights.org, are both affiliated with HSLDA. The Family Research Council describes itself as non-profit fundamentalist Christian, pro-life and pro-family, and focused on religious liberty.[104] FRC often uses alarmist language in its materials like "morally toxic public schools," a culture "at war" against family values, "sexual propaganda," and "attacks on religious freedom." Parentalrights.org, however, presents itself as secular and mainstream, including boasting of board members like former NFL player Shaun Alexander. Its goal is the passage of a Parental Rights Amendment to the U.S. Constitution, and presents fairly non-controversial statements like, "Children need to be raised by their parents, not by disconnected government officials."[105]

Home School Organizations Positioning on Religious Practice, Abuse, and CPS

Nearly all of the organizations above have clear positions on homeschooling as religious practice, the role of regulation in prevention of child neglect and abuse, and the role of child protective services. These positions come across not only in explicit sections of their websites, but also in their lobbying and research efforts.

Unsurprisingly, there are differences in these positions based on their children's or parental rights-focus and role as religious or secular organizations. The Coalition for Responsible Home Education (and the affiliated Homeschooling's Invisible Children Database) focuses on children's interests, stating "We urge policymakers to approach parents' and children's interests as equally valuable and deserving of respect."[106] Both CRHE and HIC devote large sections of their webpages to explaining the types of abuse and neglect common in homeschool cases, emphasizing how dangerous homeschooling can be in the hands of the wrong parent. CRHE says: "Homeschooling is a neutral tool that places a great deal of power in the hands of the parents… when those parents are abusive or neglectful… homeschooling is a powerful tool in the hands of their abusers, a tool that can serve to perpetuate and intensify abuse."[107] HIC emphasizes that homeschool children may be in particular danger because of their lack of access to mandatory reporters and describes in detail "themes" of abuse in their database: physical abuse, sexual abuse, imprisonment, food deprivation, medical neglect, abuse of adoptees and children with disabilities, and concealment of abduction. CRHE also takes religious practice exemptions head-on by detailing how religion can exacerbate abuse. For example, they describe how fundamentalist beliefs often encourage corporal punishment for any "rebellion" based on Biblical exhortations to use "the rod." They explain that sexual abuse may be compounded by a lack of sex education, and lead to increased shame around disclosure. Educational neglect may be exacerbated by fundamentalist ideology (like Quiverfull) in which mothers may be too overwhelmed with multiple pregnancies or caring for small children to focus on educating older children. Perhaps most notably, CRHE frames these issues with compassion and offers resources to parents who undertook the "moral mission" to homeschool their child, but are reluctant to seek help or alternatives when they realize their methods are failing.

Parental rights-focused organizations tend to use more religious practice and Fourth Amendment positioning than those that are children's rights focused. This is evident in the way they describe abuse and the role of CPS. The Family Research Council presents most of the pro-homeschool arguments on its website as protection of religious freedom. They post:

> Many who homeschool wish to teach their children that God is engaged in everyday life. For them, the school is an extension of the home. Schools should serve parents in the education of children. However, when state-run schools begin to serve a wholly secular agenda and deny parents the ability to train their children, they begin to do what the First Amendment says the state must never do: Establish religion.[108]

FRC is especially virulent in its descriptions of public school sexual education, which it describes as child abuse and "sexual propaganda." They warn parents of textbooks whose examples are "too graphic to print" and intentionally mis-gender and deride LGBTQ+ educators, describing "psychological manipulation" of children. In the rejection of comprehensive, LGBTQ+ inclusive sex education, FRC leans heavily on both religious freedom and emotional abuse argumentation:

> In public schools today, it is about enforcing conformity—conformity of feelings, attitudes, emotions, speech, beliefs and behavior. Nonconformity carries the threat of isolation—a terrifying notion to any child in school. . .[Transgender acceptance] is a denial of God's purposeful creation, which is a denial of God Himself. When government schools force Christian students to do this, it is tantamount to forced conversion.[109]

The National Home Education Research Foundation webpage includes arguments for parental rights that rest almost exclusively on Biblical theology—"God gave children to parents, not the state"— and argues against the "three spheres" theory of child protection. They also argue that any regulation of parents' right to homeschool is assuming prior bad acts, thus violating presumptions of innocent until proven guilty.[110]

Some state organizations use similar positioning in their materials. The Texas Homeschool Coalition includes a section on how to handle interactions with child protective services. While the advice is sound (i.e., ask for an explanation of charges, call a lawyer), it is surrounded by rhetoric that paints any CPS interaction as a horror for homeschoolers. This includes an anonymous story from a homeschool mother who describes the social worker as "a threat to my family" who "could make me look like a neglectful or abusive parent." THSC's blog posts tips for handling CPS interviews, calling them "a parent's nightmare come to life." They suggest that social workers rely on entrapment, comparing questioning to "George Orwell or the Soviet Union" and "the Salem witch trials." One news post is titled "Never committed abuse or neglect? Doesn't matter, under Texas state law, the state can take your children away." Other parts of the website focus on advocating for state regulations to limit the removal power of CPS and to strike homeschooling from admissible evidence in parental rights termination cases.

The Home School Legal Defense Association's webpage is perhaps the most interesting in its handling of abuse and CPS issues. While its messaging advocates strongly for religious freedom and parental rights, echoing the assertions of other writers that too many arguments for regulation focus on a minority of severely abusive or off-the-grid families,[111] HSLDA also posts comprehensive information about physical and sexual abuse, neglect, and resources for struggling parents. Of CPS, HSLDA states, "We strongly believe that when there is reliable evidence that a child is being abused or neglected, the government has a duty to intervene." They state that corporal punishment is harmful to children and offer links to alternative discipline resources. There are also materials devoted to teaching sex education and consent.

However, HSLDA's current website is not reflective of past positions. In 2013, homeschooled alumni began to call out HSLDA on various platforms, specifically accusing them of turning a blind eye to, if not outright enabling, abuse and neglect of homeschooled children.[112] The rhetoric escalated to the point that, in May 2013, HSLDA issued the following statement via Facebook:

> It has come to our attention that HSLDA has recently been accused of condoning child abuse. HSLDA does not and will not ever condone nor defend child abuse.
>
> HSLDA receives hundreds of calls each year from parents who are under investigation by CPS, often based on false, anonymous, trivial, or malicious reports. The vast majority of these are determined by CPS or a court to be unfounded and are dismissed. Because of this, we do not immediately assume that everyone who is the subject of an investigation is guilty of child abuse or neglect....We believe that every child deserves a healthy upbringing and that parents have the high honor and duty to meet that child's needs. For 30 years we have been zealously advocating for the right of thousands of parents to responsibly homeschool their children. To the extent that any statements we may have made could be misunderstood to suggest that we condone the abusive actions of some we repudiate them wholeheartedly and unequivocally.[113]

In July 2013, HSLDA added the current materials to their website.[114] However, remnants of their past stances appear. A 2011 post is still visible describing "malicious or ignorant child abuse and neglect allegations."

Even within pages dedicated to encouraging reporting of suspected abuse to authorities, HSLDA softens their stance: "If your suspicions of child abuse or neglect are based on hearsay, it is worth your time and effort to explore the situation further before taking action. . .If your suspicions are based on direct observation of the family, we still urge caution. There may be a reasonable explanation for what you have observed."[115]

Home School Organizations and Proposed Legislation

To understand some of the positions these organizations take when regulation of home education is proposed, responses to two proposals were examined, the United Nations Committee on the Rights of the Child treaty and Florida House Bill 1059. As of 2020, the UNCRC treaty has been confirmed by every country except the United States. Advocates argue that ratification could correct some of the lack of enforcement of child abuse and neglect statutes currently in existence by making children's protection a duty rather than a right of the states.[116] Opponents argue that the treaty threatens parental rights and religious freedom, explicitly warning of bans to corporal punishment and requirements to provide teens with sexual education and reproductive healthcare, regardless of parents' religious objections.[117] HSLDA has strongly opposed ratification of the UNCRC for decades. Founder Farris argues that the treaty would be unconstitutional.[118] He warns that "no family is safe from governmental intrusion" and mentions possible outlawing of corporal punishment and mandatory sex education. Most recently, HSLDA's website has called the UNCRC "an ever-present threat." There was no mention of the UNCRC found in the Coalition for Responsible Home Education's materials.

Florida House Bill 1059 (2020)[119] also drew the attention of homeschool organizations. The bill affirmed the "fundamental right of parents to direct the upbringing, education, and care of their minor children," and included provisions for education, moral and religious training, and labeled parental rights "unalienable." CRHC published multiple press releases and expressed concerns that the bill might overturn already loose home school regulations, leading to more instances of educational neglect. They argued that the bill essentially eliminated any consideration of children's rights in Florida, instead giving parents "unobstructed" rights. CRHC stated: "Children are not chattel: they are not 'owned' by their parents. Children are no one's property, to be treated or mistreated on the whim of another person."[120] CHRC was joined by the Florida Counseling Association in opposing the bill, who argued that the proposal was especially dangerous for LGBTQ+

students, and threatened the counselor-patient relationship for public school students as well.[121] Unsurprisingly, parental rights organizations, like the Florida Citizens Alliance, strongly supported the bill, using familiar arguments about sex education, forced immunization, and parental rights.[122] The bill die in Judiciary in March 2020.

Protecting Children's Rights: Suggestions and Conclusions

The rhetoric of both parental and children's rights focused homeschool organizations can help advocates for equal protection of children better understand how to frame effective arguments. One value in the analysis of these organizations is in recognizing that a few very powerful actors have controlled the narrative for nearly four decades; as home school alumni enter the public arena, they are changing the conversation about homeschooling regulation in the United States. Their arguments—through organizations like the Coalition for Responsible Home Education—may be more effective than those of professional educators and child's rights advocates who have been accused of conflicts of interest or anti-religious bias,[123] or who call for outright bans of home education.[124]

One of the first steps children's rights advocates could take is to encourage more empirical research. One of the arguments made by deregulation advocates has long been that homeschool students perform better academically than their public school peers, thus effectively shutting down attention to educational neglect.[125] However, a methodologically sound body of research does not exist to support or refute these claims. Most studies of homeschooled students' grades are flawed as these grades are often not based on the same standardized measures as the public school grades to which they are compared.[126] Other studies which show homeschoolers' high achievement in college also have limitations. While homeschool alumni perform well academically, they often report issues with relationships and goal setting, as well as social struggles based on lack of diverse experience or academic gaps from misinformation, particularly from religious-based curriculum.[127] One of the few empirically sound studies found that the sample size of homeschooled college students is limited, as homeschool alums are less likely to go to college and less likely to pursue graduate degrees than their public and private school peers.[128] These alumni also report having lower income as young adults, being less likely to volunteer, less political engagement, and lower social trust than other groups. Socioeconomic factors also complicate this research; as the economic background of homeschoolers diversifies, so should the scope of researchers seeking to understand this phenomenon.[129] Even scholars who suggest a complete ban on homeschooling[130] argue that better understanding of best practices in education benefits all students. By understanding the increasingly diverse reasons parents choose home education—opportunities for African-American students, preventing bullying, protection for LGBTQ+ students, push-back against standardized testing, etc.—advocates can work to correct societal failures to ensure diversity, protection, and equal opportunity for *all* students.[131]

Other steps for ensuring children's rights are protected are the continued expansion of homeschooling methods and access to public resources. Hybridized options, such as online public schooling and dual enrollment are increasingly popular and offer ways for students to create bonds to a shared civic society, as well as being beneficial for students with special needs.[132] Encouraging parents to explore these options might help solve many cases of educational neglect, particularly those where well-meaning parents simply do not have the energy or resources to meet their children's needs. Additionally, more states should allow homeschoolers to take part in extracurricular socialization activities as is allowed in Florida under the "Tim Tebow Law."[133] Other resources, like school psychologists, could also be made accessible to homeschool parents and students.[134] While these accommodations likely would not catch extreme cases of intentional abuse and neglect, they affirm children's "rights in trust" as well as extend the system of checks against harm by giving homeschooled students access to adults and resources beyond their parents. They are also less burdensome to parental rights advocates than the regulations suggested by scholars like Lupu, who wrote that homeschooled children should be required to have a teacher other than their parents for at least some activities, such as a coach, church official, or scout leader.[135]

These suggestions largely do not address the religious practice arguments against homeschool regulation or the harms to children that sometimes occur as a result. Homeschool alumni and children's rights advocates have pointed to the importance of raising public awareness of the outsized influence of certain extreme fundamentalist branches of homeschooling.[136] They argue that legislators, either through ignorance or fear based on extreme lobbying tactics[137] have chosen to ignore the free-rein religious exemptions have given parents to refuse to teach basic science, to under-educate girls, and to avoid child labor laws. Bartholet calls this lack of action a failure of will, and Dwyer strongly condemns lawmakers:

> States have eschewed oversight and abandoned millions of children to whatever ideological inclinations their parents might have. . . .[T]here is a pervasive attitude of avoiding confrontation with ideological extremists unless absolutely necessary. Religious groups that absolutely reject any state authority to oversee

> the way they raise "their" children are frightening to the rest of us. Many view themselves as perpetually at war with mainstream society and the state, and some are prepared to take up arms in order to win that war. Or at least we are sufficiently worried that they might do so that we cower in the face of their angry protests.[138]

Dwyer further argues that states' failure to oversee the education of homeschooled children is as egregious as ignoring physical abuse and may lead to more emotional and psychological harm in the long run.

Regulations have been suggested to require the use of science based curriculum, including sexual education, to ensure students receive instruction in basic academic subjects, and to offer financial incentives for parents who meet evaluation standards.[139] Advocates argue that most regulations that have been challenged in court have been upheld as "reasonable" restrictions to religious practice and parental rights.[140] These reasonable restrictions are generally upheld because courts rule that simply requiring exposure to other beliefs (like introducing evolution as well as creation to science students) is not the equivalent of state sanctioned religion.[141] On the other hand, some scholars warn that in addition to the cost and burden of regulation on states and parents, controlling curricular content may open the door to arguments about freedom of speech.[142]

Despite these concerns, multiple scholars have pointed to case law and viable strategies to incorporate more equal protection doctrine into protection for homeschooled children. Waddell suggests that equal protection arguments may protect girls from educational neglect by rejecting fundamentalist religious promotion of different educational standards for boys and girls.[143] Others[144] point to precedent affirming equal protection rights for minor children—rights to educational parity for children living in poor and minority districts;[145] rights of juvenile offenders;[146] and rights to educational accommodation for children with disabilities.[147] Over two decades ago, Dywer[148] drew a direct line from exceptions for religious objector parents to unconstitutional violations of children's rights to equal protection. While he argues that the strict scrutiny standard would almost certainly rule these exceptions illegitimate, he laments the difficulty of finding "next friends"[149] to bring suits for minor plaintiffs. Today, as more homeschooled alumni connect and mobilize through groups like CRHE, these "next friends" seemed poised to act, offering hope for renewed attention to equal protection argumentation.

The United States' hidden "epidemic of child abuse and neglect"[150] is certainly not limited to homeschooled children, but it may be exacerbated for them due to lack of access to resources. Yet the arguments of children's advocacy groups and scholars show that in many cases, issues of equal protection for children are moral rather than legal problems; laws are upheld but often not enforced, and states have side stepped their equal protection duties in the face of lobbying pressures.[151] These facts suggest that protecting children must go beyond education advocacy to a societal movement toward children's rights and affirmation that parental rights must account for the best interests of the child.[152] Fineman and Shepherd write:

> Fears of intruding on parental rights and destroying American individualism linger in our continuing embrace of the autonomous ideal. While some reasons for homeschooling are understandable— parents want the best start for their children and parents seek an education that is responsive to their children's needs—the answer is not to withdraw into isolation and attempt to do it alone.[153]

Our best solutions—to account for children's equal protection, parental rights, and the state's interests—must be systemic and communal rather than piecemeal and individual.

Notes

1 Elizabeth Bartholet, "Homeschooling: Parental Rights Absolutism vs. Child Rights to Education & Protection," *Arizona Law Review* 62, no. 1 (2020).
2 *Find Law.*
3 Ibid.
4 Ibid.
5 James G. Dwyer, "Religious Schooling and Homeschooling Before and After Hobby Lobby," *University of Illinois Law Review* (2016): 1409.
6 Fineman and Shepherd, "Homeschooling. . ."
7 Ibid.
8 Ira Lupu, "Home Education, Religious Liberty, and the Separation of Powers," *Boston University Law Review* 67, no. 5 (November 1987): 971–92; Ira Lupu, "The Separation of Powers and the Protection of Children," *The University of Chicago Law Review* 61, no. 4 (1994): 1317–73.
9 Fineman and Shepherd, "Homeschooling. . ."
10 Lupu, "Separation. . .," 990.
11 Joel Feinberg, "The Child's Right to an Open Future," in *Freedom and Fulfillment: Philosophical Essays*, ed. Joel Feinberg (Princeton: Princeton University Press, 1992), 76–97.
12 Georgia du Plessis, "The Legitimacy of Using the Harm Principle in Cases of Religious Freedom Within Education," *Human Rights Review* 17 (2016): 349–70.
13 Ibid.
14 Ibid.
15 Fineman and Shepherd, "Homeschooling. . .," 94.
16 Dwyer, "Religious Schooling. . .," 1411.
17 Kunzman, "Homeschooling. . ."

18 Nicholas P. Wolterstoff, *Educating for Life: Reflections on Christian Teaching and Learning*, ed. Gloria Goris Stronks, and Clarence W. Joldersma (Ada, MI: Baker Academic, 2002), 213.
19 Wisconsin v. Jonas Yoder, 406 U.S. 205 (1972).
20 Meyer v. Nebraska, 262 U.S. 390 (1923).
21 Pierce v. Society of Sisters, 268 U.S. 510 (1925).
22 Care and Protection of Charles & Others, 399 Mass. 324 (1987).
23 Runyon v. McCrary, 427 U.S. 160 (1976).
24 Lupu, "Home Education..."
25 Bartholet, "Homeschooling..."
26 Ibid.
27 Wisconsin v. Jonas Yoder, 406 U.S. 205 (1972).
28 Bartholet, "Homeschooling..."
29 Bach, "For God."
30 Ibid.
31 Home Educators Association of Virginia, (accessed February 9, 2020), https://heav.org/
32 Lupu, "Home Education..."
33 Michael Gryboski, "Future of Homeschooling: Less Religious, More Regulated?," (*The Christian Post*, February 18, 2019), https://www.christianpost.com/news/future-of-homeschooling-less-religious-more-regulated.html, para.1.
34 Ibid, para. 7.
35 Lupu, "Home Education..."
36 Ibid.
37 Burwell v. Hobby Lobby, 573 U.S. 682 (2014); Dwyer, "Religious Schooling..."
38 Reynolds v. United States, 98 U.S. 145 (1878); Bach, "For God or Grades."
39 Dwyer, "Religious Schooling..."
40 Doriane Lambert Coleman, "Storming the Castle to Save the Children: The Ironic Costs of a Child Welfare Exemption to the Fourth Amendment," *William & Mary Law Review* 47 (2005): 413–540.
41 Ibid.
42 North Carolina Child Advocacy Institute. *Child Protective Services Data Card 2002–2003*: 2005.
43 Coleman, "Storming...," 540.
44 Calabretta v. Floyd, 189 F.3d 808 (1999).
45 CRHE.
46 Coleman, "Storming..."
47 State v. Wilkerson, 247 S.E.2d 905 (1978).
48 Coleman, "Storming..."
49 Karen Augé ́, "For Some, Homeschooling Is Not about Learning. It's about Hiding Child Abuse," (*The Colorado Sun*, October 8, 2018), https://coloradosun.com/2018/10/08/homeschool-child-abuse-colorado/
50 Coleman, "Storming..."
51 Bartholet, "Homeschooling..."
52 San Antonio v. Rodriguez, 411 U.S. 1 (1973).
53 Jonathan L. V. Superior Court, 81 Cal. Rptr.3d 571 (2008); HSLDA.

54 DeShaney v. Winnebago County Department of Social Services, 489 U.S. 189, 202 (1989); Bartholet, "Homeschooling…"
55 Bartholet, "Homeschooling…"; Martha Fineman and George B. Shepherd, "Homeschooling: Choosing Parental Rights Over Children's Interests," *University of Baltimore Law Review* 46, no. 1 (2016): 64.
56 Coalition for Responsible Home Education (CRHE) (accessed February 12, 2020, https://responsiblehomeschooling.org/)
57 Robert Kunzman, "Homeschooling and Religious Fundamentalism," *International Electronic Journal of Elementary Education* 3, no. 1 (October 2010): 17–28.
58 Fineman and Shepherd, "Homeschooling…"; Homeschool Legal Defense Association (HSLDA), (accessed February 9, 2020), https://hslda.org/content/
59 CRHE.
60 Fineman and Shepherd, "Homeschooling…"
61 Ibid.
62 CRHE.
63 *Find Law,* "Child Abuse Laws," (accessed March 1, 2020, https://family.findlaw.com/child-abuse/child-abuse-laws.html).
64 Ibid.
65 Bartholet, "Homeschooling…"
66 Kunzman, "Homeschooling…"; Fineman and Shepherd, "Homeschooling…"
67 Meghan McQuiggan, Mahi Megra, and Sarah Grady, "Parent and Family Involvement in Education: Results from the National Household Education Surveys Program of 2016," *National Center for Education Statistics* (September 2017). https://nces.ed.gov/pubs2017/2017102.pdf.
68 Bartholet, "Homeschooling…"
69 McQuiggan, Megra, and Grady, "Parent and Family…"
70 Ibid.
71 Andrea Dennison, Jon Lasser, Deidre Awtry Madres, and Yasiry Lerma, "Understanding Families Who Choose to Homeschool: Agency in Context," *School Psychology* 35, no.1 (2020): 20–27.
72 Jaweed Kaleem, "Homeschooling Without God," (*The Atlantic,* March 30, 2016), https://www.theatlantic.com/education/archive/2016/03/homeschooling-without-god/475953
73 Ibid; A2Z Homeschooling, "Religious Homeschooling," (accessed March 2, 2020), https://a2zhomeschooling.com/religion/religious_homeschooling/
74 See *STEAM Powered Family,* (accessed March 2, 2020), https://www.steampoweredfamily.com/ and *Secular Homeschooling*, (last updated February 28, 2020), https://www.secularhomeschool.com/content/
75 Bartholet, "Homeschooling…"
76 Jane A. Van Galen, "Ideologues and Pedagogues: Parents Who Teach Their Children at Home," *Home Schooling: Political, Historical, and Pedagogical Perspectives*, ed. Jane A. Van Galen and M.A. Pitman (Norwood: Ablex, 1991), 63–76.
77 Brown V. Board of Education of Topeka, 347 U.S. 483 (1954); Madalyn Doucet Vicry, "Note: That Kind of Girl: Effect of Homeschooling on the Sexual Health of Women and Girls," *Georgetown Journal of Gender and Law 18* (2017): 103–129.
78 Laura J. Bach, "For God or Grades? States Imposing Fewer Requirements on Religious Home Schoolers and the Religion Clauses of the First Amendment,"

Valparaiso University Law Review 38, no. 4 (Summer 2004): 1337–98; Dennison et al., "Understanding…"; McQuiggan, Megra, and Grady, "Parent and Family…"
79 Dennison et al., "Understanding…"
80 Garvey Lundy and Ama Mazama. "'I'm Keeping My Son at Home': African American Males and the Motivation to Homeschool," *Journal of African American Males in Education* 5, no. 1 (Spring 2014): 53–74.
81 Dennison et al., "Understanding…"
82 Bartholet, "Homeschooling…"
83 Vicry, "Note…"; Kunzman, "Homeschooling…"; James G. Dwyer and Shawn F. Peters, *Homeschooling: The History and Philosophy of a Controversial Practice* (Chicago: University of Chicago Press: 2019).
84 Vicry, "Note…"; Bartholet, "Homeschooling…"
85 Ibid; Ibid; CRHE.
86 Homeschooling's Invisible Children, (accessed February 9, 2020), https://hsinvisiblechildren.org/
87 CRHE.
88 Barbara Knox, Suzanne P. Starling, Kenneth W. Feldman, Nancy D. Kellogg, Lori D. Frasier, and Suzanna L. Tiapula, "Child Torture as a Form of Child Abuse," *Journal of Child and Adolescent Trauma* 7, no. 1 (February 2014): 37–49.
89 Bartholet, "Homeschooling…"
90 Ibid.
91 HSLDA.
92 CRHE.
93 Ibid.
94 Ibid.
95 CRHE, "At-Risk Children Draft Legislation (Florida)," https://responsiblehomeschooling.org/wp-content/uploads/2017/01/At-Risk-Children-Draft-Legislation-Florida.pdf
96 Texas Homeschool Coalition, (accessed February 9, 2020), https://thsc.org/
97 HSLDA, "Homeschooling Under Your State Law: Florida," https://hslda.org/content/hs101/FL.aspx
98 Florida Parent Teacher Association, (accessed February 16, 2020), https://floridapta.org/
99 CRHE; Bartholet, "Homeschooling…"
100 Bartholet, "Homeschooling…"
101 Vicry, "Note…";
102 National Home Education Research Institute, (accessed February 17, 2020), https://www.nheri.org/
103 Homeschooling's Invisible Children.
104 Family Research Council, (accessed March 1, 2020), https://www.frc.org/
105 Parentalrights.org (accessed March 1, 2020), https://parentalrights.org/
106 CRHE.
107 Ibid.
108 Family Research Council, "Homeschooling and the Attack on Religious Freedom," para. 3.
109 Ruse, "The Plague…," para. 17, 18.

110 Marta Ray, "Sample of Child Abuse of Public School, Private School, and Homeschool Students: evidence, philosophy, and Reason," (April 10, 2017), https://www.nheri.org, para. 29.
111 Elena Silva, "The State of Homeschooling in America," (*Pacific Standard,* September 21, 2018), https://psmag.com/education/the-state-of-homeschooling-in-america
112 Joyce, "Apostates."
113 HSLDA [Facebook post]. May 7, 2013.
114 Joyce, "Apostates."
115 HSLDA.
116 Bartholet, "Homeschooling. . ."
117 Amy Rothschild, "Is America holding out on protecting children's rights?" (*The Atlantic,* May 2, 2017), https://www.theatlantic.com/education/archive/2017/05/holding-out-on-childrens-rights/524652
118 Michael Farris, "Absurdity of the U.N. Treaty on Child's Rights," (*WND,* May 4, 2009), https://www.wnd.com/2009/05/96941/
119 H.B. 1059, Florida (2020).
120 CRHE.
121 "HB 1059/SB 1634: Parental Rights," (*Resources*, February 16, 2020), https://www.flacounseling.org/resources/2020 Day at the Capitol/HB1059 Parent Rights.pdf.
122 Florida Citizens Alliance, "Bills We Support," (accessed March 1, 2020), https://floridacitizensalliance.com/liberty/2019-2020-legislative-cycle-tracking-key-bills/#support
123 Lupu, "Home Education. . ."; Bartholet, "Homeschooling. . ."
124 "Homeschooling is the most radical form of private education and potentially the most destructive to maintaining a democratic society" in George Shepherd, "Homeschooling's Harms: Lessons from Economics," *Akron Law Review* 49, no 2. (2015): 339; Fineman and Shepherd, "Homeschooling. . ."
125 Gryboski, "Future. . ."
126 Dwyer, "Religious. . ."
127 Fineman and Shepherd, "Homeschooling. . ."
128 Ray Pennings and Kathryn Weins, *Cardus Education Survey: Phase I Report (2011),* https://www.cardus.ca/research/education/reports/cardus-education-survey-phase-i-report-2011/; Bartholet, "Homeschooling. . ."
129 Bartholet, "Homeschooling. . ."
130 i.e., Fineman and Shepherd, "Homeschooling. . ."
131 Ibid.
132 Kunzman, "Homeschooling"; Silva, "The State..."
133 See https://www.homeschoolfacts.com/are-tim-tebow-laws-a-touchdown-for-homeschool-students/; Vicry, "Note. . ."; Dennison et al., "Understanding. . ."
134 Dennison et al., "Understanding. . ."
135 Lupu, "Separation. . ."
136 Vicry, "Note. . .:"
137 Bartholet, "Homeschooling. . ."
138 Dwyer, "Religious. . .," 79
139 Vicry, "Note. . .:"; Bach, "For God. . ."; Bartholet, "Homeschooling. . ."

140 Bartholet, "Homeschooling. . ."
141 Ibid.
142 Fineman and Shepherd, "Homeschooling. . ."
143 Timothy Brandon Waddell. "Bringing It All Back Home: Establishing a Coherent Constitutional Framework for the Re-regulation of Homeschooling," *Vanderbilt Law Review* 63, no. 2 (March 2010): 541–98.
144 Harris, Leslie J., and Lee E. Teitelbaum. *Children, Parents, and the Law: Public and Private Authority in the Home Schools and Juvenile Courts* (New York: Wolters Kluwer, 2020).
145 *San Antonio v. Rodriguez,* 411 U.S. 1 (1973).
146 *State v. Garcia,* 683 N.W.2d 294 (Minn. 2004).
147 *Endrew F. v. Douglas County School District Re-1,* 137S. Ct. 988 (2017).
148 Dwyer, James G., "The Children We Abandon: Religious Exemptions to Child Welfare and Education Laws as Denials of Equal Protection to Children of Religious Objectors." *North Carolina Law Review* 74 (1995–1996): 1321–478.
149 *Gardner v. Parson,* 874 F.2d 131, 137 n.10 (3rd Cir. 1989).
150 Find Law, "Child Abuse Laws," para 5.
151 Bartholet, "Homeschooling. . ."
152 Ibid; Bach, "For God..."
153 Fineman and Shepherd, "Homeschooling. . .," 96.

Bibliography

A2Z Homeschooling. "Religious Homeschooling." Accessed March 2, 2020. https://a2zhomeschooling.com/religion/religious_homeschooling/

Augé, Karen. "For Some, HomeschoolinIs Not about Learning. It's about Hiding Child Abuse." *The Colorado Sun*, October 8, 2018. https://coloradosun.com/2018/10/08/homeschool-child-abuse-colorado/

Bach, Laura J. "For God or Grades? States Imposing Fewer Requirements on Religious Home Schoolers and the Religion Clauses of the First Amendment." *Valparaiso University Law Review* 38, no. 4 (Summer 2004): 1337–98.

Bartholet, Elizabeth. "Homeschooling: Parental Rights Absolutism vs. Child Rights to Education & Protection." *Arizona Law Review* 62, no. 1 (2020). http://nrs.harvard.edu/urn-3:HUL.InstRepos:40108859

Coalition for Responsible Home Education (CRHE). Accessed February 12, 2020. https://responsiblehomeschooling.org/

Coleman, Doriane Lambert. "Storming the Castle to Save the Children: The Ironic Costs of a Child Welfare Exemption to the Fourth Amendment." *William & Mary Law Review* 47 (2005): 413–540.

Dennison, Andrea, Jon Lasser, Deidre Awtry Madres, and Yasiry Lerma. "Understanding Families Who Choose to Homeschool: Agency in Context." *School Psychology* 35, no.1 (2020): 20–27.

du Plessis, Georgia. "The Legitimacy of Using the Harm Principle in Cases of Religious Freedom Within Education." *Human Rights Review* 17 (2016): 349–70.

Dwyer, James G. "The Children We Abandon: Religious Exemptions to Child Welfare and Education Laws as Denials of Equal Protection to Children of Religious Objectors." *North Carolina Law Review* 74 (1995–1996): 1321–478.

Dwyer, James G. "Religious Schooling and Homeschooling Before and After Hobby Lobby." *University of Illinois Law Review* (2016): 1393–415.

Dwyer, James G., and Shawn F. Peters. *Homeschooling: The History and Philosophy of a Controversial Practice.* Chicago: University of Chicago Press, 2019.

Family Research Council. Accessed March 1, 2020. https://www.frc.org/

Farris, Michael. "Absurdity of the U.N. Treaty on Child's Rights." *WND*, May 4, 2009. https://www.wnd.com/2009/05/96941/

Feinberg, Joel. "The Child's Right to an Open Future." In *Freedom and Fulfillment: Philosophical Essays*, edited by Joel Feinberg, 76–97. Princeton: Princeton University Press, 1992.

Find Law. "Child Abuse Laws." Accessed March 1, 2020. https://family.findlaw.com/child-abuse/child-abuse-laws.html

Fineman, Martha and George B. Shepherd. "Homeschooling: Choosing Parental Rights Over Children's Interests." *University of Baltimore Law Review* 46, no. 1 (2016): 57–106.

Florida Parent Teacher Association. Accessed February 16, 2020. https://floridapta.org/

Gryboski, Michael. "Future of Homeschooling: Less Religious, More Regulated?" *The Christian Post*, February 18, 2019. https://www.christianpost.com/news/future-of-homeschooling-less-religious-more-regulated.html

Harris, Leslie J., and Lee E. Teitelbaum. *Children, Parents, and the Law: Public and Private Authority in the Home Schools and Juvenile Courts.* New York: Wolters Kluwer, 2020.

Heuer, William, and William Donovan. "Homeschooling: The Ultimate School Choice." *White Paper No. 170. Pioneer Institute for Public Policy Research.* Boston: Pioneer Institute for Public Policy Research, 2017.

Home Educators Association of Virginia. Accessed February 9, 2020. https://heav.org/

Home School Legal Defense Association (HSLDA). Accessed February 9, 2020. https://hslda.org/content/

Homeschooling's Invisible Children. Accessed February 9, 2020. https://hsinvisiblechildren.org/

Joyce, Kathryn. "The Homeschool Apostates." *The American Prospect*, December 4, 2013. https://prospect.org/power/homeschool-apostates/

Kaleem, Jaweed. "Homeschooling Without God." *The Atlantic*, March 30, 2016. https://www.theatlantic.com/education/archive/2016/03/homeschooling-without-god/475953

Knox, Barbara, Suzanne P. Starling, Kenneth W. Feldman, Nancy D. Kellogg, Lori D. Frasier, and Suzanna L. Tiapula. "Child Torture as a Form of Child Abuse." *Journal of Child and Adolescent Trauma* 7, no. 1 (February 2014): 37–49.

Kunzman, Robert. "Homeschooling and Religious Fundamentalism." *International Electronic Journal of Elementary Education* 3, no. 1 (October 2010): 17–28.

Lundy, Garvey, and Ama Mazama. "'I'm Keeping My Son at Home': African American Males and the Motivation to Homeschool." *Journal of African American Males in Education* 5, no. 1 (Spring 2014): 53–74.

Lupu, Ira. "Home Education, Religious Liberty, and the Separation of Powers." *Boston University Law Review* 67, no. 5 (November 1987): 971–92.

Lupu, Ira. "The Separation of Powers and the Protection of Children." *The University of Chicago Law Review* 61, no. 4 (1994): 1317–73.

McQuiggan, Meghan, Mahi Megra, and Sarah Grady. "Parent and Family Involvement in Education: Results from the National Household Education Surveys Program of 2016." National Center for Education Statistics (September 2017). https://nces.ed.gov/pubs2017/2017102.pdf

National Home Education Research Institute (NHERI). Accessed February 17, 2020. https://www.nheri.org/

North Carolina Child Advocacy Institute. *Child Protective Services Data Card 2002–2003.* 2005.

Parentalrights.org. Accessed March 1, 2020. https://parentalrights.org/

Pennings, Ray and Kathryn Weins. *Cardus Education Survey: Phase I Report (2011).* https://www.cardus.ca/research/education/reports/cardus-education-survey-phase-i-report-2011/

Ray, Marta. "Sample of Child Abuse of Public School, Private School, and Homeschool Students: Evidence, Philosophy, and Reason." (April 10, 2017). https://www.nheri.org, para. 29.

Rothschild, Amy. "Is America Holding Out on Protecting Children's Rights?" *The Atlantic,* May 2, 2017. https://www.theatlantic.com/education/archive/2017/05/holding-out-on-childrens-rights/524652

Ruse, Cathy. "The Plague of Morally Toxic Public Schools," Family Research Council, February 1, 2020. https://www.frc.org/get.cfm?i=PV20B02

Shepherd, George. "Homeschooling's Harms: Lessons from Economics." *Akron Law Review* 49, no. 2 (2015): 339–370.

Silva, Elena. "The State of Homeschooling in America." *Pacific Standard*, September 21, 2018. https://psmag.com/education/the-state-of-homeschooling-in-america

Texas Homeschool Coalition. Accessed February 9, 2020. https://thsc.org/

Van Galen, Jane A. "Ideologues and Pedagogues: Parents Who Teach Their Children at Home." In *Home Schooling: Political, Historical, and Pedagogical Perspectives,* edited by Jane A. Van Galen and M.A. Pitman, 63–76. Norwood: Ablex, 1991.

Vicry, Madalyn Doucet. "Note: That Kind of Girl: Effect of Homeschooling on the Sexual Health of Women and Girls." *Georgetown Journal of Gender and Law* 18 (2017): 103–29.

Waddell, Timothy Brandon. "Bringing It All Back Home: Establishing a Coherent Constitutional Framework for the Re-regulation of Homeschooling," *Vanderbilt Law Review* 63, no. 2 (March 2010): 541–98.

Wolterstorff, Nicholas P. *Educating for Life: Reflections on Christian Teaching and Learning*, edited by Gloria Goris Stronks, and Clarence W. Joldersma. Ada, MI: Baker Academic, 2002.

3. *On the Dole for the Homeless Soul: Religious and Sex Discrimination by Sectarian Adoption Services*

Pamela L. Morris and Susan H. Sarapin

In the United States, over half a million children are without a permanent home: 407,000 are in foster homes and 117,000 are waiting to be adopted.[1] Given this child welfare crisis, the exclusion of otherwise suitable parents who fall outside narrowly defined religious principles is counterproductive. Yet private agencies argue that "principles of non-discrimination would present them with 'an untenable choice...between their desire to help children and families and their fidelity to their religious principles,'" removing experienced and successful agencies from an overtaxed system.[2] In the United States, the government provides funding and licensure for childcare and placement for both public and private (often religiously oriented) agencies. Private agencies must be licensed by states, yet some still espouse and enact religious values in the process of placing children. Sectarian child welfare agencies often choose to turn away prospective parents who are not coreligionists or based on their preferred family structure (e.g., single parents, non-married couples, and LGBTQ couples). Currently, information about those turned away is not collected, so evidence of the problem is anecdotal through news stories and court cases. At issue in this situation are several legal conflicts involving the Free Exercise and Establishment Clauses of the First Amendment as well as the Equal Protection Clause of the Fourteenth Amendment. There is "much complication and confusion in religion clause jurisprudence by attempting to balance the separation required by the Establishment Clause with the accommodation needed for religious freedom in a highly devoted and pluralistic society."[3] The Supreme Court of the United States (SCOTUS) has not yet weighed in on discrimination by sectarian adoption agencies, and the current legal situation is murky.

Without clear legal guidelines, funding for sectarian adoption agencies may change with the political winds. The Obama-era rule, finalized in 2016 after the *Obergefell v. Windsor* SCOTUS decision regarding same-sex marriage, enforced non-discrimination for agencies receiving aid from the Department of Health and Human Services (DHHS). Faith-based organizations (FBOs) could not receive federal money if they "wished to be selective in which prospective foster or adoptive parents, or children, they would serve."[4] Several court cases, some of which are described in this chapter, were launched under this rule. In the era of growing support for non-discrimination, longstanding Catholic and other Christian child placement agencies have chosen to close rather than adhere to laws or policies that prevent them from excluding potential families based on their religious beliefs. For example, Catholic foster care and adoption agencies in Washington, D.C., Boston, the State of Illinois, San Francisco, and Buffalo have closed as a result.[5]

The Trump Administration reversed course and awarded a waiver on *state*-non-discrimination policy to South Carolina in January of 2019.[6] In addition, in November 2019, the Trump Administration announced a change to *federal* rules to preserve federal funding of faith-based adoption agencies, regardless of their views on same-sex marriage.[7] Under this new rule, the DHHS revised the 2016 rule; private entities which receive public funding and business contracts may institute discriminatory practices toward individuals predetermined to be unsatisfactory as parents.

Adding to the complexity is that the regulation of adoption is largely decentralized as a state responsibility. For example, in 2006, Catholic Charities of Boston ended adoption services because in Massachusetts all adoption agencies must be licensed by the state, whether or not they receive state dollars, and licensure depends upon the agency obeying state anti-discrimination laws.[8]

What is often lost in these political and legal battles is the human issue. Children are not goods, services, or property to be used as a resource for any organization. Religion and child welfare have been associated for much of recent history, as sectarian organizations voluntarily took on the "mission" of caring for children when others could not. For as long as this has been the case, people have questioned whether these organizations are engaged in this work for the benefit of the child or evangelism.

This chapter will first present a brief review of the role of religion in adoption, explicate the goal of establishing practicable principles regarding the best interests of the child, and present mission statements of several FBOs that contract with the government for child welfare services. Next is a review of the legal and constitutional issues, presenting several recent and ongoing court cases. Finally, the discussion proposes resolutions that meet the paramount goal: the best interests of the child.[9]

Religion and Adoption: Historically Tangled

Christian teaching commands the church to care for those who cannot care for themselves. The New Testament of the Bible states: "Religion that God our Father accepts as pure and faultless is this: to look after orphans and widows in their distress and to keep oneself from being polluted by the world" (New International Version, James 1:27). Godparents were chosen by parents to take in children should the worst happen, as it so often did in times of war, pestilence, and poverty. Legal adoption, however, was largely absent in Western Europe, due to the emphasis on primogeniture (bloodline heredity). The Church did not support adoption either, preferring that childless couples leave their legacy to the Church, and that unwanted, orphaned, or excess children be given to the Church, often as an oblation, providing "recruits or servants for the religious establishments."[10] Furthermore, this stance was "reinforced by a pious fear that Christian orphans might be adopted by non-Christian families."[11]

In the United States, early colonists largely followed these traditions. However, life in the New World was far away from relatives, established religious sites, and concerns about the inheritance of the family land. Nearer were conditions that usually left children orphaned, abandoned, and homeless.

In 1851, the State of Massachusetts became the first in the world to codify adoption into a law (An Act to Provide for the Adoption of Children), and did so with the welfare of the child in mind. England would not enact its first adoption laws until 1926. In the next twenty-five years, two dozen U.S. states followed suit. These laws arrived just in time for the fabled orphan trains, a grand experiment in providing "wholesome" families and homes (meaning Protestant farm families--a more moral climate than the cities) for 84,000 East Coast children living in asylums, in poorhouses, and on the streets.[12] In the sixty-six years the trains ran, these early state laws presided over adoptions. The orphan trains were a religious movement, and prospective parents had to provide a ministerial letter of reference.[13] Although the first adoption laws were silent on the issue of religion, it was assumed that adoptive parents were of good moral (usually Christian) standing, and judges were allowed to approve or deny adoptions as they saw fit.

The early 20th century brought influenza, world wars, and the Progressive Era. A "generation of orphans"[14] sparked a social movement that was concerned about their welfare and resulted in child-centered state and federal law and the standardization and professionalization of adoption practices.[15] Although there were some holdouts, most U.S. states passed laws legalizing adoption during this period. Although benevolent work had mostly existed in sectarian organizations, the Depression and New Deal prompted the creation of state-funded child welfare agencies and the granting of public funds to private agencies to satisfy needs that outstripped what the private entities could handle. In a mere ten-year period, between 1925 and 1935, thirty-nine states enacted or revised adoption legislation.[16]

Although not typically codified in adoption law, one philosophy that lasted through the 1970s was the pro forma matching of adoptees to potential parents—in race, appearance, culture, intelligence, and religion.[17] Placing children into homes where they could pass as biological children meant that children were chosen on the basis of race. For many years, the adoption of black children into non-black families was taboo. Although this belief subsided by the 1970s, some blacks today believe that such placements mean a loss of the child's culture and transracial adoptions remain controversial.[18] Along these lines, children were also matched to prospective parents' religious beliefs, on the assumption that the child's soul was born into a particular system of belief and should therefore stay there. Both Catholics and Jews feared the assimilation of 'their' " children into mainstream Protestantism. Matching goals were promoted by the social work field for many decades.

Beginning in the 1960s, social workers determined that to satisfy the goal of keeping children's best interests at heart, the children should be placed in adoptive families regardless of "matching" criteria; it became clear that "matched" children were not better off than others, particularly as the stigma of adoption waned and rates of international adoptions rose.[19] The decisions in *Wilder v. Bernstein* (78 Civ. 957 (S.D.N.Y, 1973)) and *Compos v. McKeithen* (341 F. Supp. 264 (E.D. La. 2971)) declared policies of racial and religious matching unconstitutional. Congress passed the Howard M. Metzenbaum Multiethnic Placement Act in 1994, which prohibited adoption agencies from turning away adoptive parents based on race.[20] This does not mean that race and religion are not considered; rather, they are discretionary instead of mandatory. For example, New York state law requires that a "child's religious faith be preserved and protected":

> Whenever a child is committed to any agency, association, corporation, institution or society, other than an institution supported and controlled by the state or a subdivision thereof, such commitment shall be made, when practicable, to

> an authorized agency under the control of persons of the same religious faith as that of the child.[21]

If the child is placed with someone of a different religion, the court must present "facts that impelled" such a decision.

One question that remains, however, is this: What, exactly, makes a good adoptive family? As we will describe in this chapter the answer is still being debated today. At times, single parents and unmarried couples were turned away (and sometimes still are). Today, LGBTQ couples face the same problems. Adoption has points of controversy that are not surprising, given the interplay between race, social issues, cultural values, and adoption practice, and other concerns.

The Best Interests of the Child

Those unfamiliar with the courtroom machinations in custody, foster-care, and adoption cases might think that the determination of the best interests of the child (BIC) is a simple task for a judge—perhaps that there is a standard list of requirements to check off to ascertain the optimal family situation for all children. In a well-known biblical case in which two women claim the same child to be their own, King Solomon decided that the love and rights of the biological mother are the relevant criteria in disputes in which the best interests of the child should be foremost on the judge's mind in determining who should have custody.[22] Unfortunately, years of child custody jurisprudence have not resulted in a clear, concretized version of the BIC standard. Although attempts to codify BIC in the U.S. began as early as the 1840s, today's BIC legal principle and the societal norms affecting it are complicated and imprecise.[23] Relationships and economic circumstances in each family are unique to that family and cannot be treated in exactly the same way as any other family. Foster, Jr. (1972) expounds:

> the controlling principle of a child's best interests is an amorphous concept which may serve as a basis for rationalization of *any* [emphasis added] result and because of an unfortunate judicial—and human—tendency to stereotype relationships.[24]

As Foster points out, BIC can be used to justify a wide variety of decisions, some of which may reflect not the best interests of the child at all, but the perspective of a judge based on his or her personal experience, prejudice, and perspective.

BIC is one of two basic rules of thumb in adjudicating custody issues; the other is the fitness of the potential or current parent.[25] The combination of these indistinct and indeterminate measures ensures an imprecise, universal solution to a multitude of unique family dynamics, leaving the family court judge with little concrete legal direction for making an extremely consequential decision; it "invites reliance by the judge on personal values."[26] Such guidelines may not be in the best interest of the child; rather, they may be in the best interest of the judge, the state, budget, and expedition. Schwartz writes: "To be sure, there are adverse consequences to a system governed by the indeterminate 'best interests' standard. These disadvantages include a lack of predictability and the disproportionate influence that the personal values and biases of judges and agency workers may wield."[27]

Overwhelmed courts employ customary judicial idioms to dispose of each case quickly, requiring much less work from the court and allowing more cases to be heard.[28] Foster, Jr., helps us understand what these shibboleths are and how they operate: "The temptation is great for overburdened courts to resort to secondary rules of thumb such as 'a natural parent is to be preferred over a stranger,' 'a mother is to be preferred over a father,' and that 'the non-custodial parent should be given liberal visitation rights.'"[29] The repercussions of recent legislation and administration policies will demonstrate how this generally accepted understanding of what is in the best interest of children has managed to disregard other variables for decades.

As an example of the courts' wavering over the meaning of BIC, consider the changes in family court custody statistics over time. As of 2011, Hughes, Jr., reported that across the United States, in the context of divorce, mothers were awarded primary custody 68–88% of the time, fathers, 8–14%, and both equally, 2–6%.[30] In 2014, mothers were awarded custody of the children about 60% of the time, indicating a trend toward joint custody.[31] Just seven years after Hughes, Jr.'s study, Kentucky became the first state to delineate joint and equal custody as the starting point, or "legal presumption," regarding custody following divorce. A default judgment of joint custody appears, on its face, to be a truly fair way to treat both the father and the mother, and yet, it is concomitantly an assumption that both parents are good and suitable parents for this specific child. If there is no mandatory examination of BIC, serious family problems might not be uncovered, and the children could end up in a dangerous home environment. BIC should be a priority over parental rights.[32]

However, according to law, there is one priority—that the child's basic human needs are met. Mnookin warned that "the court's child-protection function is to enforce minimum social standards, not to intervene coercively in an attempt to do what is best or least detrimental."[33] Continuing in that vein, Appel and Boyer expound:

> [I]n the exercise of its child protection function, the state's goal is initially not to ensure the best possible end for the child, but rather to ensure that the child's basic needs are met by the parent. In implementing this goal, courts face substantial pressure to compel conformance with societal standards of parenting. Judges must be careful to distinguish cultural or value-based differences in child-rearing practices from parental conduct that falls beneath minimally acceptable parenting standards and raises a legitimate concern about the health, safety, or welfare of the child.[34]

Next, we look at the publicly available mission statements of several FBOs that carry out adoption and foster care services on behalf of the state.

The Mission for Souls

Mission statements have been an essential management tool since the early 1980s for both for-profit and non-profit organizations, in every industry.[35] It is the most common method for communicating the organization's purpose, core values, goals, and strategic direction to all its stakeholders, including employees, customers/clients, benefactors, supervisory legal entities, vendors, and the public. The public includes investors and users of the services or goods.[36] When communicated in all its internal and external documents, the mission statement not only reminds everyone associated with the organization of its raison d'être, but also of its self-perceived or desired identity in the larger world. For faith-based organizations, balancing its identity with its fundraising needs is challenging because to receive public funds, "a faith-based organization is expected to function like any other nonprofit in promoting activities without religious intent or discrimination."[37] Thus, FBOs, particularly those who contract with the government, may struggle to define themselves when their religious ideals conflict with the state's call for equal treatment. Their mission statements often reveal how they have chosen to position themselves.

Much of the business management literature has focused on the effect of mission statements across dozens of industries on the organization's performance. In fact, most executives and researchers erroneously believe that exceptional performance results from strong, well-written, and oft-repeated mission statements. In contrast, "Little evidence exists, however, that 'proves' their [mission statements'] true value. Most studies have tended to focus almost exclusively—even obsessively—on their content. None has attempted to compare 'prescription with practice,' and only a few have tried to link findings about mission statements to any measures of performance or satisfaction."[38] To this day, despite the paucity of supportive findings, researchers continue in this vein using similar experimental designs to find almost no evidence of direct, positive, and significant relationships between mission statements and performance.[39] We believe, however, that the content of the mission statement can be valuable in another sense.

Whereas mission statements, per se, are not legally binding for an organization, they do articulate organizational priorities. Regarding faith-based adoption agencies, does the mission statement prioritize evangelism over the best interest of the child in finding a permanent, safe, and loving home or vice versa? Does the mission statement meet legal standards for an organization performing a government service, and eligible for government funding?

Eligible or not, there are good reasons to not fund a faith-based organization. Referring to *Agostini v. Felton,* 1997 and *Mitchell v. Helms,* 2000, Bielefeld and Cleveland recognized Saperstein's explanation of "a number of policy reasons to avoid direct government funding of pervasively sectarian FBOs, even though the Supreme Court held this funding to be legal if funds are used for secular purposes."[40] The public is frequently kept out of the loop because religious nonprofits tend to disclose less accountability information than larger, secular nonprofits, believing that the organization's association with a religious entity enhances its trustworthiness. That accountability is demonstrated by showing information such as the number of employees, the amount and source of donations, expenses, and the annual report. The administration and board members of the FBO may believe that "trust between donors and these organizations is already established through a religious bond. Consequently, religion-related nonprofits do not anticipate donors requesting additional accountability information."[41] Without greater disclosure, it is unclear whether the services provided warrant tax payer support.

The lack of public disclosure of accountability information has the power to negatively affect donations to the organization:

> Both corporations and nonprofits need a 'social license to operate.' They maintain the trust of important stakeholders by showing that they adhere to certain social norms and expectations of behavior. Their image, or brand, is extremely important and stakeholders, by withdrawing support as consumer or as donor/supporter, are in a position to influence their organizational success or failure.[42]

If the public trust could be augmented, the organization may not find as great a need to seek government financial support because its like-minded co-religionists would be more apt to continue donating to it, perhaps even in greater sums. To exemplify this, we next contrast mission statements (from Web sites) of several FBOs.

St. Vincent Catholic Charities and Bethany Christian Services of Michigan will be discussed within a legal case later in this chapter. Currently, both organizations' sites provide little information about prospective parents, perhaps as a result of the recent litigation. St. Vincent Catholic Charities of Michigan is an organization headquartered in Lansing, MI (stvcc.org). It offers foster-care, adoption, counseling, and immigration services. Its mission statement appears on the home page of its website: "The mission of St. Vincent Catholic Charities is the work of the Catholic Church, to share the love of Christ by performing the corporal and spiritual works of mercy." On its page about adoption, there is surprisingly scant information about the process. The foster-care page offers much more information, including the qualifications for potential foster parents ("you do not have to be Catholic"). Further information about adoption requires a call to its office or attendance at an orientation meeting. St. Vincent does provide a detailed annual report that lists the government funding, which accounts for 68.3% of its revenue. Bethany Christian Services' page (Grand Rapids, MI; bethany.org) states: "Bethany demonstrates the love and compassion of Jesus Christ by protecting children, empowering youth, and strengthening families through quality social services." No details about prospective parents are given, only the instructions to "Contact Us." Bethany's annual report is available on the site, but its accounting of its revenue is unclear. For example, one category of income in 2018 was "reimbursement for children's services" at an amount of almost $77 million. Another similarly vague category was "investments and other revenue" in the amount of just over $2 million. Government funding is not distinguished as such.

In contrast to the above two organizations, we present two mission statements which explicitly indicate the desire for religious–Christian–adoptive families. America World Adoption in McLean, VA (awaa.org), a Christian International Adoption Agency, opens its home page with a photo of three adorable children with their arms around each other. The mission statement, which also appears on the "About" page, shows up on the home page in large, bold type: "Building families according to God's design of adoption, while caring for vulnerable children around the world." This statement is then followed by a biblical quote from Jeremiah 29:11: "For I know the plans I have for you, declares the LORD, plans to prosper you and not to harm you, plans to give you a hope and a future." Its vision statement ("America World desires for every adoptable orphan to be placed in a Christian home.") makes clear its religious objectives. Christian Homes & Family Services (Abilene, TX; christianhomes.com/): "Changing lives and building Christian families through maternity, foster and adoption services." The vision statement is "A

Christian home for every child." Under requirements for adoptive parents is that both parents must be of the Christian faith and both be active members of the same church, where they both attend weekly. There is no mention of sexual orientation. The agency does not break down its financial information in such a way as to note revenue at all. It does report that the amount of money spent is $2.3 million.

Finally, we include two examples of organizations that make clear their intention to include all types of prospective parents. Family Connections Christian Adoptions (Fresno, CA; fcadoptions.org/): "Family Connections Christian Adoptions exists to assist the waiting children of the world into loving, permanent families. As a living expression of our love for Jesus Christ, we are committed to providing quality adoption services to children everywhere in need of forever homes, and to every family who welcomes them." In addition, the home page says: "FCCA operates in accordance with all state and federal non-discrimination laws and regulations. In addition, as a member of the Evangelical Council on Financial Accountability (ECFA), we are committed to ethical, responsible, and transparent financial stewardship." The site posts the 2016 annual report, which details its revenue in a pie chart. Denoting a "slice" amounting to 37.5% as government/contracts, the actual figure is not given.

The Barker Adoption Foundation (Bethesda, MD; barkeradoptionfoundation.org): "Barker provides lifelong services for all in the adoption constellation and advocates for ethical, respectful, and child-centered adoption practices." The site defines the organization's child-centered focus this way: "While we serve all members in the constellation of adoption relationships, our primary client is the child, who has no voice and often no advocate. . .The litmus test for all we do is whether we are acting in the child's best interest." And this is how the foundation expounds on its inclusiveness: "Barker values diversity of perspective, culture, race, ethnicity, religion, economic circumstances, age, sexual orientation, gender expression, and marital status. We strive to remove barriers for clients who seek our programs and services, and we value and seek diversity in our board governance structure and staff composition."

The Constitutional Issues

Although the human side of adoption is vital, legal issues are also at the forefront because:

> Adoption is a social service to serve the legal needs of the community. It is a government provided and government regulated service. It is a legal construct.

> Oversight is necessarily run by the state . . .even when it out-sources this service to private organizations, including those religiously motivated.[43]

Arriving at a legal and constitutional solution to the problem of matching enough competent parents and suitable homes for children waiting to be adopted today necessitates that we understand the foundational law that affects our implementation of foster-care and adoption services. Until gay marriage was legalized in *Obergefell v. Hodges* (2015), some state laws prevented LGBTQ adoptions because they stated that the adopting couple must be married. Others still use highly gendered language, such as "husband and wife," although this has been read to allow married same-sex couples. A key point is that LGBTQ persons are not currently a protected class, which makes the Equal Protection doctrine that protects other classes problematic. Another key point is that adoption law is regulated by state, not federal, statues. That means claims would not fall under the Religious Freedom Restoration Act (RFRA), which has largely fallen out of favor politically,[44] except as individual states have enacted statutes as a result. Therefore, we examine the First Amendment Free Exercise and Establishment Clauses as they may be used by the parties on either side of this issue and the Equal Protection Clause of the Fourteenth Amendment, as used by the sectarian adoption agencies. It is a difficult decision of equality versus neutrality, with valid claims on both sides.

Free Expression—Religious Freedom

The FBOs argue that their rights under the Free Exercise Clause are violated when state actions enforce non-discrimination statutes in adoption and foster-care placement—something that conflicts with their free exercise of religion. The current test used in Free Exercise Clause cases involving actions taken by individual states comes from the SCOTUS decision in *Employment Division v. Smith* (1990), reaffirmed as the applicable standard for states in the SCOTUS case *City of Boerne v. Flores.*[45] This case established that if a law is neutral and generally applicable but has an incidental effect (even if burdensome) on the free exercise of religion, it can still be constitutional.[46] A neutral law cannot specifically restrict religious practices, or show animus in its enactment; after *Smith*, a free exercise claim must show not just burden, but discrimination.[47] States that have anti-discrimination statutes regarding potential adoptive parents will likely meet the requirements of neutrality and general applicability and thus not be struck down by a Free Exercise claim.[48] In addition, posits Rutledge, sectarian agencies receiving state licenses for foster care and adoption are "acting as a government agent, performing a government function"[49] and, therefore, should not be given exemptions from anti-discrimination clauses. Such groups should

> give up active vocations that can be regulated by the state, or considered state action, if it intends to maintain a discriminatory stance toward homosexuals. It is a loss to free exercise that seems inevitable as the state commits more and more to principles of equality.[50]

Rutledge feels that FBOs that cling to discriminatory practices, citing religious ideals, cannot be reconciled with the principles of nondiscrimination embraced by government. Therefore, the only option is for them to leave the business of child welfare to secular organizations or FBOs which are willing to adhere to state and federal law.

Establishment Clause

Both state statutes that *allow* discrimination by FBOs and state *anti-discrimination* statutes can be contested under the Establishment Clause. The traditional test for challenges to this clause comes from *Lemon v. Kurtzman* (1971). The Lemon test states that the governmental action being challenged must (a) have a secular purpose; (b) not have a primary effect of inhibiting or promoting religion; and (c) not create excessive entanglement between the state and religion.[51]

Laws that allow FBOs to turn away parents for religious reasons are said to be protecting the free exercise of religion and this has been established as a permissible secular purpose. Therefore, the statutes would pass the first and second prongs of the Lemon test.[52] Likewise, statutes prohibiting discrimination are also generally acceptable. The third prong of the test depends on the wording of the law and how it refers to the rules, documents, beliefs, or doctrine of the organization that describes the selection of potential parents. If enforcing the state statute requires "inquiry into the laws and practices of a religious group," that would be "considered excessive entanglement" and would not pass.[53] However, laws that refer to a non-doctrinal, written organizational policy would pass. In this case, "permissive accommodation becomes relevant...where there is 'play in the joints'" between the free exercise and establishment clauses.[54]

Although it is still in use, the Lemon test has been questioned for much of its existence, particularly by SCOTUS Justices. Justice William Rehnquist in his dissent of *Wallace v. Jaffree* (1985), a case about school prayer, claimed that the test is not grounded in the history of the First Amendment and that "The three-part test has simply not provided adequate standards for deciding Establishment Clause cases...Even worse, the *Lemon* test has caused this Court to fracture into unworkable plurality opinions."[55] Fast forward to 2005, where in *Van Orden v. Perry* (constitutionality of a Ten Commandments monument), Justice Stephen Breyer in his concurrence wrote that "Lemon has had a checkered career in the decisional law of this Court."[56] Justice Antonin Scalia has also been vocal about abandoning the use of the Lemon test, in particular the first prong. In 1987, in his dissent to *Edwards* v. *Aguillard* (teaching creationism in schools) Scalia complained that the court's "embarrassing Establishment Clause jurisprudence"[57] using the Lemon test is too flexible, lacks clarity and predictability and "exacerbates the tension between the Free Exercise and Establishment Clauses."[58] In 2005, dissenting to *McCreary v. ACLU* (a Ten Commandments monument case) Scalia wrote that "as bad as the Lemon test is, it is worse for the fact that, since its inception, its seemingly simple mandates have been manipulated to fit whatever result the Court aimed to achieve."[59] Given such criticism, it seems that the likelihood of state adoption clauses may not be weighed using the Lemon test at the SCOTUS level.

Issa contends that despite the similarity of these cases to others contesting the Establishment Clause, they are at heart more complicated:

> The adoption context provides many unique interests that may not be present in a typical church-state case. For example, in the adoption context, all states claim that the promotion of the best interests of children is paramount. . .and states are constitutionally prohibited from putting the interests of the children below religious interests. . .Thus, these religious exemptions, which look like permissive accommodations, should fall because they reverse the order of interests—putting religion over children's welfare.[60]

Another constitutional promise that has been invoked by both FBOs and potential adoptive parents is Equal Protection.

Equal Protection

Equal Protection aims to prevent government from discriminating against groups of similarly situated people. In other words, that legislation should not target a group for unfair treatment. Different levels of scrutiny, or burdens of justification, are used for different legal classifications of the protected group and the importance of the right or interest; three levels of scrutiny are currently recognized.[61] Strict scrutiny is used for situations involving groups of race or national origin, and the fundamental rights of speech and religion. In this instance, the government must show a *compelling* purpose that cannot be achieved via other means in order to defend legislation. Intermediate scrutiny requires the government to show an *important* objective is being sought for the legislation. Finally, rational basis is used when stricter levels do not apply.

Examining competing Equal Protection claims puts the court in the position to decide who is more deserving of protection: FBOs, potential parents, or foster and adoptable children. To date, LGBTQ persons have not been established as a protected group under the Fourteenth Amendment that would require strict scrutiny like that of race and religion.[62] Should that occur, the issue at hand would shift to focus on this clause rather than those of the First Amendment. In the cases where courts have taken up questions of homosexuality, any Equal Protection evaluation has been only at the rational level resulting in discriminatory policies being upheld (e.g., *State Department of Health & Rehabilitative Services v. Cox*, 1993). In the case of the sectarian child welfare agencies, state regulations forcing them to adhere to anti-discrimination laws that conflict with religious views could be an argument for a violation of Equal Protection, and those laws would be subjected to strict scrutiny. In addition, it may be argued that the government has a responsibility to ensure that children "in the system" are also treated equally; that is, children are not put in an inferior position of finding a permanent home because of the policies of the organization that they have been assigned to. It is perhaps because the use of Equal Protection by both sides is possible that it is rarely used in the high-profile cases we examined.

State Laws and Court Cases

Adoption regulations in the states continue to change, especially those laws that protect either the rights of the religious agencies or the potential parents. The contesting of the constitutionality of both types of statutes is evidenced by an increase in the number of complaints filed. Twenty-nine states have statutes explicitly prohibiting discrimination of prospective foster and adoptive parents on the basis of sexual orientation or general non-discrimination statutes including California, Oregon, Wisconsin, Massachusetts, New York, Rhode Island, New Jersey, North Dakota, and Maryland.[63] Twelve states have passed laws allowing child placement agencies to turn away anyone who doesn't match their religious beliefs or moral convictions, including same-sex couples: Alabama, North Dakota, South Dakota, Virginia, Mississippi, Michigan, Texas, Kansas, Oklahoma, South Carolina, Arizona, and Tennessee.[64] Notably, this list has considerable overlap with the list of states with Religious Freedom Restoration Act (RFRA)-inspired statutes. Eight of these states have passed conscience clauses in just the past three years; the most recent, Tennessee, was passed in January 2020. A conscience clause is "a clause in an act or law providing exemptions on the grounds of conscience or belief."[65] Also called refusal clauses, they have been used by medical professionals who refuse to perform services that were legalized by the *Roe v. Wade* decision.[66] In adoption and foster care, such a clause enables placement agencies to act in accordance with their conscience without fear of government interference. The 2016 Mississippi conscience clause law was upheld by the U.S. Court of Appeals for the Fifth Circuit in *Barber v. Bryant* (860 F.3d 345 (5th Cir. 2017)). However, notable repeals of bans and conscience clauses have occurred in Arkansas (2010–2011) and Florida (overturning a prior decision that had upheld the ban in 2004), and a proposed conscience clause failed to pass in Colorado in 2018.

Several state statutes (both non-discrimination and conscience clauses) have been challenged in court, and several are still in process. We will briefly explore five such cases. Mixed signals from lower courts mean the standoff likely will not end unless the Supreme Court gets involved.

South Carolina

In January 2018, the South Carolina DHHS granted an exemption to the religious discrimination rule to Miracle Hill Ministries, which accepted only Protestant, churchgoing people to its federally funded foster-care program and required participants to sign a statement of faith. That meant Miracle Hill Ministries would be permitted to deny services to LGBTQ, Jewish, and even Catholic families wanting to foster a child despite receiving about $600,000 in public funding in 2018.[67] Just a month later, a Catholic mother of three, Aimee Maddonna, was denied an opportunity to volunteer at one of Miracle Hill's children's homes and sued the DHHS, accusing it of religious discrimination.[68] Before the case was heard in court, Miracle Hill relented and allowed Catholics to serve as volunteers and foster parents as long as they agreed to a doctrinal statement of belief. Mission Hill still will not allow Jews, Muslims or same-sex couples to foster children. South Carolina's battles are not over. In *Rogers v. United States Department of Health and Human Services,* a married lesbian couple was turned away by Miracle Hill.[69] The case (opened May 2019) is still open at the district court level. The plaintiffs cite violations of the Establishment, Equal Protection, and Due Process Clauses of the U.S. Constitution.[70]

Michigan

In 2015, Michigan passed a law allowing adoption discrimination, a law heavily favored by two private FBOs that "together facilitate 25–30% of

Michigan's foster care adoptions."[71] In 2017, the American Civil Liberties Union (ACLU) sued over the Michigan Department of Health and Human Services' contract with taxpayer-funded, state-contracted agencies, such as St. Vincent Catholic Charities and Bethany Christian Services, in *Dumont v. Gordon* (E.D. Mich., 2017). These agencies refused to place children with same-sex couples. The plaintiffs cited the Equal Protection and Establishment Clauses, claiming the following:

> . . .agencies that use religious criteria to turn away prospective parents, [cause] Plaintiffs stigmatic harm and [deny] Plaintiffs the same opportunities to work with a child placing agency that is available to every other family in Michigan seeking to adopt.[72]

The case was decided for the plaintiffs, and the Michigan Attorney General declared that adoption agencies contracting with the state can no longer decline to work with LGBT families. Bethany Christian Services opted to change its policy rather than stop serving in Michigan's foster care system. In 2018, Bethany worked with about 8% of the foster or foster-to-adopt cases in Michigan and also operates across the United States.[73] In January, 2022, the State of Michigan admitted it was bound by the SCOTUS decision in *Fulton v. Philadelphia* and allows St. Vincent Catholic Charities to continue operating.[74]

New York

The New York State Office of Children and Family Services sought to enforce a 2013 state non-discrimination statute concerning licensed adoption and foster care agencies—regardless of whether they receive any state or federal funding. The Alliance Defending Freedom sued in *New Hope Family Services v. Poole* (U.S.C.A. 2nd Circuit, 2018) on behalf of faith-based adoption provider New Hope Family Services, which refuses to serve same-sex couples, claiming the non-discrimination statute violates the agency's Free Exercise and Equal Protection rights. In March 2019, a District Court judge dismissed the case. New Hope has appealed and in November 2019, won a small victory: the 2nd Circuit Court of Appeals ruled that the agency could "keep processing adoptions while a three-judge panel considered whether the case would be reinstated."[75]

Texas

Two female Texas A&M University professors say they were denied a chance to become foster parents for refugee children because they didn't "mirror the Holy Family."[76] They sued the U.S. Department of Health and Human Services (HHS) and the U.S. Conference of Catholic Bishops (USCCB), a Catholic group contracted by the government to administer a refugee program. This case is known as *Marouf v. Azar* (391 F. Supp 3d 23 (2018)). The couple asserts violations of the Establishment Clause and the Equal Protection Clause.[77] The case is currently pending before the U.S. District Court of District of Columbia.

Pennsylvania

The City of Philadelphia learned in March 2018 that two of its foster-care providers would not accept same-sex couples to be foster parents, so the city ceased referring children to these agencies. Catholic Social Services (CSS), represented by the Becket Fund for Religious Liberty, sued the City of Philadelphia asking the court to order the city to renew the agency's contract (*Fulton v. City of Philadelphia*). CSS argued that its right to free exercise of religion and free speech entitled it to reject qualified same-sex couples because they were same-sex couples, rather than for any reason related to their qualifications to care for children.[78] The agency turned to the courts, citing its right to free speech and freedom of religion, but the courts have so far rejected its claims; a federal district court, the Third Circuit Court of Appeals, and SCOTUS have denied CSS's motions for injunctions.[79] The Third Circuit Court of Appeals ruled that the city was simply enforcing a neutral law prohibiting discrimination based on a person's sexual orientation. The judges held further that Catholic Social Services "has failed to make a persuasive showing that the City targeted it for its religious beliefs, or is motivated by ill will against its religion, rather than a sincere opposition to discrimination on the basis of sexual orientation."[80] The plaintiffs appealed to the Supreme Court, and the case was heard in November 2020.[81] Just prior to this chapter going to press, SCOTUS released its decision on June 17, 2021. We had hoped for a judgment that would decisively put an end to the controversy spelled out in this chapter; it did not. The ruling, written by Chief Justice John Roberts, was anything but definitive or momentous, and it will, most likely, be unauthoritative outside of Philadelphia. The decision handed down was not favorable for the cause of non-discrimination.

On a very technical point, the Court ruled that the Philadelphia non-discrimination requirement violated the free expression clause of the First

Amendment because it allowed exceptions to enforcement, which meant that the law is not generally enforceable.[82] Therefore, Catholic Charities, which contracts with the city to provide its services, can continue to refuse prospective parents based on the agency's foundational religious beliefs. However, Justice Alito stated in his opinion that the ruling "might as well be written on the dissolving paper sold in magic shops"[83] because the city can revise its anti-discrimination law and start over. This would force SCOTUS to rule on the bigger issues here, such as: (a) upholding *Employment Division v. Smith* (1990) and (b) providing for the non-discrimination of LBGTQ+ people, who currently do not have federal protection. But this leaves the situation still up in the air, and hundreds, if not thousands, of prospective foster and adoptive parents are denied this opportunity, until the Equality Act is passed or SCOTUS sees another nondiscrimination case without a legal flaw.

Discussion and Conclusion

We believe that FBOs which receive government aid and/or which contract with the government to handle state child welfare cases should be held to account for violation of federal nondiscrimination laws. This already includes protections for the religion of prospective parents and when Congress adds sexual orientation protection to the 14th Amendment. It will also apply if SCOTUS provides a definitive ruling in a future LGBTQ adoption discrimination case. Amid the upheaval in his state, then Massachusetts Lieutenant Governor Kerry Healy said, "I believe that any institution that wants to provide services that are regulated by the state has to abide by the laws of the state...and our antidiscrimination laws are some of our most important."[84] FBOs that do not receive aid (but which must be licensed by states to operate) are less clearly subject to federal and state laws.

FBOs should not receive government funding if they discriminate on the basis of sexual orientation, marital status, and religion. Discrimination is unconstitutional, and a waiver of maintaining nondiscriminatory policies exempts behavior that is ordinarily not permitted. The term "waiver" says it all; according to U.S. law, a waiver is "intentionally or voluntarily giving up one's recognized right."[85] In this case, the government is ceding its right to require nondiscriminatory activities and policies of faith-based agencies in the foster-care and adoption business. Harvard Law professor Martha Minow, speaking at Princeton on "Should Religious Groups be Exempt from Civil Rights Laws", said that "Always granting exemptions undermines civil rights laws...Each additional exception curtails the application of the overarching norm—and civil rights laws as a result can be too easily and thoroughly undermined."[86]

In addition to a change in policies to allow adoption by all otherwise qualified potential parents, there should be regulations about total transparency on all literature produced by these agencies, including websites. The Barker Adoption Foundation's mission statement could be used as a template for FBOs that change their modes of operation to be constitutional. Even though The Salvation Army no longer discriminates, its mission statement is confusing and could lead one to believe that their first priority is serving Jesus Christ.

We agree with others who have emphasized that the interests of the child are perhaps of more importance than any legal wrangling and the time it will take for clearer mandates.[87] Lyew writes that there is room for reform on both sides:

> Debate involving true concern for the best interest of children is rare. Commonly entangled with religious freedom arguments, advocacy for marriage equality, support for the "optimal" family. . .a child's best interest may easily be lost amongst the competing groups pushing to advance one issue or another. Children are unable to advocate for themselves, and the unfortunate, unintended consequence of the passionate, well-intentioned efforts of these groups is that a child's best interests may be pushed to the background.[88]

Lyew's point is that the many parties involved in child placement (parents, agencies, churches, judges, and so on) creates a complex web of ideals, values, and goals. Most children are unable to advocate for their own interests, and so within this web, the strand of the child can be obscured or set aside in favor of other ambitions.

Although the BIC seems like a clear enough mandate, it also may not resolve this dilemma. The goal is to place as many children with families, preferably permanently, as possible. On one hand, including all qualified parents regardless of their family structure or creed is desirable. And LGBTQ parents adopt and foster at greater rates than do heterosexual parents. As of 2016, 21.4% of same-sex couples were raising an adopted child and 2.9% fostering a child compared to 3.0% (adopted) and 0.4% (fostering) of opposite-sex couples.[89] On the other hand, forcing anti-discrimination statutes upon faith-based organizations that have been devoted to child welfare for decades (or longer, Catholic Charities opened its first U.S. orphanage in 1727) may cause those organizations to close their doors, eliminating what can be a significant amount of placement work in some geographical areas. In Philadelphia, the shuttered Catholic Social Services was serving several hundred foster children, and the closure came amid the city's urgent call for 300 more foster families to help handle the city's 6,000 foster children.[90] Here, both adoptive parents and children lost; Lyew called the closure a "profound negative impact."[91] Catholic Charities is also known for being able to find homes for hard-to-place children, and was responsible for a third of all Boston private adoptions.[92]

A definitive federal legal decision or act of Congress would be desirable that would both curb excessive litigation (a slow and expensive process) and prevent an exodus of agencies and professionals from the field. Proposals for a compromise involving conscience clauses have been put forward and, in some cases, have been enacted. In some states (such as Michigan's religious freedom adoption law),[93] when a FBO refuses to place with a family due to religious objections, the agency is required to refer the otherwise qualifying family to an agency that will accept them or at the least provide them with a list of alternative agencies. Called a disclosure requirement, this tactic was also used following *Roe v. Wade,* where healthcare providers could decline to provide the service, as long as they offered a referral to one that would.[94] We propose an additional requirement: that FBOs be required to record and disclose the number of parents rejected on the basis of their religion, and the results of referrals to alternative agencies. The success of such a compromise would depend on a thorough study of the amount of FBO placement in a particular jurisdiction and the availability of alternative agencies; no compromise should become a roadblock and prevent access to potential adoptive parents. Lyew proposes two exceptions: first, that more diligence must be taken with hard-to-place children by any agency and, second, that children of a certain age and maturity are allowed to express their own preferences about religion and same-sex couples in placement decisions.[95]

Unfortunately, writes Lyew, "this problem cannot be resolved if it continues to be a politicized issue involving religious freedom against rights for same-sex couples and vice versa, rather than a children's issue which impacts thousands of children lacking a comparably strong voice."[96]

Notes

1 "AFCARS Report," *Children's Bureau*, November 19, 2021, https://www.acf.hhs.gov/cb/report/afcars-report-28, n.p.

2 Vanessa Romo, "State-Funded Adoption Agencies in Michigan Barred From Refusing LGBTQ Parents," *NPR*, March 22, 2019, https://www.npr.org/2019/03/22/706049119/state-funded-adoption-agencies-in-michigan-barred-from-refusing-lgbtq-parents, n.p.

3 Colleen Theresa Rutledge, "Caught in the Crossfire: How Catholic Charities of Boston was Victim to the Clash between Gay Rights and Religious Freedom," *Duke Journal of Gender Law & Policy* 15 (2008): 303.
4 John Kelly, "Trump Rescinds Obama-era Rules Barring Discrimination in Foster Care, Adoption," *The Chronicle of Social Change*, September 27 2019, https://chronicleofsocialchange.org/child-welfare-2/trump-rescinds-obama-era-rules-barring-discrimination-in-foster-care-adoption/38818, n.p.
5 Andrea Picciotti-Bayer, "The Supreme Court review of Sharonell Fulton, et al. v. City of Philadelphia," *National Review*, July 29, 2019, https://www.nationalreview.com/bench-memos/the-supreme-court-review-of-sharonell-fulton-et-al-v-city-of-philadelphia/, n.p.
6 Tom Barton, "Foster-care Ruling: Victory for Religious Freedom or Bias?" *The State*, January 23, 2019, https://www.thestate.com/news/politics-government/article224958895.html, n.p.
7 Department of Health and Human Services (DHHS), "HHS Issues Proposed Rule to Align Grants Regulation with New Legislation, Nondiscrimination Laws, and Supreme Court Decisions," November 1, 2019, https://www.hhs.gov/about/news/2019/11/01/hhs-issues-proposed-rule-to-align-grants-regulation.html, n.p.
8 Maggie Gallagher, "Banned in Boston," *The Weekly Standard*, May 15, 2006, https://www.washingtonexaminer.com/weekly-standard/banned-in-boston-13329, n.p.
9 Lynne M. Kohm, "Tracing the Foundations of the Best Interests of the Child Standard in American Jurisprudence," *Journal of Law & Family Studies* 10 (2008): 337.
10 Peter Conn, *Adoption: A Brief Social and Cultural History* (Palgrave Macmillan, 2019), 47.
11 Conn, 43.
12 Carp, 5.
13 Conn, 79.
14 Conn, 49.
15 E. Wayne Carp, "Introduction," in *Adoption in America: Historical Perspectives*, ed. Wayne E. Carp, 1–26 (Ann Arbor: University of Michigan Press, 2009), 3.
16 Conn, 87.
17 Carp, 10.
Conn, 92–93.
Laura J. Schwartz, "Religious Matching for Adoption: Unraveling the Interests Behind the 'Best Interests' Standard," *Family Law Quarterly* 25, no. 2 (1991), 173.
18 Schwartz, 174–6.
19 Schwartz, 172–3.
20 Carp, 16.
21 New York Consolidated Laws, Social Services Law—SOS § 373, February 10, 2020, https://www.nysenate.gov/legislation/laws/SOS/373, n.p.
22 "King Solomon," *Jewish Virtual Library*, 2020, https://www.jewishvirtuallibrary.org/king-solomon.
23 Carp, 5.
Henry H. Foster Jr., "Adoption and Child Custody: Best Interests of the Child," *Buffalo Law Review* 22, no. 1 (1972), 1.

Lynne M. Kohm, "Tracing the Foundations of the Best Interests of the Child Standard in American Jurisprudence," *Journal of Law & Family Studies*, 10 (2008): 337.

24 Foster, Jr., 1–2.

25 Foster, Jr., 1.

26 Robert H. Mnookin, "Child-custody Adjudication: Judicial Functions in the Face of Indeterminacy," *Law and Contemporary Problems* 39, no. 3 (1972), 226.

27 Schwartz, 188.

28 Foster, Jr. 1.

29 Foster Jr., 3.

30 Robert Hughes, Jr., "Are Custody Decisions Biased in Favor of Mothers?" *Huffington Post,* June 9, 2011, https://www.huffpost.com/entry/are-custody-decisions-bia_b_870709, n.p.

31 Wayne Parker, "Key Statistics about Kids from Divorced Families," *Verywellfamily.com*, January 20, 2020, https://www.verywellfamily.com/children-of-divorce-in-america-statistics-1270390, n.p.

"Child Custody," *Justia.com*, 2018. https://www.justia.com/family/child-custody-and-support/child-custody, n.p.

32 Lauren Wallace, "What is the 'Child's Best Interest' Standard?" *LegalMatch.com*, March 6, 2018, https://www.legalmatch.com/law-library/article/childs-best-interest-standard.html, n.p.

33 Mnookin, 268.

34 Annette R. Appell and Bruce A. Boyer, "Parental Rights vs. Best Interests of the Child: A False Dichotomy in the Context of Adoption," *Duke Journal of Gender Law & Policy* 2 (1995): 64–65.

35 Ines Alegre, Jasmina Berbegal-Mirabent, Adrián Guerrero, and Marta Mas-Machuca, "The Real Mission of the Mission Statement: A Systematic Review of the Literature," *Journal of Management & Organization* 24, no. 4 (2018).

36 Christopher K. Bart, Christopher, "Sex, Lies and Mission Statements." *Business Horizons* (1997).

37 Jeffrey Yip, Edmund Twohill, Chris Ernst, and Vijayan P. Munusamy, "Leadership in Faith-based Nonprofits: The Power of Identity Boundaries to Bind and Blind," *Nonprofit Management and Leadership* 20, no. 4 (2010): 469.

38 Bart, 9.

39 Janet A. Weiss and Sandy Kristin Piderit, "The Value of Mission Statements in Public Agencies," *Journal of Public Administration Research and Theory* 9, no. 2 (1999), Isabel Maria Macedo, José Carlos Pinho, and Anabela Martins Silva, "Revisiting the Link between Mission Statements and Organizational Performance in the Non-profit Sector: The Mediating Effect of Organizational Commitment," *European Management Journal* 34, no. 1 (2016).

Valerii Dermol and Nada Trunk Širca. "Communication, Company Mission, Organizational Values, and Company Performance," *Procedia-Social and Behavioral Sciences* 238 (2018).

40 Wolfgang Bielefeld and William S. Cleveland, "Faith-based Organizations as Service Providers and their Relationship to Government," *Nonprofit and Voluntary Sector Quarterly* 42, no. 3 (2013): 478.

41 Joannie Tremblay-Boire and Aseem Prakash, "Accountability.org: Online Disclosures by US Nonprofits," *VOLUNTAS: International Journal of Voluntary and Nonprofit Organizations* 26, no. 2 (2015): 704.
42 Tremblay-Boire and Prakash, 696.
43 Rutledge, 307.
44 Brian Miller, "The Age of RFRA," *Forbes*, November 16, 2018. https://www.forbes.com/sites/briankmiller/2018/11/16/the-age-of-rfra/#f93837177bae, n.p.
45 Rutledge, 304.
46 Matthew A. Issa, "Guaranteeing Marriage Rights: Examining the Clash between Same-sex Adoption and Religious Freedom," *Georgetown Journal of Gender and Law* 18, no. 1 (2017).
Rutledge.
Patrick M. Garry, "An Equal Protection View of the First Amendment," *Quinnipiac Law Review*, 28, no. 4 (2009).
47 Garry, 826.
48 Issa, 217.
Rutledge, 303.
49 Rutledge, 304.
50 Rutledge, 305.
51 Issa, 222.
52 Issa 223.
53 Issa, 225.
54 Issa, 225.
55 *Wallace v. Jaffree*, 472 U.S. 38 (1985), 110.
56 *Van Orden v. Perry* (03–1500) 545 U.S. 677 (2005), n.p.
57 *Edwards* v. *Aguillard*, 482 U.S. 578, 640 (1987), 481.
58 *Edwards* v. *Aguillard*, 482 U.S. 578, 640 (1987), 482.
59 *McCreary County v. ACLU OF KY*, (03–1693) 545 U.S. 844 (2005), n.p.
60 Issa, 227.
61 Garry 791–92.
James G. Dwyer, "The Children We Abandon: Religious Exemptions to Child Welfare and Education Laws as Denials of Equal Protection to Children of Religious Objectors," *North Carolina Law Review* 74, no. 5 (1995): 1390–92.
62 Issa, 208.
David Rivkin and Elizabeth P. Foley, "Gay Rights, Religious Freedom and the Law," *Wall Street Journal*, April 9, 2015, https://www.wsj.com/articles/gay-rights-religious-freedom-and-the-law-1428620004, n.p.
63 Movement Enhancement Project, "Foster and Adoption Laws," June, 2022, https://www.lgbtmap.org/equality-maps/foster_and_adoption_laws.
64 John Kelly, "Trump Rescinds Obama-era Rules Barring Discrimination in Foster Care, Adoption," *The Chronicle of Social Change,* September 27 2019, https://chronicleofsocialchange.org/child-welfare-2/trump-rescinds-obama-era-rules-barring-discrimination-in-foster-care-adoption/38818, n.p.
Veronica Stracqualursi, "Tennessee Passes Bill Protecting Foster and Adoption Agencies if They Reject LGBTQ Parents for Placement," *CNN*, January 15, 2020, https://www.cnn.com/2020/01/15/politics/tennessee-adoption-foster-care-bill-trnd/index.html, n.p.

65 "Conscience clause," Oxford English Dictionary (2020), https://www.oed.com/, n.p.
66 Samantha R. Lyew, "Adoption and Foster Care Placement Policies: Legislatively Promoting the Best Interest of Children Amidst Competing Interests of Religious Freedom and Equal Protection for Same-Sex Couples," *Journal of Legislation* 42, no. 2 (2016): 196.
67 Kristian Hernandez, Pratheek Rebala, Nathanial Carey, and Mike Reicher, "Bills Supporting Religion-based Rejection Turning Parents Away from Adoption Agencies," *USA Today*, June 10, 2019, https://www.usatoday.com/story/news/investigations/2019/06/10/adoption-agencies-latest-front-religious-freedom-fight/1359072001/, n.p.
68 Hernandez, et al., n.p.
69 Nathaniel Cary, "Greenville Couple Sues Trump Administration and SC Governor Over Foster-care Practice," *Greenville News*, May 30, 2019, https://www.greenvilleonline.com/story/news/2019/05/30/greenville-sc-couple-sue-trump-administration-governor-over-miracle-hill-foster-care/1284405001/, n.p.
70 "Rogers v. Health and Human Services," ACLU. October 21, 2019, https://www.aclu.org/cases/rogers-v-health-and-human-services, n.p.
71 Lyew, 199.
72 "Dumont v. Lyon—Order Denying Motion to Dismiss," ACLU, September 14, 2018, https://www.aclu.org/legal-document/dumont-v-lyon-order-denying-motion-dismiss, 23.
73 Megan Fowler, "Despite HHS Change, Christian Foster Agencies Still Fight LGBT Requirements," *Christianity Today*, November 8, 2019, https://www.christianitytoday.com/news/2019/november/hhs-adoption-foster-change-lgbt-state-fulton-v-philadelphia.html, n.p.
74 Fowler, n.p.
75 Julie McMahon, "Can CNY Christian Adoption Agency Exclude Gays, Unmarried Couples? NY Law Faces High-profile Court Test," *Syracuse.com*, December 2, 2019, https://www.syracuse.com/news/2019/12/can-cny-christian-adoption-agency-exclude-gays-unmarried-couples-ny-law-faces-high-profile-court-test.html, n.p.
76 Lambda Legal, "Marouf v. Azar". June 2019, https://www.lambdalegal.org/in-court/cases/marouf-v-azar, n.p.
77 Lambda Legal, n.p.
78 "Fulton v. City of Philadelphia," ACLU, June 8, 2018, https://www.aclupa.org/en/cases/fulton-v-city-philadelphia, n.p.
79 Andrea Picciotti-Bayer, "The Supreme Court Review of Sharonell Fulton, et al. v. City of Philadelphia." *National Review*, July 29, 2019. https://www.nationalreview.com/bench-memos/the-supreme-court-review-of-sharonell-fulton-et-al-v-city-of-philadelphia/, n.p.
80 "Fulton v. City of Philadelphia", n.p.
81 Ariane de Vogue, "Supreme Court Takes Up Religious Liberty Dispute on Foster Care and Same-Sex Marriage," *CNN*, February 24, 2020. https://www.cnn.com/2020/02/24/politics/supreme-court-same-sex-foster-care-agency/index.html, n.p.
82 *Fulton v. Philadelphia et al.* U.S. No. 19–123 (2021) (slip opinion). https://www.supremecourt.gov/opinions/20pdf/19-123_g3bi.pdf

83 *Fulton v. Philadelphia et al.* U.S. No. 19–123 (2021) (slip opinion). (Alito, S., concurring opinion).
84 Maggie Gallagher, "Banned in Boston," *The Weekly Standard*, May 15, 2006, https://www.washingtonexaminer.com/weekly-standard/banned-in-boston-13329, n.p.
85 "Waiver," Legal Information Institute (LII), *Cornell Law School,* https://www.law.cornell.edu/wex/waiver, n.p.
86 Martha Minow, "Should Religious Groups Be Exempt from Civil Rights Laws," *Boston College Law Review* 48, no. 1, (2007): 827.
87 Issa, 209.
Lyew, 189.
88 Lyew, 194.
89 Shoshana K. Goldberg and Kerith J. Conron, "How Many Same-sex Couples in the U.S. are Raising Children?" *Williams Institute at UCLA School of Law,* July 2018, https://williamsinstitute.law.ucla.edu/wp-content/uploads/Parenting-Among-Same-Sex-Couples.pdf, n.p.
90 Catholic News Service, "Court says Philadelphia Can End Faith-based Agencies' Foster Care," CatholicPhilly.com, April 25, 2019, https://catholicphilly.com/2019/04/news/local-news/court-says-philadelphia-can-end-faith-based-agencies-foster-care/, n.p.
Monica Burke and Jared Eckert, "Philadelphia Sabotages Its Own Adoption and Foster-Care System," *The Heritage Foundation.* April 6, 2018, https://www.heritage.org/marriage-and-family/commentary/philadelphia-sabotages-its-own-adoption-and-foster-care-system, n.p.
91 Lyew, 205.
92 Rutledge, 298.
93 Lyew, 204.
94 Lyew, 203.
95 Lyew 204.
96 Lyew, 209.

Bibliography

"AFCARS Report." *Children's Bureau.* November 19, 2021. https://www.acf.hhs.gov/cb/report/afcars-report-28

Alegre, Ines, Jasmina Berbegal-Mirabent, Adrián Guerrero, and Marta Mas-Machuca. "The Real Mission of the Mission Statement: A Systematic Review of the Literature." *Journal of Management & Organization* 24, no. 4 (2018): 456–73.

Appell, Annette R., and Bruce A. Boyer. "Parental Rights vs. Best Interests of the Child: A False Dichotomy in the Context of Adoption." *Duke Journal of Gender Law & Policy* 2 (1995): 63–84.

Bart, Christopher K. "Sex, Lies and Mission Statements." *Business Horizons* November-December, (1997): 9–18.

Barton, Ryland. "Joint Custody will be the Default under New Kentucky Law." *WFPL News Louisville,* April 29, 2018. https://wfpl.org/kentucky-courts-to-grant-joint-custody-by-default-under-new-law/

Barton, Tom. "Foster-Care Ruling: Victory for Religious Freedom or Bias?" *The State.* January 23, 2019. https://www.thestate.com/news/politics-government/article224958895.html

Bielefeld, Wolfgang, and William S. Cleveland. "Faith-Based Organizations as Service Providers and Their Relationship to Government." *Nonprofit and Voluntary Sector Quarterly* 42, no. 3 (2013): 468–94.

Brodzinsky, David M., and Adam Pertman (Eds.). *Adoption by Lesbians and Gay Men: A New Dimension in Family Diversity.* New York: Oxford University Press, 2011.

Burke, Monica and Jared Eckert. "Philadelphia Sabotages Its Own Adoption and Foster-Care System." *The Heritage Foundation.* April 6, 2018. https://www.heritage.org/marriage-and-family/commentary/philadelphia-sabotages-its-own-adoption-and-foster-care-system

Carp, E. Wayne. "Introduction." In *Adoption in America: Historical Perspectives,* edited by Wayne E. Carp, 1–26. Ann Arbor: University of Michigan Press, 2009.

Cary, Nathaniel. "Greenville Couple Sues Trump Administration and SC Governor Over Foster-care Practice." *Greenville News,* May 30, 2019. https://www.greenvilleonline.com/story/news/2019/05/30/greenville-sc-couple-sue-trump-administration-governor-over-miracle-hill-foster-care/1284405001/

Catholic News Service. "Court Says Philadelphia Can End Faith-Based Agencies' Foster Care." *CatholicPhilly.com,* April 25, 2019. https://catholicphilly.com/2019/04/news/local-news/court-says-philadelphia-can-end-faith-based-agencies-foster-care/

"Child Custody." *Justia.com,* 2018. https://www.justia.com/family/child-custody-and-support/child-custody/

Conn, Peter. *Adoption: A Brief Social and Cultural History.* Palgrave Macmillan, 2019.

"Conscience clause." *Oxford English Dictionary* (2020). https://www.oed.com/

de Vogue, Ariane. "Supreme Court Takes Up Religious Liberty Dispute on Foster Care and Same-Sex Marriage." *CNN,* February 24, 2020. https://www.cnn.com/2020/02/24/politics/supreme-court-same-sex-foster-care-agency/index.html

Dean, James. "Surrendering to the State." *World Magazine,* October 24, 2019. https://world.wng.org/2019/10/surrendering_to_the_state

Department of Health and Human Services (DHHS). "HHS Issues Proposed Rule to Align Grants Regulation with New Legislation, Nondiscrimination Laws, and Supreme Court Decisions." November 1, 2019. https://www.hhs.gov/about/news/2019/11/01/hhs-issues-proposed-rule-to-align-grants-regulation.html

Dermol, Valerij, and Nada Trunk Širca. "Communication, Company Mission, Organizational Values, and Company Performance." *Procedia-Social and Behavioral Sciences* 238 (2018): 542–51.

Dowd, Rachel. "Same-sex Parenting in the U.S." *The Williams Institute, UCLA School of Law*, July 31, 2018. https://williamsinstitute.law.ucla.edu/press/same-sex-parenting/

"Dumont v. Lyon – Order Denying Motion to Dismiss." *ACLU*, September 14, 2018. https://www.aclu.org/legal-document/dumont-v-lyon-order-denying-motion-dismiss

Dwyer, James G. "The Children we Abandon: Religious Exemptions to Child Welfare and Education Laws as Denials of Equal Protection to Children of Religious Objectors." *North Carolina Law Review* 74, no. 5 (1995): 1321.

Foster Jr, Henry H. "Adoption and Child Custody: Best Interests of the Child." *Buffalo Law Review* 22, no. 1 (1972): 1–16.

Fowler, Megan. "Despite HHS Change, Christian Foster Agencies Still Fight LGBT Requirements." *Christianity Today*, November 8, 2019. https://www.christianitytoday.com/news/2019/november/hhs-adoption-foster-change-lgbt-state-fulton-v-philadelphia.html

"Fulton v. City of Philadelphia." *ACLU.* June 8, 2018. https://www.aclupa.org/en/cases/fulton-v-city-philadelphia

Gallagher, Maggie. "Banned in Boston." *The Weekly Standard*, May 15, 2006. https://www.washingtonexaminer.com/weekly-standard/banned-in-boston-13329

Garry, Patrick M. "An Equal Protection View of the First Amendment." *Quinnipiac Law Review*, 28, no. 4 (2009): 787.

Goldberg, Shoshana K. and Kerith J. Conron. "How Many Same-Sex Couples in the U.S. Are Raising Children?" *Williams Institute at UCLA School of Law.* July 2018. https://williamsinstitute.law.ucla.edu/wp-content/uploads/Parenting-Among-Same-Sex-Couples.pdf

Hernandez, Kristian, Pratheek Rebala, Nathanial Carey, and Mike Reicher. "Bills Supporting Religion-Based Rejection Turning Parents Away from Adoption Agencies." *USA Today*, June 10, 2019. https://www.usatoday.com/story/news/investigations/2019/06/10/adoption-agencies-latest-front-religious-freedom-fight/1359072001/

Hughes, Robert, Jr. "Are Custody Decisions Biased in Favor of Mothers?" *Huffington Post.* June 9, 2011. https://www.huffpost.com/entry/are-custody-decisions-bia_b_870709

Issa, Matthew A. "Guaranteeing Marriage Rights: Examining the Clash between Same-Sex Adoption and Religious Freedom." *Georgetown Journal of Gender and Law* 18, no. 1 (2017): 207.

Joyce, Kathryn. *The Child Catchers: Rescue, Trafficking, and the New Gospel of Adoption.* New York: Public Affairs, 2013.

Kelly, John. "Trump Rescinds Obama-era Rules Barring Discrimination in Foster Care, Adoption." *The Chronicle of Social Change.* September 27, 2019. https://chronicleofsocialchange.org/child-welfare-2/trump-rescinds-obama-era-rules-barring-discrimination-in-foster-care-adoption/38818

"King Solomon." *Jewish Virtual Library*. 2020. https://www.jewishvirtuallibrary.org/king-solomon

Kohm, Lynne M. "Tracing the Foundations of the Best Interests of the Child Standard in American Jurisprudence." *Journal of Law & Family Studies,* 10 (2008): 337–76.

Lambda Legal. "Marouf v. Azar". June 2019. https://www.lambdalegal.org/in-court/cases/marouf-v-azar

Lyew, Samantha R. "Adoption and Foster Care Placement Policies: Legislatively Promoting the Best Interest of Children Amidst Competing Interests of Religious Freedom and Equal Protection for Same-Sex Couples." *Journal of Legislation* 42, no. 2 (2016): 186–210.

Macedo, Isabel Maria, José Carlos Pinho, and Anabela Martins Silva. "Revisiting the Link between Mission Statements and Organizational Performance in the Non-profit Sector: The Mediating Effect of Organizational Commitment." *European Management Journal* 34, no. 1 (2016): 36–46.

McMahon, Julie. "Can CNY Christian Adoption Agency Exclude Gays, Unmarried Couples? NY Law Faces High-profile Court Test." *Syracuse.com,* December 2, 2019. https://www.syracuse.com/news/2019/12/can-cny-christian-adoption-agency-exclude-gays-unmarried-couples-ny-law-faces-high-profile-court-test.html

Miller, Brian. "The Age of RFRA." *Forbes*, November 16, 2018. https://www.forbes.com/sites/briankmiller/2018/11/16/the-age-of-rfra/#f93837177bae

Minow, Martha. "Should Religious Groups be Exempt from Civil Rights Laws." *Boston College Law Review* 48, no. 1 (2007): 781–849.

Mnookin, Robert H. "Child-custody Adjudication: Judicial Functions in the Face of Indeterminacy." *Law and Contemporary Problems* 39, no. 3 (1975): 226–93.

"Conscience clause." *Oxford English Dictionary* (2020). https://www.oed.com/

Parker, Wayne. "Key Statistics about Kids from Divorced Families." *Verywellfamily.com*, January 20, 2020. https://www.verywellfamily.com/children-of-divorce-in-america-statistics-1270390

Picciotti-Bayer, Andrea. "The Supreme Court Review of *Sharonell Fulton, et al. v. City of Philadelphia*." *National Review*, July 29, 2019. https://www.nationalreview.com/bench-memos/the-supreme-court-review-of-sharonell-fulton-et-al-v-city-of-philadelphia/

Rivkin, David and Elizabeth P. Foley. "Gay Rights, Religious Freedom and the Law." *Wall Street Journal*, April 9, 2015. https://www.wsj.com/articles/gay-rights-religious-freedom-and-the-law-1428620004

"Rogers v. Health and Human Services." *ACLU*. October 21, 2019. https://www.aclu.org/cases/rogers-v-health-and-human-services

Romo, Vanessa. "State-Funded Adoption Agencies in Michigan Barred From Refusing LGBTQ Parents." *NPR,* March 22, 2019. https://www.npr.org/2019/03/22/706049119/state-funded-adoption-agencies-in-michigan-barred-from-refusing-lgbtq-parents

Rutledge, Colleen Theresa. "Caught in the Crossfire: How Catholic Charities of Boston was Victim to the Clash between Gay Rights and Religious Freedom." *Duke Journal of Gender Law & Policy* 15 (2008): 297–314.

Saperstein, D. (2003). "Public Accountability and Faith-based Organizations: A Problem Best Avoided". *Harvard Law Review,* 116: 1353–96.

Schwartz, Laura J. "Religious Matching for Adoption: Unraveling the Interests Behind the 'Best Interests' Standard." *Family Law Quarterly* 25, no. 2 (1991): 171–92.

Stracqualursi, Veronica. "Tennessee Passes Bill Protecting Foster and Adoption Agencies if They Reject LGBTQ Parents for Placement." *CNN,* January 15, 2020. https://www.cnn.com/2020/01/15/politics/tennessee-adoption-foster-care-bill-trnd/index.html

Tremblay-Boire, Joannie, and Aseem Prakash. "Accountability.org: Online Disclosures by US Nonprofits." *VOLUNTAS: International Journal of Voluntary and Nonprofit Organizations,* 26, no. 2 (2015): 693–719.

"Waiver." *Legal Information Institute (LII),* Cornell Law School. Accessed February 11, 2020 from https://www.law.cornell.edu/wex/waiver

Wallace, Lauren "What Is the 'Child's Best Interest' Standard?" *LegalMatch.com,* March 6, 2018. https://www.legalmatch.com/law-library/article/childs-best-interest-standard.html

Weiss, Janet A., and Sandy Kristin Piderit. "The Value of Mission Statements in Public Agencies." *Journal of Public Administration Research and Theory* 9, no. 2 (1999): 193–224.

Yip, Jeffrey, Edmund Twohill, Chris Ernst, and Vijayan P. Munusamy. "Leadership in Faith-based Nonprofits: The Power of Identity Boundaries to Bind and Blind." *Nonprofit Management and Leadership* 20, no. 4 (2010): 461–72.

4. *The State of 'Writing' a Judicial Wrong: Renewing Legislative* Hesed *in* Board of Education of Kiryas Joel Village School District v. Grumet

Adrienne E. Hacker Daniels and Sergio Peña

After Rhode Island's ratification of the Constitution of the United States, May 29, 1790, President George Washington and Secretary of State Thomas Jefferson traveled to Newport, Rhode Island, arriving August 17.[1] Comporting with the oratorical norms of the time, epistolaries were delivered and addressed to the president in a formal ceremony. All this seems rather pro forma, marked by the pomp and circumstance of variations of encomium rhetoric, but the final epistolary instantiates the most historical significance, attributable to the letter's content, but more importantly "because of [the] celebrated reply" by Washington, sent a few days later from New York City.[2] The letter to which Washington responded was signed and delivered by Moses Seixas on behalf of the Hebrew congregation of Newport. Newport's synagogue is of historical import. Built in 1763 and originally known as Yeshuat Israel (and currently as Touro Synagogue), it is the oldest and still surviving synagogue in North America.[3] The heart of Seixas's letter expresses concern for the historical dearth of religious liberties accorded certain citizens:

> Deprived as we heretofore have been of the invaluable rights of free citizens, we now with a deep sense of gratitude to the Almighty disposer, of all events behold a Government erected by the majesty of the people—a Government, which to bigotry gives no sanction, to persecution no assistance—but generously affording to all liberty of conscience and immunities of Citizenship—deeming everyone, of whatever nation, tongue or language, equal parts of the great government machine.[4]

In his written reply, Washington echoes Seixas's optative discourse:

> All possess alike liberty of conscience and immunities of citizenship. It is now no more that toleration is spoken of, as if it was by the indulgence of one class of people that another enjoyed the exercise of their inherent natural rights. For happily, the Government of the United States, which gives to bigotry no sanction, to persecution no assistance, requires only that they who live under its protection should demean themselves as good citizens in giving it on all occasions their effectual support.[5]

Washington's influential response over 230 years ago, at once affirms the centrality of the free exercise of religion clause and religious liberty as codified in the First Amendment and collides with the Establishment Clause. *Everson v. Board of Education* (1947) represents the first Supreme Court case in which the Establishment Clause was applied to the states.[6] In the better part of five decades since, important Establishment Clause cases were decided, with a particularly compelling and vexing one decided in the mid-1990s. A Supreme Court case decided June 27, 1994, *Board of Education of Kiryas Joel Village School District v. Grumet* (512 U.S. 687), exemplifies the foundational import of religious liberty as articulated by Washington in tandem with the inherent complexities in its attempted reconciliations and rapprochements with the Establishment Clause and the Equal Protection Clause of the Fourteenth Amendment.[7] As Boyarin and Boyarin state, "one of the complicating aspects of *Kiryas Joel* is that religious establishment and equal-protection jurisprudence issues appear to be closely intertwined in the case."[8]

Worthy of underscoring and not going unnoticed, the first two clauses of the First Amendment read, "Congress shall make no law respecting an establishment of religion, or prohibiting the free exercise thereof,"[9] and Section 1 of the Fourteenth Amendment reads as,

> All persons born or naturalized in the United States and subject to the jurisdiction thereof, are citizens of the United States and of the State wherein they reside. No State shall make or enforce any law which shall abridge the privileges or immunities of citizens of the United States; nor shall any State deprive any person of life, liberty, or property, without due process of law, nor deny to any person within its jurisdiction the equal protection of the laws.[10]

In this 6–3 plurality decision, the Court determined that a special New York State statute, legislated to create a separate school district exclusively for children with disabilities in Kiryas Joel, was in violation of the proscription against the establishment of religion.[11] A separate school district had been legislated to accommodate the homogeneously populated village of Kiryas Joel, founded by Satmar Hasidim, an ultra-Orthodox group within Judaism.

The school district was created to provide a secular education for the special needs children of the village who were legally entitled to special education services initially established by the Federal Government as the Education for all Handicapped Children Act (EAHCA) of 1975, and then reauthorized in 1990 as the Individuals with Disabilities Education Act (IDEA).[12] At first the students' nonsectarian education was provided at Bais Rochel, a school in the village, but this space was ultimately determined to be an unconstitutional proxemic solution, as was a subsequent and intermediate short-lived solution.

As an Establishment Clause case, *Kiryas Joel* raises vexing issues in the interrelatedness between "religious establishment and equal protection jurisprudence,"[13] insofar as the "separation of the Hasidic school children inevitably comes to be seen as analogous to an acceptable or unacceptable form of racial segregation."[14] This chapter explores the intersectionality of the hopscotching legislative and judicial histories surrounding the Kiryas Joel school district case. The rhetoric in both the judicial and legislative arenas of the case reflects a muddled adjudication in tandem with a legislative imbroglio. Although one might conclude that "all's well that ends well," the "serpentine"[15] journey which reached the conclusion that the Kiryas Joel school district was ultimately deemed constitutionally valid was far from dispositive, and as ostensibly settled, its existence remains steeped in controversy.

The chapter begins with a discussion of the sociology of the Satmar Hasidim and their geographical and cultural post World War II journey, realized in large part with the incorporation of the village of Kiryas Joel; the provenance of the legal and judicial contestations; a survey of key Supreme Court precedents; an analysis of the case applying Hermagorean *stasis* theory; and the impact of disability on the education of the Satmar children.

The *Kiryas Joel* case poses unique constitutional and legislative challenges and this chapter argues, that, as much as stasis theory illuminates the case through forensic and deliberative rhetoric, the case ironically reaches its "denouement" on the side of asystatic theory, essentially with the questions of balance *(isazon)* and inconclusiveness *(aporon).*

The Genesis of a Village

The Satmar Hasidim have their geographical roots in Satu Mare, once a part of Hungary and presently a part of Romania.[16] Their leader, Grand Rebbe Joel Teitelbaum, a Holocaust survivor, emigrated from Jerusalem in 1946 to the Williamsburg section of Brooklyn, New York.[17] Many of the Satmar Hasidim who survived the concentration camps learned the Rebbe Teitelbaum survived the Holocaust and reunited with him in Brooklyn.[18] In 1975, disenchanted with the encroachment of a profane and secular New York culture corrupting the Satmar's piety, Rabbe Teitelbaum located a parcel of land in the town of Monroe in Orange County, approximately 50 miles north of New York City.[19] The land of 1.1 square miles was purchased and legally incorporated as the Village of Kiryas Joel (eponymously named for the Rebbe), with the requisite 500 residents, and in 1977 Kiryas Joel was born with unencumbered legal recognition.[20] Although the establishment of the actual village was left uncontested as a violation of the Establishment Clause, the establishment of the school district was contested, but ultimately rendered constitutional through some judicial, but mostly legislative legerdemain. However, this sleight of hand was wholly avoidable, in that the exigence which engendered the establishment of the school district was really no exigence at all, save for the misapplication of the Establishment Clause to previous SCOTUS cases.

Putting aside the legal dilemmas surrounding the Kiryas Joel Village school district, the creation of the village itself in 1977 and its continued growth has been fraught with strife and contention. Kiryas Joel is the poorest community in the United States, in spite of the fact that no one is homeless or experiences food insecurity, and crime is negligible.[21] The demographics are somewhat shocking. Of municipalities with more than 10,000 people, Kiryas Joel has the highest proportion of its residents at the poverty level.[22] As of 2011, the median age of its residents was 12 and household size 6, the lowest and the highest metrics respectively.[23] The educational data would be construed as bleak by any reasonable person. In Kiryas Joel, only 39% are high school graduates with less than 5% possessing a bachelor's degree.[24]

In his incisive essay,[25] Jonathan Boyarin delineates the series of imbricated issues raised in the *Kiryas Joel* case, including (1) the reconciliation of a village constitutionally established with clearly defined geographic boundaries to those of the presumably "unconstitutionally" established school district; and (2) the physical separation of the disabled Hasidic children from the confines of the Monroe-Woodbury school district classrooms and the ways that this might "be seen as analogous to an unacceptable form of racial segregation, clearly impacting the Equal Protection Clause." Arguably, religion cannot be the primary determinative criterion in drawing boundaries for a village or a school district, but are there political and legal consequences when use of that criterion is denied?

Navigating the Judicial and Legislative Terrain

After the 1988 decision by the New York Court of Appeals held that the Monroe-Woodbury school district was not "compelled to teach the village's disabled children"[26] at Bais Rochel, a private venue for wholly sectarian learning within Kiryas Joel, Governor Mario Cuomo signed the special state statute in 1989, Chapter 748, "making the Satmar enclave the only village in the state with the power and authority to operate its own public school system."[27] In 1992, Lawrence Kahn, State Supreme Court Justice ruled Chapter 748 unconstitutional, rendering the legislation "an attempt to camouflage with secular garments, a religious community as a public school district."[28] In 1993, Kahn's ruling was upheld in a 4–2 State Court of Appeals decision. And in 1994, SCOTUS upheld Kahn's decision.[29]

From that point forward, the New York legislature, in concert with Governor Cuomo, tried again to rewrite the law in such a way as make it appear applicable to other communities, but in reality, no other community could meet the criteria.[30] In a procedural opinion, the State Supreme Court Justice Joseph Harris, allowed the school district to stay open, and in 1995, Justice Kahn agreed that the second attempt was a charm! But with some retrograde in 1997, the New York Court of Appeals contravened Kahn, concluding that the second law is unconstitutional.[31] And in the same year, SCOTUS reversed their 1985 opinion in *Aguilar v. Felton*, deciding in *Agostini v. Felton* that students can indeed be instructed in the secular subjects within the confines of sectarian schools (like Bais Rochel). The decision was based on the conclusion that this policy did not rise to the entanglement criterion as stipulated in *Lemon v. Kurtzman*.[32]

Solidifying the school district's constitutional stature, Governor George Pataki and the New York legislature enacted a third law, with applicability to one other school district in the state of New York.[33] Not to be outdone, in 1998, Albany's State Supreme Court Justice Teresi decided that the legislature's and governor's third attempt was not a charm, with the appellate division affirming his ruling.[34] And finally, the New York Court of Appeals agreed that the third law was unconstitutional. But in a last-ditch attempt, a fourth bill did pass, with criteria seeming to pass constitutional muster, and the law has been allowed to stand.[35]

The Nascence and Progeny of an Ill-Conceived SCOTUS Decision

Under the umbrella of the contested parameters of the Establishment Clause, the other fault lines in the *Kiryas Joel* case are the interdependent spatial issues of the built environment: erected space and bordered space. As previously stated, the *Kiryas Joel* case created several fault lines specifically pertaining to the issues of disability in tandem with the issue of venue. Two

SCOTUS decisions set the preliminary stage for the decision in *Kiryas Joel.* In *Aguilar v. Felton* (1985), the Court found that paying the salaries of public school teachers to provide "remedial education to children in sectarian schools was unconstitutional."[36] Applying the Lemon test, Justice Brennan, writing for the majority, invoked the entanglement prong as delineated in *Lemon v. Kurtzman.* Interestingly, the program was established pursuant to the federal statute Title I of the 1965 Elementary and Secondary School Act, but what concerned Justice Brennan seems particularly puzzling. With the secular classes taught by public school teachers in private non-sectarian and religiously affiliated schools, Justice Brennan worries that the supervision provided by the City of New York in its administration of the Title I program to ensure that the program is not "used, intentionally or unwittingly to inculcate the religious beliefs of the surrounding parochial school" would actually engender "excessive entanglement of church and state." In essence, the actions taken to avert disentanglement (through supervision), would actually trigger entanglement (per the third prong of the Lemon test). In her dissenting opinion in Parts II and III, Justice O'Connor foreshadows her sentiments in *Kiryas Joel* by saying,

> The Court greatly exaggerates the degree of supervision necessary to prevent public school teachers from inculcating religion, and thereby demonstrates the flaws of a test that condemns benign cooperation between church and state. I would uphold Congress' effort to afford remedial instruction to disadvantaged schoolchildren in both public and parochial schools.[37]

In the companion landmark case, *Grand Rapids School District v. Ball* (1985), the Court "invalidated a community education program financed by the public school system that held classes in space leased from private schools."[38] The curriculum provided supplementary pedagogy in "remedial" and "enrichment" subjects, including reading, art, mathematics, music and physical education.[39] In a "repeat performance" with variations on the theme, Justice Brennan concluded in part, that,

> The state-paid instructors, influenced by the pervasively sectarian nature of the religious schools in which they work, may subtly or overtly indoctrinate the students in particular religious tenets at public expense. . .[40]

In sum, Justice Brennan's ineluctable conclusion is that the program, known as the Community Education and Shared Time programs "have the 'primary or principal' effect of advancing religion," and therefore violate the dictates of the Establishment Clause of the First Amendment.[41]

In this case, although Justice O'Connor sees the Shared-Time programs as constitutional and comparable to New York's Title I program, she agrees with the Court that the Community Education program is violative of the Establishment Clause given the fact that here, the teachers are parochial school teachers and pose a greater threat in their inclination to advancing religion.[42]

The Court ruled in *Zobrest v. Catalina Foothills School District* (1993) that secular teachers accommodating students in a nonsectarian venue did not violate the Establishment Clause. In the *Zobrest* case, Mr. Zobrest, who was hearing impaired since birth, needed assistance from a sign language interpreter in his Catholic high school.[43] Mr. Zobrest was entitled to disability services pursuant to the Individuals with Disabilities Act, and Justice Rehnquist held that providing an interpreter to a student in a sectarian school does not violate the Establishment Clause. The case reinforced the foundational principle of IDEA in that it provides benefits to all children in a neutral manner regardless of what type of school they attend.

In 1997, the decision in *Agostini v. Felton* overturned *Aguilar v. Felton*—mercifully I might add—and in cutting to the chase in her opinion written on behalf of the majority, Justice Connor states,

> ...We find no logical basis upon which to conclude that Title I services are an impermissible subsidy of religion when offered on campus, but not when offered off campus. Accordingly, contrary to our conclusion in Aguilar, placing full-time employees on parochial school campuses does not as a matter of law have the impermissible effect of advancing religion through indoctrination.[44]

What ensued in the *Kiryas Joel* case three years prior to *Agostini v. Felton*, to engender such a stark example of peripeteia? The maxim that "two wrongs don't make a right" applies in the *Kiryas Joel* case, exemplified by Justice O'Connor's partial dissenting and prescient opinion in *Aguilar v. Felton*. In *Aguilar*, she portends her "I told you so" opinion in *Kiryas Joel*. Granted, religious groups can be accommodated, but for Justice O'Connor, the statute creating the Kiryas Joel Village school district was invalid in its limited applicability, thereby vitiating the ethical principle of Kantian universalizability. For Justice O'Connor, the Aguilar decision—to use her phrase, "does not demand hostility to religion, religious ideas, religious people, or religious schools."[45] It is the Court's insistence on disfavoring religion in *Aguilar* that led New York to favor it here.[46] She then recommends a complete reconsideration of *Aguilar v. Felton*, realized in her majority opinion in *Agostini v. Felton*.

Taking a Classical Rhetorical Turn

In unraveling these threads, classical rhetorical principles are applied to the *Kiryas Joel* case. This methodology seems well-conceived given the ways that the Kiryas Joel dilemma careened over the better part of fifteen years. As previously stated, on a macro level, the case can best be understood by appreciating its lateral journey (in terms of co-equal branches of government) from the legislative to the legal arena and from the legal to the legislative arena multiple times—a sort of genre whiplash, and on a micro level, the interdependence of the genres within each of the two provinces.

In his *Rhetoric*, Aristotle delineates the three genres of rhetoric: deliberative, forensic and epideictic.[47] Deliberative rhetoric, taking place in a civic arena, deals with policy issues of expediency and inexpediency. Deliberative rhetoric addresses the stock issues of need, plan and practicality, deliberating about the utility of implementing a policy. Forensic rhetoric resides in the legal arena, broaching questions of accusation and defense and justice, utilizing stasis theory. And epideictic (ceremonial) rhetoric broaches questions of praise or blame and the virtuous. Each genre engages the ends of the other genres to varying degrees. As Nadeau offers, "In a forensic speech. . .the special end is justice but considerations of expediency and honor may also be very much in order."[48] And in deliberative rhetoric, the ends of the just and honorable in forensic and epideictic rhetoric respectively, are evident in and appropriately incorporated into deliberative rhetoric.[49] For example, epideictic driven topics can be incorporated into speeches under the rubrics of forensic rhetoric or deliberative rhetoric.[50] Directly addressing the *Kiryas Joel* case, in addition to the traditional stock issues, deliberative rhetoric also includes discussion of "justice and legality of a proposal," (in forensic rhetoric) as well as "considerations like honor," (in epideictic rhetoric).[51]

In his brilliant article "Rhetoric and Forensic Stasis: Reconsidering the Scope and Function of an Ancient Rhetorical Heuristic in the Aftermath of the Thomas/Hill Controversy," George Pullman examines the interface of forensic and deliberative rhetoric through the application of the "ancient rhetorical heuristic" of stasis theory. Pullman concedes that although each of the Aristotelian genres enjoys a practical cachet, they are "almost always mingle[d] in practice."[52] The benefit of a heuristic stasis is to allow "differences of opinion" to be resolved using the four "hierarchically arranged questions."[53] Aristotle's four questions are "(1) if you maintain that the act was not committed, your main task is to prove this. (2) If you maintain that the act *did no harm*, prove this. If you maintain that (3) the act was *less* than is alleged, or (4) *justified*, proves these facts, just as you would prove the act not to have been committed if you were monitoring that."[54] Although stasis theory is introduced in Aristotle's *Rhetoric*, Hermagoras is credited with having written the most significant treatment of stasis theory in the second century B.C.E.[55] Hermagoras drew from Aristotle's Rhetoric in formulating his stasis theory: (1) stochasmos-conjecture, (2) horos—definition, (3) poiotēs-quality, and (4) metalepsis-objection.[56] In other words, has an act taken place, what is it called, are there extenuating circumstances, and are there procedural anomalies?[57]

When there seems to be an inability to resolve the differences, the "unanswerable questions that disrupt communication are asystatic."[58] Hermagoras delineated four questions bereft of stasis capability:

1. Deficient (ellipse): insufficient evidence to constitute a case.
2. In balance (isazon): evidence so equally distributed on both sides that a state of balance cannot be overcome.
3. One-sided (monomeres): the weight of evidence concentrated on one side so that no real contest can take place.
4. Inconclusive (aporon): a question on which it is difficult, if not impossible, to reach a conclusion. For instance, Alexander was said to have been urged in a dream not to have confidence in dreams.[59]

Added conflicts arise when disputants argue crosswise, one on questions of fact and one on questions of value.[60] Although stasis is generally understood to be the primary province of forensic rhetoric and the canon of invention, Thomas Sloan states that "that stasis understood as the pro and con of the courtroom should be returned to the center of rhetorical instruction and that 'forensic [is] paradigmatic of rhetorical thinking itself.' "[61] Hermagoras's theory accommodated the stasiastic paradigm for all genres, since each speaking event engages a primary, predominant goal in addition to subordinated elements.

One could argue that the *Kiryas Joel* case was comparably asystatic in that resolvability of the issues seemed unachievable. The layers of unresolvability are manifold. The *Kiryas Joel* case engaged two distinct environments: the political arena (the state of New York) and the judicial arena (the Supreme Court).

Both deliberative stock issues and forensic stasis are enlisted in coming to terms with a resolution intrajudicially, intralegislatively, and ultimately between the two.

Board of Education of Kiryas Joel Village School District v. Grumet, Foundational Precepts and Dissoi Logoi

Boyarin and Boyarin note that the nexus between the "judicial opinions" and "legal commentary" resides in "the relation between identity (the nature of the subject of rights) and polity (the constituency of the state)."[62] However, Boyarin and Boyarin argue that a key, but overlooked tenet regarding political identity is the "diaspora (primary orientation elsewhere than a group's present residence) and genealogy (family and group descent and upbringing)."[63] Why is this important? The residency of the Satmar in what Boyarin and Boyarin call "satellite communities," even while Williamsburg remains a flourishing Hasidic community, are characteristically allochthonous,[64] engendering the conflict of living in a place but not being of that place until that place is transformed into one more concordant with the community's identity. In essence, the Satmar needed to make the village suit their geographical and cultural needs.

Boyarin and Boyarin base this conclusion in large part on a seminal essay by Robert Cover, "Nomos and Narrative." As Cover states, "we inhabit a nomos—a normative universe where the weakness in the hermeneutics of the law is not having taken into account what he calls 'jurisgenesis'—the 'the creation of legal meaning" must be understood "through an essentially cultural medium."[65] *Dissoi Logoi* augments stasis theory in exploring all sides of a given argument including through "particular cultural contexts (nomos),"[66] and "inherent, natural qualities (phusis)."[67] This concept comports with the notion that communities like Kiryas Joel should be allowed "to interpret the Constitution as it applies to them."[68] Similarly Abner Greene argues that latitude ought to be granted for according "public power to minority nomic communities" without imperiling the Establishment Clause and the Equal Protection Clause.[69] Greene conceives of this approach as a "partial exit" and "sovereignty as permeable" in which communities like the Satmar Hasidim can "be the recipients of public power" conditioned by adherence to the Constitution. Greene makes a very compelling point about the motto of the United States of America, *E Pluribus Unum*. With "In the Many, One," we also need to find value in the many even with that end result might entail geographical, cultural, and yes, religious separation, without negating the fundamental precepts of the country.[70] Greene ends by suggesting that individual "states may encourage such groups to join with others in creating an American common ground."[71]

In response to Greene, Ira Lupu faults Greene's concept of "permeable sovereignty" as a way "to bridge the gap between the assimilation necessary for liberal democracy and the presentation of culturally distinctive groups."[72] While maintaining their uniqueness and freedom to practice their religion, the constitutional norms still need to be abided. Lupu adduces evidence that the Satmar Hasidim in Kiryas Joel used very dubious tactics in the governance of the village.[73] Lupu claims that Kiryas Joel was founded in part on "retreat from an inhospitable surrounding community,"[74] and is unconvinced that Kiryas Joel is not an example of religiofavoritism with the resolution here a dangerous path towards "invidious discrimination and social harmony."[75]

Lupu worries that when nomic communities diverge from "contemporary political and social norms," deviations might lead to "unconstitutional repression or inequality."[76]

Eisgruber sees the 'exit' (of the school district) approach as "a clearly undesirable instance of government sponsored segregation."[77] Eisgruber notes the real contradictions within the Constitution, in that protections afforded sub-communities like the Satmar Hasidim "may offend constitutionally protected equality principles."[78] The only purpose of the school district is "social isolation," reinforcing the argument propounded by Justice Stevens in his concurring opinion. The creation of the school district is merely segregation which can jeopardize "political unity,"[79] adding,

> it encourages people to distrust (or even hate) their fellow citizens for reasons that are trivial and irrelevant--such as skin color, hair style, or dress. People seem, unfortunately, to have a natural tendency to demonize those who look different from themselves: government exacerbates that tendency when it lends its prestige to segregated institutions and ways of life.[80]

For Eisgruber, the Kiryas Joel school district is a fallible and unconstitutional response to the promulgation of diversity,[81] where assimilation does not necessarily preclude diversity, and is not reduced to a culturally denuded goal of the polity, but rather can serve as the "country's commitment to pluralism with its commitment to justice."[82]

Thomas Berg says that the statute should not have been deemed an Establishment Clause violation, especially because it created no harm to anyone else and represented no favoritism based on religion. He refers to the decision as "slouching toward secularism,"[83] which, according to Boyarin and Boyarin, was a reflection of the Supreme Court's bias.[84]

Kathleen Lockwood couches the Hasidic community's need to house education in the yeshivas and not in public schools as one based on "tradition and separatism,"[85] with little curricular focus on secular subjects of study.

The Stasis Theory of Board of Education of Kiryas Joel Village School v. Grumet

At the outset of his opinion, Justice Souter explicates the provenance of the Kiryas Joel Village school district, introducing the first question of stasis theory, "stasis stochasmos": did the 1989 N.Y. Laws, ch. 748 violate the Establishment Clause? The statute reads as follows:

> Section 1.: The territory of the village of Kiryas Joel in the town of Monroe, Orange county on the date when this act shall take effect, shall be and hereby is constituted a separate school district and shall be known as the Kiryas Joel village school district and shall have and enjoy all the powers and duties of a union free school district under the provisions of the education law.
>
> Section 2.: Such a district shall be under the control of a board of education which shall be composed of from five to nine members elected by the qualified voters of the village of Kiryas Joel, said members to serve for term not exceeding five years.
>
> Section 3.: This act shall take effect on the first day of July next succeeding the date on which it shall have become a law.[86]

In adducing evidence to support the constitutional violation embedded within the conjectural stasis (stochasmos), Justice Souter moves to "horos," to situate the violation of the Establishment Clause within the parameters of *stare decisis.*

When referencing *Aguilar v. Felton* and its companion case *School District of Grand Rapids v. Ball* (1985), Justice Souter's explication seems to provide some legal cover for the village school district, by among other facts, noting "the panic, fear and trauma [the children] suffered in leaving the confines of their own community and being with people whose ways were so different."[87] In applying the Lemon test in *Lemon v. Kurtzman* (1971), the statute, ch. 748 fails primarily on the second prong of the Lemon test. According to the criteria delineated for the Lemon test, "the statute must have a secular legislative purpose"; second, its principal or primary effect must be one that neither advances nor inhibits religion; and finally, the statute must not foster "an excessive government entanglement with religion."[88]

In what could be reasonably construed as a faulty analogy, Justice Souter locates a violative equivalency between the *Kiryas Joel* case and *Larkin v. Grendel's Den, Inc.* (1982) and *School District of Abington Township v. Schempp*, most pointedly, with the third prong of the Lemon test: entanglement of government with religion. For Justice Souter, the delegation of governmental authority in the Kiryas Joel Village school district is neither neutral nor incidental to religion.[89]

In an intriguing section towards the end of Justice Souter's opinion, he cites a passage from *Corporation of Presiding Bishops of Church of Jesus Christ of Latter-Day Saints v. Amost* (1987), in which the firing of an engineer who worked at a facility run by the Latter-Day Saints was not discriminatory under Title VII of the Civil Rights Act of 1964, and no offense to the Equal Protection statute.[90] Abiding by the Lemon test, Justice Souter cites the case with "ample room under the Establishment Clause for 'benevolent neutrality which will permit religious exercise to exist without sponsorship and without interference.' "

In terms of the third question in stasis theory, here poiotēs (or quality) "refines" the definitional limitations by locating a space where the Free Exercise Clause provides no conflict with the Establishment Clause, potentially constitutional, characterized as "benevolent neutrality." The characterization of "accommodation" is constitutional as distinguished from its unconstitutional counterpart in the "Establishment" (Clause).

The fourth tenet of stasis theory metalepsis (objection) applies in varying degrees to all the concurring opinions, in that the Kiryas Joel school district should not have been established in the manner in which it was established. In his separate concurring opinion, Justice Blackmun avers the legitimate application of the second and third prongs of the Lemon test to ch. 748 as a constitutionally invalid legislative act.

Justice Stevens' opinion, joined by Justices Blackmun and Ginsburg in concurrence, advanced interesting arguments vis-à-vis stasis theory. The legislation engendered a violation of the Establishment Clause with its effect of establishing rather than accommodating religion. This language is pertinent inasmuch as federal law mandates that children with disabilities are accommodated. Justice Stevens concedes that the children experienced "panic, fear and trauma," but posits a perplexing solution to this exigence, recommending that "the State could have taken steps to alleviate the children's fear by teaching their schoolmates to be tolerant and respectful of Satmar customs," with the added benefit of strengthening diversity. But Justice Stevens' critique also advances the argument regarding the unconstitutionality of the school district, since its boundaries are not based on geography, but rather religion. The evidence in support of this claim is that two-thirds of the children attending the Kiryas Joel schools are Hasidic children with special needs, but those children are not residents of Kiryas Joel. Justice Stevens relies as well on the precedents of *Aguilar v. Felton* (1985) and *School District of Grand Rapids v. Ball* (1985). The invalid result of the creation of the school district is favoritism and preferential treatment for one particular religion—in this case, the Satmar Hasidim.

In a precipitous turn within horos, the argument states that *Aguilar v. Felton* was decided in the dark spirit of a hostility toward religion, given no imprimatur in either the Free Exercise or Establishment Clauses. At this point in the opinion, the point is made that this conundrum in its entirety could have been averted.

Given the complexity of Establishment Clause cases and the many sub-classifications of cases,[91] the use of the Lemon test for all Establishment Clause cases is questioned and questionable in providing a "a single test, a Grand Unified Theory that would resolve the cases that may arise under a particular Clause." In short, in deciding Establishment Clause cases, one size does not fit all.

Justice Kennedy, agreeing with the conclusion of the opinion, writes a separate opinion. For him, the "vice" inherent in the Kiryas Joel school district resulted in "drawing boundaries on the basis of religion," and had the approach not been pursued in a "forbidden manner," the accommodations for the children "would have been valid." According to Justice Kennedy, New York State's statute that created the village of Kiryas Joel "had complete discretion not to enact it," but New York state chose not to go that nonviolative route. For Justice Kennedy, this legislative "discretion" accomplished nothing more than "religious gerrymandering" and cannot be abided by the Establishment Clause, with boundaries having been demarcated along "a religious line."[92]

Justice Kennedy is not offended by the homogeneous make-up of the village, populated by "co-religionists," as long as the "boundaries are derived according to neutral historical and geographic criteria." This "birds of a feather flock together" reality is not presumptively violative of the Establishment Clause, save for the way that it was realized in Kiryas Joel's school district. Justice Kennedy concedes that the *Aguilar* and *Grand Rapids* decisions "may" have been ill-conceived, but for him two wrongs do not make a right, and "one misjudgment is no excuse however, for compounding it with another."

The dissent penned by Justice Scalia, joined by Chief Justice Rehnquist and Justice Thomas, turns the majority's arguments as seen from the vantage point of stasis theory on its proverbial head. Unlike most Establishment Clause cases, Kiryas Joel involves no funding of a school classified as a private or sectarian school. Kiryas Joel is a public, co-ed school, and made no extreme or inappropriate "special adjustments to the religious needs of its students." The sole cachet, in addition to its population of children with disabilities, is that they were of the same religion— The latter merely ancillary to the issue at hand.

First, Justice Scalia disavows the distinction without a difference between the *Kiryas Joel* and *Larkin v. Grendel's Den, Inc.* cases as Justice Souter would not. Conversely, Justice Scalia sees no difference between abrogating a group's rights or an individual's rights predicated on religious beliefs. Justice Scalia demonstrates a more sympathetic sensibility to the exacerbated challenge faced by the children: their distinctiveness in their disabilities as well as in their dress and customs. For Scalia, there is nothing extraordinary about the creation of "small specialized school districts" through special legislation here as there have been for "institutionalized children." In short, no special treatment and no favoritism based on religion is triggered.

One of Justice Scalia's intriguing arguments is a refutation of one of Justice Souter's arguments, employing a hypoethetical analogy. Justice Scalia claims that Justice Souter would have no issue with this "humanitarian legislation" if the students' parents were "commune dwellers" or another homogenous group. Justice Scalia reorients the demographic, by suggesting that the children do exhibit "cultural characteristics that are accompanied by religious belief," whereby the religion is more incidental and ancillary to the defining criteria in relation to the Free Exercise and Establishment Clauses.

In another distinction without a difference argument, Justice Scalia claims the village's boundaries already existed and were deemed legally and constitutionally valid, so how could a federally protected entity (i.e. public school for disabled children) possibly be illegal? In what ways could this be construed as fruit from the poisoned tree! In Justice Scalia's thinking, the school is an accommodation—nothing more, nothing less. Relevant here is *Zorach v. Clauson* (1952), which upheld the constitutionality of a program for public school students, allowing them to leave school early to attend off-site religious education classes. Not satisfied with the rebuke of his colleagues thus far, Justice Scalia inveighs against Justice Stevens for his wholesale disrespect for and dismissiveness of the Hasidic family values and religious faith.

Conceding that *Aguilar v. Felton* and *Grand Rapids v. Ball* were ill-conceived decisions, unlike Justice Kennedy, Justice Scalia sees the creation of the school district as an appropriate solution, not mired in two wrongs make a right thinking. Although Justice Scalia found the Lemon test ineffectual, unlike Justice O'Connor's recommendation that Establishment Clause cases should be decided inductively on a case by case basis, for Justice Scalia the guiding principle should be "fidelity to the longstanding tradition of our people, which surely provide the diversity of treatment that Justice O'Connor seeks, but do not leave us to our own devices." In Justice Scalia's castigation of the majority, his final words tell all, accusing them of "turn[ing] the Establishment Clause into a repealer of our nation's tradition of religious toleration." In their brilliant distillation of the major tenets of the SCOTUS decision, Jonathan and Daniel Boyarin cite Justice Scalia's sharp dissent as a "rhetorical dismissal of the Establishment Clause,"[93] Justice Stevens's concurring opinion expressing an "almost nostalgic insistence on the handicapped children's overriding right to interact with non-Hasidic children from the surrounding area,"[94] and Justices Souter's and O'Connor's technical needle threading "which appeared to permit the school board to continue once the New York legislature rewrote the enabling legislation in terms less specific to Kiryas Joel."[95]

As challenging as the caselaw has been in providing pellucid criteria for application of the Establishment Clause most infamously and rather ineffectually with the Lemon test,[96] some scholars have looked for more luminous ways of navigating religious expression cases. Given the interdependent and synergistic issues (of religion and disability) which arose in the Kiryas Joel case, scholars have posited a compelling approach to the adjudication of cases circumscribing Free Exercise and the Establishment Clause, and that is with the application of the Equal Protection Clause of the Fourteenth Amendment. As Michael A. Paulsen says, "the religion clauses should be considered *together* and understood as advancing fundamentally *similar* interests."[97] Paulsen calls this new adjudicative model, "the equal protection of the free exercise of religion."[98] For Paulsen, the precipitative events for this novel paradigm inhered in three SCOTUS cases: *Wallace v. Jaffree*, *Aguilar v. Felton* and *Grand Rapids v. Ball*, the latter set of 1985 cases having advanced the impetus for the creation of the Kiryas Joel Village school district.[99]

Susan Gellman and Susan Looper-Friedman similarly propound a more tenable solution to the Establishment Clause conundrum, utilizing the Equal Protection Clause. Why is that? Because the heart of the issue in "government religious expression cases" is fundamentally "unequal treatment."[100] In fact, Gellman and Looper-Friedman invoke an excerpt from Justice Sandra Day O'Connor's concurring opinion in the *Kiryas Joel* case which gravitated towards an application of the Equal Protection Clause.[101] This legal paradigm is particularly apt for the *Kiryas Joel* case as evidenced by the dual, overlapping issues: religion and disability. In the 1985 SCOTUS case *City of Cleburne, Texas v. Cleburne Living Center*, the Court ruled that although an ordinance denying the Cleburne Living Center a permit "to operate a group home for individuals with intellectual disabilities"[102] unconstitutional, the Court would not "recognize persons with intellectual disabilities as a protected quasi suspect class."[103] The decision did however represent progress for individuals with intellectual disabilities looking to reside in "community-based housing."[104] In a subsequent legislative act, the Americans with Disabilities Act was enacted in 1990, strengthening "judicial protection of the rights of persons with disabilities by establishing the foundation for a heightened level of equal protection for them."[105]

	1a	1b	2a	2b	2c	3a	3b	4a
Majority - Souter, Blackmun, Stevens, O'Connor, Ginsburg	•		•			•		•
Plurality – Souter, Blackmun, Stevens, Ginsburg	•				•			
Concurrence - Blackmun	•		•					
Concurrence – Stevens, Blackmun, Ginsburg	•						•	
Concurrence - O'Connor	•				•			•
Concurrence – Kennedy	•					•		•
Dissent – Scalia, Rehnquist, Thomas		•		•		•		

Stochamos - Conjecture

1a. The Establishment Clause is violated. (*Aguilar v. Felton*; *Grand Rapids v. Ball*; *Larkin v. Grendel*; *Lemon v. Kurtzman*).

1b. The Establishment Clause is not violated. (*Witters v. Washington*; *Zobrest v. Catalina*).

Horos – Definition

2a. The issue at hand fails the Lemon test. (*Larkin v. Grendel*; *Lemon v. Kurtzman*)

2b. The issue at hand served the purpose of providing reasonable accommodations without entanglement with religion. (*Witters v. Washington*; *Zobrest v. Catalina*)

2c. The issue at hand engenders accommodations on the basis of religion and/or entanglement with religion beyond the scope of the Establishment Clause and/or Free Exercise Clause. (*Aguilar v. Felton*; *Grand Rapids v. Ball*; *Larkin v. Grendel*)

Poiotēs – Quality

3a. "Plea-for-leniency."[106]

3b. "Counterplea (claim of benefit rendered)."[107]

Metalepsis – Objection

4a. The manner in which the government acted overreached, and in doing so, it accommodated and/or established religion beyond what is constitutionally permissible. (*Larkin v. Grendel*)

Figure 4.1: This Court's got (stock) issues: A visual representation of stasis theory in the deliberative realm of the *Kiryas Joel* Court.

This visual was adapted from Ray Nadeau's model in "Hermogenes on 'Stock Issues' in Deliberative Speaking" which delineates the stock issues of deliberative speaking for writers spanning from the Classical era to the Renaissance, forming a tradition of deliberative speaking that has stayed consistent since the Renaissance. Our adaption of this model distills the various stock issues that arose in the deliberation of the Kiryas Joel Court and how those are reflected in the various opinions of the case. In their deliberations, the Justices' application of precedents reflects how previous Establishment Clause cases have formed these different stock issues which they used to develop their own conclusions based on the various factors of this case.

Disability, Education and Equal Protection

As legally dubious was the way in which the Kiryas Joel Village School District came into being, and with the Court's reconsideration of the original legal "sin" of holding secular classes in a sectarian venue which violated the Establishment Clause, the end of the legal/legislative battle does not appear to have torn the First Amendment asunder, notwithstanding the ineluctable contradictions between the Establishment Clause and the free exercise of religion. However, reconciling the case with the Equal Protection Clause of the Fourteenth Amendment might seem more legally and morally convoluted.

As anathema as the Hasidic education is the secular life, including secular education, one cannot help but feel heartened by the fact that the Kiryas Joel children would be the beneficiaries of a secular education, enhancing their lives as children with special needs. After the decision to disallow the students from attending the sectarian school within the Kiryas Joel boundaries, the children's parents deemed the experience at the Monroe-Woodbury public school venue damaging to the children on several fronts, including insensitivity to their food restrictions, serving them non-kosher meat from McDonald's, and putting children in the Christmas pageant, with one child from Kiryas Joel cast as Rudolph the Red-Nosed Reindeer.[108]

In a sense, the Hasidic community puts the Equal Protection Clause ostensibly in retrograde. From *Plessy v. Ferguson* (1896) to *Brown v. Board of Education (*1954), the community's decision can be understood with this landmark, legal backdrop as re-realizing a "separate but equal" status. David Elazar expounds upon the concept of the "covenant idea" as a key component for a flourishing "democratic government and society."[109] This "covenantal dynamic" is comprised of three terms.[110] The first is *brit*, which is Hebrew for covenant, another is *shalom*, Hebrew for peace, and the one I would like to shed more light on is *hesed*, which is Hebrew for grace or lovingkindness. Elazar notes that *hesed* doesn't fully translate with a comparable English word, but he adds that "it is best understood as the loving fulfillment of the obligations flowing from a covenant bond."[111] And it certainly hasn't gone unnoticed by Elazar that *hesed* and *Hasid* are closely aligned, in that "a person who acts in the way of *hesed* is called a *Hasid*."[112] This covenantal moral dimension supersedes the legal dimension.[113] And *hesed* as a part of the covenant, informs the *nomos* of *Dissoi Logoi*.

In her essay, "Judaism and Disability," Julia Watts Belser invokes the Jewish principle of *b'tselem elohim*, evocative of the passage in Genesis 1:27, "that God created all humanity 'in the divine image.' "[114] Although Belser concedes that this passage ought to be a wholly inclusive affirmation bereft of any exceptions, it hasn't always been construed that way, particularly for people with disabilities.[115] The parents and children of Kiryas Joel were doubly tasked with ensuring that, notwithstanding the children's disabilities and lifestyle customs (dress, hair food), that were different from the other children who were not Hasidic, still they were to be afforded their full humanity. Irrefutably that was not achieved when the children were sent to the Monroe-Woodbury school district, and one can imagine a more benevolent experience at the Kiryas Joel venue, distinguished by a genuine *hesed*.

I do think that the secular education is beneficial to the special needs children at the Kiryas Joel Village school district, and inasmuch as the curriculum was indeed secular, no violation of the Establishment Clause occurred. And the secular education should be more vigorously incorporated into the education of all Hasidic schoolchildren, whether attending a public or sectarian school. Shulem Deen's memoir *All Who Go Do Not Return*, chronicles a kind of paradoxical life as a member of the Hasidic community—whether Kiryas Joel, the Satmar community, or the Skverer Hasidic community, which was Deen's community in New Square, New York, thirty miles southeast of Kiryas Joel. New Square also lays claim to one of the poorest municipalities in the country.[116] Deen was actually expelled from New Square for heresy.[117] His poignant and eloquent memoir chronicles a painful journey of self-discovery and devastating loss. Having lived in Borough Park, Brooklyn and attended "the Skeverer yeshiva in Williamsburg, Brooklyn,"[118] Deen, as have other "reformed" Hasidim, raised alarms about the educational experiences of Hasidic children in the yeshivas. The paradox is stark, with a curricular oasis marked by study in Talmud and Torah, surrounded by a barren "secular" desert. Ironically, the girls fare better in obtaining an all-around education, including exposure to more secular subjects, since they are excluded from joining the rabbinate or becoming Jewish leaders in the community. Their distaff responsibilities upon marriage are of the highest priority, so more time can be devoted to those subjects. Here are some of the data as delineated in the 2017 report published by the non-profit organization Yaffed (Young Advocates for Fair Education), whose goal is to strengthen the secular education of students within the ultra-Orthodox yeshivas.[119] Some of the data are startling, and even shocking. From ages 7 through 12, Hasidic boys learn only the most rudimentary skills in arithmetic and English reading and writing. This part of the curriculum occurs for only 90 minutes per day, four days per week. This class time is "treated as free time for restless students," and the teachers "teaching these subjects can barely speak English themselves."[120] Once boys turn thirteen, there is absolutely no time devoted to any secular subjects including science, history, math or English, for these and other subjects of their ilk are considered profane and irrelevant to a pious, Hasidic life.[121] Most of the boys graduate without a high school diploma, and upon completing yeshiva studies, they can barely speak English, possessing only minimal skills and little financial autonomy. As Deen says, as a high school student in the yeshiva, he witnessed the students' activities in study hall consisting of practice in writing their signatures in English so that they could obtain marriage licenses.[122] The erudition and knowledge of Judaism seems eclipsed by the neglect of and disregard for the state-mandated curriculum, which applies to all New York students, whether in non-sectarian or sectarian schools. Rabbi Norman Lamm, the Orthodox President of Yeshiva University died May 31, 2020, [123] and as reported in his obituary in the New York Times, Rabbi Lamm espoused the concept of Torah U'madda, explained as "leading a life that blends rigorous adherence to Jewish law with full-throated pursuit of worldly knowledge and immersion in the wider society."[124] Hasidic communities see this idea as anathema to a pious Jewish life, leaving them vulnerable to the toxicity of a venal secular world, and eventually, leading to the erosion and the demise of Jewish communities.[125] The languages of Yiddish and Hebrew as the mainstays of communication can remain vital and vibrant and customs can be maintained with a little give and take—finding creative, nonthreatening and harmonious ways of enriching the Hasidic world with aspects of the secular and vice versa. Dipping your toes into a different body of water every now and then won't cause an inescapable immersion.

Conclusion

Examining the *Kiryas Joel* case through the lens of stock issues and stasis theory, as instantiated in deliberative and forensic rhetorical genres, reveals the challenges imposed upon adjudicating a legal case in which the marshaled arguments on either side of the question as to whether the creation of the Kiryas Joel village school district violates the Establishment Clause are equally cogent. The case is ultimately understood through two questions of asystatic theory: *isazon*, because both sides achieve a sort of legal homeostasis, and *aporon*, because the case exemplifies a web of seemingly irresolvable argument. In George Washington's reply to the Hebrew Congregation of Newport, Rhode Island, the penultimate statement reads as follows:

> May the children of the Stock of Abraham, who dwell in this land, continue to merit and enjoy the good will of the other inhabitants; while every one shall sit in safety under his own vine and fig-tree.[126]

A student of the Bible, Washington alluded to this notion on more than one occasion.[127] This depiction of " 'every man under his vine and under his fig tree' represents an era of peace and security in the past and the vision of an ideal future (I Kings 5:5; Micah 4:4; cf. Joel 2:22)."[128] Notwithstanding any perceived inconclusiveness, this is certainly a lofty goal for the special needs children of Kiryas Joel, and one definitively distinguished by *hesed.*

Notes

1 Jonathan D. Sarna, "George Washington's Correspondence with the Jews of Newport," in *To Bigotry No Sanction: George Washington and Religious Freedom* (Philadelphia: National Museum of American Jewish History, 2012), 17.
2 Sarna, "George Washington's Correspondence with the Jews of Newport," 18.
3 Ibid.
4 Ibid, 19–20.
5 Ibid, 22.
6 Christopher Thomas Anglim, *Encyclopedia of Religion and the Law in America*, 2nd ed. (Amenia, New York: Grey House Publishing, 2009), 198.
7 Board of Education of Kiryas Joel v. Grumet, 512 U.S. 687 (1994); Commonly known as the Kiryas Joel case.
8 Johnathon Boyarin and Daniel Boyarin, "Circumscribing Constitutional Identities in *Kiryas Joel*," in *Powers of Diaspora*, ed. Johnathon Boyarin and Daniel Boyarin, (Minneapolis: University of Minneapolis Press, 2002), 121.
9 T. Barton Carter, Marc A. Franklin, and Jay B. Wright, *The First Amendment and the Fourth Estate*, 6th ed. (New York: Foundation Press, 2003), 1046.
10 T. Barton Carter, Marc A. Franklin, and Jay B. Wright, *The First Amendment and the Fourth Estate*, 6th ed. (New York: Foundation Press, 2003), 1048.
11 Linda Greenhouse, "High Court Bars School District," *New York Times*, June 28, 1994.
12 For an insightful discussion of the *Kiryas Joel* case, see Laura Hempen, "Board of Education of Kiryas Joel School District v. Grumet: Accommodationists Strike a Blow to the Wall of Separation," *Saint Louis University Law Journal* 39.
13 Boyarin and Boyarin, "Circumscribing Constitutional Identities in *Kiryas Joel*," 121.
14 Ibid.
15 See Robert Healey, "Thomas Jefferson's 'Wall': Absolute or Serpentine?" *Journal of Church and State* 30, no. 3 (1988): 447: "If with no surer legal guidance we are to take up and decide every variation of this controversy ... we are likely to make the legal 'wall of separation between church and state' as winding as the famous serpentine wall designed by Mr. Jefferson."; In the same article, Healey provides a superb discussion of the legal applications and ramifications of Jefferson's metaphorical wall. For other scholars' discussions, see Underwood and Mead, "Establishment of Religion Analysis: The Lemon Test or Just Lemonade," *Journal of Law & Education* 25.
16 Louis Grumet and John Caher. *The Curious Case of Kiryas Joel.* Foreword by Judith S. Kaye (Chicago: Chicago Review Press, 2016), 2–3.

17 Israel Rubin. *Satmar: Two Generations of an Urban Island* (New York: Peter Lang, 1997), 47.
18 Rubin, *Satmar: Two Generations of an Urban Island*, 47.
19 Grumet and Caher, *The Curious Case of Kiryas Joel*, 4.
20 Ibid; It should be noted that the creation of the village itself was not without significant discord. Although having met the legal bar for incorporation, many questioned the tactics used by the proposed village's supporters/residents to achieve their ends. See Grumet and Caher, 11–28, and Fred R. Bleakley. "Torn Asunder," *Wall Street Journal*, June 1, 1994.
On January 1, 2019, Kiryas Joel officially became the town of Palm Tree, having split from the town of Monroe. In a 4–1 vote, a petition was approved allowing Kiryas Joel to annex 163.8 acres of land and secede from the town of Monroe in the overall public interest. According to the documentary City of Joel, "United Monroe blessed this secession with several conditions including no more annexations for 10 years." Oster, March. See "Kiryas Joel is now Palm Tree, the First Official US Haredi Orthodox Town," *Jewish Telegraphic Agency*, January 6, 2019, and Jesse Sweet, dir., *City of Joel* (United States: Samuel Goldwyn Films, 2018), Online.
21 Sam Roberts, "A Village with the Numbers, Not the Image, of the Poorest Place," *New York Times*, April 20, 2011. https://www.nytimes.com/2011/04/21/nyregion/kiryas-joel-a-village-with-the-numbers-not-the-image-of-the-poorest-place.html
22 Roberts, "A Village with the Numbers, Not the Image, of the Poorest Place."
23 Ibid.
24 Ibid.
25 Jonathan Boyarin, "Circumscribing Constitutional Identities in Kiryas Joel," *Yale Law Journal* 106, no. 5 (1997): 1537–70.
26 Grumet and Caher, *The Curious Case of Kiryas Joel*, 258.
27 Ibid.
28 Ibid, 259.
29 Ibid, 260.
30 Ibid.
31 Ibid.
32 Ibid.
33 Ibid, 261.
34 Ibid.
35 Ibid.
36 Anglim, *Encyclopedia of Religion and the Law in America*, 21.
37 Aguilar v. Felton, 473 U.S. 402 (1985).
38 Anglim, *Encyclopedia of Religion and the Law in America*, 252.
39 School District of the City of Grand Rapids v. Ball, 473 U.S. 373 (1985).
40 Ibid.
41 Ibid.
42 In *Wolman v. Walter*, an Ohio program wanted to provide aid to what were for the most part Catholic schools. See Anglim, 608. Six categories of aid were available including "diagnostic services with state personnel testing the individual children for specified health and educational problems," and "therapeutic services for health

and educational disabilities provided by state personnel at sites outside the parochial school." These two provisions were ruled constitutional. See Anglim, 608.

43 Zobrest v. Catalina Foothills School District, 509 U.S. 1 (1993). For an insightful comparative analysis for *Board of Education of Kiryas Joel Village School District v. Grumet* and *Zobrest*, see Underwood: "The rulings in Zobrest and Kiryas Joel demonstrate that in the K-12 educational context the wall of separation is both uneven and serpentine in character."; See also, Hempen.

44 Agostini v. Felton, 521 U.S. 203 (1997).

45 Ibid.

46 Ibid.

47 Aristotle, *Poetics and Rhetoric*, ed. by Eugene Garver (New York: Barnes & Noble Classics, 2005).

48 Ray Nadeau, "Hermogenes on 'Stock issues' in Deliberative Speaking," *Speech Monographs* 25, no. 1 (1958): 60.

49 Nadeau, "Hermogenes on 'Stock issues' in Deliberative Speaking," 62.

50 Nadeau, "Hermogenes' On Stasis: A Translation with an introduction and notes," 376.

51 Ibid, 377.

52 George L. Pullman, "Rhetoric and Forensic Stasis: Reconsidering the Scope and Function of an Ancient Rhetorical Heuristic in the Aftermath of the Thomas/Hill Controversy," *Rhetoric Society Quarterly* 25 (1995): 223.

53 Pullman, "Rhetoric and Forensic Stasis: Reconsidering the Scope and Function of an Ancient Rhetorical Heuristic in the Aftermath of the Thomas/Hill Controversy," 224.

54 Aristotle, *Poetics and Rhetoric*, ed. by Eugene Garver, 489.

55 Aristotle, *Poetics and Rhetoric*, ed. by Eugene Garver, 489; Patricia Bizzle and Bruce Herzberg, eds., *Rhetorical Tradition: Readings from Classical Times to the Present*, 2nd ed. (Boston: Bedford/St. Martin's, 2001), 32–33.

56 Ray Nadeau, "Hermogenes' On Stasis: A Translation with an Introduction and Notes," *Speech Monographs* 31, no. 4 (1964): 370.

57 Nadeau, "Hermogenes' On Stasis: A Translation with an Introduction and Notes," 370.

58 Ibid, 378.

59 Ibid.

60 Pullman, "Rhetoric and Forensic Stasis: Reconsidering the Scope and Function of an Ancient Rhetorical Heuristic in the Aftermath of the Thomas/Hill Controversy," 225.

61 Ibid, 226.

62 Boyarin and Boyarin, "Circumscribing Constitutional Identities in *Kiryas Joel*," 106.

63 Ibid.

64 Ibid, 107.

65 Robert M. Cover, "Foreword: *Nomos* and Narrative," *Harvard Law Review* 97 (1983): 11.

66 Richard A. Lanham. *A Handlist of Rhetorical Terms*, 2nd ed. (University of California Berkeley Press, 1991), 57.

67 Theresa Enos, "Dissoi Logoi (Dialexis)," in *Encyclopedia of Rhetoric and Composition: Communication from Ancient Times to the Information Age* (New York: Routledge, 1996), 197.
68 Boyarin and Boyarin, "Circumscribing Constitutional Identities in *Kiryas Joel*," 110.
69 Abner S. Greene, "Article and Response: Kiryas Joel and Two Mistakes About Equality," *Columbia Law Review* 96, no. 1 (January 1996): 86.
70 Greene, "Article and Response: Kiryas Joel and Two Mistakes About Equality," 86.
71 Ibid.
72 Ira C. Lupu, "Article and Response: Uncovering the Village of Kiryas Joel," *Columbia Law Review* 96, no. 1 (January 1996): 109.
73 Ira C. Lupu, "Article and Response: Uncovering the Village of Kiryas Joel," 112.
74 Ibid, 117.
75 Ibid, 119.
76 Ibid, 112.
77 Christopher L. Eisgruber, "Article and Response: The Constitutional Value of Assimilation," *Columbia Law Review* 96, no. 1 (January 1996): 87.
78 Christopher L. Eisgruber, "Article and Response: The Constitutional Value of Assimilation," 88–89.
79 Ibid, 95.
80 Ibid.
81 Ibid, 103.
82 Ibid, 102.
83 Thomas C. Berg, "Slouching Towards Secularism: A Comment on Kiryas Joel School District v. Grumet," *Emory Law Journal* 44, no. 2 (Spring 1995): 435.
84 Boyarin and Boyarin, "Circumscribing Constitutional Identities in *Kiryas Joel*," 105.
85 Kathleen Lockwood, "Political Power, a Religious Agenda, and the Failings of the Endorsement Test: Hasidic Educational Separatism and the East Ramapo School Board," *First Amendment Law Review* 12, no. 3 (2014): 700.
86 Board of Education of Kiryas Joel v. Grumet, 512 U.S. 687 (1994).
87 *Ibid.*
88 Lemon v. Kurtzman, 403 U.S. 602 (1971).
89 See McDaniel v. Paty, 435 U.S. 618 (1978)
90 Scott A. Merriman, *Religion and the Law in America,* vol. 1 (Santa Barbara, California: ABC-CLIO, 2007), 184–5.
91 See Conkle, 114–215.
92 Within the legal province, accommodation has a dual meaning as explained by Conkle. "Accommodation" can be granting "special protection to the exercise of religion by exempting religious conduct from legal burdens that would otherwise be applicable," or "a favoring of religion as manifested in particular contexts." See Daniel O. Conkle *Constitutional Law: The Religion Clauses,* 2nd ed., 139. As Boyarin suggests, "constitutional debates frequently turn on the degree of accommodation the state will make to the 'actual practices' of its citizens." See Boyarin and Boyarin, "Circumscribing Constitutional Identities in *Kiryas Joel*," in *Powers of Diaspora*, 109.
93 Jonathan Boyarin and Daniel Boyarin, "Circumscribing Constitutional Identities in *Kiryas Joel*," in *Powers of Diaspora* (Minneapolis: University of Minnesota Press, 2015), 126.
94 Boyarin and Boyarin, "Circumscribing Constitutional Identities in *Kiryas Joel*," 126.

95 Ibid, 127.
96 Lemon v. Kurtzman, 403 U.S. 602 (1971).
97 Michael A. Paulsen, "Religion, Equality, and the Constitution: An Equal Protection Approach to Establishment Clause Adjudication," *Notre Dame Law Review* 61, no. 3 (1986): 315.
98 Paulsen, "Religion, Equality, and the Constitution: An Equal Protection Approach to Establishment Clause Adjudication," 315.
99 Ibid, 359–62.
100 Susan Gelman and Susan Looper-Friedman, "Thou Shalt Use the Equal Protection Clause for Religion Cases (Not Just the Establishment Clause)," *Journal of Constitutional Law* 10, no. 4 (2008): 666.
101 Gelman and Looper-Friedman, "Thou Shalt Use the Equal Protection Clause for Religion Cases (Not Just the Establishment Clause)," 683.
102 Steven K. Hoge, "*Cleburne* and the Pursuit of Equal Protection for Individuals with Mental Disorders," *Journal of the American Academy of Psychiatry and the Law Online* 43, no. 4 (2015): 417.
103 Hoge, "*Cleburne* and the Pursuit of Equal Protection for Individuals with Mental Disorders," 417.
104 Ibid, 419.
105 Ibid.
106 Nadeau, "Hermogenes on 'Stock issues' in Deliberative Speaking," 375.
107 Ibid.
108 Grumet and Caher, *The Curious Case of Kiryas Joel*, 6.
109 Daniel J. Elazar, "The Political Theory of Covenant: Biblical Origins and Modern Developments," *Publius* 10, no. 4 (1980): 26.
110 Elazar, "The Political Theory of Covenant: Biblical Origins and Modern Developments," 26; See also Boyarin and Boyrain, *Powers of Diaspora*, who state "It is easy to connect the Jewish Satmar group as a further link in this chain of covenantal communities, and there are numerous reasons why it is tempting to assimilate the residents of Kiryas Joel to the pilgrim migrants to America."
111 Ibid, 27.
112 Ibid.
113 Ibid, 11.
114 Julia Watts Belser, "Judaism and Disability," in *Disability and World Religions*, ed. Darla Y. Schumm and Michael Stoltzfus (Waco, Texas: Baylor University Press, 2016), 100.
115 Julia Watts Belser, "Judaism and Disability," 101.
116 Steve Lieberman, "New Square Ranked as New York's Poorest Municipality," *The Journal News*, May 9, 2018. https://www.lohud.com/story/news/local/rockland/2018/05/09/new-square-ranked-poorest-municipality-new-york-state/591434002/; Samuel Stebbins and Michael B. Sauter, "Which Town in Your State Is the Poorest? Here Is the List," *24/7 Wall Street*, May 8, 2018. https://www.usatoday.com/story/money/economy/2018/05/08/which-town-your-state-poorest-list-financial-hardship/581103002/
117 Shulem Deen, *All Who Go Do Not Return: A Memoir* (Minneapolis, Minnesota: Grayworf Press, 2015), 5.
118 Deen, *All Who Go Do Not Return*, 30 and 25.

119 YAFFED, "*Executive Summary. Non-equivalent: The State of Education in New York City's Hasidic Yeshivas.* New York, NY: YAFFED, 2017. https://d3n8a8pro7vhmx.cloudfront.net/yaffed/pages/116/attachments/original/1504750988/Yaffed_Report_Executive_Summary_online_version.pdf?1504750988
120 YAFFED, "Executive Summary. Non-equivalent: The State of Education in New York City's Hasidic Yeshivas."
121 Shulem Deen, "Why Is New York Condoning Illiteracy?" *New York Times*, April 4, 2018. https://www.nytimes.com/2018/04/04/opinion/yeshivas-literacy-new-york.html?smid=em-share
122 Deen, "Why Is New York Condoning Illiteracy?"
123 Joseph Berger, "Norman Lamm, 92, Dies; Rescued Yeshiva U. From Brink of Bankruptcy," *New York Times.* May 31, 2020. https://www.nytimes.com/2020/05/31/obituaries/Norman-Lamm-Dead.html?smid=em-share
124 Berger, "Norman Lamm, 92, Dies; Rescued Yeshiva U. From Brink of Bankruptcy."
125 Ibid.
126 Sarna, "George Washington's Correspondence with the Jews of Newport," 22.
127 See Sarna, "George Washington's Correspondence with the Jews of Newport," 23, fn. 9.
128 "Jewish Virtual Library," *American-Israeli Cooperative Enterprise*, n.d., https://www.jewishvirtuallibrary.org/fig

Bibliography

Agostini v. Felton, 521 U.S. 203 (1997).

Aguilar v. Felton, 473 U.S. 402 (1985).

Anglim, Christopher Thomas. *Encyclopedia of Religion and the Law in America.* 2nd ed. Amenia, New York: Grey House Publishing, 2009.

Aristotle. *Poetics and Rhetoric,* edited by Eugene Garver. New York: Barnes & Noble Classics, 2005.

Balibar, Étienne. *Equaliberty.* Translated by James Ingram. Durham, NC: Duke University Press, 2014.

Belser, Julia Watts, "Judaism and Disability." In *Disability and World Religions*, edited by Darla Y. Schumm and Michael Stoltzfus, 93–113. Waco, Texas: Baylor University Press, 2016.

Berg, Thomas C. "Slouching Towards Secularism: A Comment on Kiryas Joel School District v. Grumet." *Emory Law Journal* 44, no. 2 (Spring 1995): 433–99.

Berger, Joseph. "Norman Lamm, 92, Dies; Rescued Yeshiva U. From Brink of Bankruptcy." *New York Times.* May 31, 2020. https://www.nytimes.com/2020/05/31/obituaries/Norman-Lamm-Dead.html?smid=em-share

Bizzel, Patricia and Bruce Herzberg, eds. *Rhetorical Tradition: Readings from Classical Times to the Present.* 2nd ed. Boston: Bedford/St. Martin's, 2001.

Bleakley, Fred R. "Torn Asunder." *Wall Street Journal.* June 1, 1994.

Board of Education of Kiryas Joel v. Grumet, 512 U.S. 687 (1994).

Boyarin, Jonathan. "Circumscribing Constitutional Identities in Kiryas Joel." *Yale Law Journal* 106, no. 5 (January 1997): 1537–70.

Boyarin, Jonathan and Daniel Boyarin. *Powers of Diaspora*. Minneapolis: University of Minnesota Press, 2002.

Boyarin, Jonathan and Daniel Boyarin. "Circumscribing Constitutional identities in *Kiryas Joel*." In *Powers of Diaspora*, 103–27. Minneapolis: University of Minnesota Press, 2015.

Carter, T. Barton, Marc A. Franklin, and Jay B. Wright. *The First Amendment and the Fourth Estate*. 6th ed. New York: Foundation Press, 2003.

Conkle, Daniel O. *Constitutional Law: The Religion Clauses*. 2nd ed. New York: Foundation Press, 2009.

Cover, Robert M. "Foreword: *Nomos* and Narrative." *Harvard Law Review* 97 (1983): 4–68.

Deen, Shulem. *All Who Go Do Not Return: A Memoir*. Minneapolis, Minnesota: Grayworf Press, 2015.

Deen, Shulem. "Why Is New York Condoning Illiteracy?" *New York Times*. April 4, 2018. https://www.nytimes.com/2018/04/04/opinion/yeshivas-literacy-new-york.html?smid=em-share

Eisgruber, Christopher L. "Article and Response: The Constitutional Value of Assimilation." *Columbia Law Review* 96, no. 1 (January 1996): 87–103.

Elazar, Daniel J. "The Political Theory of Covenant: Biblical Origins and Modern Developments." *Publius* 10, no. 4 (Fall 1980): 3–30.

Enos, Theresa, ed. "Dissoi Logoi (Dialexis)." In *Encyclopedia of Rhetoric and Composition: Communication from Ancient Times to the Information Age*. New York: Routledge, 1996.

Gelman, Susan and Susan Looper-Friedman. "Thou Shalt Use the Equal Protection Clause for Religion Cases (Not Just the Establishment Clause)." *Journal of Constitutional Law* 10, no. 4 (May 2008): 665–743.

Greene, Abner S. "Article and Response: Kiryas Joel and Two Mistakes About Equality." *Columbia Law Review* 96, no. 1 (January 1996): 1–86.

Greene, Abner S. "The Rehnquist Court and the First Amendment: The Apparent Consistency of Religion Clause Doctrine." *Washington University Journal of Law & Policy* 21 (2006): 225–61.

Greenhouse, Linda. "High Court Bars School District." *New York Times*. June 28, 1994.

Grumet, Louis and John Caher. *The Curious Case of Kiryas Joel*. Foreword by Judith S. Kaye. Chicago: Chicago Review Press, 2016.

Healey, Robert M. "Thomas Jefferson's 'Wall': Absolute or Serpentine?" *Journal of Church and State* 30, no. 3 (1988): 441–62.

Hempen, Laura M. "Board of Education of Kiryas Joel School District v. Grumet: Accommodationists Strike a Blow to the Wall of Separation." *Saint Louis University Law Journal* 39, no. 4 (Summer 1995): 1389–428.

Hoge, Steven K. "*Cleburne* and the Pursuit of Equal Protection for Individuals with Mental Disorders." *Journal of the American Academy of Psychiatry and the Law Online* 43, no. 4 (December 2015): 416–22.

"Jewish Virtual Library." *American-Israeli Cooperative Enterprise.* n.d. https://www.jewishvirtuallibrary.org/fig

Lanham, Richard A. *A Handlist of Rhetorical Terms.* 2nd ed. Berkeley, CA: University of California Press, 1991.

Larkin v. Grendel's Den, Inc., 459 U.S. 116 (1982).

Lemon v. Kurtzman, 403 U.S. 602 (1971).

Lieberman, Steve. "New Square Ranked as New York's Poorest Municipality." *The Journal News.* May 9, 2018. https://www.lohud.com/story/news/local/rockland/2018/05/09/new-square-ranked-poorest-municipality-new-york-state/591434002/

Lockwood, Kathleen. "Political Power, a Religious Agenda, and the Failings of the Endorsement Test: Hasidic Educational Separatism and the East Ramapo School Board." *First Amendment Law Review* 12, no. 3 (2014): 697–724.

Lupu, Ira C. "Article and Response: Uncovering the Village of Kiryas Joel." *Columbia Law Review* 96, no. 1 (January 1996): 104–20.

Lynch v. Donnelly, 465 U.S. 688 No. 82–1256 (1984).

Merriman, Scott A. *Religion and the Law in America.* 2 vols. Santa Barbara, California: ABC-CLIO, 2007.

Nadeau, Ray. "Hermogenes on 'Stock issues' in Deliberative Speaking." *Speech Monographs* 25, no. 1 (1958): 59–66.

Nadeau, Ray. "Hermogenes' On Stasis: A Translation with an Introduction and Notes." *Speech Monographs* 31, no. 4 (1964): 361–424.

Oster, March. "Kiryas Joel Is Now Palm Tree, the First Official US Haredi Orthodox Town." *Jewish Telegraphic Agency.* January 6, 2019. https://www.jta.org/quick-reads/town-of-palm-tree-becomes-first-official-u-s-haredi-orthodox-town

Paulsen, Michael A. "Religion, Equality, and the Constitution: An Equal Protection Approach to Establishment Clause Adjudication." *Notre Dame Law Review* 61, no. 3 (January 1986): 310–71.

Pullman, George L. "Rhetoric and Forensic Stasis: Reconsidering the Scope and Function of an Ancient Rhetorical Heuristic in the Aftermath of the Thomas/Hill Controversy." *Rhetoric Society Quarterly* 25 (1995): 223–30.

Roberts, Sam. "A Village with the Numbers, Not the Image, of the Poorest Place." *New York Times.* April 20, 2011. https://www.nytimes.com/2011/04/21/nyregion/kiryas-joel-a-village-with-the-numbers-not-the-image-of-the-poorest-place.html

Rubin, Israel. *Satmar: Two Generations of an Urban Island.* New York: Peter Lang, 1997.

Sarna, Jonathan D. "George Washington's Correspondence with the Jews of Newport." In *To Bigotry No Sanction: George Washington and Religious Freedom,* 17–24. Philadelphia: National Museum of American Jewish History, 2012.

School District of the City of Grand Rapids v. Ball, 473 U.S. 373 (1985).

Stebbins, Samuel and Michael B. Sauter. "Which Town in Your State Is the Poorest? Here Is the List." *24/7 Wall Street.* May 8, 2018. https://www.usatoday.com/story/money/economy/2018/05/08/which-town-your-state-poorest-list-financial-hardship/581103002/

Sweet, Jesse, dir. *City of Joel.* United States: Samuel Goldwyn Films, 2018. Online.

Underwood, Julie K. and Julie F. Mead. "Establishment of Religion Analysis: The Lemon Test or Just Lemonade." *Journal of Law & Education* 25, no. 1 (Winter 1996): 55–82.

Wallace, Karl R. "The Substance of Rhetoric: Good Reasons." *Quarterly Journal of Speech* 49, no. 3 (October 1963): 239–49.

YAFFED. "YAFFED. Young Advocates for Fair Education." YAFFED. 2020. https://yaffed.org/

YAFFED. *Executive Summary. Non-equivalent: The State of Education in New York City's Hasidic Yeshivas.* New York, NY: YAFFED, 2017. https://d3n8a8pro7vhmx.cloudfront.net/yaffed/pages/116/attachments/original/1504750988/Yaffed_Report_Executive_Summary_online_version.pdf?1504750988

YAFFED. *Non-equivalent: The State of Education in New York City's Hasidic Yeshivas.* New York, NY: YAFFED, 2017. https://d3n8a8pro7vhmx.cloudfront.net/yaffed/pages/116/attachments/original/1523680597/Yaffed_Report_online_version.pdf?1523680597

Zobrest v. Catalina Foothills School District, 509 U.S. 1 (1993).

5. *Flag on the Play: Equal Protection Clause, the Establishment Clause, and Prayer at School and School Sporting Events*

M. Elizabeth Thorpe

Joseph Kennedy was a high school assistant football coach who would take a knee on the field after each game in prayer. After some time, some players started joining him. The school district eventually contacted him and told him this behavior was in violation of district policy and he would need to cease this activity. Kennedy willfully violated the district's policy, was placed on administrative leave, and upon his next review, his contract was not renewed. Kennedy took his case to court on the basis of religious liberty and lost. The case was decided on the basis of the Establishment Clause, which prohibits Congress from establishing a state religion, but I argue it would have been a sounder argument to decide on the Equal Protection Clause, which requires the state to treat individuals in the same manner as others in the same circumstances.

An Equal Protection argument grounds that decision in the importance of a person—that is, it focuses on people as opposed to religion. Such an argument grounds the decision on the protection of people, not institutions. The Bill of Rights is meant to be a document that articulates the rights of people, not institutions. An argument that protects the rights of people as opposed to institutions is more closely aligned with our Constitution (*Citizens United* notwithstanding). The Bill of Rights, and other amendments, are written to describe how people's rights are protected. The Bill of Rights is designed to protect Christians (or Muslims, or Buddhists), not Christianity. The same goes for those who do not identify with any religion. An Equal Protection argument in church/state cases continues in that tradition, protecting the rights of people, instead of protecting the ideals and goals of institutions. An Equal Protection argument avoids creating "others" out of nonadherents to the majority religion, as Justice O'Connor noted in *Lynch v. Donnelly*. When the state supports religious displays it creates a kind of hierarchy with those who are part of that state-supported religion at the top because they

> are supported by the state, while those who are not part of that religion do not, at that moment, receive state sponsorship. The state establishes an insider/outsider situation.[1]

In 2019, the Supreme Court of the United States (SCOTUS) denied Joseph Kennedy's petition of certiorari. Kennedy, the football coach at Bremerton High School, claimed that his contract had not been renewed because he prayed on the field after games, thereby denying him his right to freely exercise his religion. In March of 2021 the U.S. Court of Appeals for the Ninth Circuit denied his appeal. The basis of the Supreme Court's denial was on questions of fact, and not necessarily an endorsement of the original Ninth Circuit Court of Appeals decision, which was that Kennedy could not support a Free Exercise case and that the school was justified in their actions because of the Establishment Clause. Still, *Kennedy v. Bremerton* engages important questions concerning rights to Free Exercise and the Establishment Clause. Specifically, the case interrogates whether state sponsorship of prayer at a school event violates the Establishment Clause. I argue that this case highlights an even more complicated issue: the relationship between the Establishment Clause and Equal Protection. In this chapter I will argue how Establishment Clause arguments create insider/outsider hierarchies while Equal Protection arguments focus on people as opposed to religion, summarize the *Kennedy* case, provide some precedent case law, and describe the application of the law. In this case, Kennedy represents an institution, or the state. This case illustrates how the Equal Protection Clause can be used to focus on the individual as opposed to systems or institutions. The Equal Protection Clause could provide greater protection for people who are not of the majority religion or who are irreligious in cases of state sponsored displays of religion from being relegated to "outsider" status as articulated in *Lynch v. Donnelly*.

This case presents an interesting example of how the Free Exercise Clause, which states that people have the right to exercise their religion freely and as they see fit, and the Equal Protection Clause, which requires that the state govern impartially, can be in tension with one another. On the one hand,

Kennedy argued that he has the right to exercise his religion freely, which is constitutionally the case. On the other hand, the Equal Protection Clause guarantees that the government will not favor one religion over another. This can cause tension around Free Exercise—if a person feels they are called to pray at state events they might see it as a necessary part of practicing their religion, but the state cannot be seen to endorse that religion with state prayer. State sponsored religion would be favoring one group and creating outsiders, which would be in violation of the Equal Protection Clause. So while there may be tension between the Equal Protection Clause and the Free Exercise Clause, it is hopefully held in check by the Establishment Clause.

The federal district court ruled against Kennedy on all counts by applying Justice Sandra Day O'Connor's endorsement test.[2] Justice O'Connor defined the endorsement test as,

> The Establishment Clause prohibits government from making adherence to a religion relevant in any way to a person's standing in the political community. Government can run afoul of that prohibition. . . [by] endorsement or disapproval of religion. Endorsement sends a message to nonadherents that they are outsiders, not full members of the political community, and an accompanying message to adherents that they are insiders, favored members of the political community. [. . .] The proper inquiry under the purpose prong of *Lemon*,[3] I submit, is whether the government intends to convey a message of endorsement or disapproval of religion.[4]

Since the Ninth Court made its decision, the SCOTUS has weighed in on the issue, deciding in Kennedy's favor. While this has been decided as a free exercise and free speech case, I maintain it is an Equal Protection issue, especially since this issue is likely to become more and more frequent.

Equal Protection and Insider/Outsider Status

The Equal Protection Clause comes from the Fourteenth Amendment which states that "No state shall make or enforce any law which shall abridge the privileges or immunities of citizens of the United States; nor shall any state deprive any person of life, liberty, or property, without due process of law; nor deny to any person within its jurisdiction the equal protection of the laws." The Fourteenth Amendment was adopted during Reconstruction to address the rights of newly freed slaves, but the Equal Protection Clause has historically been important beyond just Reconstruction. The phrase means that the government must apply the law equally and cannot create legal castes amongst its citizens.

The Fourteenth Amendment was originally written to incorporate freed slaves into the citizenry. The Equal Protection Clause is at the heart of *Brown v. Board of Education*, the case which desegregated American schools. It is also at the center of *Lawrence v. Texas*, which was a turning point in gay rights in American history for ruling that anti-sodomy laws were unconstitutional. The Equal Protection Clause, as we understand it, now guarantees that the government will not create castes or "others" among its citizenry. The state should not favor one group over another—it should treat all of its citizens equally.

This is important in the *Kennedy* case because by giving tacit approval to one religion over others, Kennedy was creating "others" out of nonadherants to the majority religion, which runs afoul of the Equal Protection Clause. It is not the job of the government to favor one group over another, and state sanctioned religious displays do exactly that.

Susan Gellman and Susan Looper-Friedman have argued that the Equal Protection Clause should be used as well as, or perhaps instead of, the Establishment Clause in church/state separation cases.[5] Equal Protection arguments are grounded in less controversial arguments because an Equal Protection argument does not depend on whether the Court takes a liberal or conservative view of the Establishment Clause. It removes that partisanship from the equation. They claim that the Equal Protection Clause clarifies the tension between religious liberty and the Establishment Clause by focusing on people as opposed to the religion. There has been a great deal of hand-wringing over government religious expression; it has rarely been couched as an Equal Protection Clause issue. William Marshall observes that there has been a variety of reasons since the *Engel v. Vitale* and *Abington School District v. Schempp* cases, for example, that prayer in school has been deemed unconstitutional. In *Engel v. Vitale* the New York State Board of Regents authorized a voluntary prayer for recitation at the beginning of each school day. A group of organizations came together and challenged the prayer on the grounds of the Establishment Clause. The Court decided that prayer in public schools (if the school is leading the prayer) is unconstitutional, even if participation is not required and the prayer is not tied to a particular religion. In *Abington v. Schempp*, Pennsylvania schools were required by law to read from the Bible at the opening of each school day. The district court ruled that this was a violation of the First Amendment, even after the district allowed a student to excuse himself. The state's Supreme Court reversed the district court's decision and held that the practice was constitutional, even though they admitted the religious character of the exercise. However, the Supreme Court of the United States ruled that public schools cannot sponsor Bible readings and recitations of the Lord's Prayer under the First Amendment's Establishment Clause.

Marshall observes that "while *Engel* and *Schempp* focus on societal harms caused by school prayer, such as sectarian divisiveness and the corruption of religion, the later cases primarily concentrate on individual harms such as coercion and alienation. This doctrinal inconsistency, then, might suggest that the constitutional case against school prayer is not as straightforward as one might think."[6] Gellman and Looper-Friedman argue that the Equal Protection Clause has several advantages over the Establishment Clause for governmental religious expression cases. First, they claim it is a more pragmatic approach for the foreseeable future. Reliance on the Establishment Clause is risky for proponents of church/state separation, and as the Courts become more conservative, the Establishment clause is on shakier and shakier ground.[7] A more socially conservative court, that is more inclined to protect conservative ideas of "religious liberty," is less inclined to protect the separation of church and state in favor of a church or religious population that can practice their religion wherever and however they see fit. Secondly, the Equal Protection Clause "speaks to the harm that is actually suffered."[8] The focus is on marginalization, not evangelism. The Equal Protection Clause approach changes the question to "whether the government is endorsing Christians, not Christianity."[9] By focusing on the Equal Protection Clause instead of the Establishment Clause, church/state cases are humanized. That is, they focus on individuals and people instead of institutions and practices. The questions are focused on people not religion, and whether the government is stratifying its citizenry. As the Court argued in *Abington,* "The State must be steadfastly neutral in all matters of faith, and neither favor nor inhibit religion. In my [Brennan's] view, government cannot sponsor religious exercises in the public schools without jeopardizing that neutrality."[10]

The traditional reasoning dealing with church/state issues comes from cases like *Engel* and *Schempp* and deals with the Establishment Clause. According to the reasoning in *Engel*, the writers of the Constitution were concerned with the conflict that could happen when religions vied with each other to obtain the government's stamp of approval.[11] The harm is to society, not to the individual. The Court reasoned that religion will inevitably be corrupted if it depends on the government for support. Here, again, the Court was not aiming to protect the individual but to protect the faith. The *Schempp* case addressed the constitutionality of saying the Lord's Prayer and Bible reading in school. *Schempp* established that government action had to have a valid secular purpose and that an action must have a "primary effect that neither advances nor inhibits religion."[12]

Equal Protection Clause questions move the focus away from sanctioning religion to favoring people. Gellman and Looper-Friedman observe that the problem with government religious expression is not that it proselytizes but that it differentiates.[13] As the Wisconsin Court argued,

> . . . the excluded pupil loses caste with his [sic] fellows, and is liable to be regarded with aversion and subjected to reproach and insult. But it is a sufficient refutation of the argument that the practice in question tends to destroy the equality of the pupils which the constitution seeks to establish and protect, and puts a portion of them to serious disadvantage in many ways.[14]

In other words, when a government engages in religious expression, the danger or injury is not that the government will draw more adherents to that religion. The danger is that the government will marginalize those who are not already adherents to that religion. Religious expression creates division where there need not be any. As SCOTUS argued in *Abington,* "When government, the Court said, allies itself with one particular form of religion, the [374 U.S. 203, 222] inevitable result is that it incurs 'the hatred, disrespect and even contempt of those who held contrary beliefs.'[15] Gellman and Looper-Friedman observe that several SCOTUS opinions have recognized just this phenomenon: nonadherents are outsiders.[16] *Lynch v. Donnelly* became famous for its "non-endorsement test" that now occupies much of Establishment Clause doctrine.[17] In this case a man objected to a creche that was a part of a Christmas display in Pawtucket, RI. The creche had been part of the city's display for decades. The SCOTUS found that, notwithstanding the religious significance of the creche, the city had not violated the Establishment Clause. Justice O'Connor wrote into her famous concurring opinion a "clarification" on how the Establishment Clause should be read. O'Connor's opinion in *Lynch v Donnelly* described how endorsing state religions created insiders and outsiders. Those who were members of the majority, or state-endorsed religion, were part of the favored, or inside group, while those who were not members were outsiders.

Lee v. Weisman is of doctrinal importance because of its inclusion of coercion in applying the Establishment Clause.[18] In this case a middle school principal had invited a local rabbi to speak and to pray at his school's graduation ceremony. A father objected and sought a restraining order, but he was denied. After the ceremony, where prayers were recited, the father sought a permanent injunction to keep clergy from delivering prayers at school ceremonies. The SCOTUS held that government involvement in this case creates "a state-sponsored and state-directed religious exercise in a public school." In the opinion, the Justices considered what "force" was. The student in question was not required to stand but was "forced" because of peer pressure. The court notes that "adolescents are often susceptible to pressure from their peers towards conformity, and that the influence is strongest in matters of social convention," making the prayer psychologically coercive, which professor of law Joanne C. Brant argues should be unconstitutional.[19] If the government is in any way making citizens feel pressured to pray then the government has crossed a constitutional boundary. But prayer that does not harass or pressure citizens is simply a matter of freedom of expression.[20]

The problem with religious expression from the government, however, is not coercion. The problem is one of "difference."[21] If a person has to pray along with saying the Pledge at a school event, non-Christian students may be made to feel they are different. Being a "real American" means submitting to the prayer. If you were Jewish or Muslim you were still an American with equal rights, but you were "sort of a variation on the theme—in fact, your very entitlement to those equal rights was because of, and dependent upon, your similarity to Christian Americans, not your equality to them regardless of similarity or difference."[22] The problem was not that you were coerced into prayer. You may not have felt forced at all. The problem is that you were differentiated by the prayer. Gellman and Looper-Friedman liken this to the problems faced by women and people of color who "report feeling like variations on the white male norm, and whose equality under the law depended on them proving their similarity to white men."[23] Similarly, Christians in the US have never had to argue they were "real" Americans.[24] So, when the government engages in Christian speech it is reinforcing that connection between Christianity and citizenship. It is creating a separation among Americans of other religions.

Even government religious speech designed to be universal or nonsectarian cannot be entirely inclusive. For one, it automatically excludes atheists and agnostics. Secondly, it likely excludes non-Christians even with attempts to make it as universal as possible. Prayers in religions other than Christianity may be in a different language or may be chanted. They may require a particular posture or may require that the sexes be separated.[25] Prayer that is simply a group of people standing with their heads bowed and listening to one person speaking is inherently not inclusive. In short, the problem is not one of inclusion or coercion but one of equality.[26] Religious expression from the government marginalizes and differentiates its citizens.

Even allowing students to be excused from religious practice does not absolve the state from their discriminatory behavior. This still creates a caste system in which non-participants are "othered" from their peers. As the Court observed in *Abington*,

> First, by requiring what is tantamount in the eyes of teachers and schoolmates to a profession of disbelief, or at least of nonconformity, the procedure may well deter those children who do not wish to participate for any reason based upon the dictates of conscience from exercising an indisputably constitutional right to be excused. Thus the excusal provision in its operation subjects them to a cruel dilemma. In consequence, even devout children may well avoid claiming their rights and simply continue to participate in exercises distasteful to them because of an understandable reluctance to be stigmatized as atheists of nonconformists simply on the basis of their request.[27]

Similarly, the Louisiana State Supreme Court argued in *Herold v. Parish Bd. Of School Directors*,

> Under such circumstances, the children would be excused from the opening exercises. . . because of their religious beliefs. And excusing such children on religious grounds, although the number excused might be very small, would be a distinct preference in favor of the religious beliefs of the majority, and would work a discrimination against those who were excused. The exclusion of a pupil under such circumstances puts him in a class by himself; it subjects him to a religious stigma; and all because of his religious belief. Equality in public education would be destroyed by such act, under a Constitution which seeks to establish equality and freedom in religious matters.[28]

A number of cases have come close to using the Equal Protection Clause as the basis for a church/state case, but they have stopped short. In *Walz v. Tax Commission*, Justice Harlan was concerned about neutrality in a case about property tax exemptions to religious organizations for properties used solely for religious worship.[29] In this case Frederick Walz, owner of some real estate in NY, brought suit against the NYC Tax Commission challenging property tax exemptions for churches. Walz claimed that the exemptions forced him, as a taxpayer, to indirectly support religious institutions. The Court held that the exemptions did not violate the Establishment Clause. The exemptions did not advance or inhibit religion and no particular religion had been singled out. Justice Harlan argued in his concurring opinion that "neutrality in its application requires an Equal Protection Clause mode of analysis."[30] Harlan's nod to the notion of Equal Protection Clause would go unheeded.

The Justice who came closest to bringing the Equal Protection Clause to bear on church/state cases was Justice Sandra Day O'Connor in the *Santa Fe* case.[31] In *Santa Fe Independent School District v. Doe* the Court took up the issue of prayer at high school football games. Prior to 1995, in Santa Fe's student council chaplain would deliver an overtly Christian prayer over the public-address system before each home game. Two families filed suit under the Establishment Clause. While the suit was pending the district adopted a new policy: student initiated and led prayer was permitted but not required and there would be two student votes—the first to determine if there would be invocations, the second to determine who would give them. The United States District Court for the Southern District of Texas ordered that the prayer had to be nonsectarian and nonproselytizing. The Court of Appeals held that this was all invalid. The Santa Fe School District took this to the Supreme Court claiming this was private, student speech not public speech and therefore not state sanctioned and not subject to the Establishment Clause. SCOTUS decided against the school district. The Court decided that the prayers were public speech authorized by a government policy and taking place on government property at government-sponsored events and that the District's policy involved both perceived and actual government endorsement of the delivery of prayer. In *Santa Fe Independent School District v. Doe*, O'Connor wrote (citing *Lynch v. Donnelly*) that "School sponsorship of a religious message is impermissible because it sends the. . . message to. . . nonadherents 'that they are outsiders, not full members of the political community and an accompanying message to adherents that they are insiders, favored members.' "[32] O'Connor understood that religious expression from a governmental body is divisive because it creates insiders and outsiders. It establishes a situation in which certain citizens are more legitimate than others because their religion is acknowledged by the government while others are not. This does not work to draw people to that religion, and the government may not be officially endorsing that religion, but in expressing religious content it allies itself with members of that religion, creating an inherent insider and outsider scenario. This gets to the heart of the Equal Protection Clause. All citizens cannot see themselves as equal if some are more legitimate because of their insider status. This is different from the Establishment Clause, which warns of a state religion. This is a focus on citizens and membership, not the religion itself.

Arguing Identity

An example of the insider/outsider that church/state cases can construct is that of *Torasco v. Watkins*. Roy Torasco was appointed to be a Notary Public but could not assume the position because he would not declare his belief in God. This clearly created a hierarchy of citizens. The state was favoring those citizens who shared a belief not just in a higher power but in the Judeo-Christian God. The state was establishing clear insiders to the point that they would only appoint those from approved religious traditions. In this case, the Court ruled in favor of Torasco. While they said he could have chosen to not pursue the position, that does not mean the state was not violating the constitution. The Establishment Clause was clearly violated. While the Court did not reason in terms of hierarchies or insider/outsider statuses, they did cite the *Everson v. Board of Education* case that said no person can be forced to adhere to a religion. In other words, no person can be forced to assume an identity, or part of an identity, that they do not choose of their own accord.

The fact that Torasco could not be forced to adhere to a particular religion or acknowledge a particular power speaks to the fact that the Constitution protects our individual identities. We are protected in that we can choose our individual persons and belief systems as our own, and that cannot be mandated by the state. This protection of the individual is as much a matter of Equal Protection as it is of Free Exercise. It is a matter of treating each individual the same under the law and gets more to the heart of the matter of treating each individual equally, based on their identity, regardless of their religion or non-adherence to a religion. This is why I argue the Equal Protection Clause protects individuals as opposed to institutions.

Rhetorically, this approach to church/state decisions has a notable impact on both argument and effect of the argument. Any time a decision on the church/state relationship is made there is some potential for a statement on identity. As I have outlined here, a decision that supports a display of religion creates outsiders and a hierarchy of citizens. However, if the state makes a decision based on the Establishment Clause and suppresses displays of religion, those members of the religious community may feel as if they are being made into outsiders. But if expressing your religion is an important part of your citizenship, that says something profound about how you view what it means to be an American. Religious displays, which are predominantly Christian, associated with citizenship, indicate that religion is a part of American identity. Being made an outsider because you cannot display your religion combines religion with citizenship, which is different than saying your religion is protected by the law.

Making decisions like these based on Equal Protection reasoning avoids these assumptions by basing the decisions on people, not religion. Your citizenship is protected because you are a person, not because of any religion you may or may not practice. Equal protection reasoning avoids arguments that identify religion with citizenship in either direction. Arguments based in the Establishment Clause and the Free Exercise Clause allow for arguments that connect religion to citizenship, which is a slippery slope for a liberal democracy. If all Americans, of all religions (or those who are not religious) are going to be equal citizens, then religion cannot be associated with citizenship.

Using the Equal Protection Clause in cases that deal with identity is not a new concept. *Brown v. Board of Education* was based on the idea that the Equal Protection Clause protected American identity.[33] In *Brown v. Board* the Court argued that education could not be separate because then students would be learning different versions of American identity, and that would be a violation of the Equal Protection Clause. The Equal Protection clause protects the person, which, in a church/state case, is different than basing the decision on religion. It has long been associated with identity. *Brown v. Board* established that the Fourteenth Amendment protects a person's identity as an American.

In the following section I will outline the details of the *Kennedy* case to show how it illustrates the tension I have outlined so far in this chapter.

Kennedy v. Bremerton—*Praying at the Game*

The *Kennedy* case presents an ideal case study in how church/state cases provide a variety of legal predicaments. On the one hand, the case was decided as an Establishment case. But on the other, it is an excellent example of how Establishment cases may well be more firmly decided as Equal Protection Clause cases in an effort to protect those that do not wish to partake in religious displays of the majority.

It is important to understand Kennedy's prayer as a part of his community. According to the Circuit Court, Bremerton School District is religiously diverse. Students there represent Christianity, Judaism, Islam, Baha'i, Buddhism, Hinduism, Zoroastrianism, and other faiths.[34] His prayer set him apart from any number of people in his community. According to Kennedy, his religious beliefs "require him to give thanks through prayers at the end of each game for the players accomplishments and the opportunity to be a part of their lives through football."[35] Kennedy felt called to take a knee at the 50 yard line after the game was over and players and coaches from opposing teams have shaken hands and offer a quiet prayer of thanksgiving for players safety and sportsmanship.[36] Kennedy was very specific that this be on the 50 yard line after the game. In other words, it had to be a public prayer. This prayer usually lasted about 30 seconds. He wore a shirt or jacket with the school logo when he prayed.[37] Eventually this practice evolved into a much more involved affair. He began giving "short motivational speeches at midfield after the games." During said speeches students and coaches for both his team and the opposing side would kneel around Kennedy, who raised a helmet from each team, and delivered a message with religious content.[38]

Kennedy acknowledged "that these motivational speeches likely constituted prayers."[39]

The district court reasoned that Kennedy was still on the job even though the game had ended and that praying while wearing the school colors in a prominent location would be understood by reasonable observers as an endorsement of religion by the school. The court also found that the district had offered him reasonable accommodations by offering to allow him to pray in a press box, away from the public eye, or within the athletic facilities or a school building, but Kennedy insisted on public prayer on the field. As such, the court dismissed Kennedy's Title VII claims.[40] Kennedy claimed this was a matter of free speech, but the district court applied the *Pickering* test and found the Kennedy was speaking as a public employee and not a private citizen, so his claims for protected speech were unwarranted.[41] The *Pickering* balancing test is when the Court assesses a public employee's constitutional protections based on a two-part test: First, the Court asks whether the employee spoke on a matter of larger societal significance or importance. If the employee was disciplined for speech on a private grievance (so, complaining about the employer), then the employer is protected. But if the employee spoke on a matter of societal concern, the Court moves on to the second prong of the test, which is the balancing prong. In this test, the Court must balance the employees' right to free speech against the employer's interest in an efficient workplace.[42]

The District first learned of Kennedy's penchant for leading prayers in 2015. This prompted an inquiry into whether Kennedy was complying with the school board's policy on "Religious-Related Activities and Practices." The policy stated that "'as a matter of individual liberty, a student may of his/her own volition engage in private, non-disruptive prayer at any time not in conflict with learning activities.'" Additionally, "'school staff shall neither encourage nor discourage a student from engaging in non-disruptive oral or silent prayer or any other form of devotional activity.'"[43] Kennedy was advised that he could continue to give inspirational talks, but they must be completely secular. Further, student religious activity and expression must be student initiated and may not be encouraged or supervised by the staff. He was further advised that if students did choose to engage in any religious activity, school staff could not take any action that a reasonable observer could perceive as an endorsement of that activity.[44] Finally, the District told Kennedy that he was

> free to engage in religious activity, including prayers, so long as it does not interfere with job responsibilities. Such activity must be physically separate from any student activity and students may not be allowed to join such activity. In order to avoid the perception of endorsement discussed above, such activity should

> either be non-demonstrative (i.e., not outwardly discernible as religious activity) if students are also engaged in religious conduct, or it should occur while students are not engaging in such conduct.[45]

Kennedy complied with the District for several weeks before requesting a religious accommodation under the Civil Rights Act of 1964. Kennedy claimed that his religious expression occurred during "non-instructional hours" at a time when his coaching duties had ceased. He admitted the prayers were audible, but argued they were not in the name of a specific religion, and that he did not encourage or discourage students from participating. He announced he would be resuming his practice of praying at the next game.[46]

Kennedy's intention to pray at the game was widely publicized, including by Kennedy himself. At the next game, Kennedy proceeded to take a knee after the game. According to Kennedy's telling of the incident, "while he was kneeling with his eyes closed, 'coaches and players from the opposing team, as well as members of the general public and media, spontaneously joined [him] on the field and knelt beside [him].'"[47] Sometime after this spectacle, "members of a Satanist religion contacted the District and said they 'intended to conduct ceremonies on the field after football games if others were allowed to.'"[48]

The District contacted Kennedy shortly after to clarify its position. It explained that it does not prohibit prayer or other religious exercise or expression by employees while on the job, but such exercise could not lead to a perception of District endorsement of religion. The District argued that as an assistant coach, he was responsible for students not just during games but also prior to and after games until players are released to their parents. He was also wearing BHS attire at an event in front of a large group of attendees who knew he was there solely by virtue of his employment.[49] The District was clear that it was willing to accommodate religious exercise that would not be seen as an endorsement. The District suggested a private location for the prayer, or that Kennedy wait until the stadium was empty before he kneel on the 50-yard line.[50] Kennedy found these suggested accommodations unacceptable and demanded to be able to pray publicly, on the field, at the end of the game. He continued to do so in spite of the District's admonitions.[51] He was eventually put on paid administrative leave.[52]

While Kennedy was on leave and not able to participate in games, BHS players did not pray on their own after the games. The only time anyone ever prayed was when they were led by Kennedy. This led the District to posit that it "'is very likely that over the years, players have joined in these activities because to do otherwise would mean potentially alienating themselves from their team, and possibly their coaches.'" The District opined that there may have been, however unintentional, a certain amount of coercion for players to join Kennedy in prayer on the field.[53] At his next review Kennedy was not rehired because he failed to follow District policy. He filed suit the following year, claiming that BSD retaliated against him for exercising his right to free speech. The Court ultimately decided against Kennedy because of Kennedy's status as a public employee and because of BSD's need to avoid an Establishment Clause violation.[54]

In the following section I will outline cases that provide important precedent to the *Kennedy* case to help to contextualize and understand it and give credence to the argument that church/state would be more adequately decided by Equal Protection arguments than Establishment arguments.

Prayer in School Precedent and the Establishment Narrative

The *Kennedy* case was not without some clear precedent, such as the *Santa Fe* case. It would seem the *Santa Fe* case would provide clear guidance for the *Kennedy* case because if students cannot lead public prayer then surely school officials are even more restricted. But Kennedy argued that he was engaged in private speech, much as the students in Santa Fe had, so the lines were not so clearly drawn. A more explicit analogy might be drawn to *Doe v. Duncanville Independent School District*. In *Duncanville* Jane Doe was a twelve-year-old who played seventh grade basketball. The girls' basketball coach regularly began or ended practice with a team recitation of the Lord's Prayer. Doe was uncomfortable with the practice but participated in order to avoid tension. John Doe, upon observing this and ascertaining that his daughter was uncomfortable, told his daughter she did not have to participate, and she resolved to stop.[55]

John Doe contacted Ed Parker, the assistant superintendent of Duncanville Independent School District (DISD) schools who told Doe that unless he had "grandparents buried in the Duncanville Cemetery he had no right" to tell him how to run his schools. Mr. Doe contacted Marvin Utecht, Ed Parker's successor, who took action to halt prayers at pep-rallies but insisted there was nothing to be done about post-game prayers. Mr. Doe went before the school board, who were disinclined to alter the practice. Jane and John doe subsequently filed a complaint against DISD for a number of objectionable religious acts and practices which allegedly occurred at DISD schools and sponsored events.[56]

Upon deciding not to participate in prayers, Doe was required by her coach to stand outside the prayer circle or not return to the locker room with the group. Her parents contended that DISD fostered "a climate in which Doe is singled out and subjected to criticism on the basis of her religious beliefs. The record shows that her fellow students asked, 'Aren't you a Christian?' and that one spectator stood up after a game and yelled, 'Well, why isn't she praying? Isn't she a Christian?' Additionally, Doe's history teacher called her 'a little atheist' during one class lecture."[57] This kind of behavior clearly created a situation in which Doe was treated differently because of the state's sanctioning of religion. It is precisely the behavior O'Connor warned about in *Lynch.*

The Does claimed a violation of the Establishment Clause and the district court found that DISD's practices violated all three prongs of the *Lemon* test. It ordered that the defendants were enjoined from permitting employees of DISD to "lead, encourage, promote, or participate in prayer with or among students during curricular or extracurricular activities, including before, during or after school related sporting events."[58] Further, the Court ordered that "due to the pervasive nature of past school prayer, Defendants are to advise students of [DISD], in writing, that under the First Amendment of the United States Constitution, prayer and religious activities initiated and promoted by school officials are unconstitutional, and that students have a constitutional right not to participate in such activities."[59]

A similar case that seems to give some guidance to the *Kennedy* case is the United States Court of Appeals 11th Circuit case *Holloman ex Rel. Holloman v. Harland.*[60] Holloman, a former student at a high school in Alabama, filed suit against his high school economics teacher, Fawn Allred, and the school principal, George Harland, because he had been punished for raising his fist during the Pledge of Allegiance and because his rights were violated by Allred's daily ritual of conducting a silent moment of prayer.[61]

Allred began her classes every day by asking "Does anyone have any prayer requests?" After noting the various requests she would hold a moment of silence, often begun by saying "Let us pray" and ended with "Amen." She never gave students the opportunity to leave the room during prayer requests or during the moment of silence.[62] The court reasoned the "praying goes sufficiently beyond the range of activities normally performed by high school teachers and commonly accepted as part of their job."[63] Prayer is not a pedagogically sound part of any curriculum. It is "not a type of act that falls within a reasonably specific category of actions that teachers are authorized to perform; there is not an easy way of abstracting away its unconstitutional aspects to arrive at a type of behavior that falls within teachers' discretionary authority."[64] The nondenominational nature of the prayer does not mitigate the circumstance. Government should be neutral between religion and nonreligion.[65] Prayer is ultimately outside of the purview of a school setting and Holloman was put in an impossible position by being asked to pray.

Perhaps the most pertinent case is *Borden v. East Brunswick Board of Education*.[66] In 2007 Marcus Borden was the head football coach at East Brunswick High School where he had been in that position since 1983. In that time he had engaged in two pre-game prayer activities: one at the team dinner, and one in the locker room when he took a knee with the players to pray.[67] In 2005, Jo Ann Magistro, the superintendent of EBSD, received a complaint from a parent about the prayer at the team dinner. Borden continued the tradition but told students that if they felt uncomfortable during the prayer, they could wait in the restroom during the team prayer at games and at the dinner. Following the September 30, 2005 game, Magistro received several more complaints from parents.[68]

On October 6th, EBSD's counsel advised Magistro and the Board of Education that the school could not "lead, encourage, or participate in student prayer." Magistro met with Borden the next day and told him that all prayer needed to be student initiated. Magistro asked counsel to provide some clear guidelines for faculty participation in student prayer.[69] Counsel advised that if "student athletes on their own decide to hold a prayer huddle before a game, after a game, or during a game, or during half-time, they have a right to do so." However,

> Neither the school district nor any representative of the school district (teacher, coach, administrator, board member, etc.) may constitutionally encourage, lead, initiate, mandate, or otherwise coerce, directly or indirectly student prayer at any time in any school-sponsored setting, including classes, practices, pep rallies, team meetings, or athletic events.
>
> Representatives of the school district, as referenced above, cannot participate in student-initiated prayer. That very issue was decided by the Fifth Circuit Court of Appeals in a decision cited with approval by the United States Supreme Court and is, therefore, the operative law of the land at this time. To quote the Court, 'If while acting in their official capacities (school district) employees join hands in a prayer circle or otherwise manifest approval and solidarity with student religious exercises they cross the line between respect for religion and endorsement of religion,' and such conduct was prohibited.[70]

That evening, Borden resigned. But on October 17, 2005 he withdrew his resignation and agreed to abide by the District's policies for the remainder of the season.

Prior to the next season, Borden emailed the co-captains of the football team and asked them to ask the players whether they would like to continue the tradition of praying at the team dinner and prior to the game.[71] He told them whatever the players decided was fine. Their response indicated that the players voted to continue the prayers, so Borden stood and bowed his head during the pre-meal prayer and remained on one knee during pre-game prayers as the season began.

In November 2005 Borden brought suit against the District and the superintendent. Borden sought "to show his respect for his players, respect for The Team Prayers, and respect for East Brunswick's football tradition by engaging in two silent acts during the Team Prayers: (i) bowing his head during grace; and (ii) taking a knee with his team in the locker room." Borden claimed the District violated his Due Process and Equal Protection Clause rights.[72] The Court was not sympathetic to Borden's claims reasoning that paragraph two of the school's guidelines prohibits a school official from "'encourag[ing], lead[ing], initiat[ing], mandat[ing], or otherwise coerc[ing]' students into prayer."[73] They note that the Supreme Court "has held that a school district is in violation of the Establishment Clause where 'the degree of school involvement makes it clear that [prayer activities] bear the imprint of the State and thus put school-age children who objected in an untenable position.'"[74]

Borden claimed the content of his speech was secular, intended to promote solidarity, help form the team into a cohesive family unit, and show respect for the players' prayers. But the content of his message was not a matter of public concern. The coach did "not perform these silent acts as a part of a broad social or policy statement of being able to take a knee or bow his head in public."[75] The form and context of his speech reinforce its non-public nature. Because these acts are not on matters of public concern he does not have a free speech right to trigger the *Pickering* balancing test.[76] This is particularly pertinent to the *Kennedy* case because Kennedy's actions were similar in that they were not on matters of public concern—they were prayers that he *chose* to make public. However, just because he chose to make a private matter public does not mean it passes the *Pickering* test because making public a private matter does not create a public forum or create a public concern out of private matters.

Borden argued that being involved in the prayers was a part of character education which was a part of his job as an educator.[77] In this, he admitted that the acts of bowing his head in prayers and taking a knee are means of teaching respect and good moral character. He also admitted his "coaching methods are pedagogic."[78] In other words, he is acting as a representative of the school district. EBHS is allowed to choose how its students are taught and what they are taught, and the district provided guidelines to Borden that were clear and in line with Constitutional precedent.

The concurring opinion went further in arguing for the problematic nature of Borden's prayer. Judge McKee argued that the players on the team were put in the "untenable position of either compromising any opposing beliefs they may have had or going on record (at the very least with their captains) as opposing their coach and perhaps a majority of their teammates."[79] McKee questions how this could foster unity, as even though the captains report the team unanimously voted to continue the traditions of prayer, the records suggest the results were very different. In the fall of 2005, a distraught parent complained to the superintendent that her son was very uncomfortable with the prayer. When asked why her son participated, the mother stated that he "'was fearful that if he did not go along with what was obviously the coach's desire he would not get playing time.'"[80] It appears that it never occurred to Borden that his tradition could be uncomfortable for some and could even deter others from playing football at all.[81] Borden is a teacher, and therefore a state actor, and failed to appreciate that not everyone may agree with his beliefs. For purposes of the First and Fourteenth Amendments any player who held opposing beliefs should not have to "'go along to get along'" by silently participating in religious practices.[82]

These cases provide an Establishment Clause narrative and describe how the state should not endorse a religion, but there is an implicit argument that needs to be made clearer. These cases all point to issues of Equal Protection Clause, as well, as they are a matter of equally protecting religious and irreligious minorities from the infringement of a religious power. Each of these cases paint a picture of state actors creating an environment in which certain people or groups are favored over others. Those that do not ascribe to the majority beliefs that the state sanctions in its outward religious display are subjected to discriminatory treatment. The state creates a stratified citizenry by favoring a group of people above another. This is a matter of Equal Protection Clause as much as it is the Establishment Clause.

Application of the Law and the Equal Protection Clause

Lynch v. Donnelly argued that the "Court has never held that political divisiveness alone was sufficient to invalidate government conduct."[83] But the actions in *Kennedy*, and these other cases, are more than just politically divisive. These actions are discriminatory. When the state supports public prayer it violates the Equal Protection Clause, not just the Establishment Clause. When the state allows state sanctioned prayer, they create outsiders, specifically those who do not partake in the state sanctioned religion, of some groups by state actors, which is not divisive; it is oppressive. State approval of a religion creates castes of people. This is a matter of the Equal Protection Clause because that is precisely what it is designed to avoid. The Equal Protection Clause is a matter of making sure the state treats all people fairly and equally, but when state actors acknowledge one religion over others, it automatically stratifies citizens. As Brennan wrote in *Lynch*, those who believe in the religion expressed by the state "receive the unique and exclusive benefit of public recognition and approval of their views."[84] This is an elevation of one belief system over another. Brennan argues in the dissent that "the effect on minority religious groups, as well as on those who may reject all religion, is to convey the message that their views are not similarly worthy of public recognition are not entitled to public support. It was precisely this sort of religious chauvinism that the Establishment Clause was intended forever to prohibit."[85] Brennan acknowledges that a function of the Establishment Clause is to keep the state from creating insider/outsider or privileged classes within the citizenry. This is also the function of the Equal Protection Clause. The *Holloman* and *Borden* cases could have been argued on the grounds of the Equal Protection Clause, creating a more solid foundation for the *Kennedy* case. In *Santa Fe v. Doe* the Court argued that deferring to the majority does nothing to protect the minority view but rather "places the students who hold such views at the mercy of the majority."[86] The Court recognized that when state actors recognize a religion those students in the minority, whether it be minority religion or those who have no religion, are automatically marginalized. The Equal Protection Clause exists to prevent exactly that kind of marginalization.

In the *Borden* case, Superintendent Magistro described phone calls she received in 2005 from parents of cheerleaders who complained that their daughters were uncomfortable during the pregame prayer. Students learned of these complaints and blamed two Jewish cheerleaders. These two young women were subsequently subject to intense anti-Semitic bullying and harassment and even threatened on a student blog. The prayer clearly created a category of "outsider" that led to a series of volatile harassments.[87] This is an example par excellence of how state religious action can marginalize those in the minority. It othered those who were in the minority and created an untenable, hostile environment that the Equal Protection Clause exists to prevent, especially in a state sanctioned environment such as a public school. The Equal Protection Clause should have been first and foremost in the minds of the Courts in the *Borden* and *Kennedy* cases. With this body of evidence in mind, let us look at the *Kennedy* case through an Equal Protection Clause lens as opposed to an Establishment one.

The Court reasoned that Kennedy was still on the job when he led these prayers at the 50-yard line. His duties as a coach or teacher had not ended even though the game had, so he was still at this point a state actor. This could easily be seen as state sanctioned religion, then, which is why the case was argued as an Establishment case. But consider the effect on people and not religion. When the state extends its approval on a particular religion, in this case Christianity, it effectively extends its approval on Christians. This is, by all accounts, a religiously diverse district. For a state actor to appear to favor one religious group over another is not just a matter of state sanctioned religion but is a matter of state sanctioned favoritism which runs afoul of the Equal Protection Clause.

Kennedy was offered the opportunity to pray in private but insisted on making his prayer public. This is important in understanding the role of the prayer in this narrative. Kennedy was not praying just as an individual, but he insisted on making the prayer a matter of public observance. In this way, he brought the state into it. He brought attention to his role as a state actor by making the prayer public at the football game. Had he prayed silently and away from the view of the public, he would not have been in a position to create insider/outsider groups, but his actions were specifically designed to register approval of a particular religion in the public eye. In this way he was clearly indicating that nonadherants to his religion were "othered" by his actions as a state representative. As the Court observed in *Abington,* "many deeply devout persons have always regarded prayer as a necessarily private experience."[88]

Students have the right to pray if it is self-initiated. Prayer in school is not outlawed; school sanctioned prayer is what is problematic. It is important to note then that once Kennedy was not leading any prayers, students did not continue praying. It appears as if the only prayer at the games in question was state sanctioned prayer—students were not interested in continuing the practice. This indicates that it was the state supporting religious groups not students. The state had created an environment in which certain religious groups were elevated above others with state support even though students had not even indicated they desired any prayer at that time. Under the Equal Protection Clause this could be discriminatory and prejudicial.

Conclusion and Future Studies

The Fourteenth Amendment was written to guarantee the citizenship rights of freed slaves but has since expanded to mean that the government cannot create a situation in which one group of its citizens is favored over another.

This is, and has been, essential in the Civil Rights Movement and the LGBTQ movement and has created a legal world in which citizens can demand fairer and more equal treatment across the board. The Equal Protection Clause means that the citizenry cannot be separated out into castes or state-sanctioned elites or inferiors, or insiders and outsiders. Establishment Clause questions, then, should be considered with an eye to the Equal Protection Clause. There are certainly good legal reasons why the state should not sanction religion, and an important part of that is that the state should not elevate groups of people over other groups. When the state approves of one religion over another, or over non-religion in general, the state tacitly approves of those members of that religion. It creates a group of insiders with its approval, which is in direct opposition to the spirit of the Equal Protection Clause.

The *Kennedy* case is part of a long string of cases dealing with prayer in school and specifically at sporting events at schools. All of these cases share similar themes. When a state actor engages in religious activity it creates an "outsider" status for students who do not wish to participate in the religious activity. Kennedy may not have intended to create tension by engaging in public prayer, but by creating a situation in which one group is favored by the state, there is an inherent "outsider" status for those who do not wish to participate. As a state actor, this is discriminatory.

Future work should seriously consider the way that the Equal Protection Clause interacts with the Establishment Clause. Legal and rhetorical scholars should ask whether these two can be considered separately at all. Focusing on the Equal Protection Clause in conjunction with the Establishment Clause humanizes the issue and brings the focus back to citizens as opposed to religious acts. This is especially important for prayer in school cases because the importance should be the value of the students. Focusing on the people emphasizes that the students are what is important to the case at hand. This does not devalue their religious expression, but emphasizes that people have inherent value, which adds to the value of religious liberty. By focusing on the value of people as opposed to just the religious expression, it also refocuses the case so that students and teachers are equally as valuable. The Equal Protection Clause focus moves the issue away from who has the right to express their religious beliefs to the fact that all expressions of identity, religious or otherwise, are valued equally.

Kennedy was a state actor when he took the field to pray. When he did so he implied that the state favored not just a religious display, but a specific religion. And favoring a religion, means favoring the religious. The government is not meant to favor any of its citizens over another. Kennedy's display was in violation of the Equal Protection Clause, as all state-sponsored prayer is. The government cannot favor religion because it cannot favor the religious. The Equal Protection Clause does not allow for that kind of favoritism among its citizens.

Notes

1 *Lynch v. Donnelly*, 465 U.S. 668 (1984).
2 Joanne C. Brant, "Sullivan Lecture 2016 Engel: Divisiveness or Coercion—A Response to Professor Marshall." *Capital University Law Review* 46 no. 3 (2018): 378.
3 The Lemon test is a test concerning the entanglement between church and state. It is threefold:
✓ The statute must have a secular legislative purpose. (Purpose Prong)
✓ The principal or primary effect of the statute must neither advance nor inhibit religion. (Effect Prong)
✓ The statute must not result in an "excessive government entanglement" with religion. (Entanglement Prong)
There are three factors to this prong:
✓ Character and purpose of institution benefited.✓ Nature of aid the state provides.✓ Resulting relationship between government and religious authority.
4 Lynch v. Donnelly.
5 Susan Gellman and Susan Looper-Friedman, "Thou Shalt Use the Equal Protection Clause for Religion Cases (Not Just the Establishment Clause." *Journal of Constitutional Law* 10, no. 4 (2008): 665–743.
6 William P. Marshall, "The Constitutionality of School Prayer: Or Why Engel V. Vitale May Have Had It Right All Along." *Capital University Law Review* 46, no. 339 (2018): 341.
7 Gellman and Looper-Friedman, 701.
8 Gellman and Looper-Friedman, 701.
9 Gellman and Looper-friedman, 703.
10 *Abington* School District *v. Schempp*, 374 U.S. 203 (1963), p. 299.
11 Marshall, 346.
12 Marshall, 347, citing ***Abington School District v. Schempp***, 374 U.S. 203 (1963).
13 Gellman and Looper-Friedman, 666.
14 *State ex rel. Weiss v. District Board of School District No. 8*, 76 Wis. 177, 200, 44 N.W. 967, 975.
15 *Abington* School District *v. Schempp*, 374 U.S. 203 (1963), p. 222.
16 Gellman and Looper-Friedman, 667.
17 Marshall, 344.
18 Marshall, 344.
19 Lee v. Weisman, 505 U.S. 577 (1992).
20 Brant, 381–97.
21 Gellman and Looper-Friedman, 670.
22 Gellman and Looper-Friedman, 670.
23 Gellman and Looper-Friedman, 670.
24 Gellman and Looper-Friedman, 670.

25 Gellman and Looper-Friedman, 671–72.
26 Gellman and Looper-Friedman, 672.
27 *Abington* School District *v. Schempp*, 374 U.S. 203 (1963), pp. 289–90.
28 *Herold v. Parish Board of School Directors*, 136 La. 1034, 1049–1050, 68 So. 116, 121.
29 Gellman and Looper-Friedman, 681.
30 *Walz v. Tax Commission of the City of New York*, 397 U.S. 664 (1970).
31 Gellman and Looper-Friedman, 682.
32 *Santa Fe Independent School Dist. v. Doe*, 530 U.S. 290 (2000).
33 M. Elizabeth Thorpe, "The Whiteness of *Brown*: The Failed Constitutive Rhetoric of *Brown v. Board of Education*." *Communication Law Review* 19, no.1 (2019): 79–99. Commlawreview.org.
34 *Kennedy v. Bremerton School District* No. 16–35801.
35 *Kennedy v. Bremerton*, p. 6.
36 *Kennedy v. Bremerton*, p. 6.
37 *Kennedy v. Bremerton*, p. 6.
38 *Kennedy v. Bremerton*, p. 6.
39 *Kennedy v. Bremerton* p. 7.
40 Brant, 378.
41 Brant, 378–79.
42 David L. Hudson, Jr.,"Pickering Connick Test." *The First Amendment Encyclopedia Presented by the John Seigenthaler Chair of Excellence in First Amendment Studies* https://www.mtsu.edu/first-amendment/article/1608/pickering-connick-test
43 *Kennedy v. Bremerton*, p. 7.
44 *Kennedy v. Bremerton*, p. 8.
45 *Kennedy v. Bremerton*, p. 8.
46 *Kennedy v. Bremerton*, p. 9.
47 *Kennedy v. Bremerton*, p. 10.
48 *Kennedy v. Bremerton*, p. 10.
49 *Kennedy v. Bremerton*, p. 11.
50 *Kennedy v. Bremerton*, p. 12.
51 *Kennedy v. Bremerton*, p. 13.
52 *Kennedy v. Bremerton*, p. 13.
53 *Kennedy v. Bremerton*, p. 14.
54 *Kennedy v. Bremerton*, p. 18.
55 *Doe v. Duncanville Independent School District*, 70 F.3d 402 (1995), 1–2.
56 *Doe v. Duncanville Independent School District*, 70 F.3d 402 (1995), 2.
57 *Doe v. Duncanville Independent School District*, 70 F.3d 402 (1995), 3.
58 *Doe v. Duncanville Independent School District*, 70 F.3d 402 (1995), 4.
59 *Doe v. Duncanville Independent School District*, 70 F.3d 402 (1995), 4.
60 *Holloman ex rel. Holloman v. Harland*, 370 F.3d 1252 (11th Cir. 2004).
61 *Holloman ex rel. Holloman v. Harland*, 370 F.3d 1252 (11th Cir. 2004), p. 1.
62 *Holloman ex rel. Holloman v. Harland*, 370 F.3d 1252 (11th Cir. 2004), p. 3.
63 *Holloman ex rel. Holloman v. Harland*, 370 F.3d 1252 (11th Cir. 2004), p. 22.
64 *Holloman ex rel. Holloman v. Harland*, 370 F.3d 1252 (11th Cir. 2004), p. 22.
65 *Holloman ex rel. Holloman v. Harland*, 370 F.3d 1252 (11th Cir. 2004), p. 26.

66 *Marcus A. Borden v. School District Of The Township Of East Brunswick; Board of Education of The Township of East Brunswick; Dr. Jo Ann Magistro, in her capacity as Superintendent, School District of the Township of East Brunswick, Appellants.* No. 06–3890.
67 *Marcus A. Borden v. School District Of The Township Of East Brunswick; Board of Education of The Township of East Brunswick; Dr. Jo Ann Magistro, in her capacity as Superintendent, School District of the Township of East Brunswick, Appellants.* No. 06–3890, p. 5.
68 *Marcus A. Borden v. School District Of The Township Of East Brunswick; Board of Education of The Township of East Brunswick; Dr. Jo Ann Magistro, in her capacity as Superintendent, School District of the Township of East Brunswick, Appellants.* No. 06–3890, p. 7.
69 *Marcus A. Borden v. School District Of The Township Of East Brunswick; Board of Education of The Township of East Brunswick; Dr. Jo Ann Magistro, in her capacity as Superintendent, School District of the Township of East Brunswick, Appellants.* No. 06–3890, p. 8.
70 *Marcus A. Borden v. School District Of The Township Of East Brunswick; Board of Education of The Township of East Brunswick; Dr. Jo Ann Magistro, in her capacity as Superintendent, School District of the Township of East Brunswick, Appellants.* No. 06–3890, pp. 9–10.
71 *Marcus A. Borden v. School District Of The Township Of East Brunswick; Board of Education of The Township of East Brunswick; Dr. Jo Ann Magistro, in her capacity as Superintendent, School District of the Township of East Brunswick, Appellants.* No. 06–3890, pp. 13–14.
72 *Marcus A. Borden v. School District Of The Township Of East Brunswick; Board of Education of The Township of East Brunswick; Dr. Jo Ann Magistro, in her capacity as Superintendent, School District of the Township of East Brunswick, Appellants.* No. 06–3890, pp. 14–15.
73 *Marcus A. Borden v. School District Of The Township Of East Brunswick; Board of Education of The Township of East Brunswick; Dr. Jo Ann Magistro, in her capacity as Superintendent, School District of the Township of East Brunswick, Appellants.* No. 06–3890, p. 21.
74 *Marcus A. Borden v. School District Of The Township Of East Brunswick; Board of Education of The Township of East Brunswick; Dr. Jo Ann Magistro, in her capacity as Superintendent, School District of the Township of East Brunswick, Appellants.* No. 06–3890, pp. 21–22. Citing *Santa Fe Indep Sch. Dist v. Doe.*, 530 U.S. 290, 305 (2000).
75 *Marcus A. Borden v. School District Of The Township Of East Brunswick; Board of Education of The Township of East Brunswick; Dr. Jo Ann Magistro, in her capacity as Superintendent, School District of the Township of East Brunswick, Appellants.* No. 06–3890, p. 32.
76 *Marcus A. Borden v. School District Of The Township Of East Brunswick; Board of Education of The Township of East Brunswick; Dr. Jo Ann Magistro, in her capacity as Superintendent, School District of the Township of East Brunswick, Appellants.* No. 06–3890, pp. 32–34.
77 *Marcus A. Borden v. School District Of The Township Of East Brunswick; Board of Education of The Township of East Brunswick; Dr. Jo Ann Magistro, in her capacity*

as Superintendent, School District of the Township of East Brunswick, Appellants. No. 06–3890, 34.
78 *Marcus A. Borden v. School District Of The Township Of East Brunswick; Board of Education of The Township of East Brunswick; Dr. Jo Ann Magistro, in her capacity as Superintendent, School District of the Township of East Brunswick, Appellants.* No. 06–3890, 35.
79 *Marcus A. Borden v. School District Of The Township Of East Brunswick; Board of Education of The Township of East Brunswick; Dr. Jo Ann Magistro, in her capacity as Superintendent, School District of the Township of East Brunswick, Appellants.* No. 06–3890, 57–58.
80 *Marcus A. Borden v. School District Of The Township Of East Brunswick; Board of Education of The Township of East Brunswick; Dr. Jo Ann Magistro, in her capacity as Superintendent, School District of the Township of East Brunswick, Appellants.* No. 06–3890, p. 58.
81 *Marcus A. Borden v. School District Of The Township Of East Brunswick; Board of Education of The Township of East Brunswick; Dr. Jo Ann Magistro, in her capacity as Superintendent, School District of the Township of East Brunswick, Appellants.* No. 06–3890, p. 58.
82 *Marcus A. Borden v. School District Of The Township Of East Brunswick; Board of Education of The Township of East Brunswick; Dr. Jo Ann Magistro, in her capacity as Superintendent, School District of the Township of East Brunswick, Appellants.* No. 06–3890, p. 59.
83 *Lynch v. Donnelly*, 465 U.S. 668 (1984), p. 684.
84 *Lynch v. Donnelly*, 465 U.S. 668 (1984), p. 701.
85 *Lynch v. Donnelly*, 465 U.S. 668 (1984), p. 701.
86 *Santa Fe* Independent School Dist. *v. Doe*, p. 12.
87 *Marcus A. Borden v. School District Of The Township Of East Brunswick; Board of Education of The Township of East Brunswick; Dr. Jo Ann Magistro, in her capacity as Superintendent, School District of the Township of East Brunswick, Appellants.* No. 06–3890, pp. 61–64.
88 *Abington* School District *v. Schempp*, 374 U.S. 203 (1963), p. 284.

Bibliography

Abington School District *v. Schempp*, 374 U.S. 203 (1963).

Brant, Joanne C. "Sullivan Lecture 2016 Engel: Divisiveness or Coercion – A Response to Professor Marshall." *Capital University Law Review* 46 no. 3 (2018): 373–98.

Brown v. Board of Education of Topeka, 347 U.S. 483 (1954).

Doe v. Duncanville Independent School District, 70 F.3d 402 (1995).

Everson v. Board of Education, 330 U.S. 1 (1947).

Gellman, Susan and Susan Looper-Friedman. "Thou Shalt Use the Equal Protection Clause for Religion Cases (Not Just the Establishment Clause." *Journal of Constitutional Law* 10 no.4 (2008): 665–743.

Herold v. Parish Board of School Directors, 136 La. 1034, 1049–1050, 68 So. 116, 121.

Holloman ex rel. Holloman v. Harland, 370 F.3d 1252 (11th Cir. 2004).

Kennedy v. Bremerton School District No. 16–35801.
Lawrence v. Texas, 539 U.S. 558 (2003).
Lee v. Weisman, 505 U.S. 577 (1992).
Lemon v. Kurtzman, 403 U.S. 602 (1970).
Lynch v. Donnelly, 465 U.S. 668 (1984).
Marcus A. Borden v. School District Of The Township Of East Brunswick; Board of Education of The Township of East Brunswick; Dr. Jo Ann Magistro, in her capacity as Superintendent, School District of the Township of East Brunswick, Appellants. No. 06–3890.
Marshall, William P. "The Constitutionality of School Prayer: Or Why Engel V. Vitale May Have Had It Right All Along." *Capital University Law Review* 46 no 339 (2018): 339–72.
Santa Fe Independent School Dist. v. Doe, 530 U.S. 290 (2000).
State ex rel. Weiss v. District Board of School District No. 8, 76 Wis. 177, 200, 44 N.W. 967, 975.
Torcaso v. Watkins, 367 U.S. 488 (1961).
Walz v. Tax Commission of the City of New York, 397 U.S. 664 (1970)

Part II. Equality and Government Endorsement of Religion

6. *Will Thomas Jefferson's Wall Come a' Tumblin' Down? Propping Up the Johnson Amendment*

JULIET DEE

On May 4, 2017, President Donald Trump issued an Executive Order, "Promoting Free Speech and Religious Liberty." He claimed that this order repealed the Johnson Amendment, although his own Justice Department quickly explained that in fact the Executive Order had left the Johnson Amendment intact. But this raises the question, *why* did President Trump issue an executive order to undermine what had been an uncontroversial amendment? President Trump appeared to want religious leaders to speak out in favor of individual political candidates without risking their tax-exempt status. If Congress had actually repealed the Johnson Amendment in accordance with President Trump's wishes, this would not merely have chipped away at the Establishment Clause's "wall of separation" between church and state; it would have demolished the "wall of separation" with the proverbial wrecking ball.

In 1954, then-Senator Lyndon Johnson introduced a campaign intervention prohibition as an amendment to Section 501(c)(3) of the Internal Revenue Code. It became known as the Johnson Amendment, which prohibits non-profit organizations such as charities, churches, or private colleges from electioneering, meaning that they may not support or oppose any political candidates. The Johnson Amendment does *not* apply to 501(c)(4) organizations such as social welfare organizations, which *are* permitted to lobby and to endorse candidates. A 501(c)(3) organization has tax-exempt status, and contributions to 501(c)(3) organizations (charities) are tax-deductible. In contrast, contributions to 501(c)(4) organizations are *not* tax-deductible.

We might frame the conflict over the Johnson Amendment as a conflict between (1) the Establishment Clause of the First Amendment, which guarantees religious freedom, and (2) the Fourteenth Amendment, which guarantees equal protection of the laws to all citizens. The tension occurs when religious leaders want to exercise their First Amendment right to electioneer, but in doing so, could be denying equal protection of the (tax) laws to members of the general public who are in effect subsidizing the religious leaders' speech because churches, synagogues, mosques and other religious institutions, being 501(c)(3) organizations, are tax-exempt.

The goal of this essay is to demonstrate the importance of the Johnson Amendment in preserving our democracy. Part of the controversy surrounding the Johnson Amendment results from the distinction between a *right* and a *privilege*. The Establishment Clause of the First Amendment guarantees that freedom of religion is a fundamental *right*. The Internal Revenue Service (IRS) has provided the *privilege* of tax-exempt status to religious organizations. Of course, if a government agency grants a privilege, it must also enforce regulations to ensure that religious institutions do not abuse the privilege. For example, religious universities cannot deny admission based on an applicant's race, as is discussed below.

Furthermore, although former President Trump never acknowledged it, some legal scholars are concerned that a hidden motive for repealing the Johnson Amendment is to allow "dark money" contributions to political candidates and political action committees (PACs) to be funneled through 501(c)(3) organizations. If this should occur, taxpayers' money could go toward subsidizing politicians whose messages the taxpayers vehemently disagree with. This would be a perverse form of compelled speech, all the more insidious because "dark money" undermines transparency in a democracy, as is discussed below.

Court Decisions and IRS Investigations Upholding the Johnson Amendment[1]

Congress first codified tax-exempt status for churches and non-profit charities in the Revenue Act of 1913. In 1934, Congress amended the exemption to exclude any churches and non-profit charities that engaged in lobbying. When Lyndon Johnson was a U.S. Senator, he proposed an amendment to the tax code, allowing tax exemptions to churches and non-profits, known as 501(c)(3) organizations, provided that they do *not* attempt to influence legislation and do *not* attempt to "participate or intervene in any political campaign on behalf of any candidate for public office." Congress passed it and President Dwight Eisenhower signed it into law; this became known as the Johnson Amendment.

The Internal Revenue Service (IRS) makes clear that leaders of 501(c)(3) organizations cannot make partisan or "electioneering" comments at official functions (as in a church service, for example). The IRS' Tax Guide for Churches and Religious Organizations includes examples of situations that violate the Johnson Amendment.

Churches receive preferential treatment compared with other charities in that the IRS does not require churches to file (1) an application for § 501(c)(3) status, (2) an annual informational return, which other non-profits are required to file to maintain their tax-exempt status, and (3) a corporate tax return (which applies to all tax-exempt nonprofits).

Congress amended the tax code as part of the Omnibus Budget Reconciliation Act of 1987 (OBRA); here, Congress added the words "in opposition to" in order to clarify that the Johnson Amendment not only prohibited support for a candidate, but also prohibited opposition to a candidate. This reflected "a Congressional policy that the U.S. Treasury should be neutral in political affairs."[2]

The IRS has thus identified twenty-nine types of nonprofits that are exempt from paying state or federal taxes. For example, labor unions, teachers' pensions and civic leagues are tax-exempt, but *only* 501(c)(3)s have a two-part benefit: (1) they do not pay taxes themselves, and (2) individuals who donate money may then deduct these donations against their income taxes. Thus, like religious institutions, charities and private colleges and universities may not endorse or oppose individual political candidates.

The IRS is quite reluctant to define terms such as "religious institution" or even "religion," because if government surveillance of a church or charity requires it to begin an analysis of the sincerity of religious beliefs, the IRS could be at risk of violating the Establishment Clause.[3] Of course, there are exceptions; for example, after the September 11, 2001 terrorist attacks, the U.S. Treasury Department froze the assets of three Muslim charities after they were identified as "specially designated global terrorists" (SDGTs), and the IRS immediately revoked their tax-exempt status. The three Muslim charities were the Holy Land Foundation, Global Relief Foundation and Benevolence International Foundation.[4]

Is Tax-Exempt Status for Churches a Right or a Privilege?

In a few cases in which the IRS has revoked tax-exempt status for religious organizations or private Christian schools, the religious organizations or schools argued that they had a *right* to tax-exempt status, whereas the IRS argued that it was a *privilege*. The IRS further argued that they had forfeited this privilege as a result of racist admission policies (refusing to admit black students to a university) or as a result of overtly campaigning for or against a political candidate, thus violating the Johnson Amendment. The idea that placing conditions on receipt of government benefits differs from direct regulation can be traced to an early doctrine of constitutional law: the *rights-privilege distinction*.[5] Law school Dean Rodney Smolla has explained that under philosopher John Locke's social contract theory, a person possesses rights from birth, as entitlements of natural law, before a government is created.[6] The government may not curtail fundamental rights such as freedom of speech or freedom to practice one's religion unless the government can show that its restrictions will serve a *compelling* state purpose.

In contrast to rights, the government can create a *privilege* by its own grace, but this means that the government may set limits on citizens' enjoyment of a privilege. Smolla explains that "Privileges are not rights, but are rather public charity. . ..The [government] may attach whatever conditions [it] pleases to the gift."[7] In other words, if tax-exempt status is a privilege, then the IRS can apply the Johnson Amendment as a means of setting limits or conditions on receipt of the privilege.

Thus, our Founding Fathers viewed freedom of religion as a fundamental right, and the IRS later provided the *privilege* of tax-exempt status to religious organizations. At the same time, however, we need the equal protection of the laws that the Fourteenth Amendment guarantees in order to ensure that our tax money does not support religious leaders' electioneering or universities' exclusion of black students, as in the cases discussed below.

Background: Litigation Involving Churches and Universities

In reality, the IRS has seldom investigated or revoked the tax-exempt status of religious organizations or churches. The IRS challenged the Christian Echoes National Ministry, Bob Jones University, Goldsboro Christian Schools, Jimmy Swaggart, Jerry Falwell, Pat Roberton's Christian Coalition and Branch Ministries, however, following blatant "electioneering" by these individuals and their organizations; these cases are discussed below.

Christian Echoes National Ministry v. United States (1972)

Reverend Billy James Hargis incorporated the nonprofit Christian Echoes National Ministry in 1951 in Oklahoma with the purpose of establishing a weekend religious magazine and weekly radio and television broadcasts; in other words, Hargis was an early "televangelist." The IRS granted Christian

Echoes tax-exempt status as a religious organization under Section 501(c)(3) in 1953. From 1961 through 1966 Christian Echoes' revenues were nearly $1 million per year. Christian Echoes appealed to its readers and viewers to write their Congressmen to stop federal aid to education, health care and public housing, abolish the federal income tax, withdraw from the United Nations, and outlaw the Communist Party in the United States, for example.

In 1966, however, the IRS revoked Christian Echoes' tax-exempt status because it had intervened in political campaigns on behalf of candidates for public office. For example, Christian Echoes attacked John F. Kennedy in 1960 and Lyndon Johnson in 1964. At Christian Echoes' annual convention, they endorsed Barry Goldwater for President. When Christian Echoes filed suit against the IRS, a federal district court held that the organization's tax-exempt status should be reinstated, at which point the IRS appealed.

The U.S. Court of Appeals for the Tenth Circuit reminded Christian Echoes that tax-exempt status was a *privilege*, not a right.[8] The appellate court explained that the Johnson Amendment served "an overwhelming and compelling government interest: that of guaranteeing that the wall separating church and state remain high and firm."[9] The Tenth Circuit thus reversed the lower court decision and upheld the IRS' decision to revoke Christian Ministries' tax-exempt status.

Bob Jones University and Goldsboro Christian Schools v. United States (1983)

Bob Jones University identified itself as a Christian school in Greenville, South Carolina; the university required its teachers to be devout Christians. Bob Jones Sr. had founded the university in 1927, and as a non-profit, the IRS granted it tax-exempt status. It did not admit any black students. In 1970 the IRS notified Bob Jones University that colleges and universities that practiced racial discrimination would lose their tax-exempt status.

In 1971 Bob Jones University began admitting black students if they were married (provided their spouses were black) but still refused to admit unmarried black students. Beginning in 1975, Bob Jones University began admitting unmarried black students, but made the following policy announcement to its students:

> There is to be no interracial dating.
> Students who are partners in an interracial marriage will be expelled.
> Students who are members of any group which advocates interracial marriage will be expelled.
> Students who date outside of their own race will be expelled.[10]

Following six years of negotiations, the IRS revoked Bob Jones University's tax-exempt status in 1976 on grounds of racial discrimination, at which point the university filed suit against the IRS.

At the same time, the IRS had revoked the tax-exempt status of Goldsboro Christian Schools in Goldsboro, North Carolina, also on grounds of racial discrimination. Goldsboro Christian Schools admitted only white students. They rationalized this by arguing that all of mankind was descended from one of Noah's three sons. According to their beliefs, blacks and Asians were descended from Ham (Hamitic), Jews were descended from Shem (Shemitic), and Caucasians were descended from Japheth (Japhethitic). They taught that cultural mixing of the races would violate Biblical precepts.[11] When Goldsboro Christian Schools sued the IRS, their case was later combined with the Bob Jones lawsuit, and the U.S. Supreme Court decided both cases together.

In considering the two cases, the U.S. Supreme Court justices began by observing that: "The exemption from taxation of money or property devoted to charitable purposes is based upon the theory that the government is compensated for the loss of revenue by its relief from financial burdens which would otherwise have to be met by other public funds."[12] The U.S. Supreme Court approached tax-exempt status as a form of subsidy; in other words, "taxpayers [were] indirect and vicarious 'donors' to [Bob Jones University]."[13] Thus, taxpayers were indirectly contributing to segregation and discrimination against black students.

The justices also explained that the government had a compelling interest in eradicating racial discrimination. Furthermore, this interest substantially outweighed any burden that losing tax-exempt status would place on the schools' exercise of their religious beliefs. Because the IRS policy was neutral and applied equally to *all* private colleges and universities, it did not violate the Establishment Clause of the First Amendment.[14] Furthermore, the government had to ensure that black students would receive equal protection of the law under the Fourteenth Amendment when they applied to college.

Jimmy Swaggart, Jerry Falwell, and Pat Robertson

In addition to private universities such as Bob Jones, the IRS has also investigated religious organizations and "televangelists." In the 1980s, Jimmy Swaggart Ministries received $150 million a year in donations and the IRS had designated it as a tax-exempt organization. Swaggart endorsed Pat Robertson for President in 1988. Because Swaggart had campaigned for Robertson in 1985 and 1986, the IRS investigated and retroactively revoked the tax-exempt status for those two years; thus, the IRS assessed Jimmy Swaggart Ministries $171,122 in back taxes and interest for 1985 and 1986.[15]

Jerry Falwell's Old Time Gospel Hour received about $47 million per year in donations in 1986 and 1987, but the IRS revoked its tax-exempt status for those two years, and fined it $50,000 for violating the Johnson Amendment. The IRS' investigation showed that Old Time Gospel Hour personnel had been working to raise funds for the "I Love America" political action committee (PAC); this PAC had been working with Falwell's Moral Majority to support certain congressional candidates. The IRS also revoked the tax-exempt status of the Liberty Federation, another one of Falwell's organizations similar to the Moral Majority.[16]

In 1986, the Christian Broadcasting Network (CBN) supported Pat Robertson's campaign for President. The IRS began an investigation of CBN that lasted for twelve years; ultimately in 1998 the IRS revoked the tax-exempt status of Pat Robertson's Christian Broadcasting Network (CBN) and fined CBN for violating the Johnson Amendment because Pat Robertson had diverted CBN's funds to support his own campaign for President in 1986 and 1987.[17] The amount of money that CBN paid was kept confidential.[18]

In 1989, Pat Robertson's Christian Coalition had filed an application for tax-exempt status. Following a ten-year battle, however, in 1999 the IRS denied it tax-exempt status because the Christian Coalition had been asking evangelical ministers to distribute pro-Republican-candidate voter guides to their congregations. For example, the Christian Coalition had played a crucial role in the Republican take-over of the U.S. Senate and House of Representatives in 1994.[19]

Branch Ministries v. Rossotti (2000)

Pat Robertson's Christian Coalition was not the only evangelical group that opposed Presidential candidate Bill Clinton in the 1992 election. For example, Pastor Daniel Little of Branch Ministries ran the Church at Pierce Creek in Binghamton, New York. The IRS had granted the church tax-exempt status in 1983. In 1992, four days before the Presidential election, Little placed full-page ads in *USA Today* and the *Washington Times*. The ads carried the headline "Christians, Beware!" and warned readers not to vote for Bill Clinton because he was pro-choice, in favor of gay rights and in favor of sex education; Little's ad claimed that Clinton's positions on issues were a violation of Biblical precepts. At the bottom of the page, the ad asked readers to send donations to the Church at Pierce Creek. In response, the IRS opened a church tax inquiry; three years later in 1995, the IRS revoked the Church at Pierce Creek's tax-exempt status because it had violated the Johnson Amendment. Branch Ministries filed suit against the IRS, arguing that the IRS had no authority to revoke its tax exemption. A federal district court granted summary judgment in favor of the IRS, at which point Branch Ministries appealed.

The U.S. Court of Appeals for the District of Columbia Circuit noted that under the Church Audit Procedures Act (1983), the IRS had the authority to grant or revoke tax-exempt status for churches. As in the earlier *Christian Echoes* case, the appellate court reminded Branch Ministries that tax-exempt status is a *privilege*, not a right; by running the full-page newspaper ads against Bill Clinton, Branch Ministries had flouted the conditions of the privilege. The D.C. Circuit noted that the Church at Pierce Creek could form a related "social welfare" organization under Section 501(c)(4) of the tax code, and this organization could in turn form a political action committee (PAC) that could participate in political campaigns.[20] In other words, Branch Ministries could avoid any burden on its free exercise of religion by using other channels (a 501(c)(4) organization) for any political speech that Reverend Little thought was crucial to its faith.

Like 501(c)(3)s, 501(c)(4)s are nonprofits that are exempt from paying federal corporate income taxes, but 501(c)(4)s may legally engage in a greater degree of political activity. Donations to 501(c)(4)s, unlike 501(c)(3)s, however, are *not* tax-deductible as charitable contributions. Attorney Jonathan Backer explains the difference and provides examples: "Prominent 501(c)(4) organizations include the Sierra Club and NARAL Pro-Choice America on the left and the National Rifle Association and the Koch brothers' Americans for Prosperity on the right."[21] The D.C. Circuit emphasized that federal campaign finance law allows 501(c)(4)s to operate PACs that solicit and distribute contributions to political candidates. After clarifying that Branch Ministries could set up a 501(c)(4) that could legally support candidates of Reverend Little's choice, the D.C. Circuit affirmed the lower court's decision that the IRS had been correct in revoking the Church at Pierce Creek's tax-exempt status.

IRS Investigation of Left-Leaning Churches

Although the IRS actions discussed above are about the evangelical "Christian right," the IRS has also issued warnings to churches that leaned politically to the left. For example, two days before the November 2004 presidential election, Nobel Peace Prize winner Archbishop Desmond Tutu was a co-celebrant at a service of the All Saints Episcopal Church in Pasadena,

California. Although Archbishop Tutu did not mention politics at all, Reverend George Regas gave a guest sermon in which he commented that George W. Bush's favorable attitude toward testing and using nuclear weapons would make Jesus very sad. Regas added:

> President [George W.] Bush has led us into war with Iraq as a response to terrorism. Yet I believe Jesus would say to [George W.] Bush and [John] Kerry, "War is itself the most extreme form of terrorism. President Bush, you have not [conveyed to the American people] the human consequences of the war in Iraq." Jesus would say, "The sin at the heart of this war against Iraq is your belief that an American life is of more value than an Iraqi life—that an American child is more precious than an Iraqi baby. . . .but God loathes war." Jesus would have said to Bush, "Mr. President, your doctrine of pre-emptive war is a failed doctrine. Forcibly changing the regime of an enemy that posed no imminent threat has led to disaster."[22]

Seven months after Regas gave this sermon, the IRS sent All Saints a letter advising them that they might not be tax-exempt as a church. In response, All Saints' tax attorney Marcus Owens wrote to the IRS saying: "It seems ludicrous to suggest that a pastor cannot preach about the value of promoting peace simply because the nation happens to be at war during an election season.[23]" Following two years of negotiations, in 2007 the IRS dropped its investigation of All Saints with the explanation that Regas' sermon was a "one-time occurrence;" furthermore, the IRS seemed to be satisfied that the church had put "policies in place to ensure that [All Saints] complies with the prohibition against intervention in campaigns for public office."[24]

Pulpit Freedom Sunday

On September 28, 2008, 33 ministers across the United States gave sermons that made specific recommendations about which political candidates their congregations should vote for. The Alliance Defense Fund (ADF) sponsored this event, called "Pulpit Freedom Sunday," as a direct constitutional challenge to the Johnson Amendment. The participating ministers videotaped their sermons and sent them to the IRS. After receiving the videotaped sermons, the IRS launched an investigation into a mega-church called the Living Word Christian Center in Brooklyn Park, Minnesota, after its minister James Hammond spoke from the pulpit to endorse Michele Bachmann for Congress.[25] The IRS also launched an investigation into Warroad Community Church in Warroad, Minnesota, after its minister Gus Booth had endorsed John McCain from the pulpit; Booth told his congregation that John McCain's positions on issues were more in line with Biblical principles than were Barack Obama's positions on issues.[26] However, the IRS later dropped both investigations.[27]

Since 2008, more than 3800 ministers have participated in Pulpit Freedom Sunday each year on a designated Sunday in September; except for the investigations into the Warroad Community Church and the Living Word Christian Center, the IRS has declined to investigate any of the participants.

Attempts to Repeal the Johnson Amendment

In 2001, U.S. Representative Walter Jones of North Carolina introduced the Houses of Worship Political Speech Protection Act (H.R. 2357), which would have repealed the Johnson Amendment, but it did not pass. Jones later introduced the Houses of Worship Free Speech Restoration Act of 2005, but it did not pass. Jones introduced a similar bill in 2007, but his bill never made it out of the Ways and Means Committee.

Nearly a decade after Jones had tried to repeal the Johnson Amendment, when Donald Trump was running for President, he spoke in a closed-door meeting to more than 50 evangelical Christian ministers and two rabbis on June 21, 2016. President Trump later recounted what he had said at the meeting:

> Why is it that the whole thing with Christianity, it's not going in the right direction? It's getting weaker, weaker, weaker from a societal standpoint? And I realized that there are petrified ministers and churches. . . . When it comes to talking about it openly or who [sic] they support or why they support somebody because he's a person who shares their values, they're petrified to do it. And I couldn't get the answer. . . .And then one day, somebody said, "They're petrified of losing their tax-exempt status." And I said, "What is that all about?" And they said it was [the Johnson Amendment.] And we are going to get rid of that, because you should have the right to speak. If we don't [get rid of the Johnson Amendment], you're going to have a continuing downward spiral. And I don't want to see that, because I've been a Christian and I love Christianity. And the evangelicals have been so incredibly supportive.[28]

When Trump introduced Mike Pence as his running mate on July 16, 2016, he also singled out evangelicals as the beneficiaries of his attack on the Johnson Amendment:

> And what we're doing—and what we're doing that I'm so proud of, so proud—and nobody else would even think about doing it— I fought very hard for it. We'll call it the Johnson Amendment, where he took away from the evangelicals—and I want to thank the evangelicals, because without the evangelicals, I could not have won this nomination. The evangelicals have been unbelievable. I dominated with the evangelicals. . . .And I said—and I said for the evangelicals,

> that we're going to do something that nobody's even tried to do. You have the Johnson Amendment, where you are just absolutely shunned if you're evangelical; if you want to talk religion, you lose your tax-exempt status. We put into the platform, that we're going to get rid of that horrible Johnson Amendment.[29]

After becoming President, Trump signed an Executive Order, "Promoting Free Speech and Religious Liberty" on May 4, 2017, during a National Day of Prayer ceremony in the Rose Garden before an evangelical Christian audience. President Trump (falsely) claimed that this order repealed the Johnson Amendment. He said: "This Executive Order directs the IRS not to unfairly target churches and religious organizations for political speech. No one should be censoring sermons or targeting pastors. In America, we do not fear people speaking freely from the pulpit; we embrace it." President Trump told the ministers that their churches would not lose their tax exemption for violating the Johnson Amendment; henceforth, they could say whatever they wanted: "This financial threat against the faith community is over. You're now in a position where you can say what you want to say."[30]

In response to President Trump's executive order, the Freedom from Religion Foundation (FFRF) filed suit against President Trump, arguing that he had no authority to veto a statute that Congress had passed and President Dwight Eisenhower had signed into law in 1954. Furthermore, FFRF argued that President Trump's Executive Order was unfairly favoring churches and religious organizations over secular non-profit charities; in other words, ministers would be free to tell their congregations whom to vote for, but secular non-profits could not do this. In its Complaint, FFRF argued that President Trump's Executive Order was "also intended to favor Christianity as the majority religion over other religions and evangelical Christianity as a voting bloc President Trump depended on over other Christian denominations."[31] In its Complaint, FFRF further argued that President Trump's "intended policy of selective non-enforcement of electioneering restrictions against churches and other religious organizations has the effect of converting these organizations into unregulated political action committees (PACs), effectively excluding billions of dollars from taxation each year."[32] FFRF concluded its Complaint by emphasizing that President Trump's Executive Order violated the Establishment Clause by giving preferential treatment to churches over secular non-profits; thus FFRF asked the court for a declaratory judgment that the executive order was unconstitutional.[33]

In July 2017, the (then) Republican-controlled House of Representatives voted 217–199 (along party lines) to pass the Free Speech Fairness Act, which directed the IRS not to revoke the tax-exempt status of churches that participate in political campaigns. The National Council of Nonprofits, a network of more than 25,000 nonprofit organizations, tried to persuade Congressmen not to include the Free Speech Fairness Act as a rider in a tax bill, but it still passed. Tim Delaney, director of the National Council of Nonprofits objected, saying: "It's now impossible for Congress and the White House to deny their objective: to politicize the trusted charitable nonprofit community by authorizing unlimited and untraceable political money to flow through the nonprofit sector to benefit partisan special interests. Charitable nonprofits are not in the business of partisan politics and are not here to be used to hide or launder political money."[34] Karen Gano, President of the Board of Directors of the National Association of State Charity Officials (NASCO), which represents 99 religious organizations and more than 5,800 charities, also sent a letter to Mitch McConnell, Paul Ryan, Chuck Schumer, Nancy Pelosi and other Congressional leaders. Gano urged them to protect the Johnson Amendment from repeal; she also cautioned them not to exploit religious and charitable organizations as "another cog in a political machine or another loophole in campaign finance laws."[35]

To echo the words of Tim Delaney and Karen Gano, many nonprofits raised concerns that repealing the Johnson Amendment would create a new dark money channel for powerful donors to funnel their money to political candidates. Indeed, "the Joint Committee on Taxation (Congress's official scorekeepers) estimated that the repeal of the Johnson Amendment would cost the government $1 billion in the first few years as the rich donated more money to religious institutions and nonprofits and got tax write-offs for doing so."[36] The Joint Committee on Taxation also estimated that repealing the Johnson Amendment would cost $2.8 billion in revenue from 2018 to 2027 (Joint Committee, 2017).

However, the corresponding tax bill in the U.S. Senate did not include the Free Speech Fairness Act. Thus in reconciling the House and Senate versions of the bill, the Senate parliamentarian deleted the Free Speech Fairness Act from the tax bill in December 2017.[37]

Arguments in Favor of Repealing the Johnson Amendment

A number of legal scholars such as Shawn Voyles, Erik Stanley and David Abbondanza have argued that Congress should repeal the Johnson Amendment on the grounds that it violates the Establishment Clause. For example, former Regent University law professor Shawn Voyles has argued that churches should be free to favor or oppose political candidates without suffering the cost of taxation. Voyles observes that from an historical standpoint, churches

> brought an end to the practice of dueling by getting prohibitions against it written into [state] constitutions....Churches were active in the effort to abolish slavery. Churches pressed for laws against gambling, prostitution and child labor. They have worked for laws advancing organized labor, women's suffrage, civil rights and family welfare.[38]

Voyles' arguments are noteworthy, but of course we must also acknowledge that churches in the South used the Bible to rationalize slavery before the Civil War, and hundreds of ministers spoke from the pulpit to oppose women's suffrage in the 1800s; in other words, church leaders have not been monolithic in leading us toward equal protection of the laws.

Attorney Erik Stanley, who represents the Alliance Defense Fund, the organization that supports Pulpit Freedom Sunday, argues that the IRS has nearly always targeted conservative Christians rather than liberal Christians in its investigations. Stanley points to Reverend Jesse Jackson's 1984 Presidential campaign:

> Going beyond simply asking ministers to endorse his campaign, Reverend Jackson called upon churches to coordinate major campaign fundraising efforts. The Jackson campaign distributed flyers and encouraged church members to bring donations for Jackson's campaign to church. Campaign offerings were then collected separately from regular church donations by many churches. [But] the IRS chose not to investigate this potential violation of the Johnson Amendment.[39]

Stanley likewise notes that when Barack Obama ran for President in 2008, Obama's minister Reverend Jeremiah Wright spoke from the pulpit in favor of Obama rather than Hillary Clinton during the Democratic primary.[40]

Stanley further argues that the U.S. Supreme Court's decision in *Citizens United v. Federal Election Commission* (2010), holding that corporations have a First Amendment right to contribute money to political candidates, creates a precedent suggesting that the Johnson Amendment should be repealed; in other words, if corporations have the right to give financial support to political candidates of their choice, then churches should have this right as well.[41] In *Citizens United,* the High Court made clear that corporations do not need to establish a 501(c)(4) organization through which to fund political candidates; rather, "a corporation may speak for itself without being forced to set up a [501(c)(4)] that requires a series of burdensome and time-consuming regulations."[42] Stanley applies the High Court's reasoning in *Citizens United* to the Johnson Amendment:

> A Section 501(c)(3) nonprofit corporation cannot be expected to give up its favorable tax treatment in order to exercise its First Amendment rights. Stated

> differently, Congress cannot condition the exercise of First Amendment rights on the surrender of tax-exempt status or benefits. Doing so runs afoul of *Citizens United*.[43]

Erik Stanley's argument in favor of applying the *Citizens United* precedent to the Johnson Amendment has indeed alarmed those who still support the Johnson Amendment.

Like Shawn Voyle and Erik Stanley, attorney David Abbondanza argues that Congress should repeal the Johnson Amendment because it discriminates against ministers based solely on the content of their speech; in other words, a content-based restriction on speech would violate the First Amendment. Abbondanza further argues that the Johnson Amendment places an "unconstitutional condition" on the church's tax-exempt status.[44]

The unconstitutional conditions doctrine holds that the government may not penalize an individual (or a church) for the exercise of a constitutional right. Furthermore, the government may not condition the availability of a government benefit on an individual's (or a church's) agreement to waive such a right. The U.S. Supreme Court outlined the concept of "unconstitutional conditions" when it held that school administrators could not refuse to renew a teacher's contract after the teacher made statements they disagreed with:

> [The government] may not deny a benefit to a person on a basis that infringes upon his constitutionally protected interest—especially, his interest in freedom of speech. For if the government could deny a benefit to a person because of his constitutionally protected speech or associations, his exercise of those freedoms would in effect be penalized.[45]

Despite the High Court's willingness to grant the teacher Robert Sindermann equal protection of the law, the "unconstitutional conditions doctrine" has a long and convoluted history, with ambiguous and inconsistent results. An example of the confusion surrounding this doctrine is the U.S. Supreme Court's decision in *Rust v. Sullivan*. In *Rust,* Justice William Rehnquist, writing for the majority, held that the government could prohibit Title X (family planning) clinics that received government funding from providing abortion counseling; in other words, if the government provided the funds, it could set limits or conditions on the speech of the doctors and nurses who staffed family planning clinics (he who pays the piper calls the tune). The High Court acknowledged that the unconstitutional conditions doctrine represented a "troubled area of our jurisprudence."[46] Former Stanford Law School Dean Kathleen Sullivan described the unconstitutional conditions doctrine as "a minefield to be traversed gingerly."[47]

Legal scholars Mark Goldfeder and Michelle Terry acknowledge Abbondanza's argument that the Johnson Amendment might create an "unconstitutional condition," in the sense that the IRS is granting the privilege of tax-exempt status only to those who give up the right of free speech,[48] but they also note the opposing arguments:

> Religious organizations [or any 501(c)(3) charity] can set aside the tax exemption and conduct business as usual, but [tax-exempt status] is only available when organizations shoulder the burden [of refraining from electioneering, as the Johnson Amendment requires]. The case law is simply unclear [on unconstitutional conditions], so resolution must come from somewhere else.[49]

Goldfeder and Terry also note that the Johnson Amendment has survived all constitutional challenges; furthermore, courts have always upheld it, as in *Christian Echoes, Bob Jones University,* and *Branch Ministries,* discussed above.[50]

Arguments for Keeping the Johnson Amendment

In 2010 in *Citizens United,* the U.S. Supreme Court held that corporations may intervene in political campaigns by contributing funds to and endorsing candidates.[51] A few years later, the High Court held that the Religious Freedom Restoration Act (RFRA) exempted closely held corporations from the Affordable Care Act's (ACA's) contraceptive mandate in *Burwell v. Hobby Lobby Stores* (2014).[52] In *Hobby Lobby,* the justices accorded great deference to the family owners of Hobby Lobby and their argument that the ACA placed too great a burden on their religious beliefs and practice by mandating that employers' health insurance coverage mandated certain types of contraceptive devices.

Attorney Jonathan Backer argues, however, that despite *Citizens United* and *Hobby Lobby,* the Johnson Amendment can survive a challenge under the Religious Freedom Restoration Act because of its key role in preventing entanglement between government and religion:

> The [Johnson Amendment] holds at bay intrusive IRS inquiry into religious... activity that would accompany engagement in partisan politics. Because the electioneering prohibition is narrowly tailored to the compelling state interest in ensuring separation between church and state, the [Johnson Amendment] can and should survive RFRA review despite the sweeping changes ushered in by *Hobby Lobby* and *Citizens United.*[53]

Backer also notes that there is no "non-invasive means for the [IRS] to permit religious organizations to electioneer while ensuring that political activity does not overtake religious activity that the [IRS] had wished to [encourage] by granting tax-exempt status."[54]

Citizens United, the Johnson Amendment and Concerns about Dark Money

Jonathan Backer explains that one outcome of the U.S. Supreme Court's *Citizens United* decision was the creation of larger political action committees known as super PACs. Super PACs may solicit unlimited funds and spend unlimited amounts of money on campaign advertising, provided that they do not directly contribute to or coordinate their efforts with individual candidates. [*Citizens United*] also enabled politically oriented 501(c)(4) organizations, known colloquially as "dark money" groups, to spend unlimited amounts of money while shielding the names of their donors.[55]

Backer cautions that without the Johnson Amendment, "groups claiming to be houses of worship could sprout up during an election season and solicit unrestricted tax-deductible contributions from the public to spend in unlimited amounts, supporting or opposing candidates for political office."[56] Backer refers to such hypothetical organizations as "God PACs," warning that they could make it even easier for a few wealthy donors to bankroll elections via such "God PACs" seeking to change the landscape of American politics.[57]

Goldfeder and Terry agree with Backer, explaining that if Congress repeals the Johnson Amendment, then Section 501(c)(3) organizations could receive tax-deductible donations, and donors would be completely shielded from disclosure of political donations, which would hinder transparency. "Donors could deduct contributions from their annual income, which creates an incentive for people to switch from giving money to super PACs (which are required to identify their donors) to 501(c)(3)s."[58]

Law professor Ellen Aprill likewise echoes these warnings about dark money and super PACs:

> Contributions to 501(c)(3) charities are deductible; contributions to PACs and non-charitable section 501(c)(4) organizations are not. [If the Johnson Amendment is repealed], many who wish to intervene in political campaigns will shift their contribution from PACs and [501(c)(4) organizations] to charities. Under our current campaign finance regime, only dollars that have been taxed can be used for political intervention.[59]

Aprill is thus drawing our attention to subtleties in our tax code that the general public may not be aware of: if we donate to religious organizations and receive a tax deduction, this is *before* we have paid taxes on this income, whereas if we donate to a political action committee, this is *after* the IRS has determined our tax liability.

Like Ellen Aprill, attorney Whitney Untiedt also warns that repealing the Johnson Amendment would exacerbate the dangers of "dark money" in politics:

> To claim that religious leaders are hamstrung by the Johnson Amendment is at best misinformed and at worst, disingenuous. Though no proponent of repeal [of the Johnson Amendment] has publicly acknowledged it as such, it certainly appears likely that at least one driving force behind the effort is to create a scheme in which unregulated "dark money" contributions to candidates and PACs can be funneled through 501(c)(3) organizations that offer tax deductions to donors. In effect, the existence of tax-deductible political donations would place the ultimate burden for financing campaigns on taxpayers themselves, to the tune of an estimated $2.1 billion in lost revenue.[60]

If taxpayers are forced to assume the burden of financing political campaigns as Whitney Untiedt suggests could happen, taxpayers would lose equal protection of the law in the sense that their hard-earned tax dollars could be used to pay for politicians whose messages are offensive or even abhorrent to them.

Backer, Aprill, Untiedt, Goldfeder and Terry thus agree that by keeping the Johnson Amendment, the IRS is guarding against "dark money" in politics. The IRS is also pursuing the compelling interest of preventing government subsidies of partisan political activity.

As an antidote to "dark money," Ellen Aprill argues that the Democracy Is Strengthened by Casting Light On Spending in Elections (DISCLOSE) Act should apply not only to PACs and 501(c)(4) organizations but to Section 501(c)(3) organizations as well, including churches. U.S. Congressman David Cicilline (D-Rhode Island) introduced the DISCLOSE Act of 2019 (H.R. 2977) that would

1. Require corporations to report campaign expenditures of $10,000 or more to the Federal Election Commission (FEC) within twenty-four hours and to disclose all campaign-related expenditures to their shareholders
2. Strengthen the ban on foreign money in political campaigns
3. Create a "stand-by-your-ad" so that PACs that are funding a political commercial must state that they "approve this message."[61]

Although the House of Representatives has passed the DISCLOSE Act, Senate Majority Mitch McConnell has refused to bring it to the floor of the Senate; thus, it has not become law.

Since the DISCLOSE Act has not passed, Whitney Untiedt urges that Congress must keep the Johnson Amendment in place; she explains that the real purpose of the Johnson Amendment is *not* to limit the free exercise of speech or religion, but merely to

> require non-profit organizations to pay for [exercising freedom of speech or religion] out of their own pockets, as everyone else is required to do under the provisions of the Internal Revenue Code.[62]

The problem of tracking "dark money" is complicated further by the fact that many Fortune 500 companies "quietly fund political efforts that are antithetical to their public stances."[63] For example, AT&T pays lip service to LBGTQ rights, but quietly funded the campaign of former North Carolina governor Pat McCrory, who signed the infamous "bathroom bill," which required transgender people to use public bathrooms corresponding to the gender on their birth certificates. Companies such as Google, AT&T, Sony, and Target, which claim to support Black Lives Matter, have PACs that directly donated to the election campaign of former Senator Kelly Loeffler of Georgia, who said she was "adamantly opposed" to Black Lives Matter.[64]

With the difficulty of tracking "dark money," Untiedt further warns that repealing the Johnson Amendment could cause trust in our system of government to be eroded beyond repair if politically-motivated donors are allowed to claim tax deductions for campaign and PAC contributions:

> Nonprofits may be forced to re-direct significant funds from mission-driven purposes to political spending in order to retain the favor of lawmakers. Do we want an America where Habitat for Humanity builds homes for low-income families, or builds a war chest for presidential campaigns?....Common sense [suggests that we] accept the Johnson Amendment's reasonable restrictions on the use of tax-deductible donations--and deregulation is a dangerous proposition indeed.[65]

An example of a 501(c)(3) organization that became politicized occurred in 2012 when Karen Handel became the new chief executive officer of the Susan G. Komen Breast Cancer Foundation. Handel opposed reproductive choice and announced that the Susan G. Komen Foundation would no longer contribute any of its funds to Planned Parenthood to pay for women's mammograms. Several top-level staff members resigned in protest, and public outrage at Handel's decision was so vehement that the Susan G. Komen Foundation's Board of Directors reversed the decision four days later. But contributions to the Susan G. Komen Foundation declined by 22% in 2013;[66] hundreds of women notified the Susan G. Komen Foundation that they would contribute directly to Planned Parenthood instead.

Discussion

As is the case in many legal tugs-of-war, there are valid arguments on both sides of the question of whether or not Congress should repeal the Johnson Amendment. Looking back over the past two centuries, we certainly would have wanted ministers and their congregations to end dueling, gambling, and child labor. We would also have wanted churches to fight for organized labor, women's suffrage, and civil rights. Of course, one might argue that if "the arc of the moral universe is long, but it bends toward justice" (as Reverend Dr. Martin Luther King had said), we would hope that churches would have fought for these causes whether or not the IRS granted them tax-exempt status because it was the right thing to do. As was mentioned above, however, the Establishment Clause does not create a monolith in which all ministers agree on what is morally "right." Before the Civil War, southern preachers were seldom abolitionists.

Legal scholars such as Shawn Voyles, Erik Stanley and David Abbondanza appear to assume that tax-exempt status for churches is a *right,* whereas the IRS and the U.S. Supreme Court appear to view tax-exempt status as a *privilege* that private universities or religious organizations must forfeit if they maintain racist admissions policies or engage in political campaigns. Voyles, Stanley and Abbondanza argue that Congress should repeal the Johnson Amendment because they view it as a violation of the Establishment Clause.

In contrast, legal scholars such as Jonathan Backer, Ellen Aprill, Whitney Untiedt, Mark Goldfeder and Michelle Terry argue that Congress should keep the Johnson Amendment intact because it comprises one of the last lines of defense against "dark money" in political campaigns. If Congress should in fact repeal the Johnson Amendment, the effect would be that many people who wish to contribute to political campaigns will shift their contributions from political action committees (PACs) to churches and charities in order to take advantage of the tax deduction. In other words, if 501(c)(3)s can support or oppose political candidates, donors will be tempted to donate to 501(c)(3)s rather than 501(c)(4)s. This is because contributions to the former are tax-deductible, whereas contributions to 501(c)(4)s (such as the National Rifle Association on the right or the Brady Campaign to Prevent Gun Violence on the left) are not tax-deductible. This is an argument that should command our attention.

One provision of the Tax Cuts and Jobs Act (TCJA) that Congress passed in 2017 was to double the standard deduction. Taxpayers can still itemize their deductions if they want to, but there is less incentive to do so now that standard deductions are higher. Whereas about 30% of taxpayers had itemized their deductions before the TCJA doubled the standard deduction, only about 10% of taxpayers now itemize their deductions.[67] In 2017, leaders of 501(c)(3) organizations expressed the fear that fewer people would donate to charities as a means of getting a tax deduction. They were correct: taxpayers itemized $54 billion less in charitable contributions in 2018 than they had in 2017.[68]

To complicate matters further, in June 2020 the U.S. Supreme Court, reversing a Montana Supreme Court decision, held that states must allow religious schools to participate in programs that provide scholarships to students attending private schools.[69] The *Espinoza* decision opens the door to more public funding of religious education. Former Education Secretary Betsy DeVos explained that now "families can use taxpayer funds to choose [private schools]. . .including faith-based schools."[70] Randi Weingarten, President of the American Federation of Teachers (AFT), said she feared that the High Court's ruling would be used "to defund and dismantle public education."[71]

In April 2020, Congress also allocated $350 billion for the Paycheck Protection Program (PPP) as part of the $2 trillion Coronavirus Aid, Relief and Economic Security (CARES) Act that it passed. The U.S. Small Business Administration (SBA) has designated churches and other religious organizations as "businesses." This means that they may receive SBA loans whether or not they provide secular social services.[72] Under the Paycheck Protection Program, businesses with fewer than 500 employees, including faith-based organizations, are eligible to receive loans of up to $10 million. The loans are in large part forgivable, so churches and other houses of worship will not be required to pay all the money back.[73] Despite the SBA's rule that would disqualify applicants with more than 500 employees, the SBA gave between $1.4 billion and $3.5 billion to the Roman Catholic Church because its lobbyists, along with other religious groups, persuaded the Trump administration to grant them "special dispensation," despite the fact that the number of their employees exceeded the 500-person cap.[74] Loan recipients included about forty Catholic dioceses that had spent hundreds of millions of dollars compensating victims of pedophile priests.[75] University of Pennsylvania law professor Marci Hamilton observed that the SBA's special consideration for Catholic, Protestant and Jewish groups has further eroded the wall between church and state: "With that erosion, religious groups that don't pay taxes have gained more access to public money."[76] Law professors Nelson Tebbe,

Micah Schwartzman and Richard Schragger have commented that the SBA's use of taxpayer money to pay for clergy salaries is something that once would have been unthinkable:

> As applied, the [Paycheck Protection Program] explicitly extends to nonprofits, including churches--with no restrictions on payment of clergy salaries. Although the aid initially takes the form of a loan, it is largely forgivable if the recipient maintains its payroll size for a sufficient period. . . .The Paycheck Protection Program violates the constitutional rule requiring the separation of church and state, and it does so on an enormous scale. . . .We are witnessing an important moment in the nation's constitutional history: the quiet demise of the already ailing separation of church and state.[77]

Legal and Policy Vice-President of the American Atheists Alison Gill has objected to the SBA's decision to include churches and other religious organizations as businesses:

> [The government] cannot spend tax dollars on prayer, on promoting religion or proselytization. That directly contradicts the Establishment Clause of the First Amendment. This is the most drastic attack on church-state separation we have ever seen.[78]

In addition to the American Atheists, other critics have charged that for the SBA to treat churches and other religious organizations as "businesses" represented a major policy change in which the Trump administration appeared to be flouting the "wall of separation" of church and state that Thomas Jefferson had called for. The Small Business Administration is thus further eroding the "wall of separation" between church and state. In doing so, it weakens the Establishment Clause by unduly favoring churches and religious organizations over atheists or agnostics, for example. Because tax money from atheists or agnostics is supporting religious organizations via the PPP, those who are not members of churches or other houses of worship are not receiving equal protection of the laws.

Taking in the larger picture, one sees that in the U.S. Supreme Court's June 2020 *Espinoza* decision, the majority approved diverting taxpayer money to religious schools in Montana. The Small Business Administration's Paycheck Protection Program blurs Thomas Jefferson's "wall of separation" between church and state. Add to this the point that legal scholars Backer, Aprill, Untiedt, Goldfeder and Terry make to the effect that the Johnson Amendment is one of our last lines of defense against "dark money" in political campaigns.

After Joe Biden won the November 2020 election, the group Americans United for Separation of Church and State called on President Biden to shore up the wall of separation and to protect and enforce the Johnson Amendment. It appears that under the Biden administration, Congress will indeed keep the Johnson Amendment intact, and our democracy will be better served. We must not allow the "wall of separation" to come a' tumblin' down.

Notes

1 The author would like to acknowledge the assistance of University of Delaware graduate student Steve Waldorf in gathering background information for this manuscript.
2 Omnibus Budget Reconciliation Act, H.R. Rep. No. 100–391 (II), 100th Congress, 1st Session, Part 2 at 1625 (1987).
3 Bruce R. Hopkins, *The Law of Tax-Exempt Organizations* (11th ed.). (Hoboken, New Jersey: John Wiley & Sons, 2018), 300.
4 Malick W. Ghachem, "Of 'Scalpels' and 'Sledgehammers:' Religious Liberty and the Policing of Muslim Charities in Britain and American since 9/11." 9 *University of California at Los Angeles Journal of Islamic & Near Eastern Law* 25, no. 27 (2009–2010).
5 William W. van Alstyne, "The Demise of the Right-Privilege Distinction in Constitutional Law." *Harvard Law Review* 81 (1968): 1439.
6 Rodney A. Smolla, *Free Speech in an Open Society* (New York: Alfred A. Knopf, 1992), 178.
7 Ibid., 179.
8 *Christian Echoes National Ministry v. United States,* 470 F. 2d 849, 857 (10th Cir. 1972).
9 Idem.
10 *Bob Jones University v. United States,* 461 U.S. 574, 580–81 (1983).
11 Ibid., Note 6 (1983).
12 Ibid., 590 (1983).
13 Ibid., 591.
14 Ibid., Note 30.
15 David E. Anderson, "Jerry Falwell's Ministry Fined for Taking Role in Politics." *Washington Post,* April 10, 1993. Retrieved May 20, 2020 from https://www.washingtonpost.com/archive/local/1993/04/10/jerry-falwells-ministry-fined-for-taking-role-in-politics/ce8c87b3-0740-4b1b-a691-df39e73064fb/
16 Idem.
17 Robert Boston, *Why the Religious Right Is Wrong about Separation of Church and State* (Amherst, New York: Prometheus Books, 2003), 198.
18 "Robertson's Network Settles IRS Dispute." *Los Angeles Times,* March 21, 1988. Retrieved May 20, 2020 from https://www.latimes.com/archives/la-xpm-1998-mar-21-me-31250-story.html
19 Thomas B. Edsall and Hanna Rosin, "IRS Denies Christian Coalition Tax-Exempt Status." *Washington Post* (June 11, 1999): A4.
20 *Branch Ministries v. Rossotti,* 211 F. 3d 137, 143 (D.C. Cir. 2000).
21 Jonathan Backer, "Thou Shalt Not Electioneer: Religious Nonprofit Political Activity and the Threat 'God PACs' Pose to Democracy and Religion," 114 *Michigan Law Review* 619, 631 (February 2016).

22 Patricia Ward Biederman and Jason Felch. "Anti-War Sermon Brings IRS Warning." *Los Angeles Times*, November 7, 2005. Retrieved May 20, 2020 from https://www.latimes.com/archives/la-xpm-2005-nov-07-me-allsaints7-story.html
23 Idem.
24 Paul Caron, "IRS Drops Investigation into Church's Anti-War Sermon; Church Demands Investigation of IRS and Apology." TaxProf Blog, September 24, 2007. Retrieved May 20, 2020 from https://taxprof.typepad.com/taxprof_blog/2007/09/irs-drops-inves.html
25 Nanette Byrnes, "Hundreds of Pastors Back Political Candidates; Defy Tax Rules." Reuters, October 7, 2012. Retrieved May 20, 2020 from https://www.reuters.com/article/us-usa-tax-pulpit/hundreds-of-pastors-back-political-candidates-defy-tax-rules-idUSBRE89700E20121008
26 Paul Walsh, "Warroad Pastor's IRS Case Closed, for Now," *Minneapolis Star Tribune*, July 29, 2009. Retrieved May 20, 2020 from http://www.startribune.com/warroad-pastor-s-irs-case-closed-for-now/52000717/?c=y&page=all&prepage=2#continue
27 Idem.
28 *Freedom from Religion Foundation v. Donald Trump*, Complaint for Declaratory and Injunctive Relief at 9, No. 17-CV-330 (U.S. District Court for the Western District of Wisconsin, filed May 4, 2017).
29 Ibid., 10.
30 Ibid., 2.
31 Ibid., 16–17.
32 Ibid., 18.
33 Ibid., 19.
34 Jacqueline Thomsen, "House Passes Measure Blocking IRS from Revoking Churches' Tax-Exempt Status over Political Activity." *The Hill*, July 19, 2018. Retrieved May 21, 2020 from https://thehill.com/policy/finance/domestic-taxes/397996-house-passes-measure-blocking-irs-from-revoking-churches-tax
35 Karen Gano, Letter from National Association of State Charity Officials to Congressional leaders, August 23, 2017. Retrieved May 21, 2020 from http://www.nonprofitlawblog.com/assets/NASCO-Letter-to-Congressional-Leaders-re-Johnson-Amendment-8.23.2017.pdf
36 Heather Long, "In Small Win for Democrats, Final Tax Bill Won't Include Provision to Allow Churches to Endorse Political Candidates." *Salt Lake Tribune*, December 15, 2017. Retrieved May 21, 2020 from https://www.sltrib.com/news/nation-world/2017/12/15/in-small-win-for-democrats-final-tax-bill-wont-include-provision-to-allow-churches-to-endorse-political-candidates/
37 Idem.
38 Shawn A. Voyles, "Choosing between Tax-Exempt Status and Freedom of Religion: the Dilemma Facing Politically-Active Churches." 9 *Regent University Law Review* 219, 226 (Fall 1997).
39 Erik W. Stanley, "A Survey of Religious Freedom for Individuals and Faith-Based Institutions: LBJ, the IRS, and Churches: The Unconstitutionality of the Johnson Amendment in Light of Recent Supreme Court Precedent." 24 *Regent University Law Review* 237, 257–258 (2011–2012).
40 Ibid., 257.

41 Ibid., 270.
42 Ibid., 272.
43 Ibid., 274.
44 David Abbondanza, "The Pulpit Initiative: Fighting to Return America's First Freedom to Her Churches." *Richmond Public Interest Law Review 12:3:*225–242, 235 (January 1, 2009).
45 *Perry v. Sindermann,* 408 U.S. 593, 597 (1972).
46 *Rust v. Sullivan,* 111 S.Ct. 1759, 1779 (1991).
47 Sullivan, Kathleen. "Unconstitutional Conditions." 102 *Harvard Law Review* 1413, 1415–16 (1989).
48 Mark A. Goldfeder and Michelle K. Terry. "To Repeal or Not Repeal: The Johnson Amendment." 48 *University of Memphis Law Review* 209, 234 (Fall 2017).
49 Ibid., 250.
50 Ibid., 238.
51 *Citizens United v. Federal Election Commission,* 558 U.S. 310 (2010).
52 *Burwell v. Hobby Lobby Stores, Inc.* 573 U.S. 682 (2014).
53 Jonathan Backer, "Thou Shalt Not Electioneer: Religious Nonprofit Political Activity and the Threat `God PACs' Pose to Democracy and Religion," 114 *Michigan Law Review* 619, 648 (February 2016).
54 Ibid., 647.
55 Ibid., 626.
56 Ibid., 628.
57 Idem.
58 Mark A. Goldfeder and Michelle K. Terry. "To Repeal or Not Repeal: The Johnson Amendment." 48 *University of Memphis Law Review* 209, 252 (Fall 2017).
59 Ellen Aprill, "Amending the Johnson Amendment in the Age of Cheap Speech." 2018 *University of Illinois Law Review Online* 1, 17 (Spring 2018).
60 Whitney Untiedt, "Lighting the Way: The Johnson Amendment Stands Strong against Dark Money in Politics." 6 *Emory Corporate Governance Accountability Review* 37, 42 (2019).
61 David Cicilline, "Cicilline Re-Introduces DISCLOSE Act." May 23, 2019. Retrieved May 23, 2020 from https://cicilline.house.gov/press-release/cicilline-re-introduces-disclose-act
62 Untiedt, 43.
63 Andrew Ross Sorkin, "Corporations Hurt Causes with Giving." *New York Times,* July 22, 2020: B1.
64 Idem.
65 Untiedt, 43–44.
66 Jamie Stengle, "Komen Sees Big Drop in 2013 Contributions." *USA Today*, January 3, 2014. Retrieved May 20, 2020 from https://www.usatoday.com/story/money/business/2014/01/03/komen-sees-big-drop-in-contributions-after-dispute/4314041/
67 Greg Rosalsky, "Charitable Giving Is Down; It Might Be Time to Reform the Charitable Deduction." National Public Radio, November 12, 2019. Retrieved May 24, 2020 from https://www.npr.org/sections/money/2019/11/12/778326512/charitable-giving-is-down-it-might-be-time-to-reform-the-charitable-deduction

68 Leslie Albrecht, "Americans Slashed Their Charitable Deductions by $54 Billion after Republican Tax-Code Overhaul." MarketWatch, July 11, 2019. Retrieved May 24, 2020 from https://www.marketwatch.com/story/americans-slashed-their-charitable-deductions-by-54-billion-after-trumps-tax-overhaul-2019-07-09
69 *Espinoza v. Montana Department of Revenue*, 591 U.S. ___ (2020).
70 Adam Liptak, "Supreme Court Gives Religious Schools More Access to State Aid." *New York Times,* June 30, 2020.
71 Idem.
72 Small Business Administration (SBA). "Faith-Based Organizations: Frequently Asked Questions Regarding Participation of Faith-Based Organizations in the Paycheck Protection Program (PPP) and the Economic Injury Disaster Loan (EIDL) Program." Retrieved May 24, 2020 from https://www.sba.gov/sites/default/files/2020-04/SBA%20Faith-Based%20FAQ%20Final.pdf
73 Tom Gjelten, "Another Break from the Past: Government Will Help Churches Pay Pastor Salaries." National Public Radio, April 6, 2020. Retrieved May 24, 2020 from https://www.npr.org/sections/coronavirus-live-updates/2020/04/06/828462517/another-break-from-the-past-government-will-help-churches-pay-pastor-salaries
74 Associated Press, "After Lobbying, Catholic Church Won $1.4 Billion in Virus Aid." (Wilmington, Delaware) *News Journal,* July 11, 2020: 5A.
75 Idem.
76 Idem.
77 Nelson Tebbe, Micah Schwartzman and Richard Schragger, "The Demise of the Wall between Church and State." *New York Times,* June 9, 2020: A23.
78 Alison Gill, Interview granted to Tom Gjelten, "Another Break from the Past: Government Will Help Churches Pay Pastor Salaries." *National Public Radio,* April 6, 2020. Retrieved May 24, 2020 from https://www.npr.org/sections/coronavirus-live-updates/2020/04/06/828462517/another-break-from-the-past-government-will-help-churches-pay-pastor-salaries

Bibliography

Abbondanza, David. "The Pulpit Initiative: Fighting to Return America's First Freedom to Her Churches." *Richmond Public Interest Law Review* 12, no. 3 (January 1, 2009): 225–42.

Albrecht, Leslie. "Americans Slashed Their Charitable Deductions by $54 Billion after Republican Tax-Code Overhaul." MarketWatch, July 11, 2019. Retrieved May 24, 2020 from https://www.marketwatch.com/story/americans-slashed-their-charitable-deductions-by-54-billion-after-trumps-tax-overhaul-2019-07-09

Anderson, David E. "Jerry Falwell's Ministry Fined for Taking Role in Politics." *Washington Post,* April 10, 1993. Retrieved May 20, 2020 from https://www.washingtonpost.com/archive/local/1993/04/10/jerry-falwells-ministry-fined-for-taking-role-in-politics/ce8c87b3-0740-4b1b-a691-df39e73064fb/

Aprill, Ellen. "Amending the Johnson Amendment in the Age of Cheap Speech." 2018 *University of Illinois Law Review Online* 1 (Spring 2018).

Associated Press, "After Lobbying, Catholic Church Won $1.4 Billion in Virus Aid." *News Journal (Wilmington, Delaware)*, (July 11, 2020): 5A.

Backer, Jonathan. "Thou Shalt Not Electioneer: Religious Nonprofit Political Activity and the Threat 'God PACs' Pose to Democracy and Religion." *Michigan Law Review* 114 (February 2016): 619.

Biederman, Patricia Ward and Jason Felch. "Anti-war Sermon Brings IRS Warning." *Los Angeles Times,* November 7, 2005. Retrieved May 20, 2020 from https://www.latimes.com/archives/la-xpm-2005-nov-07-me-allsaints7-story.html

Bob Jones University v. United States, 461 U.S. 574 (1983).

Boston, Robert. *Why the Religious Right Is Wrong about Separation of Church and State.* Amherst, New York: Prometheus Books, 2003.

Branch Ministries v. Rossotti, 211 F. 3d 137 (D.C. Cir. 2000).

Burwell v. Hobby Lobby Stores, Inc. 573 U.S. 682 (2014).

Byrnes, Nanette. "Hundreds of Pastors Back Political Candidates; Defy Tax Rules." Reuters, October 7, 2012. Retrieved May 20, 2020 from https://www.reuters.com/article/us-usa-tax-pulpit/hundreds-of-pastors-back-political-candidates-defy-tax-rules-idUSBRE89700E20121008

Caron, Paul. "IRS Drops Investigation into Church's Anti-war Sermon; Church Demands Investigation of IRS and Apology." TaxProf Blog, September 24, 2007. Retrieved May 20, 2020 from https://taxprof.typepad.com/taxprof_blog/2007/09/irs-drops-inves.html

Christian Echoes National Ministry v. United States, 470 F. 2d 849 (10th Cir. 1972).

Church Audit Procedures Act (CAPA). 26 U.S.C. Section 7611(d)(1)(A)(i) (1983).

Cicilline, David. "Cicilline Re-introduces DISCLOSE Act." May 23, 2019. Retrieved May 23, 2020 from https://cicilline.house.gov/press-release/cicilline-re-introduces-disclose-act

Citizens United v. Federal Election Commission, 558 U.S. 310 (2010).

Edsall, Thomas B. and Hanna Rosin. "IRS Denies Christian Coalition Tax-Exempt Status." *Washington Post* (June 11, 1999): A4.

Espinoza v. Montana Department of Revenue, 591 U.S. ___ (2020).

"Evangelist Jimmy Swaggart Faces Debt Collectors, IRS Tax Liens." United Press International, January 29, 1992. Available at https://www.upi.com/Archives/1992/01/29/Evangelist-Jimmy-Swaggart-faces-debt-collectors-IRS-tax-liens/5436696661200/

"FFRF Sues Trump over Church Politicking." Freedom from Religion Foundation, May 4, 2017. Available at https://ffrf.org/news/news-releases/item/29320-ffrf-sues-trump-over-church-politicking

Fitzpatrick, Michael. "Rust Corrodes: The First Amendment Implications of *Rust v. Sullivan, Stanford Law Review* 45 (November 1992): 185.

Freedom from Religion Foundation v. Donald Trump, Complaint for Declaratory and Injunctive Relief, No. 17-CV-330 (U.S. District Court for the Western District of, filed May 4, 2017).

Gano, Karen. Letter from National Association of State Charity Officials to Congressional leaders, August 23, 2017. Retrieved May 21, 2020 from http://www.nonprofitlawblog.com/assets/NASCO-Letter-to-Congressional-Leaders-re-Johnson-Amendment-8.23.2017.pdf

Ghachem, Malick W. "Of 'Scalpels' and 'Sledgehammers:' Religious Liberty and the Policing of Muslim Charities in Britain and American Since 9/11." 9 *University of California at Los Angeles Journal of Islamic & Near Eastern Law* 25, 2009–2010.

Gill, Alison. Interview granted to Tom Gjelten, "Another Break from the Past: Government Will Help Churches Pay Pastor Salaries." National Public Radio, April 6, 2020. Retrieved May 24, 2020 from https://www.npr.org/sections/coronavirus-live-updates/2020/04/06/828462517/another-break-from-the-past-government-will-help-churches-pay-pastor-salaries

Gjelten, Tom. "Another Break from the Past: Government Will Help Churches Pay Pastor Salaries." National Public Radio, April 6, 2020. Retrieved May 24, 2020 from https://www.npr.org/sections/coronavirus-live-updates/2020/04/06/828462517/another-break-from-the-past-government-will-help-churches-pay-pastor-salaries

Goldfeder, Mark A. and Michelle K. Terry. "To Repeal or Not Repeal: The Johnson Amendment." *University of Memphis Law Review* 48 (Fall 2017): 209.

Hopkins, Bruce R. *The Law of Tax-Exempt Organizations* (11th ed.). Hoboken, New Jersey: John Wiley & Sons, 2018.

Joint Committee on Taxation, Estimated Revenue Effects of the Chairman's Amendment in the Nature of a Substitute to H.R. 1, JCX-47-17 (2017).

Liptak, Adam. "Supreme Court Gives Religious Schools More Access to State Aid." *New York Times,* June 30, 2020.

Long, Heather. "In Small Win for Democrats, Final Tax Bill Won't Include Provision to Allow Churches to Endorse Political Candidates." *Salt Lake Tribune,* December 15, 2017. Retrieved May 21, 2020 from https://www.sltrib.com/news/nation-world/2017/12/15/in-small-win-for-democrats-final-tax-bill-wont-include-provision-to-allow-churches-to-endorse-political-candidates/

Omnibus Budget Reconciliation Act, H.R. Rep. No. 100–391 (II), 100th Congress, 1st Session, Part 2 at 1625 (1987).

Perry v. Sindermann, 408 U.S. 593 (1972).

Religious Freedom Restoration Act, 42 U.S.C. Section 2000bb (1994).

"Robertson's Network Settles IRS Dispute." *Los Angeles Times,* March 21, 1988. Retrieved May 20, 2020 from https://www.latimes.com/archives/la-xpm-1998-mar-21-me-31250-story.html

Rosalsky, Greg. "Charitable Giving is Down; It Might Be Time to Reform the Charitable Deduction." National Public Radio, November 12, 2019. Retrieved May 24, 2020 from https://www.npr.org/sections/money/2019/11/12/778326512/charitable-giving-is-down-it-might-be-time-to-reform-the-charitable-deduction

Rust v. Sullivan, 111 S.Ct. 1759 (1991).

Small Business Administration (SBA). "Faith-Based Organizations: Frequently Asked Questions Regarding Participation of Faith-Based Organizations in the Paycheck Protection Program (PPP) and the Economic Injury Disaster Loan (EIDL) Program." Retrieved May 24, 2020 from https://www.sba.gov/sites/default/files/2020-04/SBA%20Faith-Based%20FAQ%20Final.pdf

Smolla, Rodney A. *Free Speech in an Open Society.* New York: Alfred A. Knopf, 1992.

Sorkin, Andrew Ross. "Corporations Hurt Causes with Giving." *New York Times* (July 22, 2020): B1.

Stanley, Erik W. "A Survey of Religious Freedom for Individuals and Faith-Based Institutions: LBJ, the IRS, and Churches: The Unconstitutionality of the Johnson Amendment in Light of Recent Supreme Court Precedent." *Regent University Law Review* 24 (2011–2012): 237.

Stengle, Jamie. "Komen Sees Big Drop in 2013 Contributions." *USA Today*, January 3, 2014. Retrieved May 20, 2020 from https://www.usatoday.com/story/money/business/2014/01/03/komen-sees-big-drop-in-contributions-after-dispute/4314041/

Sullivan, Kathleen. "Unconstitutional Conditions." *Harvard Law Review* 102 (1989): 1413.

Tebbe, Nelson, Micah Schwartzman, and Richard Schragger, The Demise of the Wall between Church and State." *New York Times* (June 9, 2020): A23.

Thomsen, Jacqueline. "House Passes Measure Blocking IRS from Revoking Churches' Tax-Exempt Status over Political Activity." *The Hill,* July 19, 2018. Retrieved May 21, 2020 from https://thehill.com/policy/finance/domestic-taxes/397996-house-passes-measure-blocking-irs-from-revoking-churches-tax

Untiedt, Whitney. "Lighting the Way: The Johnson Amendment Stands Strong against Dark Money in Politics." *Emory Corporate Governance Accountability Review* 6 (2019): 37.

Van Alstyne, William W. "The Demise of the Right-Privilege Distinction in Constitutional Law." *Harvard Law Review* 81 (1968): 1439.

Voyles, Shawn A. "Choosing between Tax-Exempt Status and Freedom of Religion: The Dilemma Facing Politically-Active Churches." *Regent University Law Review* 9 (Fall 1997): 219.

Walsh, Paul. "Warroad Pastor's IRS Case Closed, for Now." *Minneapolis Star Tribune,* July 29, 2009. Retrieved May 20, 2020 from http://www.startribune.com/warroad-pastor-s-irs-case-closed-for-now/52000717/?c=y&page=all&prepage=2#continue

7. *Roadside Memorial Crosses: Highway to Healing or Crossroads of Conflict*

Amanda Reid

Roadside memorial crosses, marking the last-alive place, are erected by those grieving the loss of a friend or family member. The roadside cross in Figure 7.1 beckons the passerby's attention and encourages "Don" to rest in peace ("RIP"). These crosses are planted with a self-proclaimed authority derived from loss and longing. But state and local laws often prohibit these private memorials on public land. Nevertheless, these bans are often not enforced. This chapter analyzes the roadside memorial cross phenomenon, the tensions sparked by these crosses, and the doctrinal vacuum created by the Supreme Court's recent Establishment Clause jurisprudence. When an unauthorized roadside cross is not removed from public property, the open question is whether the selective nonenforcement of land use laws gives rise to an Establishment Clause violation. It is unclear whether courts continue to consider the primary effect on a reasonable observer or consider what message is sent to members of the community when transportation officials turn a blind eye and allow roadside crosses to remain—sometimes for years—on public property.

Under the three-part test set out in the 1971 case of *Lemon v. Kurtzman*,[1] the display of religious symbols on public property can violate the Establishment Clause if a symbol's presence conveys to a reasonable observer that the government prefers or endorses a particular religion. Establishment Clause jurisprudence aims to conciliate religious differences and to foster harmonious coexistence in a pluralistic society. The law does not demand elimination of all religious displays in the public sphere. It is only when the primary effect of a religious display conveys a message that religion, or a particular religious belief, is favored or preferred, that the law requires its removal. The law demands equal treatment and equal citizenship to individuals of all faiths.[2] At

Figure 7.1: Picture of a roadside memorial cross taken by the author in Jacksonville, Florida.

its core, the Establishment Clause guarantees equal protection for religious minorities and nonbelievers.[3]

As discussed below, the Court's most recent Establishment Clause pronouncements in *American Legion v. American Humanist Association*[4] have failed to offer meaningful guidance for policymakers and lower courts. The confused state of Establishment Clause jurisprudence has been called "a hot mess."[5] The *Lemon* test has been much maligned and criticized by courts and commentators.[6] But efforts to repudiate *Lemon* have been unsuccessful. Justice Antonin Scalia once likened the *Lemon* test to a "ghoul in a late-night horror movie" that just won't die.[7] After *American Legion*, is the *Lemon* test dead and buried—or will it be resurrected? If the *American Legion*'s historico-traditional approach is unavailing, lower courts may need to return to the *Lemon* test. For policymakers and lower courts, it is frustratingly unclear what test is appropriate to use when evaluating roadside memorial crosses. The *American Legion* Court has made a messy area of the law now even messier.

Roadside Memorial Cross Phenomenon

The instinct to memorialize the dead has ancient roots. However, the instinct to memorialize road deaths is a modern phenomenon.[8] Roadside memorial crosses are erected by those grieving the loss of a loved one—often memorializing a traffic fatality of a teenager or young adult.[9] Marking the last-alive place with a roadside memorial cross is a mushrooming phenomenon. As scholars Jennifer Clark and Ashley Cheshire note, "Spontaneous roadside memorials in Texas were rare and perhaps even nonexistent in the years before World War II . . . ."[10] In a small Texas town, near the Arkansas border, author Jane Stern observed a string of memorials: "There seem to be roadside grave markers every mile."[11] The modern roadway has become a deathscape punctuated with mementos and mourning.[12] Photographer Peter Warzel described roadside crosses as "ubiquitous in the American countryside."[13]

This ubiquity of roadside crosses speaks to the dangers of our automobile culture. Traffic fatalities are a leading cause of death.[14] Sadly, nearly 40,000 people die each year in automobile crashes in the United States, and a disproportionate number are teenagers and young adults.[15] But the public doesn't perceive the roadway as a dangerous place.[16] The unexpectedness of road deaths often causes shock and complicated grief. Those experiencing complicated grief have trouble accepting the loss.

Grief can create an ambiguous state where one feels torn between acknowledging the pain and denying the deceased's absence.[17] Grief, especially from the loss of a child, spurs a powerful ache to maintain a bond with the departed. A roadside memorial simultaneously maintains a connection with the deceased, while also affording closure in the grieving process.[18] The memorial marks the absence and reminds passersby that a loved one is absent.[19] Sanctifying the last-alive place allows for a spatial fix to anchor a connection with the departed.[20] The death marker also serves as a warning to others: this cautionary function creates meaning for an otherwise meaningless death.[21]

Roadside memorials serve to both proclaim the deceased's absence and give meaning to their death. Each memorial is a unique and idiosyncratic reflection of unique and idiosyncratic grief. While no two memorials are the same, as a phenomenon, scholars have identified common elements, and the most obvious shared feature is a dominant cross. One survey of memorials in Texas found that more than 93% included a cross.[22] Some researchers posit that the cross is used as a generic symbol of death, rather than a symbol of religion.[23] The nontraditional placement of a cross on the roadside is outside the confines of the church and is thus in "outright opposition to conventional religion."[24] For some, this flouting of conventional religion undercuts the roadside cross's religious meaning. There are those who suggest the cross is used as a matter of cultural integration rather than an act of religious expression.[25] But as each cross is an idiosyncratic expression, it is difficult to know the meaning of each roadside cross.

Researchers have studied roadside memorials across the globe and across cultures.[26] Roadside memorials are found throughout the Americas, Europe, and Australasia.[27] Despite religious and cultural differences in these regions, there appears to be a common impetus to remember the last-alive place along the roadside. Some scholars suggest the common impetus is an implicit critique of modernity—our modern car culture and modern death practices.[28] These senseless deaths are at the hands of modern car technology, and evidence of these deaths are swiftly erased from the roadway.[29] Without a memorial, other drivers may never know of the tragedy at that site. Individually, the memorial is a plea to not forget the departed.[30] Collectively, the phenomenon reflects a tension between our fragility and our technology.[31] The roadside memorial becomes a tangible manifestation of grief and a critique of the anonymity of modern road culture.

Tensions Sparked by Roadside Crosses

As discussed below, recent newspaper accounts reflect the range of community responses to these memorials. In response, state and local policymakers are grappling with how to regulate spontaneous roadside memorials.[32] Some states ban private memorials entirely, a number of states encourage them when placed in a safe location, and a few states provide official memorials instead of private ones.[33] Some states have no policy, thus leaving it to cities and municipalities to craft rules. For example, a small town in New Mexico recently changed its ordinance because the blanket ban was not being enforced.[34] The city's ordinance now permits roadside memorials that meet time, size, and placement restrictions.

In jurisdictions where private memorials are prohibited, grieving families continue to erect them. One grieving wife told a local San Diego reporter, "I know it's illegal. I know it's against policy. I know you're not supposed to have roadside memorials."[35] But she, like many other memorial-makers, erected a wooden cross out of a self-proclaimed authority derived from loss and longing.[36] When highway workers removed the memorial, the wife told the reporter she was "crushed." After learning about news media attention, a transportation official reached out to the wife to apologize for the "insensitivity my maintenance crews have shown towards the memorial of your late husband." The official said he would instruct all field supervisors to "make sure this behavior is never repeated again."

Roadside memorials continue to proliferate along the roadway, even when they are not allowed.[37] This proliferation is due in part to a lack of enforcement of land use regulations. Thus, while many state and local laws prohibit these private memorials, transportation officials often do not enforce the ban. In Florida, local transportation officials often don't enforce the law, as a reporter noted, "to avoid the delicate and emotional issue of taking down a marker in memory of somebody who was killed."[38] Some transportation officials have an unwritten policy to turn a blind eye to memorials unless a complaint is made, or it is a traffic hazard.[39]

While initially sympathetic to the loss, complaints can come from some in the community who resent the manifestation of private grief on public property. There are a variety of reasons for the resistance to private memorials: they can be an unwanted reminder of trauma and tragedy; they can create traffic safety concerns; they can deteriorate into sun-faded, rain-soaked eyesores; and they can reflect an impermissible union of church and state. Public officials face the challenge of balancing the interests of the community with the grieving process of the bereaved.[40] The decision to retain or remove a roadside memorial puts local policymakers in a double bind.[41] When officials do enforce the prohibition and remove roadside crosses, that can trigger powerful emotional responses from grieving friends and family. As researchers observe, "enforcement efforts become a public relations disaster, especially if memorial builders choose to take their plight to the public via the media."[42] The stories below illustrate that the choice to either retain or remove a memorial can create divisiveness in a community.

Community discord sparked by roadside memorial crosses is exemplified in news reports from a small town in Georgia.[43] A family maintained a roadside cross for eighteen-year-old Dylan for over five years. Caring for this memorial gave the family great comfort. But some neighbors resented the memorial and sent an anonymous letter: "It is very unfortunate that you lost your son and grandson. The residents who live off Harry Driggers Boulevard have lost loved ones just like you. You burden us with your make-shift memorial in our backyard. It is down right despicable to remember your loved one this way. . . . It has been 5 years—get on with your life. We are tired of sharing your pain."[44] In response to the letter, Dylan's sister told a local reporter, "It's already painful enough that we lost him. And then for someone to send a letter that is just so heartless." A local reporter reached out to neighbors to ask if the memorial was a problem, and one said "No, not at all." This story illustrates how some in the community want crosses removed, while others do not object to them.[45]

A similar story unfolded in Florida when a resident's complaint prompted officials to remove a cross that was erected for nineteen-year-old Zach. Zach's grandmother told a local reporter that the cross "just brings us comfort."[46] In explaining the importance of the memorial she said it allows her to "talk to Zach and talk to God and do what we need to do." After the family's story received media attention, more than 500 residents signed a petition to keep a teenager's memorial cross standing. This story reinforces that community members can have conflicting opinions on whether a cross should remain or be removed.

In addition to talking with local news outlets, community members have also expressed their views online. A blog post, titled "Roadside Memorials: Meaning and Rules Behind Them," had a comment that underscores another source of tension caused by these private expressions of loss and longing: an unwanted reminder of tragedy.[47] The post by Linda shared her family's experience:

> My sister was killed when a man driving the opposite direction crossed over the centerline causing a head on collision. Both died at the scene. The location of the crash is just down the road from my sister's house, where her husband remains living. One of her daughters and family live close by. The negligent driver's family placed a cross with his name inscribed on it; his family lives 30 miles away and can likely avoid the area. My sister's husband, daughter, granddaughters, and son-in-law pass the site whenever they go somewhere and return. A daily reminder that he killed her there. As we are all still grieving — his family, too—ours feel like we've been slammed against the wall again, and for those who pass his name daily at the exact place he killed my sister, it is insult to injury.

This story illustrates how these memorials can be a source of vicarious trauma for others in the community.[48]

In Pennsylvania, twenty-one-year-old Alexandra was killed when a SUV hit her motorcycle.[49] Alexandra's parents found deep solace in maintaining a 12-foot roadside memorial cross as a tribute and cautionary reminder. Eight years later, the cross was removed and replaced with an anonymous note titled "You Do Not Own This Space." The note continued:

> Roadside memorials have become so numerous, and so distracting and dangerous, that more and more states are trying to regulate them. They are dangerous distraction to rubberneckers on already hazardous roads. Highway officials also complain the memorials frequently get in the way of road crews cutting grass or clearing snow. Left unchecked, the practice would eventually leave the highways littered with crosses, flags, flowers, etc. These items are legally considered

> abandoned refuse and can be simply picked up and taken by anyone who has a mind to. Those who place them believe that they retain possession and are effectively making a private claim to public property through adverse possession. This runs afoul of the laws.

A similar story was reported in Australia, with a self-confessed vandal who promised to continue removing roadside memorial crosses.[50] After removing one cross, the local resident left a note saying, in part, "Authorities should not allow this to happen anywhere. So I will continue to take out any other crosses that I pass."[51] These stories reflect the self-help to which some in the community will resort when local officials turn a blind eye to these crosses.

When officials do remove crosses, that enforcement can provoke the ire of grieving families. In Indiana, a father was "devastated" when his homemade memorial to Gabriella, his twenty-three-year-old daughter, was removed by local transportation officials ten months after she died along the interstate.[52] Gabriella ran out of gas along the roadway, and when she was outside her car she was killed by another motorist. In explaining the meaningfulness of the memorial, Gabriella's dad said, "We weren't able to have a showing because of the nature of the accident. She was hit going 70 miles an hour. I wanted a place to memorialize her memory." A spokesperson for the Indiana Department of Transportation explained that memorials are allowed to remain if they aren't too close to the roadway and aren't a distraction. Here, the spokesperson explained, Gabriella's memorial was "pretty close to the interstate," and "there was Styrofoam flying around and just a bunch of stuff on the side [of] the road that is distracting to drivers and maybe not safe for the motorists." Driver distraction and traffic hazards are common transportation concerns. In a survey of transportation officials, 70% reported that roadside memorials were considered a safety hazard in their state.[53]

In Florida, a family pleaded for the return of a six-foot memorial cross, erected where Paul died in a motorcycle crash two years before.[54] Paul's nine-year-old son told a local reporter, "Somebody stole my dad's cross." As the son explained, "It meant a lot to me because it had a lot [of] love in it and had a lot of things that meant to me." The family soon learned that local transportation officials removed the memorial because it was on the state right-of-way. Under Florida law, private memorials are not allowed, but a family can elect an official state memorial through the Florida Department of Transportation's memorial marker program.[55] Like Florida's official sign program, a number of states offer official markers in lieu of private memorials.[56]

In trying to balance the differing interests of community members, state and local governments have adopted a hodgepodge of policies for roadside memorials.[57] Some states have official polices, whereas others don't and thereby leave it up to local governments. Some jurisdictions allow private memorials, whereas other localities allow only official markers. And notwithstanding an official policy, research shows that in communities where private memorials are prohibited, the ban is regularly not enforced.[58] Around the country, roadcrews promptly remove unauthorized advertisements and political signs, but often turn a blind eye to roadside memorials.[59] In acknowledging this selective nonenforcement, a reporter once observed, "in probably no other area of public life does public practice diverge so dramatically from official policy."[60] To craft and enforce an appropriate policy, policymakers are asked to decide if these crosses are an important milestone on the road to emotional recovery or are a crossroad of conflict.

Establishment Clause Seeks to Minimize Religious Divisiveness That Fuels Social Conflict

The Founders of this nation were mindful of the dangers of entangling religion and government. In the words of the Supreme Court, the union "tends to destroy government and to degrade religion."[61] For the benefit of both the church and the state, the First Amendment provides, in pertinent part, that "Congress shall make no law respecting an establishment of religion." The display of a religious symbol on public property has been found to violate the Establishment Clause if the symbol's presence conveys to a reasonable observer that the government prefers or endorses a particular religion.

Under the three-part test set out in *Lemon v. Kurtzman*,[62] the government violates the Establishment Clause if it impermissibly endorses religion by having either the primary purpose or effect of conveying a message that religion or a particular religious belief is favored or preferred.[63] Establishment Clause jurisprudence seeks "to foster a society in which people of all beliefs can live together harmoniously."[64] The law does not demand elimination of all religious displays in the public sphere. The law demands elimination of a religious display that, in the words of Justice Sandra Day O'Connor, "sends a message to nonadherents that they are outsiders, not full members of the political community, and an accompanying message to adherents that they are insiders, favored members of the political community."[65] The Establishment Clause is about keeping government out of religion; it isn't necessarily about keeping religion out of the public sphere.[66] The law demands equal treatment and equal citizenship to individuals of all faiths.[67] Establishment Clause thus guarantees equal protection for religious minorities and nonbelievers.[68]

In balancing Establishment Clause interests, the Supreme Court evaluates the constitutionality of a religious display based on its context, setting, and history. Sometimes a Decalogue on public property is permissible and sometimes it isn't. Sometimes a crèche on public grounds is permissible and sometimes it isn't. In 1984, the Supreme Court in *Lynch v. Donnelly* rebuffed a challenge to a city's inclusion of a Nativity scene in its annual Christmas display. Applying the *Lemon* test, the Court held that notwithstanding the religious significance of the Nativity scene, the display did not violate the Establishment Clause.[69] The Court noted that the Nativity scene—surrounded by Santa's house, reindeer, candy-striped poles, a Christmas tree, carolers, cutout figures representing a clown, an elephant, and a teddy bear, hundreds of colored lights, and a large banner that read "Seasons Greetings"—had been included in the city's annual celebration for over forty years without evidence of political friction or divisiveness. The Court emphasized that the Constitution does not require complete separation of church and state; the Constitution affirmatively mandates accommodation, not merely tolerance, of all religions, and forbids hostility toward any faith. Anything less, according to the Court, would require the "callous indifference" that was not intended by the Establishment Clause.[70]

Five years later, in *County of Allegheny v. ACLU*, the Court held that a Nativity scene did violate the Establishment Clause.[71] The crèche was placed on the grand staircase of the county courthouse, and no figures of Santa or other decorations surrounded it. Unlike the crèche in *Lynch*, nothing in the context of this display detracted from the crèche's religious message. Here, the crèche stood alone as the single element of the display on the grand staircase. According to the Court, the county chose to celebrate Christmas in a way that had the effect of endorsing a patently Christian message: Glory to God for the birth of Jesus Christ.[72] This endorsement of a religious message violated the Establishment Clause.

Sixteen years later, the Court heard two separate cases to considered whether the display of a Ten Commandments monument violated the Establishment Clause. In one case, a 5-4 majority voted to remove newly erected Decalogue displays in Kentucky,[73] and in the other case another 5-4 majority voted to retain a forty-year-old Decalogue display in Texas.[74] Justice Stephen Breyer was the swing vote in both cases. In Texas, the longstanding display was among seventeen monuments and twenty-one historical markers located on the grounds of the state capitol. Justice Breyer emphasized that the Texas display had been there for years, without controversy, and was surrounded by other secular displays.[75] The totality of the display's context, setting, and uncontroversial tenure suggested no endorsement of religion. In Kentucky, on the other hand, the displays' context and controversial history suggested an impermissible endorsement of religion. In Kentucky, the Ten Commandments were displayed on the walls of two county courthouses. Initially, the displays included only the Decalogue, but after lawsuits were filed challenging the displays, government officials added other texts like the Magna Carta, the Declaration of Independence, and the Bill of Rights. According to the Court, belated attempts to contextualize the text did not mitigate the religious purpose in posting the display or temper its sectarian message. The government violates the Establishment Clause when its "ostensible object is to take sides" for a religious purpose.[76] A display's history and context illuminate whether a "predominantly" sectarian or secular message is communicated. The display in the abstract—crèche, Decalogue, or Latin cross—is not determinative: "under the Establishment Clause detail is key."[77] It is details like a display's context, setting, and tenure that have been determinative.

The Supreme Court has not yet addressed the phenomenon of erecting roadside memorial crosses for those killed along the roadway. But one Circuit Court of Appeals has. In 2010, the Tenth Circuit held that 12-foot white crosses erected by a non-profit organization to memorialize fallen highway patrol officers violated the Establishment Clause.[78] Photos of these crosses are below in Figure 7.2. The Utah Highway Patrol Association, with the permission of Utah state authorities, erected and maintained a number of memorial crosses on public land. The crosses stood twelve-feet high with six-foot horizontal cross-bars. On the horizontal cross-bar, the fallen trooper's name, rank, and badge number were printed in large letters. Immediately beneath the biographical information hung a large depiction of the highway patrol's official "beehive" symbol. Below that, the year the trooper died and a small plaque with the trooper's picture were included.

Applying the *Lemon* test, the Tenth Circuit concluded that these memorials had the effect of conveying to a reasonable observer that the state was endorsing Christianity. Under *Lemon*'s first prong, the state had a plausible secular purpose in allowing the memorial crosses, namely to honor fallen troopers and to promote safety on the state's highways. While the state did not act with the purpose of favoring religion, the effect prong is a separate inquiry, or else, as the Tenth Circuit observed, "this second prong would be rendered meaningless."[79] The purpose in erecting a display can thus differ from the display's effect on the reasonable observer.[80] The context and setting affect whether the display conveys a predominantly secular or sectarian message.[81] Here, according to the Tenth Circuit, while the purpose was secular, the effect was to convey a predominantly sectarian message.[82] First, the memorials used the Latin cross, the "preeminent" symbol of Christianity. Second, these symbols stood alone on public land, as opposed to being part

Figure 7.2: Photos of 12-foot memorial crosses erected to honor fallen highway patrol officers in Utah (Images taken from published court opinion in *American Atheists, Inc. v. Davenport*, 637 F.3d 1095 (10th Cir. 2010)).

of a contextualizing display with other symbols. Third, the crosses conspicuously bore the imprimatur of the Utah Highway Patrol, a state agency. Thus, reasonable motorists driving by a memorial were bound to see a 12-foot cross standing alone on public property with an agency's insignia. The Tenth Circuit held that these memorial crosses had the impermissible effect of conveying to a reasonable observer that the state prefers or otherwise endorses Christianity.

While the Supreme Court has not yet addressed the roadside cross phenomenon, the Court has addressed the display of a Latin cross on public property. The 2019 case preserving the Bladensburg Peace Cross is the Court's latest attempt to thread the needle between endorsing religion and signaling hostility toward religion.[83] As Professor Michael McConnell noted, "By narrowly focusing on already-established symbols, the decision was able to situate itself in the moderate middle of the religious-symbol culture wars."[84] In Maryland, a Latin cross stands 40 feet above a busy roadway. A photo of the cross is below in Figure 7.3. The cross was erected in 1925 as a memorial to area soldiers who died serving in World War I. Justice Samuel Alito, writing for the majority, held that the Peace Cross did not violate the Establishment Clause. As evidence of the difficulty this case posed, the fractured Court issued six separate opinions in addition to the majority.[85]

While the Latin cross is undoubtedly a symbol of Christianity, the Court explained that the cross can take on an added secular meaning when it is used in a war memorial.[86] And this particular longstanding memorial has now become a "prominent community landmark," such that its removal today would manifest "a hostility toward religion that has no place in our Establishment Clause traditions."[87] The Court then instructed that the "passage of time gives rise to a strong presumption of constitutionality," and that "retaining established, religiously expressive monuments, symbols, and practices is quite different from erecting or adopting new ones."[88] In evaluating these established monuments, a plurality of the Court abandoned the *Lemon* test for a "more modest approach" that "looks to history for guidance."[89] This historico-traditional approach offers a "presumption of constitutionality" for "longstanding monuments, symbols, and practices."[90] In his concurrence, Justice Breyer emphasized that new memorials would not receive this presumption: "A newer memorial, erected under different circumstances, would not necessarily be permissible under this [history and tradition] approach."[91] In addition to the monument's age, Justice Breyer also emphasized the previous lack of controversy: "the Cross has stood on the same land for 94 years, generating no controversy in the community until this lawsuit was filed."[92] Longstanding monuments that haven't generated

Figure 7.3: Photo of the Bladensburg Peace Cross in Maryland (Image taken from the Appendix in *American Legion v. American Humanist Association*, 139 S. Ct. 2067 (2019)).

controversy are presumptively constitutional. But what about new memorials that do generate controversy?

Doctrinal Uncertainty for Evaluating Roadside Memorial Crosses

The Supreme Court's most recent Establishment Clause pronouncements have created more doctrinal uncertainty in an already confused area of the law. In *American Legion*, a plurality of four Justices (Alito, Roberts, Breyer, and Kavanaugh) rejected the *Lemon* test when considering longstanding monuments. Justice Clarence Thomas wrote separately to amplify that he would overrule *Lemon* in "all contexts."[93] And Justice Neil Gorsuch called the *Lemon* test "a misadventure"[94] that is "now shelved."[95] With these six votes (plurality of four plus Justices Thomas and Gorsuch), the *Lemon* test appears dead-letter.[96] Justice Elena Kagan joined Parts I, II–B, II–C, III, and IV of the Court's opinion, but importantly she withdrew from the portion of the opinion that abandoned *Lemon*—thus turning that portion into a plurality. She wrote a concurring opinion that appeared to offer a lifeline to *Lemon*: "Although I agree that rigid application of the *Lemon* test does not solve every Establishment Clause problem, I think that test's focus on purposes and effects is crucial in evaluating government action in this sphere—as this very suit shows. I therefore do not join Part II–A. I do not join Part II–D out of perhaps an excess of caution."[97] So, what's the state of the law?[98] Does Justice Kagan's withdrawal from the portions of majority opinion abandoning *Lemon* preserve the test in any way? As previously noted, Justice Scalia colorfully likened *Lemon* to a "ghoul in a late-night horror movie that repeatedly sits up in its grave and shuffles abroad, after being repeatedly killed and buried."[99] Is *Lemon* dead-letter now or not?

In post-*American Legion* caselaw, the viability of *Lemon* appears very much unsettled. In a copyright case in 2020, Justice Thomas wrote in a footnote, "this Court has not overruled *Lemon v. Kurtzman*, 403 U.S. 602 (1971), which pronounced a test for evaluating Establishment Clause claims."[100] Justice Alito and Justice Breyer joined Justice Thomas' dissent in the copyright case; however, Justice Breyer expressly did not join the footnote discussing the test for Establishment Clause claims.[101] The Justices' divergence on this point underscores the fact that the *Lemon* test is in limbo.

Notwithstanding the *Lemon* question, today it seems safe to say that a majority of the Court will ratify longstanding practices (like legislative prayer)[102] and longstanding monuments (like the Bladensburg Peace Cross).[103] But it isn't clear how old the monument needs to be, or how long ago the practice needs to have been established, to generate the presumption of constitutionality.[104] The gist seems to be that the Court doesn't want to encourage removals that smack of hostility to religion. As the Court stated, "A government that roams the land, tearing down monuments with religious symbolism and scrubbing away any reference to the divine will strike many as aggressively hostile to religion."[105] The government should strive to maintain the current equilibrium.[106] The Court aims to calm religious tensions, not inflame them. But new items added to the landscape are different. The unanswered question under current jurisprudence is how we are to evaluate new memorials and new practices.

As noted above, the roadside cross phenomenon is a modern development, and researchers posit that the phenomenon is driven by a need to respond to modern road culture and modern death practices.[107] For this new practice of erecting new memorials, what test will lower courts use to evaluate Establishment Clause questions?[108] If the Founding Era historical record is silent on roadside crosses, of what help is a historico-traditional approach? If the historico-traditional approach is unavailing, might courts reanimate *Lemon*?

The 1971 *Lemon* test's reign has been marked by its opportunistic invocation and its resilience after near death experiences.[109] In the wake of *American Legion*'s doctrinal uncertainty, will courts re-enlist the services of *Lemon*'s hypothetical reasonable observer for new memorials? If so, what would such an observer conclude in light of the selective failure to enforce the law? Transportation officials regularly turn a blind eye to these memorials. Does selective nonenforcement send a message of the government's religious preference? Does selective nonenforcement of land use laws give rise to equal protection concerns? Is selective nonenforcement "taking sides" in a way the Establishment Clause seeks to prevent?

The Supreme Court has observed that permanent displays on public property are best understood as government speech, rather than purely private speech of the memorial-maker.[110] And allowing monuments to remain on public property suggests some amount of approval of the message: "It certainly is not common for property owners to open up their property for the installation of permanent monuments that convey a message with which they do not wish to be associated. And because property owners typically do not permit the construction of such monuments on their land, persons who observe donated monuments routinely—and reasonably—interpret them as conveying some message on the property owner's behalf."[111] The open question is whether the government has tacitly accepted these memorials by selectively not enforcing land use laws.

Regulating roadside memorials can put local officials in a "Catch-22" double bind. Local news accounts from a small town in California crystalize the challenge for policymakers.[112] A grieving mother erected a 5-foot cross on a public roadway in memory of her nineteen-year-old son, Anthony. A local resident complained to city officials, and the cross was removed because it violated local signage laws. Two days later, after Anthony's mother pleaded with city officials, the cross was restored. A city official told the complainant that the family "is very upset," and the compromise solution was to restore the cross for another month or so. That deadline came and went, and the cross was still on the public roadway. The complainant then enlisted the assistance of the American Humanist Association to negotiate (or litigate if necessary) the cross's removal. The American Humanist Association's letter to city officials said, "Unquestionably, the city's selective enforcement of its signage ordinance and its displays of the Christian cross on government property violates the state and federal Constitutions and must therefore be removed immediately."

This emotionally charged story garnered local and national media attention.[113] The mother told reporters, "It's so petty and sad that they have to complain over removing a cross." She explained: "It's his personal preference that he was Christian. What's wrong with having a cross up?"[114] The cross was a source of comfort for her and others who knew her son. When faced with removing the cross, she said "It's like I'm losing my son again, pretty much." After the city officials removed the mother's cross, six new crosses were erected by others in the community. Signs on the new crosses included messages like, "What happened to Freedom," "RIP Anthony," "What if this was your Child?," and "To each his own."[115] After the family's one cross was removed, six more appeared in its stead: local policymakers are in a tough spot. Local governments are caught between the grieving who want a memorial to remain—indefinitely—and the few vocal community residents who want it removed.

Conclusion

Establishment Clause jurisprudence seeks to "avoid that divisiveness based upon religion that promotes social conflict."[116] The purpose of the Establishment Clause is to provide equal protection for religious majorities, religious minorities, and nonbelievers. *American Legion* teaches that longstanding and established memorials are presumptively constitutional. Justice Breyer was impressed that the Bladensburg Peace Cross hadn't created any controversy for over ninety years.[117] The Court's Establishment Clause jurisprudence aims to minimize divisiveness and promote tolerance. Going around removing established displays opens the door to more disputes and more debates. The urge to purge all religious displays would open a proverbial can of worms, and a great purge would bespeak hostility to religion. It risks roiling up tensions in a religion-culture war; it risks starting disputes about monuments that don't currently exist. The Court would rather let sleeping monuments lie. The *American Legion* Court has adopted a pragmatic approach. Managing monuments prospectively is less divisive than revisiting old monuments. But within this approach is an implicit acknowledgment that such displays are predominantly religious—or else why would it be hostile to religion to remove them.

While the Court's pragmatic let-old-monuments-lie approach has its appeal, it is weak constitutional guidance for lower courts and policymakers. What do we do with new displays? In particular, how do we evaluate roadside memorial crosses? Newly erected crosses don't seem to fit within the Court's presumption for longstanding displays. But it isn't clear how old is old enough to trigger the presumption—five years, ten years, or fifty years? And what's the test for new displays that don't trigger the presumption? Is

Lemon dead-letter in all contexts, like Justice Thomas urged in *American Legion*? Or is *Lemon* resurrected for any instances when the presumption of constitutionality doesn't apply? Moreover, is the failure to equally enforce a road sign ban, by turning a blind eye to these crosses, an equal protection violation?

In adopting its historico-traditional approach, the Court further muddied an area of the law judges have denominated "a hot mess" and a "jurisprudence in shambles."[118] As illustrated above with local news reports, roadside crosses ignite raw emotions. Establishment Clause jurisprudence seeks to minimize social tensions, not provoke them. But doctrinal uncertainty invites litigation and fuels social conflict. As Professor McConnell noted, doctrinal uncertainty has spurred "continual litigation in the lower courts with unpredictable results, heightening rather than dampening the sectarian divide between religious and nonreligious, Christian and non-Christian."[119] Rather than keeping the peace, the Supreme Court is inviting division. The Court has made the law less clear, not more clear. The jurisprudential hot mess is now even messier.

Notes

1 Lemon v. Kurtzman, 403 U.S. 602 (1971).
2 Town of Greece v. Galloway, 572 U.S. 565, 615 (2014) (Kagan, J., dissenting) ("Our Constitution promises that they may worship in their own way, without fear of penalty or danger, and that in itself is a momentous offering. Yet our Constitution makes a commitment still more remarkable—that however those individuals worship, they will count as full and equal American citizens. A Christian, a Jew, a Muslim (and so forth)—each stands in the same relationship with her country, with her state and local communities, and with every level and body of government. So that when each person performs the duties or seeks the benefits of citizenship, she does so not as an adherent to one or another religion, but simply as an American.").
3 Caroline Mala Corbin, "Nonbelievers and Government Speech," *Iowa Law Review* 90, no. 1 (2012): 379 (arguing "the Establishment Clause can be viewed as essentially functioning as an Equal Protection Clause for nonbelievers"); Alan E. Brownstein, "Harmonizing the Heavenly and Earthly Spheres: The Fragmentation and Synthesis of Religion, Equality, and Speech in the Constitution," *Ohio State Law Journal* 51, no. 1 (1990): 103 (suggesting "the establishment clause has become a de facto substitute for an independent equal protection analysis of the treatment of religious minorities by the state").
4 American Legion v. American Humanist Association, 139 S. Ct. 2067 (2019).
5 Kondrat'yev v. City of Pensacola, 903 F.3d 1169, 1179 (11th Cir. 2018) (Newsom, J., concurring in the judgment) ("The Court's Establishment Clause jurisprudence is, to use a technical legal term of art, a hot mess.").
6 *American Legion*, 139 S. Ct. at 2081 ("The [*Lemon*] test has been harshly criticized by Members of this Court, lamented by lower court judges, and questioned

by a diverse roster of scholars."). *See also* Adrienne E. Hacker-Daniels, "Is It Too Heavy of A Constitutional Cross To Bear? Making Sense Of The Decision in American Legion v. American Humanist Association," *First Amendment Studies* (April, 2020): 7 ("Although the Lemon test has been the predominant application to Establishment Clause cases, over its almost five decades, it has been marginalized, losing its legal heft and luster, providing, as stated in Van Orden v. Perry, "merely a guide and not a binding precedent," and virtually moribund in the Peace Cross case.").

7 Lamb's Chapel v. Ctr. Moriches Union Free Sch. Dist., 508 U.S. 384, 398 (1993) (Scalia, J., concurring in the judgment).

8 Charles O. Collins and Charles D. Rhine, "Roadside Memorials," *Omega* 47, no. 3 (2003): 223.

9 Amanda Reid, "Private Memorials on Public Space: Roadside Crosses at the Intersection of the Free Speech Clause and the Establishment Clause," *Nebraska Law Review* 92, no. 124 (2013): 126.

10 Jennifer Clark and Ashley Cheshire, "RIP By The Roadside: A Comparative Study of Roadside Memorials in New South Wales, Australia, and Texas, United States," *Omega* 48, no. 3 (2004): 214.

11 Jane Stern, "Roadside Memorials," *The Paris Review*, June 1, 2017, https://www.theparisreview.org/blog/2017/06/01/roadside-memorials/.

12 Clark and Cheshire, "RIP By The Roadside," 205.

13 Peter Warzel, "On the Haunting Beauty of Roadside Crosses in New Mexico," *Catapult*, September 11, 2018, https://catapult.co/stories/roadside-crosses-descanso-crucitas-peter-warzel.

14 The World Health Organization reports that the number of annual road traffic deaths has reached 1.35 million, and road traffic injuries are now the leading killer of people aged 5–29 years. "Global Status Report on Road Safety 2018," *World Health Organization*, accessed May 17, 2021, https://www.who.int/violence_injury_prevention/road_safety_status/2018/en/.

15 "Traffic Safety Facts Annual Report Tables, Motor Vehicle Traffic Fatalities and Fatality Rates, 1899–2017," *National Highway Traffic Safety Administration*, accessed May 17, 2021, https://cdan.nhtsa.gov/tsftables/tsfar.htm.

16 Reid, "Private Memorials on Public Space," 131–32.

17 Thomas Fuchs, "Presence in Absence: The Ambiguous Phenomenology of Grief," *Phenomenology and the Cognitive Sciences* 17, no. 1 (2018): 44.

18 Amanda Reid, "Place, Meaning, and the Visual Argument of the Roadside Cross," *Savannah Law Review* 2, no. 1 (2015): 272–76.

19 Avril Maddrell, "Living with the Deceased: Absence, Presence and Absence-Presence," *Cultural Geographies* 20, no. 4 (2013): 501–22.

20 Collins and Rhine, "Roadside Memorials," 228; Maddrell, "Living with the Deceased," 507.

21 Mirjam Klaassens, Peter Groote, and Paulus P. P. Huigen, "Roadside Memorials from a Geographical Perspective," *Mortality* 14, no. 2 (2009): 198–99.

22 Clark and Cheshire, "RIP By The Roadside," 207. Note that in the Netherlands, only one quarter (23%) of surveyed Dutch roadside memorials had a cross. Mirjam Klaassens, Peter D. Groote, and Frank M. Vanclay, "Expressions of Private Mourning in Public Space: The Evolving Structure of Spontaneous and Permanent Roadside Memorials in the Netherlands," *Death Studies* 37, no. 2 (2013): 154.

23 Clark and Cheshire, "RIP By The Roadside," 213.
24 Jennifer Clark and Majella Franzmann, "Authority from Grief, Presence and Place in the Making of Roadside Memorials," *Death Studies* 30, no. 6 (2006): 583.
25 Collins and Rhine, "Roadside Memorials," 229.
26 Lucyna Przybylska, "Memorial Crosses in Poland: A Commonplace and Contested Element of Public Roads," *Geografie*, 120, no. 4 (2015): 507–26 (Poland); Olga Nešporová and Irina Stahl, "Roadside Memorials in the Czech Republic and Romania: Memory versus Religion in Two European Post-Communist Countries," *Mortality* 19, no. 1 (2014): 22–40 (Czech Republic and Romania); Erik Cohen, "Roadside Memorials in Northeastern Thailand," *Omega* 66, no. 4 (2013): 343–63 (Thailand); Mirjam Klaassens, Peter Groote, and Paulus P. P. Huigen, "Roadside Memorials from a Geographical Perspective," *Mortality* 14, no. 2 (2009): 187–201 (Netherlands); Anna Petersson, "Swedish Offerkast and Recent Roadside Memorials," *Folklore* 120, no. 1 (2009): 75–91 (Sweden); Holly Everett, "Roadside Crosses and Memorial Complexes in Texas," *Folklore* 111 (2000): 91–118 (United States).
27 Clark and Cheshire, "RIP By The Roadside," 206.
28 Ibid. 216.
29 Reid, "Place, Meaning, and the Visual Argument of the Roadside Cross," 284–85.
30 Jon K. Reid and Cynthia L. Reid, "A Cross Marks the Spot: A Study of Roadside Death Memorials in Texas and Oklahoma," *Death Studies* 25 no. 4 (2001): 341–56.
31 Kate V. Hartig and Kevin M. Dunn, "Roadside Memorials: Interpreting New Deathscapes in Newcastle, New South Wales," *Australian Geographical Studies* 36, no. 1 (1998): 5–20.
32 Collins and Rhine, "Roadside Memorials," 236.
33 Reid, "Private Memorials on Public Space," 149–55.
34 Charles Dunlap, "Council Approves Ordinance for Roadside Memorials," *The Mexico Ledger*, October 29, 2019, https://www.mexicoledger.com/news/20191029/council-approves-ordinance-for-roadside-memorials
35 Dave Downey, "Caltrans Apologizes, Says Highway Wrong Place for Memorials," *The San Diego Union-Tribune*, September 13, 2007, https://www.sandiegouniontribune.com/sdut-caltrans-apologizes-says-highways-wrong-place-for-2007sep13-story.html
36 Clark and Franzmann, "Authority from Grief, Presence and Place in the Making of Roadside Memorials," 584.
37 George E. Dickinson and Heath C. Hoffmann, "Roadside Memorial Policies in the United States," *Mortality* 15, no. 2 (2010): 156–57.
38 Lisa J. Huriash, "Memorials Create Dilemma for Cities," *Sun Sentinel*, February 25, 2012, https://www.sun-sentinel.com/sfl-memorials-create-dilemma-for-cities-20151202-story.html
39 Dickinson and Hoffmann, "Roadside Memorial Policies in the United States," 160–62.
40 Reid, "Private Memorials on Public Space," 143–44.
41 Chris Ross, "Roadside Memorials: Public Policy vs. Private Expression," *American City & County* 113, no. 5 (1998): 53, https://www.americancityandcounty.com/1998/05/01/roadside-memorials-public-policy-vs-private-expression/ ("Removing unofficial markers is a sensitive issue.").

42 Collins and Rhine, "Roadside Memorials," 241.

43 " 'Get On With Your Life' Community Rallies Behind Mom Who Received Letter To Remove Son's Memorial," *Action News Jax*, April 29, 2019, https://www.actionnewsjax.com/news/local/brunswick-community-stands-by-mother-asked-to-take-down-son-s-memorial/944616674/. A similar story unfolded in a small town in Vermont. Jackie Pascale, "Stories of the Cross: A Devastating Reminder—For Some, A Cross Can Make Them Relive A Tragedy; For Others, It Can Be A Way To Move On," *NBC5*, November 26, 2019, https://www.mynbc5.com/article/stories-of-the-cross-a-devastating-reminder/29989771.

44 Zahra Mulroy, "Neighbours Send Cold-Hearted Letter To Grieving Family About Memorial For Young Son," *Mirror*, May 3, 2019, https://www.mirror.co.uk/news/us-news/neighbours-send-cold-hearted-letter-14974666.

45 Public opinion survey research shows that drivers are "fairly divided on the issue." Richard Tay, "Drivers' Perceptions and Reactions to Roadside Memorials," *Accident Analysis and Prevention* 41, no. 4 (2009): 669.

46 James Sparvero, "Roadside Cross For Palm Bay Teenager Might Be Removed After Complaint," *WKMG News 6*, April 15, 2019, https://www.clickorlando.com/news/2019/04/16/roadside-cross-for-palm-bay-teenager-might-be-removed-after-complaint/.

47 Jenny Goldade, "Roadside Memorials: Meaning and Rules Behind Them," *Frazer Consultants*, June 28, 2017, https://www.frazerconsultants.com/2017/06/roadside-memorials-meaning-and-rules-behind-them/.

48 Reid, "Place, Meaning, and the Visual Argument of the Roadside Cross," 278–79.

49 Alexis Hobbs, "Couple Who Lost Daughter in Car Accident Find Her Roadside Memorial Replaced With Horrible Note," *Woman's Day*, September 3, 2015, https://www.womansday.com/life/news/a51810/couple-who-lost-daughter-in-car-accident-find-her-roadside-memorial-replaced-with-horrible-note/.

50 Marta Pascual Juanola, " 'This Is Not A Cemetery': Vandals Steal Mandurah Roadside Memorial, Leave Angry Note Behind," *WA Today*, April 17, 2019, https://www.watoday.com.au/national/western-australia/this-is-not-a-cemetery-vandals-steal-mandurah-roadside-memorial-leave-angry-note-behind-20190417-p51f5h.html.

51 Carla Hildebrandt, "Self-Confessed Mandurah Roadside Memorial Vandal Plans To Continue Cross Crusade," *WA Today*, May 10, 2019, https://www.watoday.com.au/national/western-australia/self-confessed-mandurah-roadside-memorial-vandal-plans-to-continue-cross-crusade-20190509-p51ltj.html.

52 Stephanie Wade, "Grieving Father Upset After Daughter's Roadside Memorial Removed," *RTV6 Indianapolis*, January 23, 2020, https://www.theindychannel.com/news/working-for-you/grieving-father-upset-after-daughters-roadside-memorial-removed.

53 Dickinson and Hoffmann, "Roadside Memorial Policies in the United States," 161.

54 Melissa Eichman, "Hernando Family Says Missing Roadside Memorial Found," *Bay News 9*, January 2, 2020, https://www.baynews9.com/fl/tampa/news/2020/01/02/hernando-family-hoping-for-return-of-missing-roadside-memorial#.

55 "Office of Maintenance: Memorial Markers," *Florida Department of Transportation*, accessed May 17, 2021. https://www.fdot.gov/maintenance/memorialmarkers.shtm.

56 Reid, "Private Memorials on Public Space," 150–51.

57 Ibid. at 149–55.
58 Collins and Rhine, "Roadside Memorials," 237; Dickinson and Hoffmann, "Roadside Memorial Policies in the United States," 161.
59 Ian Urbina, "As Roadside Memorials Multiply, A Second Look," *New York Times.com*, February 6, 2006, https://www.nytimes.com/2006/02/06/us/as-roadside-memorials-multiply-a-second-look.html.
60 Ross, "Roadside Memorials," 51.
61 Engel v. Vitale, 370 U.S. 421, 431 (1962). As the Supreme Court has stated: "The history of governmentally established religion, both in England and in this country, showed that whenever government had allied itself with one particular form of religion, the inevitable result had been that it had incurred the hatred, disrespect and even contempt of those who held contrary beliefs. That same history showed that many people had lost their respect for any religion that had relied upon the support for government to spread its faith. The Establishment Clause thus stands as an expression of principle on the part of the Founders of our Constitution that religion is too personal, too sacred, too holy, to permit its 'unhallowed perversion' by a civil magistrate." *Engel*, 370 U.S. at 431–32.
62 Lemon v. Kurtzman, 403 U.S. 602 (1971).
63 County of Allegheny v. American Civil Liberties Union, 492 U.S. 573, 593 (1989).
64 "The Religion Clauses of the Constitution aim to foster a society in which people of all beliefs can live together harmoniously, and the presence of the Bladensburg Cross on the land where it has stood for so many years is fully consistent with that aim." American Legion v. American Humanist Association, 139 S. Ct. 2067, 2074 (2019).
65 Lynch v. Donnelly, 465 U.S. 668, 688 (1984) (O'Connor, J., concurring).
66 Michael W. McConnell, "No More (Old) Symbol Cases," *Cato Supreme Court Review* (2018–2019): 101 ("The Establishment Clause is all about reducing the government's power to influence the national religious culture—not about reducing (or increasing) the role of religion. The best way for government's role to be minimized is for the governmental sphere to conform, in general, to the public culture as it has developed over time. That sphere is a mixture of the secular and the religious.").
67 Town of Greece v. Galloway, 572 U.S. 565, 615 (2014) (Kagan, J., dissenting) ("Our Constitution promises that they may worship in their own way, without fear of penalty or danger, and that in itself is a momentous offering. Yet our Constitution makes a commitment still more remarkable—that however those individuals worship, they will count as full and equal American citizens. A Christian, a Jew, a Muslim (and so forth)—each stands in the same relationship with her country, with her state and local communities, and with every level and body of government. So that when each person performs the duties or seeks the benefits of citizenship, she does so not as an adherent to one or another religion, but simply as an American.").
68 Corbin, "Nonbelievers and Government Speech," 379; Brownstein, "Harmonizing the Heavenly and Earthly Spheres," 103.
69 Lynch v. Donnelly, 465 U.S. 668 (1984).
70 *Lynch*, 465 U.S. at 673.
71 County of Allegheny v. American Civil Liberties Union, 492 U.S. 573 (1989).
72 *County of Allegheny*, 492 U.S. at 601–02.
73 McCreary County v. American Civil Liberties Union, 545 U.S. 844 (2005).

74 Van Orden v. Perry, 545 U.S. 677 (2005) (plurality announced by Chief Justice Rehnquist, in which Justices Scalia, Kennedy, and Thomas joined; Justice Breyer concurred in the judgment).
75 *Van Orden*, 545 U.S. at 701 (Breyer, J., concurring in the judgment) ("Here the tablets have been used as part of a display that communicates not simply a religious message, but a secular message as well. The circumstances surrounding the display's placement on the capitol grounds and its physical setting suggest that the State itself intended the latter, nonreligious aspects of the tablets' message to predominate. And the monument's 40-year history on the Texas state grounds indicates that that has been its effect.").
76 *McCreary County*, 545 U.S. at 860.
77 Ibid. 867.
78 American Atheists, Inc. v. Davenport, 637 F.3d 1095 (10th Cir. 2010).
79 Ibid. 1119–20.
80 Ibid. 1123 ("the designers' purpose in creating the displays at issue in this case may not always coincide with the displays' likely effect on the reasonable observer").
81 *Van Orden*, 545 U.S. at 702 (Breyer, J., concurring).
82 The Tenth Circuit stated: "Here, we conclude that the cross memorials would convey to a reasonable observer that the state of Utah is endorsing Christianity. The memorials use the preeminent symbol of Christianity, and they do so standing alone (as opposed to it being part of some sort of display involving other symbols). That cross conspicuously bears the imprimatur of a state entity, the UHP, and is found primarily on public land." *American Atheists, Inc.*, 637 F.3d at 1121.
83 "The Religion Clauses of the Constitution aim to foster a society in which people of all beliefs can live together harmoniously, and the presence of the Bladensburg Cross on the land where it has stood for so many years is fully consistent with that aim." *American Legion*, 139 S. Ct. at 2074.
84 McConnell, "No More (Old) Symbol Cases," 97.
85 The majority opinion written by Justice Alito was joined by Chief Justice Roberts and Justices Breyer, Kagan, and Kavanaugh, which included a partial plurality without Justice Kagan. Justices Breyer, Kagan, and Kavanaugh each wrote separate concurring opinions. Justice Thomas and Justice Gorsuch each filed an opinion concurring in the judgment. And Justice Ginsburg filed a dissenting opinion.
86 *American Legion*, 139 S. Ct. at 2076 (noting "the cross's widespread resonance as a symbol of sacrifice in the war").
87 Ibid. 2074 (quoting Van Orden v. Perry, 545 U.S. 677, 704 (2005) (Breyer, J., concurring in the judgment)).
88 Ibid. 2085.
89 Ibid. 2087 (plurality) (Part II D).
90 Ibid. 2081–82 (plurality) (Part II A) (counseling "against efforts to evaluate such [static monument] cases under *Lemon* and toward application of a presumption of constitutionality for longstanding monuments, symbols, and practices").
91 Ibid. 2091 (Breyer, J., concurring).
92 Ibid. 2091 (Breyer, J., concurring).
93 Ibid. 2097 (Thomas, J., concurring in the judgment) ("I would take the logical next step and overrule the *Lemon* test in all contexts.").

94 Ibid. 2101 (Gorsuch, J., concurring in the judgment) ("As today's plurality rightly indicates in Part II–A, however, *Lemon* was a misadventure.").
95 Ibid. 2102 (Gorsuch, J., concurring in the judgment).
96 McConnell, "No More (Old) Symbol Cases," 96–97 ("[I]n spite of the appearance of a fractured Court, the justices broke 7-2 on the narrow question of already-established symbols and 6-3 on the broader question of *Lemon*. That supermajority, including two of the liberal justices, will go far to legitimate the decision in the eyes of the public and to insulate it against future challenge and from nitpicking by lower courts.").
97 *American Legion*, 139 S. Ct. at 2094 (Kagan, J., concurring in part).
98 McConnell, "No More (Old) Symbol Cases," 104 ("Using the standard methodology for identifying the holding of a case where there are multiple opinions but no majority, it is clear that, despite Justice Kagan's choice 'out of perhaps an excess of caution' not to join Sections II-B and II-D, the Alito opinion commands a solid majority of six votes. I cannot imagine a lower court thinking, after this, that the *Lemon* test is good law.").
99 Lamb's Chapel v. Ctr. Moriches Union Free School District, 508 U.S. 384, 398 (1993) (Scalia, J., concurring in the judgment).
100 Georgia v. Public.Resource.Org, Inc., 140 S. Ct. 1498, 1520 n.6 (2020) (Thomas J., dissenting).
101 *Id.* at 1513 ("Justice Thomas, with whom Justice Alito joins, and with whom Justice Breyer joins as to all but Part II–A and footnote 6, dissenting.").
102 Town of Greece v. Galloway, 572 U.S. 565 (2014); Marsh v. Chambers, 463 U.S. 783 (1983).
103 American Legion v. American Humanist Association, 139 S. Ct. 2067 (2019). *See also* Salazar v. Buono, 559 U.S. 700 (2010) (plurality opinion) (remanding case addressing Latin cross on federal land honoring World War I soldiers).
104 *American Legion*, 139 S. Ct. at 2102 (Gorsuch, J., concurring in the judgment) ("How old must a monument, symbol, or practice be to qualify for this new presumption [of constitutionality]?"). *See also* McConnell, "No More (Old) Symbol Cases," 99 ("The Court provides no definition of what it means, but presumably the term "established" refers to monuments or practices that were erected without significant controversy and remained in place for some period of time—not necessarily lengthy—before the litigation started to generate controversy (absent evidence that the lack of opposition was due to intimidation). It is impossible to predict how many cases, if any, will fall close to that line.").
105 *American Legion*, 139 S. Ct. at 2084–85.
106 McConnell, "No More (Old) Symbol Cases," 97 ("[*American Legion*] allows religiously expressive sleeping dogs to lie. But it does not green-light attempts by present and future officeholders to interject new religious symbols as a type of religious-identity politics.").
107 Clark and Cheshire, "RIP By The Roadside," 206.
108 McConnell, "No More (Old) Symbol Cases," 106 ("The death of *Lemon* is therefore welcome. The main question is what will take its place.").
109 Lamb's Chapel v. Ctr. Moriches Union Free School District, 508 U.S. 384, 399 (1993) (Scalia, J., concurring in the judgment) ("The secret of the *Lemon* test's survival, I think, is that it is so easy to kill."); *American Legion*, 139 S. Ct. at 2080

("As Establishment Clause cases involving a great array of laws and practices came to the Court, it became more and more apparent that the Lemon test could not resolve them.").

110 Pleasant Grove City, Utah v. Summum, 555 U.S. 460, 470 (2009).

111 Ibid. 471.

112 Kimberly Winston, "Calif. City Torn By Multiple Fights Over Public Crosses," *WashingtonPost.com*, March 11, 2014, https://www.washingtonpost.com/national/religion/calif-city-torn-by-multiple-fights-over-public-crosses/2014/03/11/7e46013c-a956-11e3-8a7b-c1c684e2671f_story.html

113 "Mom Who Lost Son in Fatal Crash To Remove Cross Memorial After Atheist Group Complains," *CBS Los Angeles*, March 6, 2014, https://losangeles.cbslocal.com/2014/03/06/mom-who-lost-son-in-fatal-crash-to-remove-cross-memorial-after-atheist-group-complains/

114 Jonathan Lloyd, Jacob Rascon, and Tony Shin, "Mother Removes Cross Memorial After Dispute With Atheist Rights Group," *NBC Los Angeles*, March 6, 2014, https://www.nbclosangeles.com/news/local/lake-elsinore-atheists-group-demands-cross-removal-american-humanist-association-devaney-memorial-religion-church-state/1992042/

115 Ibid.

116 *Van Orden*, 545 U.S. at 698 (Breyer, J., concurring in the judgment).

117 *American Legion*, 139 S. Ct. at 2091 (Breyer, J., concurring) ("the Cross has stood on the same land for 94 years, generating no controversy in the community until this lawsuit was filed")

118 Utah Highway Patrol Ass'n v. Am. Atheists, Inc., 132 S. Ct. 12, 13 (2011) (Thomas, J., dissenting from a denial of a petition for writ of certiorari).

119 McConnell, "No More (Old) Symbol Cases," 96.

Bibliography

Action News Jax. "'Get on with your life' Community Rallies Behind Mom Who Received Letter to Remove Son's Memorial." April 29, 2019. https://www.actionnewsjax.com/news/local/brunswick-community-stands-by-mother-asked-to-take-down-son-s-memorial/944616674/.

American Legion v. American Humanist Association, 139 S. Ct. 2067 (2019).

American Atheists, Inc. v. Davenport, 637 F.3d 1095 (10th Cir. 2010).

Brownstein, Alan E. "Harmonizing the Heavenly and Earthly Spheres: The Fragmentation and Synthesis of Religion, Equality, and Speech in the Constitution." *Ohio State Law Journal* 51, no. 1 (1990): 89–174. http://hdl.handle.net/1811/64032.

CBS Los Angeles. "Mom Who Lost Son in Fatal Crash To Remove Cross Memorial After Atheist Group Complains." March 6, 2014. https://losangeles.cbslocal.com/2014/03/06/mom-who-lost-son-in-fatal-crash-to-remove-cross-memorial-after-atheist-group-complains/.

Clark, Jennifer, and Ashley Cheshire. "RIP By The Roadside: A Comparative Study of Roadside Memorials in New South Wales, Australia, and Texas, United

States." *Omega* 48, no. 3 (May 2004): 204–21. https://doi.org/10.2190/3RED-6H7D-PNNC-URT7.

Clark, Jennifer, and Majella Franzmann. "Authority from Grief, Presence and Place in the Making of Roadside Memorials." *Death Studies* 30, no. 6 (September 2006): 579–99. https://doi.org/10.1080/07481180600742574.

Cohen, Erik. "Roadside Memorials in Northeastern Thailand." *Omega* 66, no. 4 (June 2013): 343–63. https://doi.org/10.2190/OM.66.4.e.

Collins, Charles O., and Charles D. Rhine. "Roadside Memorials." *Omega* 47, no. 3 (November 2003): 221–44. https://doi.org/10.2190/1654-01N2-2A3C-GQ9C.

Corbin, Caroline Mala. "Nonbelievers and Government Speech." *Iowa Law Review* 90, no. 1 (2012): 347–415. https://repository.law.miami.edu/cgi/viewcontent.cgi?article=1047&context=fac_articles.

County of Allegheny v. American Civil Liberties Union, 492 U.S. 573 (1989).

Dickinson, George E., and Heath C. Hoffmann. "Roadside Memorial Policies in the United States." *Mortality* 15, no. 2 (July 2010): 154–67. https://doi.org/10.1080/13576275.2010.482775.

Downey, Dave. "Caltrans Apologizes, Says Highway Wrong Place for Memorials." *The San Diego Union-Tribune*, September 13, 2007. https://www.sandiegouniontribune.com/sdut-caltrans-apologizes-says-highways-wrong-place-for-2007sep13-story.html.

Dunlap, Charles. "Council Approves Ordinance for Roadside Memorials." *The Mexico Ledger*, October 29, 2019. https://www.mexicoledger.com/news/20191029/council-approves-ordinance-for-roadside-memorials.

Eichman, Melissa. "Hernando Family Says Missing Roadside Memorial Found." *Bay News 9*, January 2, 2020. https://www.baynews9.com/fl/tampa/news/2020/01/02/hernando-family-hoping-for-return-of-missing-roadside-memorial#.

Engel v. Vitale, 370 U.S. 421 (1962).

Everett, Holly. "Roadside Crosses and Memorial Complexes in Texas." *Folklore* 111 no. 1 (2000): 91–118. https://doi.org/10.1080/001558700360906.

Florida Department of Transportation. "Office of Maintenance: Memorial Markers." Accessed May 17, 2021. https://www.fdot.gov/maintenance/memorialmarkers.shtm.

Fuchs, Thomas. "Presence in Absence: The Ambiguous Phenomenology of Grief." *Phenomenology and the Cognitive Sciences* 17, no. 1 (2018): 43–63. https://doi.org/10.1007/s11097-017-9506-2.

Georgia v. Public.Resource.Org, Inc., 140 S. Ct. 1498 (2020).

Goldade, Jenny. "Roadside Memorials: Meaning and Rules Behind Them." *Frazer Consultants*, June 28, 2017. https://www.frazerconsultants.com/2017/06/roadside-memorials-meaning-and-rules-behind-them/.

Hacker-Daniels, Adrienne E. "Is It Too Heavy of A Constitutional Cross To Bear? Making Sense of The Decision in American Legion v. American Humanist Association."

First Amendment Studies (April 2020): 1–12. https://doi.org/10.1080/21689725.2020.1742762.

Hartig, Kate V., and Kevin M. Dunn. "Roadside Memorials: Interpreting New Deathscapes in Newcastle, New South Wales." *Australian Geographical Studies* 36, no. 1 (1998): 5–20. https://doi.org/10.1111/1467-8470.00036.

Hildebrandt, Carla. "Self-Confessed Mandurah Roadside Memorial Vandal Plans to Continue Cross Crusade." *WA Today*, May 10, 2019. https://www.watoday.com.au/national/western-australia/self-confessed-mandurah-roadside-memorial-vandal-plans-to-continue-cross-crusade-20190509-p51ltj.html.

Hobbs, Alexis. "Couple Who Lost Daughter in Car Accident Find Her Roadside Memorial Replaced With Horrible Note." *Woman's Day*, September 3, 2015. https://www.womansday.com/life/news/a51810/couple-who-lost-daughter-in-car-accident-find-her-roadside-memorial-replaced-with-horrible-note/.

Juanola, Maria Pascual. "'This Is Not A Cemetery': Vandals Steal Mandurah Roadside Memorial, Leave Angry Note Behind." *WA Today*, April 17, 2019. https://www.watoday.com.au/national/western-australia/this-is-not-a-cemetery-vandals-steal-mandurah-roadside-memorial-leave-angry-note-behind-20190417-p51f5h.html.

Klaassens, Mirjam, Peter D. Groote, and Frank M. Vanclay. "Expressions of Private Mourning in Public Space: The Evolving Structure of Spontaneous and Permanent Roadside Memorials in the Netherlands." *Death Studies* 37, no. 2 (2013): 145–71. https://doi.org/10.1080/07481187.2011.641137.

Klaassens, Mirjam, Peter Groote, and Paulus P. P. Huigen. "Roadside Memorials from a Geographical Perspective," *Mortality* 14, no. 2 (2009): 187–201. https://doi.org/10.1080/13576270902808068.

Lamb's Chapel v. Ctr. Moriches Union Free School District, 508 U.S. 384 (1993).

Lemon v. Kurtzman, 203 U.S. 602 (1971).

Lloyd, Jonathan, Jacob Rascon, and Tony Shin. "Mother Removes Cross Memorial After Dispute With Atheist Rights Group." *NBC Los Angeles*, March 6, 2014. https://www.nbclosangeles.com/news/local/lake-elsinore-atheists-group-demands-cross-removal-american-humanist-association-devaney-memorial-religion-church-state/1992042/

Lynch v. Donnelly, 465 U.S. 668 (1984).

Maddrell, Avril. "Living with the Deceased: Absence, Presence and Absence-Presence." *Cultural Geographies* 20, no. 4 (April 2013): 501–22. https://doi.org/10.1177/1474474013482806.

Marsh v. Chambers, 463 U.S. 783 (1983).

McConnell, Michael W. "No More (Old) Symbol Cases," *Cato Supreme Court Review* (2018–2019): 91–118. https://www.cato.org/sites/cato.org/files/2019-09/cato-supreme-court-2019-6.pdf.

McCreary County v. American Civil Liberties Union, 545 U.S. 844 (2005).

Mulroy, Zahra. "Neighbours Send Cold-Hearted Letter to Grieving Family about Memorial for Young Son." *Mirror*, May 3, 2019. https://www.mirror.co.uk/news/us-news/neighbours-send-cold-hearted-letter-14974666.

National Highway Traffic Safety Administration. "Traffic Safety Facts Annual Report Tables, Motor Vehicle Traffic Fatalities and Fatality Rates, 1899–2017." Accessed May 17, 2021. https://cdan.nhtsa.gov/tsftables/tsfar.htm.

Nešporová, Olga, and Irina Stahl. "Roadside Memorials in the Czech Republic and Romania: Memory versus Religion in Two European Post-Communist Countries." *Mortality* 19, no. 1 (2014): 22–40. https://doi.org/10.1080/13576275.2013.870543.

Pascale, Jackie. "Stories of the Cross: A Devastating Reminder – For Some, a Cross Can Make Them Relive a Tragedy; For Others, It Can Be a Way to Move On." *NBC5*, November 26, 2019. https://www.mynbc5.com/article/stories-of-the-cross-a-devastating-reminder/29989771.

Petersson, Anna. "Swedish *Offerkast* and Recent Roadside Memorials." *Folklore* 120, no. 1 (2009): 75–91. https://doi.org/10.1080/00155870802647841.

Pleasant Grove City, Utah v. Summum, 555 U.S. 460 (2009).

Przybylska, Lucyna. "Memorial Crosses in Poland: A Commonplace and Contested Element of Public Roads." *Geografie* 120, no. 4 (2015): 507–26. https://doi.org/10.37040/geografie2015120040507.

Przybylska, Lucyna, Justyna Liro, Grażyna Holly, and Ewa Klima. "Inscriptions on Roadside Memorials in Poland." *Death Studies*, 44, no.7 (2020): 419–29. https://doi.org/10.1080/07481187.2019.1626944.

Reid, Amanda. "Private Memorials on Public Space: Roadside Crosses at the Intersection of the Free Speech Clause and the Establishment Clause." *Nebraska Law Review* 92, no. 124 (2013): 124–84. https://digitalcommons.unl.edu/nlr/vol92/iss1/5/.

Reid, Amanda. "Place, Meaning, and the Visual Argument of the Roadside Cross." *Savannah Law Review* 2, no. 1 (2015): 265–300. https://works.bepress.com/amanda_reid/16/.

Reid, Jon K., and Cynthia L. Reid. "A Cross Marks the Spot: A Study of Roadside Death Memorials in Texas and Oklahoma." *Death Studies* 25, no. 4 (2001): 341–56. https://doi.org/10.1080/07481180125931.

Ross, Chris. "Roadside Memorials: Public Policy vs. Private Expression." *American City & County* 113, no. 5 (1998): 50–53. https://www.americancityandcounty.com/1998/05/01/roadside-memorials-public-policy-vs-private-expression/.

Salazar v. Buono, 559 U.S. 700 (2010).

Sparvero, James. "Roadside Cross for Palm Bay Teenager Might Be Removed after Complaint." *WKMG News 6*, April 15, 2019. https://www.clickorlando.com/news/2019/04/16/roadside-cross-for-palm-bay-teenager-might-be-removed-after-complaint/.

Stern, Jane. "Roadside Memorials." *The Paris* Review, June 1, 2017. https://www.theparisreview.org/blog/2017/06/01/roadside-memorials/.

Tay, Richard. "Drivers' Perceptions and Reactions to Roadside Memorials." *Accident Analysis and Prevention* 41, no. 4 (2009): 663–69. https://doi.org/10.1016/j.aap.2009.03.006.

Town of Greece v. Galloway, 572 U.S. 565 (2014).

Urbina, Ian. "As Roadside Memorials Multiply, A Second Look." *New York Times.com*, February 6, 2006. https://www.nytimes.com/2006/02/06/us/as-roadside-memorials-multiply-a-second-look.html.

Utah Highway Patrol Ass'n v. Am. Atheists, Inc., 132 S. Ct. 12 (2011).

Van Orden v. Perry, 545 U.S. 677 (2005).

Wade, Stephanie. "Grieving father upset after daughter's roadside memorial removed." *RTV6 Indianapolis*, January 23, 2020. https://www.theindychannel.com/news/working-for-you/grieving-father-upset-after-daughters-roadside-memorial-removed.

Warzel, Peter. "On the Haunting Beauty of Roadside Crosses in New Mexico." *Catapault*, September 11, 2018. https://catapult.co/stories/roadside-crosses-descanso-crucitas-peter-warzel.

Winston, Kimberly. "Calif. City Torn By Multiple Fights Over Public Crosses." *WashingtonPost.com*, March 11, 2014. https://www.washingtonpost.com/national/religion/calif-city-torn-by-multiple-fights-over-public-crosses/2014/03/11/7e46013c-a956-11e3-8a7b-c1c684e2671f_story.html.

World Health Organization. "Global Status Report on Road Safety 2018." Accessed May 17, 2021. ISBN: 9789241565684. https://www.who.int/violence_injury_prevention/road_safety_status/2018/en/.

8. *The Recognition of Religiosity: Taze Gibson, Jehovah's Witnesses, and the Selective Training and Service Act of 1940*

DAVID R. DEWBERRY AND PAT ARNESON

When the United States goes to war, draftees who are morally opposed to taking up arms also go to battle. However, their fight is a far different one from soldiers who serve without objection in the military. Those who seek an exemption from fighting abroad may find themselves fighting at home for the equal recognition of their voices, beliefs, and freedoms. Such people are, at best, popularly referred to as conscientious objectors. At worst, they are called traitors and un-American.

Taze Hamrick Gibson was born in Meridian, Mississippi, and was a faithful Jehovah's Witness throughout his entire life. Gibson registered as required under the Selective Training and Service Act of 1940. The Act gave the President of the United States the authority to draft soldiers for training and service following the declaration of war against Germany in World War II. Gibson received a letter in October 1942 from the local board of the Selective Service system in El Dorado, Arkansas, where he was living. That letter would be the start of a four-year battle that Gibson would fight for his right to be treated equally to soldiers from other religions who objected to serving in the military. In this chapter we examine the conflict between equal protection under the law and the freedom of religion that Taze Hamrick Gibson, a Jehovah's Witness, experienced when he fought for his rights during World War II.

First, we outline the origins and beliefs of Jehovah's Witnesses. An overview of the Selective Training and Service Act of 1940 follows, which provides context for the classification of Jehovah's Witnesses in World War II.

We review Gibson's case, discussing how his right to equal protection and right to freedom of religion were in conflict with one another. Government employees were working from a legal paradigm, while Gibson was approaching the situation from a communicative paradigm. We argue that Gibson and all the other Jehovah's Witnesses around the world deserve to have their voices heard and to be treated equally with non-Jehovah's Witnesses under the law.

The Origins and Beliefs of Jehovah's Witnesses

Charles Taze Russell began the Watchtower Bible and Tract Society, popularly referred to as Jehovah's Witnesses, in Pittsburgh, Pennsylvania in 1872. Russell was unsatisfied with the various orthodox Christian doctrines of the time and organized the Watch Tower Bible and Tract Society to express his understanding of the Bible. Initially, his followers were called "Russellites" but in 1931 they came to be known as Jehovah's Witnesses.[1] Since then, the group has grown worldwide with more than 8.5 million members.[2]

Jehovah's Witnesses identity fifteen "basic beliefs" that shape their religion.[3] These include a recognition that the Bible is inspired by the word of God (Jehovah); that Jesus is the son of God and the Holy Trinity does not exist; and that the Old and New Testaments of the Bible are literal, although there are some aspects that are figurative. Jehovah's Witnesses believe that paradise was lost when Adam and Eve, tempted by Satan, disobeyed God in the Garden of Eden. Paradise will be restored following the Battle of Armageddon, when Jesus and God's Angels will wage war on Satan and his demons.[4]

Members of Jehovah's Witnesses are certain that people, such as themselves, who believe in and obey God will live in paradise on Earth following Armageddon. Every person who is baptized as a Jehovah's Witness is considered by the church to be a minister.[5] Joe Knox explained, "The importance of public ministry to the Jehovah's Witness cannot be overstated.. . . Witnesses are simply not regarded as Witnesses in good standing unless they engage in evangelism."[6] Evangelism is a dominant marker of their faith. To convert people to their ministry, Witnesses go door to door to discuss their religion.

Members of the Jehovah's Witnesses actively engage in face-to-face witnessing activities. The practice of Jehovah's Witnesses' door-knocking is due to the belief that the only way to reach people is by talking with them face-to-face. Information alone about the group would not persuade other people to attend a congregational meeting.[7] During their door-to-door proselytizing, Jehovah's Witnesses point to current events such as "war, famine, environmental pollution, genocide, and international terrorism" as evidence "that the end of the world is imminent and that a New Kingdom is about to be inaugurated" in the battle of Armageddon.[8] This proselytizing is the *sine qua non* of being a Jehovah's Witnesses.

The drive to convert other people to their faith is so strong that Jehovah's Witnesses have described ministering as "returning to a place where they have encountered difficulties, believing that it is their missionary duty to do so."[9] Witnesses persist, regardless of people who do not answer the door, who will not talk with them, or who argue with them about faith. Ironically, "this very consistency in exalting their faith has played a large part in arousing public anger against the group."[10]

Similar animosity is also directed toward Jehovah's Witnesses because they are seen as un-American. Knox writes, "the refusal of the Jehovah's Witnesses to perform some of the most basic rituals of citizenship has led champions of Americanism to cast them as unpatriotic and even seditious."[11] Jehovah Witnesses refuse to salute the flag, which they believe is a violation of the ten commandments' prohibition on graven images. Further, they refuse to engage in military service or to fight in any wars of human origin.[12] An example of such a war is World War II, which saw the first peace time draft in the United States.

Selective Training and Service Act of 1940

Although the United States had not yet entered World War II, there was a growing sense during the 1930s that the nation needed to increase and strengthen the military.[13] In response, the Selective Training and Service Act of 1940 was passed by Congress and signed into law by President Franklin D. Roosevelt. The Act was passed on September 16, 1940 to "provide for the common defense by increasing the personnel of the armed forces of the United States and providing for its training."[14]

The 1940 Selective Training and Service Act was based in large part on the 1917 Selective Service Act. There were some minor differences (e.g., ages at which men were required to register), but many similarities. For example, each man was required to serve for twelve consecutive months and then remain in the reserves for ten years or until he turned forty-five years old, draftees were identified by lottery, and draft numbers were included in capsules that were drawn from a bowl.

However, there were some differences between the two conscription Acts. Information on conscientious objectors is included in both Acts. They use parallel language related to ordained ministers and theology students.

However, one difference is that theology students were required to be enrolled in theology school "for more than one year prior to the date" of the 1940 Act.[15] This requirement was not included in the 1917 Act. In addition, Jehovah's Witnesses were not often granted a ministerial exemption from the Selective Training and Service Act of 1940.

Section 5(g) of the 1940 Act specifically relates to conscientious objectors. Men could file for exemption from service if "by reason of religious training and belief, [he] is conscientiously opposed to participation in war in any form. Any such person claiming such exemption ... whose claim is sustained ... [may] be assigned to noncombatant service ... [or] assigned to work of national importance, under civil direction."[16] The Act identifies a process for filing an appeal, including a hearing and board recommendations.

In addition to conscientious objectors, the 1917 Selective Service Act included exemptions from training and service for several other groups of people. These included "regular or duly ordained ministers of religion, students who at the time of the approval of this Act are preparing for the ministry in recognized theological or divinity schools" and any person "who is found to be a member of any well-recognized religious sect ... whose existing creed or principles forbid its members to participate in war in any form and whose religious convictions are against war or participation therein in accordance with the creed or principles of said religious organizations."[17] These statements exempted some members of religions. Members of Jehovah's Witnesses were required to file an appeal for exemption from training and service.

The 1917 Act included noncombatant service, stating "no person so exempted shall be exempted from service in any capacity that the President shall declare to be noncombatant."[18] During World War I conscientious objectors served in noncombatant roles and were part of the military. These roles included serving as fire fighters or in psychiatric hospitals.[19] In 1917, if a conscientious objector refused to participate in any way, he was imprisoned. If guards perceived him as being insincere, his imprisonment might include being given less food, solitary confinement, hard labor, or even physical abuse.[20]

The 1940 Act altered the exemptions that were given. Three classes of people were singled out: aliens, ministers, and conscientious objectors. Aliens living in the United States who had no intention of becoming an American citizen were required to register for the draft but were exempt from service. Ministers who were "regular or duly ordained" and "students who are preparing for the ministry in theological or divinity schools" were also exempt from service.[21] Conscientious objectors, men who refused to participate "in war in any form," were reclassified in 1940 and no longer exempt from service.[22]

In 1940, conscientious objectors were assigned to noncombatant roles in the military (e.g., medical units) or tasked with performing "work of national importance under civilian direction."[23] National service included being placed in Civilian Public Service Camps, also known as "work camps."[24] Jehovah's Witnesses referred to these camps as "Satan's tools."[25] At these camps, draftees largely continued projects that originated with the Civilian Conservation Corps, a voluntary work relief program that employed men during the Great Depression. Many of these camps were funded by churches and religious organizations. In the work camps men were either not paid at all or received a small allowance.[26] Each man had to find a sponsor to pay $35 a month in order to cover the expense to house and feed them.[27]

While the national service option made the 1940 Act "more liberal" than the 1917 Act, the 1940 version failed in one key regard.[28] The 1940 Act failed "to recognize the conscientious scruples of a substantial number of persons ... [including] those willing to fight in some circumstances and thus not opposed to 'participation in war in any form' but unwilling to engage in the type of struggle for which the draft was invoked."[29] This perceived inconsistency caused a conundrum for some local draft boards.

Classifying Jehovah's Witnesses

The Selective Training and Service Act of 1940 presented a problem for Jehovah's Witnesses, and Jehovah's Witnesses presented a problem for local draft boards in each state.[30] At issue was the statute's classification system. The local boards who implemented the legislation, as well as members of the general community, were often antagonistic toward men who appealed their classification. Jehovah's Witnesses were no exception. Most Jehovah's Witnesses requested exemption from service as a minister of the Jehovah's Witnesses religion.

Should Jehovah's Witnesses Be Classified as Conscientious Objectors?

Shawn Francis Peters wrote that the Jehovah's Witnesses' "unorthodox faith and practices often befuddled the men who had been given the task of classifying them."[31] As a result, some local draft boards classified Jehovah's Witnesses as conscientious objectors whereas other local boards refused such a classification. Regardless, Jehovah's Witnesses objected to being classified as conscientious objectors for two reasons.

First, Jehovah's Witnesses did not believe themselves to be conscientious objectors. Pacifists oppose all instances of war and despite popular misconceptions, Jehovah's Witnesses are not pacifists. They are willing and ready to fight in the battle of Armageddon alongside God and his Son, neither of whom they deem to be pacifists.[32] Jehovah's Witnesses believe there are just wars based on their faith in what is righteous. The most recent just battles were "those fought by the Israelites in the books of Judges and Joshua."[33] While these Holy battles were just wars, Jehovah's Witnesses did not perceive World War II to warrant fighting against their "brothers" in other countries.

The second reason Jehovah's Witnesses objected to conscientious objector status was due to the national service provision of the Selective Training and Service Act of 1940. Jehovah's Witnesses believed that the requirement that conscientious objectors perform national service at work camps interfered with their religious obligations. Work camps prevented them from proselytizing, a fundamental practice of their religion.

Should Jehovah's Witnesses Be Classified as Ministers?

Given their covenant with God to witness, Jehovah's Witnesses sought exemption from combative, noncombative, and national service roles. Since they could not in good faith call themselves conscientious objectors, Jehovah's Witnesses "claimed exemption as an ordained minister."[34] The fight over who was to be classified as a minister was the major issue Jehovah's Witnesses faced under the 1940 Act for two reasons.

First, to claim ministerial status the 1940 Act required registrants to be an ordained minister or a student already enrolled for a year in a theological school. However, Jehovah's Witnesses believe that one does not need to be ordained by men to be a minister who spreads the word of God. They believe "the only One who can give the real authority to preach the Word of God is Jehovah himself, even as he gave it unto His Son (Isa. 61:1, 2)."[35]

All members of Jehovah's Witnesses who are baptized are considered ordained ministers. Baptism is not a sacrament, but "a public declaration that one has already dedicated oneself to Jehovah."[36] Prior to baptism, a believer becomes a "disciple," and carefully studies the Bible to gain "an accurate knowledge of Jesus and Jehovah God (John 17:3)."[37] Baptism, or ordination, is generally held at conventions or assemblies of Jehovah's Witnesses. In a person's public declaration of faith, believers "unreservedly dedicate themselves to Jehovah."[38] Disciples are baptized in an immersion pool and one's service to God has begun. Jehovah's Witnesses declare that this process is their procedure for ordination and ministry and is comparable to that of ministers of other religions.

Second, those who have been baptized in the faith are identified as baptized publishers. The term "publisher" was used instead of minister in that Witnesses follow their commission from the church to publicize their beliefs.[39] "Publishers are typically each required to report at least one hour per month to be counted as a 'regular publisher.' "[40] If a person fails to report witnessing activity for one month, the person is termed "irregular" and those who fail to report for six consecutive months are classed as "inactive."[41] This understanding of a "minister" was not reflected in the 1940s common use of the term, which prompted members of draft boards to quickly deny Jehovah's Witnesses requests to be awarded a ministerial exemption.[42]

In an attempt to help resolve this issue, General Lewis Hershey, the Director of the Selective Service, developed criteria in 1942 and 1943 to determine who was indeed a minister and who was not among the Jehovah's Witnesses. In 1942, Hershey said that any Jehovah's Witnesses who spent more than eighty hours a month could claim 4-D or ministerial status.[43] In 1943, Hershey said that any Witness who spent more than 150 hours a month proselytizing was considered a "pioneer publisher" or full time minister.

For Jehovah's Witnesses, however, pioneer publishers were not seen as any different than "publishers," who in 1942 averaged 14.7 hours each month proselytizing.[44] Jehovah's Witnesses believed they were being unfairly denied the ministerial exemption, but the Selective Service disagreed. The government's argument was that the ministerial exemption was not denied because of religious beliefs, but because of the full time occupational nature of ministerial work, which reflected the exemption status for other types of full time work (e.g., agriculture work).[45] Since Jehovah's Witnesses who were pioneer publishers often worked secular jobs in addition to proselytizing, local boards denied many Jehovah's Witnesses the ministerial exemption. This included Taze Hamrick Gibson.

Taze Hamrick Gibson

Taze Hamrick Gibson had been prepared by his father to be a minister ever since he could remember.[46] He completed eight years of elementary school and one year of high school before leaving at the age of 16. In addition to his public education, Gibson received education in divinity school, taking a course of study in the ministry.[47] Gibson was living in El Dorado, Arkansas, when he registered for the draft at age 18 as required by law and was assigned number 12064.[48]

In October 1942, the local draft board notified twenty-year-old Gibson that his number had been drawn. The board sent Gibson a questionnaire that asked his name, address, occupation, education, family status (single, married, children, etc.), criminal background, and whether he was an alien, conscientious objector, or minister.[49] On the Selective Service questionnaire, Gibson wrote:

> The job I am now working at is minister of religion. I do the following kind of work in my present job: Preaching the Kingdom of God for which Jesus taught his followers to pray (Matthew 6:10). I have also worked at the following occupations other than my present job, during the past 5 years: Farm laborer, farming from 1934 to 1940. My usual occupation, or the occupation for which I am best fitted, is ministry work.. . . I am a minister of religion. I do customarily serve as a witness. I have been a minister of Jehovah's Witnesses since June 1938. I have been formally ordained. My ordination was performed on September 9, 1938, by Brother Miller at Birmingham, Alabama. I am a student preparing for the ministry in a theological or divinity school. I am attending the Watchtower Bible and Tract Society, which was established before September 16, 1939, and is located at 117 Adams Street, Brooklyn, New York.[50]

Gibson indicated that he preached 175 hours a month, or approximately 44 hours a week.[51] This was more than the 150 hours that Hershey would later require for a pioneer publisher. Gibson claimed classification IV-D under Section 5(d): "Ministers of religion or divinity students."[52]

Gibson's local draft board was Selective Service Local Board No. "A" of Union County, Arkansas, made up of A.P. Reynolds (chair), E. H. Mellor, and B. R. McClanahan.[53] On November 6, 1942 the board denied Gibson's request for exemption. Gibson was ranked as Class I-A: "Available; fit for general military service."[54] Gibson filed an appeal to the Selective Service Appeal Board No. 2 located in Little Rock, Arkansas.[55] On May 8, 1943 the appeal board, chaired by S. C. Vinsonhaler, reconsidered Gibson's request and, instead of awarding him a ministerial exemption, classified him as Class IV-E: "Conscientious objectors available only for civilian work of national importance."[56] Gibson's request for a ministerial exemption had once again been denied.

On September 1, 1943 Gibson was notified to appear on September 22, 1943 for a pre-induction physical examination. He was found to be physically fit and was accepted for civilian service. Gibson then appealed to Arkansas' Director of the Selective Service, E. L. Compere, asking him to "appeal the determination to the President of the United States" and to stop Gibson's induction process.[57]

While Gibson was waiting for the state appeal board's decision, on January 3, 1944 *Falbo v. United States* was decided.[58] In that case, a Jehovah's Witness was classified as a conscientious objector but believed he should have been classified as a minister. Falbo thought the board misclassified him and refused to report to an induction because he was under no obligation to follow a "mistaken order."[59] The Court ruled against Falbo saying he could have petitioned for a legal review of his classification only after completing the entire induction process, which was to be completed at an induction camp. Consequently, Falbo was found guilty of failing to go through the induction process. Gibson sought to avoid the barrier Falbo met when Gibson appealed his classification.[60]

Gibson interpreted the *Falbo* decision as requiring him to report to camp to exhaust his administrative remedies.[61] Gibson did not dispute that had no intention "to submit to the camp's jurisdiction or authority."[62] All of Gibson's actions were directed toward finishing the administrative process and obtaining exempt status under the 1940 Act. Gibson's efforts were undoubtedly guided by Hayden C. Covington, the legal counsel for the Watch Tower Bible and Tract Society, who argued Falbo's case and nearly two dozen other cases involving Jehovah's Witnesses (including Gibson's) before the Supreme Court. Hayden later brought his considerable legal experience with the Selective Service system to the aid of Muhamad Ali, who was drafted during the Vietnam War.

The state appeal board declined to appeal Gibson's classification to the President and did not stop Gibson's induction process. On May 23, 1944 Gibson was assigned to a civilian public service camp. Summer passed and on August 8, 1944 Gibson was mailed "an order to report for work of national importance" and instructed to appear at the Local Board in Carlinville, Illinois on August 21, 1944, which he did. He was then "sent to the public service camp at Hill City, South Dakota."[63] Gibson dutifully followed the law despite his repeated insistence that he had been misclassified. Upon his arrival in Illinois, he boarded a train that traveled for two days to a work camp in far western South Dakota.

Once Gibson arrived at the camp, he sought out the camp director and camp physician, but both were away. Gibson stayed at the camp for three days without performing any work until the physician and camp director returned. When the camp director returned, Gibson immediately talked with him. Gibson handed over a typed written history of his efforts to be classified as a minister of religion and explained that it was a violation of his conscience to remain at the camp. He explained his job was to spread the "gospel of God's Kingdom, which must be proclaimed to all nations."[64] Gibson's letter highlighted the unequal and unfair treatment he received. He wrote, "Now who but a prejudiced person would deny me the rights guaranteed every individual by the Constitution of the United States."[65] Gibson concluded his letter by explaining that he followed every order and every law that was not in conflict with God's law.

The camp director then explained if Gibson left the camp, he would be arrested. Gibson responded that his arrest would "not be the first time a Christian had been punished for following Christ Jesus, who was also punished."[66] Gibson asked the camp director to provide a statement showing that he had reported to the camp on August 23, 1944. He requested verification that the administrative process of induction was completed but that he did not perform any work. Gibson was provided with this statement on August 28 and he then left the camp to return to his ministerial work.[67] He headed to Indiana to resume his duty of proselytizing. Just over three months later, the Federal Bureau of Investigation arrested Gibson for leaving the camp.

Due Process, Equal Protection, and Freedom of Religion

Local draft boards refused to consider many of the arguments presented by Jehovah's Witnesses in seeking a ministerial exemption.[68] While many denials were based on the unique nature and beliefs of Jehovah's Witnesses, some denials were based on anti-Jehovah's Witnesses sentiment.[69] People were angry at Jehovah's Witnesses, who refused to fight "when there is widespread support and patriotism for the war," especially after the bombing of Pearl Harbor.[70] While Jehovah's Witnesses denounced Adolf Hitler in their publications, what people saw were "religious zealots who proclaimed their religion to be above one's patriotism to one's country."[71]

Rather than exempting Jehovah's Witnesses based on ministerial classification, local boards sometimes classified Jehovah's Witnesses as conscientious objectors. In response, Jehovah's Witnesses refused to report to the work camps. Those who failed to report were arrested. Between 1940 and 1945, 3,992 Jehovah's Witnesses were convicted for ignoring orders related to induction or work of national importance.[72] Nathan T. Elliff writes, "This accounted for about one out of every three such convictions of every character and about three out of every four convictions involving persons professing some type of religious or conscientious objection."[73] Furthermore, Jehovah's Witnesses received longer prison sentences than other groups who violated the 1940 Act.[74] If sentenced to jail, parole boards were hesitant to release Jehovah's Witnesses back to their communities out of fear of public anger that Jehovah's Witnesses were allowed to preach while other fathers and sons were off fighting or serving in work camps.[75] Some parole boards offered to release Jehovah's Witnesses if they promised not to proselytize, but Jehovah's Witnesses would refuse. Mulford Q. Sibley and Philip E. Jacob explain, "This Jehovah's Witness policy was frequently criticized by objector and civil-liberties organizations on the ground that it constituted a clear violation of the principle of religious freedom."[76]

While it was possible for Jehovah's Witnesses to appeal their status as a conscientious objector to seek a ministerial exemption, they first had to report to the work camps. Sibley and Jacob write,

> The objector must first obey the order and complete the administrative process (by reporting to the Army or Civilian Public Service, as the case might be) and then petition for a writ of habeas corpus. At this point, the problem of classification can be raised, but not before. Since many objectors and practically all Jehovah's Witnesses, could not in good conscience 'complete the administrative process,' they were limited to a hearing on the simple question of disobedience of a local board. In the hearing or trial for failure to obey a local-board order, the sole question at issue was whether the objector did in fact disobey the order [to report to the camp]. Since the objector would usually not deny that disobedience—and would sometimes indeed proclaim it in stentorian tones—the disposal of his case was relatively simple.[77]

At every turn Jehovah's Witnesses experienced lack of due process, denial of equal protection under the laws, and the absence of freedom of religion.

The Due Process Clause in the U.S. Constitution states, "No person shall . . . be deprived of life, liberty, or property, without due process of law." In the Fifth Amendment, the Due Process Clause applies to federal crimes and federal criminal prosecutions. In the Fourteenth Amendment, the Due Process Clause guarantees due process of law in state criminal prosecutions. This clause prevents states from enacting laws that "discriminate in an unreasonable and unjustified manner."[78] That amendment also prohibits states from denying "to any person within its jurisdiction the equal protection of the laws."[79] Neither Amendment protected Gibson.

On December 2, 1944, Gibson was arrested for violating the Selective Training and Service Act of 1940.[80] He was indicted for leaving the camp and his trial began on February 13, 1945. Gibson requested the case be dismissed, as the Act deprived him of his constitutional rights. The court refused his request and he pled not guilty to the charges based on his belief that he was misclassified and therefore not required to stay at the camp. Gibson ran into two related problems: who had jurisdiction over the work camp in which he was charged with desertion, and the lack of a full and fair hearing on his appeal for exemption from the 1940 Selective Training and Service Act.

The first problem Gibson faced was the question of who had jurisdiction regarding legal infractions in work camps during a time of war. Time passed while Gibson continued to seek a hearing on his case. He reported to a work camp as required by law and by his interpretation of the *Falbo* ruling. The courts have the responsibility of reviewing "draft board decisions when a full and fair hearing has been denied; the decision is arbitrary, capricious and unreasonable on an issue of fact; or the decision is contrary to law."[81] Gibson's appeal to overrule the draft board decision required him to "(1) Exhaust all administrative appeals; (2) obey order to report for induction; (3) submit to mental and physical examination; (4) do everything required up to, but not including, the taking of the oath" of service.[82] He did everything he was supposed to do.

Gibson reported to the camp and submitted to his physical examination but did not take the oath. Gibson was quickly found guilty of deserting the camp and sentenced to five years in prison to be served in the Federal Correctional Institution at Sandstone, Minnesota.[83] Gibson appealed to the U.S. Circuit Court of Appeals for the 8th Circuit, who affirmed the conviction on June 15, 1945.[84] He then appealed to the U.S. Supreme Court.

The U.S. Supreme Court heard Gibson's appeal while he was in prison. At issue was the timeline for completing the administrative process for selection and the effect that had upon Gibson's right to challenge the validity of his classification in the criminal proceedings.[85] Lawyers for the United States argued that when Gibson boarded the bus transporting him to a work camp he "became subject to the camp's jurisdiction, and ... doing this irrevocably ... [prevented him] from defending against the charge of desertion on the ground that his classification was invalid."[86] They asserted that when Gibson boarded the bus to begin his journey to a camp, the government shifted jurisdiction over him to the director of the camp; Gibson disagreed. Gibson asserted that he was following the court's ruling in *Falbo* and was required to go to the camp and abide by the law up to the point of taking an oath.

Justice Wiley Blount Rutledge Jr. delivered the Supreme Court's decision. No draft registrant who "becomes subject to the 'jurisdiction' of a work camp under the Selective Service procedure ... forfeits his right to defend against a charge of desertion or other breach of duty, on the ground that his classification was invalid."[87] The Court continued, "Unlike the man 'actually inducted,' the person classified IV-E remains a civilian" who is subject to "civil penalties and [a civil] mode of trial for violating duties."[88] No person can be deprived of his right to defense for invalid classification by the local draft board. On December 23, 1946 the U.S. Supreme Court in *Gibson v. United States* granted Gibson a new trial in the U.S. District Court of the Western District of Arkansas. The Supreme Court ruled that the district judge's refusal to allow Gibson to present his evidence demonstrating misclassification deprived him of due process as guaranteed under the Fourteenth

Amendment.[89] Gibson would now be able to tackle the primary problem, the issue of his classification.

From the beginning, Gibson only sought a full and fair hearing on his claim of exemption from the Selective Service. On May 12, 1948 Judge John E. Miller ruled that when Gibson registered under the 1940 Selective Training and Service Act he claimed "to be a duly ordained minister of religion, and he submitted proof in the form of statements and affidavits of Jehovah's Witnesses stating that they recognized him as performing the duties and functions of an ordained minister."[90] Gibson never wavered from the claim for exemption as a minister of religion.

When Gibson was classified as IV-E, and during the time his appeal was refused by Compere and Lewis, he continued to work full time as a Jehovah's Witnesses minister. Judge Miller ruled the state "refused and failed to consider the proof submitted by plaintiff in support of his contentions, and that they acted contrary to and in violation of Section 622.44 of the Selective Service Regulations and opinion No. 14 of the Selective Service National Headquarters concerning Jehovah's Witnesses."[91] The court ruled that the state discriminated against Gibson "contrary to the due process clause of the 5th Amendment," which "deprived him of the procedural rights of due process to a full and fair hearing by a fair and unprejudiced board contrary to the due process clause of said constitution."[92] The state offered no evidence to dispute Gibson's claims that he was a minister of religion.[93]

Gibson prevailed in his hearing for exempt status on May 12, 1948. He was finally provided due process and equal protection of the laws. World War II had ended over two years earlier. Gibson navigated the rampant anti-Jehovah's Witness hostility and the unfair treatment of people who implemented the 1940 Selective Training and Service Act. While he was successful in his efforts to gain a ministerial exemption, his case tells us much about the importance of communication in First Amendment cases.

Communication and the First Amendment

The precipitating factors that foster conflicts between equal protection and freedom of religion originate in a communicative encounter—what words mean to whom, how negotiation occurs, why certain values are privileged, and so forth. Jehovah's Witnesses were often treated as enemies of the state and treasonous during World War II. "Perhaps as many as 100,000 claimed CO [conscientious objector] status. Six thousand went to prison as COs, 5,000 of whom were Jehovah's Witnesses."[94] Members of other religions were, perhaps understandably so, opposed to Jehovah's Witnesses who requested exemption; Jehovah's Witnesses were also hostile against members of other religions during World War II. However, they still deserved to be heard in a society with a liberal understanding of free speech.

Knox observes that "although 125 religious groups objected to military service in the 1940s and 1950s, the position of Jehovah's Witnesses was unique. In 1955, one legal scholar reported that their approach was 'at complete variance with the position of the other 124 types of religious objectors.' "[95] While Jehovah's Witnesses are unique, we are reminded of John Stuart Mill's famous quote, "If all mankind [of 124 religions] minus one, were of one opinion, and only one person [Jehovah's Witnesses] were of the contrary opinion, mankind would be no more justified in silencing that one person, than he, if he had the power, would be justified in silencing mankind."[96]

Communicative encounters should be the focus of our—communication and rhetorical scholars'—attention. As David R. Dewberry and Catherine L. Langford write, "A scholarly approach to free expression often benefits from the recognition of the rhetorical and/or mediated spectacle of the individual(s) who are at the heart of First Amendment jurisprudence."[97] They assert that legal arguments and processes relating to free speech ironically censor the actual free speech that sparked controversy. Instances of free speech (e.g., ministering/proselytizing to members of one's community) and the message that is to be conveyed in a context are overshadowed by the public and legal discourse over the applicability of the First Amendment.[98] The emphasis is too often on a static definition within a static law rather than on the persons negotiating the meaning of legal definitions.

David R. Dewberry and Pat Arneson differentiate two dominant paradigms for studying free speech: scholars may approach an issue by working within a legal paradigm, or within a communicative paradigm.[99] A legal paradigm is one in which "specialized information and language" is used to argue whether legally something "could" legally be said.[100] On the other hand, a communicative paradigm focuses "on the content of the ideas communicated and not the [legal] ability to express those communications."[101] The value of the communicative paradigm is that it allows scholars to examine "power issues and relations" and "to recognize the contextuality and subjectivity of the practice and application of free speech."[102] As such, a "communicative paradigm does not readily address or employ First Amendment jurisprudence but still addresses issues of free speech."[103]

The two paradigms provide different insights on public discourse surrounding controversial speech. G. Thomas Goodnight's influential essay on "The Personal, Technical, and Public Spheres of Argument," helps explain how interpretive differences arise.[104] Arguments in the personal sphere are similar to a debate between two friends—there are no formal rules or restrictions. In the technical sphere, arguments are governed by formal rules such as publishing in academia or hearings in the courts. Arguments in the public sphere resemble instances of public deliberation. The legal paradigm resembles argument within the technical sphere and the communicative paradigm resembles argument with the public sphere. In our initial formulation, we believed that the personal sphere was not relevant to our argument because we did not envision how the personal sphere had any "basis in civics."[105] The case of Taze Gibson allows us to reconsider that and to include the spirit of the personal sphere into a communicative paradigm for examining free speech.

The personal sphere is one where argument and debate is informal and ephemeral, and only affects those involved (recall that Goodnight's example was of two friends in a bar). The topic of the discussion may be a "public issue" (i.e., matters outside the two persons) or a "private issue" (i.e., matters within the relationship).[106] Further, David Zarefsky explains that one of the prerequisites for discussion in the (inter-)personal sphere is a preexisting relationship.[107] However, even though there is no existing relationship or there is a refusal to engage with another, there still remains a need to be heard. And that is exactly what happened with Taze Gibson. The U.S. government failed to recognize and hear Gibson, as a person and as a devout Jehovah's Witness. Gibson attempted to explain himself and his position, but the other side was not willing to listen.

Communication scholars generally recognize interpersonal communication as an umbrella term used for forms of face-to-face dyadic communication. Two recognized types of interpersonal communication are conversation and dialogue. As W. Barnett Pearce observed, within the variety of dyadic exchanges and encounters "[s]ome communication events which have all the properties of conversation, are simply 'strategic' [rhetorical]. That is, one's own ideas or positions on issues are never put 'at risk' of being changed in the conversation; one's own behavior is controlled by interests and relationships outside the conversation."[108] An objective understanding of the other person and a focus on control in the interaction are often associated with the use of strategies of persuasion within an interpersonal context.

Dialogue is the second primary approach to interpersonal communication. Kenneth N. Cissna and Rob Anderson recognize a distinction between conversation ("in which participants merely exchange messages back and forth") and dialogue, which is intersubjective and open.[109] In contrast to rhetoric, an important characteristic of dialogue is that this mode of communication emphasizes listening as necessary for the co-construction of meaning. This did not happen for Gibson, who endeavored greatly to be heard while government employees refused to engage in any meaningful dialogue. As such, the government employees easily engaged in conversation designed to maintain meaning within the status quo.

There are two dominant threads of dialogue scholarship: prescriptive dialogue and descriptive dialogue. Dialogic thinking, present in most forms of dialogue, "is a broader philosophical stance informing a procedural approach to create an open interactive communication environment in which the views and interests of others are recognized and respected."[110] Scholars who work prescriptively recommend the enactment of "certain behaviors of speaking and listening that are manifest and enacted (or not) . . . and that can even be taught and improved."[111] This approach to dialogue is similar to conversation. Working toward a description of dialogue, scholars recognize that the phenomenon of dialogue is possible in human interaction but is rarely actualized in everyday discourse. Communicators must hold "an intention of openness to the other, both in being real about oneself and being receptive to [meeting] the other."[112] In descriptive dialogue one sees connections, examines assumptions, learns through inquiry, and creates shared meanings.[113] Gibson was working from a descriptive or open dialogic stance, while government employees were engaged in interpersonal conversation with him.

While the 1917 Act exempted persons whose religion did not allow participation in war, by 1940 such an option was no longer available. The perceived urgency and rise of complex government bureaucracy led to a perception that people must fit into one of the predetermined categories. The meaning of categories was not open to interpretation.

After nearly five years of going through the machinations of the court trying to gain a classification that was always already his, Gibson was given a ministerial exemption. Gibson first received his notification letter in October 1942 and his case was closed on May 12, 1948, over two years after the end of the war. The only consolation Jehovah's Witnesses receive is somewhat ironic: the so-called unpatriotic and unorthodox religious group is one of the true defenders of the First Amendment's protection of the freedom of religion.

Conclusion

A number of themes and issues are evident in the forgoing discussion of Jehovah's Witnesses and the Selective Training and Service Act of 1940. Jehovah's Witnesses were treated unequally with respect to members of other religions in the World War II draft. Gibson did not receive equal protection of the laws; to do so would require him to not exercise his freedom of religion. His struggle to achieve equal protection under the law in the United States is just one example of the prosecution and persecution that Jehovah's Witness face. Unfortunately, the challenges that Gibson faced in the United States continue to be a common occurrence for Jehovah's Witnesses throughout the world.

Two barriers stopped Gibson from receiving the rights guaranteed to him in the Constitution. The first issue is related to citizens' right to freedom of religion. The problem stemmed from the general public as members of dominant Christian religions who labeled the beliefs and practices of Jehovah's Witnesses as idiosyncratic and abnormal. Labeling Jehovah's Witnesses as an illegitimate religious organization led to members of that religion being denied equal protection of the laws. In turn, Jehovah's Witnesses' reticence to communicate about their religion with members of other religions (aside from their proselytizing activities) also contributed to Gibson's rights being denied by government entities.

A second issue that limited Gibson's rights is related to the approach to interaction that members of the government took when working on his case. Recognizing the potential conflicts between approaching a case from a legal paradigm or a communicative paradigm aids in reasoning about miscommunication.[114] This is especially true when a person's right to equal protection and freedom to practice religion comes into conflict with persons not open to appreciating difference. When a person's perspective is not heard—in Gibson's case when the evidence he offered related to being a minister was disregarded—he exercised his right to move the dispute to the court. Doing so addresses the symptoms rather than the cause of a conflict, thus overburdening our court system. When working from a legal paradigm to the First Amendment communication scholars are missing the "human dimension" by not considering the person.[115] This in and of itself is a major concern for us.

Consequently, this chapter demonstrates the value of examining interpersonal communication within First Amendment controversies, rather than focusing on public discourse or the rhetoric of judicial discourse, which are mainstays in First Amendment scholarship. As such, this paper touts the virtues of examining free speech issues from a speech perspective. We recommend looking at the human dimension of freedom of religion cases—listening to people and their experiences and considering how they interacted in a given situation. Whatever impact Jehovah's Witnesses would have had on the effort in World War II is unknowable, however their effort fighting for their rights at home is knowable and progress has been made. Yet, Jehovah's Witnesses continue to fight for their human rights abroad.

Members of Jehovah's Witnesses continue to challenge persecution around the world. Jehovah's Witnesses' activities are banned in 34 countries.[116] As of July 2020, there are 107 Jehovah's Witnesses imprisoned for their religious activities and status as conscientious objectors around the globe.[117] One country that is actively persecuting Jehovah's Witnesses is the Russian Federation, previously the Union of Soviet Socialist Republics (USSR).

Although the USSR did not vote in favor of the United Nations' Universal Declaration of Human Rights in 1948, by the late 1980s and early 1990s, the Russian Federation, the state recognized as the legal successor to the Union of Soviet Socialist Republics (USSR), actively participated in constructing "almost all the international human rights instruments negotiated through the UN system."[118] At the 1993 Vienna World Conference on Human Rights, Russia even voted in favor of establishing a UN High Commissioner for Human Rights. However, by the turn of the 21st century, leaders had once again become increasingly critical of the UN's human rights policies as exemplified in Russia's 2014 annexation of Crimea. In a 2017 United Nations Security Council meeting, Evgeny Zagaynov of the Russian Federation asserted he "shared the concerns of those who feared that human rights might be used as a means to exert power over other countries."[119] Many of today's Russian diplomats are taking positions similar to those taken in the 1940s. Two decades into the 21st century, human rights abuses have again become systemic, and specifically affect members of Jehovah's Witnesses.

As of June 17, 2020, in Russia there are 32 Jehovah's Witnesses who are imprisoned, 24 under house arrest, 153 are not allowed to travel, and 353 are under investigation.[120] In separate interviews, Gibson's son and granddaughter both pointed to the ongoing persecution in Russia.[121] Gibson's granddaughter explains: "They have been arresting men and women there for peacefully meeting together to worship, or even having any of our literature. Often the men are beaten in prison and given harsh sentences. A lot of the property owned by Jehovah's Witnesses has also been confiscated by the Russian government. And this was a country that a couple years ago we could meet together peacefully and worship with no issues."[122] She recognizes that Russia's changing human rights position on the Jehovah's Witnesses could very well happen again in the United States. She writes, "We are fully prepared for what happened in the United States 100 years ago, and what is happening in Russia now, to happen here [in the United States] again."[123] While Jehovah's Witnesses have fought hard to defend their religious beliefs and practices in the United States, they continue this fight abroad. Jehovah's Witnesses simply want their religion to be treated as equal with other religions.

Notes

1 J. A. W., "Religious Freedom and the Jehovah's Witnesses," *Virginia Law Review* 34 (1948): 77.
2 "How Many of Jehovah's Witnesses Are There Worldwide?" JW.org, accessed on December 25, 2019, https://www.jw.org/en/jehovahs-witnesses/faq/jehovah-witness-beliefs/.
3 "What Do Jehovah's Witnesses Believe?" JW.org, accessed on December 25, 2019, https://www.jw.org/en/jehovahs-witnesses/faq/jehovah-witness-beliefs/.
4 "What Is God's Purpose for the Earth?" JW.org, accessed on December 25, 2019, https://www.jw.org/en/library/books/good-news-from-god/why-did-god-create-the-earth/.
5 Julien Cornell, "Exemption from the Draft: A Study in Civil Liberties," *The Yale Law Journal* 56 (1947): 264.
6 Joe Knox, "Jehovah's Witnesses as Un-Americans? Scriptural Injunctions, Civil Liberties, and Patriotism," *Journal of American Studies* 4 (2013): 1097.
7 Supreme Court of the United States, Transcript of Record: *Taze Hamrick Gibson v. The United States of America*, 329 U.S. 338 (1946), 61.
8 John Smith, *Encyclopedia of Religion in America*, s.v. "Jehovah's Witnesses" (Washington, DC: CQ Press, 2010), 1106–07.
9 Julien Cornell, "Exemption from the Draft: A Study in Civil Liberties," *The Yale Law Journal*, 56 (1947): 264.
10 Francis H. Heller, "A Turning Point for Religious Liberty," *Virginia Law Review* 29 (1943): 443.
11 Joe Knox, "Jehovah's Witnesses as Un-Americans? Scriptural Injunctions, Civil Liberties, and Patriotism," *Journal of American Studies* 4 (2013): 1081–108, 1082.
12 Michael Corbett and Julia Mitchell Corbett, *Politics and Religion in the United States* (New York: Garland Publishing, Inc., 1999), 110.
13 Martin Folly and Niall Palmer, *The A to Z of U.S. Diplomacy from World War I through World War II* (Lanham: Scarecrow Press, 2010), 309.
14 Selective Training and Service Act of 1940, 885, https://govtrackus.s3.amazonaws.com/legislink/pdf/stat/54/STATUTE-54-Pg885a.pdf.
15 Selective Training and Service Act of 1940, 888, https://govtrackus.s3.amazonaws.com/legislink/pdf/stat/54/STATUTE-54-Pg888a.pdf.
16 Selective Training and Service Act of 1940, 889, https://govtrackus.s3.amazonaws.com/legislink/pdf/stat/54/STATUTE-54-Pg889a.pdf.
17 Selective Service Act of 1917, 78, https://govtrackus.s3.amazonaws.com/legislink/pdf/stat/40/STATUTE-40-Pg78.pdf.
18 Selective Service Act of 1917, 76, https://govtrackus.s3.amazonaws.com/legislink/pdf/stat/40/STATUTE-40-Pg76.pdf.
19 Melvin Gingerich, *Service for Peace: A History of Mennonite Civilian Public Service* (Akron, PA: Mennonite Central Committee, 1949), 147, 213.

20 C. Henry Smith, *Smith's Story of the Mennonites* (Newton, KS: Faith and Life Press), 545.
21 Selective Training and Service Act of 1940, https://govtrackus.s3.amazonaws.com/legislink/pdf/stat/54/STATUTE-54.pdf.
22 Cornell, "Exemption," 258.
23 Selective Training and Service Act of 1940, https://govtrackus.s3.amazonaws.com/legislink/pdf/stat/54/STATUTE-54.pdf.
24 Cornell, "Exemption," 266.
25 Cynthia Hastas Morris, "Arkansas's Reaction to the Men Who Said 'No' to World War II," *The Arkansas Historical Quarterly* 43 (1984): 153–77; Francis H. Heller, "A Turning Point for Religious Liberty," *Virginia Law Review* 29 (1943): 441.
26 Morris, "Arkansas's Reaction," 167; Albert N. Keim, *The CPS Story: An Illustrated History of Civilian Public Service* (Brattleboro, VT: Good Books, 1990), 94.
27 Morris, "Arkansas's Reaction," 167.
28 Morris, "Arkansas's Reaction," 155.
29 Cornell, "Exemption," 267.
30 Mulford Q. Sibley and Philip E. Jacob, *Conscription of Conscience: The American State and the Conscientious Objector, 1940–1947* (Ithaca: Cornell University Press, 1965), 31.
31 Shawn Francis Peters, *Judging Jehovah's Witnesses: Religious Persecution and the Dawn of the Civil Rights Revolution* (Lawrence: University Press of Kansas, 2000), 263.
32 "Why Jehovah's Witnesses Are Not Pacifists," Watchtower Online Library, https://wol.jw.org/en/wol/d/r1/lp-e/1951080#h=5.
33 Knox, "Jehovah's Witnesses," 1101.
34 Cornell, "Exemption," 264.
35 Cornell, "Exemption," 264.
36 "Should I Dedicate My Life to God and Be Baptized?" https://www.jw.org/en/library/books/bible-study/what-is-baptism/.
37 "Becoming an Ordained Minister—God's Way!" Watchtower Online Library, https://wol.jw.org/en/wol/d/r1/lp-e/1988448
38 "Becoming an Ordained Minister."
39 Cornell, "Exemption," 264.
40 "Report Field Service Accurately," *Our Kingdom Ministry*, September 1988, 3, https://wol.jw.org/en/wol/d/r1/lp-e/201988328
41 "Helping Irregular Publishers," *Our Kingdom Ministry*, December 7, 1987, https://wol.jw.org/en/wol/d/r1/lp-e/201987447; "Keep the Word of Jehovah Moving Speedily," *Our Kingdom Ministry*, October 1, 1982, https://wol.jw.org/en/wol/d/r1/lp-e/201982361.
42 Knox, "Jehovah's Witnesses," 1101.
43 Morris, "Arkansas' Reaction," 164n35.
44 Nathan T. Elliff, "Jehovah's Witnesses and the Selective Service Act," *Virginia Law Review* 31 (1945): 815.
45 Elliff, "Jehovah's Witnesses," 816.
46 Supreme Court of the United States, Transcript of Record, 61. Taze Hamrick Gibson's legal cases related to his claim for exempt classification include: *Gibson v. United States* 149 F.2d 751 (8th Cir. 1945), https://casetext.com/case/gibson-v-united-states-21; *Gibson v. United States*, 329 U.S. 338 (1946),

https://supreme.justia.com/cases/federal/us/329/338/#T6; G *Gibson v. Reynolds*, 77 F. Supp. 629 (W.D. Ark. 1948), https://casetext.com/case/gibson-v-reynolds.
47 *Gibson v. Reynolds*, 77 F. Supp. 629 (W.D. Ark. 1948).
48 Supreme Court of the United States, Joint Brief for Petitioners: *Taze Hamrick Gibson v. The United States of America*, 5.
49 Supreme Court of the United States, "Appendix to Brief for Petitioner," 3A.
50 *Gibson v. Reynolds*, 77 F. Supp. 629 (W.D. Ark. 1948), 631; United States Circuit Court of Appeals for the Eighth Circuit, Appendix to Brief for Petitioner: *Taze Hamrick Gibson v. The United States of America*, 3A.
51 Cornell, "Exemption," 264.
52 Anne Yoder, "Military Classifications for Draftees," *Swarthmore College Peace Collection*, https://www.swarthmore.edu/library/peace/conscientiousobjection/MilitaryClassifications.htm.
53 *Gibson v. Reynolds*, 77 F. Supp. 629 (W.D. Ark. 1948).
54 Yoder, "Military Classifications."
55 *Gibson v. Reynolds*, 77 F. Supp. 629 (W.D. Ark. 1948).
56 *Gibson v. Reynolds*, 77 F. Supp. 629 (W.D. Ark. 1948), 631; Yoder, "Military Classifications."
57 *Gibson v. Reynolds*, 77 F. Supp. 629 (W.D. Ark. 1948), 631.
58 *Falbo v. United States*, 320 U.S. 549 (1944).
59 *Falbo v. United States*, 320 U.S. 549 (1944), 550.
60 "*Gibson v. United States*," *United States Reports: Cases Adjudged in The Supreme Court at October Term, 1946*, vol. 329 (Washington: U.S. Government Printing Office, 1947), 342. Google books.
61 "*Gibson v. United States*," *United States Reports*, 342.
62 "*Gibson v. United States*," *United States Reports*, 342.
63 *Gibson v. Reynolds*, 77 F. Supp. 629 (W.D. Ark. 1948), 631.
64 Supreme Court of the United States, "Appendix to Brief for Petitioner," 9.
65 United States Circuit Court of Appeals for the Eighth Circuit, "Appendix to Brief for Petitioner: *Taze Hamrick Gibson v. The United States of America*," 18A.
66 Supreme Court of the United States, "Joint Brief for Petitioners," 8.
67 *Gibson v. Reynolds*, 77 F. Supp. 629 (W.D. Ark. 1948).
68 Sibley and Jacob, *Conscription of Conscience*, 335.
69 Knox, "Jehovah's Witnesses," 1101.
70 Knox, "Jehovah's Witnesses," 1090.
71 Morris, "Arkansas' Reaction," 158.
72 Elliff, "Jehovah's Witnesses," 811.
73 Elliff, "Jehovah's Witnesses," 811.
74 Knox, "Jehovah's Witnesses," 1101.
75 Sibley and Jacob, *Conscription of Conscience*, 385–86.
76 Sibley and Jacob, *Conscription of Conscience*, 386.
77 Sibley and Jacob, *Conscription of Conscience*, 345.
78 "3.2 The Due Process and Equal Protection Clauses," *Criminal Law*, https://saylordotorg.github.io/text_criminal-law/s07-02-the-due-process-and-equal-prot.html.
79 3.2 The Due Process and Equal Protection Clauses."
80 *Gibson v. Reynolds*, 77 F. Supp. 629 (W.D. Ark. 1948).
81 Cornell, "Exemption," 272.

82 Thomas L. Dalrymple, "Selective Service Act: Proper Procedure for Challenging Validity of Draft Classification," *Michigan Law Review* 44 (1946): 875.
83 *Gibson v. Reynolds*, 77 F. Supp. 629 (W.D. Ark. 1948).
84 *Gibson v. United States*, 149 F.2d 751 (8th Cir. 1945).
85 *Gibson v. United States*, 329 U.S. 338 (1946).
86 "*Gibson v. United States*," *United States Reports* 352.
87 "*Gibson v. United States*," *United States Reports*, 356.
88 "*Gibson v. United States*," *United States Reports*, 357.
89 *Gibson v. United States*, 329 U.S. 338 (1946).
90 *Gibson v. Reynolds*, 77 F. Supp. 629 (W.D. Ark. 1948), 632.
91 *Gibson v. Reynolds*, 77 F. Supp. 629 (W.D. Ark. 1948), 632.
92 *Gibson v. Reynolds*, 77 F. Supp. 629 (W.D. Ark. 1948), 632.
93 *Gibson v. Reynolds*, 77 F. Supp. 629 (W.D. Ark. 1948).
94 L. William Yolton, "Conscientious Objection," in *Protest, Power, and Change: An Encyclopedia of Nonviolent Action from ACT-UP to Women's Suffrage*, eds. Roger S. Powers, William B. Vogele, Christopher Kruegler and Ronald M. McCarthy (New York: Routledge, 1997/2011), 127.
95 Knox, "Jehovah's Witnesses," 129.
96 John Stuart Mill, *On Liberty* (London: John W. Parker and Son, 1859), 33.
97 David R. Dewberry and Catherine L. Langford, "Silencing Spectacles: Freedom of Speech on Trial," *Free Speech Yearbook* 46 (2012): 104.
98 Dewberry and Langford, "Silencing Spectacles," 104.
99 David R. Dewberry and Pat Arneson, "Based in and Focused on Argumentation: Communicative and Legal Approaches to Free Speech and the First Amendment," *Concerning Argument: Selected Papers from the Fifteenth NCA/AFA Conference on Argumentation 2007*, ed. Scott Jacobs (Washington, DC: National Communication Association, 2009), 158–65.
100 Dewberry and Arneson, "Based in and Focused on," 161.
101 Dewberry and Arneson, "Based in and Focused on," 163.
102 Dewberry and Arneson, "Based in and Focused on," 163–64.
103 Dewberry and Arneson, "Based in and Focused on," 158.
104 G. Thomas Goodnight, "The Personal, Technical, and Public Spheres of Argument: A Speculative Inquiry into the Art of Argumentation," *Journal of the American Forensic Association* 18 (1982): 214–27.
105 Dewberry and Arneson, "Based in and Focused on," 162.
106 Amy Janan Johnson, Dale Hample, and Ioana A. Cionea, "Understanding Argumentation in Interpersonal Communication: The Implications of Distinguishing Between Public and Personal Topics," *Communication Yearbook* 38 (2014): 145.
107 David Zarefsky, "Goodnight's 'Speculative Inquiry' in Its Intellectual Context," *Argumentation & Advocacy* 48 (2012): 211–15.
108 W. Barnett Pearce, "Creating Places for Dialogic Argument in the National Conversation," in *Argumentation and Values: Proceedings of the SCA/AFA Conference on Argumentation*, ed. Sally Jackson (Backlick, VA: Speech Communication Association, 1995): 244.

109 Kenneth N. Cissna and Rob Anderson, "Dialogic Rhetoric, Coauthorship, and Moments of Meeting," in *Dialogue and Rhetoric*, ed. Edda Weigand (Philadelphia, PA: John Benjamins Publishing Co., 2008): 42.
110 Jim Macnamara, "Organizational Listening: Addressing a Major Gap in Public Relations Theory and Practice," *Journal of Public Relations Research* 28, no. 3/4 (2016): 148.
111 Cissna and Anderson, "Dialogic Rhetoric," 41.
112 Cissna and Anderson, "Dialogic Rhetoric," 42.
113 Linda Ellinor and Glenna Gerard, *Dialogue: Rediscover the Transforming Power of Conversation* (New York: John Wiley, 1998), qtd. in W. Barnett Pearce and Kimberly A. Pearce, "Combining Passions and Abilities: Toward Dialogic Virtuosity," *Southern Communication Journal* 65, no. 2/3 (2000): 164.
114 Dewberry and Arneson, "Based in and Focused on."
115 Shawn Francis Peters, "Chuck Smith, Review of Judging Jehovah's Witnesses: Religious Persecution and the Dawn of the Rights Revolution," *Journal of Church and State* 44 (2002): 166.
116 "Countries Where Jehovah's Witnesses' Activities are Banned," RadioFreeEurope, February 7, 2019, https://www.rferl.org/a/countries-where-jehovahs-witnesses-activities-are-banned/29757419.html.
117 "Jehovah's Witnesses Imprisoned for Their Faith—By Location," Jehovah's Witnesses, https://www.jw.org/en/news/legal/by-region/world/jehovahs-witnesses-in-prison-2/.
118 Human Rights Committee, "The UN, Human Rights and Russia: Part I, United Nations Association of the United States of America, May 14, 2018, http://www.unanca.org/news-events/news/1122-the-un-human-rights-and-russia-pt1.
119 "Security Council Must Take Human Rights into Account in All Deliberations, Secretary-General Stresses during Thematic Debate," Security Council Meeting, United Nations, April 18, 2017, https://www.un.org/press/en/2017/sc12797.doc.htm.
120 "Imprisoned for Their Faith," Jehovah's Witnesses, https://www.jw.org/en/news/legal/by-region/russia/jehovahs-witnesses-in-prison/.
121 Names redacted out of respect, telephone interview by first author, April 1, 2020.
122 Name redacted out of respect, Facebook Messenger interview by first author, March 4, 2020.
123 Name redacted out of respect, Facebook Messenger interview by first author, March 4, 2020.

Bibliography

"3.2 The Due Process and Equal Protection Clauses," *Criminal Law*, https://saylordotorg.github.io/text_criminal-law/s07-02-the-due-process-and-equal-prot.html.

"Becoming an Ordained Minister—God's Way!" Watchtower Online Library, https://wol.jw.org/en/wol/d/r1/lp-e/1988448

Cissna, Kenneth N. and Rob Anderson, "Dialogic Rhetoric, Coauthorship, and Moments of Meeting," in *Dialogue and Rhetoric*, ed. Edda Weigand (Philadelphia, PA: John Benjamins Publishing Co., 2008).

Corbett, Michael and Corbett, Julia Mitchell. *Politics and Religion in the United States* (New York: Garland Publishing, Inc., 1999).

Cornell, Julien. "Exemption from the Draft: A Study in Civil Liberties," *The Yale Law Journal* 56 (1947): 258-275.

"Countries Where Jehovah's Witnesses' Activities are Banned," RadioFreeEurope, February 7, 2019, https://www.rferl.org/a/countries-where-jehovahs-witnesses-activities-are-banned/29757419.html.

Dalrymple, Thomas L. "Selective Service Act: Proper Procedure for Challenging Validity of Draft Classification," *Michigan Law Review* 44 (1946): 874-876.

Dewberry, David R. and Arneson, Pat. "Based in and Focused on Argumentation: Communicative and Legal Approaches to Free Speech and the First Amendment," *Concerning Argument: Selected Papers from the Fifteenth NCA/AFA Conference on Argumentation 2007*, ed. Scott Jacobs (Washington, DC: National Communication Association, 2009), 158–165.

Dewberry, David R. and Langford, Catherine L. "Silencing Spectacles: Freedom of Speech on Trial," *Free Speech Yearbook* 46 (2012): 97-106.

Elliff, Nathan T. "Jehovah's Witnesses and the Selective Service Act," *Virginia Law Review* 31 (1945): 811-834.

Ellinor, Linda and Gerard, Glenna. *Dialogue: Rediscover the Transforming Power of Conversation* (New York: John Wiley, 1998), qtd. in W. Barnett Pearce and Kimberly A. Pearce, "Combining Passions and Abilities: Toward Dialogic Virtuosity," *Southern Communication Journal* 65, no. 2/3 (2000): 161-175.

Falbo v. United States, 320 U.S. 549 (1944).

Folly, Martin and Palmer, Niall. *The A to Z of U.S. Diplomacy from World War I through World War II* (Lanham: Scarecrow Press, 2010).

Gibson v. Reynolds, 77 F. Supp. 629 (W.D. Ark. 1948).

"*Gibson v. United States*," *United States Reports: Cases Adjudged in The Supreme Court at October Term, 1946*, vol. 329 (Washington: U.S. Government Printing Office, 1947).

Gingerich, Melvin. *Service for Peace: A History of Mennonite Civilian Public Service* (Akron, PA: Mennonite Central Committee, 1949).

Goodnight, G. Thomas. "The Personal, Technical, and Public Spheres of Argument: A Speculative Inquiry into the Art of Argumentation," *Journal of the American Forensic Association* 18 (1982): 214–227.

Heller, Francis H. "A Turning Point for Religious Liberty," *Virginia Law Review* 29 (1943): 440-459.

"Helping Irregular Publishers," *Our Kingdom Ministry*, December 7, 1987, https://wol.jw.org/en/wol/d/r1/lp-e/201987447

"How Many of Jehovah's Witnesses Are There Worldwide?" JW.org, accessed on December 25, 2019, https://www.jw.org/en/jehovahs-witnesses/faq/jehovah-witness-beliefs/.

Human Rights Committee. "The UN, Human Rights and Russia: Part I, United Nations Association of the United States of America, May 14, 2018, http://www.unanca.org/news-events/news/1122-the-un-human-rights-and-russia-pt1.

"Imprisoned for Their Faith," Jehovah's Witnesses, https://www.jw.org/en/news/legal/by-region/russia/jehovahs-witnesses-in-prison/.

J. A. W. "Religious Freedom and the Jehovah's Witnesses," *Virginia Law Review* 34 (1948): 77.

"Jehovah's Witnesses Imprisoned for Their Faith—By Location," Jehovah's Witnesses, https://www.jw.org/en/news/legal/by-region/world/jehovahs-witnesses-in-prison-2/.

Johnson, Amy Janan, Hample, Dale and Cionea, Ioana A. "Understanding Argumentation in Interpersonal Communication: The Implications of Distinguishing Between Public and Personal Topics," *Communication Yearbook* 38 (2014): 145-173.

"Keep the Word of Jehovah Moving Speedily," *Our Kingdom Ministry*, October 1, 1982, https://wol.jw.org/en/wol/d/r1/lp-e/201982361.

Keim, Albert N. *The CPS Story: An Illustrated History of Civilian Public Service* (Brattleboro, VT: Good Books, 1990).

Knox, Joe. "Jehovah's Witnesses as Un-Americans? Scriptural Injunctions, Civil Liberties, and Patriotism," *Journal of American Studies* 4 (2013): 1081-1108.

Macnamara, Jim. "Organizational Listening: Addressing a Major Gap in Public Relations Theory and Practice," *Journal of Public Relations Research* 28, no. 3/4 (2016): 146-169.

Mill, John Stuart. *On Liberty* (London: John W. Parker and Son, 1859).

Morris, Cynthia Hastas. "Arkansas's Reaction to the Men Who Said 'No' to World War II," *The Arkansas Historical Quarterly* 43 (1984): 153–177.

Pearce, W. Barnett. "Creating Places for Dialogic Argument in the National Conversation," in *Argumentation and Values: Proceedings of the SCA/AFA Conference on Argumentation*, ed. Sally Jackson (Backlick, VA: Speech Communication Association, 1995): 242-249.

Peters, Shawn Francis. *Judging Jehovah's Witnesses: Religious Persecution and the Dawn of the Civil Rights Revolution* (Lawrence: University Press of Kansas, 2000).

Peters, Shawn Francis. "Chuck Smith, Review of Judging Jehovah's Witnesses: Religious Persecution and the Dawn of the Rights Revolution," *Journal of Church and State* 44 (2002): 166-167.

"Report Field Service Accurately," *Our Kingdom Ministry*, September 1988, 3, https://wol.jw.org/en/wol/d/r1/lp-e/201988328.

"Security Council Must Take Human Rights into Account in All Deliberations, Secretary-General Stresses during Thematic Debate," Security Council Meeting, United Nations, April 18, 2017, https://www.un.org/press/en/2017/sc12797.doc.htm.

Selective Training and Service Act of 1940, https://govtrackus.s3.amazonaws.com/legislink/pdf/stat/54/STATUTE-54-Pg885a.pdf.

"Should I Dedicate My Life to God and Be Baptized?" https://www.jw.org/en/library/books/bible-study/what-is-baptism/.

Sibley, Mulford Q. and Philip E. Jacob, *Conscription of Conscience: The American State and the Conscientious Objector, 1940–1947* (Ithaca: Cornell University Press, 1965).

Smith, C. Henry. *Smith's Story of the Mennonites* (Newton, KS: Faith and Life Press).

Smith, John. *Encyclopedia of Religion in America*, s.v. "Jehovah's Witnesses" (Washington, DC: CQ Press, 2010), 1106–1107.

Supreme Court of the United States, Joint Brief for Petitioners: *Taze Hamrick Gibson v. The United States of America.*

Supreme Court of the United States, Transcript of Record: *Taze Hamrick Gibson v. The United States of America*, 329 U.S. 338 (1946).

United States Circuit Court of Appeals for the Eighth Circuit, Appendix to Brief for Petitioner: *Taze Hamrick Gibson v. The United States of America.*

"What Do Jehovah's Witnesses Believe?" JW.org, accessed on December 25, 2019, https://www.jw.org/en/jehovahs-witnesses/faq/jehovah-witness-beliefs/.

"What Is God's Purpose for the Earth?" JW.org, accessed on December 25, 2019, https://www.jw.org/en/library/books/good-news-from-god/why-did-god-create-the-earth/.

"Why Jehovah's Witnesses Are Not Pacifists," Watchtower Online Library, https://wol.jw.org/en/wol/d/r1/lp-e/1951080#h=5.

Yoder, Anne. "Military Classifications for Draftees," *Swarthmore College Peace Collection*, https://www.swarthmore.edu/library/peace/conscientiousobjection/MilitaryClassifications.htm.

Yolton, L. William. "Conscientious Objection," in *Protest, Power, and Change: An Encyclopedia of Nonviolent Action from ACT-UP to Women's Suffrage*, eds. Roger S. Powers, William B. Vogele, Christopher Kruegler and Ronald M. McCarthy (New York: Routledge, 1997/2011).

Zarefsky, David. "Goodnight's 'Speculative Inquiry' in Its Intellectual Context," *Argumentation & Advocacy* 48 (2012): 211–215.

Part III. Equal Protection and the Religious Freedom Restoration Act

9. Burwell v. Hobby Lobby *(2014): How Rhetorical Strategies Invoking Religious Freedom Harm Women and LGBTQ+ Persons*

Skye de Saint Felix

Women's access to proper healthcare, including preventative screenings, contraception, abortion, and other reproductive healthcare services, are fundamental for women's autonomy.[1] Currently, a litany of conservative policies work to make women's reproductive healthcare, especially abortion and contraception, inaccessible and illegal.[2] While many factors can deter women from accessing care (e.g. stigma, lack of clinics or providers nearby, fears of deportation, and many others), this chapter focuses on how cost, corporate freedom, and insurance issues deny women necessary health services. A new set of healthcare restrictions emerged when corporations, namely Hobby Lobby, Mardel, and Conestoga, argued that providing their employees insurance coverage for contraceptives violated their rights to religious freedom. After numerous lower courts ruled against the companies in question, typically arguing that they did not have the rights to religious freedom under the Religious Freedom Restoration Act of 1993 (RFRA) since they were not people, the Supreme Court agreed to hear the case.

Burwell, Secretary of Health and Human Services, et al. v. Hobby Lobby Stores, Inc., et al. (2014) became a landmark case that privileged religious freedom over women's rights by ruling that *corporations* have access to personhood rights that protect free religious exercise. The ruling allowed businesses like Hobby Lobby to deny insurance coverage for contraceptives to its employees.[3] But a key factor for this ruling begins in 2010 with the Women's Health Amendment to the Patient Protection and Affordable Care Act (ACA), colloquially known as Obamacare. The Women's Health Amendment enacted a contraceptive mandate, which required companies with over fifty full-time employees to provide healthcare plans with "preventive care and screenings" for women without "any cost sharing requirements."[4] Part of this mandate included access to twenty contraceptive methods approved by The Food and Drug Administration (FDA). Hobby Lobby objected to four methods, citing a religious belief that they were abortifacients, abortion-inducing drugs, in their lawsuit against Health and Human Services (HHS). The four methods in question were two emergency contraceptives (ECs), ella and Plan B, and two types of intrauterine devices (IUDs), copper and hormonal IUDs, which provide long term birth control that typically lasts three to five years. The Supreme Court of the United States (SCOTUS) stated that four of the twenty methods "may have the effect of preventing an already fertilized egg from developing any further by inhibiting its attachment to the uterus."[5] On June 30, 2014, the Court upheld that the contraceptive mandate "substantially burdened [Hobby Lobby's] exercise of religion and HHS had not... proved that the mandate was the 'least restrictive means' of furthering a compelling governmental interest."[6]

A 5-4 SCOTUS majority ruled that the Court had a responsibility to uphold the RFRA, which they argued renders the contraceptive mandate unlawful. Five male justices determined the case's outcome in favor of corporate religious liberty; the only three women on the Court were in the dissent alongside Justice Beyer. To assess how this ruling was argued and its effects, I use this chapter to investigate rhetorics shaping the ruling. First, I discuss the *Hobby Lobby* case, including its context and specific rhetorical and legal standards. I argue that "corporate rights," to which Justice Ruth Bader Ginsburg dissented, gave personhood liberties to corporations, and privileged their interests over their employees. The case raises questions of who is considered a person under the law and who is allowed to access basic human rights such as healthcare. In this section of the paper, I discuss how personhood rhetorics, specifically ones that grant humanity to corporations and to fetuses, are commonly used by anti-choice groups to curtail abortion and contraception access; they contribute to a reality where women have limited personhood rights that can be curtailed by the so-called personhood rights of corporations and zygotes. Second, I argue that this case employs incrementalism, a common strategy used in anti-abortion cases and discrimination against LGBTQ+ people that works by chipping away rather than directly challenging people's rights. This chapter examines how *Hobby Lobby* contributes to a body of reasoning (scholarly, social, and legal), which favors the religious "right" of a closely-held corporation over an individual right to equal protection under the law. I conclude with a discussion of how women and LGBTQ+ people are disproportionately affected by religious freedom precedents and how the *Hobby Lobby* aftermath is far from over.

At the heart of this chapter is a discussion of the gendered consequences of how we frame cases involving women's rights and importantly, how they provide a stepping stone for corporations to apply the logic more broadly. This chapter echoes an essential point of feminism: the right to control one's body and make their own reproductive choices is essential to gender equality.[7] While it is true that *Burwell v. Hobby Lobby* (2014) is a case of many issues—insurance and healthcare coverage, public health, women's rights and gender equity, corporate personhood, religious liberty, class, labor and employment rights, workplace discrimination—women's rights are diminished and denied when we refer to this as a "religious freedom" case, instead of an attack on women's bodily autonomy and personal rights. Women's rights are often overlooked in Constitutional law. Maya Manian explains that even when courts rule in favor of women's rights, it is often framed as upholding freedoms, rather than supporting women specifically. For instance, *Griswold v. Connecticut* (1965) granted contraceptive rights for married couples under "marital privacy," and *Roe v. Wade* (1973) granted the right to abortion based on "doctor's rights" and "the right to privacy."[8] In fact, Mary Ziegler acknowledges that "rarely do progressive activists explain why sexual liberty should be protected."[9] When we fail to foreground women's rights to sexual liberty or personal agency, we open the door for state regulation and suppression of sexual expression, which makes it easier to enact gender-based discrimination in healthcare and employment practices as evidenced in *Hobby Lobby*. As Justice Ginsburg explains in her dissent, women's full participation in economic, social, and political life are at stake, but the Court continues to ignore or act ambivalent about women's autonomy.[10]

Hobby Lobby *and the ACA's Contraceptive Mandate*

In 2014, Hobby Lobby was a for-profit corporation, with 514 stores in 41 states and over 13,000 employees across the nation. Although it was not classified as a religious organization, the company said it operated under Christian values and principles.[11] *Hobby Lobby* (2014) represents two lawsuits—one filed by Hobby Lobby's CEO and founder David Green (and his family), who included his affiliated businesses like Mardel in his lawsuit, and one filed by Conestoga's owner and operator, Norman Hahn (and his family). These companies argued that they should not have to comply with the birth control mandate because it violated their "sincere Christian beliefs that life begins at conception."[12] To be clear, the ACA does not require that companies provide insurance to any of their employees, but if they do provide insurance, it has to be equal for men and women.[13]

Birth control is used for more than pregnancy prevention. Many women use birth control like IUDs to help with hormonal imbalances, menstruation, endometriosis, and other women's reproductive health concerns.[14] Still, Green and Hahn opposed the use of emergency contraceptives and IUDs because, to them, they cause abortions. Emergency contraceptives and IUDs are not abortifacients.[15] Put simply, if a woman wanted an abortion, neither ECs nor IUDs would work.[16] The only connection to abortion is that they can help prevent a future need to have an abortion. But Green and Hahn argued that fertilization represents life, even without implantation. Although it is medically inaccurate to describe contraceptives as abortifacients, the Court upheld that it was enough for Green to *believe* the medications caused abortion. Using the Free Exercise Clause of the First Amendment and the Religious Freedom Restoration Act's (RFRA) (1993) ruling that "governments shall not substantially burden a person's free exercise of religion,"[17] Green argued that Hobby Lobby's religious liberty was violated and that their business practices would face a substantial burden if they were fined for noncompliance with the birth control mandate.[18]

To better understand the other side of the debate, let us consider why the contraceptive mandate was included in the ACA. Senator Barbara Mikulski of Maryland created the Woman's Health Amendment (also known as the Mikulski Amendment) to address the health disparities between men and women's access to care. She cites the fact that many insurance companies treat womanness as a pre-existing condition, with millions of women "uninsured during their prime reproductive years, despite the fact that the average woman spends about 30 years trying not to get pregnant and three years either trying to get pregnant, being pregnant, or immediately post-partum." Coupled with the fact that 98% of sexually active American women have used birth control at some point in their lives, Mikulski and her sixty-one Senate colleagues saw the public interest in birth control as compelling, and necessary to include full coverage for women's preventative health in the ACA.[19]

Shortly after the Mikulski Amendment was enacted, conservatives worked to repeal its power through "conscience" legislation. In 2012, the Senate denied a "conscience amendment," which would have allowed employers or insurance providers to deny coverage in the name of "religious beliefs or moral convictions."[20] Conscience or refuse clause laws can especially hinder women's reproductive choices because emergency contraception is a time-sensitive matter. If pharmacies or pharmacists turn women away or lie about not having medication in stock because they do not want to dispense it, women are placed in a difficult and urgent position, especially if they have to travel or pay more for their medicine after they were initially denied. The right to refuse supports moral and religious superiority that tells women their behaviors and bodies should be regulated. Then-Tenth Circuit judge Gorsuch, who ruled in Hobby Lobby's favor of a lower-level court version of the case, said,

> All of us face the problem of complicity. All of us must answer for ourselves whether and to what degree we are willing to be involved in the wrongdoing of others. For some, religion provides an essential source of guidance both about what constitutes wrongful conduct and the degree to which those who assist others in committing wrongful conduct themselves bear moral culpability.[21]

Religious refusals further expanded in January 2018, when the Trump administration created the Conscience and Religious Freedom Division within the HHS Office of Civil Rights with the explicit goal of creating and strengthening conscience objections in health care.[22]

While conscience legislation primarily targets the two emergency contraceptives that Hobby Lobby opposed coverage of, it is important to also analyze what happens when women cannot access long term contraception, the other two forms of the contraceptive mandate. Long-acting reversible contraceptives (LARCs) like IUDs and hormonal implants are becoming more popular among women, especially because they dramatically reduce the likelihood of user error, such as forgetting to take a pill or taking it at sporadic times of day. They are the most effective form of contraception. But without insurance, LARCs can be incredibly expensive, costing in the hundreds or thousands for insertion and removal.[23] LARCs allow women to visit the doctor less often and can help with conditions like anemia, endometriosis, acne, fatigue, dysmenorrhea, and even cancer. Given this, it is difficult to imagine how limiting access to LARCs and ECs does not create a substantial or undue burden on women's reproductive decisions, which of course, also affects their economic and familial decisions.[24]

Women are prioritized in this chapter primarily because women are the ones most directly impacted by *Hobby Lobby*. But the case also affects our social understandings of women and gender. Neil S. Siegel and Reva B. Siegel argue that the Court's opinion focused on "material considerations, not on the creation of social meanings" or on the "individual female employees."[25] When women's rights are pitted against religious rights, it mischaracterizes the rights of women as inherently immoral and an undue burden to business operations. Framing contraception as immoral distorts that fact that many women use contraception *to* act responsibly. Thus, when the Court ruled that there was a "compelling interest" in free religious exercise, women were left asking, "What about compelling interests in *our* humanity?" So although the Court did affirm that birth control is a compelling interest, it did not outweigh corporate religious interests. Siegel and Siegel explain that what should be deemed compelling are the "core concerns of the community in promoting public health and facilitating women's integration in the workplace" and the concerns of those who benefit from the contraceptive mandate, including "bodily integrity, personal autonomy, and equal citizenship."[26]

It is clear that there are many factors, interests, and rhetorics shaping the *Hobby Lobby* ruling, but two primary concerns were gravely overlooked—effects on women (and later LGBTQ+ persons) and how contraception is a public health issue. In what follows, I investigate two primary rhetorical strategies, personhood and incrementalism, that have political and social effects beyond *Hobby Lobby*. In addition to religious liberty for corporations, personhood and incrementalism strategies significantly undermine women and LGBTQ+ access to healthcare, while subordinating their humanity. Neither personhood nor incremental strategies began with *Hobby Lobby*, but both contribute to new lines of reasoning for healthcare cases. Similarly, both strategies are built on and contribute to a larger history of demonizing women and LGBTQ+ persons because their right to bodily decisions are deemed immoral and unworthy of state protection.

Who Gets to Be a Person Under the Law? The Personhood Movement's Assault on Women

Hobby Lobby set a dangerous precedent for who and what can be considered a person, and is therefore entitled to the rights of "persons." In 2011 at an Iowa State Fair, then-presidential candidate Mitt Romney said, "Corporations are people, my friend," which sparked a litany of polarizing responses. Some believed he was "socially tone deaf" and did not understand average Americans, while others believed he was referring to the fact that corporations are often considered people under statutory and regulatory laws.[27] In some ways, religious freedom for corporations was the next step in a chain of cases giving for-profit entities personhood rights: *Citizens United v. Federal Election Commission* (2010) granted free speech to corporations,[28] *New York Times Co. v. Sullivan* (1965) granted freedom of the press,[29] corporations have the right to assembly (because they are considered free associations with free assembly rights), and they also maintain the right to petition through a multi-billion dollar lobbying industry.[30] But do these First Amendment freedoms mean that corporations are *people*? Personhood is an essential rhetorical frame for this case, because the RFRA upheld a *person's* free exercise of religion. *Hobby Lobby* therefore raised the following questions: Are corporations people? Can corporations exercise religion? If so, can they enforce their beliefs on their employees? Does corporate personhood outweigh women's personhood/lives?

The Court included Hobby Lobby in the RFRA's definition of persons, which extended the legal application of corporate personhood, and ultimately, corporate power. But since this was the first time that corporate personhood and religious exemptions were legally tied, many were unconvinced that corporations deserve personhood rights. Lawyers in *Burwell v. Hobby Lobby* argued to extend the logic that allows nonprofits to legally exercise religion as justification for granting religious freedoms to corporations. But HHS and Justice Ginsburg stated that Hobby Lobby lost rights to personhood when they defined themselves as corporations instead of general partnerships or sole proprietors.[31] Ginsburg stated the distinction between the two "is hardly obscure. Religious organizations exist to foster the interests of persons subscribing to the same religious faith," but for-profit corporations do not. In fact, employees at a corporation are not from one religious community and it would be illegal to hire based on religious-based criteria.[32] In her dissent, Ginsburg distinguished between "natural persons" and "artificial legal entities." Citing *Trustees of Dartmouth College v. Woodward* (1819), Ginsburg reiterated Chief Justice Marshall's definition of a corporation as an "artificial being, invisible, intangible, and existing only in contemplation of law." On this basis, HHS argued that Hobby Lobby and other companies should not be able to sue for RFRA violations, and that as owners, Green and Hahn should not be able to sue because the government regulations only affect corporations.[33] In addition, Ginsburg also cited Justice Stevens' assertion in *Citizens United v. Federal Election Commission* (2010) that corporations "have no consciences, no beliefs, no feelings, no thoughts, no desires."[34] By these definitions, for-profit companies cannot exercise religious beliefs and are distinguished from their owners, directors, and shareholders.

Jessica White explains how the personhood standard in *Hobby Lobby* is defined (even by Justice Alito) as protecting the rights of owners, shareholders, *and* employees. Alito began his argument citing the "people (including shareholders, officers, and employees)," but concluded by stating that protecting corporations "protects the religious liberty of the humans who own and control those companies."[35] White explains that this rhetorical shift privileged the owners above all other persons in the company, making shareholders and employees secondary. She argues, "rhetorically speaking, the Court's paternalistic move marked a synechdochic translation whereby the owners stood in for the totality of the corporate person, even though legally, the corporate person had been defined as constituting all three of the elements (owners, shareholders, AND employees)."[36] The owner's religious beliefs became the beliefs of the company, making the *and* an *or*. Therefore, if the "owner(s) subscribe(s) to either a pro-Life or pro-Choice hermeneutic on a legal issue, the corporation will follow suit."[37] Since Hahn and Green had religious objections to contraception and abortion, so did Hobby Lobby. By protecting the beliefs of the owners, employees are framed as unworthy of equal protection.

How Personhood Rhetoric Affects Women

Corporate personhood and the general expansion of the personhood movement creates hierarchies between various entities deemed "people," often positioning women at the bottom. Women of childbearing capacity already pay about 68% more for healthcare than men will in their entire lifetime.[38] This fact, coupled with the reality that women are not paid as much as men, is already a significant burden on women's healthcare that compounds when women are denied access to birth control. In addition, it is unsafe for women with certain medical conditions to carry children, and denying contraception and abortion ignores circumstances like financial instability or rape. In some situations, the four types could be an answer to the least restrictive means test and the Court's "compelling interest" in birth control.[39]

While expanding the definition of person to include corporations has limited women's access to birth control, expanding the rights of personhood to fetuses threatens abortion rights. Like corporate personhood, fetal personhood is a rhetorical construction based on certain religious doctrines that at best make abortion a sin, and at worst a form of murder. It also means punishing women for their choices and for being "bad," negligent, and promiscuous women who use abortion as a form of birth control. The murder frame makes women's choices unethical and selfish, but also criminal. Attempting to access abortion care can result in incarceration, deportation, or losing one's children.[40] This is, in part, because fetal personhood justifies banning abortion even in early stages of gestation and demonizes all abortions.[41] In addition, considering IUDs and ECs as abortifacients manipulates our public understandings of abortion to also ban contraceptive methods that prevent the need for future abortions.

Fetal personhood also pits women against the unborn, creating a dichotomy that asks the public to determine whose rights deserve protection. Because of this, Von Hagel and Mansbach argued that "many in the pro-life movement view [*Hobby Lobby*] as a victory in their struggle to limit—and eventually eliminate—the right to abortion."[42] The irony of expanding personhood to corporations and day-old zygotes is that it retracts women's personhood. As Dahlia Lithwick warns, "Turning everything and anything into a 'person' ultimately also serves to turn persons into things." Furthermore, she explains that *Hobby Lobby* is such a worrisome case because it fused "together two of the most dangerous right-wing civil rights obsessions of our times: the ambition of large, for-profit corporations to see themselves as people, with faith, convictions, and consciences, and the attempts of citizens, using their own science and their own facts, to declare when legal personhood begins, and then impose universal laws based on those beliefs."[43] This paved the way for personhood to begin whenever someone says it does and promotes using religious personhood to justify curtailing other people's fundamental rights to healthcare.

Neither corporations nor zygotes have been birthed from a human being. They cannot be considered "natural" or "persons," yet are afforded human rights. Personhood movements are also dangerous for women because they are aimed at writing and passing legislation at both state and federal levels. Jennifer Jorczak explains how *Hobby Lobby* promotes gender discrimination by ignoring the certain circumstances women face in their workplace, with insurance, and with reproductive health. She states, "This supposedly equal application of equal protection leads to inequitable results; by ignoring gender differences when evaluating gender discrimination, courts are contributing to the continued subordination of subordinate groups."[44] Tara Zabehi explains that denying women contraceptive access is the "equivalent to depriving individuals of their employee benefits that are covered under federal law" and is a clear example of gender-based discrimination.[45] This opens the door for denying women social security, minimum wage, or altering hiring processes because of religious freedom. Because *Hobby Lobby* privileged the First Amendment rights of corporations, this ruling stoked fears that its application would continue "gender and race discrimination in the workplace,"[46] and jeopardize LGBTQ+ employment protections. If a corporation thinks homosexuality or being genderqueer is a sin, and paying their salary supports this "lifestyle," then corporations could claim religious freedom to fire or refuse to hire LGBTQ+ employees. After all, *Hobby Lobby* demonstrated that rights can be reversed to favor discrimination.

A Key Case in "Radical Incrementalism"

Legal scholar Jessica Mason Pieklo called the *Hobby Lobby* case a clear example of "radical incrementalism," a strategy used to rollback contraceptive rights under intentionally deceptive frames, instead of trying to criminalize the right directly.[47] Incrementalism, the tactic of eroding rights in steps or increments, is commonly used in cases involving gender equity. Most notably, anti-choice advocates work to make abortion illegal by first making it inaccessible through state restrictions and Targeted Regulation of Abortion Provider (TRAP) laws that shut down clinics. These kinds of state restrictions are easier to pass than repealing *Roe v. Wade*, and work to make rights legal in name only. To be fair, incrementalism strategies can also help *gain* rights for minorities, but here I focus on how they are used to chip away women's rights.

Ainsworth and Hall explain that incremental legal strategies are typically predicated on the "recognition that overturning Supreme Court decisions is difficult, making major changes to federal laws is difficult, and making sustained change to any policy takes time."[48] Polarizing social issues are especially difficult to change because a majority vote is required, which often means lots of lobbying efforts. Incrementalism has the advantage of being minor, so eroding key freedoms, like the right to access contraceptives guaranteed in *Eisenstadt v. Baird* (1972), *appears* less severe. Ainsworth and Hall argue that the guise that it is "just a minor change" makes a policy shift "seem quite reasonable on [its] face" and is more difficult to oppose.[49] This strategy can also falsely write a decision as neutral or in the case of *Hobby Lobby*, can act as if this case was merely about religious freedom instead of also about a denial of women's bodily autonomy. As a clear case of "radical incrementalism," *Hobby Lobby* did not strike down the entire birth control mandate or work outside of the RFRA, but it "set the path for future courts to do so."[50]

One way incrementalism works is by introducing new actors into the narrative. For instance, Von Hagel and Mansbach explain that most conversations about abortion and contraception discuss women and fetuses, and sometimes doctors. But *Hobby Lobby* expanded the conversation by increasing the number of stakeholders in reproductive rights to include employers. Empowering employers to have a direct or active role in women's reproductive health is a relatively new tactic that uses incrementalism to make contraception (and abortion) rights inaccessible.[51] Women's agency is eroded when the interests of doctors, pharmacists, nurses, politicians, employers, insurance companies, parents, immigration officers, and others are taken into consideration. When incrementalism allows for a litany of new stakeholders, these parties can inaccurately claim that they are burdened by a legal standard.

For instance, allowing corporations and employers to interfere with reproductive autonomy is not only inappropriate, but inapplicable given the distinction between religious beliefs and religious exercise. *Employment Division, Department of Human Resources of Oregon v. Smith* (1990) explains that '"exercise of religion' often involves not only belief and profession but the performance of (or abstention from) physical acts."[52] While the Greens and Hahns argued that the mandate would force their hand on contraception, scholars such as Leslie Griffin point out that the store owners were not forcing employers to use contraception and were not dispensing the medication themselves. She writes, "It is still not clear, for example, why providing insurance coverage involves the exercise of religion."[53] And since the birth control mandate applies generally and does not target a specific religious group, it could not be considered a First Amendment violation. Similarly, the Third Circuit denied the Greens and Hahns claims that the birth control mandate violated the RFRA because it requires no actions by the owners, just the corporations.[54] Corporations and owners cannot forbid a woman from spending her wages on contraceptives herself. In the same vein, Ginsburg explained that decisions "to claim benefits under the plans are made not by [corporations], but by the covered employees"; this cannot substantially burden the religious exercise of corporations or owners.[55]

Incrementalism is also particularly dangerous in *Hobby Lobby* because it allowed for those who supported denying women rights the opportunity to frame this decision as narrow. It applied to "closely-held corporations," which sounds limiting on its face, but ignores the reality that over 90% of corporations are closely-held, meaning that over half of the company's shares are held by just a few individuals.[56] The idea that the ruling would only apply narrowly to corporations is, as Ginsburg explained, a rhetorical charade; "Although the Court attempts to cabin its language to closely held corporations, its logic extends to corporations of any size, public or private."[57] She added that the ruling "invites for-profit entities to seek religion-based exemptions from regulations they deem offensive to their faith," which could extend well beyond contraceptives.[58]

Justice Ginsburg warned that religious liberty could be used to object beyond contraceptives "to blood transfusions (Jehovah's Witnesses); antidepressants (Scientologists); medications derived from pigs, including anesthesia, intravenous fluids, and pills coated with gelatin (certain Muslims, Jews, and Hindus); and vaccinations (Christian Scientists, among others)."[59] Physician-assisted suicide could be in jeopardy. Some Satanists filed a lawsuit saying that forcing a woman to have an ultrasound before getting an abortion violated their religious freedom.[60] Although the Court said the ruling only applied to birth control and did not allow for people to "cloak illegal discrimination as religious practice,"[61] the following examples will show how

LGBTQ+ persons have been affected by this ruling. This is, of course, deeply dehumanizing, but also targets a group of people who already have fewer employment protections and consumer services, and are less likely to have insurance coverage that meets all of their healthcare needs.[62]

*A Post-*Hobby Lobby *World: Deepening Discrimination against Women and LGBTQ+*

Health and Human Services' concerns that *Hobby Lobby* would lead to greater gender inequity were validated after a number of cases used religious freedom to justify denying healthcare and/or employment to women and LGBTQ+ people. Religious freedom was mobilized as a legal precedent (when cases would explicitly reference *Hobby Lobby*) and in public memory, where cases did not cite *Hobby Lobby,* but communicated similar arguments about a company's right to religious liberty. How this is case is remembered, legally and publicly, continues to shape our understandings of religious freedom and the tension between company and employee rights. First, I discuss cases where *Hobby Lobby* was explicitly cited or its standards (such as a "substantial burden" on religious exercise) were invoked.

Shortly after *Hobby Lobby,* other cases have tested the influence and precedent of this case. *Perez v. Paragon Contractors* (2014) investigated children labor by the Fundamentalist Church of Jesus Christ of Latter-day Saints, but since the church had a "religious vow not to discuss church matters," they argued that it would be a substantial burden to testify. Judge David Sam used *Hobby Lobby's* substantial burden standard to dismiss the case, citing that required testimonies were not the "least restrictive means of furthering that compelling government interest."[63] To try and sidestep *Hobby Lobby's* ruling, President Obama created a policy in 2015, which would grant contraceptive coverage to employees when employers refused. The company merely had to fill out a form to HHS stating objection and the government would get a third-party insurer to cover the employee at no additional cost. But the form proved to be a controversial ask.[64] As shown, some institutions have capitalized on the ambiguity of the "substantial burden" and "least restrictive means" standards to escape government regulation or scrutiny.

In another case, Wheaton College was allowed to claim religious exceptions from the birth control mandate, although they legally could not obtain an exemption unless they filled out a government form. Calling the form a "substantial burden," they were able to claim exemption despite the new HHS provision under Obama. Little Sisters of the Poor, a congregation of Catholic women, also claimed the same protections as Wheaton College, citing the form as a burden. Here, it is clear that the "substantial burden" murkiness allows religious organizations, or groups that claim newfound religion, to argue that just about any and all actions can create a substantial burden. These cases are also supported by conservative lobbying groups like the Becket Fund for Religious Liberty, which seeks to expand the *Hobby Lobby* decision.[65] Creating a web of rulings that stretch *Hobby Lobby*'s influence demonstrates how incrementalism breeds legal discrimination, one case at a time.

While this paper prioritizes the effects on women's humanity and bodily autonomy who were targeted *in* the ruling, LGBTQ+ were heavily targeted *after* the ruling. In 2016, fears that LGBTQ+ discrimination would increase in a post-*Hobby Lobby* world manifested as a conservative Christian business fired a transgender employee, Aimee Stephens, for wanting to "dress as a woman," which they argued would violate their dress code. Citing a belief that gender transitions violate biblical teachings, R.G. & G. R. Harris Funeral Homes was able to deny employment to Stephens (who had no protections under federal law) by arguing that not firing Stephens would be a "substantial burden" on their religious exercise.[66] Under President Obama's administration, HHS expanded the understanding of "sex discrimination" to include gender identity and sexual orientation. But not all courts agreed with this move towards inclusion.[67] As shown through Stephens' case, allowing businesses to practice discrimination based on religious beliefs makes our government "powerless to enforce laws to protect all Americans against the harms of discrimination."[68] Next, I discuss instances where this case emboldened different employers or service providers to discriminate more freely.

Another prominent SCOTUS case, *Masterpiece Cakeshop, Ltd. v. Colorado Civil Rights Commission* (2018), ruled in a 7-2 decision that a Colorado baker could refuse to make a cake for a same-sex couple's wedding. While this case was primarily concerned with the First Amendment and *Hobby Lobby* assessed both the First Amendment and the RFRA, the reasoning behind the rulings overlaps. Both Hobby Lobby and Masterpiece Cakeshop were allowed to practice discrimination under religious objections. Although the two cases are intertwined in these ways, *Hobby Lobby* is not mentioned or cited in *Masterpiece Cakeshop*. The (perhaps strategic) lack of connection highlights the elusive power of incrementalism; failing to discuss cases together obscures the systematic nature of attacks on LGBTQ+ and women's rights. Moreover, LGBTQ+ discrimination in the name of religion is commonplace in religiously-affiliated hospitals, particularly Catholic hospitals that deny healthcare to transgender patients and deny tubal ligations and other safe contraceptive procedures to women. In one highly publicized case at Dignity

Health, the hospital refused to give a transgender man a hysterectomy, calling it a "sterilization" rather than gender-affirming care.[69] And in 2020, the Supreme Court heard arguments about whether Philadelphia could exclude a Catholic agency from its foster care system, citing a religious refusal to work with gay couples.[70]

While *Hobby Lobby* regulated employers' rights to limit contraceptive coverage, an issue that will likely be affected by this case is coverage for LGBTQ+ medications like PrEP, a drug used to prevent HIV infection. PrEP, or pre-exposure prophylaxis, is not just a drug for those in the LGBTQ+ community, but gay and bisexual men use it at the highest rates.[71] Contraception, STIs, and HIV prevention are clear public health issues, but the Court's decision that these interests are not "compelling" enough or the "least restrictive means" of meeting a community goal, subject medicines like PrEP to employer denial. Similar to LARCs, PrEP can be very expensive, up to $2,000 for a 30-day supply.[72] If employers and insurance companies refuse to cover PrEP because of a religious objection, not only does the likelihood of HIV transmission increase and endanger public health, but we also communicate to LGBTQ+ persons that their health is not worth protecting.

Women and those who use contraceptives are still facing difficulty accessing this form of healthcare post-*Hobby Lobby.* Many states have policies that require insurance providers to cover contraception if they cover other prescriptions, but have exceptions for religious employers or insurances. In July 2020, a 7-2 Supreme Court decision upheld the Trump administration's regulation that allows employers to deny birth control coverage and Obama's contraceptive mandate if they cite religious or moral objections. This decision could lead to as many as 126,000 women losing contraceptive coverage from their employers.[73] The Supreme Court's ruling was one of the latest decisions in a long-standing public debate over employers' ability to interfere with the healthcare of their employees.

Hobby Lobby also illustrates how the definition of a "religious employer" can be manipulated and stretched as any company could claim that an action violates their religious freedom. Conscience-clause laws and or religious refusal clauses can apply to a range of services and prescriptions, including emergency contraception and more recently, medicines such as mifepristone that would help women who have miscarried.[74] In 2020, the post-*Hobby Lobby* reproductive rights landscape was characterized by forty-six states that allowed health care providers to refuse abortion services, twelve states that allowed contraception refusals, and eighteen which allowed sterilization refusals.[75] It is also important to note that when abortion is highly regulated and inaccessible for so many women, contraceptive rights become even more crucial. Sometimes refusal is illegal (although Jessica Valenti states that few pharmacists fear consequences) and sometimes it is state-sanctioned. This has also given rise to activist groups like Pharmacists for Life International, a group of anti-choice pharmacists who organize to deny women's access to contraceptives.[76] With corporations, pharmacists, and insurance providers using moral superiority as a justification to control women's reproductive health, women's fundamental personhood continues to take a backseat to a litany of factors and actors.

Even some supporters of religious freedom argue that *Hobby Lobby* weakens the concept. Leslie Griffin explains that it is against the RFRA to impose one's religion on another person and begs the question of which religions and religious practices deserve protection. Griffin argues that "religious freedom is best protected when the Constitution and laws are interpreted to advance a shared political and legal system based on common values rather than religious ones."[77] And Jessica Mason Pieklo asks us to consider the religious freedom of the *employees*. Their rights to be free from religious discrimination and to make their own choices when it comes to religious practices (or lack thereof) were severely omitted from the debate.[78] Similarly, those who felt that it was unjust to impose economic consequences on (rich) corporations overlooked the economic impositions and burdens that *Hobby Lobby* imposed on women.

Conclusion

It is important that we do not simply remember *Hobby Lobby* as a "religious freedom" case and continue to overlook its effects on employee humanity and rights. This case shaped our understandings of who and what is considered a legal person. Corporate personhood furthers hierarchies between "people," subordinating employees, namely women and LGBTQ+ people. Justice Alito called for the protection of owners, but Jorczak argues that this "protection should never be extended to corporations to the detriment of human beings."[79] Legalizing discrimination under the guise of religious freedom not only dehumanizes groups of people by labeling their choices "sinful" or "immoral," but also denies them equal protection under the law. In addition, expanding the definition of personhood fuels the anti-choice personhood movement that works to rollback abortion rights and encourages punishment for women's choices. Rhetorics of personhood and incrementalism work together here to rollback social advances for women and the LGBTQ+ community.

Moreover, the rulings in *Hobby Lobby* greatly aggrandized corporate power. First, owner beliefs did not have to be rooted in scientific fact (i.e., supporting the belief that contraceptives are abortifacients even though the assertion is medically inaccurate). This dangerous precedent enables employers to deem a litany of behaviors "immoral," opening the door for numerous forms of discrimination. Second, employers were granted privileges despite the fact that they were not being asked by the government to actively *do* anything. They were instead asked *not to interfere* with a government-issued mandate that helped alleviate gender discrimination in the workplace. The Court's decision privileges owners to the detriment of their employees by allowing them to create their own interpretations of a "substantial burden."

In addition to contextualizing corporate personhood, *Hobby Lobby* elucidates the rhetorical functions of incrementalism. As a strategy, incrementalism's deceptive power masquerades the systemic attack on women and LGBTQ+ persons. For instance, there is a surprising lack of connection between contemporary religious liberty cases and *Hobby Lobby.* Many, like the Colorado baker case, discuss religious freedom to object to a business' services, but do not stress *Hobby Lobby's* influence. But creating a web of cases (even if they do not explicitly reference each other) against women and the LGBTQ+ community creates numerous institutional barriers that deny them access to bodily autonomy. Making these connections helps us understand how we got here, and can help prevent these rulings from being seen in isolation. Isolation leads to arguments that the cases are not that severe or do not change much in our legal landscape. As incrementalism shows, seeing lines of reasoning as new and narrow ignores how they build on each other to create an environment hostile to reproductive rights, bodily autonomy, and inclusive workplaces.

Depleting access to contraceptives, PrEP, hormone therapies, and other forms of gendered care is also a public health issue. Women's wellbeing is improved when they have access to reproductive healthcare. Not only does this give them agency and control over their lives, but it also leads to greater social, political, economic, and gender equity. Workplaces also benefit. Not only is a company more attractive to potential employees if they provide healthcare (i.e., 83% of women said they want their employers' insurance to cover the full range of reproductive healthcare, including abortion and contraception), but Mary Alice Carter, Jen Stark & Sonja Spoo explain that many consumers pay attention to a company's values when choosing where to put their dollars.[80] Similarly, LGBTQ+ people benefit from access to PrEP, hormone therapies, and similar treatments that acknowledge their humanity. Tackling the HIV epidemic, for instance, leads to less transmission and people living longer, healthier lives.[81] While the individual rights of employees are clearly important, public health likewise suffers when cases like *Hobby Lobby* allow for healthcare discrimination.

The incremental trend of making rights legal in name, but inaccessible, works to regulate rights out of existence. Moving forward, the rhetorically constructed personhood of corporations and zygotes cannot continue to outweigh the actual humanity of living, breathing people. Unmasking the rhetorical power of personhood, incrementalism, and cloaking discrimination as religious freedom helps expose the oppression of women and LGBTQ+ persons. And it is important to remember that if we are going to achieve gender equality, basic human rights cannot be tied to one's employment or subjected to the beliefs of their employer.

Notes

1 I recognize that women are not the only people who need access to contraception and do not wish to be exclusionary in my language. However, *Hobby Lobby* was ruled in terms of "women's access to contraception," and I have adopted the same frames for this chapter.
2 Alisa Von Hagel and Daniela Mansbach, *Reproductive Rights in the Age of Human Rights: Pro-life Politics from Roe to Hobby Lobby* (New York: Palgrave Macmillan, 2016), 20.
3 Burwell v. Hobby Lobby Stores, Inc., 573 U.S.___ (2014).
4 Patient Protection and Affordable Care Act, Pub. L. No. 111–148, 124 Stat. 119 (2010) (codified as amended primarily in scattered sections of 42 U.S.C.), 15.
5 Burwell v. Hobby Lobby (2014), 2.
6 Ibid., 2.
7 Neil S. Siegel and Reva B. Siegel, "Compelling Interests and Contraception," *Connecticut Law Review* 47, no. 4 (2015): 1025.
8 Maya Manian, "Response: Griswold, Geduldig, and Hobby Lobby: The Sex Gap Continues," *University of Miami Law Review* 69, Caveat 17 (2015): https://lawreview.law.miami.edu/the-sex-gap-continues/
9 Mary Ziegler, "The (Non-Right) to Sex," *University of Miami Law Review* 69 (2015): 668.
10 Burwell v. Hobby Lobby (2014), 2.
11 Tara Zabehi, "Burwell v. Hobby Lobby Stores, Inc.: Creating Power for Corporations at the Cost of Changing Women's Lives," *The Journal of Business, Entrepreneurship & the Law* 9, no. 1 (May 2016): 1.
12 Burwell v. Hobby Lobby (2014), 2.
13 Jessica Mason Pieklo, "'Hobby Lobby' Is Just the Beginning: A Flood of Corporate Religious Objections Is Coming," *Rewire,* July 1, 2014, https://rewire.news/article/2014/07/01/hobby-lobby-just-beginning-flood-corporate-religious-objections-coming/
14 Helena Kopp Kallner, "Benefits of Reversible Contraception," *National Center for Biotechnology Information* 7 (2018): 3.

15 Laura Pelucchini, "Hobby Lobby Case: What Religious Liberty Can Do to Personal Freedom," *Sapienza Legal Papers* 3, no. 1 (2014): 20.
16 ECs can only prevent implementation, which does not fit the medical definition of an abortion. Medically, an abortion refers to the intentional termination of a pregnancy. Fertilization and implementation have to occur before a person is pregnant, so methods to prevent fertilization and implementation are not abortions.
17 Religious Freedom Restoration Act, 42 U. S. C. §§2000bb–1–4 (1993), 1.
18 While the tax may seem like a financial burden, Yvette Ann Walker points out that a penalty is not an imposition because "preservation of the taxation system is a compelling government interest of the highest order." Yvette Ann Walker, "More Than Human: Modern Expansion of Corporate Personhood Rights in Hobby Lobby," *Review of Law and Social Justice* 24, no. 2 (2015): 327.
19 Jennifer Jorczak, "Not Like You and Me: Hobby Lobby, The Fourteenth Amendment, And What the Further Expansion of Corporate Personhood Means for Individual Rights," *Brooklyn Law Review* 80, no. 1 (2014): 285–300.
20 Burwell v. Hobby Lobby (2014) (Ginsburg, R.B., dissenting), 6.
21 Hobby Lobby Stores, Inc., et al. v. Sebelius, et al., No. 12–6294 (2013),78.
22 Sandra H. Johnson, "Conscience and Religious Freedom Division Marks Its First Anniversary with Action," *Hastings Center Report* 49, no. 2 (2019): 4.
23 Doctors must also be trained to handle LARCs, which can create problems for women even with insurance to find ones in-network or closely located.
24 Kallner, "Benefits of Reversible Contraception," 3.
25 Siegel and Siegel, "Compelling Interests and Contraception," 1036.
26 Ibid., 1025.
27 "Jorczak, "Not Like You and Me," 286.
28 Citizens United v. Fed. Election Comm'n, 558 U.S. 310, 340–43 (2010).
29 N. Y. Times Co. v. Sullivan, 376 U.S. 254, 264 (1964).
30 "Jorczak, "Not Like You and Me," 287.
31 Burwell v. Hobby Lobby (2014), 2.
32 Burwell v. Hobby Lobby (2014) (Ginsburg, R.B., dissenting), 16.
33 Ibid., 2.
34 Burwell v. Hobby Lobby (2014) (Ginsburg, R.B., dissenting), 14.
35 Burwell v. Hobby Lobby (2014), 18.
36 Jessica L. White, "Hermeneutics, Rhetoric, and Paternalism in Abortion Law: An Analysis of *Burwell v. Hobby Lobby, Inc*," M.A. thesis, (California State University, Long Beach, 2016), 78.
37 Ibid., 79.
38 Zabehi, "Cost of Women's Lives," 14.
39 Burwell v. Hobby Lobby (2014), 40.
40 For more on women's reproductive punishments see: Jeanne Flavin, *Our Bodies, Our Crimes: The Policing of Women's Reproduction in America* (New York: NYU Press, 2010).
41 Sara Hayden, "Revitalizing the Debate between <Life> and <Choice>: The 2004 March for Women's Lives," *Communication and Critical/Cultural Studies* 6, no. 2 (2009): 114.
42 Von Hagel and Mansbach, *Reproductive Rights in the Age of Human Rights,* 1.

43 Dahlia Lithwick, "Un-People," *Slate,* December 3, 2013, https://slate.com/news-and-politics/2013/12/hobby-lobby-and-corporate-personhood-the-alarming-conservative-crusade-to-declare-everything-except-people-a-legal-person.html
44 Jorczak, "Not Like You and Me," 298.
45 Zabehi, "Cost of Women's Lives," 15.
46 Ibid., 14.
47 Pieklo, "Hobby Lobby is Just the Beginning."
48 Scott H. Ainsworth and Thad E. Hall, *Abortion Politics in Congress: Strategic Incrementalism and Policy Change* (New York: Cambridge, 2011), 10.
49 Ibid., 12.
50 Pieklo, "'Hobby Lobby' Is Just the Beginning."
51 Von Hagel and Mansbach, *Reproductive Rights in the Age of Human Rights,* 3.
52 *Employment Division, Department of Human Resources of Oregon v. Smith*, 494 U.S. 872 (1990), 877.
53 Leslie Griffin, "Hobby Lobby: The Crafty Case that Threatens Women's Rights and Religious Freedom," *Hastings Constitutional Law Quarterly* 42, no. 4 (2015): 674.
54 Jorczak, "Not Like You and Me," 308.
55 Burwell v. Hobby Lobby (2014) (Ginsburg, R.B., dissenting), 23.
56 Sarah Kliff, "Here's What a 'Closely-held Corporation' is," *Vox,* June 30, 2014, https://www.vox.com/2014/6/30/5857084/heres-what-a-closely-held-corporat ion-is
57 Burwell v. Hobby Lobby (2014) (Ginsburg, R.B., dissenting), 19.
58 Ibid., 20.
59 Burwell v. Hobby Lobby (2014) (Ginsburg, R.B., dissenting), 33–34.
60 Griffin, "Hobby Lobby: The Crafty Case," 691.
61 Burwell v. Hobby Lobby (2014), 6.
62 Griffin, "Hobby Lobby: The Crafty Case," 687.
63 Jeffrey Toobin, "On Hobby Lobby, Ginsburg Was Right," *New Yorker,* September 30, 2014, https://www.newyorker.com/news/daily-comment/hobby-lobbys-troubl ing-aftermath
64 Laura Bassett, "White House Finds Way Around Hobby Lobby Birth Control Decision," *Huffington Post,* July 10, 2015, https://www.huffpost.com/entry/white-house-birth-control_n_7771004
65 Toobin, "On Hobby Lobby, Ginsburg Was Right."
66 Emma Green, "Why Religious Employers Can Fire Trans People, According to a Michigan Court," *The Atlantic,* August 18, 2016, https://www.theatlantic.com/politics/archive/2016/08/in-michigan-its-totally-legal-to-fire-trans-people-for-their-gender-identity/496559/
67 Ibid.
68 Kate Opalewski, "Disappointing Ruling Allows Discrimination Against Transgender People," *Pride Source,* August 17, 2016, https://pridesource.com/article/77668-2/
69 Emily London and Maggie Siddiqi, "Religious Liberty Should Do No Harm," *Center for American Progress,* April 11, 2019, https://www.americanprogress.org/issues/religion/reports/2019/04/11/468041/religious-liberty-no-harm/
70 Adam Liptak, "Supreme Court to Hear Case on Gay Rights and Foster Care," *New York Times,* February 24, 2020, https://www.nytimes.com/2020/02/24/us/supreme-court-gay-rights-foster-care.html

71 Tim Fitzsimons, "PrEP Use Jumps to 35 Percent among Gay and Bi Men at Risk of HIV," *NBC News,* March 7, 2019, https://www.nbcnews.com/feature/nbc-out/prep-use-jumps-35-percent-among-gay-bi-men-risk-n980516
72 Shefali Luthra and Anna Gorman, "Rising Cost of PrEP to prevent HIV Infection Pushes it out of Research for Many," *NPR,* June 30, 2018, https://www.npr.org/sections/health-shots/2018/06/30/624045995/rising-cost-of-prep-a-pill-that-prevents-hiv-pushes-it-out-of-reach-for-many
73 Adam Liptak, "Supreme Court Upholds Trump Administration Regulation Letting Employers Opt Out of Birth Control Coverage," *New York Times,* July 8, 2020, https://www.nytimes.com/2020/07/08/us/supreme-court-birth-control-obamacare.html
74 Mara Gordon and Sarah McCammon, "A Drug That Eases Miscarriages Is Difficult For Women To Get," *NPR,* January 10, 2019, https://www.npr.org/sections/health-shots/2019/01/10/666957368/a-drug-that-eases-miscarriages-is-difficult-for-women-to-get
75 Guttmacher Institute, "Refusing to Provide Health Services."
76 Jessica Valenti, *The Purity Myth: How America's Obsession with Virginity in Hurting Young Women* (Berkeley: Seal Press, 2010), 136–37.
77 Griffin, "Hobby Lobby: The Crafty Case," 642.
78 Pieklo, "'Hobby Lobby' Is Just the Beginning."
79 Jorczak, "Not Like You and Me," 321.
80 Mary Alice Carter, Jen Stark and Sonja Spoo, "Why Businesses Should Support Reproductive Healthcare," *Rewire,* January 29, 2020, https://rewire.news/article/2020/01/29/businesses-should-support-reproductive-rights/
81 American Medical Association, "AMA Adopts New Public Health Policies to Improve Health of Nation," *AMA,* June 13, 2019, https://www.ama-assn.org/press-center/press-releases/ama-adopts-new-public-health-policies-improve-health-nation-3

Bibliography

Ainsworth, Scott H., and Thad E. Hall. *Abortion Politics in Congress: Strategic Incrementalism and Policy Change.* New York: Cambridge, 2011.

American Medical Association. "AMA Adopts New Public Health Policies to Improve Health of Nation." *AMA,* June 13, 2019. https://www.ama-assn.org/press-center/press-releases/ama-adopts-new-public-health-policies-improve-health-nation-3.

Bassett, Laura. "White House Finds Way Around Hobby Lobby Birth Control Decision." *Huffington Post,* July 10, 2015. https://www.huffpost.com/entry/white-house-birth-control_n_7771004.

Carter, Mary Alice, Jen Stark, and Sonja Spoo. "Why Businesses Should Support Reproductive Healthcare." *Rewire,* January 29, 2020. https://rewire.news/article/2020/01/29/businesses-should-support-reproductive-rights/.

Fitzsimons, Tim. "PrEP Use Jumps to 35 Percent among Gay and Bi Men at Risk of HIV." *NBC News,* March 7, 2019. https://www.nbcnews.com/feature/nbc-out/prep-use-jumps-35-percent-among-gay-bi-men-risk-n980516.

Gordon, Mara, and Sarah McCammon. "A Drug That Eases Miscarriages Is Difficult for Women to Get." *NPR,* January 10, 2019. https://www.npr.org/sections/health-shots/2019/01/10/666957368/a-drug-that-eases-miscarriages-is-difficult-for-women-to-get.

Green, Emma. "Why Religious Employers Can Fire Trans People, According to a Michigan Court." *The Atlantic,* August 18, 2016. https://www.theatlantic.com/politics/archive/2016/08/in-michigan-its-totally-legal-to-fire-trans-people-for-their-gender-identity/496559/.

Griffin, Leslie. "Hobby Lobby: The Crafty Case that Threatens Women's Rights and Religious Freedom." *Hastings Constitutional Law Quarterly* 42, no. 4 (2015): 641–94.

Guttmacher Institute. "Refusing to Provide Health Services." *Guttmacher Institute,* February 1, 2020. https://www.guttmacher.org/state-policy/explore/refusing-provide-health-services.

Hayden, Sara. "Revitalizing the Debate between <Life> and <Choice>: The 2004 March for Women's Lives." *Communication and Critical/Cultural Studies* 6, no. 2 (2009): 111–31.

Johnson, Sandra H. "Conscience and Religious Freedom Division Marks Its First Anniversary with Action." *Hastings Center Report* 49, no. 2 (2019): 4–5.

Jorczak, Jennifer. "Not Like You and Me: Hobby Lobby, The Fourteenth Amendment, and What the Further Expansion of Corporate Personhood Means for Individual Rights." *Brooklyn Law Review* 80, no. 1 (2014): 285–321.

Kallner, Helena Kopp. "Benefits of Reversible Contraception." *National Center for Biotechnology Information* 7 (2018): 1–8.

Kliff, Sarah. "Here's What a 'Closely-held Corporation' is." *Vox,* June 30, 2014. https://www.vox.com/2014/6/30/5857084/heres-what-a-closely-held-corporation-is.

Liptak, Adam. "Supreme Court to Hear Case on Gay Rights and Foster Care." *New York Times,* February 24, 2020. https://www.nytimes.com/2020/02/24/us/supreme-court-gay-rights-foster-care.html.

Liptak, Adam. "Supreme Court Upholds Trump Administration Regulation Letting Employers Opt Out of Birth Control Coverage." *New York Times,* July 8, 2020. https://www.nytimes.com/2020/07/08/us/supreme-court-birth-control-obamacare.html.

Lithwick, Dahlia. "Un-People." *Slate,* December 3, 2013. https://slate.com/news-and-politics/2013/12/hobby-lobby-and-corporate-personhood-the-alarming-conservative-crusade-to-declare-everything-except-people-a-legal-person.html.

London, Emily, and Maggie Siddiqi. "Religious Liberty Should Do No Harm." *Center for American Progress,* April 11, 2019. https://www.americanprogress.org/issues/religion/reports/2019/04/11/468041/religious-liberty-no-harm/.

Luthra, Shefali, and Anna Gorman. "Rising Cost of PrEP to Prevent HIV Infection Pushes It Out of Research for Many." *NPR,* June 30, 2018. https://www.npr.org/sections/health-shots/2018/06/30/624045995/rising-cost-of-prep-a-pill-that-prevents-hiv-pushes-it-out-of-reach-for-many.

Manian, Maya. "Response: Griswold, Geduldig, and Hobby Lobby: The Sex Gap Continues." *University of Miami Law Review* 69, Caveat 17 (2015): https://lawreview.law.miami.edu/the-sex-gap-continues/.

Opalewski, Kate. "Disappointing Ruling Allows Discrimination Against Transgender People." *Pride Source,* August 17, 2016. https://pridesource.com/article/77668-2/.

Pelucchini, Laura. "Hobby Lobby Case: What Religious Liberty Can Do to Personal Freedom." *Sapienza Legal Papers* 3, no. 1 (2014): 19–26.

Pieklo, Jessica Mason. "'Hobby Lobby' Is Just the Beginning: A Flood of Corporate Religious Objections Is Coming." *Rewire,* July 1, 2014. https://rewire.news/article/2014/07/01/hobby-lobby-just-beginning-flood-corporate-religious-objections-coming/.

Siegel, Neil S., and Reva B. Siegel. "Compelling Interests and Contraception." *Connecticut Law Review* 47, no. 4 (2015): 1025–43.

Toobin, Jeffrey. "On Hobby Lobby, Ginsburg Was Right." *New Yorker,* September 30, 2014. https://www.newyorker.com/news/daily-comment/hobby-lobbys-troubling-aftermath.

Valenti, Jessica. The Purity Myth: How America's Obsession with Virginity in Hurting Young Women. Berkeley: Seal Press, 2010.

Von Hagel, Alisa, and Daniela Mansbach. *Reproductive Rights in the Age of Human Rights: Pro-life Politics from Roe to Hobby Lobby.* New York: Palgrave Macmillan, 2016.

Walker, Yvette Ann. "More Than Human: Modern Expansion of Corporate Personhood Rights in Hobby Lobby." *Review of Law and Social Justice* 24, no. 2 (2015): 297–327.

White, Jessica L. "Hermeneutics, Rhetoric, and Paternalism in Abortion Law: An Analysis of *Burwell v. Hobby Lobby, Inc.*" M.A. thesis, California State University, Long Beach, 2016.

Zabehi, Tara. "Burwell v. Hobby Lobby Stores, Inc.: Creating Power for Corporations at the Cost of Changing Women's Lives." *The Journal of Business, Entrepreneurship & the Law* 9, no. 1 (May 2016): 1–22.

Ziegler, Mary. "The (Non-right) to Sex." *University of Miami Law Review* 69 (2015): 631–84.

10. Burwell v. Hobby Lobby *and the Supreme Court's Three-Sphere Monte*

JOSEPH SERY

On March 23, 2010, the Patient Protection and Affordable Care Act (ACA) was signed into law by President Obama following a contentious and highly partisan political process. The comprehensive health care reform includes provisions for preventative services, mental health and addiction resources, pregnancy and maternity care, pre-existing conditions, state and federal Health Insurance Exchanges, in addition to many more components.[1] Upon its implementation, the legislation was inundated with numerous legal challenges in the lower courts followed by landmark decisions issued by the Supreme Court. Many of the cases targeted the potential Achilles heel of the ACA: the individual mandate requiring persons to purchase health insurance which was narrowly upheld by the Supreme Court.[2] Whereas these attempts to undermine the ACA were ultimately unsuccessful, others targeting specific provisions garnered more favorable results. One such case, *Burwell v. Hobby Lobby*, will be the focus of this essay.

One of the reasons that the *Hobby Lobby* case proved to be a catalyst for public argument is due to the multitude of issues within its scope: the free exercise of religion, corporate personhood, and women's rights and public health, and the ACA, to name a few. Issuing the opinion of the Court in a 5-4 vote, Justice Samuel Alito focused his argument on the legal implications of the Religious Freedom Reformation Act of 1993 (RFRA) which, among other legal guarantees, prohibits the "Government [from] substantially burden[ing] a person's exercise of religion even if the burden results from a rule of general applicability" unless the Government "demonstrates that application of the burden to the person—(1) is in furtherance of a compelling governmental interest; and (2) is the least restrictive means of furthering that compelling governmental interest."[3] The crux of ***Burwell v. Hobby Lobby*** centers on a small provision established by the ACA which mandates that employee-sponsored healthcare services must provide twenty forms of contraception at no cost to employees. According to the Green family, owners of Hobby Lobby and Mardel (a Christian bookstore chain), and the Hahn family, owners of Conestoga Wood Specialties (a lumber company that consolidated their case with the Greens), four of the twenty contraceptives qualify as abortifacients—i.e. drugs that induce abortion. The contraceptives in question include two forms of intrauterine devices (IUD), Ella, and "Plan-B," the latter is available over-the-counter. The devout Christian owners of these companies argued that these contraceptives destroy life and violate the moral conscience established by their faith, and thus providing them is tantamount to sin.

Agreeing with the petitioners, the opinion of the Court argued that the contraceptive provisions established by the ACA are incompatible with the provisions established by the RFRA. The key issues addressed by the opinion of the Court attend to the following line of argument: (a) the RFRA guarantees individuals the free exercise of religion unless the government has a compelling interest that doesn't substantially burden said citizens; (b) closely held for-profit corporations qualify as persons that may exercise their "sincerely held religious beliefs"; (c) the contraceptive coverage requirement established by the ACA creates a "substantial burden" on the exercise of religion; (d) the government lacks a "compelling interest" in requiring all forms of birth control to be covered; and (e) there are less restrictive means of addressing the requirement to provide "preventative care and screenings," including contraception, than inducing a corporate healthcare provider to violate their religious conscience.

Drawing upon Thomas Goodnight's idea of the "three spheres of argumentation," this essay argues that Justice Alito's majority opinion engaged in a rhetorical sleight of hand as he shifted the grounds of argument depending on what suited his rhetorical needs at the moment. Akin to the street hustle game known as the three-card monte, wherein a "mark" attempts to locate a particular playing card while the dealer engages in deception so as to misdirect the mark's attention, Justice Alito relied upon the personal sphere of religious belief in order to undermine the medical consensus from the technical sphere concerning contraception and public health. As a result, the arguments deployed in response are nullified due to the fact they operate in the wrong sphere. Perhaps more importantly, the concerns of the public sphere are downplayed in order to make the decision appear to be uncomplicated and inevitable. *Hobby Lobby* underscores the significant rhetorical challenge when navigating multiple spheres of discourse and the problems that arise when absent a point of *stasis*. In order to advance this idea, I will first provide an overview of Goodnight's argument and its applicability to the *Hobby Lobby* decision. With this theoretical framework established, I then address the conflict between the personal and technical spheres at play within the decision while also stressing the minimization of the public concerns. Given the ACA's concern with public health, the decision needed to frame the issue in terms of the personal sphere as a rhetorical maneuver to shift the grounds from the public to the personal. Finally, I suggest a turn toward the pragmatic tradition, particularly John Dewey and Richard Rorty, as a way to move forward after *Hobby Lobby*, emphasizing the important role of the judiciary in responding to and shaping public dialogue.

The Interplay of Argumentative Spheres

The *Hobby Lobby* decision occupies an interesting rhetorical position in that it simultaneously engages multiple spheres of argument at once. In his germane essay, "The Personal, Technical, and Public Spheres of Argument: A Speculative Inquiry into the Art of Public Deliberation," G. Thomas Goodnight delineated three distinct yet interconnected rhetorical spaces for managing uncertainty.[4] Responding to and expanding upon his intellectual predecessors, including Habermas,[5] Arendt,[6] Dewey,[7] and others, Goodnight posited that "the public sphere is being steadily eroded by the elevation of the personal and technical groundings of argument"[8] and in so doing made the case for a revitalized public discourse that acknowledges the encroachment of the personal and technical spheres. As I will argue, the *Hobby Lobby* decision navigates all three of these rhetorical spaces and reflects, in part, Goodnight's concern over the waning presence of public deliberation and the role the Supreme Court plays therein. Before that, however, one must first understand the qualities that distinguish each sphere and where they manifest in the decision.

First, the personal sphere constitutes the most ephemeral realm of argument. Likened to two strangers arguing at an airport bar, Goodnight noted how these arguers rely upon tacit assumptions on what qualifies as sound argumentation based on previous experience and social norms. The quality of the argument is determined only by the participants involved who, having no preparation save for their own intellectual and rhetorical background that can be pulled into the conversation at a moment's notice, tend to rely heavily on their personal beliefs and opinions whether informed or not. Although the discussion may carry on beyond that moment by others, the substantive argument ends when the individuals part ways. These arguments may or may not have a lasting impact on them, but the likelihood is small given the limited amount of exposure and interest from such interlocutors. It is important to note that in the personal sphere of argument that which qualifies as support and induces judgment requires "the most informal demands of evidence, proof sequences, claim establishment, and language use."[9] What constitutes a "good" argument is dependent upon the range of experiences, beliefs, values, and expectations that are particular to the individual. There may be an implied negotiation between the interlocutors, but the personal sphere is nonetheless individualistic and idiosyncratic. Technical argument may find its way into such discussions, but the personal sphere is best characterized by its reliance upon opinions grounded in personal knowledge. Within the *Hobby Lobby* decision, this is most evident in the majority opinion's continuous reiteration of the sincerely held beliefs of the Hahn and Green families concerning the four forms of contraception at issue. Their position is justified because it is personally, if sincerely, held.

Unlike the personal sphere, the technical sphere is most often populated by academics and experts arguing within their respective fields of knowledge. Interlocutors "[bring] together a considerable degree of expertise with the formal expectations of scholarly argument."[10] Moreover, "The technical arguments are judged by referees as worthy of preservation."[11] Depending on the topic, there exist an array of argumentative standards and expectations that help to validate knowledge claims. For example, physicists, anthropologists, psychologists, and theologians each are guided by different norms of argumentation from which they derive authority, but all are guided by the precepts dictated by the reigning scholarly expectations in their respective field. Unlike the personal sphere, technical argumentation seeks to "advance a special kind of knowledge."[12] In short, the technical sphere is where experts argue with fellow experts with little or no concern about how their views would be reflected in the personal or public spheres. *Hobby Lobby* intersects two primary technical fields: law and medicine. Clearly law is the most obvious as the Supreme Court is a collection of legal experts arguing about the intricacies of the Constriction, legal precedent, and the legislative statutes upon which they frame their decisions. In addition, the issue before the Court is inextricably linked to the technical issue of birth control medicine and the scientific arguments behind it. The two spheres, however, have different standards of argument and when translated to the legal realm, medical expertise is abandoned or ignored.

Finally, the public sphere of argument represents those spaces wherein issues of general interest and public concern are argued. They may be informed by the personal or the technical spheres, but these are only pertinent "insofar as they are made congruent with the practices of public forums."[13] Unlike the personal sphere, which is more "informal and fluid," and the technical sphere, which relies upon specialized expertise, the public sphere relies upon a "tradition of argument such that its speakers would employ common language, values, and reasoning so that [a] disagreement could be settled to the satisfaction of all concerned."[14] In addition, "Most characteristically, though, the interests of the public realm—whether represented in an appropriate way or not—extend the stakes of argument beyond private needs and the needs of special communities to the interests of the entire community."[15] Going beyond the scope of the personal and technical spheres, the public sphere contains distinct expectations that are informed by various "customs, traditions, and requirements for arguers"[16] that help to drive forward the unique arguments that occupy the rhetorical space. Concerning *Hobby Lobby*, at least two particular issues of public argument are present. The two specific issues represent the clash between religion and women's reproductive rights that represent competing moral claims and the role that they play in public life. These are captured in the "substantial burden" facing the company owners and the "compelling government interest" in offering a broad spectrum of contraceptives for women.

Noted earlier, Goodnight worried that the public sphere is in danger on two fronts. He emphasized the growing power of the technical sphere, which has only continued since the original publication of the essay, and noted that technical advancements and the arguments that have spurred them on have not satisfied the expectations of the public sphere. Instead, they are used to supplant, supersede, or even tyrannize public deliberation.[17] This is not to say that the technical sphere is unimportant to public discourse, but Goodnight felt that public leaders are failing in their obligation to "provide parameters for scientific argument"[18] so that it may better serve the public sphere. Similarly, the personal sphere invaded the public by way of a focus on personal experience over communal values. As such, "political speakers present not options but personalities, perpetuating government policy by substituting debate for an aura of false intimacy."[19] One would be hard pressed to argue that this trend has not continued, especially with the advent of social media and the cult of personality that dominates contemporary politics.

The decline of the public sphere is a common theme amongst contemporary scholars. Alan McKee noted five particular issues that have contributed to this diminishment: trivialization, commercialization, spectacle, fragmentation, and apathy.[20] Rhetoricians have been quick to take up these issues and others as they investigate the purported deterioration. David Levasseur and Diana Carlin cited a predominance of egocentric arguments as the most significant contributing factor to a deficient public sphere.[21] Contrasting such pessimism, some rhetorical scholars are also quick to promote the hopeful possibilities of the public. Gerard Hauser, for example, acknowledged such civic potential in *Vernacular Voices: The Rhetoric of Publics and Public Spheres* and cited both the discursive shifts that have occurred and also the possibility for extended engagement regarding contemporary issues.[22] The public may be lost, but that does not presuppose it cannot be found.

Whereas Goodnight focused on the distinct qualities of each individual sphere, what happens when a discourse touches on all three simultaneously? Reflecting on Goodnight's essay, Edward Schiappa adopted a Foucauldian understanding of the spheres of argument, going so far as to suggest that "the manner in which we draw distinctions among the different spheres may, itself, contribute to the decline of public discourse."[23] Schiappa's "radical stance" argued that there are no true differences in the way that the spheres reflect knowledge production save "for the way they enact different power/knowledge relations."[24] He aptly used the example of abortion, which occupies all rhetorical spaces in the personal decision and private autonomy, the medical and legal technical expertise framing it, and the aspects of morality that bring it into the public sphere. He carried this one example into a broader discussion of sexism writ large. Calling upon argumentation scholars "to question the *oppositions* implied by certain discursive practices,"[25] Schiappa encouraged the scrutinization of the rhetorical tensions at play within and between the spheres of argument.

It is in this spirit that I approach the *Hobby Lobby* decision as it embodies the personal, technical, and public spheres in various ways. In doing so, I hope to complement the already compelling scholarship addressing the case. Much has already been made within the legal studies community as scholars have addressed a myriad of different dimensions the case has impacted. Scholars have investigated such issues as the impact the decision has and will have on reproductive rights and public health,[26] the role of science in legal decision-making,[27] the enduring problem of what constitutes a "substantial burden,"[28] potential legal challenges,[29] and rhetorical power of dissent as a vehicle for public activism,[30] amongst others. Examining the decision through the competing and contrasting spheres of argument elucidates the various ways in which a particular sphere is adopted, thus shifting the grounds of argument and minimizing the rhetorical potency of the opposition. The majority opinion especially benefited from these rhetorical shifts and the lack of *stasis* they require.

In doing so, the decision reflects an important failure from the Supreme Court because, in many ways, they are the *embodiment* of the public sphere. As Justice Robert Jackson noted in *Brown v. Allen*, “We are not final because we are infallible, but we are infallible only because we are final.”[31] Not only are they the final word when it comes to the law, they are also the fount from which public discourse flows. As a result, they have a special obligation both to the institution of law and the public discourse surrounding it. Just because they are, de facto, a realization of the public sphere does not mean every decision necessarily serves that purpose well. The stakes are all the higher when complex, politically-charged issues must be decided. When it comes to Supreme Court decisions and their place within the public sphere of argument, perhaps we ought to stray away from evaluating them as either right or wrong, which is often the case following contentious cases, and instead focus on whether decisions have a better or worse impact on public deliberation.

The Shifting Spheres of Hobby Lobby

The first and most obvious act of rhetorical sleight of hand is exhibited in the clash between sincerely held religious belief and medical science. The crux of the decision rests upon the Hahn and Green families believing that the four forms of contraception function as abortifacients; that is, they induce abortion following the fertilization of an egg. Rather than relying upon the First Amendment’s Free Exercise Clause (even though it remains central to the case), Justice Alito fixated on the RFRA. As passed, the Act reads:

> Prohibits any agency, department, or official of the United States or any State (the government) from substantially burdening a person’s exercise of religion even if the burden results from a rule of general applicability, except that the government may burden a person’s exercise of religion only if it demonstrates that application of the burden to the person: (1) furthers a compelling governmental interest; and (2) is the least restrictive means of furthering that compelling governmental interest.[32]

The impetus behind this legislation includes various moments in legal history, but the two most significant are arguably *Wisconsin v. Yoder* and *Employment Division, Department of Human Resources of Oregon v. Smith*. In *Wisconsin v. Yoder*, an Amish family challenged a state mandate that required Amish children to attend school outside of the Amish community until they reached sixteen years old despite such an education violating their religious beliefs.[33] The state’s argument was framed as a compelling interest in the role education plays in preparing students to become independent citizens and neutral in relation to religious beliefs since the education was compulsory for every youth. Siding with Yoder, Chief Justice Burger held that the state had not produced a convincing argument and the alternative vocational education received in an Amish community satisfied the general state interest. Moreover, Chief Justice Burger stressed the importance of the *sincerity* of religious beliefs held by the Amish and the longstanding tradition that it upheld. The defense of sincerity would become central to *Hobby Lobby.*

The second important case and the impetus behind RFRA was *Employment Division, Department of Human Resources of Oregon v. Smith.*[34] The case concerned two employees who ingested peyote as part of a religious ceremony. Both were fired for misconduct per the regulations on consuming illicit drugs. The Supreme Court upheld their termination, speculating that not to do so would lead to all manner of exceptions to valid laws and "civic obligations of almost every conceivable kind."[35] The case struck a bold new precedent that rejected the interpretation of the Free Exercise Clause articulated in *Yoder* by favoring majority-driven legislation as opposed to "the more recent traditions of the Court [that] acknowledge the central importance of protecting minority rights in a majority culture and take on, as a proper function of the judiciary, the job of protecting certain religious freedoms of individuals that are burdened by otherwise valid laws."[36] The public's negative response to *Smith* was swift and fierce. Franklyn Haiman noted how the decision united organizations that were often "bitter opponents," such as "religious groups across the entire spectrum, from the mainstream to the fringes, along with organizations like the ACLU and legal groups."[37] Despite a temporary challenge by the Supreme Court in *City of Boerne v. Flores*, which found RFRA unconstitutional by way of states' rights,[38] RFRA was resuscitated via the Religious Land Use and Institutionalized Persons Act of 2000.[39] Among other things, RLUIPA circumvented the Supreme Court's federalism challenge and reinstated the supremacy of RFRA that carries forward today.

Returning to *Hobby Lobby* and its invocation of the legitimacy of the families' beliefs, Justice Alito continuously reiterated their importance as the ultimate factor in legitimizing their case. He asserted at the outset, "The owners of the businesses have religious objections to abortion, and *according to their religious beliefs* the four contraceptive methods at issue are abortifacients. If the owners comply with the HHS mandate, *they believe* they will be facilitating abortions."[40] Later, he restated the point that these families "believe that life begins at conception and that it would violate their religion to facilitate access to contraceptive drugs or devices that operate after that point."[41] Noting that "no one has disputed the sincerity of their religious beliefs,"[42] Justice Alito also addressed the added layer of corporate personhood underlying the case by stressing that it is "difficult as a practical matter to ascertain the sincere 'beliefs' of a corporation."[43] These are by no means the only references to the families' belief systems—there are a dozen more scattered throughout the decision in addition to Kennedy's concurring opinion. Clearly, the sincerely held religious beliefs of the families are the cornerstone of the decision; without it, the families could not claim a "substantial burden" as they make no objections to the other forms of contraception.

Yet, the issue of whether or not the four contraceptives induce abortion or anything like it is not supported by the medical community. In the context of the case, the term "abortifacient" is meant to indicate a contraceptive that interrupts an otherwise viable pregnancy when a fertilized egg implants in the uterus. The contraceptives under review include two intrauterine devices and two forms of emergency contraception. Concerning the emergency contraceptives, in an amicus brief submitted by multiple medical organizations, including the American College of Obstetricians and Gynecologists, they asserted that Plan B and Ella, the two contraceptives involved in the case, are not abortifacients: "At the outset, we note that, as discussed below, there is no scientific evidence that emergency contraceptives available in the United States and approved by the FDA affect an existing pregnancy. . .None, therefore, is properly classified as an abortifacient."[44] The brief also stressed the important difference between pregnancy prevention and pregnancy termination.

Investigating the research defending this position, Meredith Rachel Mandell emphasized the various ways in which the contraceptives have been misrepresented. Concerning Ella, the arguments claiming it functions as an abortifacient likely rely upon the misuse of the product because "when used at the recommended dose and timing for emergency contraception,"[45] it does not impact post-fertilization implantation. Plan B is also misinterpreted, albeit in a different way. She argued that the false impression has been perpetuated due to the FDA requiring the manufacturer to include a potential implantation effect on the packaging without justification. The medical consensus, however, "suggests that there is no meaningful scientific evidence proving that Plan B interferes with the implantation of a fertilized egg."[46] The two IUDs differ little in the scientific agreement. The argument against ParaGard, an IUD that releases copper so as to destroy sperm before it reaches the egg, utilized data research that relies upon "a very small set of data" that is "almost 20 years old."[47] The other IUD is perhaps the most susceptible to criticism as "there is not full scientific agreement" and whether or not it impacts an already fertilized egg and may do so " in rare instances," but this was advanced in only a single analysis of the current literature.[48] In sum, only one out of the four contraceptives challenged in the case *might* qualify under the loose definition of abortifacient in certain circumstances.

One should not overlook the importance of the term "abortifacient" as well. As public controversies go, abortion is arguably on the top of the list of the most heated and ideologically driven. The medical community does not associate the term "abortion" with the prevention of a fertilized egg from implanting. "There is only one drug approved to induce abortion," wrote Jamie Manson. "It is called RU-486 (mifepristone) and is not on the FDA's list of approved contraception. It is available only by prescription and no employer is forced to pay for it as part of an employee health plan."[49] This is yet another sleight of hand in order to associate the contraceptives with the already heated, ideologically driven issue of abortion writ large. The term is loaded and helps spur support for the Hahns and Greens, making it appear as if the government is forcing them to participate in the practice. Overall, however, the scientific community disagrees with the religious beliefs of the Hahns and Greens. One may hold beliefs, even sincerely, that are incorrect on the merits in which they are categorized. These arguments, however, went unheeded as Justice Alito shifted the grounds of argument to the personal sphere rather than the technical sphere where "the subject matter and consequences of the dispute are up to the participants involved."[50] In *Hobby Lobby*, personal opinion of the private sphere supplants the grounds of the scientific evidence of the technical sphere. Thus, the private sphere of argument is privileged in Supreme Court doctrine and displace the medical/technical sphere.

As a rhetorical turn, the reliance upon belief, which does not have the same epistemological threshold in the medical community, is a clever, albeit deceptive, pivot that shifts the argument from the technical sphere of medicine to the personal sphere of religious conviction. In many ways, it illustrates a combination of Marcus Paroske's "epistemological filibuster" and Leah Ceccarelli's "fairplay wedge," both of which are bad faith strategies to foster scientific controversy so as to legitimize or delegitimize governmental action. Describing his term, Paroske wrote, "An 'epistemological filibuster'' occurs when one side in a science policy controversy exploits uncertainty over how thoroughly to deliberate as a means to preclude the resolution of that issue in government action."[51] In other words, because there is a degree of uncertainty, no matter how small or unsubstantiated, government action is delayed. For example, one may argue that there is not complete agreement within the scientific community about the human contribution to climate change, so carbon-tax legislation is shelved until unanimity can be achieved (knowing full well that it cannot). The anti-vaxx movement utilizes a similar strategy as the debunked essay linking vaccinations to autism and the anecdotal evidence provided by supporters is used to invalidate the overwhelming consensus in the medical community.

The fairplay wedge, on the other hand, enables government action. Deriving the term from a strategy deployed by the Discovery Institute, Ceccarelli highlighted their desire "to 'defeat scientific materialism' and 'replace materialistic explanations with the theistic understanding that nature and human beings are created by God.'"[52] In short, religious ideas are given the same platform—in this case, "teaching the controversy" about evolution vs. intelligent design—as accepted scientific ideas for the sake of fairness. *Hobby Lobby* highlights the uncertainty of the epistemological filibuster and the enabling of government action via the fairplay wedge to legitimize the religious beliefs concerning the contraceptives over the technical position of the scientific community. Justice Alito captured this sentiment when arguing that "HHS and the principle dissent in effect tell the plaintiffs that their beliefs are flawed. For good reason, we have repeatedly refused to take such a step,"[53] but there is a marked difference between beliefs about the metaphysical aspects of life and personhood compared to the beliefs about how contraception actually works.

Justice Alito rhetorical prestidigitation regarding the relationship between law and science is not the only example of his shift away from the technical sphere and to the personal sphere of argument. Favoring the religious beliefs of the plaintiffs also required the majority to ignore a different technical issue in the rules guiding the invocation of scientific opinion as a guide for legal decision-making. The Federal Rules of Evidence includes a provision guiding judges on how and when to admit scientific expertise, in addition to determining the role it should play in the case. Rule 702 is an attempt to guard against "junk science,"[54] reminiscent of the dangers of the aforementioned epistemological filibuster and fairplay wedge. As the quality and legitimacy of scientific expertise on legal issues grew throughout the 20th century, the legal system needed to address the scope and influence it ought to have when hearing testimony and deciding cases. As Mandell noted, the original rule was more lenient to bad science but, following the 1993 decision in *Daubert v. Merrell Down Pharmaceuticals, Inc.*, refined what constitutes "valid science" including the techniques used, supporting publications, the regulatory standards, and whether or not there is acceptance in the broader scientific community.[55] Judges remain the final arbiters on what ought to be admitted as valid science per the standards established, but to ignore the scientific community altogether illustrates another way in which Justice Alito shifted the grounds of argument, this time away from the technical guidelines long established within the legal community.

The turn away from accepted science strays from some earlier freedom of religion jurisprudence, albeit the Establishment Clause rather than the Free Exercise Clause. Although *Hobby Lobby* is only tertiarily concerned with the Establishment Clause, as Justice Ginsburg's dissent noted, there nonetheless exists precedent promoting science over religious belief. Establishment Clause cases often engage issues of government support of religious beliefs/organizations,[56] public displays of religion on government property,[57] and the role/presence of religion in public schools.[58] One case, however, contributes to how one thinks about the details in *Hobby Lobby*; namely, *Epperson v. Arkansas*, the 1968 case that addressed whether or not the teaching of evolution can be prohibited in public schools.[59] The Supreme Court sided in favor of evolution and argued that the government must remain neutral, yet not prevent religious thinking. Years later, the issue was revisited by a lower court with the rhetorical twist of "intelligent design" replacing "creationism" in order to create distance from religion and adopt a more secular posture, although the defendants were ultimately unsuccessful in their attempt to teach intelligent design.[60] Both cases dealt with the clash between religion and science, a prominent theme in the arguments offered in *Hobby Lobby*, and both challenged the legitimacy of religious belief masquerading as legitimate science.

Unlike the many other First Amendment or RFRA claims of sincerely held religious belief, *Hobby Lobby* is unique in that it extends the capacity of religious belief to corporate entities. Although the idea was made (in) famous in the Supreme Court's landmark *Citizens United v. Federal Election Commission* decision in 2010,[61] the idea of corporate personhood has roots in 19th century jurisprudence. As Thom Hartmann noted, the idea germinated from a misreporting of *Santa Clara County v. Southern Pacific Rail Road* where the argument did not appear in the opinion but has nonetheless been read into it.[62] Despite its specious background, the Supreme Court nonetheless defended corporate personhood nearly a century later,[63] which would go on to serve as precedent in *Citizen's United* and shortly after in *Burwell v. Hobby Lobby*. As Mitt Romney would say in his presidential campaign, the current standard is that "corporations are people, my friend."[64]

The legal precedent established in *Citizens United* and the ensuing cases laid the groundwork for *Hobby Lobby*. "The first question that we must address," wrote Justice Alito, "is whether this provision applies to regulations that govern the activities of for-profit corporations like Hobby Lobby, Conestoga, and Mardel."[65] In answering this question, he created a false dichotomy: either give up the right to seek judicial protection of their religious liberty or forgo the benefits, available to their competitors, of operating as corporations. Such a rhetorical turn assumes the extension of religious beliefs at the outset; one's for-profit business, which enjoys various benefits and protections granted by the federal government, is inseparably connected from the religious identity of the owners. Justice Alito would later elaborate upon this position, claiming that "A corporation is simply a form of organization used by human beings to achieve desired ends. . .And protecting the free-exercise rights of corporations like Hobby Lobby, Conestoga, and Mardel protects the religious liberty of the humans who own and control those companies."[66] On various occasions, Justice Alito attempted to frame Hobby Lobby and the other companies as occupying a distinct class. They are not publicly traded corporations, "and it seems unlikely that the sort of corporate giants to which HHS refers will often assert RFRA claims."[67] Note, he did not say they do not have the ability, but predicts that they simply won't take the same path as the Hahns and the Greens. Speculating about future legal challenges is a prominent theme in the majority decision as Justice Alito argued that the precedent established will not be abused as Justice Ginsburg claimed in her dissent. Since the decision, numerous cases have been moving through the lower courts with employers requesting similar if not more extreme exemptions. Even the act of filling out the exemption form and submitting it to the insurance provider has been argued to be too great a burden.

Justice Alito also confronted the profit-making motive driving such corporations, but suggests that this "flies in the face of modern corporate law" as it assumes they "pursue profit at the expense of everything else." Offering various counter examples of "hybrid corporate forms" that may have a "dual-purpose," Justice Alito broke down the distinction between non-profit and for-profit companies. Doing so serves at least two purposes. The first is to reinforce the jurisprudence established in *Citizens United* concerning corporate personhood. The second connects for-profit corporations, which are not extended exceptions for the contraception mandate (save for those policies that were "grandfathered in"), with non-profits, which the HHS allowed for exceptions without contest. He argued that "The Hahns believe that they are required to run their business 'in accordance with their religious beliefs and moral principles'" and that through the corporate connection to their employees' insurance plans, "it is immoral and sinful for [them] to intentionally participate in, pay for, facilitate, or otherwise support these drugs." Paraphrasing the arguments from HHS, Justice Alito asserted that RFRA was never intended "to apply to for-profit corporations because it is difficult as a practical matter to ascertain the sincere 'beliefs' of a corporation."[68] Much like the inability to ascertain the sincerity of personal religious beliefs,

Justice Alito similarly stressed the inability to assess the sincerity of their corporate manifestation. Interestingly, Justice Alito relied on the technical sphere of legal argument to build support for the legitimacy of corporate personhood and, once that had been established, returned to the personal sphere of religious belief.

In response, Justice Ginsburg called attention to an important figure left out of the conversation: the employee. In her dissent, Justice Ginsburg asserted that the decision "would deny legions of women *who do not hold their employers' beliefs* access to contraceptive coverage that the ACA would otherwise secure."[69] While the beliefs of the owners and, by extension, their corporations dictate the Court's decision, the religious beliefs of the employees are ignored entirely despite the direct impact it will have on their lives. Drawing from Chaffee's famous characterization of the harm principle, Justice Ginsburg characterized the situation as an example of "[y]our right to swing your arms ends just where the other man's nose begins."[70] Suggesting the majority opinion is purposefully misinterpreting precedent and legal statutes, she argued that "the exercise of religion is characteristic of natural persons"[71] and to suggest it applies to corporate entities is disingenuous. Unlike non-profit religious organizations, which are granted exemptions from the contraception mandate, corporate entities are not created with the purpose of advancing "interests of persons subscribing to the same religious faith."[72] Overall, the corporations in question are trying to get all of the benefits of incorporation without adhering to their broader social responsibilities.

In her dissent, Justice Ginsburg also warned of the potential ramifications created by the precedent the *Hobby Lobby* decision established. One such impact was the Department of Health and Human Services under President Trump expanding the breadth of exemptions, including which organizations ought to be afforded exemptions and on what grounds they could be justified. Regarding the latter, appeals may be made based on moral conviction that need not be restricted to religious conviction. The *Hobby Lobby* decision also helped pave the way for future decisions, most notably *Little Sisters of the Poor Saints Peter and Paul Home v. Pennsylvania*.[73] The 2020 decision was long in the making with the original litigation taking place in 2013. In the most recent and likely final decision on the issue, the Supreme Court held in favor of the Little Sisters in a 7-2 decision, although Justice Elena Kagan authored a concurring opinion joined by Justice Stephen Breyer. The majority's decision was based largely on technical grounds concerning the role of the Health Resources and Services Administration and the need to defer to their judgment via the legal standard known as Chevron deference. Importantly, the case differs from *Hobby Lobby* in that the concerned parties represented a non-profit religious organization, not a corporate entity. Nonetheless, the judgment may be used in future cases to further expand the scope of religious and moral exemptions and the power of RFRA to justify them.

Justice Ginsburg, joined by Justice Sonia Sotomayor, again dissented from the opinion of the court. Although she drew heavily from the technical sphere of law to ground her arguments and levy criticisms upon the majority decisions, the heart of her dissents relied upon arguments that are most fitting in the public sphere, namely, the compelling interest of the government to uphold reproductive rights specifically and women's equality generally. One of the potential dangers of the decisions issued by the majority is its impact on public discourse. The public, already caustically divided on ideological lines, draws upon divisive cases, which in turn impacts their discursive practices. *Hobby Lobby* has added fuel to the fire and provided them with a way of discussing the scope of religious belief beyond anything previously imagined. Whereas the history of the Free Exercise and Establishment Clauses viewed these protections as a shield against government intervention, the current interpretation of RFRA and its extension to corporations now positions religious belief as a sword able to attack legislation and previously accepted social responsibilities. Mary Ann Glendon argued that legal vocabulary has become increasingly influential for the citizenry: "This 'legalization' of popular culture is both cause and consequence of our increasing tendency to look to law as an expression and carrier of the few values that are widely shared in our society: liberty, equality, and the ideal of justice under law."[74] She continued, "Legal discourse has not only become the single most important tributary to political discourse, but it has crept into the languages that Americans employ around the kitchen table, in the neighborhood, and in their diverse communities of memory and mutual aid."[75] Given the role that law plays in political and public culture, it is inseparably connected with contemporary discourse. *Hobby Lobby* has elevated the power and significance of the personal sphere of religious belief such that technical arguments are superseded. Consequently, the quality of public discourse suffers.

Rather than reflecting upon how the Supreme Court should have decided *Hobby Lobby*, which is inevitably bound to ideological priorities and interpretive frameworks, perhaps a better consideration is how to move forward in a productive, humanistic manner. What does *Hobby Lobby* tell us about the challenges embedded in judiciary and what rhetorical resources are available as an effective remedy? Clearly, relying upon the personal sphere to determine issues of public concern that rely upon scientific knowledge is insufficient. Moreover, danger resides in giving expertise—the technical sphere—supremacy over public issues imbued with moral commitments, a point stressed by Goodnight and reinforced by the sordid history of medicine in the United States. After all, Justice Oliver Wendell Holmes, Jr. drew from the reigning scientific consensus of the day when he argued for forced sterilization in *Buck v. Bell*, infamously captured in the phrase, "Three generations of imbeciles is enough."[76] Expertise should be used as a useful guide and a contributing voice in a broader discourse, but to give it free reign will no doubt create an entirely new set of legal, moral, and rhetorical problems. How, then, can these competing spheres of influence be put into conversation so as to inform, yet not dominate the decision-making process? I suggest a turn to pragmatism as useful guide to help navigate through the present rhetorical situation.

Negotiating the Tensions: A Pragmatic Response

Considered the only distinct school of philosophy to emerge out of the United States, pragmatism has a rich intellectual history. Much like rhetoric, pragmatism has had its ups and downs in terms of reputation and support as the core tenets have gone in and out of fashion in response to the ever-changing intellectual climate. Also like rhetoric, it is difficult to pin down a single definition that satisfies all who subscribe to it. Most, however, would agree that pragmatism shirks the Cartesian view of epistemology and acknowledges the inevitability of uncertainty. Instead of resigning to solipsism or unfettered skepticism, pragmatism resonates with rhetoric in that both recognize the imperative to act based on incomplete and imperfect knowledge. Following Robert Danisch, pragmatism begins "by rejecting the speculative concerns of traditional philosophy and searching for a philosophy of action," which he argued "is tied inextricably to rhetoric."[77] Pragmatism addresses "the need for practical methods designed to improve American life and create responsible agents of change," which requires "focusing on concrete communicative practices instead of abstract ideas" and the facilitation of "rhetorical strategies for binding communities together and granting individuals a voice in the affairs of those communities."[78] But there are better and worse ways to do so, thus the challenge becomes how one can cultivate the former and avoid the latter.

Amongst the many thinkers who have populated the pragmatic tradition, John Dewey is arguably the most useful in such a task, not only due to his prolific writing and immense influence, but, more importantly, because he was first and foremost dedicated to constructing a healthy public life. While his writings on political theory, education, psychology, and many other topics certainly work toward this end, an often-overlooked text may be particularly useful for examining the implications and legacy of the *Hobby Lobby* decision. Written in 1934, *A Common Faith* is one of the precious few of Dewey's works that directly confronted the relationships between science, religion, and society. Dewey acknowledged the important role that religion plays in people's lives and society writ large as it feeds a yearning for an individual to experience "something beyond itself and so its own unification depends upon the idea of the integration of the shifting scenes of the world into that imaginative totality we call the Universe."[79] He noted the "moral and practical"[80] components of faith, which ultimately contribute to our shared public lives. Such faith, however, must not be untethered to the physical world in which we live because there is a danger that it may "convert the idealism of action into a system of beliefs about antecedent reality."[81] As such, the intellectual resources at hand must not be considered enemies of religion, but valuable resources: "Understanding and knowledge also enter into a perspective that is religious in quality. Faith in the continued disclosing of truth through directed cooperative human endeavor is more religious in quality than is any faith in a completed revelation."[82] Dewey called for a kind of "faith in intelligence"[83] akin to religious faith. Alas, this position is often viewed as an attempt to undermine religious belief, thus pitting the intellectual pursuits of science and religion at odds. Keep in mind, Dewey wrote this work in the wake of the Scopes "monkey trial" and other public controversies involving the clash between science and religion.

Yet, Dewey was not calling for a scientific mindset to replace ideas rooted in faith; after all, he described his faith in democracy in terms that would later reverberate in Robert Bellah's work on civil religion.[84] As a pragmatist, he was also skeptical of the search for truth that defined the analytic tradition against which he was arguing. Dewey instead sought collaboration; the idea that religion can benefit from a scientific methodology and science can benefit from the kind of spirit and moral fortitude that define religion. When Dewey was writing, as in the present day, the two often treat each other with disdain, although science is more willing to budge when new ideas are introduced that help to explain the world better. Fundamentalism, on the other hand, is rooted in "an irreducible minimum of belief so fixed in the advance that it can never be modified."[85] There are important moments in history when religion opened the door to science to the benefit of all involved, but only after great struggle. The Catholic Church long resisted heliocentrism and, later, evolution, but both have been folded into the Catechism without a disruption to their core beliefs. These moments cannot be forced, however; they must be borne out of thoughtful communication and rich dialogue in the public sphere so as to move toward what Dewey calls "passionate intelligence."[86] In the *Hobby Lobby* decision, such a mindset is all but absent and violates the original spirit of the First Amendment's protection of religion; namely, that it should serve as a shield from government intrusion and not a sword to strike down anything that challenges fundamentalism. Dewey once described the public as lost, but, contra Walter Lippmann, thought it could be redeemed through the arts of communication and deliberation. The Supreme Court, the emblem of law in the United States, must lead by example.

Dewey's most vocal supporter throughout the second wave of pragmatism, Richard Rorty, echoed some of these sentiments. Although he was far less sympathetic to science, often brushing aside Dewey's commitment to the scientific method as errant thinking, he nonetheless embraced a similar idea of community and the role that rhetoric must play therein. Moreover, his ideas may help us figure out *how* to go about moving forward. In *Contingency, Irony, and Solidarity*, Rorty highlighted the need for imagination and "the imaginative ability to see strange people as fellow sufferers."[87] Such an imagination—the ability to conceive of the lives of others, even those markedly different from you—is imperative in a diverse democratic community. Both religion and science must take heed of this advice. Rorty's critique of science offered it a place at the table so long as it serves as "a model of human solidarity,"[88] a point with which Dewey would no doubt agree. Religion must share the same obligation toward solidarity in a liberal society. Yet, solidarity will not be found, it must be *created*. One vital way in which this can be achieved is inherently discursive. Rhetoric is positioned especially well to respond to this call as it is not so much concerned with that which is, but rather that which *can be*. Rorty called for the need to begin "speaking differently," rethinking the discourses that have led to the untenable positions that put people and institutions at odds rather than bring them together.

The inherited language of the Supreme Court reflects this idea well. Dominated by a legalese that allows for the rationalization through a pastiche of constitutional interpretation (of which there is no standard), statutes young and old, and the occasional choose-your-own adventure approach to precedent. The result is a hermeneutic that can be used to serve the conclusion of a decision rather than the other way around. Even though decisions are crafted with strategic intentionality, they are treated as if they are the objectively correct interpretation. Not all decisions are colored by such gymnastic reasoning, yet many of the most contentious, most divisive, most impactful decisions engage in some form of intellectual chicanery. What is lost in the wake is the role the Supreme Court plays in shaping public dialogue.

There is no simple answer to resolve this dilemma. Law is set up as a zero-sum game with a winner and a loser, and to undermine the legal tradition as we have it challenges the very foundation of law. While that may be the case, we can still acknowledge the faults in the system. In response, I suggest we take heed of James Boyd White's characterization of law as "a way in which we use an inherited language to talk to each other and to maintain a community,"[89] then there must be a way in which legal discourse can be improved. White noted, "Every legal speech is made from a defined position, to a defined audience, in a defined language. The law always assumes a speaker and audience located in the context it defines. This is how it makes a world and makes it real."[90] Moreover, these arguments never remain in the realm of the particular for very long. Perhaps the most miraculous and compelling element of the rhetorical function of legal culture is its ability to constantly fluctuate between the particular and the general, rooted in the moment yet always poised to transcend it. Again, White captured this notion well:

> [I]t is the constitution of a world by the distribution of authority within it; it establishes the terms on which its actors may talk in conflict or cooperation among themselves. The law establishes roles and relations and voices, positions from which and audiences to which one may speak, and it gives us speakers the materials and methods of a discourse. It is a way of creating a rhetorical community over time. It is this discourse, working in the social context of its own creation, this language in the fullest sense of the term, that *is* the law. It makes us members of a common world.[91]

The process of judgment involves particular audiences as well as universal audiences, both of which require rhetorical insight and nuance in order to be successful. To argue to and for a narrow, particular audience would only preach to the choir and often judges are more interested in spreading the good word. They are less pastors and more proselytizers.

Often, however, judges and legal thinkers remain uninterested in going beyond the technical sphere of law. As such, they do not acknowledge their role in shaping public dialogue on the most important matters that shape our collective lives. Both Dewey and Rorty stressed the necessity of creative intelligence that leans into the challenges of contingency rather than trying to reason out of them. Creativity and the judicial act of creation is also central concern for White. In *Heracles' Bow*, he called attention to the "acknowledgement of inconsistency and tension, the openness to ambiguity and uncertainty,"[92] suggesting law is a creative practice of composition with many interrelated aspects combining to produce something akin to a work of art, rather than mere dogmatic rules or a pseudo-objective decision. White perceived law and language to be "living material" that is used to create meaning;[93] a community practice of defining and redefining itself through the law.[94] In this regard, legal discourse provides a vital *constitutive* function that shapes and reshapes a communal identity within the public sphere. Legal and political institutions are an important rhetorical lens through which a society views and creates a shared community. The essential yet fragile role of judges is to produce a strong foundational discourse that balances between the pragmatic needs of a given society while simultaneously illuminating a path for moral and cultural development. More importantly, it does so through argumentation and discourse, rather than force, for "only persuasion, and persuasion of the sincere and authentic kind by which community is established, can work."[95]

An important question remains: what does such creative, pragmatic judgment look like? While there is no simple answer, especially when complex issues that require complex responses are at stake, one important idea from the rhetorical tradition offers insight—rhetorical invention. The term has a rich history, with important touchstones spread throughout the history of rhetoric, and often evokes an ability to manage contingencies and draw from an array of ideas so as to make the most effective argument. Those with a sensitivity to rhetorical invention have the capacity to think differently and, perhaps more importantly, *speak* differently. Katie Gibson's analysis of Justice Ginsburg's rhetorical legacy captured this sentiment well as it articulated the various limitations imposed upon legal reasoning and the ways in which the boundaries of legal judgment may be expanded in a meaningful way. Gibson noted three rhetorical commitments that contribute to the obduracy of Supreme Court decisions, objectivity, abstraction, and closure, which have "served to defend an in ideology of conservative constitutionalism and to protect the patriarchal status quo."[96] Objectivity concerns ways in which legal judgment positions itself as "disinterested and apolitical"[97] in order to obscure the rhetorical agency and subjectivity inherent to legal judgment. Abstraction is called upon to separate the decisions and the ramifications that they sow from the persons they directly impact. "The rhetorical commitment to abstraction, *demands that the general rule governs all* while rendering the lives and experiences of many women inconsequential and invisible."[98] Finally, closure speaks to those models of legal judgment, particularly textual originalism, that view the Constitution as "all-encompassing and unchanging."[99] According to this model of interpretation, the judiciary must be tethered to the document in its original manifestation as opposed to those theories that view it as a living document that changes with the public it judges.

Tracing these three issues through a series of cases both preceding and during Justice Ginsburg's time on the Supreme Court, Gibson stressed the important ways in which these rhetorical strategies have framed problematic decisions throughout the court's history and Justice Ginsburg's rhetorical ingenuity in combatting them. In many ways, she has championed the creative intelligence espoused by Dewey and Rorty, representing how and why it is important to "challenge discursive practices that render women voiceless and disqualify their legitimacy as participants in public discourse and political practice."[100] One important way in which she has done this in her opinions and dissents is to call attention to the lived experiences of those impacted by the amazing power of the courts decisions, thus challenging the trope of abstraction. This devotion to challenging the prevailing norms of legal discourse is important not only because context matters, but also the fact that legal discourse shapes and is shaped by everyday life. As Austin Sarat and Thomas R. Kearns aptly capture,

> Law seeks to colonize everyday life and give it substance, to capture it and hold it in its grasp, to attach itself to the solidity of the everyday and, in so doing, to solidify it further. But because everyday life is a force in motion and a clash of forces that never fully reveal themselves, law can never fully capture or organize the everyday. Law does not just happen *to* the everyday; it is produced and reproduced *in* everyday encounters.[101]

A return to the everyday aspects of law, to the "complexities of difference, context, and lived experience,"[102] stretches the scope of law to include the many voices who may weigh in, whether they be those of women long silenced by the judicial process, medical professionals who can speak to the saliency of an opinion concerning their expertise, religious communities who object to various expectations required of them to participate in commercial life, or the citizenry writ large. As a result, the judiciary is in a better position to confront their role in shaping public discourse. Moreover, an expanded set of discursive resources allows for a more robust rhetorical invention and a path to creative intelligence in the law. As Gibson characterized Justice Ginsburg, her ability to speak differently is not a detriment to her legal acumen but one of her greatest strengths.

The *Hobby Lobby* decision has its fair share of supporters and detractors, both of which focus on particular aspects of the decision that merit praise or blame. While these opinions may range from nuanced to self-serving, they nonetheless focus on the details of the case at hand. Such work is good and important, but it also operates within a system of discourse that tends to ignore the public sphere of argumentation and the important role that the Supreme Court plays therein. The decision itself fails in this task by focusing so heavily on the personal sphere of belief as the crux of the opinion while ignoring the vital contribution of the technical sphere and the chorus of voices from the medical community who challenge the basis of such belief. But to rely solely on the technical sphere also fails to escape the discursive limitations imposed upon the decision-making process. As it stands, religious liberty and reproductive equality remain at odds and the decision only serves to reinforce such animosity. These tensions, however, are vital issues of public concern that merit a more robust, more thoughtful, more rhetorical examination that might require new ways of talking to and recognizing others. While not the end point, the Supreme Court should certainly serve as a guide for such public discourse.

Notes

1 Affordable Care Act.
2 *National Federation of Independent Business v. Sebelius.*
3 Affordable Care Act,. §§2000bb-1(a), (b).
4 Goodnight, "Spheres of Argument," 251–264.
5 Habermas, *Structural Transformation of the Public Sphere*; Habermas, "The Public Sphere."
6 Arendt, *The Human Condition.*
7 Dewey, *The Public and Its Problems.*
8 Goodnight, "Spheres of Argument," 258.
9 Goodnight, "Spheres of Argument," 255.
10 Goodnight, "Spheres of Argument," 255.
11 Goodnight, "Spheres of Argument," 255.
12 Goodnight, "Spheres of Argument," 255.
13 Goodnight, "Spheres of Argument," 255.
14 Goodnight, "Spheres of Argument," 255.
15 Goodnight, "Spheres of Argument," 255.
16 Goodnight, "Spheres of Argument," 256.
17 For example, see Easterly, *The Tyranny of Experts*, wherein the author outlines the various ways in which Western economics has attempted to "fix" issues pertaining to global poverty yet ignore the various extraneous issues that would likely arise in the public sphere of deliberation.
18 Goodnight, "Spheres of Argument," 257.
19 Goodnight, "Spheres of Argument," 259.
20 McKee, *The Public Sphere.*
21 Levasseur and Carlin, "Egocentric Argument."
22 Hauser, *Vernacular Voices.*
23 Schiappa, "Spheres of Argument," 47.
24 Schiappa, "Spheres of Argument," 48.
25 Schiappa, "Spheres of Argument," 52.
26 Blum, "Restoring the Parameters"; Kissling, "No Justice, No"; Von Hagel and Mansbach, *Reproductive.*
27 Kahn, "Neuroscience, Sincerity, and the Law,"; Mandell, "Scientific Opinion."
28 Helfand, "The Substantial Burden Puzzle."
29 Matthews, "Reverse Hobby Lobby."
30 Rand, "Fear the Frill."

31 *Brown v. Allen*, 343.
32 Religious Freedom Restoration, codified at 42 U.S.C. § 2000bb through 42 U.S.C. § 2000bb-4.
33 *Wisconsin v. Yoder*.
34 *Human Resources of Oregon v. Smith*.
35 *Human Resources of Oregon v. Smith*, 494.
36 Nussbaum, *Liberty of Conscience*, 157.
37 Haiman, *Religious Expression*, 103.
38 *City of Boerne v. Flores*.
39 Religious Land Use and Institutionalized Persons Act.
40 *Hobby Lobby*, 2 (emphasis added).
41 *Hobby Lobby*, 14.
42 *Hobby Lobby*, 29.
43 *Hobby Lobby*, 29.
44 Brief for Physicians for Reproductive Health.
45 Mandell, "Scientific Opinion," 105.
46 Mandell, "Scientific Opinion," 104.
47 Mandell, "Scientific Opinion," 109.
48 Mandell, "Scientific Opinion," 110.
49 Manson, "What an Abortifacient is."
50 Goodnight, "Spheres of Argument," 256.
51 Paroske, "Science Policy Controversies," 151.
52 Ceccarelli, "Manufactured Scientific Controversy," 208.
53 *Hobby Lobby*, 37.
54 Mendell, "Scientific Opinion," 93.
55 Mendell, "Scientific Opinion," 93.
56 For example, *Everson v. Board of Education*; *Torcaso v. Watkins*; *Braunfeld v. Brown*; *Gallagher v. Crown Kosher*; *Lemon v. Kurtzman*.
57 For example, *Marsh v. Champers*; *Lynch v. Donnelly*; *McCreary County v. American Civil Liberties Union*; *Van Orden v. Perry*.
58 For example, *Engel v. Vitale*; *School District of Abington Township v. Schempp*; *Stone v. Graham*.
59 *Epperson v. Arkansas*.
60 *Kitzmiller v. Dover Area School District*.
61 *Citizens United v. Federal Election Commission*.
62 Hartmann, *Unequal Protection*, 41.
63 *First National Bank of Boston v. Bellotti*.
64 Rucker, "Mitt Romney Says."
65 *Hobby Lobby*, 16.
66 *Hobby Lobby*, 18.
67 *Hobby Lobby*, 29.
68 *Hobby Lobby*, 29.
69 *Hobby Lobby*, Ginsburg dissenting, 7 (emphasis added).
70 *Hobby Lobby*, Ginsburg dissenting, 8.
71 *Hobby Lobby*, Ginsburg dissenting, 14.
72 *Hobby Lobby*, Ginsburg dissenting, 16.
73 *Little Sisters of the Poor v. Pennsylvania*.

74 Glendon, *Rights Talk*, 3.
75 Glendon, *Rights Talk*, 3.
76 *Buck v. Bell.*
77 Danisch, *Necessity of Rhetoric*, 3.
78 Danisch, *Necessity of Rhetoric*, 3.
79 Dewey, *A Common Faith*, 19.
80 Dewey, *A Common Faith*, 20.
81 Dewey, *A Common Faith*, 24
82 Dewey, *A Common Faith*, 26.
83 Dewey, *A Common Faith*, 26.
84 Bellah, "Civil Religion in America."
85 Dewey, *A Common Faith*, 39.
86 Dewey, *A Common Faith*, 79.
87 Rorty, *Contingency, Irony, and Solidarity*, xvi. Elsewhere I have made a similar call for imagination, especially in the realm of judicial decision-making. See Sery, "Literary Imagination."
88 Rorty, *Objectivity, Relativism, and Truth*, 39.
89 White, *When Words Lose Their Meaning*, 273.
90 White, *When Words Lose Their Meaning*, 266.
91 White, *When Words Lose Their Meaning*, 266.
92 White, *Heracles' Bow*, 124.
93 White, *Heracles' Bow*, 126.
94 White, *Heracles' Bow*, 225.
95 White, *Heracles' Bow*, 20
96 Gibson, *Legacy of Dissent*, 4.
97 Gibson, *Legacy of Dissent*, 7.
98 Gibson, *Legacy of Dissent*, 8.
99 Gibson, *Legacy of Dissent*, 9.
100 Gibson, *Legacy of Dissent*, 105.
101 Sarat and Kearns, "Editorial Introduction," 7–8
102 Gibson, *Legacy of Dissent*, 119.

Bibliography

Arendt, Hannah. *The Human Condition*. Chicago: University of Chicago Press, 1958.

Bellah, Robert "Civil Religion in America." *Daedalus* 96, no. 1 (1967): 1–21.

Blum, John D. "Restoring the Parameters of Public Health in a Time of Hobby Lobby and Ebola: The Case for a Wellness Account." *Belmont Law Review* 2 (2015): 119–48.

Braunfeld v. Brown, 366 U.S. 599 (1961).

Brown v. Allen, 344 U.S. 443 (1953).

Buck v. Bell, 274 U.S. 200 (1927).

Burwell v. Hobby Lobby, 573 U. S. _____ (2014).

Ceccarelli, Leah. "Manufactured Scientific Controversy: Science, Rhetoric, and Public Debate." *Rhetoric & Public Affairs* 14, no. 2 (2011): 195–228. doi: 10.1353/rap.2010.0222.

Citizens United v. Federal Election Commission, 558 U.S. 310 (2010).
City of Boerne v. Flores, 521 U.S. 507 (1997).
Danisch, Robert. *Pragmatism and the Necessity of Rhetoric*. Columbia, SC: University of South Carolina Press, 2007.
Dewey, John. *The Public and Its Problems*. Athens, OH: Swallow Press/Ohio University Press Books, 1927.
Dewey, John. *A Common Faith*. New Haven: Yale University Press, 1934.
Easterly, William. *The Tyranny of Experts: Economics, Dictators, and the Forgotten Rights of the Poor*. New York: Basic Books, 2013.
Employment Division, Department of Human Resources of Oregon v. Smith, 494 U.S. 872 (1990).
Engel v. Vitale, 370 U.S. 421 (1962).
Epperson v. Arkansas, 393 U.S. 97 (1968).
Everson v. Board of Education, 330 U.S. 1 (1947).
First National Bank of Boston v. Bellotti, 435 U.S. 765 (1978).
Gallagher v. Crown Kosher, 366 U.S. 617 (1961).
Gibson, Katie L. *Ruth Bader Ginsburg's Legacy of Dissent: Feminist Rhetoric and the Law*. Tuscaloosa: University of Alabama Press, 2018.
Glendon, Mary Ann. *Rights Talk: The Impoverishment of Political Discourse*. New York: Knopf, 1991.
Goodnight, G. Thomas, "The Personal, Technical, and Public Spheres of Argument: A Speculative Inquiry into the Art of Public Deliberation." In *Contemporary Rhetorical Theory: A Reader*, edited by John Louis Lucaites, Celeste Michelle Condit, and Sally Caudill, 251–64. New York: Guilford Press, 1999.
Habermas, Jürgen. *The Structural Transformation of the Public Sphere: An Inquiry into a Category of Bourgeois Society*. Cambridge: MIT Press, 1989.
Habermas, Jürgen. "The Public Sphere." In *Contemporary Political Philosophy: An Anthology* edited by Robert E. Goodin and Philip Pettit. Oxford: Blackwell Publishers, 1997.
Hagel, Alisa Von and Mansbach, Daniela. *Reproductive Rights in the Age of Human Rights*. New York: Palgrave Macmillan, 2016.
Haiman, Franklyn S. *Religious Expression and the American Constitution*. East Lansing: Michigan State University Press, 2003.
Hartmann, Thom. *Unequal Protection: How Corporations Became "People" – And How You Can Fight Back*. Oakland: Berret-Koehler Publishers, 2010.
Hauser, Gerard. *Vernacular Voices: The Rhetoric of Publics and Public Spheres*. Columbia: University of South Carolina Press, 1999.
Helfand, Michael A. "The Substantial Burden Puzzle." *University of Illinois Law Review* (2016): 1–9. https://ssrn.com/abstract=2791081.
Kahn, Jonathan. "Neuroscience, Sincerity, and the Law." *Bergen Journal of Criminal Law and Criminal Justice* 3, no. 2 (2015): 203–20. doi:10.15845/bjclcj.v3i2.908.

Kissling, Elizabeth A. “No Justice, No Pill/Know (Reproductive) Justice, Know the Pill.” *Women’s Reproductive Health* 3, no. 2 (2016): 109–12. doi: 10.1080/23293691.2016.1196085.

Kitzmiller v. Dover Area School District, 400 F. Supp. 2d 707 (M.D. Pa. 2005).

Lemon v. Kurtzman, 403 U.S. 602 (1971).

Levasseur, David G. and Carlin, Diana B. “Egocentric Argument and the Public Sphere: Citizen Deliberations on Public Policy and Policymakers.” *Rhetoric & Public Affairs* 4, no. 3 (Fall 2001): 407–31. https://www.jstor.org/stable/41940589

Little Sisters of the Poor Saints Peter and Paul Home v. Pennsylvania, 591 U.S. _____ (2020).

Lynch v. Donnelly, 465 U.S. 668 (1984).

Mandell, Meredith Rachel. “When Religious Belief Becomes Scientific Opinion: Burwell v. Hobby Lobby and the Unraveling of Federal Rule 702.” *Northwestern Journal of Law and Social Policy* 12, no. 1 (2016): 92–118. https://scholarlycommons.law.northwestern.edu/njlsp/vol12/iss1/4

Manson, Jamie. “What an Abortifacient is – and What it Isn’t.” *National Catholic Reporter*, February, 20, 2012. https://www.ncronline.org/blogs/grace-margins/what-abortifacient-and-what-it-isnt

Marsh v. Champers, 463 U.S. 783 (1983).

Matthews, Kaili E. “Reverse Hobby Lobby: The Satanic Temple’s Fight against Indoctrination Abortion Laws.” *Rutgers Journal of Law and Religion* 19, no. 3 (2018): 383–397.

McCreary County v. American Civil Liberties Union, 545 U.S. 844 (2005).

McKee, Alan. *The Public Sphere: An Introduction.* Cambridge: Cambridge University Press, 2005.

National Federation of Independent Business v. Sebelius, 567 U.S. 519 (2012).

Nussbaum, Martha C. *Liberty of Conscience: In Defense of America’s Tradition of Religious Equality.* New York: Basic Books, 2008.

Paroske, Marcus. “Deliberating International Science Policy Controversies: Uncertainty and AIDS in South Africa.” *Quarterly Journal of Speech* 95, no. 2 (2009): 148–70. Doi: 10.1080/00335630902842053.

Patient Protection and Affordable Care Act, 42 U.S.C. § 18001 et. seq. (2010).

Rand, Erin J. “Fear the Frill: Ruth Bader Ginsburg and the Uncertain Futurity of Feminist Judicial Dissent.” *Quarterly Journal of Speech* 101, no. 1 (2015): 72–84. doi: 10.1080/00335630.2015.994898.

Religious Freedom Restoration Act of 1993, Pub. L. No. 103–141, 107 Stat. 1488 (1993).

Religious Land Use and Institutionalized Persons Act, Pub.L. 106–274 (2000).

Rorty, Richard. *Contingency, Irony, and Solidarity.* Cambridge: Cambridge University Press, 1989.

Rorty, Richard. *Objectivity, Relativism, and Truth.* Cambridge: Cambridge University Press, 1991.

Rucker, Philip. "Mitt Romney Says 'Corporations are People.'" *The Washington Post*, August 11, 2011. https://www.washingtonpost.com/politics/mitt-romney-says-corporations-are-people/2011/08/11/gIQABwZ38I_story.html.

Sarat, Austin and Thomas R. Kearns. "Editorial Introduction." In *Law in Everyday Life*, edited by Austin Sarat and Thomas R. Kearns, 1–20. Ann Arbor: University of Michigan Press, 1995.

Schiappa, Edward. "'Spheres of Argument' as *Topoi* for the Critical Study of Power/Knowledge." In *Spheres of Argument: Proceedings of the Sixth SCA/AFA Conference on Argumentation*, edited by Bruce E. Gronbeck, 47–56. Annandale, VA: Speech Communication Association, 1989.

School District of Abington Township v. Schempp, 374 U.S. 203 (1963).

Sery, Joseph. "Law, Literature, and the Literary Imagination: Toward a Rhetorical Understanding of Martha Nussbaum's 'Poet Judge.'" *Communication Law Review* 17, no. 1 (2017): 1–22.

Stone v. Graham, 449 U.S. 39 (1980).

Torcaso v. Watkins, 367 U.S. 488 (1961).

Van Orden v. Perry, 545 U.S. 677 (2005).

White, James Boyd. *Heracles' Bow: Essays on the Rhetoric and Poetics of the Law.* Madison: University of Wisconsin Press, 1985.

White, James Boyd. *When Words Lose Their Meaning: Constitutions and Reconstitutions of Language, Character, and Community.* Chicago: University of Chicago Press, 2004.

Wisconsin v. Yoder, 406 U.S. 205 (1972).

11. *Prejudice, Politics, and Privilege: The Evolution of Religious Freedom in the United States and Its Disparate Impact on Native Americans*

Jason Zenor

In 2016, several of the tribes of the Great Sioux Nation filed another injunction in court to stop the building of the Dakota Access Pipeline as previous attempts had been unsuccessful. The tribes had been in a long legal, as well as political, fight with the company and federal government to stop the construction of the oil pipeline through their ancestral lands. But, the 2016 injunction took a new approach—the Cheyenne River Sioux tribe argued that the pipeline would put a substantial burden on its ability to practice its religion in violation of the Religious Freedom Restoration Act of 1993 (RFRA). The tribe claimed that the finished pipeline would fulfill the prophecy that a 'black snake' will destroy its land by leaking out crude oil.[1] Legal analysts felt that the chances of this argument prevailing was quite low since RFRA's 'substantial burden' requirement did not intend to protect against the building of a pipeline. Moreover, in 2009, the Navajo Nation had failed in a similar RFRA claim when it challenged the building of a ski resort that would spray artificial snow (containing trace amount of human waste) on sacred lands.[2]

As predicted, the Sioux tribes' RFRA claim against the Dakota Access Pipeline did fail. A federal court held that the tribe was late with its claim and that there were already a bridge and a road over the disputed lands as well as natural gas pipelines nearby. But it was the court's analysis of the religious exercise claim that was more revealing. The court questioned the sincerity of the religious claim altogether, dismissing the prophecy as being created only a few decades earlier when those roads were built. The tribe believed that the prophecy was like any other prophecy that had been passed down by religious elders and that the outcome of the case was just more proof that American courts do not understand tribal religions.[3] After the case failed, the Trump Administration approved the pipeline and it was completed in 2017. Unfortunately, the prophecy should not have been so quickly dismissed as the pipeline has leaked several times since it went into operation.[4]

Around the same time as the Dakota Access Pipeline case was in the courts, another case about religious freedom was being argued. In *Masterpiece Cakeshop*,[5] a baker, who was a devout Christian refused to make a specialty wedding cake for a same-sex couple because his religious beliefs did not support same-sex marriage. The State of Colorado fined him for violating the state's anti-discrimination laws. The baker sued the state claiming that it was a violation of his free exercise rights and several amicus briefs were written in support of him, including the U.S. Justice Department of the Trump Administration.[6] In the end, The U.S. Supreme Court ruled in favor of the baker holding that the state was hostile to his religious beliefs when it fined him.[7]

These cases illustrate how majority and minority religions are still treated differently, both politically and legally. The tribe in the Dakota Access Pipeline case cited RFRA, which was passed to protect religious minorities, specifically Native American religions who had been discriminated against for centuries. But the federal court was suspicious of the tribes' claims of a religious prophecy, while in *Masterpiece Cakeshop*, the U.S. Supreme Court was sympathetic to a devout Christian's claim that baking a cake for a same-sex wedding would substantially burden his right to free exercise of religion. The centrality that baking and selling a cake has to religion was never in question. The sincerity of the Christian belief was simply assumed as if baking cakes for same-sex marriage has been central to Christianity for time immemorial. Whereas the tribes had the burden of proof for showing that their religious beliefs were sincere, historical and documented. Moreover, these cases went beyond the legal argument and into politics, with the baker having the political backing of the Trump Administration, while the tribes did not. In the end, RFRA failed to fulfill to its original cause of protecting a religious minority, but did protect the more politically powerful Christian majority.

Accordingly, this chapter demonstrates how the Judeo-Christian religious practices have been long been privileged both politically and legally in the U.S.. First the chapter outlines how Native Americans have long been denied the right to practice their religions. Next the chapter recounts the 20th century expansion of legal protections for minority religions. Then the chapter details the U.S. Supreme Court's shift in limiting constitutional protection of free exercise led to several Congressional acts protecting religious freedom for minority religions. Then the chapter examines how Christian groups utilized statutory protections of religion to discriminate against the LGBT community, while Native American groups were still having to justify the sincerity of their religious practices in court. Finally, the chapter argues that constitutional protections need to evolve to either truly protect all religious practices or to balance the rights of religious practice with other rights.

Long History of Suppressing Native American Religious Rights

The First Amendment's protection of religious liberty is thought to reflect the quintessential American value of 'religious tolerance.' But history shows that the adoption of the First Amendment was a response to religious intolerance going back to the earliest days of the British colonies. The Charter of the Rhode Island (Providence Plantation) colony is often used as an example of the earliest form of religious tolerance in the colonies. But, Roger Williams' (and others') move to a new land was a function of his banishment from the Massachusetts Bay Colony as the Puritans did not tolerate any political or religious dissent, even from other Christian denominations.[8]

Even with the adoption of the First Amendment, the ideal of religious tolerance was not a reality in practice. In the first few decades of the nation, several states still had official religions and/or laws discriminating against people from different religions, such as Catholicism and Judaism. The Nation's founders are often praised and quoted for their support of religious tolerance in the creation of a secular government.[9] But when President George Washington wrote a letter to a Jewish synagogue about the acceptance of religious liberty in the new nation, he explicitly singled out "the Children of the Stock of Abraham" as the recipients of such liberty.[10] The new nation may have protected religious dissent, but it was "often limited to Christian groups."[11]

While early Americans may have debated the acceptance of different monotheistic religions, there was little question to the 'savagery' of Native American tribes and their religious practices.[12] This notion was even embedded into common law with the notorious Marshall Trilogy,[13] the foundation of modern Federal Indian Law. In these cases, the U.S. Supreme Court enshrined the Doctrine of Discovery as the legal justification for the federal government's plenary powers over all tribes and reservations.[14] Chief Justice John Marshall argued that the "character and religion" of tribes were subservient to the "superior genius of Europe." Thus, the European (and then

American) proselytizing was "ample compensation" for the taking of ancestral lands.[15]

From early contact, European missionaries attempted to convert Native Americans to Christianity.[16] In the 19th century, the federal government had a new national policy—the complete assimilation of Native Americans—socially, politically, and culturally.[17] This meant tribes were removed from their ancestral homes and forced to live on reservations, an act that was supported by Christian missionaries who felt it was needed to civilize tribal members.[18] When the tribes attempted to fight back, the government responded with harsher laws to destroy their culture and identity, including banning spiritual practices such as sun dances.[19] Removal acts would also take individual tribal members away from their communities and put them into Christian boarding schools. The stated goal of such schools was to "kill the Indian, save the man."[20]

Free Exercise Clause in the 20th Century

It was not until the mid-20th century that the U.S. Supreme Court created a legal test for the Free Exercise Clause. Prior to WWII, the First Amendment's protection of religious practices did not apply to the states. But, during the civil rights era, the Warren Court made 'free exercise' into a fundamental right. This meant any government action that created a substantial burden to religion had to survive strict scrutiny. However, when Native Americans went to the court seeking protection for their religious practices, they did not receive the same protections as their Christian counterparts.

Strict Scrutiny for Christian Minorities

In *Sherbert v. Verner (1963)*,[21] a Seventh-Day Adventist was fired because she refused to work on Saturdays, which she considered to be the day of the Sabbath. When she applied for unemployment benefits, the government denied it despite her religious claim, which was a protected exemption under state law. The U.S. Supreme Court ruled in favor of the plaintiff holding that the government had burdened the free exercise of religion by forcing her to decide between her religion and her entitled unemployment benefits. The Court held that when the government forces such a burden, the government action must serve a compelling state interest and the law must be narrowly tailored.[22]

In *Wisconsin v. Yoder (1972)*,[23] an Amish community refused to send its children to school past the age of sixteen, which violated compulsory education laws requiring schooling to the age of eighteen. The U.S. Supreme Court ruled in favor of the Amish and their religious objection as it was a sincere belief and the government had not shown any harm to not having the extra years of schooling. The Court found that laws "offend the constitutional requirement for governmental neutrality if [they] unduly burden[] the free exercise of religion."[24]

In both cases, the U.S. Supreme Court protected members of minor Christian sects who objected to the laws of the Christian majority. Most other Christians did not object to compulsory school to the age of 18. Most other Christians recognized the Sabbath as being on Sunday not Saturday (thus many communities had Blue Laws that forbade commercial activity on Sunday).[25] But, the beliefs of the Amish and Seventh Day Adventist were never questioned as being valid and sincere as they were in service of the Christian God.

In the case of *Church of the Lukumi Babalu Aye, Inc. v. Hialeah (1993)*,[26] the U.S. Supreme Court examined a case involving the religious practices of Santeria, a pantheistic religion that originated with West African slaves who were brought to Cuba. The religion combines aspects of the Yorubo religion with Roman Catholicism and includes healing rituals using herbs and animals. The City of Hialeah, Florida passed a law that barred animal slaughter, but made several exceptions, including for Kosher practices. In passing the law, council members made it clear that law was intended to stop the Santeria religious practice of animal sacrifice. The Court found that the law was not facially neutral since it was aimed at the religious practice. Thus, it overturned law because it did not survive strict scrutiny as there was no compelling state interest in stopping the animal sacrifice.[27]

Rational Basis for Native Americans

The U.S. Supreme Court has examined several cases dealing with the religious practices of Native Americans. In each of the following cases, tribes lost as the Court did not apply the strict scrutiny test, differentiating between the claims of Native Americans and previous cases involving Christian religions.

In *Bowen v. Roy (1986)*,[28] a Native American family refused to use a Social Security number for their daughter when applying for food stamps because, according to their religious beliefs, using the number would rob the daughter of her soul and not allow her to become a holy person. Despite it being a sincere religious belief, the Court denied the family's right claiming that the Social Security law itself and the requirement that it be used on government forms were facially neutral and did not discriminate based on beliefs.[29]

In *Lyng v. Northwest Cemetery Protective Association (1988)*,[30] the U.S. government sought to construct a road through national forest lands that would be used to remove timber. In reviewing the plan, the U.S. Forest Service determined that it would have an adverse impact to the tribal religious practices on sacred lands in the park, but the government went through with the plan anyway. The U.S. Supreme Court concluded that the action did not violate the First Amendment as Native American tribes were not coerced into violating their religion- they were just not allowed to practice on the sacred lands. The Court stated that it did not want to place government land into religious servitude. In the end, the government interest in managing land outweighed the burden on religious practice.[31]

It was not until the late 20th century that Congress recognized that previous government prohibitions on tribal religious practices did not comport with First Amendment protections.[32] In 1978, Congress passed the American Indian Religious Freedom Act (AIRFA) to protect "sacred lands for tribal use, possession of sacred objects, and the freedom to worship through ceremonials and traditional rites."[33] AIRFA required that the government had to consider the effect that its actions had on tribal religious practices and had to do so in consultation with tribes.[34]

But, the AIRFA did not provide for any penalties if the government did not follow the law. Thus in this era, courts often ruled against tribes' assertion of religious rights, upholding government regulations on collecting eagle feathers,[35] a dam flooding sacred burial grounds,[36] and allowing tourists to use a sacred site for skiing.[37] Therefore, Congress had to amend AIRFA in 1994 to give more protection on land rights and other religious practices for Native Americans.[38]

In 2000, Congress passed the Religious Land and Institutionalized Persons Act of 2000 (RLUIPA), which prohibited land use regulations from imposing a substantial burden on the exercise of religion.[39] These laws and additional laws like RFRA now require the government to apply strict scrutiny. Nevertheless, the land uses cases are often still decided in favor of the government with public land management cited as a compelling state interest and ability for a Native American litigant to show a substantial burden is difficult if they can still practice their rituals[40]

The Insincerity of Courts in Finding No Burden on Native American Religion

Native American religious practices can be difficult for outsiders to comprehend as there is great variation in religious practices among the hundreds of tribes in the U.S. But, one common trait among all tribes is a connection between religious practice and the lands they once called home.[41] This connection to land and spirituality is fundamental to Native American culture and to lose such connection undermines the very essence of their identity:

> Tribal cultures, from the time of their creation, have been formed, shaped, and renewed in relationship with mountains, mesas, lakes, rivers, and other places that are imbued with the spirituality, history, knowledge, and identity of the people.[42]

Yet, when a religious practice was tied to land, courts have held that the practice could simply take place elsewhere.[43] Since Native Americans were not being jailed or fined for their religious practices, nor were they being denied a government entitlement, courts felt that there was not a substantial burden to the practice of their religion. Courts see Native American connection to land as spirituality, rather than an exercise of a religious practice.[44] Unfortunately for tribal members, many of the sacred ancestral lands are held by others as private property, national parks open to the public, or federal land not open to the public.

Lyng and other land use cases illustrate the U.S. legal system's implicit bias in favor of Judeo-Christian religions. U.S. law protects religious beliefs and practices as the 'freedom of conscience' is the central value of free exercise clause.[45] But the legal system is less open to protecting specific property where it takes place. This can be tied to the fact that there are very few places in the U.S. that would be considered sacred in the Judeo-Christian religions (one exception would be Mormon sites). Churches can be moved and even cemeteries can be move, because the connection to the land is not inherent. Thus, in American jurisprudence there was not a strong precedent for protecting land for religious purposes. This was even less protection when the sacred land is not owned by the religious adherents.[46]

In protecting minority Christian sects, the U.S. Supreme Court was quick to shower them with praise as being beneficial to society.[47] But for religions outside of the Judeo-Christian tradition, the Court was not so open. When it came to cases arising from Christian practice, courts rarely required an actual showing of centrality- it was just assumed. However, when it came to cases arising from Native American religious practices, courts have forced tribes to show the centrality of the practice. Courts often dismissed other Native American religious practices as being insincere, while accepting the common practices of the Judeo-Christian religions. For example, ingesting of plants was often classified as an illegal drug use, while during the prohibition, sacramental wine was exempt.[48]

A Legal Loss and a Political Win for Free Exercise of Religion

In 1990, the U.S. Supreme Court decided the case of *Employment Division v. Smith*.[49] The plaintiffs in the case had been fired from their jobs as drug rehabilitation counselors. They were also members of the Native American church (a religion that combines aspects of Christianity with traditional tribal religious practices). A practice of the church was to ingest peyote, which was classified as an illegal drug at the time. The employers believed that employees' use of hallucinogenic drugs undermined their status as counselors. When the plaintiffs applied for unemployment benefits, they were denied because they had been fired from their jobs for work misconduct. The plaintiffs argued that this was a violation of their free exercise rights as peyote was part of their religion and sued the state.

The U.S. Supreme Court upheld the government action stating that the state laws were generally applicable and facially neutral.[50] The Court feared that accommodating a minority religion would be preferring one religion over another. In the opinion, the Court did not explicitly overturn the *Sherbert* requirement that the government could not substantially interfere with a person's ability to practice sincere religious beliefs. Instead, Justice Scalia differentiated *Sherbert* arguing that it involved the additional right of the parent. Scalia also differentiated the case from *Yoder*, where the act of recognizing the Sabbath on Saturday was not illegal, whereas the use of drugs in *Smith* was illegal. Scalia cited several other cases where religious acts were stopped if they were illegal including violating child labor laws,[51] not paying taxes,[52] and dodging the draft.[53] He also argued that if a strict scrutiny test was to be used in free exercise cases, it must be applied equally to all religious actions.[54] But such a test would result in a dysfunctional legal system. All sorts of laws- from child neglect laws to environmental laws to traffic laws- could then be challenged as a violation of religious beliefs.[55]

With the ruling in *Smith*, many religious practices- beyond Native Americans' practices- were in jeopardy. The government would have just to show that the law was facially neutral and generally applicable, which is usually easy for the government to do. Theoretically, after the case, an orthodox Jew could be forced to buy non-Kosher food if the government required as a matter of health or food safety policy. A Sikh could be forced to remove their turban on an airplane if it was believed to be a public safety threat. An Amish community could be forced to have Internet access if was government policy to modernize the nation.

As a result, the *Smith* decision received broad political backlash. Disparate groups such as the ACLU, American Humanist Association, the

Christian Legal Society, and Southern Baptists formed the 'Coalition for the Free Exercise of Religion' in order to lobby Congress to act.[56] The Native American Civil Rights Movement separately proposed that Congress pass a specific act to protect tribal religious practices such as ingesting peyote, using eagle feathers, and preserving sacred lands.[57]

Congress did act by passing the Religious Freedom Restoration Act (RFRA) in 1993.[58] The act claimed to turn the legal protections of religious exercise back to the *Sherbert* test by requiring that any government action that substantially burdened religious practices had to survive strict scrutiny. RFRA spells out "exercise of religion" to be *any* religious exercise, moving beyond the previous requirement that the practice had to be central to the religion. RFRA was a rare bipartisan success, passing 97-3 in the Senate with very little outside objection.[59] Though *Smith* was the impetus for RFRA, not all of the religious concerns of Native Americans were part of the law. In fact, Congress explicitly stated in passing RFRA "[p]re-Smith case law makes it clear that strict scrutiny does not apply to government actions involving only management of internal Government affairs or the use of the Government's own property."[xl]

When a case pertaining to the use of hallucinogenic drugs came back to the U.S. Supreme Court, the religious practice was not dismissed as insincere this time. In *Gonzales v. O Centro Espirita Beneficente Uniao Do Vegetal (2006)*,[60] the Court examined a case about a New Mexican church based on a Brazilian religion. One of the church's religious practices was to have members, including children, ingest the hoasca tea. But the tea was listed a Substance I Controlled Drug and was illegal under federal law. When a shipment of the tea was seized at the border, the church sued the federal government claiming that the action violated RFRA. The Court ruled in favor of the church as the government action did not survive strict scrutiny as required by RFRA. Furthermore, RFRA amendments explicitly protected other religious uses of hallucinogenic drugs, such as peyote. However, the case did not legalize possession the drug, if only lifted the temporary restraining order for this church in this case.[61]

Religious Right Exploits RFRA Laws

When RFRA was debated and passed, it was not even considered that the law would be used to discriminate against protected classes.[62] In the first few years of RFRA enactment, cases were rare and the few that happened dealt with secular issues.[63] But the timing of law and politics created a volatile mix. In *City of Boerne v. Flores (1997)*,[64] the U.S. Supreme Court invalidated

RFRA's jurisdiction over states. So, in response, Congress passed RULIPA and several other laws to fill the gap. Additionally, twenty states passed their own RFRA laws. But, for the states, the impetus of these laws was not just the *Flores* case- the main driver was the expansion of civil rights for the LGBTQ community.

The LGBTQ Community Finds Legal Protections in Court

During the 1980s, half of U.S. states considered consensual acts of sodomy to be a crime. The U.S. Supreme Court upheld these laws as constitutional because states could regulate morality.[65] Moreover, the Reagan Administration, which was supported by the Religious Right, was unresponsive to the needs of the gay community suffering during the AIDS epidemic. When large cities tried to pass regulations protecting the LGBTQ community from discrimination in housing, religious conservatives began to argue that it was a violation of their freedom of religion.[66]

Then, in 1996, the U.S. Supreme Court overturned a Colorado law that barred homosexuals and bisexuals being designated as a protected class. The Court found the law to be a violation of equal protection and that it was passed with animus towards the class of persons.[67] This led to the U.S. Supreme Court decision in *Lawrence v. Texas (2003),*[68] which held that anti-sodomy laws were unconstitutional as they too violated equal protection. In the majority opinion, Justice Kennedy stated that discrimination against the LGBTQ community was parallel to racial discrimination, thus unprotected. But, in dissent, Justice Scalia argued that these laws could have been considered a "reasonable effort to preserve traditional American moral values."[69]

In 1993, the Hawaii Supreme Court held that the state's bar on same-sex marriage did not survive strict scrutiny.[70] In response to the case, the State of Hawaii amended their constitution to allow the state to only recognize a marriage of opposite sex couples. Similarly, the U.S. Congress passed The Defense of Marriage Act in 1996, defining marriage as between a man and a woman for all federal purposes and allowed states not to recognize same-sex marriages licensed in other states.[71]

In the 2000s, the Massachusetts[72] and Iowa[73] State Supreme Courts also ruled that same-sex couples had the right to marry. This time state legislatures across the nation moved to stop the expansion of same-sex marriage and by the end of the decade half of U.S. states had constitutional amendments narrowing the rights to marry.[74] Then the U.S. Supreme Court decided U.S. v Windsor (2013)[75] overturning the federal Defense of Marriage Act. Finally, in Obergefell v Hodges (2014),[76] the Court declared the right to marriage as a fundamental right for all persons. Once again Justice Kennedy found similarities between discrimination based on race and discrimination based on sexual orientation.

The Religious Right Circles the Wagons

By comparing defenders of same-sex marriage to racists, the Court only further enraged the Religious Right. The fear was that these cases would allow for any and all religious objections from conservatives to be constitutionally barred. Thus, the U.S. Supreme Court's decisions forced the Religious Right to turn to legislatures to preserve traditional laws that promoted their religious beliefs. The religious right's political lobbying was able to get many state legislatures to pass more expansive RFRA laws that often explicitly allowed for discrimination of the LGBTQ community.[77] In the five years after *Obergefell*, twenty-one states passed revised RFRA laws. Only, nineteen U.S. states have protection against discrimination of members of the LGBT community- with an overlap of only four states having both a RFRA law and explicit LGBTQ protections.[78]

The second RFRA movement was part of a cultural war rather than any overarching legal principles. Despite the courts' explicit statements about religious freedoms, twenty-one states still felt a need to pass RFRA laws to protect conservatives who did not agree with the legalization of same-sex marriage (and other LGBTQ rights). The notable part of the state RFRA laws was that they were housed in anti-discrimination language- protecting Christians against discrimination. But, most of these states had never passed laws protecting discrimination on the basis of sex, race or sexual orientation until they were forced to.[79]

Eventually, the backlash against the state RFRAs became too politically toxic and states turned away from them (Georgia's Governor did not sign the bill and Indiana had to amend its RFRA). So, when state legislation would not grant protection for discrimination against the LGBTQ community, proponents turned to the courts and the sweeping legal protection of federal RFRA.[80] In *Burwell v. Hobby Lobby (2014)*,[81] the U.S. Supreme Court held that a closely-held corporation could not be forced to provide insurance that pays for contraceptives because it violates the company's religious beliefs, which are protected by federal RFRA.

But, the origins of the federal RFRA was to protect minorities who had difficulty getting exemptions in the legislative process demanded by *Smith*.[82] Religious minorities often lack the political power to convince legislatures that their unique religious practices deserve protection.[83] But, instead of being used to protect religious minorities, it is the politically powerful religious majority that seized upon the federal RFRA to protect itself from judicial decisions of *Lawrence* and *Obergefell.*

The political shift of the religious freedom debate may be best illustrated in the switch in the U.S. Supreme Court- an institution that claims to be above politics. In 1990, Justice Scalia penned the majority opinion in *Smith* that held that free exercise claims could not win against facially neutral and generally applicable laws. He also signed onto the majority opinion in *Flores* in 1997, which argued that RFRA was an "intrusion on every level of government."[84]

But, almost a quarter century later, Justice Scalia signed on to the majority in *Hobby Lobby v. Burwell* which holds that closely-held corporations do not have to follow a federal law that violates their religious beliefs. The dissenting opinion in the *Hobby Lobby* case was written by Justice Ruth Bader Ginsburg who was heavily influenced by Justice Scalia's opinion in *Smith.* She feared that religious objection would allow people to ignore generally applicable laws like anti-discrimination and equal pay.

What had changed over the twenty-four years? It may have been the passage of RFRA convinced Scalia that the legislative process had provided for strict scrutiny protection, thus it was acceptable. But, if we look at the laws being threatened mentioned by Justice Scalia and Justice Ginsburg respectively, then the politics of it all becomes clear. In *Smith*, Justice Scalia mentions concerns for the legality of compulsory military service, drug laws, and equal protection. In the *Hobby Lobby* case, Justice Ginsburg mentions the threats to discrimination laws, required vaccines, and equal pay. These lists seem to reflect the laws supported by the conservatives and progressives respectively. As one author speculated:

> Justice Scalia may not have wanted to support the right of Native Americans to smoke peyote in contravention of state law but did want to support the right of evangelical Christian owners of a family corporation to refuse to pay for contraceptive health insurance as required by the ACA, a law with which he profoundly disagreed, both legally and personally.[85]

The Insincerity of Contemporary Religious Freedom

"Religious sincerity" has been a part of free exercise jurisprudence for close to a century.[86] Traditionally, courts have stated that they would not delve into the content of the religious belief or judge on its merit. As Justice Jackson warned in United States v. Ballard (1944), when it comes to religions that are not Judeo Christian, non-believers "are likely not to understand and are almost certain not to believe."[87]

But, courts would judge on whether the party's claim to a religious belief was sincere as a question of fact based on the evidence of religious practice.[88] But in the U.S. Supreme Court case *Hobby Lobby v. Burwell,* both the majority and the dissent stated that the sincerity of belief can no longer be a factor for courts to interpret.[89] Seemingly, any party can now make any religious claim and it will not be questioned.

But, the neutral analysis of religious claims has not been consistent. A clear privilege is being granted to claims of Christian practice—there is an assumption of sincerity. As mentioned earlier, Native American claims in the U.S. Supreme Court have never been successful. But, even post-RFRA, where it seems all religious claims are respected, Native American religious claims always seem to be questioned, more so when it comes to land use.

Ingesting drugs as a religious practice is protected, but in many ways this fits the religious majority's view of religion. It is analogous to communion and the drinking of sacramental wine. Native Americans are granted a religious accommodation when it comes to possessing the feathers of protected eagles. But, they are not allowed to kill the eagle themselves -they must get them from the government.[90] The Trump Administration supported the Ramapough Lenape Indians' RULIPA claim against the town of Mahwah, NJ. The town claimed that the tribe was violating zoning laws by having a prayer site in a residential area. But, the tribe was using the spot for prayer and it owns the property.[91]

But, with other religious claims, the right to free exercise is not so clear. Native American requests to protect the sanctity of ancient, sacred lands is dismissed. As long as the tribes can still access the place, then there is no substantial burden.[92] A 'Black Snake' prophecy is questioned and ultimately dismissed because it lacks the historical record that major religions' prophecies would have.[93] In these cases, courts consider whether the land use is a substantial burden and attempt to balance the competing interests of the parties.[94] Yet, a corporation can claim that it cannot provide coverage for its employees' birth control and a baker can claim that it cannot create a cake for a same-sex wedding. The U.S. Supreme Court did not even question if these were sincere religious beliefs. In the end, it is clear that there is a privilege toward religious practices that resemble the familiar Judeo-Christians practices and it is embedded in the law of religious accommodation. Moving forward, laws need to do more to fulfill the promise of equal protection of all religions. This means either protecting all religious beliefs that are burdened or moving back to a balancing test for religious accommodation, including for Christianity.

Conclusion

The Religious Right argues that they are the minority in a secular nation and that their individual rights must be protected. But over the last forty years, their political power has been quite evident in all branches of government at every level. For example, in 2017, President Trump signed an Executive Order on Religious Liberty promising to protect all religions, while at the same passing a travel ban that he called a "Muslim Ban" while he was a candidate. At the same time, the Religious Right has been privileged by a legal protection that was originally intended to protect a religious minority, such as Native Americans, whose rights were put in question by the decision in *Smith.*

But, RFRA expanded the protection of religious exercise well beyond *Sherbert*. After RFRA, religious exercise could not to be substantially burdened unless the government had a compelling state interest and the law was narrowly tailored. This is very difficult for the government to establish. RFRA now essentially protects any religious practice against all government regulation- as any government burden is substantial. Moreover, in *Burwell v. Hobby Lobby (2014),* the U.S. Supreme Court extended this religious protection to a corporation. It appears the Court will also no longer examine the centrality or the sincerity of the belief—a party must merely *claim* that there was a burden to religion in order to prevail. This was exactly what Justice Scalia warned against in *Smith,* individuals are now "a law unto themselves." Yet, as the example of the Sioux challenge of the Dakota Access Pipeline or the Navajo Nation's challenge to a ski resort on sacred lands show us, free exercise of religion for all has not been fully realized.

Notes

1 Ellen Gilmer, "Pipeline foes pivot to religious freedom," *Energy & Economics News* (Feburary, 9, 2017). https://www.eenews.net/stories/1060049828.
2 Ibid.
3 Britain Eakin, "Tribe denied religious injunction against Dakota Access Pipeline," *Court Service News* (March 7, 2017). https://www.courthousenews.com/tribe-denied-religious-injunction-dakota-access-pipeline.
4 Morgan Winsor, "Over 380,000 gallons of oil spill from Keystone Pipeline in North Dakota," *ABC News* (November 1, 2019). https://abcnews.go.com/US/380000-gallons-oil-spill-keystone-pipeline-north-dakota/story?id=66683075.

5 138 S.Ct. 1719 (2017).
6 Jess Bravin, "Trump Administration backs baker who refused to make wedding cake for gay couple." *Wall St. Journal* (September 8, 2017). https://www.wsj.com/articles/trump-administration-backs-baker-who-refused-to-make-wedding-cake-for-gay-couple-1504843234.
7 Masterpiece Cakeshop v. Colorado Civil Rights Commission, 138 S.Ct 1719 (2017).
8 Thomas J. Cleary, "In Impartiality We Trust: A Commentary on Government Aid and Involvement with Religion," 2 *Southern New England Law Journal (Roundtable Symposium)* 2 (2007): 120.
9 Ibid at 173.
10 George Washington, "From George Washington to the Hebrew Congregation in Newport, Rhode Island," (August, 18 1790). https://founders.archives.gov/documents/Washington/05-06-02-0135.
11 Boerne v. Flores, 521 U.S. 507, 551 (1997) (O'Connor, J., dissenting).
12 Kenneth Davis, "America's True History of Religious Tolerance," *Smithsonian Magazine* (October, 2010). https://www.smithsonianmag.com/history/americas-true-history-of-religious-tolerance-61312684.
The Declaration of Independence states that "All men are created equal," but goes on to state that Native Americas are "the merciless Indian Savages, whose known rule of warfare, is an undistinguished destruction of all ages, sexes and conditions." Thomas Jefferson, "Declaration of Independence," (July 4, 1776). https://www.archives.gov/founding-docs/declaration-transcript.
13 Frank Pommersheim, *The Broken Landscape: Indians, Indian Tribes and the Constitution* (Oxford: Oxford Press, 2012). DOI:10.1093/acprof:osobl/9780199915736.003.0004.
14 Ibid.
15 Johnson v. M'Intosh, 21 U.S. 543 (1823): 573.
16 Carol Higham, " Christian Missions to Native Americans," *Oxford Research Encyclopedia* (2016). https://oxfordre.com/americanhistory/view/10.1093/acrefore/9780199329175.001.0001/acrefore-9780199329175-e-323.
17 Jason Gubi, "The Religious Freedom Restoration Act and Protection of Native American Religious Practices," *The Modern American* (Fall 2008): 73–79.
18 Scott A. Taylor, "The Native American Law Opinions of Judge Noonan: Do We Hear the Faint Voice of Bartólome De Las Casas?" *University of St. Thomas Law Journal* 1 (2003): 183.
19 "Governing the Court of Indian Offenses," 17 U.S.C 105 (1883). See original text at: https://rclinton.files.wordpress.com/2007/11/code-of-indian-offenses.pdf.
20 Jason Gubi "The Religious Freedom Restoration Act and Protection of Native American Religious Practices," *The Modern American* (Fall 2008): 74.
21 374 U.S. 398.
22 Ibid at 406.
23 406 U.S. 205.
24 Ibid at 220.
25 Marc Stern et al., "Faith Under Democracy: What Have Religious Believers Gained? What Have They Lost?" *Georgetown Journal Law & Public Policy, Vol. 1* (2003): 262. Braunfeld v. Brown, 366 U.S. 599 (1961).
26 508 U.S. 520.

27 Ibid at 546.
28 476 U.S. 693.
29 Ibid at 700.
30 485 U.S. 439.
31 Ibid at 451.
32 American Indian Religious Freedom Act (AIRFA), 42 U.S.C. §1996 (1978).
33 Ibid.
34 Ibid.
35 United States v. Top Sky, 547 F.2d 486, 488 (9th Cir.1976) .
36 Seqouyah v. Tennessee Valley Authority, 620 F.2d 1159, 1165 (6th Cir. 1980).
37 Wilson v. Block, 708 F.2d 735, 737–38 (C.A.D.C. 1983).
38 1994 Amendments to AIRFA, Public Law No 103–344, codified at 42 U.S.C. § 1996 a (b)(1) (1994).
39 42 U.S.C.A. § 2000cc(a)(1) (West 2020).
40 Allison M. Dussias, "Friend, Foe, Frenemy: The United States and American Indian Religious Freedom," *Denver University Law Review* 90 (2012): 404.
41 Joel Brady, "Land Is Itself a Sacred, Living Being": Native American Sacred Site Protection on Federal Public Lands Amidst The Shadows of Bear Lodge," *American Indian Law Review* 24 (2000): 153.
42 Kristen A. Carpenter, "A Property rights approach to Sacred Sites cases: Asserting a Place as Indians as non-owners," *UCLA Law Review* 52 (2005): 1063.
43 Ibid at *77.*
44 Navajo Nation v. U.S. Forest Service, 535 F.3d 1058 (9th Cir. 2008), cert. denied, 129 S. Ct. 2763 (2009).
45 Wallace v. Jaffree, 472 U.S. 38, 50 (1985): 50.
46 James Dohnalek, "Native American Religious Accommodations, National Parks, and the Cutter Test," 15 *University of St. Thomas Law Journal* 15 (2019): 715.
47 Jason Gubi, "The Religious Freedom Restoration Act and Protection of Native American Religious Practices," *The Modern American* (Fall 2008): 74.
48 Volstead Act, ch. 85, tit. II, sec. 3, 41 Stat. 305 (1920).
49 Employment Division, Department of Human Resources of Oregon v. Smith, 494 U.S. 872 (1990).
50 Ibid at 879.
51 Prince v. Massachusetts, 321 U.S. 158 (1944).
52 United States v. Lee, 455 U.S. 252 (1982).
53 Gillette v. United States, 401 U.S. 437 (1971).
54 Employment Division v. Smith, 494 U.S. 872 (1990): 888.
55 Ibid.
56 Brian Miller, "The Age of RFRA," *Forbes* (November 16, 2018). https://www.forbes.com/sites/briankmiller/2018/11/16/the-age-of-rfra/#49c44ac577ba.
57 Clinton Oxford, "Failing Native American Prisoners: RLUIPA & the Dilution of Strict Scrutiny," *Georgia Journal of Law & Modern Critical Race Perspective* 9 (2017): 208.
58 42 U.S.C. §§ 2000bb–2000bb-4.
59 U.S. Senate, Roll Call Vote No. 331, 103d Cong. (October 27, 1993), http://www.senate.gov/legislative/LIS/roll_call_lists/roll_call_vote_cfm.cfm?&congress=103&session=1&vote=00331.

60 546 U.S. 424.
61 Id. at 427.
62 Amanda Holpuch, "Religious Freedom Restoration Act: How a Legislative 'miracle' Got Discriminatory," *The Guardian* (April 2, 2015). https://www.theguardian.com/us-news/2015/apr/02/religious-freedom-restoration-history.
63 Ibid.
64 521 U.S. 507.
65 Bowers v. Hardwick, 478 U.S. 186 (1986).
66 Linda C. McClain, "From Romer v. Evans to United States v. Windsor: Law as a Vehicle for Moral Disapproval in Amendment 2 and the Defense of Marriage Act," *Duke Journal Gender Law & Policy* 20 (2013): 385.
67 Romer v. Evans, 517 U.S. 620 (1996).
68 539 U.S. 558.
69 Romer v. Evans, 517 U.S. 620: 651 (Scalia, J. dissenting).
70 Baehr v. Lewin, 74 Haw. 530 (1993).
71 Defense of Marriage Act (DOMA) of 1996, Pub. L. No. 104–199, 1996 U.S.C.C.A.N. (110 Stat.) 2419, invalidated by United States v. Windsor, 570 U.S. 744, 769–71 (2013).
72 Goodridge v. Department of Public Health, 798 N.E.2d 941 (Mass. 2003).
73 Varnum v. Brien, 763 N.W.2d 862 (Iowa 2009).
74 Brian K. Miller, "Reconciling Religious Freedom and LGBT Rights: The Perils and Promises of Masterpiece Cakeshop," *George Mason University Civil Rights Law Journal* 29 (2019): 274.
75 United States v. Windsor, 570 U.S. 744 (2013).
76 Obergefell v. Hodges, 135 S. Ct. 2584 (2015).
77 Brian K. Miller, "Reconciling Religious Freedom and LGBT Rights: The Perils and Promises of Masterpiece Cakeshop," *George Mason University Civil Rights Law Journal* 29 (2019): 245
78 Ibid at 255.
79 Brian K. Miller, "Reconciling Religious Freedom and LGBT Rights: The Perils and Promises of Masterpiece Cakeshop," *George Mason University Civil Rights Law Journal* 29 (2019): 255.
80 Ira Lupu, "Moving Targets: Obergefell, Hobby Lobby, and the Future of LGBT Rights," *Alabama Civil Rights & Civil Liberties Law Review* 7 (2015): 59.
81 Burwell v. Hobby Lobby, 573 U.S. 682 (2014).
82 Michael Helfand, "A New Age for Religious Minorities?," *University of Illinois Law Review Online* (2017): 13.
83 Michael A. Helfand, "Identifying Substantial Burdens," *Illinois Law Review* (2016): 1778.
84 City of Boerne v. Flores, 521 U.S. 507 (1997): 508.
85 Martha Swartz, "Justice Scalia Was Right: We've Gone Too Far in Protecting the Exercise of Religious Beliefs," *Temple Law Review Online* 89 (2017): 22.
86 United States v. Ballard, 322 U.S. 78 (1944).
87 United States v. Ballard, 322 U.S. 78 (1944): 93.
88 Nathan S. Chapman, "Adjudicating Religious Sincerity," *Washington Law Review*92 (2017): 1188.
89 573 U.S. 682, 771 (Ginsburg, J., dissenting).

90 Luke Goodrich, "Sex, Drugs, and Eagle Feathers: An Empirical Study of Federal Religious Freedom Cases," *Utah Law Faculty Scholarship* (2017): 67.
91 Sarah Masslin Nir, "Native Americans Finds Interesting Ally in N.J. Fight: Trump Administration," *New York Times* (April 22, 2019). Available at https://www.nytimes.com/2019/04/22/nyregion/ramapough-lenape-indians-mahwah-nj.html.
92 Navajo Nation v. U.S. Forest Service, 535 F.3d 1058 (9th Cir. 2008), cert. denied, 129 S. Ct. 2763 (2009); Snoqualmie Indian Tribe v. F.E.R.C., 545 F.3d 1207, 1210 (9th Cir. 2008).
93 Ellen Gilmer, "Pipeline Foes Pivot to Religious Freedom," *Energy & Economics News* (Feburary 9, 2017). https://www.eenews.net/stories/1060049828.
94 Allison M. Dussias, "Friend, Foe, Frenemy: The United States and American Indian Religious Freedom," *Denver University Law Review* 90 (2012): 401.

Bibliography

American Indian Religious Freedom Act Amendments of 1994, Public Law 103-344, codified at 42 U.S.C. § 1996 a (b)(1) (1994).

American Indian Religious Freedom Act, 42 U.S.C. (1978), §1996.

Baehr v. Lewin, 74 Haw. 530 (1993).

Bowen v. Roy. 476 U.S. 693 (1986).

Bowers v. Hardwick, 478 U.S. 186 (1986).

Brady, Joel. ""Land Is Itself a Sacred, Living Being": Native American Sacred Site Protection on Federal Public Lands Amidst the Shadows of Bear Lodge." *American Indian Law Review* 24, no. 1 (1999): 153.

Bravin, Jess. "Trump Administration Backs Baker Who Refused to Make Wedding Cake for Gay Couple." *The Wall Street Journal*. Dow Jones & Company, September 8, 2017. https://www.wsj.com/articles/trump-administration-backs-baker-who-refused-to-make-wedding-cake-for-gay-couple-1504843234.

Burwell v. Hobby Lobby, 573 U.S. 682 (2014).

Carpenter, Kristen A. "A Property Rights Approach to Sacred Sites Cases: Asserting a Place for Indians as Nonowners." *UCLA L. Rev.* 52 (2004): 1061.

Chapman, Nathan S. "Adjudicating Religious Sincerity." *Wash. L. Rev.* 92 (2017): 1185.

Church of Lukumi Babalu Aye, Inc v. Hialeah508 U.S. 520 (1993).

City of Boerne v. Flores, 521 U.S. 507 (1997).

Cleary, Thomas. "In impartiality we trust: a commentary on government aid and involvement with religion." In *S. New Eng. Roundtable Symp. LJ*, vol. 2, p. 113. 2007.

Davidson, Donald. "Essays on Actions and Events." *Oxford: Clarendon*, 2001. https://bibliotecamathom.files.wordpress.com/2012/10/essays-on-actions-and-events.pdf.

Davis, Kenneth C. "America's true history of religious tolerance." *Smithsonian Magazine* (2010).

Defense of Marriage Act of 1996, Pub. L. No. 104-199, 1996 U.S.C.C.A.N. (110 Stat.) 2419.

Dohnalek, James. "Native American Religious Accommodations, National Parks, and the Cutter Test." *U. St. Thomas LJ* 15 (2018): 715.

Dussias, Allison M. "Friend, Foe, Frenemy: The United States and American Indian Religious Freedom." *Denv. UL Rev.* 90 (2012): 347.

Eakin, Britain. "Tribe Denied Religious Injunction to Dakota Access Pipeline." *CNS*, March 7, 2017. https://www.courthousenews.com/tribe-denied-religious-injunction-dakota-access-pipeline/.

Ellen Gilmer, "Pipeline foes pivot to religious freedom," *Energy & Economics News* (February, 9, 2017). https://www.eenews.net/stories/1060049828.

Employment Division, Department of Human Resources of Oregon v. Smith, 494 U.S. 872 (1990).

Establishment Clause Unaffected, U.S.C. 42, §§ 2000bb -- 2000bb-4.

Gillette v. United States, 401 U.S. 437 (1971).

Gilmer, Ellen. "Pipeline Foes Pivot to Religious Freedom." *E & E News*, (2017). https://www.eenews.net/stories/1060049828.

Gonzales v. O Centro Espirita Beneficente Uniao Do Vegetal. 546 U.S. 418 (2006).

Goodrich, Luke W., and Rachel N. Busick. "Sex, Drugs, and Eagle Feathers: An Empirical Study of Federal Religious Freedom Cases." *Utah Law Faculty Scholarship.*

Goodridge v. Department of Public Health, 440 Mass. 309 (2003).

Gubi, Jason. "The religious freedom restoration Act and protection of Native American religious practices.", 73-79. Mod. Am. 4 (2008): 73.

Helfand, Michael A. "Identifying Substantial Burdens." *U. Ill. L. Rev.* (2016): 1771.

Helfand, Michael. "A New Age for Religious Minorities." *U. Ill. L. Rev.* Online (2017): 1.

Higham, Carol L. "Christian missions to american indians." In *Oxford Research Encyclopedia of American History.* 2016.

Holpuch , Amanda. "Religious Freedom Restoration Act: How a Legislative 'Miracle' Got Discriminatory." *The Guardian.* Guardian News and Media, April 2, 2015. https://www.theguardian.com/us-news/2015/apr/02/religious-freedom-restoration-history.

Johnson v. M'Intosh, 21 U.S. 543 (1823).

Lawrence v Texas. 539 U.S. 558 (2003).

Lupu, Ira C. "Moving Targets: Obergefell, Hobby Lobby, and the Future of LGBT Rights." *Ala. CR & CLL Rev.* 7 (2015): 1.

Lyng v. Northwest Indian Cemetery Protective Association 485 U.S. 439 (1988).

Masterpiece Cakeshop v. Colo. Civil Rights, 138 S. Ct. (2018).

McClain, Linda C. "From Romer v. Evans to United States v. Windsor Law as a Vehicle for Moral Disapproval in Amendment 2 and the Defense of Marriage Act." *Duke J. Gender L. & Pol'y* 20 (2012).

Miller, Brian K. "Reconciling Religious Freedom and LGBT Rights: The Perils and Promises of Masterpiece Cakeshop." *Geo. Mason UCRLJ* 29 (2018): 245.

Miller, Brian. "The Age of Rfra." *Forbes*. Forbes Magazine, November 16, 2018. https://www.forbes.com/sites/briankmiller/2018/11/16/the-age-of-rfra/#49c44ac577ba.

Navajo Nation v. U.S. Forest Service, 535 F.3d 1058 (2008).

Nir, Sarah Maslin. "Native Americans Find Surprising Ally IN N.J. Fight: Trump Administration." *The New York Times*. The New York Times, April 22, 2019. https://www.nytimes.com/2019/04/22/nyregion/ramapough-lenape-indians-mahwah-nj.html.

Obergefell v. Hodges, 135 S. Ct. 2584(2015).

Office of Indian Affairs. "Governing the Court of Indian Offenses," 17 U.S.C 105 (1883).

Oxford, Clinton. "Failing Native American Prisoners: RLUIPA & the Dilution of Strict Scrutiny." *Geo. JL & Mod.* Critical Race Persp. 9 (2017): 203.

Pommersheim, Frank. "Broken landscape: Indians, Indian tribes, and the constitution." *Oxford University Press*, 2009.

Prince v. Massachusetts, 321 U.S. 158 (1944).

Protection of Land Use as Religious Exercise Act, 42 U.S.C., § 2000cc(a)(1) .

Romer v. Evans, 517 U.S. 620 (1996).

Roundtable Symp. LJ, vol. 2, p. 113. 2007.

Sequoyah v. Tennessee Valley Authority, 620 F.2d 1159 (1980).

Sherbert v. Verner. 374 U.S. 398 (1963).

Snoqualmie Indian Tribe v. F.E.R.C., 545 F.3d 1207, 1210 (2008).

Stern, Marc. "Faith under Democracy: What Have Religious Believers Gained - What Have They Lost" *Georgetown Journal of Law & Public Policy* 1 (2002): 249.

Swartz, Martha. "Justice Scalia Was Right: We've Gone Too Far in Protecting the Exercise of Religious Beliefs." *Temp. L. Rev.* Online 89 (2017): 22.

Taylor, Scott A. "The Native American Law Opinions of Judge Noonan: Do We Hear the Faint Voice of Bartolome De Las Casas." *U. St. Thomas LJ* 1 (2003): 148.

United States Senate. "Roll Call VOTE 103rd Congress - 1ST Session." *U.S. Senate*. January 16, 2020. http://www.senate.gov/legislative/LIS/roll_call_lists/roll_call_vote_cfm.cfm?&congress=103&session=1&vote=00331.

United States v. Ballard, 322 U.S. 78 (1944).

United States v. Lee, 455 U.S. 252 (1982).

United States v. Top Sky, 547 F.2d 486 (1976).

United States v. Windsor, 570 U.S. 744 (2013).

Varnum v. Brien, 763 N.W.2d 862 (2009).

Volstead Act, ch. 85, tit. II, sec. 3, 41 Stat. 305 (1920).

Wallace v. Jaffree, 472 U.S. 38, 50 (1985).

Washington, George. "Founders Online: From George Washington to the Hebrew Congregation in Newport ..." *National Archives and Records Administration*.

Wilson v. Block, 708 F.2d 735 (1983).

Winsor, Morgan. "Over 380,000 gallons of oil spill from Keystone pipeline in North Dakota." *ABC News 1* (2019).
Wisconsin v. Yoder. 406 U.S. 205 (1972).

Part IV. Religious Freedom v. Equality in American Culture

12. *Equal Protection Excess: Visualizing the Effects of Christian Nationalism*

Diana Isabel Martínez, Jamila Cupid, and Robert Mejia

Images of mothers and children detained near the northern Mexico border have circulated widely. These photographs capture objects—shoes, pads on the floor, aluminum foil blankets, fencing, overcrowding, and waiting—that break from the visual commonplaces of human decency. Over time, a plethora of newspaper and magazine articles have reported that detention centers are overcrowded and constitute unsanitary living conditions. Detention centers, such as the one in McCallen, Texas, are "notorious for putting detainees in cage-like rooms," "separating parents from their children," and withholding medical care from ill and dying patients. Immigrants know this facility as " 'the icebox' and 'the dog pound.' "[1] Given the ubiquity of these short- and long-term centers scattered around the U.S., the government is creating generational trauma that will have profound impacts later in life.[2] The effects of being separated from one's family, having to endure abuse, neglect, and assault, will affect entire populations extensively, and it occurs with the full force of the law.

These horrific conditions expose the human rights abuses that occur with support of the law. Though the policies affecting migrants have long existed, the circumstances described above became more publicly known after the 2016 election, particularly how many protections—such as due process and equal protection under the law—that might have been perceived as a hallmark of the system of government in place in the U.S. quickly and seamlessly eroded under the new administration. The images of migrants in detention centers, their stories, and the effects of the application of the law, are readily available in plain sight through a quick google search. Regardless of which organization takes the picture, it is clear that people are held in overcrowded places without access to basic sanitation, endure physical and sexual assault, forced sterilization, with some even losing their lives. The images are pervasive, easily shared on social media, and they present the public with an obligation to help the people who are, quite literally, trapped in cages. The images also perform a public display of law enforcement, of enacting a "zero tolerance" policy toward immigration patterns.

Popular magazines, such as *Time*, responded to this humanitarian crisis by taking an image of a crying toddler looking up at a border agent arresting her mother and superimposing the crying toddler next to the president.[3] Responses to these images have varied somewhat, depending on how a particular audience chooses to interpret the images. Whether these photographs move people out of outrage or satisfaction, they are significant in that they have stirred the country into a conversation about the nature of immigration.

What these images help to illuminate is that, while the law allegedly aims to protect the nation's citizens, in practice, citizenship provides more rights for some and not others. Hector Amaya's term "citizenship excess" explains the excesses or slippages in meaning through the additional benefits that citizens enjoy and "deficiencies" imposed on people who, despite having a claim to a territory, fall outside of the ruling class' definition of citizen.[4] Amaya's work discusses Mexican nationals who never migrated but lost rights due to the 1848 Treaty of Guadalupe Hidalgo despite meeting the criteria of citizenship as established by the 14th Amendment. This differential treatment highlights the uneven distribution of legal protection—not on the basis of citizenship—but rather because the law is designed to benefit those with citizenship excess: white, male, Christian. The effects of this phenomenon are visible in the clash between due process, equal protection, and religious freedom.

Using Amaya's concept of citizenship excess, this project contends that a link exists between excess, due process, equal protection, and religious freedom, one that directly supports Christian nationalism, and the elements of this relationship may be derived through publicly observable images of immigration. To prove our claim, this essay will identify elements of the visual rhetoric that, although identifying human rights abuses, frame immigrants as deficient, how these deficiencies resonate with Christian nationalism, and result in the perpetuation of citizenship excess (that then ties in with an excess in due process and equal protection law). The material consequences of Christian nationalism emphasizing these deficiencies over human rights abuses, not only highlights the tension between ethics and the law; a critical visual analysis of images of immigrant children illustrates contradictory rhetorical aesthetics that enable these images to stand in for Christian nationalists *and* human rights activists, which highlights the importance of reckoning with how visual rhetoric exposes the limits of legal imagination and the implications this holds for those in "deficiency." By combining Roland Barthes' insights on how the photograph both resonates with and resists cultural expectations, Kenneth Burke's exploration of the intertextual nature of representation, and Michael Lechuga's analysis of representations of migrant vernacular discourses, we show how representations of immigrant suffering legitimate the human rights abuses of the law and uphold the politics of Christian nationalism.

Overlapping Spaces of Latina/o/x Studies, Immigration, and Religion

Studies on immigration, violence on the border, and visuality explore the complex practices that disempower communities and make their experiences known, and the literature emphasizes the need for more work in this area. E. Johanna Hartelius' edited collection accounts for the discursive elements of U.S. immigration and attends to the language in immigration discourse and the standpoint from whom this discourse is communicated.[5] J. David Cisneros discusses important issues such as what it means to say that the border crossed us, instead of the popular discourse that Mexican immigrants crossed over to the United States.[6] The discursive effects of the border results in material, and often deadly, consequences. Nina Maria Lozano explores the gendered violence on the border,[7] Leandra Hinojosa Hernández and Sarah De Los Santos Upton analyze gendered violence in the Américas,[8] and Michelle A. Holling adds to this conversation of feminicidios and violence.[9] Unrelated to Latina/o/x immigration, Robert Hariman and John Louis Lucaites' analyze Nick Ut's 1972 photograph of a nine-year-old girl fleeing napalm to illustrate what makes photographs iconic.[10] Kevin Michael DeLuca discusses the confrontational and unorthodox rhetoric of environmental activists, arguing that images can be generative and shift public understanding of issues.[11] These studies reveal the porosity of the visual medium and the varied discursive elements of images that go beyond the simplistic representations of migration in the media. What is missing is an analysis of how these images serve as a means of making laws public, and this chapter considers the intersection between equal protection and religious freedom in relationship with Christian nationalism.

Christian nationalism refers to an American ideology that "idealizes and advocates a fusion of Christianity and American civic life."[12] The intent of this fusion is, as Philip Gorski argues, "to make citizenship in one the mark of citizenship in the other, to purge all those who lack the mark, and to expand the borders of the kingdom as much as possible, by violent means if necessary."[13] Though Gorski cautions that Christian nationalism ought to be understood as distinct from civil religion—as civil religions "recognize the importance of an institutional separation between church and state"—civil religionists believe that "it is of vital importance" for the borders of church and state to overlap.[14] What this means in the U.S.-context is that Christian nationalism benefits from the political and legal victories of American civil religionists.

Indeed, constitutional protections that should ostensibly apply to all peoples (citizens and non-citizens alike), such as the establishment and free exercise clause, have been inconsistently applied, often contingent upon the religious affiliation of the affected parties. As Ruth Bader Ginsburg argued in her dissent of *Burwell v. Hobby Lobby Stores, Inc.* (2014), the courts uneven application of the establishment and free exercise clause means that particular religious affiliations (i.e., Christian nationalism) affect the interpretation and application of the law—such as freedom of speech, equal protection, and due process—resulting in the superseding of the rights of those who do not belong to that faith system.[15] This is all to say that Christian nationalism serves as the standard by which populations are measured in relation to the distribution of political, economic, and social benefits of citizenship (i.e., citizenship excess). Those groups which are categorically denied membership in Christian nationalism are defined as deficient. This is particularly true of Latin American immigrants.

What this discussion on the relationship between Christian nationalism and the law illustrates is that the protections offered by the First, Fifth, and Fourteen Amendment are not guaranteed to bodies deemed having citizenship deficiencies. Amaya discusses how the law has helped to uphold policies and the constitutionality of laws that have worked to perpetuate racism.[16] This is further illustrated in *Brandenburg v. Ohio*, which upheld the freedom of speech rights of the KKK; while seemingly a treatise on the constitutional value of speech, it also codified spaces for hate speech to occur. It is no surprise then that vagueness in the law or the use of abstractions such as "speech" can be manipulated, and this is the case in conceptions of naturalization, immigration, and citizenship. Some of the deficiencies of citizenship are readily available in the "conflicted jurisprudence" regarding "undocumented immigrants' protection under the First Amendment."[17] Gabriella M. D'Agostini states:

> A few judicial opinions have found that the First Amendment covers undocumented immigrants, arguing that denying them this protection contravenes the intent behind the Equal Protection principle. But the Supreme Court has

> at least implied that the First Amendment does not apply to undocumented immigrants by interpreting the text of "the people" in certain amendments as meaning strictly U.S. citizens.[18]

In other words, citizens have the right to hate speech, as evidenced by legal jurisprudence, green card holders have limited free speech access (as they ultimately cannot vote), and undocumented immigrants speak at their own risk with no guaranteed protections.

Beyond uncertain boundaries of jurisdiction, migrant bodies experience vulnerabilities ripe for human rights violations that are possible within legal means. Barbara A. Frey and X. Kevin Zhao examine the human rights implications of immigration laws and their enforcement in the United States; they explain that "the use of deportation and mandatory detention against noncitizens" as not "the criminalization *of* human rights violations, but criminalization *as* a human rights violation."[19] Claiming that international law generally considers citizens and noncitizens as deserving of "general equality," the practice of "mandatory detention violates the non-discrimination norm emanating from international law."[20] One way that this issue entered legal discourse was through the concept of "aggravated felony," which began through the Anti-Drug Abuse Act of 1988 that allowed for deportations based on "serious crimes such as murder and the trafficking of drugs or weapons," and has expanded to include nonviolent offenses.[21]

The trend of trampling on migrants' human rights has gone as far-reaching as entering sacred spaces. D'Agostini traces the history of ICE, which was established by the Homeland Security Act of 2002 for "identifying, apprehending, and removing noncitizens from the United States when they violate U.S. immigration law," and how this history also includes the tactic of "immigration raids, also known as immigration sweeps, to apprehend large groups of undocumented immigrants at certain locations."[22] These strategies, D'Agostini notes, were amplified through the 45th administration's executive order, most commonly known as the "zero-tolerance" enforcement of immigration law.[23] Despite internal policies stating "that officers should avoid apprehending undocumented immigrants at 'sensitive locations,' such as schools, hospitals, places of worship, or places of civil ceremonies," ICE officers have done just that.[24] Are there ever any sacred spaces for immigrants and their citizen allies to enjoy? If not, it seems that by extension, citizens' "excess" is trampled on for some by the state, and therein lies the judicial possibility. Exploring the excesses enjoyed by citizens who attend religious gatherings and the deficiencies and uncertainties evident in the law, it is necessary to consider how these practices are articulated in publicly available discourse, particularly how they are perpetuated visually.

Citizenship Excess v. Deficiencies and Equal Protection/ Christian Nationalism v. Human Rights Abuses

While the law most obviously offers a discourse for interpreting acts, so too do photographic images offer discursive resources for thinking through the legality of events. Photographs can do this by attracting attention and stirring emotions through violating reality, visual metaphor, parody, and point of view.[25] As Jonathan Crary argues, particular visual regimes govern not just how an image should be constructed but also the ideological effects of that which is being represented.[26] As it pertains to Christian nationalism, the sanctity of the child *and* the responsibility of the parent stands front and center. The consequence of this centering children is perhaps most profoundly felt in humanitarian crises, as it reduces the complexity of immigration to a problem of parenting choices. Since immigrants are often denied any other form of communication, the *image* literally stands in for *and* judges them. The effect of this photographic displacement is that the image speaks for the individual and invites the viewer to pass judgment, potentially silencing the photographed individual in the process.[27] The semiotic consequence of this photographic displacement is that the producer of the signifier (the photograph) often carries more communicative power than the individual captured within the image (the referent), and renders some individuals as undeserving of the rights and privileges of citizenship excess.

Just as not all citizens are recognized equally under the law,[28] from the perspective of the photographer, not all "referents" are created equal as some possess the communicative capacity to be rhetorically framed in ways amenable to the ideological interests of the photographer. As Rakiya Omaar and Alex de Waal argue: "The camera can't lie, we are told. But anyone who has watched a Western film crew in an African famine will know just how much effort it takes to compose the 'right' image. Photogenic starving children are hard to find, even in Somalia."[29] If, as Messaris states, "in a medium that can reproduce the look of reality, the best way to get attention is to violate it,"[30] which occurs when an "unexpected, odd, or confusing image" is presented to an audience to grab their attention,[31] this means that the representation of humanitarian crises often constitutes the violation of the very subjects for whom we are purported to be caring for: "Reduced to nameless extras in the shadows behind Western aid workers or disaster tourists, the grieving, hurting and humiliated human beings are not asked if they want to be portrayed in this degrading way."[32] This, of course, begs the question of how do we represent the disaster without reproducing the disaster?[33]

This critical visual analysis puts the law and what is legal on display, exhibits elements in conjunction with Christian nationalism, but also points to moments of possibility. Images operate as a composite of discrete rhetorical elements that can be assembled and reassembled towards particular political and legal ends.[34] Dissecting these discrete elements means analyzing what is innate to the image (punctum), the cultural resonance of the image (studium), and how the image circulates.[35] We are compelled by the terminology of the punctum and studium as means for thinking through how a single photographic detail (i.e., the punctum) can operate metonymically, which "paradoxically, while remaining a 'detail,' it fills the whole picture."[36] Though Barthes believed these "details" to just happen to be there and that it was "not possible to posit a rule of connection between the *studium* and the *punctum*,"[37] we agree with the criticism that there is nothing innate to the image that escapes culture.[38] As Laura Mulvey argues, images pose "questions of the ways the unconscious (formed by the dominant order) structure ways of seeing and pleasure in looking."[39] So though photographic accidents may occur (i.e., an element of the image that evaded the awareness of the photographer), the content (what was captured) and form (how it was captured) always reveal the ideological choices made by the photographer.

This recognition of harm and understanding of due process is no less true of the now-iconic 2018 image of a two-year old Honduran child crying as her mother is being searched by the U.S. Border Patrol. Though the child was one of many who were stopped by US Border Patrol agents on June 12 as they crossed the Rio Grande into Texas, the image of this child looking up in agony as her mother is searched by an ICE officer became "the face of 'zero tolerance.' "[40] Moore would receive the 2018 World Press Photo of the year, and the image would become "the human face" of the 45th administration's " 'zero-tolerance' immigration policy."[41] Since Moore took other pictures that night, including several more of the child, the photograph warrants further analysis to better understand the rhetorical work of the photograph's studium and punctum. This is especially pertinent for, as our analysis discusses, the form and content of the iconic image would transform as it circulated.

If, as Hariman and Lucaites argue, an image obtains iconic status when it appears in "print, electronic, or digital media that are widely recognized and remembered, are understood to be representations of historically significant events, activate strong emotional identification or response, and are reproduced across a range of media genres or topics,"[42] then the following analysis is that of understanding what happens to Latinx suffering when it is made iconic. How suffering is imagined matters for the criminal justice system is built upon the regulation of harm. The legal system does not minimize harm, but rather serves as a political mechanism for transferring suffering and pleasure from some bodies to others. As Lisa Cacho argues, the disparity in burden of proof thresholds between whites and people of color illustrates "how the criminal justice system has not only conferred a permanent victim status to whiteness but in doing so also demands violence against the black or brown body."[43] Thus, how harm is imagined matters. Accordingly, our analysis is structured as follows: (1) we consider a less circulated image of the humanitarian crisis to illustrate why alternative representations failed to resonate with the U.S. cultural imaginary regarding immigration; (2) we analyze how the now-iconic image of the two-year-old Honduran girl resonated with this U.S. cultural imaginary; (3) we demonstrate how the image transformed for a final time, when its iconicity was cemented on the cover of *Time* magazine.

Taking the Picture: The Translation of Suffering and Christian Nationalism

As argued earlier, Christian nationalism carries with it legal and political benefits and as such operates as the de facto civil religion of the United States. Even if one does not identify as a Christian nationalist, the cultural patterns of innocence, suffering, and salvation, are a part of mainstream American culture. This phenomenon is apparent in the representation of the Southern border immigration crisis as illustrated by the iconic image of the two-year-old Honduran girl crying as her mother is detained by U.S. border patrol. But first, it is necessary to examine the events leading to the selection of the iconic image as well as the range of available images that were not selected by media outlets to represent the Southern border immigration crisis.

On June 12, as border patrol agents were searching Central American refugees before putting them into buses to be sent to detention centers, Pulitzer Prize-winning photographer John Moore, who has spent a decade covering immigration, was present taking photographs for Getty Images.[44] Though Moore took numerous pictures that night, his attention was captured by a mother and her child, who were the last to be processed for detainment.[45] As he watched this family, the agents had the mother put down her daughter so that they could search the woman against a vehicle.[46] At that moment, as the mother was being searched, the two-year-old Honduran girl broke into tears.[47] Moore felt that what he was witnessing would transform popular understanding of the government's family separation policy; since the searches were taking "only a few seconds," Moore quickly dropped to his knees to photograph the girl at her level.[48] Recounting these events—and comparing them against alternative images captured—matters for our understanding of how a humanitarian crisis is transformed into terms amenable to Christian nationalism at the moment of its being photographed, and the consequences of this transformation.

As noted above, Moore is a Pulitzer Prize-winning photographer who has spent the past ten years covering immigration. Indeed, just the day prior, on June 11, Moore had taken photographs of Central American refugees departing an immigration-processing center in McAllen, Texas. Notably, several of Moore's photos from June 11 included families with their children, including one of a man holding a child as he walks, looking down dejected (see Figure 12.1).[49] Likewise, the night of June 12, Moore had taken several other photographs of parents with their children, including one of the two-year-old Honduran girl being held by her mother.[50] Each of these photographs captures the harms of the humanitarian crisis occurring at the U.S.-Mexico border. Yet, it is the iconic image that matters for it is the one that is "widely recognized and remembered" as the most powerful representation of historical events.[51] This means that images can operate metonymically to transform existing symbolic structures or synecdochally to sustain existing symbolic structures.[52] The event (i.e., the humanitarian crisis at the U.S.-Mexico border) exists. What this section will illustrate is how Christian nationalism intersects with the operationalization of the law—not just a reiteration of the law, but how it is carried out in practice and why. The selection of which image to remember the event is indicative of these principles.

The first image, for the sake of our analysis, is of a man carrying a child as they depart an immigration-processing center in McAllen, Texas (see Figure 12.1). A reverse google image search returns only fifteen uses of this image: CNN, Chicago Tribune, San Diego Union Tribune, Getty Images, and a handful of other smaller media outlets. The caption for this image provides no information about the individuals photographed, only that: "Central American immigrant families depart ICE Custody, pending fugue immigration court hearings on June 11, 2018 in McAllen, Texas. Thousands of undocumented immigrants continue to cross into the U.S., despite the current administration's recent 'zero tolerance' approach to immigration policy."[53] Viewers have no information on the relationship between any of the individuals captured by this photograph.

When analyzing this image, we must keep in tension that which is brought by the event itself (the punctum) and that which is brought by the photographer (the studium). Barthes believed that the punctum operated as a "partial object [and thus] to give examples of punctum is [. . .] to give myself up."[54] Though Barthes believed the punctum to operate on a private

Figure 12.1: Image of man carrying child. McAllen, TX, June 11, 2018. (Photo Title: "Undocumented Immigrants Go To Court For Deportation Hearings." Photo Credits: John Moore/Getty Images News/Getty Images.)

personal level, understanding which "partial objects" resonate, and which don't, matters for as Stuart Hall argued, the resonance of a message, in our case this image, is contingent upon the relation of the relative subject position of the viewer vis-à-vis the message and message sender.[55] In this case, though Moore is a talented photographer, bending the punctum of this image into terms amenable to the tastes of his Christian nationalist audience would have been difficult. By the punctum, we mean those elements that are beyond the control of the photographer. This daytime photograph of refugees dejectedly leaving an immigration-processing center does not resonate with the U.S. cultural imaginary regarding immigration as something that occurs at an unincorporated national border. Likewise, neither does the crowd of tired, dejected men resonate with images of Central American men as violent criminals—which alongside Latin lovers are the only roles granted Latinos in American culture.[56] What Moore attempts to capture and emphasize with this photograph is the lone child. Nonetheless, this child resists being transformed into a studium, for the child appears to refuse to play the role of a docile victim: this child stares directly at the camera. Though it is difficult to discern what emotions the child may have been experiencing at this moment, the ambiguity of this glance is precisely the point: it resists easy translation into terms amenable to the U.S. cultural imaginary. Further emphasizing the photograph's "difficulty," it is taken at a slight leftward tilt, likely a byproduct of attempting to take a picture as one is moving in the middle of a crowd.

The combined effect of this photograph in terms of what it captures (i.e., punctum), and how that punctum resists easy translation into the studium, means that ultimately a Christian nationalist ideology rendered the image illegible to mainstream journalistic and news reading audiences. The fourteenth amendment makes a distinction between the due process protections afforded to rights versus privileges.[57] As non-citizens, the photographed individuals have limited access to the due process protections afforded to rights—for even refugee claims are contingent upon being recognized as a refugee.[58] This means that the due process protections afforded to non-citizens operate in line with the comparatively weaker protections offered to privileges. A defiant child being carried by a man does not fit within the U.S. cultural imaginary regarding what constitutes a legitimate victim, and thus, a refugee. The deficiency of citizenship goes unquestioned in this image. As illegitimate victims, the purchase of their citizenship is limited to that of their home nation.

Becoming an Icon: Christian Nationalism and the Distillation of Suffering

If Christian nationalism found the other images to be lacking in acceptable suffering—and thus undeserving of legal protection—this begs the question of what form of migrant suffering would be found amenable and to what ends. Because Christian nationalism defines citizenship in terms of one's ethnic and religious status, the legal protections offered by citizenship are already categorically denied to migrants. The legal prospects of migrants are already determined in advanced—they do not belong, they are not getting asylum. This means that, to be legible to Christian nationalism, the selected image must capture not what it means to be a citizen but what it means to be a refugee.

The second image for our analysis, that of the now-iconic two-year-old Honduran girl, fits firmly within the U.S. cultural imaginary. In contrast to the photograph of the child being carried by a man (see Figure 12.1), a reverse google image search returns over 1,000 uses of this two-year old's image (see Figure 12.2). Though not necessarily unique for Moore's photographs, the caption for this image is heavily detailed and includes information that is useful for the photograph's subsequent transformation into an icon:

> MCALLEN, TX - JUNE 12: A two-year-old Honduran asylum seeker cries as her mother is searched and detained near the U.S.-Mexico border on June 12,

> 2018 in McAllen, Texas. The asylum seekers had rafted across the Rio Grande from Mexico and were detained by U.S. Border Patrol agents before being sent to a processing center for possible separation. Customs and Border Protection (CBP) is executing the Trump administration's "zero tolerance" policy towards undocumented immigrants. U.S. Attorney General Jeff Sessions also said that domestic and gang violence in immigrants' country of origin would no longer qualify them for political asylum status.[59]

Like the photograph (as we will argue), this caption resonates strongly with the Christian nationalist imaginary regarding Latin America, immigration, and citizenship: crossing a treacherous national border, subsequently being detained by border patrol, "legitimate" victims fleeing corrupt nations, and seeking salvation in the United States.

As with the caption for this image, there is much about the photograph's punctum that makes it amenable to the U.S. cultural imaginary. The mix of harsh lighting (likely from flashlights and patrol vehicles), and lack of daylight, has the effect of producing long, disorienting shadows that complement the sense of anxiety and fear that one would imagine the mother and child to be experiencing in this photograph. This framing helps to create a sense of

"All the News That's Fit to Print"

The New York T

VOL. CLXVII . . . No. 57,993 © 2018 The New York Times Company NEW YORK, THURSDAY, JUNE 14, 2018

Detained Near the Border

A 2-year-old Honduran girl cried as her mother was searched near the U.S.-Mexico border. The House speaker, Paul D. Ryan, told Republicans on Wednesday that his compromise on immigration legislation had the support of President Trump. Page A16.

Figure 12.2: Image of two-year-old Honduran asylum seeker crying as her mother is searched by an immigration officer. McAllen, TX, June 12, 2018. (Photo Title: Border Patrol Agents Detain Migrants Near US-Mexico Border. Photo Credit: John Moore/ Getty Images News/Getty Images.)

identification with the people in the photograph, but it is only the child who is featured as a whole person, and thus the only individual worthy of the privilege of legal protection. This work is by design, for though Moore had taken numerous photographs that night—most at standing level—he opted to kneel so that he could photograph this child at eye level[60]; in essence, Moore's decision encourages us to interpret the events from the perspective of this child. Hence, the emotional state of this child matters, for since she is positioned as the primary figure for identification, it is her tears that frame the events captured by the photograph. In essence, the child figures as a metaphor for understanding the humanitarian crisis at the border *and* the legal harm to be rectified. The problem, however, is that as Burke argues, metaphors easily slip into synecdoche (representation) or metonymy (reduction).[61] That is, in offering us an understanding of the humanitarian crisis from the perspective of a child, viewers may understand this perspective as one amongst many (synecdoche) or as a replacement for all other perspectives (metonymy). The differences between the two (synecdoche and metonymy) matter for synecdoche is inherently conservative, as it complements the viewers existing worldview, whereas metonymy is inherently transformative, as it replaces the viewers existing worldview.[62] To be clear, we should not understand conservative or transformative as corresponding to existing political parties but rather from the relative perspective of the viewer. A conservative reading would simply mean that it reinforces the worldviews of the viewer (whether Christian nationalist or otherwise), whereas as a transformative reading would simply mean that the view has changed (again, whether from a conservative or liberal perspective).

Whether one reads the image in synecdochal or metonymic terms hinges to some extent on the subject position of the viewer. As Hall argued, the interpretation of a message depends on the relative correspondence between the viewer and the message.[63] For audiences that lack a connection to Latinidad, the perspective of the child will dominate as the audience will lack the necessary cultural knowledge to fill in the gaps of the image: that is, they will be unable to fully appreciate and understand the perspective of the photographically incomplete mother. For audiences that possess a connection to Latinidad, they will be able to fill in these gaps and thus understand this image as one possible representation amongst many. The consequence is that this image may operate transformatively for non-Latinx audiences and conservatively for Latinx audiences. Since our interest is the effect that these images have on the political imaginary, this transformative effect matters for the framing of the humanitarian crisis in terms of a crying child certainly makes for an emotionally powerful image, but also has the effect of ironically depoliticizing the crisis. What this image suggests is that all the child needs is her mother (whom is being searched and unable to comfort her). Had the child not been crying, the image would have (sadly) lacked the same emotional weight for many audiences. This may be why what so many audiences have found detestable about the detention centers is not that refugees are being detained but rather that families are being separated. Indeed, Obama is considered more humanitarian than 45 precisely because Obama detained families together. Though this distinction matters—especially for the child—the fact remains that immigrants, whether refugees or not, should never be detained.

Being an Icon: The Christian Nationalist Essence of Suffering

The rhetoric of Christian nationalism reaches its logical conclusion in its iconic construction of what it means to be a refugee. As we have already argued, there were multiple images of migration that could have been selected to represent the southern border humanitarian crisis. The collective sum of these images articulate what Lechuga argues maps the

> multiple and decentered discursive praxis, performed and mediated, that (1) illuminates the landscapes of citizenship and belonging, (2) locates dominant discourses emerging from within those landscapes; and (3) draws attention to discourse that mobilizes a fluid and immediate critique against State power.[64]

These alternative images did not serve the interests of Christian nationalism, and thus the selected icon resonates with and is transformed to serve the purposes of the dominant discourse on immigration policy that emerged from this perspective. This is not to suggest that the crying child is compliant, as her tears are directed at the officer and not her mother; but as the image is transformed, the immigration policy that gave rise to this situation is erased and reduced to an interpersonal conflict between the girl and 45.

Indeed, a curious thing began to happen as the image of this two-year-old Honduran girl crying began to circulate: the picture began to lose its context. As the photograph circulated, more and more of the image became cropped. This decontextualization initially occurred through the circulating of the image without relevant caption detail. This practice frequently occurs as images become iconic, for as Cara Finnegan argues, captions can have the effect of removing images "from the realm of the iconic, universal suffering by giving us concrete information [that] locates the picture in space and time."[65] By extension, the removal or transformation of the caption can dislocate the picture from a specific time and space, thus enabling it to enter the realm of the iconic. The question of interest for us is not that the image became iconic, but rather how the essence of suffering was distilled as it became iconic. To answer this question, we must return to Barthes' notion of the punctum, that is, what it is about this image that pricked the audiences' interest.

As already noted, much about the punctum of the photograph of the two-year-old Honduran girl resonated with the U.S. cultural imaginary regarding immigration: the darkness, the disorienting lights, the reference to the U.S.-Mexico border, and more. There were, however, multiple variations of the image in circulation as Moore took several photos of the child that night. Some images featured the girl crying as her mother is being searched by a border patrol officer. Other photos, however, were taken with the girl crying as her mother appears to be talking with the border patrol officer; in those images, the mother and officer are only photographed from the waist down (so that we do not see their upper body). Regardless of the image used, however, the child always remained at the center. This illustrates that what resonated with the audience was not necessarily the act of detention but rather the crying child herself. Moore had hoped that the image of the child would serve as a vehicle for giving new meaning to our understanding of the family separation policy,[66] and the image succeeded more than he could have imagined. For in centering the girl as the focal point for our understanding of the family separation policy, Moore had transformed the humanitarian crisis from a geopolitical issue involving multiple countries, international and domestic policy, and affecting a range of communities and family configurations. In its place, Moore had transformed the humanitarian crisis into a parental problem: the care and comfort of this child. Though this child's care and comfort matters, the political implications of this framing have repercussions for both the child, her mother, and the larger refugee crisis.

This problem becomes clearer when we consider the exact moment in which the distillation of the image was completed, and the subsequent essence of suffering it offered: when an image of the crying two-year-old Honduran asylum seeker appeared on the June 2, 2018 cover of TIME magazine.[67] For the cover, all that remains of the original photograph is that of the crying child. Every other element of the original image is removed. In its place is a pure red background and an image of 45, emotionlessly staring down at the crying child, and the words "Welcome to America." The message is clear, 45 has made the child cry. Though the image presents 45 as the source of this child's tears, however, the proposed solution is both limited and ambiguous, contingent upon the interpretation of various audiences. A progressive reader may fill in the gaps and perceive 45 as a stand-in for family separation policies. A Christian nationalist, on the other hand, may fill in the gaps differently, and interpret this as an instance of child abandonment: where is the mother?

Regardless of the interpretation offered, however, the solution is this: comfort the child.

Because the comfort of the child—abstracted from the broader geopolitics of immigration—this image and its implicit solution offered represent a poverty of legal and political imagination. As mentioned, Obama's record on immigration is controversial for many Latinx organizations and communities. Obama is appreciated for his work in implementing the Deferred Action for Childhood Arrivals program (DACA), which enabled undocumented youth to remain in the United States as long as they met specific requirements (such as no criminal record) and continued to renew their registration with the federal government every two years. Nonetheless, Obama was also referred to as "the deporter-in-chief" by Janet Murguía, president of the National Council on La Raza (NCLR) due to the 2.8 million undocumented immigrants who were deported during his presidency (at the time, more immigrants were deported under his presidency than any other president).[68] Likewise, DACA was an expensive program for immigrants ($495 fee every two years), failed to provide a path to citizenship, had no enduring power (as it was an executive order), and worked to create a national registry that could be abused by subsequent presidents.[69] In essence, though DACA offered some relief for undocumented immigrants, it is flawed policy as it replaced one form of precarity with another. As it pertains to the *Time* magazine cover, by situating 45 as the reason for this child's tears, the solution proposed is a nostalgia for the policies of a prior administration that, though better, were legally and politically limited. Though liberal and conservative readers may desire different policies—those that allow undocumented immigrants to remain versus those that force undocumented immigrants to leave—the legal and political imaginary remains limited to one of keeping the child from crying. If the child's tears are stilled, whether through the reuniting families in detention centers, reinstating DACA (which has no path for citizenship), or deporting families together, as long as the child is not crying, then the humanitarian crisis fades from public consciousness.

Conclusion

The law is an interpretive document contingent upon the cultural imaginary of the state and its citizens. What constitutes a legitimate harm and adequate due process will vary according to what has been done and to whom.[70] The concept of citizenship excess, as coined by Amaya, offers a useful analytic for thinking through the legal and political consequences of this cultural imaginary. As Amaya argues, citizenship excess refers to those judiciary and extra-judiciary benefits conferred onto those who are recognized as legitimate citizens.[71] Though non-citizens are technically granted access to the same constitutional rights as citizens (such as due process and protection from theft, loss of life, and other harms) as long as non-citizens remain within the jurisdiction of the United States, the very right to be within U.S. jurisdiction is always precarious for non-citizens. This is especially so for undocumented immigrants, as to petition the courts for legal protection would necessarily mean to signal to the courts that one has violated the law (by definition of being undocumented). Similarly, the notion of citizenship excess can be applied to those who legally possess citizenship but are socially defined as conditional citizens by virtue of their distance from Christian nationalism. Examples of this differential treatment for those who are perceived as illegitimate citizens include: Racial profiling, stop and frisk, and laws such as Arizona SB 1070 (which allows law enforcement officers to demand proof of citizenship whenever an "an officer detains a person on suspicion of a state law crime [e.g., traffic stop]").[72] This means that though the law grants equal protection to citizens and non-citizens alike, non-citizens and "conditional" citizens alike are denied access to the benefits of citizenship excess.

This means that legal scholars must recognize how the imaginary, specifically the imaginary of Christian nationalism, affects legal and political decisions. That is, as we argue, we must understand how the notion of Christian nationalism refers to both a specific political movement as well as what Raymond Williams calls a structure of feeling that extends beyond the confines of a specific political movement.[73] By this, we mean that the iconography of Christian nationalism—white, Christian, sanctity of children, protestant work and family ethic, etc.—is so entrenched within the United States that one's claim to citizenship is to some extent modulated by one's proximity to the affective politics of Christian nationalism. Recognizing this means that it is not enough to analyze the judicial rhetoric of a particular law or policy, but we must also analyze those cultural forms that influence the interpretation of those laws and policies. Iconic images, we argue, are one such site where notions of citizenship, harms, due process, and other judicial concepts are made legible—and thus interpretable—for the U.S. public.

In making the argument that legal scholars must analyze cultural forms for their impact on our judicial imaginary, we have offered Barthes' notions of the punctum and studium, Burke's master tropes, and Lechuga's mapping of migrant vernacular discourses as useful analytical tools. Though we disagree with Barthes' assessment of the punctum as a personal, private response that operates beyond culture, we nonetheless find the punctum as a useful concept for understanding how the referent of a given photograph resonates with or resists the ideological interests of the photographer. Because the punctum exists at least partially beyond the control of the photographer, we must interrogate why certain representations can enter the realm of the iconic and others remain relegated to the realm of the exception. These are not innocent decisions, for as Finnegan argues, iconic images are those that can transcend space and time.[74] This means that those images—i.e., those images that lack the right punctum—are condemned to a specific context and denied the possibility of participating in a larger public debate. For the non-citizens and "illegitimate" citizens contained within the photograph, this has the effect of foreclosing their concerns from the cultural imaginary. This is because their interests are deemed so specific and unique that there is no meaningful contribution deemed to be made to larger (i.e., Christian nationalist) concerns. That said, such representation serves as a double-bind for, as we argue, the cost of becoming an icon means that, to be heard, marginalized populations must give up that which they hold dear: the two-year-old girl becomes an icon at that moment in which she loses her mother.

In conclusion, we have demonstrated that photographs play an essential role in the legal and political imaginary. The notion of harms and due process is core to the U.S. judicial system, but these legal concepts do not exist outside of the imaginary. Instead, what constitutes a legitimate harm and what constitutes adequate due process are contingent upon the state and public's ability to imagine the pain and suffering of another. Failing to take the imaginary seriously means that even progressive legal scholars will continue to operate in the realm of the possible; though some may interpret this as a pragmatic decision as it is better to make incremental change than none at all, as our analysis of the iconic image of the two-year-old Honduran girl demonstrates, these pragmatic decisions often resonate with Christian nationalism and thus are vulnerable to regressive politics. Likewise, the notion of citizenship excess—which refers to the unearned benefits of citizenship for white populations—reminds us that the things we are often told are not possible are in fact possible, for some. It is precisely because these things have proven to be possible for some that we should imagine them to be possible for all. Granting Moore the benefit of doubt, it is entirely possible that he genuinely believed that taking the photograph of this two-year-old Honduran girl would transform the law and policy governing the immigration debate. It did: family separation policies are no longer enforced, *except when such separation is "clearly necessary for the safety and well-being of the child"*[75]; which, consistent with our analysis regarding the racial political imaginary, is to say, it did not—deportations and family separations continue to this day.[76] This is no fault of the two-year-old Honduran girl. We wonder what possibilities might have emerged, however, had the image of the man carrying the child been allowed to circulate instead? What possibilities might emerge were we to share the hope of a child, starring at those who would stand in her *and* her family's way, when it appears as though all hope is lost.

Notes

1 Debbie Nathan, "A 5-Year-Old Girl in Immigrant Detention Nearly Died of an Untreated Ruptured Appendix," The Intercept, https://theintercept.com/2018/09/02/border-patrol-immigrant-detention-medical-neglect-texas/, para 3.
2 Benedict Carey, "Reuniting and Detaining Migrant Families Pose New Mental Health Risks," *New York Times*, https://www.nytimes.com/2018/06/22/health/migrant-families-immigration-detention.html.
3 The decision to refer to the previous president as 45 is a political decision in protest of the prior administration. Other scholarly works have done the same (e.g., Sarah De Los Santos Upton, Diana Isabel Bowen, and Leandra Hinojosa Hernández, "Nepantla Activism in *Braiding Borders + Trenzando Fronteras*," in *Latina/o/x Communication Studies: Theories, Methods, and* Practice, eds. Leandra Hinojosa Hernández, Diana I. Bowen, Sarah De Los Santos Upton, and Amanda R. Martinez (Lanham, MD: Lexington Books, 2019), 229–50.
4 Hector Amaya, *Citizenship Excess: Latinas/os, Media, and the Nation* (New York, NY: New York University Press, 2013).
5 E. Johanna Hartelius, *The Rhetorics of US Immigration: Identity, Community, Otherness* (University Park, PA: The Pennsylvania State University Press, 2015).
6 J. David Cisneros, *The Border Crossed Us: Rhetorics of Borders, Citizenship, and Latina/o Identity* (Tuscaloosa, AL: The University of Alabama Press, 2013).
7 Nina M. Lozano, *Not One More!: Feminicidio on the Border* (Columbus, OH: The Ohio State University Press, 2019).
8 Leandra Hinojosa Hernández and Sarah De Los Santos Upton, *Challenging Reproductive Control and Gendered Violence in the Américas: Intersectionality, Power, and Struggles for Rights* (Lanham, MD: Lexington Books, 2019).
9 Michelle A. Holling, "'So My Name is Alma, and I Am the Sister of ...': A Feminicidio Testimonio of Violence and Violent Identifications," *Women's Studies in Communication* 37, no. 3 (2014).
10 Robert Hariman and John Louis Lucaites, *No Caption Needed: Iconic Photographs, Public Culture, and Liberal Democracy* (Chicago, IL: The University of Chicago Press, 2007).
11 Kevin Michael DeLuca, *Image Politics: The New Rhetoric of Environmental Activism* (New York, NY: Routledge, 2005).
12 Joshua T. Davis and Samuel L. Perry, "White Christian Nationalism and Relative Political Tolerance for Racists," *Social Problems* 68, no. 3 (2021): 513.
13 Philip Gorski, *American Covenant: A History of Civil Religion from the Puritans to the Present* (Princeton, NJ: Princeton University Press, 2017), 17.
14 Gorski, 17.

15 Burwell v. Hobby Lobby Stores, Inc., 573 US 682 (2014). See also City of Boerne v. Flores, 521 US 507 (1997); Employment Division, Department of Human Resources of Oregon, et al., Petitioners v. Alfred L. Smith et al., 494 US 872 (1990).
16 Amaya, *Citizenship.*
17 Gabriella M. D'Agostini, "Treading on Sacred Land: First Amendment Implications of ICE's Targeting of Churches," *Michigan Law Review* 118, no. 2 (2019): 326.
18 D'Agostini, 326–27.
19 Barbara A. Frey and X. Kevin Zhao, "The Criminalization of Immigration and the International Norm of Non-discrimination: Deportation and Detention in US Immigration Law," *Law and Inequality: A Journal of Theory and Practice* 29, no 2 (2011).
20 Frey and Zhao, 280.
21 Frey and Zhao, 296–98.
22 D'Agostini, "Treading," 319.
23 D'Agostini, 319.
24 D'Agostini, 320.
25 Paul Messaris, *Visual Persuasion: The Role of Images in Advertising* (Thousand Oaks, CA: Sage, 1997).
26 Jonathan Crary, *Techniques of the Observer: On Vision and Modernity in the Nineteenth Century* (Cambridge, MA: MIT Press, 1992).
27 Gayatri C. Spivak, "Can the Subaltern Speak?," in *Marxism and the Interpretation of Culture,* eds. Cary Nelson and Lawrence Grossberg (Urbana: University of Illinois Press, 1988), 271–313.
28 Lisa Marie Cacho, "The Presumption of White Innocence," *American Quarterly* 66, no. 4 (2014).
29 Rakiya Omaar and Alex de Waal, "Disaster Pornography from Somalia," Center for Media Literacy, www.medialit.org/reading-room/disaster-pornography-somalia, para. 2.
30 Messaris, *Visual Persuasion*, 5.
31 Mark R. Stoner and Sally J. Perkins, *Making Sense of Messages: A Critical Apprenticeship in Rhetorical Criticism* (Boston, MA: Houghton Mifflin Company, 2005), 306.
32 Omaar and Alex de Waal, "Disaster," para. 4.
33 Maurice Blanchot, *The Writing of the Disaster*, trans. Ann Smock (Lincoln, NE: University of Nebraska Press, 1980/1995).
34 Gillian Rose, *Visual Methodologies* (Thousand Oaks, CA: Sage, 2016).
35 Cara A. Finnegan, "Social Engineering, Visual Politics, and the New Deal: FSA Photography in Survey Graphic," *Rhetoric & Public Affairs* 3, no. 3 (2000).
36 Roland Barthes, *Camera Lucida: Reflections on Photography* (New York, NY: Hill and Wang, 1980/1982), 45.
37 Barthes, 42.
38 Laura Mulvey, "Visual Pleasure and Narrative Cinema," in *Media and Cultural Studies: Keyworks*, eds. Meenakshi Gigi Durham and Douglas M. Kellner (Malden, MA: Blackwell Publishing, 1975/2006): 342–52; Rose, *Visual.*
39 Mulvey, "Visual," 343.

40 Madison Park and Kyle Almond, "This 2-Year-Old Has Become the Face of 'Zero Tolerance,'" *CNN*, https://www.cnn.com/interactive/2018/06/us/crying-girl-john-moore-immigration-cnnphotos/.
41 Park and Almond.
42 Hariman and Lucaites, *No Caption*, 27.
43 Cacho, "The Presumption," 1085.
44 Park and Almond, "This."
45 Ibid."
46 Ibid.
47 Ibid.
48 Ibid.
49 Ibid.
50 Ibid.
51 Hariman and Lucaites, *No Caption*, 27.
52 Emily Winderman, Robert Mejia, and Brandon Rogers, "'All Smell Is Disease': Miasma, Sensory Rhetoric, and the Sanitary-Bacteriologic of Visceral Public Health," *Rhetoric of Health & Medicine* 2, no. 2 (2019).
53 John E. Moore, "Undocumented Immigrants Go to Court for Deportation Hearings," Getty Images, https://www.gettyimages.fi/detail/news-photo/central-american-immigrant-families-depart-ice-custody-news-photo/971859424.
54 Barthes, *Camera*, 43.
55 Stuart Hall, "Encoding/Decoding," in *Media and Cultural Studies: Keyworks*, eds. Meenakshi Gigi Durham and Douglas M. Kellner (Malden, MA: Blackwell Publishing, 1980/2006): 163–73.
56 David Stamps, "Is It Really Representation? A Qualitative Analysis of Asian and Latino Characterizations in Broadcast Television," *American Communication Journal* 21, no. 1 (2019).
57 "Due Process," Cornell Law School Legal Information Institute, accessed September 26, 2020, https://www.law.cornell.edu/wex/due_process, para 11.
58 U.S. Department of Homeland Security, "DHS and DOJ Issue Third-Country Asylum Rule," https://www.dhs.gov/news/2019/07/15/dhs-and-doj-issue-third-country-asylum-rule.
59 John E. Moore, "Border Patrol Agents Detain Migrants near Us-Mexico Border," Getty Images, https://www.gettyimages.com/detail/news-photo/two-year-old-honduran-asylum-seeker-cries-as-her-mother-is-news-photo/973077552.
60 Park and Almond, "This."
61 Kenneth Burke, *A Grammar of Motives* (Berkeley, CA: University of California Press, 1945/1969).
62 Hayden White, *Metahistory: The Historical Imagination in Nineteenth-Century Europe* (Baltimore, MD: John Hopkins University Press, 1973).
63 Hall, "Encoding/Decoding."
64 Michael Lechuga, "Mapping Migrant Vernacular Discourses: Mestiza Consciousness, Nomad Thought, and Latina/o/x Migrant Movement Politics in the United States," *Journal of International and Intercultural Communication* 13, no. 3 (2020): 263.
65 Finnegan, "Social," 345.
66 Park and Almond, "This."

67 TIME Magazine, June 2, 2018. https://time.com/magazine/us/5318226/july-2nd-2018-vol-192-no-1-u-s/
68 Amanda Sakuma, "Obama Leaves Behind a Mixed Legacy on Immigration," *NBC News*, https://www.nbcnews.com/storyline/president-obama-the-legacy/obama-leaves-behind-mixed-legacy-immigration-n703656.
69 Anti-Defamation League, "What Is DACA and Who Are the Dreamers?," ADL, https://www.adl.org/education/resources/tools-and-strategies/table-talk/what-is-daca-and-who-are-the-dreamers.
70 Cacho, "The Presumption"; Gerald R. Smith, "Of Malice and Men: The Law of Defamation," *Valparaiso University Law Review* 27, no. 1 (1992); David van Mill, "Freedom of Speech," The Stanford Encyclopedia of Philosophy, https://plato.stanford.edu/archives/sum2018/entries/freedom-speech/.
71 Amaya, *Citizenship.*
72 Billy Peard, "SB 1070 in 2018: What Are Our Rights?" ACLU, https://www.acluaz.org/en/news/sb-1070-2018-what-are-our-rights.
73 Raymond Williams, *Marxism and Literature* (Oxford: Oxford University Press, 1978).
74 Finnegan, "Social."
75 The White House. "Executive Order on the Establishment of Interagency Task Force on the Reunification of Families." https://www.whitehouse.gov/briefing-room/presidential-actions/2021/02/02/executive-order-the-establishment-of-interagency-task-force-on-the-reunification-of-families/. The 45th administration established a similar policy, with an executive order "to stop separating families except in cases where there is concern that the parent represents a risk to the child." Southern Poverty Law Center, "Family Separation – A Timeline," SPLC, https://www.splcenter.org/news/2022/03/23/family-separation-timeline.
76 The ACLU and National Immigrant Justice Center report that family separation practices continued to exist well after the end of 45's "zero tolerance" policy. Immigration officials simply included claims of alleged gang affiliations, alleged drug offenses, and other alleged offenses as satisfying the child safety and well-being criteria. See: Southern Poverty Law, "Family"; National Immigrant Justice Center, "The Biden Administration Routinely Separates Immigrant Families," NIJC, https://immigrantjustice.org/staff/blog/biden-administration-routinely-separates-immigrant-families

Bibliography

Amaya, Hector. *Citizenship Excess: Latinas/os, Media, and the Nation.* New York, NY: New York University Press, 2013.

Anti-Defamation League. "What Is DACA and Who Are the Dreamers?" ADL. https://www.adl.org/education/resources/tools-and-strategies/table-talk/what-is-daca-and-who-are-the-dreamers.

Barthes, Roland. *Camera Lucida: Reflections on Photography.* New York, NY: Hill and Wang, 1980/1982.

Blanchot, Maurice. *The Writing of the Disaster.* Translated by Ann Smock. Lincoln, NE: University of Nebraska Press, 1980/1995.

Burke, Kenneth. *A Grammar of Motives.* Berkeley, CA: University of California Press, 1945/1969.

Burwell v. Hobby Lobby Stores, Inc., 573 US 682 (2014).

Cacho, Lisa Marie. "The Presumption of White Innocence." *American Quarterly* 66, no. 4 (2014): 1085–90.

Carey, Benedict. "Reuniting and Detaining Migrant Families Pose New Mental Health Risks." *New York Times.* https://www.nytimes.com/2018/06/22/health/migrant-families-immigration-detention.html.

Cisneros, J. David. *The Border Crossed Us: Rhetorics of Borders, Citizenship, and Latina/o Identity.* Tuscaloosa, AL: The University of Alabama Press, 2013.

City of Boerne v. Flores, 521 US 507 (1997).

Crary, Jonathan. *Techniques of the Observer: On Vision and Modernity in the Nineteenth Century.* Cambridge, MA: MIT Press, 1992.

D'Agostini, Gabriella M. "Treading on Sacred Land: First Amendment Implications of ICE's Targeting of Churches." *Michigan Law Review* 118, no. 2 (2019): 315–43.

Davis, Joshua T., and Samuel L. Perry. "White Christian Nationalism and Relative Political Tolerance for Racists." *Social Problems* 68, no. 3 (2021): 513–34.

De Los Santos Upton, Sarah, Diana Isabel Bowen, and Leandra Hinojosa Hernández. "Nepantla Activism in *Braiding Borders + Trenzando Fronteras.*" In *Latina/o/x Communication Studies: Theories, Methods, and Practice*, edited by Leandra Hinojosa Hernández, Diana I. Bowen, Sarah De Los Santos Upton, and Amanda R. Martinez, 229–50. Lanham, MD: Lexington Books, 2019.

DeLuca, Kevin Michael. *Image Politics: The New Rhetoric of Environmental Activism.* New York, NY: Routledge, 2005.

"Due Process." Cornell Law School Legal Information Institute. Accessed September 26, 2020. https://www.law.cornell.edu/wex/due_process.

Employment Division, Department of Human Resources of Oregon, et al., Petitioners v. Alfred L. Smith et al., 494 US 872 (1990).

Finnegan, Cara A. "Social Engineering, Visual Politics, and the New Deal: FSA Photography in Survey Graphic." *Rhetoric & Public Affairs* 3, no. 3 (2000): 333–62.

Frey, Barbara A., and X. Kevin Zhao. "The Criminalization of Immigration and the International Norm of Non-discrimination: Deportation and Detention in US Immigration Law." *Law and Inequality: A Journal of Theory and Practice* 29, no 2 (2011): 279–312.

Gorski, Philip. *American Covenant: A History of Civil Religion from the Puritans to the Present.* Princeton, NJ: Princeton University Press, 2017.

Hall, Stuart. "Encoding/Decoding." In *Media and Cultural Studies: Keyworks*, edited by Meenakshi Gigi Durham and Douglas M. Kellner, 163–73. Malden, MA: Blackwell Publishing, 1980/2006.

Hariman, Robert, and John Louis Lucaites. *No Caption Needed: Iconic Photographs, Public Culture, and Liberal Democracy*. Chicago, IL: The University of Chicago Press, 2007.

Hartelius, E. Johanna. *The Rhetorics of US Immigration: Identity, Community, Otherness*. University Park, PA: The Pennsylvania State University Press, 2015.

Hernández, Leandra Hinojosa, and Sarah De Los Santos Upton. *Challenging Reproductive Control and Gendered Violence in the Américas: Intersectionality, Power, and Struggles for Rights*. Lanham, MD: Lexington Books, 2019.

Holling, Michelle A. "'So My Name is Alma, and I Am the Sister of . . .': A Feminicidio Testimonio of Violence and Violent Identifications." *Women's Studies in Communication* 37, no. 3 (2014): 313–38.

Lechuga, Michael. "Mapping Migrant Vernacular Discourses: Mestiza Consciousness, Nomad Thought, and Latina/o/x Migrant Movement Politics in the United States." *Journal of International and Intercultural Communication* 13, no. 3 (2020): 257–73.

Lozano, Nina M. *Not One More!: Feminicidio on the Border*. Columbus, OH: The Ohio State University Press, 2019.

Messaris, Paul. *Visual Persuasion: The Role of Images in Advertising*. Thousand Oaks, CA: Sage, 1997.

van Mill, David. "Freedom of Speech." The Stanford Encyclopedia of Philosophy, https://plato.stanford.edu/archives/sum2018/entries/freedom-speech/.

Moore, John E. "Border Patrol Agents Detain Migrants near Us-Mexico Border." Getty Images. https://www.gettyimages.com/detail/news-photo/two-year-old-honduran-asylum-seeker-cries-as-her-mother-is-news-photo/973077552.

Moore, John E. "Undocumented Immigrants Go to Court for Deportation Hearings." Getty Images. https://www.gettyimages.fi/detail/news-photo/central-american-immigrant-families-depart-ice-custody-news-photo/971859424.

Mulvey, Laura. "Visual Pleasure and Narrative Cinema." In *Media and Cultural Studies: Keyworks*, edited by Meenakshi Gigi Durham and Douglas M. Kellner, 342–52. Malden, MA: Blackwell Publishing, 1975/2006.

Nathan, Debbie. "A 5-Year-Old Girl in Immigrant Detention Nearly Died of an Untreated Ruptured Appendix." The Intercept. https://theintercept.com/2018/09/02/border-patrol-immigrant-detention-medical-neglect-texas/.

National Immigrant Justice Center, "The Biden Administration Routinely Separates Immigrant Families," NIJC, https://immigrantjustice.org/staff/blog/biden-administration-routinely-separates-immigrant-families

Omaar, Rakiya, and Alex de Waal. "Disaster Pornography from Somalia." Center for Media Literacy. www.medialit.org/reading-room/disaster-pornography-somalia.

Park, Madison, and Kyle Almond. "This 2-Year-Old Has Become the Face of 'Zero Tolerance.'" *CNN*. https://www.cnn.com/interactive/2018/06/us/crying-girl-john-moore-immigration-cnnphotos/.

Peard, Billy. "SB 1070 in 2018: What Are Our Rights?" ACLU. https://www.acluaz.org/en/news/sb-1070-2018-what-are-our-rights.

Rose, Gillian. *Visual Methodologies*. Thousand Oaks, CA: Sage, 2016.

Sakuma, Amanda. "Obama Leaves Behind a Mixed Legacy on Immigration." *NBC News*. https://www.nbcnews.com/storyline/president-obama-the-legacy/obama-leaves-behind-mixed-legacy-immigration-n703656.

Smith, Gerald R. "Of Malice and Men: The Law of Defamation." *Valparaiso University Law Review* 27, no. 1 (1992): 39–93.

Southern Poverty Law Center, "Family Separation – A Timeline," SPLC, https://www.splcenter.org/news/2022/03/23/family-separation-timeline

Spivak, Gayatri C. "Can the Subaltern Speak?" In *Marxism and the Interpretation of Culture*, edited by Cary Nelson and Lawrence Grossberg, 271–313. Urbana: University of Illinois Press, 1988.

Stamps, David. "Is It Really Representation? A Qualitative Analysis of Asian and Latino Characterizations in Broadcast Television." *American Communication Journal* 21, no. 1 (2019): 1–12.

Stoner, Mark R., and Sally J. Perkins. *Making Sense of Messages: A Critical Apprenticeship in Rhetorical Criticism*. Boston, MA: Houghton Mifflin Company, 2005.

The White House. "Executive Order on the Establishment of Interagency Task Force on the Reunification of Families." https://www.whitehouse.gov/briefing-room/presidential-actions/2021/02/02/executive-order-the-establishment-of-interagency-task-force-on-the-reunification-of-families/

U.S. Department of Homeland Security. "DHS and DOJ Issue Third-Country Asylum Rule." https://www.dhs.gov/news/2019/07/15/dhs-and-doj-issue-third-country-asylum-rule.

White, Hayden. *Metahistory: The Historical Imagination in Nineteenth-Century Europe*. Baltimore, MD: John Hopkins University Press, 1973.

Williams, Raymond. *Marxism and Literature*. Oxford: Oxford University Press, 1978.

Winderman, Emily, Robert Mejia, and Brandon Rogers. " 'All Smell Is Disease': Miasma, Sensory Rhetoric, and the Sanitary-Bacteriologic of Visceral Public Health." *Rhetoric of Health & Medicine* 2, no. 2 (2019): 115–46.

13. *If It Was Never About the Cake, What Was It About? How Members of the Public Framed the* Masterpiece Cakeshop v. Colorado Civil Rights Commission *Supreme Court Ruling*

ANN E. BURNETTE AND REBEKAH L. FOX

When Charlie Craig and David Mullins walked into the Masterpiece Cakeshop in Lakewood, Colorado, in 2012, they had no idea that their request for a wedding cake would ultimately be such a tall order. The couple planned to be married in Massachusetts, where same-sex marriages were legal, and return to Colorado to celebrate their marriage. Their bakery order and Masterpiece Cakeshop owner Jack Phillip's refusal to fill that order based on religious objections would spark a landmark Supreme Court ruling. Since the ruling, the case has been used to justify grounds for refusing service based on religious beliefs. Legal scholars and activists have noted that this conflict is a point of contestation for both freedom of expression and freedom of religion with potentially far-reaching implications. While the questions of law are disputed in the courtroom, the definitions and premises of the public debate are deliberated in the court of public opinion. We examine the public discourse around the debate as represented by newspaper editorials and letters to the editor in five major national newspapers. We find four themes within this editorial content: (1) characterizing warriors in a cultural war, (2) defining "expression" and how it applies to this case, (3) explaining what it means to be open for business, and (4) offering future projections and pragmatic solutions. These editorial themes provide a lens through which we can understand how citizens and opinion leaders have framed the conflicts among religious freedom, freedom of expression, and marriage equality.

These rhetorical interpretations of this ruling will have a profound impact on future legal and political debates.

Narrative of the Event

According to David Mullins, he and his fiancé, Charlie Craig, visited the Masterpiece Cakeshop in July 2012 "with a bunch of ideas" about the cake they wanted to celebrate their wedding.[1] Phillips responded, "Sorry, guys, I don't make cakes for same-sex weddings."[2] While Phillips offered to sell other items in his bakery, Mullins and Craig left the shop. Mullins and Craig recalled feeling "shocked," "mortified," "embarrassed" and "degraded"; Phillips recounted that the couple "swore at me, flipped me off, and stormed out."[3] Mullins and Craig posted their account of their experience on social media; both the couple and Phillips described receiving threats and other forms of harassment as the incident garnered attention. Mullins and Craig obtained their cake from another bakery and filed a complaint with the Colorado Civil Rights Commission (CCRC) arguing that Phillips had, under the state's public accommodations law, illegally discriminated against them. The CCRC decided in favor of Mullins and Craig and ordered Masterpiece Cakeshop to provide cakes for same-sex marriages and take a series of steps within two years to come into compliance with Colorado law.

With the help of Alliance Defending Freedom, Phillips appealed the decision to the Court of Appeals. Meanwhile, the American Civil Liberties Union joined the CCRC in representing Mullins and Craig. The Court of Appeals upheld the state's decision, ruling that the act of baking a wedding cake was part of the expected conduct of Phillips's bakery rather than an exercise of free speech or religion. The Supreme Court of Colorado declined to hear an appeal. As the parties to the suit prepared to take their case to U.S. Supreme Court, the U.S. Department of Justice supported Phillips. Civil rights organizations including the NAACP Legal Defense Fund and the Southern Poverty Law Center supported Mullins and Craig.

Many observers were curious about the role that particular Supreme Court Justices would play. Justice Neil Gorsuch had joined the Court in April 2017, and Court observers viewed the *Masterpiece* case as a test of his conservative beliefs.[4] Justice Anthony Kennedy was also under the spotlight; his opinions in *Romer v.* Evans (1996), *Lawrence v. Texas* (2003), *United States v. Windsor* (2013), and *Obergefell v. Hodges* (2015), had broadly supported LGBTQ rights. Kennedy's reputation as a swing vote on the Court between liberal and conservative jurisprudence invited scrutiny of his function in the *Masterpiece* decision.

The Court handed down its ruling on June 4, 2018. In a 7-2 opinion authored by Kennedy, the Court ordered a reversal of the decision of the Colorado Civil Rights Commission. The majority found that the CCRC had demonstrated hostility toward Jack Phillips's religion. Justices Ruth Bader Ginsburg and Sonia Sotomayor dissented and argued that the CCRC had ruled appropriately in the case.[5] Concerned parties quickly moved in to spin the decision in a favorable light. The American Civil Liberties Union argued that "The court reversed the Masterpiece Cakeshop decision based on concerns unique to the case but reaffirmed its longstanding rule that states can prevent the harms of discrimination in the marketplace, including against LGBT people."[6] Meanwhile, U.S. Attorney General Jeff Sessions held that the decision was a defense of First Amendment religious protections against government discrimination.[7]

Many Americans saw the case as yet another clash in the culture war and felt invested in the outcome. In one show of concern, people gathered at the Masterpiece Cakeshop bakery when the ruling was handed down. Supporters of Phillips carried balloons in celebration and were met with a sign on the locked door of the bakery from Phillips, who said that he was in New York and thanked people for his support.[8]

The issues in the *Masterpiece Cakeshop* case continued to resonate after the ruling. Playwright Bekah Brunstetter, a writer and producer for the NBC series "This Is Us," wrote a play called "The Cake," which featured a North Carolina baker who refused to bake a wedding cake for a lesbian couple. The baker cited her Christianity as the reason for her refusal, despite the fact that one of the brides is the daughter of her late best friend. While Brunstetter said she started the play before the *Masterpiece Cakeshop* case, her work received attention because of the obvious similarities between her play's plot and the *Masterpiece* case.[9] The arguments in *Masterpiece Cakeshop* also motivated some businesses to reexamine and rearticulate their business philosophy. Yelp capitalized on the conflict the case represented by starting an "Open to All" campaign. The online review company added a category that let businesses be marked as open to customers of any race, ethnicity, national origin, sex, religion, disability, sexual orientation, gender identity or gender expression.[10] Yelp claimed that the feature would "help protect consumers from discrimination."[11] The company said the purpose of the campaign was to "build awareness and understanding of the importance of nondiscrimination laws and defend the bedrock principle that when businesses open their doors to the public, they should be Open to All."[12]

First Amendment and Other Legal Scholars Grapple with the Ruling

The decision in the *Masterpiece Cakeshop* case left First Amendment and legal scholars plenty of room to discuss the Supreme Court's reasoning and potential implications of the ruling. The decision had been anxiously awaited because, it was thought, the ruling would give clear guidance in similar cases. In one of the amicus briefs (later published in the Cato Supreme Court Review), Professor of Law and Public Policy Thomas Berg summed up the potential contribution of the ruling when he asked "When does a commercial product or service—for example, creating a cake—embody a message such that the Free Speech Clause protects a business against being compelled to provide it?"[13] However, the Court's 7-2 ruling was based on the narrow argument that the Colorado Civil Rights Commission had shown "hostility" toward the cake baker's religious beliefs. Thus, the Court's decision did not provide guidance that could be used in similar cases, and was seen by some legal scholars as "kicking the can down the road."[14] Reflecting on this lack of guidance, Brian Miller wrote:

> The Court's minimalist holding seems completely unaware of its own fraught role in fomenting this divide, and its stirring calls for toleration are hardly comforting given that the opinion leaves too many questions unanswered. In the aftermath of Masterpiece, religious business owners, LGBT persons, and state policy makers are all in the dark regarding their legal standing.[15]

As the can is being kicked down the road, scholars are debating a wide range of related issues including the current state of anti-discrimination protections,[16] marriage equality and LGBTQ + rights,[17] accommodations of religion,[18] and even the overall state of democracy.[19] One theme that tends to surface in much of this writing is the difficulty associated with what the actual issue is and how it manifests in the framing of the case. If the case is framed as "freedom of religion v. freedom from discrimination,"[20] "freedom of religion versus freedom to live life as one wishes,"[21] or "a collision of liberty and equality,"[22] different aspects of the clash come forward.

Just as there are many ways to frame the issue, scholars are suggesting a variety of solutions. Some scholars are working to offer solutions that they think might transcend the dichotomy of protecting religion versus protecting (or preventing compelled) speech. For example, seeking legislative accommodations,[23] or adopting a stance of symmetric constitutionalism[24] have been put forward, as well as the development of a detailed "roadmap" offered by law professor Robert Rains in the *Vermont Law Review*. Rains suggests that any government official must offer the same services for same-sex couples that are available for other couples unless the service can be performed immediately by another government official without delay or inconvenience to the couple and without significant expense to the public.[25] For private businesses, Rains recommends that those who provide "public accommodations (wedding chapels, florists, photographers, bakers, seamstresses, etc.) must accommodate the entire public" unless doing so contradicts "sincerely held religious beliefs" or compels a vendor "to explicitly endorse same-sex marriage."[26] Rains admits, "Unquestionably, the compromise above would leave many people, on both sides of our cultural/religious divide, unhappy, and leave many questions to be litigated."[27]

With such a complex topic, it should not be a surprise that many people on both sides are struggling with what the case means. It should also not be a surprise that traditional and social media are shaping the debate in powerful ways. In his 2019 article "Wedding Cakes, Equality, and Rhetorics of Religious Freedom" in *First Amendment Studies*, Issac West explored how "religious freedom is articulated in conservative publics"[28] by examining three conservative news outlets—Breitbart, Fox News, and Glenn Beck's *The Blaze*—and how they covered a separate but related 2013 case out of Oregon, wherein a cake shop was fined by the state after its owners refused to make a wedding cake for a lesbian couple. West was particularly interested in how "individual and social dramas are crafted and circulated in conservative media ecosystems"[29] and how the individual case comes to function as a synecdoche that dramatizes complex legal issues.

This chapter seeks to contribute to a better understanding of how citizens, as opposed to legal or academic scholars, are coming to terms with the *Masterpiece* ruling by examining the views contested in the public sphere in the form of opinion pieces and editorials in five of the largest U.S. newspapers. We selected editorial content including opinion pieces by invited authors, letters to the editor, and newspaper editorials to provide an analysis of citizens' voices as opposed to the legal analysis traditionally provided in law reviews, or the commentary given by elected officials. We analyzed editorial content appearing in *USA Today*, *New York Times*, *The Wall Street Journal*, *Los Angeles Times* and the *New York Post*, starting with the day the Supreme Court announced it would hear the case (June 26th, 2017), through when the decision was handed down (June 4th, 2018). We also included editorial content through the end of 2018 as part of the initial framing period.

Analysis of Editorial Content

We categorized the editorial content into four main areas: (1) characterizing warriors in a cultural war, (2) defining "expression" and how it applies to this case, (3) explaining what it means to be open for business, and (4) offering future projections and pragmatic solutions. In this section, we briefly explain the content in each section along with the subsections that emerged, and provide direct quotes from the editorials for illustration purposes.

Characterizing Warriors in a Cultural War

The first category, "characterizing warriors in a cultural war," reflects the opinion of those authors who hold that the stakes are high and the battle is being waged between (mostly) two groups—those who hold traditional Christian beliefs, and those who fight for more progressive values. Some authors focused on the *nature of the event in the cakeshop*, others focused on *the character of those in the "cultural war,"* and some tried to characterize *the nature of the ruling itself.*

What Is the Nature of the Event in the Cakeshop?

Some members of the public were interested in classifying the type of action that took place in the cakeshop itself. This seemed like an important topic for the authors because if they could assign intent in the moment of the event, it would seem they would also know where to place blame. For example, one author asked:

> Would a Jewish baker be required to create a cake for a Nazi event? Would a black baker be required to create a cake for the Ku Klux Klan? Is an artist required to paint a portrait of someone he or she does not like? Surely there are other bakers who would accommodate the couple's request, and insisting that this particular baker do it appears to be a spiteful act.[30]

Some authors dismissed the larger First Amendment issues at stake by pointing out that the other side is overreacting. One author argued that "progressives appear bent on making a literal federal case out of every cake in America."[31] Jack Phillips himself seemed to downplay the magnitude of the event when he wrote:

> The two men who came into my shop that day were living out their beliefs. All I did was attempt to live out mine. I respect their right to choose and hoped they would respect mine. They did not. And, considering all of the hate mail, obscene calls and death threats my family has received since I was sued, a lot of

> other people don't see tolerance as a two-way street, either. But the Constitution does. The First Amendment defends my right to create custom cake art that is consistent with my faith, while declining requests that ask me to celebrate events or messages that conflict with my faith. As a cake artist, I can live out my faith in my day-to-day life, and make that faith the basis for my creative decisions.[32]

The different interpretations of the event suggested profoundly different responses to the *Masterpiece* ruling.

The Character of Those in the Fight

Perhaps not surprisingly, some of the most pointed rhetoric appeared in editorials dedicated to explaining the character of the enemy in the fight. In addition, authors offered heartfelt characterizations of themselves. Maybe because the topic of free speech and free religion is very personal and people who are attempting to influence others through editorials recognize the power of personal testimony, we also saw people amplifying their own ethos as a persuasive tactic.

It is fairly common for letters to the editor to include ad hominem attacks of the people with whom the authors disagree. The following quote intensified the ad hominem attack by using language that speaks directly to the reader:

> Or, in other words, if SCOTUS upholds the lower-court ruling, it will empower unelected civil-rights commissions — which are typically stacked with hard-left authoritarians — to decide when your religious actions are appropriate. How could any honest person believe this was the Constitution's intent? There was a time, I'm told, when the state wouldn't substantially burden religious exercise and would use the least restrictive means to further compelling interests. Today, the state can substantially burden a Christian because he has hurt the wrong person's feelings.[33]

Rather than simply making ad hominem attacks, some of the editorials were more specific about what the other side misunderstands, or how narrow-minded they are. One author wrote, "In this era of identity politics, some have been programmed to reflexively side with the person making accusations of status-based discrimination, all in an effort to empower the state to coerce a minority of people to see the world their way."[34] Another author wrote:

> In the closely watched Masterpiece Cakeshop case, the Supreme Court dealt a blow against the small-mindedness that so often characterizes the self-appointed minders of social justice in America. In his majority opinion, Kennedy honed in on the blatant bias of Colorado's bias police, who apparently blanch at anything that doesn't accord with their blinkered, thoughtless progressivism.[35]

Tying together the idea that there is a cultural war and those on the other side are just spouting off their "standard" lines of reasoning, one author wrote:

> The hostility to Mr. Phillips and his beliefs isn't unusual. The rhetoric Justice Anthony Kennedy condemned—and cited as examples of constitutionally impermissible animus--is often heard from antagonists who attempt to ruin religious believers. Comparisons to racism and Nazism such as the Colorado commission made are standard for left-liberal culture warriors.[36]

Beyond the claims that the other side just doesn't get it is the assumption that the other side is made up of bullies, the intolerant, hypocrites, etc. For example, one person argued, "Progressives engage in culture-war bullying when religious liberty would stand in the way of their social views."[37] Or, from the opposite view, an observer wrote:

> The inability to get along because of fundamental differences in defining what makes us good people is one of the chief reasons for discrimination, slaughter and genocide. As the governor of Indiana, Mike Pence attributed the failure of his proposed Religious Freedom Restoration Act to intolerance toward evangelicals. Yet a quick glance at Christian-backed legislation is enough to reveal who the intolerant ones are. Mr. Pence's desire to discriminate while cloaked in his religion made him an evangelical hero, holding the second-highest office in the land.[38]

Again, we saw some authors calling out what they perceived as hypocrisy:

> Conservative Christians have significantly altered the way in which they engage in many culture war issues. The most current Supreme Court term epitomizes this fundamental shift: More and more often, conservative Christians are pitching arguments built on liberal legal doctrines -- especially First Amendment precedents that emphasize broad individual rights. . . This legal strategy has proved effective, and there are some broader public benefits, as some evidence suggests that evangelicals are learning to value the rights of others. But this court term has also uncovered a weakness in the new attitude about rights. It is evident in the Muslim travel ban case. Simply put, conservative Christians are much less likely to extend the same religious-freedom rights to Muslims that they claim for themselves. . . . Reciprocity is vital to building political support. In the long run, the political effectiveness of conservative Christians' rights claims is likely to be affected by their commitment to the rights of others, too.[39]

The alternative to the argument that the other side is wrong, for whatever reason, is the argument that the author's side is right because they are reasoned in their arguments. One appeal that emerged in this area was the argument that "I am on the other side, but I'm not like the others over there." For example, one author distanced himself from the idea of the cultural war all together when he wrote:

> My side — the socially conservative, evangelical Christian side — supposedly won a major victory Monday when the U.S. Supreme Court ruled in favor of a Colorado baker who declined to make a wedding cake for a gay couple. But it doesn't feel like a win to me. But as someone who once fought in that cultural war, and who now regrets it, I still hold out hope that we can learn to respect and value those whose beliefs and experiences are different than our own. It's the Christian thing to do. The American thing to do. The right thing to do.[40]

Another author denounced warrior language altogether in an effort to make the claim that Christians should be more like ambassadors to other communities, with the goal of avoiding clash. He wrote:

> This is not to say Christians should never claim our legal rights, as the Colorado baker did before the Supreme Court. The Constitution protects the free exercise of our religion. We can claim this right when needed. The Bible records that Paul the Apostle claimed his legal rights as a Roman citizen when a mob demanded his arrest. My hope is this: If we Christians will take seriously the commands to pray for our persecutors, to love our enemies, and to "live such good lives among" our unbelieving neighbors, if we will posture ourselves as ambassadors rather than warriors, then we might avoid many of the conflicts that would require the claiming of legal rights. Christians are called to be ambassadors to the LGBTQ community while embracing Scripture's authority.[41]

The last example in this section is from an author who was voicing frustration about this case in particular, but also about the larger persecution by other Christians. He wrote:

> Ever since I was a teenager, I've felt like a Christian being persecuted by other Christians. The endless hate crimes (last month two men in Denver were stabbed because they were holding hands), the constant introduction of antigay "religious freedom" legislation, the eternal discussion about personal rights versus freedom of speech — it all just makes me weary to the bone. I'm made wearier because religion is being used as a shield.[42]

As a final dimension of characterizing the warriors in a cultural war, these texts included the opinions of those who were seeking to capture the essence of the ruling itself. Often editorials that were about the essence of the case worked to reduce the complexity of the issue. For example, one author asked us to scratch below the surface to get to the essence of the debate when he wrote, "The bakery's argument is among the most radical to come before the Supreme Court in recent years. When you scratch below the surface, the case poses the following question: Is there a constitutional right to discriminate?"[43]

One author of a *New York Times* letter to the editor was Gene Robinson, a retired Episcopal bishop and the first openly gay Episcopal bishop. He took issue with *New York Times* op-ed columnist David Brooks's comment, "It's just a cake."[44] Robinson responded, "No, it's just dignity. Like the people of color, the disabled and other minorities before them, L.G.B.T. citizens seek to be accorded the same public dignity available to everyone else."[45] Robinson stipulated, "If this baker also refused to bake cakes for couples living together before marriage, or divorcés getting remarried—biblical sins—perhaps I would buy the baker's religious argument."[46] However, Robinson pointed out that Jack Phillips, in refusing to provide a wedding cake for a same-sex couple, "sets this 'sin' above all others and seeks not 'religious freedom' but permission to discriminate."[47]

Responding to the same editorial as Robinson, another author challenged the notion that the case was "just about a cake" and employed both a historical analogy and sarcasm. She wrote that she was "shocked" by David Brook's column, including his assertion that "it is just a cake."[48] She noted that by Brooks's logic, "Rosa Parks's seat was just a seat; she really should have had a nice conversation with those who were trying to get her to the back of the bus and maybe those white supremacists would have come around."[49]

Some letters and editorials announced clearly the values that were essentially at stake in the case, but argued that most readers may have interpreted the case incorrectly. Replying to an editorial written in support of Jack Phillips, one author wrote, "I am in the minority who applauds the writers' defense of the baker, Jack Phillips."[50] However, this letter writer noted, other people have "focused on freedom of expression, but the case is not just about expression. It is, indeed, about discrimination. But not in the way it has often been construed."[51] The writer asked the audience to consider that "There are many, such as myself, who have come to the conclusion that God is real and that He has certain basic expectations of us."[52] The writer noted, "Though we tolerate others who do not believe as we do, capitulation in support of an immoral situation is a violation of integrity that comes with consequences."[53] This led the letter writer to conclude that, "Individuals like Mr. Phillips may be truly between a rock and a hard place when someone demands a service supporting something that they consider immoral," and that "To force someone to abandon his livelihood or to completely avoid a major aspect of his profession on account of trying to live a moral life is absolutely discrimination."[54]

In one of its lead editorials, *The New York Times* seemed to agree with the idea that the case was clearly about discrimination but asserted that First Amendment scholars, not necessarily those charged with discrimination, were wrong. The editorial noted, "Some free-speech advocates argue that this case is simply a matter of deciding which sorts of expression merit First Amendment protection and which do not."[55] The editors posed the question of whether vendors such as caterers, florists, photographers, and calligraphers can argue that their services should be protected by the First Amendment. The *Times* warned, "If the justices rule for Mr. Phillips, they will be hard-pressed to find a clear limiting principle. And that would render public-accommodations laws like Colorado's effectively meaningless."[56] The editors argued:

> This, of course, is precisely the objective of the rear-guard action undertaken by religious objectors who, thwarted in their efforts to prevent gay couples from enjoying the rights and benefits that flow from marriage, are now invoking their own constitutional rights to avoid treating those same couples equally in the marketplace. But equality, and human dignity, are what the cake shop case comes down to. Justice Arthur Goldberg understood this more than 50 years ago in a 1964 case involving a challenge to the Civil Rights Act's ban on discrimination in public accommodations. Discrimination "is not simply dollars and cents, hamburgers and movies," he wrote in a concurring opinion. "It is the humiliation, frustration and embarrassment that a person must surely feel when he is told that he is unacceptable as a member of the public." The discrimination in that case was based on race; in 2017, it's hard to see how the same logic does not apply to discrimination based on sexual orientation.[57]

The clarity that marked the editorials before the ruling seemed to fall away after the ruling, leaving authors to suggest that no one really won and that the issue was unresolved. For example Bob Fredericks in the *New York Post* noted, "the decision also did not permanently settle the clash between LGBTQ rights and religious freedom, an issue that's bound to continue dividing Americans and lead to future court cases on multiple levels."[58] Fredericks observed that other analysts who have weighed in on the ruling have judged that the decision "offered small victories for those on all sides of the issue."[59] For instance, he wrote, "Religious-liberty advocates got another expansion of the Free Exercise Clause, which has been championed by President Trump and his evangelical base, who don't want to be forced into actions, like providing employees birth control, if it violates their religious beliefs."[60] Yet, Fredericks noted, the decision does not resolve the LGBTQ equality issues nor the free speech issues of the case and those questions will need to be resolved by lower courts and the advocacy of American citizens.[61] Other authors also acknowledged a small victory for the time being, but argued that the overall issue was unresolved. For example, Rich Lowry asserted that the "Court will eventually have to return to this topic. But for now, it's done the right thing—any day that officious bureaucrats who want to chase religion from the public square are slapped down is a good day for America."[62]

Defining Pivotal Words or Concepts

The Supreme Court, legal scholars, and members of the general public all seemed to be working to locate the meaning of certain terms such as "expression," or trying to determine if the point of disagreement is with the message being communicated or the identity of the individuals involved.

Some authors pointed out that the cake itself is a type of expression and should be protected by the First Amendment. For example, Louise Melling wrote, "In the bakery's argument, the cake is the expression, and the Constitution protects its refusal of service because the cake is expressive." She asked whether that refusal should be protected "simply because the refused service was artistic and expressive? By this logic, the Constitution could protect the right of a hairdresser who refuses to cut the hair of Muslims or a hotel that won't host an interfaith wedding."[63] The *Wall Street Journal* wrote, "Custom cakes can be construed as artistic expression, which is protected by the First Amendment. And weddings for many people are religious celebrations, and participation—or abstention—is itself an act of expression."[64] In one of several editorials written by Jack Phillips himself, he argued, "My work at the cake shop is more than a way to make a living. Designing each wedding cake is an expressive act, as I create an artistic centerpiece that announces a couple's union as a marriage and tells part of their story."[65] In this piece he identified himself as a "cake artist" and concluded, "My perspective and beliefs are inseparable from the work I create."[66]

Alternatively, some authors pointed to the exact opposite conclusion about expression. One letter to the editor warned that Phillips's position, "requires that we view designing a cake—any cake—as a form of speech."[67] The writer noted, "The facts of the case don't involve any specific message written on the cake or depiction of a same-sex couple, so it's the act of designing the cake regardless of any specific content on the cake."[68] The writer then observed that if designing a cake is speech, then the baker could refuse to serve other customers, including biracial couples, Muslims, or Jews. He concluded, "If that is speech, then others who produce creative but utilitarian works, such as gardeners, florists, chefs, architects, software engineers and the like, are likewise free to discriminate. The Supreme Court should recognize the absurdity of the baker's position."[69]

A subset of the expression debate is the distinction that some authors draw between baking a custom cake ("creating," "designing," etc.) versus selling any other baked good in the cake shop. For example, one person wrote, "I agree it would be discrimination if it was a cake that had already been made. However, the baker is being asked to create the cake, and it is a cake to be used in a ceremony that violates his religious beliefs."[70] David

Harsanyi argued that the *Masterpiece* case was not a challenge of marriage equality itself but that much of the reporting of the case framed it as a contest between "the tolerant and the closed-minded."[71] Noting that many headlines focus on the Phillips' refusal to serve a gay couple, Harsanyi wrote:

> A person with only passing interest in this case might be led to believe that Phillips is fighting to hang a "No Gays Allowed" sign in his shop. In truth, he never refused to serve a gay couple. He didn't even really refuse to sell David Mullins and Charlie Craig a wedding cake. Everything in his shop was available to gays and straights and anyone else who walked in his door. What Phillips did was refuse to use his skills to design and bake a unique cake for a gay wedding.[72]

Jack Phillips made a similar argument when he wrote:

> Designing a wedding cake is a very different thing from, say, baking a brownie. When people commission such a cake, they're requesting something that's designed to express something about the event and about the couple. What I design is not just a tower of flour and sugar, but a message tailored to a specific couple and a specific event — a message telling all who see it that this event is a wedding and that it is an occasion for celebration. In this case, I couldn't. What a cake celebrating this event would communicate was a message that contradicts my deepest religious convictions, and as an artist, that's just not something I'm able to do, so I politely declined.[73]

Inextricably related to the question about expression was the question about what exactly Phillips was disagreeing with during his refusal at the cakeshop. Was he disapproving of the message that would be implicitly carried in the cake or the personal identity of the customers? One author grappled with this when he wrote:

> If those playing down the importance of the Masterpiece Cakeshop ruling are wrong, those overstating it are also off base. *Family Guy* creator Seth MacFarlane claimed that "It's a shorter walk than we think, particularly today, from 'I won't bake them a cake because they're gay' to 'I won't seat him here because he's black.'" This wildly mischaracterizes Mr. Phillips's position. The Masterpiece proprietor serves all customers, regardless of sexual orientation, but he can't in good conscience communicate all messages or celebrate all events. He is motivated by his Christian belief that marriage unites husband and wife, not his customer's identity.[74]

Alternatively, Harsanyi drew a clear distinction between the identity of the gay couple and the cake carrying the message. He wrote, "If a couple had asked him to design a specialty cake that read 'Congrats on the abortion, Jenny!' I'm certain he would have refused them as well, even though abortions are legal. It's not the people; it's the message."[75]

Explaining What It Means to Be Open for Business

One of the contentious questions of the *Masterpiece* case was: what does it mean to be open for business? Many argued that the understanding of a business as part of an open marketplace determines the way any business should be conducted. In this framing, proprietors should not discriminate against customers or clients.

Some observers argued that Constitutional prohibitions of discrimination left no room for business practices to differentiate among customers. Louise Melling in the *L.A. Times* noted, "If the Constitution exempts the bakery from the law's bar on discrimination—either because the discrimination is motivated by religion or because it is attached to an expressive service—it would mean that the Constitution protects discrimination."[76] Jonathan Goldstein applied this principle to Phillips directly, saying that if Phillips "adapts generally most or all of the attributes of a business open to the public (and it is undisputed that he did so), then his business behavior would be subject to a panoply of state laws, including in Colorado's case, its antidiscrimination law."[77] Goldstein concluded that Phillips had not been discriminated against because of his religious beliefs; rather, "He was found to have been operating a business generally open to the public and then to have discriminated against the gay couple in violation of the Colorado law."[78] *USA Today* made the same argument in their editorial:

> First Amendment rights to practice religion and free speech are fundamental protections, but they are not unlimited. Philips has an absolute right to his religious beliefs against gay marriage, but when the practice of those beliefs infringes on the rights of others to equal treatment, it goes too far.
>
> In this country, when you open a business and sell to the public, you agree to abide by public accommodation laws.[79]

Commenters including Montel Williams drew a parallel between Masterpiece Cakeshop not serving gay wedding customers and racial discrimination practices targeted by the Civil Rights Movement. Williams noted, "It wasn't long ago, in our history, when politicians and business owners made similar religious liberty arguments to justify segregation in businesses."[80] He added, "Businesses open to the public must be open to everyone on the same terms. That's not a novel concept. It's ripped from the playbook of civil rights warriors like Dr. Martin Luther King."[81]

In addition to the categorical arguments about what practices need to be constitutionally protected, some advocates pointed out that if business owners exercised complete license in determining which customers they could ethically serve, adherents of various faiths would decline to serve different clients on the basis of religious objection. Bob Denmark wrote to the editor of the *Wall Street Journal*, "If we allow the sellers' religious beliefs to dictate who they serve, rather than what they serve . . . then some Catholic cake bakers might not bake wedding cakes for those who were divorced."[82] He asked, "where would we draw the line on who could buy these wedding cakes?" and concluded, "Everyone has the right to select a business that allows them to act according to his own faith, conscience and sacred honor, but once he opens his doors to the public, he must serve the people who come through those doors."[83]

Another drawback of trying to protect a moral value system in deciding what clients to serve is that businesspeople may not be able to deduce accurately which customers "deserve" service and which do not. "An unfortunate consequence of judging and categorizing people based on what they look like and who they love, and then refusing to serve them based on a belief system," wrote Jan MacMichael in the *Los Angeles Times*, "is that you may very well be inadvertently serving whose less obvious behavior you would abhor if you knew about it."[84] MacMichael mused, "I wonder how many wedding cakes Masterpiece Cakeshop has baked for pornographers, domestic abusers, and others."[85] MacMichael approached this dilemma from a Christian standpoint and concluded, "It not only feels better when we leave the judging to God, it also takes a great weight off our shoulders."[86] Philip Guiral, who identifies as Christian, wrote, "It's people like Phillips who make it difficult to explain my Christian faith."[87] Guiral explained, "We are told that only God can judge what's in a man's heart, yet Phillips judges every sinner who enters his shop (by the way, we are all sinners) and decides who gets his business."[88] He noted, "It's not a sin to bake a cake, no matter the customer. Using Christianity to justify discrimination is not what God intended."[89]

The advocates concluded, whether for constitutional, practical, or religious reasons, Phillips should have consented to provide the wedding cake. On the other side of the debate, people including Phillips argued that business owners should not have to abandon or violate their religious beliefs in order to do business. In this view, the marketplace should be considered another venue for people to live their faith. Phillips argued that in operating his business, "I am always mindful of whether God is pleased with what I create."[90] He explained, "even though I serve all people, I can't design cakes that celebrate events or express messages that conflict with my faith. It's also why I've declined requests to create cakes that celebrate Halloween or memorialize a divorce."[91] Phillips argued that his business practices, like other aspects of his life, are an expression of his faith. "To understand my decision, you must understand my faith. I've been a follower of Jesus Christ for most of my adult life" he explained.[92]

Robert George defended Philips's assertion that a business proprietor should not have to choose between their religious conviction and their business. In *The New York Times*, George proclaimed, "Business owners and others have no obligation under the Constitution, nor can one be imposed by statute, to confine their religion to the private domain."[93] "On the contrary," George added, "they have the constitutional right to proclaim and act on their religious beliefs in the public domain, including in the domain of commerce."[94] In making his case, George explicitly noted that this principle was true for people of all faiths.

For some, the important question in determining how to conduct business hinged on the definition of a cake as a product or an artistic expression. Phillips himself made this distinction when he wrote, "If asked to design a cake that celebrates an event or expresses a message in conflict with my faith, I'm obliged as a matter of conscience to decline"[95] In such an instance, Phillips said he would "still offer those customers anything else in my shop and tell them that I'd gladly create a cake for a different occasion."[96] For Phillips, the distinction lies in the fact that baking a wedding cake was a form of artistic expression. He explained, "What a cake celebrating this event would communicate was a message that contradicts my deepest religious convictions, and as an artist, that's just no something I'm able to do, so I politely declined."[97] One of Phillips's supporters echoed, "I agree it would be discrimination if it was a cake that had already been made" and added, "However, the baker is being asked to create the cake, and it is a cake to be used in a ceremony that violates his religious beliefs."[98] In this view, the cake was a form of expression rather than a good to be exchanged in the marketplace.

Counterarguments to this view also emerged. One response was that the business of selling a wedding cake was essentially a service rather than a form of expression, to refuse service to customers was discriminatory. Louise Melling in the *Los Angeles Times* took this view, claiming that Colorado's anti-discrimination law "pertains to the refusal of service, not the artistry of cakes."[99] In this light, the law "does not compel the bakery or any other business that opens its doors to the public to make a particular product."[100] These arguments were grounded in the assumption that a wedding cake is a good or commodity that is offered for sale like any other product. Some observers posed a slippery slope argument to illustrate the difficulties of treating the wedding cake business an instance of artistic expression. If wedding cakes are considered artistic expressions rather than commodities, what other wedding services or supplies could constitute expression? Adam Winkler in the *Los*

Angeles Times noted, "Florists, invitation printers, dressmakers, caterers and makeup artists could all claim the goods they provide are as deserving of protection as a wedding cake."[101]

Finally, some rejected the notion that a good or service that consisted of artistic expression deserved protection in this instance. "Just as speech by a business open to the public is not protected when it communicates discrimination," Melling noted in the *Los Angeles Times*, "discrimination by a business should not be protected simply because the refusal is of a service that involves speech or expression."[102]

Offering Pragmatic Solutions and Future Projections

A final theme of rhetorical framing involved making sense of what could happen as a result of the *Masterpiece Cakeshop* decision. This included pragmatic strategies that could reduce or obviate the conflict inherent in the case as well as projections about what the future would hold, given the ruling in the case.

In order to allow commercial transactions to run smoothly for both proprietors and customers, letter writer Laurie Adami proposed that businesses that "choose to cater to any and all types of couples should post rainbows in their shop windows to let customers know they are open and supportive."[103] After all, she reasoned, "What newlyweds want to buy a wedding cake from a baker who wishes them ill?"[104] In the same vein, Yelp announced that it would add its "Open to All" feature in its "More Business Info" area to allow businesses to identify themselves as "open to all . . . regardless of race, ethnicity, national origin, sex, religion, disability, sexual orientation, gender identity, or gender expression."[105] David Hendershot suggested that, rather than trying to legislate that business owners not discriminate by requiring business owners to serve events or customers that violate their beliefs, society should tolerate the "possibility of gay people having to find another baker."[106] Dienyih Chen identified Jack Phillips as the problem in the transaction and wrote that Phillips was "in the wrong line of business."[107] According to Chen, Phillips "should have worked as a preacher serving his God, or as a bona fide artist creating masterpieces while exercising his artistic license—not a baker in the guise of both professions."[108]

Observers also sought to understand the significance of the ruling in terms of its effect on future legal and business issues. Jack Phillips proclaimed that "the Supreme Court ruled that the government was wrong to punish me for living out my faith. It also made clear that the government must respect my religious beliefs about marriage."[109] He added, "How the issue plays out for others, we'll have to wait and see. But given the court's ruling in my case,

I'm optimistic."[110] Other supporters of the decision celebrated the fact that Court found for Phillips. Ryan Anderson observed that "antidiscrimination policy is supposed to be a shield" and posited, "It has been transformed into a sword, used to coerce people into affirming a sexual orthodoxy."[111] In this frame, the *Masterpiece Cakeshop* decision served to protect religious liberty.

Some of those who agreed with the decision were less sanguine about whether the ruling would afford much defense of religious rights. The *Wall Street Journal* editorialized, "Perhaps the best that can be said is that florists, make-up artists, photographers and other people of faith have lived to fight another day" and concluded, "A ruling against Mr. Phillips would have been catastrophic for religious liberty, but the majority's muddle provides only gossamer protection."[112] Barry McDonald warned that the decision might be a sign that so-called religious freedom laws "could be deemed to violate the Equal Protection Clause rights of same-sex couples were they to be denied services under them."[113]

Those who disagreed with the decision expressed disappointment in the ruling and its negative effect on LGBTQ rights. Jennifer Finney Boylan wrote, "Masterpiece is a defeat—a qualified defeat, to be sure, and a defeat that may well be revisited. But a bigger defeat is having to have one's rights as a citizen challenged, discussed and put forth for debate in the first place. This is not just a matter of dignity. It's a matter of common sense."[114] Silas House lamented, "But the Supreme Court decision will fuel the fires of this particular battle in the culture wars. People like Mr. Phillips believe their religious liberty trumps everyone else's, and surely it overrules my own since I am a gay man."[115]

Erick Rassbach, of The Becket Fund for Religious Liberty, tried to strike a conciliatory tone when he wrote, "Americans should take the Supreme Court's ruling as a broad suggestion that we should try to get along. Dialing down the societal hostility surrounding religion will go a long way towards ensuring that we remain united in diversity."[116]

Conclusions

Beyond the salient topics that emerged in our analysis of the editorial content surrounding the Masterpiece Cakeshop we identify several things that are noteworthy for those interested in religious freedom and free speech. First, not all First Amendment test cases end up being test cases at all. In the case of Masterpiece Cakeshop, the court agreed to hear the case based on free speech, and then ruled narrowly based on the Colorado Civil Rights Commission's "hostility" toward the defendant. But the narrowness of the ruling and the lack of clear guidance for future court cases somehow falls out of most of the discussions in the public discourse surrounding the ruling. What looked like a victory or felt like a loss, really wasn't either one.

Second, just as with many cases where religion and speech are pitted against one another, people seem to be very personally vested, whether they are part of the case or not. There is so much left to debate and decide concerning the clash of these two rights in the marketplace, it is no wonder the editorial content about the case is so vociferous. As the coverage of the editorial content shows, people are connecting with a range of ideological, philosophical, and practical matters related to the case. Because of this, it is likely that we will see Masterpiece used to support multiple, and likely completely different viewpoints in future cases.

Third, because the ruling affects how people run small businesses and their roles and responsibilities to protect against discrimination, and because those roles and responsibilities are still unclear, tensions (and opportunities) still exist. In other words, this case clearly affects how we interpret anti-discrimination guidelines, but it also effects how people are positioned to make or lose money, and that complicates matters. As Issac West writes, "Conflicting constitutional principles are intrinsic parts of living together in a heterogeneous society, but interactions in an economic market are subject to specific rules and regulations because of the pernicious effects that flow from segregated marketplaces."[117]

Fourth, Masterpiece points to the conflicts inherent in locating the place where one individual's rights end and another's begin. A similar conflict is expressed in whether a pharmacist who opposes abortion can refuse to dispense abortifacient medications.[118]

We identify four themes we see in the public commentary about the *Masterpiece* ruling: (1) characterizing warriors in a cultural war, (2) defining "expression" and how it applies to this case, (3) explaining what it means to be open for business, and (4) offering future projections and pragmatic solutions. While these themes focus on various aspects of the *Masterpiece* decision, we also note that there are some consistent elements that tie these themes together. First, all the themes reveal a sense of urgency as advocates must jump in quickly to define the terms of the debate. One reason for this is the time frame of the texts we studied. We evaluated discourse that appeared as the case was taken up by the Court and in the immediate aftermath of the decision. Partisans on each side wanted to get the first chance to spin the decision in the way that supported their beliefs. Another reason for this urgency might also be the nature of the ruling itself. *Masterpiece Cakeshop* was not a sweeping defense of either religious protection or LGBTQ rights;

rather, the Court ruled on a narrow question. Nevertheless, advocates on both sides of this issue did not want the opportunity afforded by a Supreme Court ruling to pass without asserting their interpretations of the greater issues. A second similarity among these themes is that the reactions to the ruling illustrate the space between the law and perceptions of an ideal society. As noted above, the ruling was not a clear-cut ruling on the vexing competing interests of religious freedoms, the dangers of discrimination, and the logic of the marketplace. But the commentators we evaluated were eager to stake out their own vision of how society should balance or privilege these elements. From a legal standpoint, the *Masterpiece* decision created static that will need to be resolved through future judicial rulings and legislation. But, in the meantime, citizens want answers and direction as they navigate these issues. A third similarity among these themes is the force of the language in all of them. The ruling could be spun in a positive or negative way; in a clear-cut or nuanced way; or in a fearful or hopeful way. The rhetoric during this period shows us the language people are using as the come to terms with the issues raised by the ruling. This in turn gives us insight into the way that subsequent debates will be framed.

Future Directions

Scholars interested in clashes of freedom of religion and freedom of speech will be at no loss moving into the future. The Masterpiece ruling will likely be applied to other types of services that will be considered expressive speech (florists, photographers, etc.), in fact, it already has, but it is likely to also be cited in cases that may seem unrelated. How churches navigate staying open during pandemics in the face of pandemic protocols, while protecting religious expression is another example of the clash between the establishment clause and free expression.

As citizen-scholars interested in making a difference in society, we have opportunities. As those trained in the rhetorical tradition, we are uniquely positioned to contribute to the debate about what constitutes communication, and expression. As those trained in argumentation, we can identify and explain argumentation themes and strategies as they play out in the public arena. As First Amendment scholars we can explore the tension among First Amendment rights and draw from historical interpretations to illuminate contemporary conflicts. Our challenge as citizens is to use our scholarly position to bring underrepresented voices into the discussion, particularly as it applies to anti-discrimination legislation, without marginalizing, co-opting, or commodifying these voices in the process.

Notes

1 Savage, "Baker's Refusal Goes to High Court; Citing His Religious Views, a Colorado Man Declined to Make a Wedding Cake for a Same-Sex Couple."
2 Ibid.
3 Ibid.
4 Brown, "Masterpiece Cakeshop: A Formula for Legislative Accommodations of Religion."
5 For a more complete analysis of the justices' arguments see Rains, 2017; Russo, 2018; Murry, 2019.
6 Moore, "Supreme Court rules baker can refuse to make gay wedding cake."
7 Ibid.
8 Turkewitz, "As Cake Case Passed Through the Courts, Colorado Was Changing."
9 McNulty, "Rupp Again Is Icing on 'The Cake'; The Mostly Satisfying Play About a Woman Reluctant to Bake for a Lesbian Couple Is Like Sugary Comfort Food."
10 Deabler, "Yelp Adds 'Open to All' Feature After Gay Wedding Cake Snub."
11 Ibid.
12 Ibid.
13 Berg, "Religious Freedom and Nondiscrimination," 139.
14 Russo, Kicking the Can down the Road in Masterpiece Cakeshop: Is Finding a Happy Medium Possible, or Will the Solution Remain Half-Baked?" 399.
15 Miller, "Reconciling religious Freedom and LGBT Rights: The Perils and Promises of Masterpiece Cakeshop," 246.
16 Anderson, "Disagreement is not always discrimination: On Masterpiece Cakeshop and the Analogy to Interracial Marriage"; Berg "Religious Freedom and Nondiscrimination;" Alexander "The Masterpiece Cakeshop decision and the clash between nondiscrimination and religious freedom."
17 Miller, "Reconciling Religious Freedom and LGBT Rights: The Perils and Promises of Masterpiece Cakeshop," 246; Griffin, "Religious Freedom, Human Rights, and Peaceful Coexistance."
18 Brown, 2019.
19 Hart.
20 Ebin and Price, "The Great American Rights Bake Off: Freedom of Religion v. Freedom from Discrimination," 588.
21 Russo, Kicking the Can down the Road in Masterpiece Cakeshop: Is Finding a Happy Medium Possible, or Will the Solution Remain Half-Baked," 441.
22 Murray, "Inverting Animus: Masterpiece Cakeshop and the New Minorities," 257.
23 Brown, "Masterpiece Cakeshop: A Formula for Legislative Accommodations of Religion."
24 Price, "Symmetric Constitutionalism: An Essay on Masterpiece Cakeshop and the Post-Kennedy Supreme Court," 1273.
25 Rains, "Icing on the Wedding Cake: Same-Sex Marriage and Religious Objections—Is There an Accommodation that Will Make Everyone Equally Happy (or Unhappy)?," 224.
26 Ibid.
27 Ibid,, 225.
28 West, "Wedding Cakes, Equality, and Rhetorics of Religious Freedom," 4.

29 Ibid., 2.
30 "The Cake Was Not a First Amendment Issue." *New York Time.*
31 "Double Religious Jeopardy" *New York Times*
32 Phillips, "Here's why I can't custom-design cakes for same-sex weddings."
33 Harsanyi, "Cake-bakers have the right to draw a line in the icing.
34 Harsanyi, "Cake-bakers have the right to draw a line in the icing."
35 Lowry, "Supreme Court ruling is a win for religious freedom."
36 Harsanyi, "Cake-bakers have the right to draw a line in the icing.
37 "Double Religious Jeopardy," *Wall Street Journal.*
38 House, "The Masterpiece Decision Isn't Harmless."
39 Lewis, "The Right Now Loves Free Speech."
40 Swarens, "We All Lost in Supreme Court Samesex Wedding Case."
41 John S. Dickerson, letter to the editor, *USA Today.*
42 House, "The Masterpiece Decision Isn't Harmless."
43 Melling, "Right to Discriminate?"
44 Quoted in Robinson, letter to the editor.
45 Robinson, letter to the editor.
46 Ibid.
47 Ibid.
48 Hart, letter to the editor.
49 Ibid.
50 Holladay, letter to the editor.
51 Ibid.
52 Ibid.
53 Ibid.
54 Ibid.
55 "The Cake Was Not a First Amendment Issue."
56 Ibid.
57 Ibid.
58 Fredericks, "Gay Wedding Cake Decision Isn't All Bad for LGBTQ Community: Analyst."
59 Ibid.
60 Ibid.
61 Ibid.
62 Lowry, "Supreme Court Ruling Is a Win for Religious Freedom."
63 Melling, "Right to Discriminate?"
64 "Let Them Not Bake Cake."
65 Phillips, "The Supreme Court Let Me Live My Faith Again."
66 Ibid.
67 Gaul, letter to the editor.
68 Ibid.
69 Ibid.
70 Tonty, letter to the editor.
71 Harsanyi, "Cake-Bakers Have the Right to Draw a Line in the Icing."
72 Ibid.
73 Phillips, "Here's Why I Can't Custom-Design Cakes for Same-Sex Weddings."
74 Anderson, "Discrimination Law Isn't Supposed to 'Punish the Wicked.'"

75 Harsanyi, "Cake-Bakers Have the Right to Draw a Line in the Icing."
76 Melling, "Right to Discriminate?"
77 Goldstein, letter to the editor.
78 Ibid.
79 "Let Them (Gay Couples) Eat Cake."
80 Williams, "Masterpiece Cakeshop Reminds Me of Jim Crow."
81 Ibid.
82 Denmark, letter to the editor.
83 Ibid.
84 MacMichael, letter to the editor.
85 Ibid.
86 Ibid.
87 Guiral, letter to the editor.
88 Ibid.
89 Ibid.
90 Phillips, "Here's Why I Can't Custom-Design Cakes for Same-Sex Weddings."
91 Ibid.
92 Ibid.
93 George, "Colorado Made the Masterpiece Case Easy for the Court."
94 Ibid.
95 Phillips, "Supreme Court Decision Says My Faith Is Welcomed Back in America."
96 Ibid.
97 Ibid.
98 Tonty, letter to the editor.
99 Melling, "Right to Discriminate?"
100 Ibid.
101 Winkler, "Does a Bakery Have Free-Speech Rights?"
102 Melling, "Right to Discriminate?"
103 Adami, letter to the editor.
104 Ibid.
105 Deabler, "Yelp Adds 'Open to All' Feature After Gay Wedding Cake Snub."
106 Hendershot, letter to the editor.
107 Chen, letter to the editor.
108 Ibid.
109 Phillips, "The Supreme Court Let Me Live My Faith Again."
110 Ibid.
111 Anderson, "Discrimination Law Isn't Supposed to 'Punish the Wicked.'"
112 "The Supreme Court's Half-Baked Cake."
113 McDonald, "Actually the Baker in Supreme Court Masterpiece Ruling Lost, It Only Looked Like He Won."
114 Boylen, "After Masterpiece, It's Time to Change the Constitution."
115 House, "The Masterpiece Decision Isn't Harmless."
116 Rassbach, "Cake Decision 'A Big Win for All Americans.'"
117 West, "Wedding Cakes, Equality, and Rhetorics of Religious Freedom," 13.
118 Gilchrist, "Supreme Court Rejects Pharmacists' Refusal to Fill Appeal."

Bibliography

Adami, Laurie S. Letter to the editor. *Los Angeles Times* (March 11, 2018). http://www.latimes.com/.

Alexander, Klint W. "The Masterpiece Cakeshop Decision and the Clash between Nondiscrimination and Religious Freedom." *Oklahoma Law Review, 71(4),* (2018).

Anderson, Ryan T. "Disagreement Is Not Always Discrimination: On Masterpiece Cakeshop and the Analogy to Interracial Marriage." *The Georgetown Journal of Law & Public Policy, 16,* pp. 123–145. (2017).

Anderson, Ryan T. "Discrimination Law Isn't Supposed to 'Punish the Wicked': The Antireligious 'Animus' Justice Kennedy Rejected Is Common Among Culture Warriors of the Left." *Wall Street Journal* (June 6, 2018). http://www.wsj.com/.

Anderson, Ryan T. "Discrimination Law Isn't Supposed to 'Punish the Wicked'; The Antireligious 'Animus' Justice Kennedy Rejected Is Common Among Culture Warriors of the Left." *Wall Street Journal* (June 6, 2018). http://www.wsj.com/.

Berg, Thomas C. "Masterpiece Cakeshop: A Romer for Religious Objectors." *Cato Supreme Court Review*, pp. 139–170. (2017).

Berg, Thomas C. "Religious Freedom and Nondiscrimination." *Loyola University Chicago Law Journal, 50(1)*, pp. 181–209. (2018).

Boylan, Jennifer Finney. "After Masterpiece, It's Time to Change the Constitution." *New York Times* (June 4, 2018). http://www.nytimes.com/.

Brown, Matthew A. "Masterpiece Cakeshop: A Formula for Legislative Accommodations of Religion." *Akron Law Review, 53(1),* pp. 176–216. (2019).

Brown, Ruth. "Supreme Court Will Take Case on Baker Who Refused to Sell Wedding Cake to Gay Couple." *New York Post* (June 26, 2017). http://www.nypost.com/.

Chen, Dienyih. "Letter to the Editor." *Los Angeles Times* (December 6, 2017). http://www.latimes.com/.

Deabler, Alexandra. "Yelp Adds 'Open to All' Feature After Gay Wedding Cake Snub." *New York Post* (August 1, 2018). http://www.nypost.com/.

Denmark, Bob. "Letter to the Editor." *Wall Street Journal* (December 20, 2017). http://www.wsj.com/.

Ebin, Chelsea, and J. Ricky Price. "The Great American Rights Bake Off: Freedom of Religion v. Freedom from Discrimination." *New Political Science* (2019): 588–603.

Feldman, Stephen M. "Having Your Cake and Eating It Too: Religious Freedom and LGBT Right." *Wake Forest Journal of Law & Policy, 140,* pp. 35–62. (2018).

Fredericks, Bob. "Gay Wedding Cake Decision Isn't All Bad for LGBTQ Community: Analyst." *New York Post* (June 4, 2018). http://nypost.com/.

Gaul, Timothy J. "Letter to the Editor." *The New York Times* (December 10, 2017). http://www.nytimes.com/.

George, Robert P. "Colorado Made the Masterpiece Case Easy for the Court." *The New York Times* (June 4, 2018). http://www.nytimes.com/.

Gilchrist, Allison. "Supreme Court Rejects Pharmacists' Refusal to Fill Appeal." *Pharmacy Times* (July 5, 2016). https://www.pharmacytimes.com/view/supreme-court-rejects-pharmacists-refusal-to-fill-appeal.

Goldstein, Jonathan. "Letter to the Editor." *Wall Street Journal* (December 10, 2017). http://www.wsj.com/.

Griffin, Leslie C. "Religious Freedom, Human Rights, and Peaceful Coexistence." *Loyola University Chicago Law Journal, 50(1)*, pp. 76–105. (2018).

Guiral, Philip. "Letter to the Editor." *Los Angeles Times* (December 6, 2017). http://www.latimes.com/.

Harsanyi, David. "Cake-Bakers Have the Right to Draw a Line in the Icing." *New York Post* (June 30, 2017). http://nypost.com/.

Hart, Brooke Magid. "Letter to the Editor." *The New York Times* (December 10, 2017). http://nytimes.com/.s

Hart, James. "When the First Amendment Compels an Offensive Result: Masterpiece Cakeshop, Ltd. v. Colorado Civil Rights Commission." *Louisiana Law Review. 79(2)*, pp. 419–439. (2018).

Hendershot, David. "Letter to the Editor." *Los Angeles Times* (December 6, 2017). http://www.latimes.com/.

Holladay, Nathan. "Letter to the Editor." *The New York Times* (December 10, 2017). http://nytimes.com/.

House, Silas. "The Masterpiece Decision Isn't Harmless." *The New York Times* (June 5, 2018). http://www.nytimes.com/.

Lewis, Andrew. "The Right Now Loves Free Speech." *New York Times* (June 27, 2018). http://www.nytimes.com/

Lowry, Rich. "Supreme Court Ruling Is a Win for Religious Freedom." *New York Post* (June 4, 2018). http://www.nypost.com/.

MacMichael, Jan. "Letter to the Editor." *Los Angeles Times* (March 11, 2018). http://www.latimes.com/.

McDonald, Barry P. "Actually the Baker in Supreme Court Masterpiece Ruling Lost, It Only Looked Like He Won." *USA Today* (June 8, 2018). http://www.usatoday.com/.

McNulty, Charles. "Rupp Again Is Icing on 'The Cake'; The Mostly Satisfying Play About a Woman Reluctant to Bake for a Lesbian Couple Is Like Sugary Comfort Food." *Los Angeles Times* (October 6, 2018). http://www.latimes.com/.

Melling, Louise. "Right to Discriminate?" *Los Angeles. Times* (December 4, 2017). http://www.latimes.com/.

Miller, Brian K. "Reconciling Religious Freedom and LGBT Rights: The Perils and Promises of Masterpiece Cakeshop." *George Mason University Civil Rights Law Journal, 29(3)*, pp. 245–274. (2018).

Moore, Mark. "Supreme Court Rules Baker Can Refuse to Make Gay Wedding Cake." *New York Post* (June 4, 2018). http://www.nypost.com/.

Murray, Melissa. "Inverting Animus: Masterpiece Cakeshop and the New Minorities." *The Supreme Court Review* 2018, no. 1 (2019): 257–97.

Phillips, Jack. "Here's Why I Can't Custom-Design Cakes for Same-Sex Weddings." *USA Today* (December 4, 2017). http://www.usatoday.com/.

Phillips, Jack. "The Supreme Court Let Me Live My Faith Again: The Justices Affirmed That I Don't Have to Violate My Beliefs to Work as a Cake Artist." *Wall Street Journal* (June 7, 2018). http://wsj.com/.

Phillips, Jack. "Supreme Court Decision Says My Faith Is Welcomed Back in America: Cake Artist Jack Phillips." *USA Today* (June 4, 2018). http://www.usatoday.com/.

Price, Zachary S. "Symmetric Constitutionalism: An Essay on Masterpiece Cakeshop and the Post-Kennedy Supreme Court." *Hastings Law Journal, 70*, pp. 1273–1316. (2018).

Rains, Robert, E. "Icing on the Wedding Cake: Same-Sex Marriage and Religious Objections—Is There an Accommodation That Will Make Everyone Equally Happy (or Unhappy)?" *Vermont Law Review, 42(2)*, pp. 191–225. (2017).

Rassbach, Eric. "Cake Decision 'A Big Win for All Americans.'" *USA Today* (June 4, 2018). http://www.usatoday.com/.

Robinson, Gene. "Letter to the Editor." *The New York Times* (December 10, 2017). http://nytimes.com/.

Russo, Charles J. "Kicking the Can Down the Road in Masterpiece Cakeshop: Is Finding a Happy Medium Possible, or Will the Solution Remain Half-Baked." *U. Dayton L. Rev.* 44 (2018): 399.

Savage, David G. "Baker's Refusal Goes to High Court; Citing His Religious Views, a Colorado Man Declined to Make a Wedding Cake for a Same-Sex Couple." *LA Times* (September 25, 2017). http://www.latimes.com/.

Swarens, Tim. "We All Lost in Supreme Court Samesex Wedding Case." *USA Today*, (June 4, 2018). http://usatoday.com/.

The New York Times. "The Cake Was Not a First Amendment Issue." (December 2, 2017). http://www:nytimes.com/.

Tonty, Don. "Letter to the Editor." *Los Angeles Times* (March 11, 2018). http://www.latimes.com/.

Turkewitz, Julie. "As Cake Case Passed Through the Courts, Colorado Was Changing." *The New York Times* (June 6, 2018). http://www.nytimes.com/.

USA Today. "Let Them (Gay Couples) Eat Cake." (June 4, 2018). http:www.usatoday.com/.

Wall Street Journal. "Let Them Not Bake Cake: Does Gay Marriage Trump the Right to Religious Expression?" (December 3, 2017). http://www.wsj.com/.

Wall Street Journal. "The Supreme Court's Half-Baked Cake: Kennedy Saves a Baker from Anti-religious Bias He Said Couldn't Happen." (June 4, 2018). http://www.wsj.com/.

West, Isaac. "Wedding Cakes, Equality, and Rhetorics of Religious Freedom." *First Amendment Studies, 53*, pp. 1–21, (2019).

Williams, Montel. "Masterpiece Cakeshop Reminds Me of Jim Crow. We Can't Create New 2nd-Class Citizens." *USA Today* (December 5, 2017). http://www.usatoday.com/.

Winkler, Adam. "Does a Bakery Have Free-Speech Rights? Business Wants the Same Protections as You and I." *Los Angeles Times* (March 4, 2018). http://www.latimes.com/.

14. *Up in the Air: Media Access and Religious Freedom*

MARK WARD SR.

Admirers called him "Fighting Bob." And as pastor of Trinity Methodist Church in Los Angeles, Robert Shuler preached from more than just a wooden pulpit. In 1926, his church obtained a license to operate radio station KGEF, exhorting Angelenos to "Keep God Ever First." Soon, Shuler's electrifying radio sermons won a mass audience as he fulminated against corruption in the city government and police force. His anti-vice campaign, supported by the city's Protestant clergy, led to the sacking of the police chief and a libel suit against Shuler by the mayor. As the vitriol rose and civic discourse declined, the Federal Radio Commission ruled in 1931 that Trinity's use of the airwaves did not serve the public and revoked its license to broadcast. The church sued the agency and, represented by the American Civil Liberties Union, took its case for free speech all the way to the Supreme Court. There the justices declared in 1932 that the public interest trumps that of the broadcaster and upheld the Commission's action.[1]

In his day, Shuler raged against bootleggers as the leading threat to public morality and against New Dealers as the leading edge of liberalism. Today the heirs to Fighting Bob decry abortion and the "gay agenda" as evidence of moral decay and castigate the Democratic Party as the stalking horse for socialism. The level of rage and polarization in American political discourse has reached new heights. Yet in contrast to Shuler, today's moral crusaders have virtually unlimited access to the airwaves. In the present era of media deregulation, they have formed vast religious media conglomerates.[2] They broadcast daily over hundreds of radio stations and on television networks carried by every major cable and satellite operator.[3] More Americans listen to religious radio and watch religious television each month than attend church.[4] And the religious media conglomerates and nationally syndicated religious programmers repackage their content for on-demand streaming via every digital media platform, increasing their audiences by an order of magnitude.[5]

As a policy, media deregulation and its attendant legal framework have never been cast in terms of equal protection. What policymaker would openly argue that equal protection should be repealed? Rather, media deregulation has been framed as an economic policy to foster market efficiencies that will respond to consumer demand. Nevertheless, as opponents point out, media deregulation implicates larger democratic assumptions of equal participation in a shared public sphere over the media airwaves. The story of religious broadcasting illustrates how federal communications policy has evolved, from protecting equal access for people and ideas to participate in a limited but common media space, to sanctioning privatized media spaces where people are free to speak (and monetize) ideas as they please. The concept of equal protection has shifted from ensuring public access to a finite public space, to fostering private access to proliferating private spaces. In theory, everyone can access these media spaces—for example, as sites to exercise their religious freedoms. Yet despite this illusion of choice, the laws of media economics dictate that only a shrinking number of interests can own these spaces. This new concept of equal protection has profound implications for democratic life, as people migrate to media enclaves without ever needing to engage people who are different from themselves.

Trees, Air, and the Public Interest

The contrast between Fighting Bob Shuler in the 1920s and 30s, and his heirs nearly a century later, illustrates a fundamental question that has confronted federal communications policymakers since the dawn of radio: When the government allocates the nation's airwaves, a scarce public good, is the public interest served by licensing an operator who broadcasts only a single viewpoint? Put another way, can the public interest in access to diverse information and opinion be balanced against the rights of broadcasters to freedom of speech under the First Amendment? Nowhere has this dilemma been more contested than in the matter of religious speech over the airwaves. Across the decades, policymakers have confronted numerous questions: Do single-faith radio stations provide religious education or propaganda? Do they have an obligation to air opposing viewpoints? Does it serve the public interest when religious broadcasters attack other faiths? Or stir up faith-based political movements? Does on-air fundraising take unfair advantage of listeners and viewers?

These and other questions—some ultimately decided by the Supreme Court—begin with a simple distinction: trees or air. The medium for print communications is paper whose source, trees, is not historically seen as subject to the laws of economic scarcity. Trees are renewable and, as a practical matter, no one can monopolize the supply of paper. Thus, the contents of newspapers, magazines, and books are generally free from regulation with exceptions only in matters such as defamation and mail fraud. By contrast, radio, television, and wireless communications are carried over the air—which would seem even more infinite than trees. Yet the actual medium that carries their signals is electromagnetic waves. These waves vary in frequency from infinitely short to infinitely long. But only a finite portion of this spectrum, called "radio waves," is usable for broadcast and wireless communications. In other words, usable waves are scarce and could in theory be monopolized. For that reason, radio waves are public property, like a street or a sidewalk, and allocated by the Federal Communications Commission (FCC). The agency grants licenses to use specific radio wave frequencies on the condition that licensees serve the "public interest, convenience, and necessity."

Therein lies the rub. The "public interest standard," enshrined more than eighty years ago under the Communications Act of 1934, has never been concretely defined.[6] Instead, the "public interest, convenience, and necessity" is a living standard whose interpretation varies with changes in media technology, public expectations, and politics. Thus, the Supreme Court in 1932 upheld the revocation of a politically crusading preacher's radio station license—while today, religious radio networks relentlessly broadcast Christian Right politics over hundreds of stations.[7] And though the Supreme Court in 1969 ruled that a religious station was required under the FCC's Fairness Doctrine to broadcast opposing viewpoints, the doctrine was repealed in 1987 after the Reagan administration declared that market forces best determine the public interest—birthing conservative talk radio in the process.[8] Until the 1950s, the major networks banned on-air fundraising by religious programs, and decades later Congress investigated televangelists after a series of sensational financial scandals in 1987–1988.[9] Yet after Congress deregulated media ownership restrictions in the 1990s, the "electronic church" is now dominated by a handful of religious media conglomerates that annually generate revenues of hundreds of millions of dollars, without oversight, through traditional broadcasting and on-demand digital streaming.[10] And the National Religious Broadcasters, an association founded in the 1940s to lobby for greater media access, nevertheless opposed the "net neutrality" rule—which gave startup streaming services the same media access as the conglomerates—that was adopted in 2015 during the Obama years but repealed in 2018 by the Trump-era FCC.[11]

Given the exponential growth of digital media options, the very idea that anyone could monopolize the media today seems absurd (although the net neutrality debate has recently drawn public attention to the increasingly oligopolistic structure of the media industries). Indeed, since the rise of FM radio in the 1970s, the cable revolution of the 1980s, and the advent of direct broadcast satellite television and radio service in the 1990s—and of course, the spread of the Internet in the 21st century—a generation of policymakers and scholars have asked whether the notion of "spectrum scarcity" is obsolete.

Nevertheless, one of the most stunning and impactful, if unnoticed, victories of the evangelical movement is securing virtually unfettered access to the media. Such a development was contested as early as the 1920s and as recently as the 1980s, when the FCC could (and did) shut down religious broadcasters for violations of the Fairness Doctrine. Since then, as ethnographer Lydia Bean concluded in her field studies of American and Canadian churches, evangelicals in the United States have adopted a politically partisan identity—while their northern counterparts have not—because only in the United States does the Christian Right possess the mass media to broadcast its message directly to the faithful.[12]

Other studies have shown that American evangelicalism, as a social system, features three tiers: a macro level of national parachurch institutions and their mass-mediated representations that disseminate subcultural norms, a meso level of Sunday sermons and other congregational discourses that structure local deliberation and joint social action, and a micro level of natural spontaneous talk and private role enactments that reproduce the norms.[13] The "electronic church," made possible by virtually unhindered media access for religious speech, is the linchpin that holds the evangelical movement together as a coherent and enduring transdenominational subculture.[14] One in four Americans identifies with this movement, making evangelical Protestantism the nation's single largest religious tradition.[15] Today, a majority of Protestants identify as "born again/evangelical."[16] And to the present point, one in five adults consume religious media on a daily basis.[17] Today's electronic church encompasses a dozen television networks carried by every major satellite service and cable operator, ten national radio networks, and some 3,000 radio stations—fully one-fifth of the nation's total AM and FM outlets—that air religious teaching, talk, or music.[18] How did the current balance between media access and religious freedom evolve? Where is it headed? What are the implications for the doctrine of equal protection as it relates to the public airwaves? For answers, the present study examines a century of the sometimes contentious, sometimes cozy, but often changing intersection of religion, media, and the public interest.

Deciding What Radio Would Be

The prehistory of broadcasting in the United States can be sketched in a series of milestones: the invention of the electric telegraph in 1835; the decision by Congress to privatize telegraph services in 1844, a key precedent for later private ownership of broadcast facilities; the discovery of electromagnetic waves in 1864; the first wireless radio-wave telegraph in 1895; the first wireless voice transmission in 1906; the sinking of the *Titanic* in 1912, which prompted the first radio licensing law; the nationalization and technological standardization of radio during World War I; and the re-privatization of radio in 1920.[19] From the 1890s onward, "wireless" was viewed as a means to improve telegraphy, a form of point-to-point "narrowcasting." But even before U.S. entry into World War I, nascent ideas of "broadcasting," of marketing the wireless receiver as a "radio music box," were being floated.[20] By 1920, a radio craze was in full swing and hobbyists nationwide were building homemade receiving sets. In November of that year, to generate a market for its factory-made sets, Westinghouse launched KDKA-AM/Pittsburgh, America's first radio station with regularly scheduled commercial programming. Soon, KDKA was competing with other stations to score radio "firsts" and transmitted the first religious broadcast, a vespers service aired live from a Pittsburgh church, on January 2, 1921. Radio was so new that, to prevent disruption of the service, the KDKA engineers donned choir robes.[21]

At the time, operators could not transmit radio signals without a license from the federal Department of Commerce. The agency sought to police the airwaves and prevent operators from interfering with one another. But as the number of stations multiplied, attempts at regulation proved impractical and in 1926 were successfully challenged in court by broadcasters. Yet all parties recognized that, if the public could not receive clear signals over their expensive new radio sets, the fledgling industry would choke on its own growth. One proposal advocated by religious, educational, and labor groups would promote free speech by classifying radio as a "common carrier," similar to existing telephone companies (and similar to how Internet service providers would have been classified under the now-repealed 2015 net neutrality rules). Thus, anyone could purchase time to transmit a radio message in the same way that anyone could purchase time to make a phone call.

Such a scheme, however, would give station operators no control over message content and was opposed by the National Association of Broadcasters. The lobby argued that without control, broadcasters could not generate the revenues to invest in technological improvements (again, an argument replayed ninety years later in the net neutrality debate). Congress reached a compromise with the Radio Act of 1927. Stations would not be common carriers but instead would be granted, by a newly created Federal Radio Commission (FRC), a short-term renewable license to use a designated radio frequency. Yet in a bow to free-speech advocates, any license would be granted on the condition that the broadcaster serve the "public interest, convenience, and necessity." Failure to meet that standard could result in the license being revoked and the frequency reassigned to another licensee.[22] Ironically, that same public interest standard soon became, as Fighting Bob Shuler discovered, the weapon wielded against advocates of free speech when they sought to operate radio stations of their own. Though radio stations of the day were commercially owned by private interests that earned a profit, the licenses they held were regarded legally as public trusts and not as permits to set up private media spaces.

Radio, Religion, and Regulation

The impact of the new regulations, promulgated by the FRC, on operators of religious stations was immediate. Before passage of the 1927 law, more than 60 of the 732 stations on the air were operated by religious groups, many of them local churches that only broadcast their Sunday worship services.[23] Unable to afford the new requirements to use professional broadcast equipment and trained operators, about half of the stations licensed to religious organizations relinquished their licenses. Many religious stations that remained on the air were associated with national ministries that could raise the funds to sustain a radio outreach; these included KFUO-AM/St. Louis (Lutheran Church Missouri Synod), KTBI-AM/Los Angeles (Bible Institute of Los Angeles), KFSG-AM/Los Angeles (Church of the Foursquare Gospel), and WMBI-AM/Chicago (Moody Bible Institute).

WMBI illustrates how early religious broadcasters grappled with the ambiguities of the new public interest standard. Evangelicals, who would soon come to dominate the medium, faced a conundrum: they were unwilling, as the price for access to the public airwaves, to dilute their gospel message or share their radio pulpits with "liberal" preachers. Chicago's Moody Bible Institute was founded by evangelist Dwight Lyman Moody, who in the 1870s pioneered modern organizational methods for mass citywide crusades and became an international celebrity.[24] As early as 1921 his namesake institute discussed launching a radio station. Yet its heritage of face-to-face evangelism, together with the new medium's increasing association with worldly entertainment and the biblical admonition that Satan is "the prince of the power of the air" (Ephesians 2:2), caused officials to hesitate. By 1925, however, donors were already sending unsolicited gifts for construction of a radio station and the decision was made to move ahead.[25]

A license was secured from the federal Department of Commerce in 1926 but, to the station's dismay, the inaugural WMBI broadcast was cut short due to interference when another Chicago station launched service the same day on the same frequency. The two stations worked out a satisfactory division of airtime. Yet a few months later, in 1927, the newly created Federal Radio Commission announced that all licenses would be reviewed and that stations could only remain on their current frequencies for sixty days while hearings were held in Washington.

WMBI station engineer Henry Crowell, whose father chaired the Institute's board of trustees, traveled to the hearings in Washington and suggested that the agency "allocate a small number of wave channels to be used jointly by educational and religious stations ... not at the remote ends of the present band, but where they would be of service to the average listener with their present receiving sets."[26] The FRC permitted WMBI to continue operating beyond the sixty-day limit but indicated that the station ultimately would be required to share time on the same frequency with several other stations. Crowell then made a second trip to Washington for a private meeting with the federal commissioners, who agreed that WMBI was "operating in the interests of public convenience, interest, and necessity." The agency later approved a new wavelength assignment to be shared with only one other station and even authorized a power increase to 5,000 watts. Yet a year later, in 1928, when Congress passed legislation to equalize the number of radio stations allowed in different regions of the country, Chicago was way over the limit. WMBI was assigned a new wavelength, shared by two other stations, and classified as a "limited time" facility. When WMBI appealed in 1929 for a new frequency assignment, the station faced an unexpected roadblock when another religious station in Chicago was disqualified from seeking a new wavelength. The FRC further proposed that religious stations be classified as "propaganda outlets" which benefitted only a small segment of the public and thus be permitted only limited broadcast hours at the remote end of the AM radio band.

This time, Moody Bible Institute President James Gray went to Washington, D.C., to testify at an FRC hearing. He pointed out that WMBI was operated as a nondenominational, educational radio outlet with programs that appealed to both religious and non-religious listeners. Strong propaganda and direct financial appeals were avoided. Slanderous statements attacking other religious viewpoints were prohibited. Guest speakers were chosen with care and strictly warned against careless comments. As a result, no formal complaint had ever been lodged against WMBI. The station lost its case for a new wavelength, but the federal commissioners went on record in 1930 to commend WMBI for its professional organization. A year later, in 1931, the agency affirmed that WMBI was operating in the public interest and would be safe as long as its license was not directly challenged by another station.

This was no small victory. In Canada, regulators were so appalled by radio preachers who broadcast attacks on other religious viewpoints, that they banned "single-faith" stations altogether.[27] And in the same year that the FRC praised WMBI for its evenhanded approach, the agency revoked the license of Fighting Bob Shuler for his vitriolic attacks on politicians, Jews, Catholics, and other evangelists. In weighing Shuler's free-speech claim against the public interest, the Supreme Court upheld the FRC. "[If] one in possession of a permit to broadcast in interstate commerce," the justices ruled, "may ... offend the religious susceptibilities of thousands, inspire political distrust and civic discord ... then this great science [of radio], instead of a boon, will become a scourge, and the nation a theater for the display of individual passions and the collision of personal interests."[28] The contrasting cases of WMBI and KGEF thus illustrate how federal communications policymakers at the dawn of radio accommodated religious speech on the public airwaves. Religious broadcasters could be granted media access provided they stuck to religious education, to positively preaching their religious messages, and not violate the public trust by negatively attacking others.

Industry Self-Regulation and the Mainline Cartel

WMBI became an influential arbiter of midcentury evangelical popular music and culture, and today is the flagship for a national network of more than eighty stations and translators whose programming is carried by another 900 affiliates.[29] In contrast, when his radio license was revoked, Shuler turned to politics, winning more than 560,000 votes as the Prohibition Party candidate in the 1932 election for U.S. Senate from California. The case of KGEF, however, is today remembered only among historians of broadcasting and communications law. Far better known is the controversy over Father Charles Coughlin and his anti-Semitic, anti-New Deal, anti-democratic radio preaching during the 1930s and 40s.[30] His case, however, differed from Shuler's in key respects. Where Shuler owned a local radio station, Coughlin's outreach was syndicated on stations nationwide. Thus, where Shuler's preaching ran afoul of the FRC's public interest standard and led to revocation of his license, Coughlin's broadcasts prompted local stations and the nascent radio networks, NBC and CBS, to consider programming standards and regulate themselves to prevent FRC intervention. Lastly, though a Catholic priest, Coughlin was refused airtime not because of his religious message but because he became a political demagogue who only happened to be a member of a religious order.

The story of broadcast industry self-regulation begins in World War I. After America entered the conflict in 1917, the government as a security measure nationalized radio, which then consisted of numerous experimental stations. To bolster public support, a federal Committee on Public Information (CPI) was formed to saturate the nation with pro-war propaganda. Radio was seen as a "miracle" technology, a "magic bullet" to sway the masses. As public relations pioneer Edward Bernays later recalled, the idea of the CPI was to create a "total environment" that would "control and regiment the masses according to our will without their knowing about it."[31]

This magic-bullet theory of radio persisted through the 1920s and 30s. As it pertained to religion on the air, fears over the purportedly hypnotic power of radio made station owners and the newly formed NBC and CBS networks sensitive to controversy. After all, stations held their licenses only on a year-to-year basis. And evangelicals, publicly scorned as "fundamentalists" after their humiliation at the Scopes Monkey Trial of 1925—the first live news event broadcast nationally via radio—were controversial.[32] So was on-air fundraising—which evangelicals, who had "separated" from the "modernist" Protestant denominations, had to do in order to purchase radio airtime. Thus, NBC in 1928, and CBS in 1931, adopted a policy of refusing to sell airtime for religious programs and instead donated free "sustaining time" to the representative national bodies of the Protestant, Catholic, and Jewish faiths. The two networks canceled the paid programs of evangelical broadcasters, who in turn had no access to sustaining time because they were not members of the Federal (later National) Council of Churches.[33]

Only when the upstart Mutual Broadcasting System launched in 1934, and needed funds to compete with its established rivals, could evangelicals purchase network airtime. The ensuing decade was a "golden age" as Charles Fuller's *Old Fashioned Revival Hour*, Percy Crawford's *Young People's Church of the Air*, and other syndicated programs aired coast-to-coast over hundreds of Mutual stations and amassed audiences of up to twenty million weekly listeners.[34] For the first time, evangelicalism became a coherent transdenominational subculture as the faithful nationwide listened to the same popular radio preachers and the same gospel music.[35] Yet by the early 1940s, this visibility also generated opposition. Influential public-interest groups such as the Institute for Education by Radio pushed Mutual to roll back paid religious programming. Alarmed, evangelicals set aside their historic independence and formed the National Association of Evangelicals (NAE) to lobby for media access.[36] The fairest way to accommodate religious speech over the airwaves, the new group argued, was a "free market" in which airtime was equally available for purchase by all comers who could act responsibly and uphold the public trust.[37] Yet in 1944 Mutual effectively ended paid religious programs, prompted largely by advertisers who complained of audience turnover when programs they sponsored followed religious broadcasts.

Because 95%[38] of all AM stations at the time were affiliated with a network—whether NBC, CBS, or Mutual—evangelical broadcasters were shut out. The networks and the mainline denominations, represented by the Federal Council of Churches, had formed a "cartel" that controlled Protestant broadcasts.[39] Yet this cartel proved short-lived. The ABC radio and television network, which was founded in 1945, decided four years later to take preachers' money. Billy Graham, then a rising media star, in 1950 debuted his *Hour of Decision* radio program on ABC. Fuller and Crawford immediately bought time on the upstart network and in 1949–50 even launched weekly ABC television broadcasts. Meanwhile, the NAE formed an affiliate, the National Religious Broadcasters (NRB), to focus on media access. With television creating vast new schedules that had to be filled, NRB's free-market argument gained ground. By the mid 1950s, NBC and CBS rescinded their policies against selling time for religious programs. The final nail in the cartel's coffin was a 1960 decision by the FCC that stations could receive public-interest credit for selling, not just donating, time for religious programs. By the end of the 1970s, the practice of donating airtime virtually disappeared, and the National Council of Churches reversed its historic opposition to paid time. Due in no small part to its media visibility, evangelical Protestantism came to be recognized as a major expression of Christian faith beside mainline Protestantism and Catholicism. In the evolving balance between media access and religious freedom, a kind of "disestablishment" occurred. A "wall of separation" between church and network arose, as network gatekeepers no longer favored one established expression of Protestant faith. Instead, the "free religious marketplace" came to the airwaves.

Deciding What's Fair over the Air

As successor to the FRC, the Federal Communications Commission was established as a permanent agency under the Communications Act of 1934. In turn, the new law permanently enshrined the "public interest, convenience, and necessity" standard for licensing broadcasters. As the new FCC interpreted that standard through the lens of the prevailing magic-bullet theory of mass communication, it declared in 1941 that radio stations may not editorialize and must be politically neutral. During World War II, however, radio reporters provided crucial coverage of battlefield news. And as the concept of "broadcast journalism" emerged, stations and networks lobbied the FCC for the same editorial privileges as print journalists. The agency responded in 1949 by promulgating the Fairness Doctrine. Broadcasters could editorialize and could air opinion programs. But should any member of the public request time to express an opposing viewpoint, equal time must be provided at no charge.

Yet what if a religious station sold time to programs that preached particular religious viewpoints? Must it provide equal time for those of a different doctrine, or from a different religion altogether, for a rebuttal? Potentially, a religious station could be compelled to split its daily schedule, giving half to paying programs and the other half to dissenters free of charge. Religious broadcasters feared this would void their ministries and, being dependent on selling airtime for programs rather than selling advertisements, jeopardize their financial viability.

Several developments during the 1950s and 60s gave rise to these fears. After the FCC suspended licensing of new radio stations during World War II, the agency stepped up licensing in the postwar years and permitted commercially operated religious stations. As network radio declined with the advent of television, radio preachers could turn to these stations for reliable media access and reliable listeners. The stations, typically with weak signals in small or rural markets, received reliable income that insulated them from ratings competition. Meanwhile, in the 1950s syndicated radio evangelists including Billy Graham, Billy James Hargis, and Carl McIntire became leading voices in the national anti-communist movement. Though their sermons against Soviet-style atheism had a religious basis, their message intersected with the politics of McCarthyism. Graham's *Hour of Decision* aired on some 800 stations, Hargis's *Christian Crusade* on 500, and McIntire's *Twentieth Century Reformation Hour* on 600 outlets.[40]

Application of the Fairness Doctrine to religious programming was put to the test in 1964. In one of his programs that year, Hargis discussed a book by journalist Fred Cook that portrayed Republican presidential candidate Barry Goldwater as a conservative extremist. Cook then went to a local Pennsylvania station, WGCB-AM owned by Red Lion Broadcasting, that aired the Hargis broadcast and requested equal time to rebut the preacher's negative assessment of his book. When WGCB refused and the FCC ruled that the station had failed its public interest obligation, Red Lion Broadcasting sued the agency on free-speech grounds. Ultimately, the Supreme Court in 1969 unanimously sided with the FCC, declaring that a "licensee has no constitutional right to be the one who holds the license" and "[t]here is nothing in the First Amendment which prevents the Government from requiring a licensee to share his frequency with others" since "the right of the viewers and listeners, not the right of the broadcasters ... is paramount."[41] Armed with this ruling, the FCC in 1973 cited the Fairness Doctrine in shutting down McIntire's flagship radio station.

Nevertheless, with the rise of the New Christian Right in the 1970s, the number of religious radio stations tripled during the decade from less than three hundred to more than a thousand.[42] Repealing the Fairness Doctrine became the top priority of the National Religious Broadcasters. The lobby ultimately won the day with the 1980 election of Ronald Reagan. The new Republican-led FCC in 1981 ditched the "trusteeship model" of broadcasting, ruled that the market best determines the public interest, and in 1987 rescinded the Fairness Doctrine. The following year, conservative talk radio was born as *The Rush Limbaugh Show* entered national syndication. Evangelical Christian talk radio also emerged as a genre with the 1982 debut of *Talk-Back with Bob Larson* and the 1983 launch of *Point of View* with Marlin Maddoux. Both shows aired daily on more than 200 stations, with Larson bringing a shock-jock format of sensational guest interviews and Maddoux offering a live, issue-oriented, call-in format.[43]

The decision of the Reagan-era FCC to repeal the Fairness Doctrine was not directly related to the concerns of religious broadcasters. Even before Reagan took office, a drive to reduce government regulations gained steam with the deregulation of the trucking and airline industries under the Democratic administration of Jimmy Carter. Given the rise of FM radio in the 1970s and cable television in the 1980s, federal communications policymakers had grounds to question whether the electromagnetic spectrum was still a scare public good capable of being monopolized. Abandoning the trusteeship interpretation of the public interest standard, in favor of letting the market decide, fit the deregulatory tenor of the times and has not been substantively challenged since. As for the balance between media access and religious free speech, the upshot is simple. Even when televangelists such as Jerry Falwell and Pat Robertson mobilized political movements that far exceeded what Fighting Bob Shuler and Billy James Hargis could ever have imagined—and even when a series of sensational televangelist scandals in 1987–88 exposed gross financial fraud—media access for religious speech remained, and still remains, sacrosanct. The advent of today's media landscape, with public airwaves converted to single-opinion private media spheres, came into view.

Consolidating the Gospel

The Reagan Revolution may have ended in 1992 with the election of Democrat Bill Clinton to the presidency. Yet the drive to deregulate could not be stopped. In the 1994 midterm elections, reenergized Republicans touted their conservative Contract with America in taking over the House of Representatives for the first time in forty years. Two years later Clinton, a centrist Democrat, announced in his 1996 State of the Union address that "the era of big government is over." In communications policy, the emergence of personal computing, the Internet, and digital technology gave rise to a growing feeling. The Communications Act of 1934, virtually untouched for sixty years, was said to reflect a vanished world of spectrum scarcity and analog technology. Democrats and Republicans agreed that America needed an overhaul of its basic communications law and the Telecommunications Act of 1996 was the result.

Lawmakers recognized, however, that the usable electromagnetic spectrum was still finite, unregulated allocation of frequencies by market forces would be chaos, and broadcasters were already heavily invested in their licensed wavelengths. Thus, the old standard of "public interest, convenience, and necessity" remained. Then, too, politicians of the 1990s were committed to the principle that, while consumers might pay subscription fees for cable and direct-broadcast satellite service, free over-the-air service must be preserved. Since traditional broadcasters paid the government nothing for the use of their assigned frequencies, they were obligated to provide the public with radio and television services for free. Local stations also provided local news, weather, public affairs programming, advertising, and emergency alerts that cable and satellite channels could not.

To safeguard local television, the FCC in the 1980s and 90s decreed in a series of rulemakings that local cable operators must provide channel space at no charge to local over-the-air stations. This "must carry" rule was a top priority of the National Religious Broadcasters as it preserved audience access for hundreds of locally-owned religious TV stations.[44] Nevertheless, the Telecommunications Act required stations to convert from analog to digital broadcasting within ten years (though the FCC later extended the deadline). Most independent, locally-owned religious stations could not afford the multimillion-dollar cost of conversion and many sold out to religious TV networks.[45] At the same time, the 1996 law allowed cable companies to own local systems covering up to 30% of the country. Soon, a cable industry that was once a hodgepodge of local franchises became today's handful of nationwide multi-system cable operators. In this new dispensation, religious television has assumed an oligopolistic structure. The major players are the Trinity Broadcasting Network and Daystar Television Network, followed by a half dozen or so lesser players.[46] Trinity and Daystar have the power to secure channel space on all major cable and satellite operators, and both networks also own dozens of local stations across the country. They then sell their nationwide media access to celebrity televangelists, from Joel Osteen to the Billy Graham Evangelistic Association, who can afford the millions of dollars required to purchase national program time.

In radio, broadcasters complained they were hamstrung by stringent limits on how many stations they could own. Under the old doctrine of preventing monopolization of the public airwaves, as recently as 1985 the cap was seven AM and seven FM outlets—and only one AM and FM per market. Many local stations were losing money because, broadcasters argued, their inability to scale up put them at a disadvantage in competing with other media for local advertising. Thus, between 1985 and 1994 the FCC had gradually raised the national ownership cap from 14 to 40—until the 1996 Telecommunications Act eliminated the cap altogether. The impact was immediate. In 1996 alone, some 2,157 stations changed hands.[47] A year later, station ownership in 86% of the nation's fifty largest media markets was heavily or moderately concentrated, compared to 18% prior to the new law.[48] Within six years, more than 40% of U.S. radio stations were under new ownership and the total number of radio station owners fell 33%.[49] By 2002, at least twenty-one radio groups owned more outlets than the pre-1996 limit of forty stations. These groups acquired more than 2,600 stations and by 2002 owned about one out of every five radio stations in the nation.[50]

Among the twenty-one largest radio groups in 2002 were evangelical broadcasters Salem Media Group, American Family Association (AFA), and Educational Media Foundation (EMF). As these consolidators went to work, the number of network-owned religious stations in the fifty largest markets quickly increased.[51] Celebrity preachers, with the funds and production values to secure network airtime, expanded their outreach while lesser-known programs declined or went off the air.[52] Today, Salem owns 115 stations, including seventy-three in the twenty-five largest media markets, and distributes its talk, news, and music programming to 3,100 affiliates in more than 300 media markets.[53] AFA's American Family Radio operates nearly 200 noncommercial FM stations that air news/talk and boasts 1,200 news affiliates.[54] In the Contemporary Christian Music (CCM) radio genre, EMF operates two networks, K-LOVE and Air1, that control more than 650 noncommercial FM stations and translators.[55] These two networks, along with rival Christian Satellite Network and its 450 stations and translators, together dominate the CCM format.[56]

From Past to Present

In the present era of media ownership deregulation and industry consolidation, the religious television and radio industries have also followed the laws of media economics and, since the 1996 Telecommunications Act, become oligopolies. Size matters because media content, once produced or acquired, can then be distributed at relatively low cost. Today, however, expanded distribution means far more than traditional broadcast channels. Religious media conglomerates have the resources to repackage their media content, stream it on demand, and drive audience traffic in the tens of millions to mobile apps and streaming channels.[57] The new conglomerates have also expanded heavily into print media and e-commerce. As centralized sources for religious education and devotional materials—as well as online church directories, pastoral job referrals, clergy professional journals, even choir robes and communion cups—they are now de facto "denominations" for historically independent evangelicals.[58]

Thus, religious freedom is conceived not merely as access to the public airwaves for religious speech. Rather, religious freedom is now the implicit freedom to own media structures that compete with secular media structures. Prior to the Telecommunications Act of 1996, listeners and viewers of evangelical radio and television heard an eclectic mix of preachers who each purchased airtime on independent local stations. In turn, these stations operated on a "dollar for a holler" basis, scheduling daily programs as they saw fit. By contrast, industry consolidation and the emergence of dominant national networks means that religious speech on the airwaves is now a centralized and homogenized echo chamber. Messaging "from a Christian perspective" is spread—through preaching programs, talk shows, and in hourly and nightly newscasts—by the same celebrity speakers broadcasting daily at the same times nationwide to a national audience of the faithful.[59] Evangelicals and their media programming "talk so much of 'the Christian worldview' because they believe in it—but also because it is a powerful rhetorical strategy" that "curtails debate, justifies hardline politics, and discourages sympathetic voters from entertaining thoughts of moderation or compromise."[60]

Yet there is an irony. Before the cable revolution of the late 1980s, when consumers had limited media options, the model for media evangelism was appealing to the broad masses. The televangelism genre amassed a combined audience of twenty million weekly viewers.[61] Jerry Falwell, Pat Robertson, and James Dobson became prominent figures in the public square. Jim Bakker built a Christian theme park whose six million annual attendees followed only Disney World and Disneyland.[62] And when Bakker and fellow televangelists Oral Roberts and Jimmy Swaggart were caught up in sensational scandals, the news was intensely covered by mainstream media. Yet in 2010 when Marcus Lamb, founder of the Daystar Television Network, confessed to adultery—on live television—and alleged a multimillion-dollar blackmail plot against him, the episode passed unnoticed.[63] Why? Today's vast proliferation of media options has fragmented national audiences. Religious broadcasting is now a niche medium, largely seen and heard only by the faithful. The digitized and deregulated "electronic church" may be bigger than ever but, compared to a generation ago, is more out of the public eye and without any public scrutiny.

As successive eras have confronted the balance between media access and religious freedom, the maxim that "elections have consequences" is abundantly evident. Radio dawned in the 1920s, the final decade of Republican dominance before the Democratic New Deal. Pro-business administrations privatized broadcasting. And rather than classifying radio as a common carrier like the telephone, policymakers set it on a path of commercial development. Religious speech was permissible so long as it did not tarnish the new medium. Then, during the era of Democratic dominance between the 1930s and 1970s, policymakers took an expansive view of the public interest standard. For religious speakers, the era was bookended by the Supreme Court's 1932 *Trinity* decision and 1969 *Red Lion* ruling. Free speech on the airwaves had its limits; the interest of the public superseded that of the broadcaster. Religious speech must be civil and fair. Finally, when the New Deal coalition waned in the 1980s and the public began to see government as the problem rather than the solution, federal communications policy again changed. The market, not Washington bureaucrats, was deemed the best mechanism to determine the "public interest, convenience, and necessity." With media channels no longer seen as a scarce good, the airwaves were no longer a trust to be stewarded by licensees but a natural resource for broadcasters to develop in response to consumer demand. And if consumers want, and are willing to support, religious programming then let that demand be supplied—without unduly burdensome restrictions on media ownership that would artificially stifle providers.

If federal communications policy has effectively swung to unrestricted media access for privatized religious speech, could it someday swing back to the historic interpretation of the public interest standard? Reinstatement of the Fairness Doctrine, mooted in years past by some Democratic lawmakers, has been dead letter for more than a decade.[64] Media mergers in fact accelerated during the Obama Administration as Comcast acquired NBC Universal, Charter Communications acquired Time Warner Cable, Microsoft acquired Skype and LinkedIn, Facebook acquired Instagram and WhatsApp, Disney Corporation acquired Lucasfilm, and AT&T acquired DirecTV, Time Warner, and T-Mobile. Since then, landmark mergers under the Trump Administration include Viacom's acquisition of CBS Corporation, Disney's acquisition of 20th Century Fox, and T-Mobile's acquisition of Sprint. As media "megalopolies" continue to grow with government blessing, the possibility that comparatively smaller religious media conglomerates would be singled out and broken up is remote. Nor does it seem likely that Congress would turn back the clock and legislate anything approaching the stringent media ownership caps that existed prior to the 1996 Telecommunications Act.

What then of religious conservatives' own fears that, as their positions on LGBTQ rights and other social issues become "politically incorrect," their speech will be censored? Alleged suppression of conservative views by social media platforms became a hot topic in 2020 after Twitter appended a fact-check to a racially charged Donald Trump tweet.[65] For its part, the National Religious Broadcasters claim that "Facebook, Google, Amazon, and Apple are information monopolies, and all have committed viewpoint suppression against ... Christian content."[66] Similar fears that government could get into the act and censor religious speech are founded on a 1983 Supreme Court precedent. In that case, Bob Jones University cited a religious basis (albeit a position disavowed by other evangelicals) for banning interracial dating and marriage. However, justices denied its First Amendment claim and sided with an IRS holding that racial discrimination is not "charitable" and the school was not entitled to the federal benefit of a tax exemption.[67] In 2020, the high court declared that discrimination on the basis of sexual orientation and gender identity is barred under the Civil Right Act of 1964.[68] Could the FCC someday rule that anti-LGBTQ speech, even if religiously based, violates its public interest standard and deny religious broadcasters the federal benefit of a license?

Other First Amendment jurisprudence argues against such a prospect. The right of religious organizations to make employment decisions on the basis of religious belief has long been established and was specifically upheld with regard to religious broadcasters in a 1998 federal court decision.[69] More broadly, a string of Supreme Court decisions has ruled that governments may not discriminate against religious organizations or speakers in disbursing generally available public benefits. Cases range from playground equipment grants and private school subsidies, to allocations of public-university activity fees and use of public-school classrooms after hours by outside groups.[70]

Nevertheless, FCC procedures remain in place that permit anyone to invoke the public interest standard and object to renewal of a radio or television station's eight-year license.[71] And because network programming today is produced at a flagship station and digitally distributed for nationwide rebroadcast and streaming, denying the license of a flagship would effectively cripple operations. Yet, successful license challenges on the basis of broadcast content are exceedingly rare. The FCC is cautious in this area—and in the matter of religious content, has good reason. When the agency considered (and subsequently denied) a 1975 petition to freeze licensing of religious stations, a rumor arose that arch atheist Madalyn Murray O'Hair was involved. Over the next twenty years the FCC received thirty million pieces of protest mail until it stopped counting. Nearly half a century later, the agency's website still alerts the public that the rumor is untrue.[72] Were the FCC to propose an actual rulemaking that would deny licenses to religious broadcasters on a viewpoint basis, public protest would be immense. For the 1 in 4 Americans who call themselves evangelicals, the electronic church is not just entertainment; it is the institution that shapes and disseminates their shared identity, culture, and way of life.[73]

Then, too, the electronic church today is less about faces and more about corporations. The conglomerates are savvy multimillion-dollar media operations. Gone is the organ music, hymn-singing choirs, shouted sermons, and eccentric personalities. Nor is there room on network program schedules for the anti-Semitism of a Fighting Bob Shuler and Charles Coughlin, the McCarthyism of a Billy James Hargis and Carl McIntire, the racism of a Bob Jones, the "name-it-and-claim-it" antics of a Reverend Ike and Ernest Angley, the bathetic on-air fundraising of an Oral Roberts and Jim Bakker, and even the shrill flag-waving of a Jerry Falwell and Pat Robertson. They have been replaced by the high production values and soothing pop psychology of a Joel Osteen and T. D. Jakes, the chatty talk shows of a Mike Huckabee (now on Trinity Broadcasting) and Jim Daly (successor to James Dobson at Focus on the Family), and the inoffensive audience-tested sounds of the Contemporary Christian music genre.

Having lost the culture war, evangelicals have switched from offense to defense. For them, "religious freedom" is chiefly the liberty to be left alone and retreat unmolested into the comfortable "parallel universe" of their subculture.[74] (Catholics also now have their own vast electronic church in the Eternal Word Television Network.[75]) Religious programming is no longer syndicated on secular stations but aired over religious networks that, in a world of 900 channels and unlimited media on demand, is seen and heard only by the faithful.[76] Who among today's religious media figures is even known to the general public, much less a lightning rod for public controversy and FCC action? Absent the concept of spectrum scarcity that anchored the original public interest standard, there is now a new Fairness Doctrine—not providing equal time for opposing viewpoints but allowing every viewpoint to amass its own private media sphere.

Conclusion

In the year 2021, religious broadcasting will have marked a century since the first religious broadcast on January 2, 1921. If the past one hundred years has shown anything, it has shown that—as in other areas of American law and public policy—the balance between public interest and the First Amendment rights of religious speakers is not a fixed point. Rather, that balance is "up in the air" as successive generations negotiate their own solutions in accord with their own times and their own technologies. Today, most observers may agree and even lament that American civil discourse is now more polarized than ever as partisans battle over a host of culture-war grievances. Yet powerful interests, religious as well as secular, profit from such discord. Religious speech may not be mainstream media fare, but religious speakers now own mainstream media entities. Trinity Broadcasting reports annual revenues topping $100 million, Daystar Television claims more than $200 million in assets, and publicly-traded Salem Media Group generates revenues of nearly $300 million per year.[77] As such, the interests of today's religious media conglomerates coincide with the interests of the media industries as a whole—to maintain the status quo and keep possession of the sprawling media empires in which they have invested hundreds of millions of dollars.

Thus, the present era of federal communications policy is built on a new doctrine of equal protection. Historically, equal protection meant guarding access for people and ideas to be heard over the scarce good of the public airwaves. In contrast, the government today sanctions "equal access" for anyone to bid on and acquire media spaces for essentially private use. Yet barriers to entry are high as media programming is costly to produce or purchase. Once created or acquired, however, the cost is about the same whether the content is broadcast on one outlet, or a hundred, or a thousand—or is streamed on demand over millions of devices. The gap between media oligarchs and also-rans grows ever larger. In practical terms, the new "equal" protection doctrine inherently favors the powerful who can afford media access. Equal protection, whether of religious speech or any other expression over the airwaves, thereby becomes a commodity that is bought and paid for. In this privatized and conglomerated media sphere, those with the most money have the most say.

Notes

1 A scholarly study of Shuler has yet to be written, with the exception of a 1975 master's thesis: Charles Edward Orbison, "'Fighting Bob' Shuler and KGEF: The Silencing of a Radio Crusader" (master's thesis, University of North Texas, 1975), https://digital.library.unt.edu/ark:/67531/metadc798063/m2/1/high_res_d/1002773405-Orbison.pdf. For further background see Cecilia Rasmussen, "Mixing Fire, Brimstone, and Politics," *Los Angeles Times* (Los Angeles, CA), November 23, 1997, https://www.latimes.com/archives/la-xpm-1997-nov-23-me-56920-story.html; and D. J. Waldie, "Cathedrals of the Air: Sister Aimee, Fighting Bob, and Early L.A. Radio," *KCET*, June 24, 2016, https://www.kcet.org/shows/lost-la/cathedrals-of-the-air-sister-aimee-fighting-bob-and-early-la-radio. For the Supreme Court decision see *Trinity United Methodist Church, South, v. Federal Radio Commission*, No. 5661, 62 F.2d 850 (1932).

2 Mark Ward Sr., "A New Kind of Church: The Religious Media Conglomerate as a 'Denomination,'" *Journal of Media and Religion* 17, nos. 3/4 (2018), 117–33; and Mark Ward Sr., "Air to the Kingdom: Religion and the Soul of Radio," in *Radio's Second Century: A Reader*, ed. John Allen Hendricks (New Brunswick, NJ: Rutgers University Press, 2020), 137–53.

3 Mark Ward Sr., "Major Networks and Personalities," in *The Electronic Church in the Digital Age: Cultural Impacts of Evangelical Mass Media, Vol. 1*, ed. Mark Ward Sr. (Santa Barbara, CA: Praeger, 2016), 255–84.

4 "More People Use Christian Media Than Attend Church," Barna Group, March 14, 2005, https://www.barna.com/research/more-people-use-christian-media-than-attend-church/

5 Mark Ward Sr., "Digital Religion and Media Economics: Concentration and Convergence in the Electronic Church," *Journal of Religion, Media, and Digital Culture* 7, no. 1 (2018): 90–120.

6 See Stuart N. Brotman, "Revisiting the Public Interest Standard in Communications Law and Regulation," Brookings Institution, March 23, 2017, https://www.brookings.edu/research/revisiting-the-broadcast-public-interest-standard-in-communications-law-and-regulation/

7 Mark Ward Sr., "'From a Christian Perspective': News/talk in Evangelical Mass Media," in *News on the Right: Studying Conservative News Cultures*, eds. Anthony M. Nadler and A. J. Bauer (New York, NY: Oxford University Press, 2020), 17–46.

8 Heather Hendershot, *What's Fair on the Air? Cold War Right-wing Broadcasting and the Public Interest* (University of Chicago Press, 2011).
9 Mark Ward Sr., "Air of the King: Evangelicals and Radio," in *Evangelical Christians and Popular Culture: Pop Goes the Gospel, Vol. 1,* ed. Robert H. Woods Jr. (Santa Barbara, CA" Praeger, 2013), 101–18; and Mark Ward Sr., *Air of Salvation: The Story of Christian Broadcasting* (Grand Rapids, MI: Baker Books, 1994).
10 Ward, "A New Kind of Church"; and Ward, "Digital Religion and Media Economics."
11 "NRB Board Unanimous against Internet Power Grab," National Religious Broadcasters, February 24, 2015, http://nrb.org/news-room/press_center/jmp/nrb-board-unanimous-against-Internet-power-grab/
12 Lydia Bean, *The Politics of Evangelical Identity: Local Churches and Partisan Divides in the United States and Canada* (Princeton, NJ: Princeton University Press, 2016).
13 Mark Ward Sr., "The Dangers of Getting What You Wished For: What Do You Say to Evangelicals?," in *Constructing Narratives in Response to Trump's Election: How Various Populations Make Sense of an Unexpected Victory,* eds. Shing-Ling S. Chen, Nicole Allaire, and Zhuojun Joyce Chen (Lanham MD: Lexington, 2018), 61–81; and Mark Ward Sr., "Television Transcendent: How the Electronic Church Constructs Charismatic Leadership as a Norm of American Religious Life," in *Leadership through the Lens: Interrogating Production, Presentation, and Power,* ed. Creshema Murray (Lanham, MD: Lexington, 2018), 131–49.
14 Mark Ward Sr., "Give the Winds a Mighty Voice: Evangelical Culture as Radio Ecology," *Journal of Radio and Audio Media* 21, no. 1 (2014): 115–33.
15 "America's Changing Religious Landscape," Pew Research Center, May 12, 2015, https://www.pewforum.org/wp-content/uploads/sites/7/2015/05/RLS-08-26-full-report.pdf; and Robert D. Putnam and David E. Campbell, *American Grace: How Religion Divides and Unites Us* (New York, NY: Simon and Schuster, 2012).
16 "In U.S., Decline of Christianity Continues at Rapid Pace," Pew Research Center, October 17, 2019, https://www.pewforum.org/2019/10/17/in-u-s-decline-of-christianity-continues-at-rapid-pace/
17 "More People Use Christian Media Than Attend Church."
18 Ward, "Major Networks and Personalities."
19 The preeminent single-volume history is Christian H. Sterling and John Michael Kittross, *Stay Tuned: A History of American Broadcasting,* 3rd ed. (Mahwah, NJ: Erlbaum, 2002).
20 Legend has it that David Sarnoff, who would later become the powerful president of the Radio Corporation of America, was a young telegraph operator for the American Marconi Company in 1916 when he wrote a memo to his superiors that wireless sets could be sold as a "radio music box." See Tom Lewis, *Empire of the Air: The Men Who Made Radio* (New York, NY: HarperCollins, 1991); Scott Woolley, *The Network: The Battle for the Airwaves and the Birth of the Communications Age* (New York, NY: HarperCollins, 2016); and Sterling and Kittross, *Stay Tuned.*
21 Ward, *Air of Salvation;* Mark Ward Sr., *The Lord's Radio: Gospel Music Broadcasting and the Making of Evangelical Mass Culture, 1920–1960* (Jefferson, NC: McFarland, 2017); Ben Armstrong, *The Electric Church* (Nashville, TN: Thomas Nelson, 1979); and Barry Siedell, *Gospel Radio* (Lincoln, NE: Good News Broadcasters, 1971).
22 Brotman, "Revisiting the Public Interest Standard."
23 Sterling and Kitross, *Stay Tuned.*

24 Bruce J. Evensen, *God's Man for the Gilded Age: D. L. Moody and the Rise of Modern Mass Evangelism* (New York, NY: Oxford University Press, 2003).
25 The account of Moody Bible Institute and the founding of WMBI is drawn from Gene Getz, *MBI; The Story of Moody Bible Institute* (Chicago, IL: Moody Press, 1986); Ben Armstrong, *Religious Broadcasting Sourcebook* (Morristown, NJ: National Religious Broadcasters, 1978); Armstrong, *The Electric Church;* Siedell, *Gospel Radio;* Ward, *Air of Salvation;* and Ward, *The Lord's Radio.*
26 Getz, *MBI,* 166.
27 Richard T. Brooks, "The 'Canadian Electric Church': The Development of Single-faith Broadcasting in Canada" (doctoral dissertation, McMaster University, 2003), https://macsphere.mcmaster.ca/bitstream/11375/11845/1/fulltext.pdf.
28 *Trinity United Methodist Church, South, v. Federal Radio Commission,* No. 5661, 62 F.2d 850 (1932).
29 Ward, *The Lord's Radio.*
30 On Coughlin, see Alan Brinkley, *Voices of Protest: Huey Long, Father Coughlin, and the Great Depression* (New York, NY: Knopf, 1982); and Donald Warren, *Radio Priest: Charles Coughlin, the Father of Hate Radio* (New York, NY: The Free Press, 1996).
31 Edward L. Bernays, *Propaganda* (1928; reprint Brooklyn, NY: IG Publishing, 2005), 71.
32 On the Scopes trial see Edward Larson, *Summer for the Gods: The Scopes Trial and America's Continuing Debate over Science and Religion* (New York, NY: Basic Books, 2008).
33 On the controversy over sustaining time see Ward, *Air of Salvation;* Tona J. Hangen, *Redeeming the Dial: Radio, Religion, and Popular Culture in America* (Chapel Hill, NC: University of North Carolina Press, 2002); Arthur Hugh Matthews, *Standing Up, Standing Together: The Emergence of the National Association of Evangelicals* (Carol Stream, IL. National Association of Evangelicals, 1992); and Garth Rosell, *The Surprising Work of God: Harold John Ockenga, Billy Graham, and the Rebirth of Evangelicalism* (Grand Rapids, MI: Baker Academic, 2008).
34 Daniel P. Fuller, *Give the Winds a Mighty Voice: The Story of Charles E. Fuller* (Waco, TX: Word, 1972); and Dan D. Crawford, *A Thirst for Souls: The Life of Evangelist Percy B. Crawford, 1902–1960* (Selinsgrove, PA: Susquehanna University Press, 2010).
35 Ward, "Give the Winds."
36 Matthews, *Standing Up.*
37 The argument that Christian church bodies, by accepting paid time as the norm, thus forfeited their standing to oppose commercialization of radio is made in Robert S. Fortner, "The Church and the Debate over Radio, 1919–1949," in *Media and Religion in American History,* ed. Wm. David Sloan (Northport, AL: Vision Press, 2000), 230–43.
38 Sterling and Kittross, *Stay Tuned.*
39 Roger Finke and Rodney Stark, *The Churching of America, 1776–2005: Winners and Losers in Our Religious Economy* (Brunswick, NJ: Rutgers University Press, 2005).
40 Hendershot, *What's Fair on the Air?*
41 *Red Lion Broadcasting Co. v. Federal Communications Commission,* 395 U.S. 367 (1969).

42 Ward, "Air to the King."
43 Ward, "'From a Christian Perspective'"; and J. Gordon Melton, Phillip Charles Lucas, and Jon R. Stone, *Prime-time Religion: An Encyclopedia of Religious Broadcasting* (Phoenix, AZ: Oryx, 1997).
44 "NRB-Commissioned Report Bolsters Case for Must Carry," National Religious Broadcasters, January 17, 2014, http://nrb.org/news-room/articles/nrb-commissioned-report-bolsters-case-for-must-carry/
45 Bradley E. Schultz, "The Economic Response of Religious Television Stations to Digital Implementation," *Journal of Communication and Religion* 28, no. 2 (2005): 307–25; Bradley E. Schultz, "The Effect of Age and Background of Religious Broadcasting Executives on Digital Television Implementation," *Journal of Media and Religion* 1, no. 4 (2002): 217–29; and Bradley E. Schultz, "The Effects of Digital Environments on Religious Television Stations," *Journal of Communication and Religion* 23, no. 1 (2000): 50–71.
46 Ward, "A New Kind of Church"; Ward, "Air to the Kingdom."
47 Mark Fratrik, *Radio Transactions 2001: Where Did All the Deals Go?* (Chantilly, VA: BIA Financial Networks, 2002).
48 Bruce E. Drushel, "The Telecommunications Act of 1996 and Radio Market Structure," *Journal of Media Economics* 11, no. 3 (1998): 3–20.
49 Christopher H. Sterling, "The Telecommunications Act of 1996," in *Museum of Broadcast Communications Encyclopedia of Radio, Vol. 3,* ed. Christopher H. Sterling (Chicago, IL: Fitzroy Dearborn, 2004), 1382–84; and George Williams and Scott Roberts, "Radio Industry Review 2002: Trends in Ownership, Format, and Finance," *Media Ownership Working Group Paper #11* (Washington, DC: Federal Communications Commission, 2002).
50 Peter DiCola and Kristin Thomson, *Radio Deregulation: Has It Served Citizens and Musicians?* (Washington, DC: Future of Music Coalition, 2002).
51 Mark Ward Sr., "Consolidating the Gospel: The Impact of the 1996 Telecommunications Act on Religious Radio Ownership," *Journal of Media and Religion* 11, no. 1 (2012): 11–30.
52 Mark Ward Sr., "Dark Preachers: The Impact of Radio Consolidation on Independent Religious Syndicators," *Journal of Media and Religion* 8, no. 2 (2009): 79–96.
53 "About Salem Media Group," Salem Media Group, accessed March 11, 2020, https://salemmedia.com/about-us/
54 "Find Your Local AFR Station," American Family Radio, accessed March 11, 2020, https://afr.net/station-finder/; "About," American Family News Network, August 29, 2018, https://onenewsnow.com/general/about
55 "Educational Media Foundation," Educational Media Foundation, accessed March 11, 2020, https://www.emfbroadcasting.com/
56 "Radio Stations," Christian Satellite Network, accessed March 11, 2020, https://csnradio.com/stations/
57 Ward, "Digital Religion and Media Economics."
58 Ward, "A New Kind of Church."
59 Ward, "'From a Christian Perspective.'"
60 Molly Worthen, *Apostles of Reason: The Crisis of Authority in American Evangelicalism* (New York, NY: Oxford University Press, 2014), 261.

61 Daniel K. Williams, *God's Own Party: The Making of the Christian Right* (New York, NY: Oxford University Press, 2010), 178.
62 Charles E. Shepard, *Forgiven: The Rise and Fall of Jim Bakker and the PTL Ministry* (New York, NY: Atlantic Monthly Press, 1989).
63 Mark Ward Sr., "Televangelism, Audience Fragmentation, and the Changing Coverage of Scandal," in *Scandal in a Digital Age,* eds. Hinda Mandell and Gina Masullo Chen (New York, NY: Palgrave MacMillan, 2016), 53–68.
64 Jim Abrams, "Senate Bars FCC from Revisiting Fairness Doctrine," *Fox News,* February 26, 2009, https://www.foxnews.com/wires/2009Feb26/0,4670,FairnessDoctrine,00.html
65 For example, see Brian Fung, "Twitter Labeled Trump Tweets with a Fact Check for the First Time," *CNN Business,* https://www.cnn.com/2020/05/26/tech/twitter-trump-fact-check/index.html. At issue is whether an "interactive computer service" that alters or removes information provided by a third-party user thus becomes a "publisher" and liable for its treatment of the material on its platform. Section 230 of the 1996 Communications Decency Act (CDA) provides immunity when a service, acting in good faith, alters or removes material it deems offensive or obscene. After Twitter labeled a Trump tweet with a fact-check on May 26, 2020, two days later the President signed an *Executive Order on Preventing Online Censorship.* The order directs federal agencies to follow what the order claims to be the original intent of the CDA and thus to narrowly interpret online platforms' immunity as applying only to treatment of "harmful" material and not political speech. See "Executive Order on Preventing Online Censorship," *The White House,* accessed in July 15, 2020, https://www.whitehouse.gov/presidential-actions/executive-order-preventing-online-censorship/.
66 "NRB Project for Digital Free Speech," National Religious Broadcasters, accessed July 11, 2020, http://nrb.org/digitalfreespeech.
67 *Bob Jones University v. United States,* 461 U.S. 574 (1983).
68 *Bostock v. Clayton County*, 590 U.S. ___ (2020).
69 *Lutheran Church-Missouri Synod v. FCC,* 141 F.3d 344 (D.C. Cir. 1998).
70 On playground equipment grants see *Trinity Lutheran Church of Columbia, Inc. v. Comer*, 582 U.S. ___ (2017). On private school subsidies see *Espinoza v. Montana Department of Revenue*, 591 U.S. ___ (2020). On public-university activity fees see *Rosenberger v. Rector and Visitors of the University of Virginia*, 515 U.S. 819 (1995). On public-school classrooms after hours by outside groups see *Lamb's Chapel v. Center Moriches Union Free School District*, 508 U.S. 384 (1993).
71 See "License Renewal Applications for Radio Broadcast Stations," Federal Communications Commission, accessed July 11, 2020, https://www.fcc.gov/media/radio/broadcast-radio-license-renewal; "License Renewal Applications for Broadcast Television Stations," *Federal Communications Commission*, accessed July 11, 2020, https://www.fcc.gov/media/television/broadcast-television-license-renewal; and "Public Participation in the License Renewal Process," *Federal Communications Commission*, accessed July 11, 2020, https://www.fcc.gov/sites/default/files/public-participation-license-renewal-process.pdf.
72 "Untrue: Religious Broadcaster Ban Rumor," *Federal Communications Commission*, accessed July 11, 2020, https://www.fcc.gov/media/radio/religious-broadcast-ban-rumor

73 Ward, "Give the Winds."
74 Daniel Radosh, *Rapture Ready: Adventures in the Parallel Universe of Evangelical Pop Culture* (New York, NY: Scribner, 2008).
75 See "Eternal Word Television Network," accessed July 15, 2020, https://www.ewtn.com/. The EWTN Global Catholic Network airs on 11 television channels with a potential reach of 350 million households in nearly 150 countries. EWTN radio programming is carried via satellite and by more than 500 affiliated local AM and FM stations worldwide. Further, EWTN operates a book publishing division, while its news division operates the Catholic News Agency and published the *National Catholic Register.*
76 The figure of 900-plus television programming networks is reported by NCTA: The Internet and Television Association, "Cable's Story," accessed July 15, 2020, https://www.ncta.com/cables-story.
77 On Trinity Broadcasting and Daystar Television see "Thirty Leading Religious Broadcasters," NPR, April 1, 2014, https://www.npr.org/2014/04/01/297331252/thirty-leading-religious-broadcasters; and on Salem see "Annual Report," accessed March 11, 2020, https://investor.salemmedia.com/sec-filings/annual-reports/content/0001193125-19-072280/0001193125-19-072280.pdf

Bibliography

"About Salem Media Group." Salem Media Group, accessed March 11, 2020. https://salemmedia.com/about-us/

Abrams, Jim. "Senate Bars FCC from Revisiting Fairness Doctrine." *Fox News.* Feb. 26, 2009. https://www.foxnews.com/wires/2009Feb26/0,4670,FairnessDoctrine,00.html

"America's Changing Religious Landscape." Pew Research Center. May 12, 2015. https://www.pewforum.org/wp-content/uploads/sites/7/2015/05/RLS-08-26-full-report.pdf;

"Annual Report." Salem Media Group, accessed March 11, 2020. https://investor.salemmedia.com/sec-filings/annual-reports/content/0001193125-19-072280/0001193125-19-072280.pdf

Armstrong, Ben. *Religious Broadcasting Sourcebook.* Morristown, NJ: National Religious Broadcasters, 1978.

Armstrong, Ben. *The Electric Church.* Nashville, TN: Thomas Nelson, 1979.

Bean, Lydia. *The Politics of Evangelical Identity: Local Churches and Partisan Divides in the United States and Canada.* Princeton, NJ: Princeton University Press, 2016.

Bob Jones University v. United States, 461 U.S. 574 (1983).

Bostock v. Clayton County, 590 U.S. ___ (2020).

Brinkley, Alan. *Voices of Protest: Huey Long, Father Coughlin, and the Great Depression.* New York, NY: Knopf, 1982.

Brooks, Richard T. "The 'Canadian Electric Church': The Development of Single-faith Broadcasting in Canada." Doctoral dissertation, McMaster University, 2003.

Brotman, Stuart N. "Revisiting the Public Interest Standard in Communications Law and Regulation." Brookings Institution. March 23, 2017. https://www.brookings.edu/research/revisiting-the-broadcast-public-interest-standard-in-communications-law-and-regulation/

Crawford, Dan D. *A Thirst for Souls: The Life of Evangelist Percy B. Crawford, 1902–1960.* Selinsgrove, PA: Susquehanna University Press, 2010.

DiCola, Peter, and Kristin Thomson. *Radio Deregulation: Has it Served Citizens and Musicians?* Washington, DC: Future of Music Coalition, 2002.

Drushel, Bruce E. "The Telecommunications Act of 1996 and Radio Market Structure." *Journal of Media Economics* 11, no. 3 (1998): 3–20.

"Educational Media Foundation." Educational Media Foundation, accessed March 11, 2020. https://www.emfbroadcasting.com/

Edward L. Bernays. *Propaganda.* 1928; reprint Brooklyn, NY: IG Publishing, 2005.

Espinoza v. Montana Department of Revenue, 591 U.S. ___ (2020).

"Eternal Word Television Network." Eternal Word Television Network, accessed July 15, 2020. https://www.ewtn.com/.

Evensen, Bruce J. *God's Man for the Gilded Age: D. L. Moody and the Rise of Modern Mass Evangelism.* New York, NY: Oxford University Press, 2003.

"Executive Order on Preventing Online Censorship." *The White House,* accessed in July 15, 2020, https://www.whitehouse.gov/presidential-actions/executive-order-preventing-online-censorship/.

"Find Your Local AFR Station." American Family Radio, accessed March 11, 2020. https://afr.net/station-finder/; "About," American Family News Network, Aug. 29, 2018, https://onenewsnow.com/general/about

Finke, Roger, and Rodney Stark, *The Churching of America, 1776–2005: Winners and Losers in Our Religious Economy.* Brunswick, NJ: Rutgers University Press, 2005.

Fortner, Robert S. "The Church and the Debate over Radio, 1919–1949." In *Media and Religion in American History,* edited by Wm. David Sloan, 230–43. Northport, AL: Vision Press, 2000.

Fratrik, Mark. *Radio Transactions 2001: Where Did All the Deals Go?* Chantilly, VA: BIA Financial Networks, 2002.

Fuller, Daniel P. *Give the Winds a Mighty Voice: The Story of Charles E. Fuller.* Waco, TX: Word, 1972.

Fung, Brian. "Twitter Labeled Trump Tweets with a Fact Check for the First Time." *CNN Business,* accessed July 15, 2020, https://www.cnn.com/2020/05/26/tech/twitter-trump-fact-check/index.html.

Getz, Gene. *MBI: The Story of Moody Bible Institute.* Chicago, IL: Moody Press, 1986.

Hangen, Tona J. *Redeeming the Dial: Radio, Religion, and Popular Culture in America.* Chapel Hill, NC: University of North Carolina Press, 2002.

Hendershot, Heather. *What's Fair on the Air? Cold War Right-wing Broadcasting and the Public Interest.* University of Chicago Press, 2011.

"In U.S., Decline of Christianity Continues at Rapid Pace." Pew Research Center. October 17, 2019, https://www.pewforum.org/2019/10/17/in-u-s-decline-of-christianity-continues-at-rapid-pace/

Lamb's Chapel v. Center Moriches Union Free School District, 508 U.S. 384 (1993).

Larson, Edward. *Summer for the Gods: The Scopes Trial and America's Continuing Debate over Science and Religion*. New York, NY: Basic Books, 2008.

Lewis, Tom. *Empire of the Air: The Men Who Made Radio*. New York, NY: Harper Collins, 1991.

"License Renewal Applications for Radio Broadcast Stations." Federal Communications Commission, accessed July 11, 2020. https://www.fcc.gov/media/radio/broadcast-radio-license-renewal.

"License Renewal Applications for Broadcast Television Stations." Federal Communications Commission, accessed July 11, 2020. https://www.fcc.gov/media/television/broadcast-television-license-renewal.

Lutheran Church-Missouri Synod v. FCC, 141 F.3d 344 (D.C. Cir. 1998).

Matthews, Arthur Hugh. *Standing Up, Standing Together: The Emergence of the National Association of Evangelicals*. Carol Stream, IL. National Association of Evangelicals, 1992.

Melton, J. Gordon, Phillip Charles Lucas, and Jon R. Stone. *Prime-time Religion: An Encyclopedia of Religious Broadcasting*. Phoenix, AZ: Oryx, 1997.

"More People Use Christian Media Than Attend Church." Barna Group. March 14, 2005. https://www.barna.com/research/more-people-use-christian-media-than-attend-church/

NCTA: The Internet and Television Association. "Cable's Story," accessed July 15, 2020. https://www.ncta.com/cables-story.

"NRB Board Unanimous against Internet Power Grab." National Religious Broadcasters. February 24, 2015. http://nrb.org/news-room/press_center/jmp/nrb-board-unanimous-against-Internet-power-grab/

"NRB-Commissioned Report Bolsters Case for Must Carry." National Religious Broadcasters. January 17, 2014. http://nrb.org/news-room/articles/nrb-commissioned-report-bolsters-case-for-must-carry/

"NRB Project for Digital Free Speech." National Religious Broadcasters, accessed July 11, 2020. http://nrb.org/digitalfreespeech

Orbison, Charles Edward. "'Fighting Bob' Shuler and KGEF: The Silencing of a Radio Crusader." Master's thesis, University of North Texas, 1975.

"Public Participation in the License Renewal Process." Federal Communications Commission, accessed July 11, 2020. https://www.fcc.gov/sites/default/files/public-participation-license-renewal-process.pdf.

Putnam, Robert D., and David E. Campbell. *American Grace: How Religion Divides and Unites Us*. New York, NY: Simon and Schuster, 2012.

"Radio Stations." Christian Satellite Network, accessed March 11, 2020. https://csnradio.com/stations/

Radosh, Daniel. *Rapture Ready: Adventures in the Parallel Universe of Evangelical Pop Culture*. New York, NY: Scribner, 2008.

Rasmussen, Cecilia. "Mixing Fire, Brimstone, and Politics." *Los Angeles Times* (Los Angeles, CA). November 23, 1997. https://www.latimes.com/archives/la-xpm-1997-nov-23-me-56920-story.html

Red Lion Broadcasting Co. v. Federal Communications Commission, 395 U.S. 367 (1969).

Rosell, Garth. *The Surprising Work of God: Harold John Ockenga, Billy Graham, and the Rebirth of Evangelicalism*. Grand Rapids, MI: Baker Academic, 2008.

Rosenberger v. Rector and Visitors of the University of Virginia, 515 U.S. 819 (1995).

Schultz, Bradley E. "The Effects of Digital Environments on Religious Television Stations." *Journal of Communication and Religion* 23, no. 1 (2000): 50–71.

Schultz, Bradley E. "The Effect of Age and Background of Religious Broadcasting Executives on Digital Television Implementation." *Journal of Media and Religion* 1, no. 4 (2002): 217–29.

Schultz, Bradley E. "The Economic Response of Religious Television Stations to Digital Implementation." *Journal of Communication and Religion* 28, no. 2 (2005): 307–25.

Shepard, Charles E. *Forgiven: The Rise and Fall of Jim Bakker and the PTL Ministry*. New York, NY: Atlantic Monthly Press, 1989.

Siedell, Barry. *Gospel Radio*. Lincoln, NE: Good News Broadcasters, 1971.

Sterling, Christopher H. "The Telecommunications Act of 1996." In *Museum of Broadcast Communications Encyclopedia of Radio, Vol. 3,* edited by Christopher H. Sterling, 1382–84. Chicago, IL: Fitzroy Dearborn, 2004.

Sterling, Christian H., and John Michael Kittross. *Stay Tuned: A History of American Broadcasting* (3rd ed.). Mahwah, NJ: Erlbaum, 2002.

"Thirty Leading Religious Broadcasters." NPR. April 1, 2014. https://www.npr.org/2014/04/01/297331252/thirty-leading-religious-broadcasters

Trinity Lutheran Church of Columbia, Inc. v. Comer, 582 U.S. ___ (2017).

Trinity United Methodist Church, South, v. Federal Radio Commission, No. 5661, 62 F.2d 850 (1932).

"Untrue: Religious Broadcaster Ban Rumor." Federal Communications Commission, accessed July 11, 2020. https://www.fcc.gov/media/radio/religious-broadcast-ban-rumor

Waldie, D. J. "Cathedrals of the Air: Sister Aimee, Fighting Bob, and Early L.A. Radio." *KCET.* June 24, 2016. https://www.kcet.org/shows/lost-la/cathedrals-of-the-air-sister-aimee-fighting-bob-and-early-la-radio.

Ward Sr., Mark. *Air of Salvation: The Story of Christian Broadcasting*. Grand Rapids, MI: Baker Books, 1994.

Ward Sr., Mark. "Dark Preachers: The Impact of Radio Consolidation on Independent Religious Syndicators," *Journal of Media and Religion* 8, no. 2 (2009): 79–96.

Ward Sr., Mark. "Consolidating the Gospel: The Impact of the 1996 Telecommunications Act on Religious Radio Ownership." *Journal of Media and Religion* 11, no. 1 (2012): 11–30.

Ward Sr., Mark. "Air of the King: Evangelicals and Radio." In *Evangelical Christians and Popular Culture: Pop Goes the Gospel, Vol. 1,* edited by Robert H. Woods Jr., 101–18. Santa Barbara, CA: Praeger, 2013.

Ward Sr., Mark. "Give the Winds a Mighty Voice: Evangelical Culture as Radio Ecology." *Journal of Radio and Audio Media* 21, no. 1 (2014): 115–33.

Ward Sr., Mark. "Major Networks and Personalities." In *The Electronic Church in the Digital Age: Cultural Impacts of Evangelical Mass Media, Vol. 1,* edited by Mark Ward Sr., 255–84. Santa Barbara, CA: Praeger, 2016.

Ward Sr., Mark. "Televangelism, Audience Fragmentation, and the Changing Coverage of Scandal." In *Scandal in a Digital Age,* edited by Hinda Mandell and Gina Masullo Chen, 53–68. New York, NY: Palgrave MacMillan, 2016.

Ward Sr., Mark. *The Lord's Radio: Gospel Music Broadcasting and the Making of Evangelical Mass Culture, 1920–1960.* Jefferson, NC: McFarland, 2017.

Ward Sr., Mark. "A New Kind of Church: The Religious Media Conglomerate as a 'Denomination.'" *Journal of Media and Religion* 17, nos. 3/4 (2018): 117–33.

Ward Sr., Mark. "Digital Religion and Media Economics: Concentration and Convergence in the Electronic Church." *Journal of Religion, Media, and Digital Culture* 7, no. 1 (2018): 90–120.

Ward Sr., Mark. "Television Transcendent: How the Electronic Church Constructs Charismatic Leadership as a Norm of American Religious Life." In *Leadership through the Lens: Interrogating Production, Presentation, and Power,* edited by Creshema Murray, 131–49. Lanham, MD: Lexington, 2018.

Ward Sr., Mark. "The Dangers of Getting What You Wished For: What Do You Say to Evangelicals?" In *Constructing Narratives in Response to Trump's Election: How Various Populations Make Sense of an Unexpected Victory,* edited by Shing-Ling S. Chen, Nicole Allaire, and Zhuojun Joyce Chen, 61–81. Lanham MD: Lexington, 2018.

Ward Sr., Mark. "Air to the Kingdom: Religion and the Soul of Radio." In *Radio's Second Century: A Reader,* edited by John Allen Hendricks, 137–53. New Brunswick, NJ: Rutgers University Press, 2020.

Ward Sr., Mark. "'From a Christian Perspective': News/talk in Evangelical Mass Media." In *News on the Right: Studying Conservative News Cultures,* edited by Anthony M. Nadler and A. J. Bauer, 17–46. New York, NY: Oxford University Press, 2020.

Warren, Donald. *Radio Priest: Charles Coughlin, the Father of Hate Radio.* New York, NY: The Free Press, 1996.

Williams, Daniel K. *God's Own Party: The Making of the Christian Right.* New York, NY: Oxford University Press, 2010.

Williams, George, and Scott Roberts. "Radio Industry Review 2002: Trends in Ownership, Format, and Finance." In *Media Ownership Working Group Paper #11.* Washington, DC: Federal Communications Commission, 2002.

Woolley, Scott. *The Network: The Battle for the Airwaves and the Birth of the Communications Age.* New York, NY: HarperCollins, 2016.

Worthen, Molly. *Apostles of Reason: The Crisis of Authority in American Evangelicalism.* New York, NY: Oxford University Press, 2014.

15. *The War on Christmas: Conspiracy Rhetoric and Political Correctness*

Logan Spence

Since 2015, conservative media has used the Starbucks annual holiday cups as a consistent talking point to reify the decade old right-wing conspiracy of the War on Christmas.[1] The War on Christmas is a conspiracy theory that holds its origins in mainstream conservative media outlets such as Fox News, InfoWars, and PragerU that tells conservative audiences that Christmas is constantly under attack by the allusive progressives. For almost two decades, conservative media, especially Fox News, have obsessively perpetuated the War on Christmas conspiracy to their assumed conservative audience which posits that political correctness is attacking the Christian foundations and assumptions of America.[2] For the War on Christmas theorists, 'political correctness' is equated to equal protections and a shadowy group of progressives who use political correctness (equal protections) to undermine and replace the religious freedoms of America.[3] The theory originated in John Gibson's book *The War on Christmas: How the Liberal Plot to Ban the Sacred Christian Holiday is Worse than You Thought*, but the conspiracy did not acquire political legitimacy until Bill O'Reilly's show circulated and perpetuated the narrative in 2004.[4] As the U.S. Supreme Court began using its judicial power to expand the 14th Amendment to recognize historically marginalized groups and eliminate discrimination, the Religious Right saw their religious freedoms, in relation to the 1st Amendment, simultaneously diminished to make way for expanded equal protection laws. As such, conservative media uses the War on Christmas to fearmonger about how American Christians are losing their religious practices in favor of expanding equal protection laws.

The rhetoric of the War on Christmas shares similarities with rhetorics of conspiracy theories. Conspiracy rhetoric and conspiracism have long been defined through the "paranoid style," where an audience feels a sense of pseudo-persecution from a conspiratorial world that is ran by an evil force that exists to consume and replace the paranoid.[5] In the paranoid style, as I conceive it, "the feeling of persecution is central, and it is indeed systematized in grandiose theories of conspiracy" (Hofstadter 4). While conspiracies can exist, conspiracy *theories* are understood as the anxiety and alienation of (currently) nonexistent conspiracies.[6] Hofstadter's paranoid style was limited only to fringe political groups (e.g., the John Birch Society and Anti-Mason groups) and did not consider how the paranoid style can be used by mainstream political groups.[7] While the paranoid style of the War on Christmas falls within the lines of the fringe right, the conspiracy also penetrates mainstream conservative discourse. As such, the War on Christmas' paranoid style relies more on subtextual conspiracy rather than the overt fantastical logical leaps posited by the paranoid style.[8] For instance, conspiracies, such as the 9/11 Truther conspiracy, will often portray themselves as a social critique of the elites rather than as a fantastical portrayal of historical events that requires massive logical leaps to draw up their conspiratorial conclusions.[9] In this way, the subtextual conspiracy of the War on Christmas persists because theorists are criticizing what is assumed to *already be* the norm—political correctness running amuck.

The confrontation in question revolves around religious freedom vs. equal protections. In the War on Christmas framework, the 'dogma of political correctness' is 'infringing' on the freedoms of God-Fearing Americans (especially conservative Christians). The War on Christmas constructs the rhetorical battlefield between the legal and dialectical tension of religious rights vs. equal protections. In my chapter, I argue that the War on Christmas utilizes subtextual conspiracy rhetoric to reframe and manipulate its conservative audience into seeing the religious freedom vs. equal protections tension as a new establishment that wishes to replace religious freedom with equal protections for marginalized groups. Toward that end, I will describe subtextual conspiracy rhetoric and then utilize this framework to analyze the rhetoric of the War on Christmas to demonstrate how theorists in right-wing media to see how their arguments formulate the religious freedom vs. equal protections conflict. Finally, I will conclude with some implications of the War on Christmas' subtextual conspiracy rhetoric. I should be clear that to be concise, I will only cite representative texts to the broader conspiracy because each text, especially for conspiracy theories, are fragments of a broader contextual narrative.[10] While each text may be unique, they all utilize similar language to achieve the same political goals—delegitimizing the recognition of equal protections and protecting religious freedom.

Conspiracies as a Subtextual Genre

Conspiracy rhetoric has been examined by several rhetorical scholars, all articulating variations of conspiracies and how people construct and use them. For instance, rhetorical scholars have illustrated how conspiracies function as a battle between agents and their sources to identify their side as pragmatic while framing the other side as fantastical.[11] My analysis suggests that the War on Christmas is a subtextual conspiracy because the War on Christmas presents itself as a rational social critique. This section will illustrate conspiracy as a rhetorical genre and will begin this section with a description of the rhetorical features of the paranoid style and their relation to conspiracy theories. Next, I will illustrate how the paranoid style becomes subtextual to a mainstream political audience and the three components to subtextual conspiracies: anti-establishment, a critique of a dominant mythic framework, and a broad political and ideological appeal.[12]

Conspiracy as Paranoid Style

Conspiracies rely upon the style of their presentation and not necessarily the contents of the conspiracy because the content is often irrational and illogical. Hofstadter (2008) defined conspiracy through the paranoid style where the conspiracy theorists constantly project a pseudo-persecution complex onto themselves and others and where an abstract evil group is plotting in the historical background to destroy the known world.[13] "The clinical paranoid sees the hostile and conspiratorial world in which he feels himself to be living as directed specifically *against him*" (Hofstadter 4). Moreover, a conspiratorial attack on the man is an attack on the entire nation and ideology and that imagined attack leads to the paranoid *style* or "distorted style" that is a "possible signal that may alert us to a distorted judgment, just as in art an ugly style is a cue to fundamental defects of taste" (6). The world becomes a theater and all events within that theater functions as a sinister plot (motivated by the illusive puppeteers behind the scenes) to subjugate the paranoid in a dark new world.

The paranoid style serves three different functions: political conflicts, demonization, and social denunciation.[14] The paranoid style is introduced in the midst of unfathomed conflict between opposing groups. When a group of people (typically a dominant group) feels that their culture or way of life is in danger, that group will often times manufacture conflict with other groups to validate their fears and justify systemic violence against the imaginary group. Since the paranoid style relies on the existence of an abstract villain in the grand narrative, the conflict must be one where compromise is not possible. The paranoid style must also demonize their enemies (scapegoats) because that demonization provides the paranoid with easy answers to complicated situations. Thirdly, the paranoid style is also used to denounce and condemn certain behaviors, even if a scapegoat does not exist within the conspiracy theory.

Limits to the Paranoid Style

Liberally borrowing from clinical psychology, the 'paranoid style' was designed to articulate the conspiratorial thinking of fringe groups—particularly on the Right.[15] "Of course, the term 'paranoid style' is pejorative, and it is meant to be; the paranoid style has a greater affinity for bad causes than good" (Hofstadter 5). However, under this framework, the paranoid style limits the perspective to only inane people that are beyond rationality.[16] The paranoid style (as Hofstadter admitted) is designed to condemn the irrational on the fringes and neglects the rationalization among conspiracy theorists that are not in the fringes. As Goodman and Poulakos (1981) asserted, "since the 'paranoid style' no longer can be said to characterize only political extremists, a theory of conspiracy discourse must account for the usefulness of this appeal to mainstream speakers and audience" (300). To understand how the paranoid style translates to a mainstream audience, Shepard developed the subtextual conspiracy.

Subtextual Conspiracies

Where the paranoid style articulates the appeal and rhetorical tactics of conspiracy theories of the fringe right, the subtextual conspiracy explains how rational people end up as conspiracy theorists.[17] The subtextual conspiracy is often referred to as the cultural sociological approach to conspiracy because it emphasizes the rationality of conspiracy theories rather than the thinking of inane persons. From a cultural sociological perspective, conspiracy theories act as a protest against the establishment. Where previous research in conspiracy rhetoric emphasizes "narrative, ideology, and anti-elitism," subtextual conspiracy rhetoric takes those assumptions further by applying them to mainstream groups rather than isolating them to the fringe right. (Shepard 122). Since subtextual conspiracies rely upon narratives and ideologies, conspiracy theorists must also utilize ideographs to condition their audience into "a vocabulary of concepts that function as guides, warrants, reasons, or excuses for behavior and belief" (McGee 6). The use of ideographs is paramount for conspiracy theorists because certain words and phrases instigate fear and anger within the audience toward an undefined powerful group.

Subtextual conspiracy rhetoric frames conspiracies as a social critique against political and social institutions. There are three components of subtextual conspiracies: anti-establishment, critique of a dominant mythic framework, and appeal to broad political interests.

Subtextual conspiracies must utilize anti-establishment rhetoric and messages.[18] Since conspiracies and the paranoid style are rooted in populist movements, subtextual conspiracies have an antagonistic attitude toward institutions rather than emphasize one group or person (e.g., the Anti-Mason group). "In this sense, conspiracy rhetoric can function as a partisan wedge for anyone rallying against a dominant regime" (Shepard 122). Since subtextual conspiracies often project anti-establishment messages, conspiracies also act as critiques of argumentative presumptions. For most forms of argumentation, presumption in debates assumes that a point stands until reason and evidence is brought to the discussion that meets the threshold to absolve its good standing (e.g., burden of proof). Subtextual conspiracies reject that presumption lies on the side of the establishment. "In other words, conspiracy theories are less about a battle for presumption in an argumentative exchange, and more about the idea that those in power should not have presumption at all" (123).

As such, subtextual conspiracies are prone to ideographs and ideographic language. "Ideographs are one-term sums of orientation, the species of 'God' or 'Ultimate' term that will be used to symbolize the line of argument the meanest sort of individual *would* pursue" (McGee 7). They are a common rhetorical strategy used in subtextual conspiracies because they do not rely on the presumption of those 'in power' to cue certain emotions within the audience.[19] In this way, ideographs are used as a means of gaining a measure of control because certain phrases and words (ideographs) possess 'obvious' or 'self-evident' meanings that are outside the boundaries of logical observations. Each keyword works together as a series of propositions to justify an ideology, which often go unquestioned.

The use of ideographs in conspiracies can be seen in the Nazi *Jewish Question* conspiracy because it utilizes Ultimate God terms to construct an imagined establishment that is deserving of 'critique' (the Jews). The Nazi *Jewish Question* conspiracy utilizes the ideograph <Jews> to eliminate all presumption from academic sources that illustrate disagreements with their claims. Since academia is controlled by the <Jews>, all academic work is deemed false and corrupt by nature. The use of <Jews> abolishes all logical observation because the ideograph is self-evident to those that understand its 'obvious' meaning. Once the audience hears certain ideographs, they are primed to abolish presumption in their claims because the series of ideographs, like subtextual conspiracy rhetoric, lies outside logical observation. Effectively, subtextual conspiracies ask their audience to constantly question everyone and everything (except the groups in which they subscribe) and always assume those in power are lying and are out to subvert the people.

Critique of the Myth

The subtextual conspiracy must also critique the nation's dominant mythic framework.[20] National mythic frameworks are often used to illustrate the national identity of country and its ideals. These myths establish the identity and meaning of a nation. For instance, the United States is defined as the Land of the Free where the people of the United States are provided with the general freedoms needed to live prosperous lives compared to those in other nations. The myth of the Land of the Free becomes the myth that provides the US with meaning as a nation. Myths provide people with ordered behaviors that are consistent with the myth and country's ideals. However, a scapegoat is always needed to maintain those myths. Subtextual conspiracies acts as a reaction to perceived oppression as the theorists assume that they are the scapegoats in that myth. The conspiracy critiques the myth to reshape it into a new world and social order that is "based around a new narrative, featuring amplified descriptions of gods and devils, heroes and villains" (Shepard 123).

Ideological Appeal

Finally, the subtextual conspiracy must attempt to appeal to audiences in a broad ideological landscape rather than just an isolated group.[21] The conspiracy appeals to other groups because the theory grounds itself in politics that *appear* within the realm of reasonable politics. The conspiracy must position itself against a long-term pattern that, on the surface, does exist to appeal to a wider audience. The attack cannot be too specific. The target must be broad enough to remain relevant long after the conspiracy was created. Shepard (2018) also asserted that the ideological appeal to a wider audience often distinguishes between 'true' believers and those that merely sympathize with the movement. However, the subtextual conspiracy relies upon the paranoid style because one cannot attempt to appeal to a wider audience without the existence of a fringe group that perpetuated the conspiracy *a priori* to the subtextual conspiracy. The fringe conspiracy must exist *a priori* to the subtextual conspiracy because the latter attempts to make the former more palatable for those not in the know.

Dialectical Tension between the 1st and 14th Amendments: Expanding and Retracting Circumferences

Before turning to my analysis, I will briefly illustrate the connection between the law and culture because that connection is integral for understanding the War on Christmas as a conspiracy. As Burke (1969) articulated, people understand their reality by locating the scene within a particular context of varying scope.[22] The choice of terms constructs the circumference for what will eventually become 'second-nature' to people. Moreover, the construction of a circumference always implies a *reduction* of scope because humans define the world in terms of other words (reducing the universe to language and symbols). However, that 'second-nature' eventually leads to the defined circumference's antithesis to become the former's point of departure because new terms and material conditions provide new qualifications or proofs for that accepted circumference.

For instance, the U.S. Supreme Court (and the entire U.S. political system) was part of a system designed to institute White supremacy, misogyny, transphobia, homophobia, and xenophobia as the main circumference within American discourse. However, as time progressed, the Supreme Court began to use that same system to expand the rights of those groups that were subjected to that circumference because the 1st Amendment allowed the establishment group (e.g., Religious Right) to violate the 14th Amendment. People on the outside of the circumference found ways to persuade the Court to alter its borders to recognize the rights of various groups. The expansion of the 14th Amendment as a point of departure is interpreted as a reduction of the 1st Amendment rights of some groups because they can no longer rely upon the assumption of 'free speech' to justify violations of the 14th Amendment. As such, the Religious Right often perceives recent Supreme Court decisions to expand the 14th Amendment as an attack on them because it dialectically reduces the circumference of the 1st Amendment that was once 'second-nature' to them.

As a subtextual conspiracy, the War on Christmas is a broad narrative that possesses an abundance of texts that remain consistent to the conspiracy's structure and language. My analysis will examine texts that highlight the broad points and arguments constructed by the War on Christmas theorists because most, if not all, of the texts in this grand narrative perpetuate the same rhetoric of control.[23] Each text is a fragment of a larger narrative because they utilize similar language that unites their religiously conservative audience into believing the social critique of the imagined establishment (political correctness). My analysis will be sectioned off between the three tenets of subtextual conspiracy rhetoric: Anti-establishment, critique of the dominant mythic form, and appeal to broad ideological agents.

Anti-establishment Wars: Political Correctness Strikes Back

For the Religious Right, their religious practices are being subverted to appeal to the growing establishment of equal protections. While not all religious people are homophobic, religion has often been the premise by which homosexuality was made illegal in America and by which same-sex marriage was denied. However, Supreme Court cases like *Lawrence v. Texas* (which decriminalized homosexuality), *Engel v. Vitale* (which denied public schools the ability to force students to do religious prayers), *Roe v. Wade*, *Bostock v. Clayton County* (which denied employers the right to fire employees for being gay for transgender), and *Obergefell v. Hodges* (which legalized same-sex marriage) created the impression that a growing force of <political correctness> has been working to undermine the religious practices of the God fearing.[24] These Supreme Court decisions expanded the circumference of the 14th Amendment at the expense of reducing the circumference of the 1st Amendment. The America that once allowed Christians to deny LGBTQ people the right to exist and marry is slowly being taken away from them to appeal to the new establishment of secular <political correctness>. Even when the Supreme Court rules in favor of the Religious Right, like the recent Supreme Court decision that upheld the Trump administration's policy to allow employers to deny contraceptives in their health insurance policies to their employees, the fact that the religious practices of American Christians need to be defended in the Supreme Court indicates to *them* that <political correctness> is becoming the new establishment.[25] No longer are American Christians granted unquestioned immunity for their religious practices. The 'second-nature' of the 1st Amendment's (especially religious freedoms) circumference was reaching its point of departure. The stripping of political and legal power from the Religious Right over time and the need to defend their historically unquestioned practices challenges the symbolic world for the Religious Right as they begin to see the cultural and political changes in America as a conspiracy of the <politically correct> establishment.

For its theorists, the War on Christmas is a tool to critique what they believe to be the new establishment, political correctness. More specifically, the War on Christmas presents itself as a 'final defense' for the one tradition the Religious Right *feels* like they have left, Christmas. The War on Christmas theory posits that the reduction of the 1st Amendment's circumference has been gradual, but the <progressives> want to eliminate Christmas as the final assault on their religious freedoms. The Religious Right sees the new cultural policies as a growing encroachment on their religious freedoms and the War on Christmas is simply the final stage of that imagined conflict. The War on Christmas theory posits that the expansion of the 14th Amendment's circumference must eliminate Christmas to finalize their new hegemony.

As a subtextual conspiracy theory, the subjects of the War on Christmas assume that political correctness is the establishment of modern America and those in power are using political correctness to force corporations and people to no longer say "Merry Christmas" in favor of equal protections. In Bill O'Reilly's original segment on the War on Christmas conspiracy, O'Reilly asserted that Christmas is "taking flak" all throughout America because there were no religious floats during the Macy's Thanksgiving Day Parade (though O'Reilly referred to the parade as the holiday parade).[26] The New York City Christmas Tree is now referred to as the Holiday Tree and Christian symbols are no longer present in public schools. Finally, corporations are 'no longer saying Merry Christmas' to their customers out of fear of political correctness.

As O'Reilly (2004) wrote, "Secular <progressives> realize that America as it is now will never approve of gay marriage, partial birth abortion, euthanasia, legalized drugs, income redistribution through taxation, and many other <progressive> visions because of religious opposition" (para. 3). In O'Reilly's argument, the War on Christmas is a social critique of what the Religious Right perceives as the establishment of <political correctness>. Conservative media figures, like O'Reilly, use ideographs (e.g., <progressive>, <the Left>, <political correctness>) to illustrate an abstract and imagined power structure that conditions their religiously conservative audience into believing that Christianity is now an oppressed group under the hegemonic system of <political correctness>. Conservatives perceive the expansion of the 14th Amendment as part of the new establishment because that expansion necessitates the reduction of the 1st Amendment, which they held as 'second-nature.' As their circumference is reduced to make way for the expansion of the 14th Amendment, the Religious Right begins to feel like they are being subjected to a new hegemony. As such, the War on Christmas provides the Religious Right with a narrative that assumes that this change is part of a grand conspiracy to undermine the 'second-nature' lifestyle of Christian, God-Fearing Americans.

During another Fox News segment after the previously mentioned Supreme Court decisions, Lou Dobbs's guest, Pastor Robert Jeffress, asserted that Christianity is under attack by the <Left> and, worst of all, they banned the phrase Merry Christmas.[27] Political pundits at Fox News utilize ideographs to construct a social reality in the minds of their audience to assume that political correctness now has political and cultural presumption. The use of ideographs constructs a strawperson understanding of progressive politics, which then allows the Religious Right, through subtextual conspiracy rhetoric, to eliminate all presumption of progressive arguments (regardless of their argumentative validity).

Far-Right radio host Dennis Prager constructed similar arguments but took the premise of the War on Christmas much further by claiming that the <Left> not only wants to secularize society, but they also want to remove Christmas as a national holiday in America.[28] Prager's video, in his infamous YouTube propaganda channel entitled PragerU, portrays the <Left> as an inane group that use distorted arguments to subvert Religious Rights for the betterment of equal protections. Moreover, the video goes to great lengths to use simple visuals to present the <Left> as a militant group that is beyond reason. At one point in the video, an abstract <Leftist> laughs at a religious conservative only to transform into a military personal holding an AR-15. Near the end of the video, the abstract <Leftist> beats up Santa Claus and kicks the speech bubble that stated, "Merry Christmas." Throughout the video, Prager represents the <Left> as a violent group that will stop at nothing to take away religious freedoms in favor of equal protections.

War on Christmas theorists use ideographs like <progressives>and the <Left> to condition their audience to emotionally react to an imagined 'enemy establishment' as a dominating force that exerts its power onto the Religious Right's Christmas traditions. Since the War on Christmas uses ideographs to misrepresent and strawperson progressive politics as an oppressive regime, the Religious Right only sees the dialectical legal tension of religious freedom and equal protections in one direction rather than as a complicated legal conflict. As America becomes more diverse, the Religious Right begins to demand simple answers to their increased anxieties of their recent recognition of the Other. The Religious Right sees the increase of equal rights for marginalized groups as the <Left> taking 'their' country away from them and right-wing outlets alleviate those anxieties by using ideographs to construct an imagined establishment to entrench those fears in a never ending loop to deny the need to recognize the Other.

That fear was exemplified in the theatrics of the Kim Davis incident where a clerk in Kentucky was jailed and held in contempt for denying marriage licenses to gay couples over her religious objections to the *Obergefell v. Hodges* decision.[29] However, after five days of being held in contempt and tremendous political pressure from the Religious Right and elected Republican officials, Davis was released from jail to a roaring crowd.[30] At the release, Mike Huckabee, alongside Senator Ted Cruz, visited Davis to demonstrate his support for her and to condemn the tyrannical practices of <political correctness>. Davis would go on to encourage the Religious Right in the crowd and on TV to continue 'the fight' because 'God was on their side.' Davis became the symbol for the Religious Right as her arrest 'confirmed' what the Religious Right *thought* was 'true,' that Christianity was under attack by the establishment of <political correctness> and anyone that defies the new establishment will be cast as literal political prisoners (like Civil Right activists). For the Religious Right, Davis was simply practicing her religion and her arrest was the establishment coming in to stop that practice to maintain equal protections.

The Subtextual Conspiracy Against the Dominant Myth of Collectivism

The second component of the War on Christmas—as a subtextual conspiracy—functions as a critique of the dominant mythic format of the nation. Like the creation of an imagined establishment, the War on Christmas conspiracy theorists construct America's 'new' mythic form, a collectivist and diversity myth that replaced the individualism of the past. Where David Griffin used his 9/11 Truther conspiracy to critique the American Exceptionalism myth as always assuming America to be in the right, the War on Christmas conspiracy does the exact opposite by critiquing the collectivist myth which supposedly assumes that America is always in the wrong (e.g., racism and colonialism).[31]

In this framework, the <Left's> obsession with expanding the circumference of equal protections and diversity is designed to trick American Christians into believing that they are bigoted for simply being Christian. The Supreme Court's decisions of *Lawrence v. Texas*, *Engel v. Vitale*, *Roe v. Wade*, *Bostock v. Clayton County*, and *Obergefell v. Hodges* gives cause to people who identify with the Religious Right to reflect upon their own beliefs and practices in relation to discrimination and their American identity. That the highest court in the nation has sided against them is interpreted as a denial of their rights and frames their relation to an American identity in the negative. As Gramsci (1971) asserted, "Cultural policy will above all be negative, a critique of the past; it will be aimed at erasing from the memory and at destroying."[32] As discriminatory religious practices are eliminated or deemed unconstitutional (the reduction of the 1st Amendment's circumference), the Religious Right may interpret these rulings as a signal that the legal system is favoring the identities of the people seeking protection through the 14th Amendment rather than their identify that has traditionally found safe harbor in the 1st Amendment. The expansion of the 14th Amendment to recognize marginalized groups (the point of departure) articulates the reduction of the 1st Amendment's circumference of religious freedom that once allowed the Religious Right to violate equal protection laws. The dialectic between the 1st and 14th Amendments' circumferences conditions the Religious Right to see the reduction in religious freedoms as an attack on them in favor of a <collectivist> myth.

For instance, during a Christmas segment on Tucker Carlson's show, Carlson interviewed right-wing YouTube media pundit, Dave Rubin from *The Rubin Report*, about a Huffington Post piece that supposedly claimed that the original Christmas animated film *Rudolf the Red Nose Reindeer* promoted bigotry.[33] Rubin asserted that the <Left> ruins all classic American Christmas stories, like Rudolf, by 'constantly' finding 'problematic' themes in them and characterize all Americans as bigots for enjoying those stories. The 'new' growing American myth of <collectivism> is transforming the American myth of individualism and that transformation requires Christmas to be eliminated to finalize the institutionalization of the <collectivist> myth.

One strategic response is to frame <progressive> arguments as absurd. For the Religious Right, <progressives> attempt to achieve the finality of the <collectivist> mythic transformation by characterizing all Christmas stories and traditions as bigoted. Framed in this way enables people who identify with the Religious Right to *feel* like they can never truly escape this new encroaching <collectivist> myth because the <Left> constantly bears their criticism down against anyone that remotely strays from the mythic format. The 'constant' dismantling of Christmas traditions and practices are perceived as the continued manifestation of the reduction of the 1st Amendment's circumference for the sake of expanding the 14th Amendment's circumference. However, the Religious Right frames <progressive> arguments as absurd and inane because that framing provides them with confirmation their opponents are incompetent and illogical to achieve any form of power. As such, when the Religious Right sees the absurd arguments by <progressives> from conservative media, they become relieved because the imagined new hegemony they fear becomes less scary and threatening than they thought. The War on Christmas must present <progressives> as massive and overwhelmingly powerful while simultaneously being weak and fragile.

The phrase "Happy Holidays" is one example War on Christmas theorists suggest the <Left> have asserted cultural dominance. The earlier cited PragerU video asserted that the phrase Happy Holidays is a recent development in American discourse that was forced upon Americans by the <Left> in conjunction with recent Supreme Court decisions to eliminate discriminatory practices on religious grounds (though framing the argument through a cultural lens than a legal lens).[34] The War on Christmas theory also presents <progressives> as already dominating American institutions and <progressives> will often make things up for the sake of taking over America and that began with the creation of "Happy Holidays." The Religious Right perceives Happy Holidays as a growing trend constructed by the <Left> to undermine American's religious freedoms until they are positioned to eliminate Christmas altogether to finalize the transformation. As such, the War on Christmas theory posits that the *developing* infiltration of <progressive> hegemony, that is also somehow already the new hegemony, will make up language and rules to undermine the religious freedoms of the Religious Right.

For the War on Christmas theorists, America used to be a country of Christian values and practices that emphasized the myth of the Individual, but the <Left> redefined America's national mythic format into a <collectivist> one that forced Christians to recognize other non-Christians and marginalized groups. Rather than being a common phrase that has been around since the mid-1800s, Happy Holidays is perceived by the Right as the <Left's> attempt to 'fix' America through inclusion and, in turn, exclude them. For Prager, American's have always said Merry Christmas, but the continued transformation into a <collectivist> myth robs the Religious Right from their religious freedoms to enjoy their lives without needing to recognize the Other. While most right-wing pundits will qualify their assertions that America is a 'melting pot,' they will also be sure to remind the audience that America has *always been* a Christian nation and the new mythic form of <collectivism> (expansion of the 14th Amendment's circumference) robs America of its true nature, religious freedom (reduction of the 1st Amendment's circumference). There was a time when the Religious Right did not need to acknowledge the existence of other people in America because they followed the myth of individualism rather than the <collective>. Since the <collectivist> myth is seen as an emphasis on equal protections, the Religious Right is conditioned to see any and all forms of equal protections as an institutional assault on religious freedoms because it detracts from the myth of individualism.

Appealing to Broader Political Interests: Liberals Can Join in the War

The War on Christmas remains prominent because of its appeal to those outside of conservative groups. While proponents of the War on Christmas blame the conspiracy on <progressives>, the conservative pundits always clarify that it is the <far Left> that has brought about the new establishment and the <collectivist> myth. This would explain why the War on Christmas is often attributed to Bill O'Reilly and not Gibson because, unlike O'Reilly (who blamed the War on Christmas on an amorphous progressive group), Gibson (as his book title explicitly states) directly targeted liberals and Democrats. Moreover, the War on Christmas theorists also posit that the <collectivist> myth simply takes their equal protections too far, even for liberals to take seriously. During a Fox News comedy session, the show mocked recent complaints about the Christmas song "Baby, It's Cold Outside" by constructing a parody advertisement for a Christmas music album titled, *I'm Dreaming of an Ultra-P.C. Christmas* that repurposes old classic American songs using politically correct titles.[35] For instance, the classic Christmas song "White Christmas" was renamed to "White (Privilege) Christmas, You Stupid Racist." While these parody songs mock the <collectivist> myth, the parody also serves a dual purpose, to frame equal protections as absurd. In this way, the obsession with equal protections ruins Christmas even for liberals. Effectively, conservative media engages in the strawperson of the <politically correct> <Left> to recruit liberals into the War on Christmas subtextual conspiracy.

Returning to the Fox News segment between Tucker Carlson and Dave Rubin, I labeled Rubin as a right-wing pundit. However, Rubin would likely take umbrage with my labeling because he *publicly* labels himself as a classical liberal.[36] Rubin's public identification as a liberal provides the War on Christmas' characterization of <progressives> with more credibility because his criticisms of the <far Left> frames all forms of equal protections as absurd. Moreover, during another segment on Fox News, the segment invited both a far-right pundit and an executive of a 'Pro-Hillary Clinton Super PAC' to talk about how there is a war against Christmas and how progressives forced Americans to say Happy Holidays over Merry Christmas.[37] As the liberal stated, he can agree with the far-right on the assertion that there is a war against Christmas because the <far Left> have forced their absurd <political correctness> onto all Americans by replacing religious freedom with equality dogma. The Religious Right can use 'liberals' as a springboard to laugh at the strawperson <progressive>. Effectively, the strawperson of the <Left> can be made more possible because even liberals have said they cannot stand the <Left> due to their obsession with <political correctness>.

This logic frames <progressives> as absurd because they believe *everything* is bigoted. Those who advocate for equal protections will always be seen in an absurdist lens because the War on Christmas conspiracy only provides their audience with the strawperson arguments. Like in Prager's video, the strawperson inclusiveness argument for Happy Holidays is framed as ridiculous because accepting the inclusiveness argument means they 'must' accept the premise (at least in their heads) that there are tenants of Christian practices that are 'problematic.' The inclusiveness argument is absurd to Prager (2016) because "who is being excluded when one wishes someone Merry Christmas?" Prager and the Religious Right cannot properly address the inclusiveness argument because they can only address the strawperson inclusiveness argument. That strawperson becomes the rallying call for all potential War on Christmas subjects because the strawperson is the establishment designed to oppress the rights of Christians. Since the strawperson is framed to assume that everything related to Christianity is bigoted, the Religious Right sees these 'critiques' as an attack on them and their practices. For the Religious Right, they feel they cannot do anything with their religion without the <politically correct> establishment coming down and telling them that they are wrong and racist for thinking otherwise and this premise can even make liberals sympathetic.

However, the appeal to liberals possesses additional functions. For liberals, the caricature of the <far Left> brings anxieties within their political movement because they do not want to be associated with socialists and communists (as the Democrats have a long tensions of their far-left counterparts).[38] If liberals defend or remain silent about the <politically correct> <Leftist>, then liberals look as if they are condoning the attack on Christmas in favor of equal protections. As Herman and Chomsky (2002) wrote, "Liberals at home, often accused of being pro-Communist or insufficiently Anti-Communist, are kept continuously on the defensive in a cultural milieu in which anticommunism is the dominant religion."[39] Moreover, while liberals may disagree with conservatives on a wide variety of issues, liberals do value the marketplace of ideas to see which ideas will win out in that competition. As a result, liberals can be sympathetic to the War on Christmas conspiracy because the <Leftist> brings anxieties within liberals from a coalition standpoint and from a principled standpoint. Liberal anxieties are exacerbated further by the War on Christmas because the theory positions liberals to either pick a side—the expansion of the 14th Amendment or the reduction of the 1st Amendment—or at least be sympathetic with the movement. The War on Christmas, as a subtextual conspiracy, opens the doors for conservative and religious Democrats to partake in the fight against what they believe to be the establishment of the <far Left> and <political correctness>.

The Ideographic Dog Whistle and Acknowledging the Dialectic of Freedom

In this chapter, I articulated subtextual conspiracy rhetoric and how the subtextual conspiracy theory will oftentimes utilize ideographic language to spread a conspiratorial message to a mainstream audience rather than just a small fringe political group. After I illustrated my subtextual conspiracy and ideographic rhetorical framework, I articulated the rhetorical tactics used by the War on Christmas through the framework of the subtextual conspiracy theory. In my analysis, I found that the War on Christmas theorists strategically use the political conflict between religious freedom vs. equal protections by placating on the fears of the Religious Right through ideographic language. Moreover, the War on Christmas theorists will often frame their coverage of <progressive> arguments as absurd and irrational tactics to eliminate Christmas as a national holiday in America to condition their conservative audience to never take progressives seriously.

After examining the subtextual conspiracy rhetoric of the War on Christmas, I must now illustrate why my analysis matters in political discourse. I will articulate how my analysis will allow us to proceed with the complicated conversation and conflict between religious freedoms vs. equal protections. As a summary, the War on Christmas subtextual conspiracy showcases the dangers of unsubstantiated conspiracies and how an unidentified and abstract villain can lead to further acts of hate and violence. Furthermore, I wish to illustrate one way to alleviate the dangerous of the War on Christmas because I think the effects of this decade long conspiracy will continue to further poison political discourse in America. Simply put, I argue that the best way to fix the effects of the War on Christmas conspiracy, both sides must recognize the dialectic.

Recognition of the Dialectic

I believe the best step to ameliorate the political poison of the War on Christmas conspiracy theory is for both sides to recognize the dialectic rather than *only* seeing the relationship between religious freedom vs. equal protections as a one-way direction. I argue that much of the political tension is exacerbated by progressives who *only* see the expansion of the 14th Amendment's circumference and conservatives that *only* see the reduction of the 1st Amendment's circumference and the antidote is the recognition of the dialectic. Now, I should briefly clarify this position as it may be viewed as a contradiction within my analysis. As I articulated, the War on Christmas theorists posit that the expansion of the 14th Amendment by the Supreme Court invariably reduces the 1st Amendment of the Religious Right. While this may indicate that the Religious Right views this tension as a dialectic rather than in one direction, I believe Burke provides a contextualization that elucidates this possible contradiction.

As Burke argued, to refer to something as a group is to reduce them because referring to them in other terms reduces them *from* a universal circumference.[40] However, that universal circumference is often omitted because, ironically, that universal circumference does not explain enough as it explains too much. Since conservatives already believe the expansion of the 14th Amendment's circumference to be the new establishment, that establishment becomes their new universal circumference. The expansion of that circumference can be omitted from their calculations because it has become grounds for *all* motives to *them*.

This omission can also be seen among progressives within this tension. With the exception of conservatives, most Americans do not care whether one says Merry Christmas or Happy Holidays because the language is either indistinguishable or irrelevant to their lives.[41] Moreover, data has indicated that more Americans are beginning to celebrate Christmas less like a religious holiday and more as a cultural holiday because many Americans are *culturally* Christian and not *religiously* Christian.[42] As such, their *cultural* connection to Christmas manifests into their universal circumference and any interpellation into Christian iconicity during Christmas is also omitted from their logical calculations. That apathy becomes the universal circumference for most Americans as it grounds all their motives (civic religiosity). As such, the reduction of the 1st Amendment's circumference becomes omitted from the progressives' calculous because their motives are grounded in their apathy toward that particular component of religious freedom (Happy Holidays vs. Merry Christmas).

As Burke articulated, a 'pure' being is the same as a 'Not-being' because the agent and the act are always bound by a scene. As Burke asserted, "One may expect to encounter the paradox of purity whenever he finds what we have called elsewhere the 'withiness of withiness,' or the 'atop the atop' " (36). Every act must come at the cost of the act's negation because what is 'good' for one act is 'bad' in another act. Since the concept of a 'pure' act is a paradox, one can see the Religious Right's pure religious freedom as a paradox because the existence of a pure freedom is equated to the lack of freedom. Unregulated religious freedom would allow people to use that freedom to undermine the freedoms of other groups. Marginalized groups would be at the whim of the Religious Right because their freedom to exist would be hampered by a community using their 'pure' freedom to halt and actively harm the freedoms of minorities.

While I may side with the progressive angle in this tension, I wish to impart this message to the reader regardless of which side they are on; begin seeing the tension between the 1st and 14th Amendment as a dialectic. Progressives must recognize that the 14th Amendment's expansion will always come at the cost of another's freedom of speech or religion. For progressives, recognizing this tension as a dialectic illustrates Burke's notion of the paradox of purity and provides progressives with a more consequentialist perspective on this issue. Since pure religious freedom is itself a paradox, I think that recognition of the dialectic between the 1st and 14th Amendment, in relation to the War on Christmas, allows progressives to effectively advocate for their positions from a consequentialist perspective. Since the expansion of the 14th Amendment is inevitably going to lead to the reduction of other people's 1st Amendment rights, progressives should embrace that logic rather than omitting it from their arguments under their apathetic presuppositions. Progressives should argue that while the expansion of the 14th Amendment will reduce some people's religious freedoms, that cost is negligible because that trade-off leads to massive harm reduction for *everyone.*

Through Burke's circumference and paradox of purity, one can see the appropriate way to engage in this legal tension, recognition of the dialectic. Moreover, one should look at this dialectic of freedom through a dramatist approach. For instance, one must ask, which agent (or group agent) is *utilizing their agency*, under the scene of 'freedom,' to exert harm against another agent's scene of freedom? This abstract argument would address the fears that consumes the Religious Right that their culture is being erased by political correctness because the latter's scene of freedom becomes the 'withness of withiness' of the universal circumference of the former. This would also provide legislators and advocacy groups with an argumentation form for determining the appropriate reduction of freedom that leads to the least amount of harm to a broader group because it recognizes the paradox of purity and allows groups to negotiate freedom within various circumferences. If progressives counteract the subtextual conspiracy through a dramatist lens, the Religious Right would be forced to either acknowledge the psychological harm of their paradox of purity or admit they wish to harm others if it means preserving their culture.

Notes

1 Rachel Sugar, "How Starbucks's Annual Holiday Cup Became a Battleground for the Heart and Soul of America," *Vox*, November 2, 2018, https://www.vox.com/the-goods/2018/11/2/18052550/starbucks-holiday-cup-explained-2018-controversies.
2 Christopher Duerringer, "The 'War on Christmas': Counterpublicity or Hegemonic Containment?," *Southern Communication Journal* 78, no. 4 (2013): 311–25, https://doi.org/10.1080/1041794x.2013.792866; John Gibson, *The War on Christmas: How the Liberal Plot to Ban the Sacred Christian Holiday Is Worse Than You Thought* (Sentinel Trade, 2006).
3 Parker Molloy, "A War on Christmas Story: How Fox News built the Dumbest Part of America's Culture War," *Media Matters for America*, accessed on December 23, 2019. https://www.mediamatters.org/war-christmas/war-christmas-story-how-fox-news-built-dumbest-part-americas-culture-war; Fox News, "Christmas in America," *Fox News*, December 2016, video, 8:06, https://www.youtube.com/watch?v=cRNgoC5eEV4.
4 Daniel Denvir, "A Short History of the War on Christmas: How Everyone from Bill O'Reilly to Jon Stewart Became a Co-Conspirator in an Annual Farce," *Politico Magazine*, December 16, 2013, https://www.politico.com/magazine/story/2013/12/war-on-christmas-short-history-101222.
5 Richard Hofstadter, *The Paranoid Style in American Politics* (New York: Vintage Books, 2008), 4; Thomas Goodnight and John Poulakos, "Conspiracy Rhetoric: From Pragmatism to Fantasy in Public Discourse," *The Western Journal of Speech Communication* 45, 299–316, https://doi.org/10.1080/10570318109374052.
6 Daniel Pipes, *Conspiracy: How the Paranoid Style Flourishes and Where It Comes From* (New York: The Free Press, 1997), 21.
7 Goodnight and Poulakos, 299.
8 Ryan Neville-Shepard, "Paranoid Style and Subtextual Form in Modern Conspiracy Rhetoric," *Southern Communication Journal* 83 (2018): 119–32, https://doi.org/10.1080/1041794X.2017.1423106.
9 Ibid., 124–5.
10 Michael McGee, "The 'Ideograph': A Link Between Rhetoric and Ideology," *The Quarterly Journal of Speech* 66, no. 1 (1980): 1–16.
11 Goodnight and Poulakos, 306–10.
12 Shepard, 122–4.
13 Hofstadter, 3.
14 Shepard, 121.
15 Hofstadter, 3–4.
16 Shepard, 121.
17 Ibid., 122.
18 Ibid., 122.
19 McGee, 6.
20 Shepard., 123.
21 Ibid., 123.

22 Kenneth Burke, *A Grammar of Motives* (Berkeley, University of California Press: 1969), 77.
23 McGee, 6.
24 "Lawrence v. Texas." *Oyez*. Accessed July 19, 2020. https://www.oyez.org/cases/2002/02-102; "Obergefell v. Hodges." *Oyez*. Accessed July 19, 2020. https://www.oyez.org/cases/2014/14-556; "Engel v. Vitale." *Oyez*. Accessed July 23, 2020. https://www.oyez.org/cases/1961/468; "Bostock v. Clayton County." *Oyez*. Accessed July 23, 2020. https://www.oyez.org/cases/2019/17-1618; "Roe v. Wade." *Oyez*. Accessed July 24, 2020. https://www.oyez.org/cases/1971/70-18.
25 Adam Tiptak, "Supreme Court Upholds Trump Administration Regulation Letting Employers Opt Out of Birth Control Coverage," *The New York Times*, July 8, 2020, https://www.nytimes.com/2020/07/08/us/supreme-court-birth-control-obamacare.html.
26 Bill O'Reilly, "Christmas Under Siege: The Big Picture," *Fox News*, December 24, 2004, https://www.foxnews.com/story/christmas-under-siege-the-big-picture.
27 Fox Business, "Is the War on Christmas Finally Over?," *Fox Business*, December 23, 2016, video, 4:28, https://www.youtube.com/watch?v=D-lA8EK8UIg.
28 PragerU. "Just Say 'Merry Christmas,'" *PragerU*, November 2016, video, 5:25, https://www.youtube.com/watch?v=mwVpTYez82w.
29 Alan Blinder & Tamar Lewin, "Clerk in Kentucky Chooses Jail Over Deal on Same-Sex Marriage," *The New York Times*, September 3, 2015, https://www.nytimes.com/2015/09/04/us/kim-davis-same-sex-marriage.html.
30 David Weigel, Abby Phillip, and Sarah Larimer, "Kim Davis Released from Jail, Ordered Not to Interfere with Same-Sex Marriage Licenses," *The Washington Post*, September 8, 2015, https://www.washingtonpost.com/news/post-nation/wp/2015/09/08/judge-orders-kentucky-clerk-kim-davis-released-from-jail/.
31 Shepard, 126.
32 Antonio Gramsci, *Selections from the Prison Notebooks*, trans. Quintin Hoare and Geoffrey Smith (New York: International Publishers, 1971), 263–4.
33 Fox News, "Are Progressives Missing the Point of 'Rudolf'?," *Fox News*, November 2018, video, 3:13, https://www.youtube.com/watch?v=QUY005iH3go.
34 PragerU. "Just Say 'Merry Christmas,'" *PragerU*, November 2016, video, 5:25, https://www.youtube.com/watch?v=mwVpTYez82w.
35 Fox News, "MeToo Movement Puts Christmas Classic on Ice," *Fox News*, December 2018, video, 5:28, https://www.youtube.com/watch?v=ljL212kcDZI.
36 PragerU, "Why I Left the Left," *PragerU*, February 2017, video, 4:22, https://www.youtube.com/watch?v=hiVQ8vrGA_8.
37 Fox News, "Is President Trump Winning the War on Christmas?," *Fox News*, video, 6:23, https://www.youtube.com/watch?v=HGHjbD3XcUs.
38 Mike Davis, *Prisoners of the American Dream: Politics and Economy in the History of the U.S. Working Class* (New York: Verso, 2018).
39 Edward Herman and Noam Chomsky, *Manufacturing Consent: The Political Economy of the Mass Media* (New York: Pantheon Books, 2002), 29.
40 Burke, 98.
41 Public Policy Polling Admin, "Only Trump Voters Care About Merry Christmas/Happy Holidays Debate," *Public Policy Polling*, December 19, 2017, https://www.publicpolicypolling.com/polls/trump-voters-care-merry-christmas-happy-holidays-debate/.

42 Pew Research Center, "Celebrating Christmas and the Holidays, Then and Now," *Pew Research Center Religion & Public Life*, December 18, 2013, https://www.pewforum.org/2013/12/18/celebrating-christmas-and-the-holidays-then-and-now/#religious-observance-of-christmas.

Bibliography

"Bostock v. Clayton County." *Oyez.* Accessed July 23, 2020. https://www.oyez.org/cases/2019/17-1618

"Engel v. Vitale." *Oyez.* Accessed July 23, 2020. https://www.oyez.org/cases/1961/468

"Lawrence v. Texas." *Oyez.* Accessed July 19, 2020. https://www.oyez.org/cases/2002/02-102

"Obergefell v. Hodges." *Oyez.* Accessed July 19, 2020. https://www.oyez.org/cases/2014/14-556

"Roe v. Wade." *Oyez.* Accessed July 24, 2020. https://www.oyez.org/cases/1971/70-18

Bill O'Reilly, "Christmas Under Siege: The Big Picture," *Fox News*, December 24, 2004, https://www.foxnews.com/story/christmas-under-siege-the-big-picture

Blinder, Alan and Lewin, Tamar. "Clerk in Kentucky Chooses Jail Over Deal on Same-Sex Marriage," *The New York Times.* September 3, 2015, https://www.nytimes.com/2015/09/04/us/kim-davis-same-sex-marriage.html

Burke, Kenneth. *A Grammar of Motives.* Berkeley: University of California Press: 1969.

Davis, Mike, *Prisoners of the American Dream: Politics and Economy in the History of the U.S. Working Class.* New York: Verso, 2018.

Denvir, Daniel. "A Short History of the War on Christmas: How Everyone from Bill O'Reilly to Jon Stewart Became a Co-Conspirator in an Annual Farce," *Politico Magazine.* December 16, 2013, https://www.politico.com/magazine/story/2013/12/war-on-christmas-short-history-101222

Duerringer, Christopher. "The 'War on Christmas': Counterpublicity or Hegemonic Containment?" *Southern Communication Journal* 78, no. 4 (2013): 311-25.

Enten, Harry. "White Evangelicals Love Trump. Religious Voters? Not So Much," *CNN.* January 1, 2020, https://www.cnn.com/2020/01/01/politics/evangelical-support-trump/index.html

Fox Business, "Is the War on Christmas Finally Over?" *Fox Business*, December 23, 2016, video, 4:28, https://www.youtube.com/watch?v=D-lA8EK8UIg

Fox News, "Are Progressives Missing the Point of 'Rudolf'?" *Fox News*, November 2018, video, 3:13, https://www.youtube.com/watch?v=QUY005iH3go

Fox News, "Is President Trump Winning the War on Christmas?" *Fox News*, video, 6:23, https://www.youtube.com/watch?v=HGHjbD3XcUs

Fox News. "Christmas in America," *Fox News*, December 2016, video, 8:06, https://www.youtube.com/watch?v=cRNgoC5eEV4

Gibson, John. *The War on Christmas: How the Liberal Plot to Ban the Sacred Christian Holiday Is Worse Than You Thought.* Sentinel Trade, 2006.

Goodnight, Thomas and Poulakos, John. "Conspiracy Rhetoric: From Pragmatism to Fantasy in Public Discourse," *The Western Journal of Speech Communication* 45, 299-316.

Gramsci, Antonio, *Selections from the Prison Notebooks*, trans. Quintin Hoare & Geoffrey Smith. New York: International Publishers, 1971.

Harry Brewis, *The War on Christmas: A Measured Response [BACKER VERSION] [YOUTUBE VERSION [VINMEO IS WEIRD]*, *hbomberguy*, video, 50:10, This video is only available, at the time of writing, to those that back Brewis on his monthly Patreon account.

Herman, Edward and Chomsky, Noam. *Manufacturing Consent: The Political Economy of the Mass Media*. New York: Pantheon Books, 2002.

Hofstadter, Richard. *The Paranoid Style in American Politics*. New York: Vintage Books, 2008.

McGee, Michael. "The 'Ideograph': A Link Between Rhetoric and Ideology," *The Quarterly Journal of Speech* 66, no. 1 (1980): 1-16.

Molloy, Parker. "A War on Christmas Story: How Fox News built the Dumbest Part of America's Culture War," *Media Matters for America*. Accessed on December 23, 2019. https://www.mediamatters.org/war-christmas/war-christmas-story-how-fox-news-built-dumbest-part-americas-culture-war; Fox News

Neville-Shepard, Ryan. "Paranoid Style and Subtextual Form in Modern Conspiracy Rhetoric," *Southern Communication Journal* 83, no. 2 (2018): 119-32.

Owen, Tess. "Breitbart, Stormfront, and Shapiro: How Man Convicted of Painting Swastikas on Synagogue Says He Got Radicalized," *Vice*. May 28, 2019. https://www.vice.com/en_us/article/kzmnaz/breitbart-stormfront-and-ben-shapiro-how-21-year-old-convicted-of-painting-swastikas-on-synagogue-says-he-got-radicalized

Pew Research Center, "Celebrating Christmas and the Holidays, Then and Now," *Pew Research Center Religion & Public Life*, December 18, 2013, https://www.pewforum.org/2013/12/18/celebrating-christmas-and-the-holidays-then-and-now/#religious-observance-of-christmas

Pipes, Daniel. *Conspiracy: How the Paranoid Style Flourishes and Where it Comes From* New York: The Free Press, 1997.

PragerU, "Why I Left the Left," *PragerU*, February 2017, video, 4:22, https://www.youtube.com/watch?v=hiVQ8vrGA_8

PragerU. "Just Say 'Merry Christmas,'" *PragerU*, November 2016, video, 5:25, https://www.youtube.com/watch?v=mwVpTYez82w

Public Policy Polling Admin, "Only Trump Voters Care About Merry Christmas/Happy Holidays Debate," *Public Policy Polling*, December 19, 2017, https://www.publicpolicypolling.com/polls/trump-voters-care-merry-christmas-happy-holidays-debate/

Sugar, Rachel. ""How Starbucks's Annual Holiday Cup Became a Battleground for the Heart and Soul of America," *Vox*. November 2, 2018, https://www.vox.com/the-goods/2018/11/2/18052550/starbucks-holiday-cup-explained-2018-controversies

Thompson, Krissah and Koncius, Jura, "Trump Vowed to End the 'War on Christmas.' Here's How the White House is Decorated This Season," *The Washington Post.* November 27, 2017, https://www.washingtonpost.com/lifestyle/style/trump-vowed-to-end-the-war-on-christmas-heres-how-the-white-house-is-decorated-this-season/2017/11/27/8a18aa3e-cfbb-11e7-a1a3-0d1e45a6de3d_story.html

Tiptak, Adam. "Supreme Court Upholds Trump Administration Regulation Letting Employers Opt Out of Birth Control Coverage," *The New York Times.* July 8, 2020, https://www.nytimes.com/2020/07/08/us/supreme-court-birth-control-obamacare.html

Vigdor, Neil. "Judge Orders Alex Jones and Infowar to Pay $100,000 in Sandy Hook Legal Fees," *The New York Times.* December 31, 2019, https://www.nytimes.com/2019/12/31/us/Alex-Jones-sandy-hook.html

Weigel, David, Phillip, Abby, & Larimer, Sarah. "Kim Davis Released from Jail, Ordered Not to Interfere with Same-Sex Marriage Licenses," *The Washington Post.* September 8, 2015, https://www.washingtonpost.com/news/post-nation/wp/2015/09/08/judge-orders-kentucky-clerk-kim-davis-released-from-jail/

Weiser, Benjamin and Watkins, Ali. "Cesar Sayoc, Who Mailed Pipe Bombs to Trump Critics, Is Sentenced to 20 Years," *The New York Times.* August 5, 2019, https://www.nytimes.com/2019/08/05/nyregion/cesar-sayoc-sentencing-pipe-bombing.html

Contributors

Pat Arneson (Ph.D., Ohio University) is Professor Emerita at Duquesne University, and Past Editor of *Communication Law Review*. She earned the Franklyn S. Haiman Award for Distinguished Scholarship in Freedom of Expression, and the James Madison Prize for Outstanding Free Speech Scholarship. Pat was the first woman Laureate Fellow of the International Communicology Institute, and has published several award-winning books.

Jennifer J. Asenas (Ph.D., University of Texas at Austin) is Chair and Professor of Communication Studies, and Director of Rhetorical Research for the Center for First Amendment Studies at California State University, Long Beach. She is the Book Review Editor of NCA's *First Amendment Studies* and *Communication and Democracy*.

Ann E. Burnette (Ph.D., Northwestern University) is Minnie Stevens Piper Professor and Regents' Teaching Professor in the Department of Communication Studies at Texas State University. She is a recipient of the James Madison Prize in First Amendment Studies.

Jamila A. Cupid (Ph.D., Howard University) is Assistant Professor of Public Relations at Pepperdine University. She studies international and intercultural public relations in the areas of campaigns, branding, relationship building, and digital media. She is also a business communication and digital media strategist for young professionals.

Juliet Dee (Ph.D., Temple University) is Associate Professor of Communication at the University of Delaware. She has served as Director of the Legal Studies Program at the University of Delaware, as Editor of *Free Speech Yearbook* (an NCA journal), and is co-author of *Mass Communication Law in a Nutshell* (2020).

David R. Dewberry (Ph.D., Denver University) is Professor of Communication at Rider University. He served as Editor of *Communication Law Review* and *First Amendment Studies.* He has earned the Franklyn S. Haiman Award for Distinguished Scholarship in Freedom of Expression, the James Madison Prize for Outstanding Free Speech Scholarship, and the Richard S. Arnold Prize for First Amendment Scholarship.

Rebekah L. Fox (Ph.D., Purdue University) is a Professor of Communication Studies at Texas State University, former editor of the *Communication Law Review* and recipient of the James Madison Prize in First Amendment Studies.

Adrienne E. Hacker Daniels (Ph.D., University of Wisconsin-Madison) is Professor of Communication and Rhetorical Studies and A. Boyd Pixley Professor of Humanities at Illinois College. Her major areas of research include the First Amendment, religious communication/interfaith dialogue. and the rhetoric of drama. She has published in the journal *First Amendment Studies,* and has contributed book chapters to *Regulating Social Media: Legal and Ethical Implications, A Communication Perspective on Interfaith Dialogue,* and *Urban Communication Reader IV: Cities as Communicative Change Agents.* She also has a published edited volume, *Communication and the Global Landscape of Faith.*

Kevin A. Johnson (Ph.D., University of Texas at Austin) is Professor of Communication Studies and Director of the Center for First Amendment Studies at California State University, Long Beach. He is the journal Editor of the National Communication Association's (NCA) *First Amendment Studies* and *Communication and Democracy.*

Diana Isabel Martínez, (Ph.D., University of Texas at Austin) is Associate Professor of Communication at Pepperdine University. Her research explores physical and psychological borderlands, a term coined by Gloria Anzaldúa to describe spaces of social, political, and cultural struggle. Her work has appeared in communication journals, including *Western Journal of Communication* and *Communication Quarterly.* Her book, *Rhetorics of Nepantla, Memory, and the Gloria Evangelina Anzaldúa Papers,* was published by Lexington Books in 2022.

Robert Mejia, (Ph.D., University of Illinois) is Communications Manager at A New Way of Life Reentry Project. His work focuses on transforming the narrative surrounding incarcerated and formerly incarcerated people and spans the intersections of media, technology, and race, class, and gender. His research has appeared in *Communication and Critical/Cultural Studies,*

Critical Studies in Media Communication, and *Rhetoric of Health and Medicine*, and other academic outlets.

Pamela L. Morris (Ph.D., Purdue University) is Associate Professor of Communication Studies at Indiana University-Purdue University Columbus. Her research interests include new media, media law, and human trafficking. She teaches and advocates for media literacy, and is a former IT project manager.

Sergio Peña (B.A., Illinois College) is pursuing a Master's degree in Communication Arts and Sciences at the Pennsylvania State University where he currently serves as an Effective Speech Teaching Assistant. His research primarily focuses on the rhetoric of queer hegemony through media representations of drag artistry. He has presented his research at the Central States Communication Association.

Amanda Reid (J.D., Ph.D., University of Florida) is Associate Professor at the University of North Carolina at Chapel Hill. She teaches in the Hussman School of Journalism and Media, and in the UNC School of Law. Her previous work has appeared in notable outlets including the *William and Mary Bill of Rights Journal*, *Nebraska Law Review*, and *International Journal of Communication.*

Skye de Saint Felix (Ph.D., University of Maryland) specializes in rhetoric and gender. Skye helps run the Rosenker Center for Political Communication and Civic Deliberation at the University of Maryland, working specifically with an archival recovery project called *Recovering Democracy Archives.* She has recently published in *Women's Studies in Communication*, *Feminist Media Studies*, and *World Medical and Health Policy.*

Susan H. Sarapin, (Ph.D., Purdue University) is Associate Professor of Communication at Troy University in Alabama. Her long-term focus has been on the effects of viewing crime drama on the public's understanding of the justice system, and a recent emphasis has been on measuring the real negative financial and health effects on Black citizens living on streets named for Confederate soldiers or living near Confederate monuments on public property in the Deep South.

Joseph Sery (Ph.D., University of Pittsburgh) is Associate Professor of Communication at Christopher Newport University. His research focuses on the intersection between rhetoric, politics, and jurisprudence and appears in several journals and edited volumes. He is also affiliated with the Pre-Law Program and teaches a course on the First Amendment.

Lindsey A. Sherrill (Ph.D., The University of Alabama) is Assistant Professor of Business Communication at the University of North Alabama. Before a decade-long career in wholesale management, Lindsey spent several years writing for small-town newspapers. Lindsey's research has appeared in notable outlets including *Journal of Broadcast & Electronic Media, Communication Research,* and *Journalism Studies.* She is also a homeschool alum.

Logan S. Spence (M.S., Illinois State University) is a Ph.D. student at Ohio University School of Communication Studies, specializing in conspiracy theory communication and rhetoric. Further reading of his research may be found in his peer reviewed essay in *Southern Communication* Journal entitled, "Rhetorical Denialism: The Melancholic Affect of Conspiracy Rhetoric and Ideological (C)Kynicism."

M. Elizabeth Thorpe (Ph.D., Texas A&M University) is Associate Professor of Communication at SUNY-Brockport. Her research engages issues surrounding the constitution of national identity, legal rhetoric, and free speech. Her research has appeared in notable outlets including *Communication Law Review*, *First Amendment Studies*, and *Atlantic Journal of Communication.* She regularly teaches courses in argumentation and debate, political rhetoric, freedom of expression, and rhetorical theory.

Mark Ward Sr. (Ph.D., Clemson University) is Professor of Communication at the University of Houston-Victoria. He has authored, coauthored, or edited seven books, including *The Electronic Church in the Digital Age,* and published more than 40 scholarly articles and essays. His honors include the Digital Religion Research Award and multiple Article of the Year awards from the Religious Communication Association. In 2018 he was named his institution's scholar of the year.

Jason Zenor (J.D., University of South Dakota) is Associate Professor in the School of Communication, Media & the Arts at SUNY-Oswego where he teaches courses in Mass Media & the Law, Media & Politics and American Indian Sovereignty. He is author of several articles appearing in notable journals including *Communication Law & Policy*, *Denver Law Review*, and *Southwestern Law Review.* Prof. Zenor has earned the Franklyn S. Haiman Award for Distinguished Scholarship in Freedom of Expression, and a NCA Distinguished Publication Award in Communication and Law.

Index

FRONTIERS IN POLITICAL COMMUNICATION

General Editors
Mitchell S. McKinney and Mary E. Stuckey

At the heart of how citizens, governments, and the media interact is the communication process, a process that is undergoing tremendous changes as we embrace a new millennium. Never has there been a time when confronting the complexity of these evolving relationships been so important to the maintenance of civil society. This series seeks books that advance the understanding of this process from multiple perspectives and as it occurs in both institutionalized and non-institutionalized political settings. While works that provide new perspectives on traditional political communication questions are welcome, the series also encourages the submission of manuscripts that take an innovative approach to political communication, which seek to broaden the frontiers of study to incorporate critical and cultural dimensions of study as well as scientific and theoretical frontiers.

For more information or to submit material for consideration, contact:

editorial@peterlang.com

To order other books in this series, please contact our Customer Service Department:

peterlang@presswarehouse.com (within the U.S.)
orders@peterlang.com (outside the U.S.)

Or browse online by series:

WWW.PETERLANG.COM

www.ingramcontent.com/pod-product-compliance
Ingram Content Group UK Ltd.
Pitfield, Milton Keynes, MK11 3LW, UK
UKHW020838290926
15470UKWH00004B/1417

9 781433 167690